LOUIS

Dom JEAN L

Dom FRANÇOIS VAN

and LOUIS COGNET, Priest at Clermont-Ferrand

HISTORY OF CHRISTIAN SPIRITUALITY

I

THE SPIRITUALITY OF THE NEW TESTAMENT AND THE FATHERS

Uniform with this volume

A HISTORY OF CHRISTIAN SPIRITUALITY, Vol. II
The Spirituality of the Middle Ages

A HISTORY OF CHRISTIAN SPIRITUALITY, Vol. III
Orthodox Spirituality and
Protestant and Anglican Spirituality

THE SPIRITUALITY OF THE NEW TESTAMENT AND THE FATHERS

LOUIS BOUYER

THE SEABURY PRESS • NEW YORK

TO

HANS URS VON BALTHSAR

Second paperback printing

1982

The Seabury Press
815 Second Avenue
New York, N.Y. 10017

Originally published as
La Spiritualité du Nouveau Testament et des Pères

English translation by Mary P. Ryan

Library of Congress Catalog Card Number: 63-16487
ISBN: 0-8164-2372-5

Printed in the U.S.A.

PREFACE

WHAT is spirituality in general and Christian spirituality in particular? In what sense has it a history? These are questions that must be answered before we enter on our work. Any solution that we may arrive at here implies the adoption of a definite point of view. And it is better to admit this fact frankly and explain why this point of view has been adopted. Hence this introduction.

Pourrat, in the first of his four volumes on *Christian Spirituality*, distinguishes "spirituality" or "spiritual theology" not only from "dogmatic theology which teaches what must be believed", but also from moral theology which, according to him, teaches only "what must be done or avoided so as not to sin mortally or venially". "Spirituality", on the contrary, includes "ascetic theology" which has "as its object the exercises to which every Christian who aspires to perfection must devote himself", together with "mystical theology" which is concerned with "extraordinary states... such as the mystical union and its secondary manifestations...".

These distinctions, it must be admitted, are not very satisfactory. Is it possible to define Christian morality by a merely negative idea: to "avoid sin"? Is aiming at perfection a matter of choice for the Christian? Furthermore, is the mystical life to be reduced to the "extraordinary"? Once we are aware of these objections, what remains of classifications that ignore them? In fact, when we study Pourrat's extremely rich work, we have difficulty in finding anything in it corresponding to the categories he has named. From one end to the other of the four volumes, we are plunged into a medley of dogmatic or moral considerations and psychological analyses, a medley in which the boundaries laid down at the outset are constantly transgressed.

Must we conclude, then, that spirituality can be nothing more than an indistinct notion, a more or less chance admixture of Christian doctrines and religious psychology?

More recent works have tried to purify Pourrat's concept by reducing it to religious psychology. One immediate consequence of this has been the fad for studies in comparative spirituality which delight in emphasizing the relationships between Christian spirituality and non-Christian spiritualities. But the authors do not always seem to have considered whether they might not be creating a good part of these analogies or similarities in ignoring, from the outset, everything that might be specific either to Christianity or to some other religion. The great danger, here as elsewhere, lies in erecting —usually unconsciously—some cherished rough-and-ready method into a norm of judgment. So Christian spirituality as spirituality is emptied of everything that is specifically Christian. And then the door is opened to all kinds of facile syncretisms. . . .

Phenomenology has produced a healthy reaction in this regard by reminding us that, in the concrete, it is impossible to separate subjective psychology from the objects towards which it is oriented. A work such as that in which Rudolf Otto compares Eckhart and Sankara, even though written by a Protestant of "liberal" a-dogmatic tendencies, has already brought out clearly how impossible it is to set up a serious comparison between spiritualities without taking account of the dogmas presupposed by each.

Are we then brought back to an amorphous idea of spirituality, combining doctrinal considerations and psychological analyses without following any definite rules or making some merely artificial distinction between them? Not in the least, to our way of thinking.

Christian spirituality (or any other spirituality) is distinguished from dogma by the fact that, instead of studying or describing the objects of belief as it were in the abstract, it studies the reactions which these objects arouse in the religious consciousness. But, rightly, it does not entertain the pseudo-scientific, and in fact wholly extravagant, prejudice that the understanding of the objects polarizing the religious consciousness is essentially foreign to an understanding of this consciousness itself. On the contrary, spirituality studies this consciousness only in its living relationship with these objects, in its real apprehension, as Newman said, of what it believes. Dogmatic theology, therefore, must always be presupposed as the basis of spiritual theology, even though the latter concerns itself with the data of the former only under the relationship that they entertain with the religious consciousness.

We still need to indicate the place of spiritual theology in relation to moral theology. There can be no question of taking out of moral theology what is called the perfection of the Christian ideal, since there can be no morality worthy of the name which is not wholly built up on a study of the final end of human life. Consequently, it is not by its concern with perfection that spirituality is to be distinguished from morality. But, while the latter examines all human acts in reference to their ultimate end, whether this reference be explicit or not, spirituality concentrates on those in which the reference to God is not only explicit but immediate. It concentrates, that is, above all on prayer and on everything connected with prayer in the ascetical and mystical life—in other words, on religious exercises as well as religious experiences.

Since human life is characterized by unity of consciousness, and since this unity is found to be enhanced, as it were, as soon as there is any reference to God, it goes without saying that we cannot make strict distinctions between studies in spirituality and studies in moral theology. Just as a truly Christian morality is never really external to dogmatic theology, so spirituality is located far more within the heart of morality than alongside it. But, although it can never be separated from the whole moral problem, spirituality constitutes a sufficiently specific part of moral theology—by reason of its formal object as well as the method required by this object—to demand special treatment.

But here the question comes up: how can we speak of a *history* of Christian spirituality? Is Christian morality, which we find so closely connected with spirituality, also capable of development?

To this we must answer that, while the morality of various human acts is not capable of basic change, once the lights of reason and faith have been given, yet the way of theorizing about these acts certainly has developed. Do not even the dogmas, the formulas in which the Christian faith is expressed, themselves have a history? Furthermore, however little we wish to reduce spirituality to religious psychology, there is no denying the close connection between them. So we cannot deny the importance of the changes brought to human psychology by the development of civilization during twenty centuries, however unalterable are the basic constituents of that psychology. And therefore we must expect Christian spirituality also to have a history, in function both of the history of doctrine and of psychological development.

It is no less important, from the first, clearly to set out what seem to us to be the definite limits to these historical variations in Christian spirituality. If it is born of the meeting between Christian revelation and human psychology, its own variations cannot exceed the limits of the variations of its constituents. Now, while there is a history of dogmas, the content of Christian revelation remains unchangeable throughout. And while there is a development in human psychology, still the continuity, the permanence of the existential characteristics of the human soul remain no less important—are even far more important—than anything about it that may change. There can, therefore, be great contrasts in the outward appearances of Christian spirituality in different times and different places. But, while one or other secondary problem can, in one or another age, assume primary importance, the essential problem and the major elements of its solution never change. It is, therefore, only with the greatest reservations that we can speak of Christian spiritualities in the plural. In the domain of spirituality as in that of dogma, the prejudice is legitimate that taxes anything too novel with being simply a deviation or degeneration. This is a truth which has been not infrequently ignored in the course of the last half-century, and one which it is the more important to emphasize in undertaking the present work.

Whence came this novel insistence on Christian spiritualities? It seems to have originated from the restoration of the religious orders in the nineteenth century, after their suppression during the French Revolution. Very rightly, these restorations were not intended merely to reconstruct the great religious bodies of the past, but also to recapture the best of their spirit. Thus Benedictine or Jesuit, Carmelite or Franciscan spirituality came to be defined by reciprocal opposition. In these attempts, recourse was had to history, but little attention was paid to the fact—indisputable, none the less—that no holy founder or reformer of a religious order ever had the idea of establishing a special spirituality more or less strictly distinct from any other. Rather we should consider how St Teresa, the great Carmelite, sought spiritual direction from Franciscans or Jesuits without asking anything other than a doctrine that was fully Catholic and fully lived up to!

However, once special spiritualities for various religious orders had been rebuilt in this rather artificial way, everyone became eager to have a spirituality all his own, unlike that of anyone else. So efforts were made to construct a spirituality for the diocesan clergy, as a kind of *ersatz* religious spirituality for men who, by the nature of things, had none of of their own—an undertaking which would have been very surprising to Bérulle or Olier: as if these men of the Church had need of anything other than the spirituality of the Church herself!

Catholic Action, itself specialized, has taken the same road, and, along the same lines, "Jociste", "Jaciste", "Jéciste", etc., spiritualities have been constructed, carefully distinguished from one another. Now we have arrived at a spirituality for laymen, in opposition to all kinds of "religious" spiritualities and, above all, to that of "monks", as if monks were anything else, in being monks, than baptized Christians eager to carry out all the requirements of their baptism! This is not to deny the fact that many factors—the different surroundings in which a person lives, the different historical circumstances in which he may find himself; different vocations, each bound up with what is most unique in each personality—will, quite legitimately and in any case inevitably, cause variations in the concrete application of the Gospel to a human life. But it remains none the less true that there has never been but one Gospel. Again, in our age as in every age, there are people who are innocently convinced that any humanity worthy of the name was born yesterday and that it can have nothing (or nothing important and worthy of attention) in common with the humanity of the past. But those who entertain such notions soon appear, in actual fact, incapable of concern for what is most fundamental, most permanent—in other words, most human—in man. The defenders of these "new men" who are not the "new man" of the Gospel regularly reveal themselves as tyrants and, finally, as murderers of the man of all times, the true man.

Our history of Christian spirituality, then, cannot be a history of different spiritualities, imagined as each self-contained, but succeeding one another in a more or less ascending line of progress. It will be the history of the problem always newly posed in a dynamic humanity and a changing civilization—the problem of how to apply as integrally as possible to the life of the soul (and so, above all, also how to comprehend as authentically as possible, how to apprehend in as real a way as possible) the Gospel of Jesus Christ, "the same yesterday, today and for ever".

The present work, in other words, will be neither simply a "literary history of religious sentiment" nor a collection of biographies or monographs on "schools of spirituality". All this material, certainly, will constantly be discussed in these volumes. But it will be studied only in connection with the Christian spiritual problem of all ages, as it is raised, as it is understood, as attempts are made to solve it, from one age to another. And so this history will be, in the final analysis, the search for, and the bringing to light of, the integral witness of tradition and of Christian experience to the whole concrete reality of "life in Christ Jesus".

TABLE OF CONTENTS

Part Two

THE FATHERS

FOREWORD TO VOLUME ONE

IT would be difficult for me, on the threshold of this study, to list the names of all those to whom I have reason to be grateful.

In connection with its remote inspiration alone, I should have to make up a lengthy list of all those who helped me discover the spiritual importance of the Fathers as coming immediately after the New Testament, and of those who aided me to penetrate the authentic riches of the New Testament itself: from Newman's *The Church of the Fathers* to *La vie spirituelle d'après les Pères des trois premiers siècles*, by G. Bardy. As for scientific works, the footnotes on each page will indicate those to which I owe most. I cannot leave unmentioned the pioneer work of P. Pourrat, P.S.S., whose analyses remain not only valuable, but invaluable. And I cannot forbear expressing my admiration and gratitude for the wonderful little book of Fr Viller, S.J., in the translation made and provided with notes by Fr Karl Rahner, S.J., which has proved one of the most useful of handbooks.

I have dedicated this volume to my colleague in the priesthood and very dear friend, Hans Urs von Balthasar, because his works have provided a particular inspiration to enter into the enduring life of these ancient texts. I owe a great deal also to innumerable friendly conversations with Dom Jean Leclercq and Fr Louis Cognet, conversations in which the profound unity of viewpoint which caused us to undertake together this *History of Christian Spirituality* was strengthened and defined.

PART ONE

Christian Origins

I

THE LEGACY OF JUDAISM

THE celebrated phrase of Pius XI: "Spiritually we are all Semites", is the best introduction to any history of Christian spirituality. We cannot enter upon such a study by any way other than that of Judaism as it was at the origins of Christianity. But it is no easy task to describe objectively the Jewish spirituality of the beginning of the first century.[1]

The Old Testament, the Hebrew Bible, has, doubtless, preserved for us the essential nourishment of Jewish piety then as today. But our modern study of the Bible, critical and historical as it is, may be as much of an obstacle as an aid when we try to understand the Bible as the Jews who were Christ's contemporaries understood it. Their perspectives were in no way ours. They took the Hebrew Bible as a finished whole. In other words, the basis or heart of their reading was the Pentateuch and what we call the "historical books"—for them "the Torah" and "the first prophets". This corresponded to the liturgy of the synagogue, which is reflected in the arrangement of our Bibles much more faithfully than we usually imagine. And it was also the context of this liturgy, especially that of its great feasts, which provided devout Jews with their basic interpretation of the Scriptures.[2]

Bible and Liturgy in Judaism

These feasts were commemorations, or had become such in the distant past. But they implied something quite different from fidelity to pious memories—the assurance that, in these creative and redemptive events, God had manifested himself to his people and for

[1] It is impossible to point to a single over-all study of this subject which is really satisfactory. See, however, the chapter by A. Tricot, "The Jewish Religion", Introductory Sect. II, ch. I, *Introduction à la Bible*, vol. II, *Le Nouveau Testament*, ed. by A. Robert and A. Feuillet, Desclée, Paris, 1959.

[2] See Oesterly and Box, *Religion and Worship of the Synagogue*, London, 1911, pp. 81–93; R. G. Finch, The *Synagogue Lectionary and the New Testament*, London, 1939, pp. 1–40; I. Elbogen, "Torah (the Reading of)", in the *Universal Jewish Encyclopedia*, vol. X, pp. 273ff.

them. More than that, these celebrations, giving rhythm to the reading of the sacred books, in some way re-actualized these divine acts. The Passover recalled the deliverance from the yoke of slavery to foreign powers, the "passing" of the Lord here below, which had caused his own to "pass" from slavery to freedom, from darkness to light, from death to life. At the same time, it reawakened in them the sense of their election and of the divine intervention which had confirmed the communion of his faithful with one another at the same time as with their God. Pentecost, or the "Feast of Weeks", bringing the people spiritually back to Sinai, renewed the covenant in the gift of the divine law and its acceptance in faith and love. The Feast of Tabernacles renewed in them their sense of themselves as a people set apart, separated from other peoples, uprooted in the eyes of the world, established only in the dwelling of faith. Did they not each year resume for some days the life of the desert, the life of tent-dwelling nomads, "pilgrims and travellers who have here no abiding city, but seek that which is to come"?

To these three great feasts of ancient origin, feasts calling for a journey to Jerusalem, was added a group of complementary feasts, less focal, but also full of teaching. The Feast of Expiations, with its fasts and purifying libations, its basic ritual of bloody sacrifices, emphasized the holiness of God and the sin of man, and also the mystery that it is God himself who by sacrifice purifies man so that he may approach him. The Feast of Purim recalled the fact that God's victories and deliverances are not of one time only, but of all times: striking down the conquering Persian of yesterday as the Egyptian of long ago. And, finally, the Feast of the Dedication of the Temple, restored under the Machabees, maintained the people in the assurance that the God of heaven, today as yesterday, willed to dwell here below, invisible but always present with his people.[3]

The Covenant and the Divine Holiness

This liturgical reading of the Bible made it above all a sacred history, and a history with continuing relevance and timeliness. The Jewish religion was essentially biblical, but this is to say that it was above all the religion of the Covenant: the Covenant of the Exodus and of Sinai; that is, a covenant based on the free gratuitous divine choice, but in return requiring that man gives himself wholly over to God, with his entire life. In this Covenant, the holiness of God blazes out, as an exigency that only he can render his own capable of bearing; and yet it is the source of an unshakable trust.

[3] See I. Elbogen, *Der jüdischen Gottesdienst in seiner geschichtlicher Entwicklung*, 3rd ed., Frankfurt am M., 1931.

not only in the divine power, in his strong hand and outstretched arm always ready to save his people, but also in the intimacy, the gracious nearness of the God whom the heavens and the heaven of heavens cannot contain, who none the less condescends to make himself the companion of his people here below.[4]

This twofold and inseparable character of the God of holiness, that is, of incomparable majesty, and also of fidelity, of merciful tenderness—aroused a piety unlike any other. Here adoration and love, the highest and purest religion, the most intimate and most exalting trust are perfectly blended, as in the prayer of the *Shema*, the most familiar of prayers to every Israelite:

> Hear, O Israel: the Lord our God is the only Lord; blessed be the glorious Name of His Kingdom for the ages of ages! And you shall love the Lord your God with your whole heart, with your whole soul and with your whole thought. . . .[5]

This is in no way the product of some abstract metaphysics, but of the very concrete belief in a God manifested in history: the living God, the personal God, who has loved those whom he has chosen and will never desert them. Nothing is more explicit in this regard than the other great prayer of Israel, the *Shemoneh Esreh*, the Eighteen Blessings, called simply "The Prayer".

> O Lord, You will open my lips and my tongue shall declare Your praises.
> You are blessed, O Lord our God and the God of our Fathers, the God of Abraham, the God of Isaac, the God of Jacob; the great, powerful and terrible God, the Most High God. Rewarder of Your faithful servants, master of all things; You who remember Your mercies to our fathers, who will give a redeemer to their children's children, for the sake of Your Name, in Your love; the king, willing to aid, who saves and protects: You are blessed, O Lord, the shield of Abraham. . . .[6]

The Torah and Holiness

To this Jewish piety, the teaching of the great prophets, succeeding one another from the eighth century on, doubtless did not stand out in the particular relief which critical exegesis has restored to it. Devout Jews absorbed the prophetic teaching diffused throughout the sacred history that had in turn been illuminated by Amos

[4] On the origins and importance in Israel of this notion of the covenant, see J. Pedersen, *Israel, its Life and Culture*, London, 1926, pp. 263–310.

[5] On the *Shema* and its recitation, see David Hedegard, *Seder R. Amram Gaon*, pt I, Lund, 1951, pp. 36ff.

[6] See David Hedegard, *op. cit*, pp. 70ff.

and Osee, Isaias and Jeremias. In return, such Jews were much more aware than are we of everything that the exceptional personalities of the prophets themselves owed to a collective, age-long experience which they had doubtless refined, but which they stood out from without ever breaking with. Again, "our Fathers", for Israel, were above all the patriarchs, and chiefly Abraham: the first to whom the Word of the election and the covenant had made itself heard, the first who had believed and who, justified by this faith, had yielded to the requirements that are the counterparts of the divine promises. And "the Prophet" above all was Moses, seen not only as the lawgiver, but as he in whom and by whom the divine arm had been manifested.[7]

For while Moses was indeed the man of the Torah, it is the bias of later Christian polemics that causes us to reduce the Torah to what we put under the heading of Law. To the devout Israelite, the Mosaic Torah was something quite other than a yoke. Or, rather, it was already that dear yoke, that light burden, of which Christ was to speak. Its primary aspect was never lost sight of, its aspect of grace, of communion, of covenant with God, which made the revelation of the Torah the corollary of the revelation of the divine Name.[8] On Horeb, indeed, the Lord had begun by disclosing his Name to Moses, that is to say, in some sort handing over to him his life, his being, in his Holiness itself.[9] And the Torah, given on the same sacred mountain,[10] was the consequence of that initial gift: a demand for holiness, doubtless, but above all a witness to the covenant concluded between the Holy One and his people: "Be ye holy as I am holy."[11]

It is impossible to understand what the Torah meant to Israel if we do not begin by fathoming what was included in their idea of this holiness.[12] Here more than ever is confirmed the living, the concrete character of the Israelite religion. Holiness is not an idea that can be defined. It is the fruit of an experience: an experience which is the distillation of a longer history. And it was this history which provided the basis for the inspiration of the last prophets, while they finally gave that history its shape.

God is holy, first of all, because he is the God of the sky and the God of the wild mountain, the God of the lightning. That is to say,

[7] See the special numbers of the review *Les Cahiers sioniens* devoted to these two personalities.

[8] On this point, see, for example, Lauterbach, *Rabbinic Essays*, Cincinnati, 1951, pp. 268ff. Cf. the excellent remarks of L. Gillet, *Communion in the Messiah*, London, 1942, pp. 60–1.

[9] Exod. 3. 13–14. On the divine Name and the importance of its revelation, see E. Jacob, *Théologie de l'Ancien Testament*, Neuchâtel-Paris, 1955, pp. 33ff.

[10] Exod. 19. 20. [11] Lev. 11. 44; 19. 2; 20. 7.

[12] See E. Jacob, *op. cit*, pp. 69ff.

he is the living God above all, but also the Inaccessible: the Sovereign, the wholly Other. But nowhere do we find an experience and an inspired teaching which elucidates this holiness as in Israel. Here, with a quite decisive clarity, holiness appears as something entirely other than a merely material grandeur. It is not enough to say that it both terrifies and fascinates, that it kills and gives life. Isaias has expressed it better than anyone else: sovereign greatness, at once moral and physical, incomparable elevation, not only above mortals but above everything and every being[13]—grandeur, however, such as inspires both total trust and absolute obedience. It is the grandeur at once of the inflexible justice proclaimed by Amos and the infinite mercy promised by Osee.[14] The two unite, indeed, in the experience, intimately personal and yet common to the whole people, of an Encounter. Here, like the Ancients on the mountain, his own believe that they see Someone, but Someone before whom, instantaneously, they prostrate themselves astonished still to be alive after having seen this Living One.[15] Yet, like Moses, having seen him without dying, a man is no longer the same: wherever he goes, he carries with him his reflection.[16] As with Isaias, a burning coal taken from the altar has purified the lips that were unclean[17] and they can sing, as in the prayer of the Eighteen Blessings, the hymn of the Seraphim:

> You are holy, and Your Name is Holy, and the Holy Ones praise You unceasingly, for You are God, the King, great and Holy; blessed be You, O Lord: God! King! Holy One!

Above all a mysterious God, he is the Living One who gives life, but he does not give life to his own without having them go through inexplicable trials to gain it, without purifying them as gold is tried in a furnace. This is the God of Isaias, but also and above all the God of Jeremias: the God who asks a man's heart so that he may inscribe his Law in it, but who cannot do so unless he has circumcised this heart—that is, humiliated and broken it,[18] must he not, according to the final word of Ezechiel, in the place of a heart of stone, put in our breast a real heart of flesh?[19]

Whence this singular intimacy with the God of heaven, who none the less wills to dwell in a tent among the tents of his own;[20] who does not even disdain to have his Name dwell in the sanctuary of

[13] See L. Bouyer, *The Meaning of Sacred Scripture*, Notre Dame, 1958, pp. 68ff.
[14] *Ibid.* pp. 52ff.
[15] Exod. 24. 9–11. [16] Exod. 34. 29. [17] Is. 6. 5–7.
[18] Cf. Jer. 4. 4 and Psalm 50. 19. See L. Bouyer, *op. cit.*, pp. 87–90.
[19] Ezech. 36. 26. [20] Exod. 25–26 and Num. 10. 15ff.

stone in which men will yet always be tempted to enclose it.[21] But it is in the obscure cloud that he dwells, even if this cloud impregnates everything it touches with his inaccessible light.[22] And, above all, it is with the humiliated, the proscribed, those whom he paradoxically seems to have abandoned, that he establishes himself as if in his chosen sanctuary: when his glorious Presence has deserted an empty temple in which a degraded cult was carried on, a cult unaware that it had already lost its whole object when it thought that it had at last materialized it. . . .[23]

Morality and Mysticism

We can, therefore, speak both of morality and mysticism in describing this piety of Israel, but the two terms are inadequate. The ritual of expiations and the whole meaning with which it became charged little by little—a meaning which was to become completely explicit with the Epistle to the Hebrews—unites both elements.[24] Or, rather, it makes us feel as though here we were dealing with an experience apart, which eludes all categories.

The content of the "sins" that Israel felt the need to expiate periodically in order to remain in favour with its God certainly appears to have been as moralistic as possible: sins are forms of disobedience to the "ten words" of Sinai. Violations of the justice with regard to the neighbour without which no one could be acceptable in the Lord's sight are here put on the same level as idolatry, the profanation of the divine name or that of the Sabbath.[25] Or, we should rather say, unfaithfulness to God is seen to involve injustice towards men, or what comes to the same thing, such injustice is seen to imply such infidelity. But this amounts to saying that, while religion appears at first entirely moralized, morality here has wholly taken on a directly religious significance. We must never be mistaken as to the word of the prophet Osee, that the Lord prefers mercy to sacrifices.[26] Mercy, or better the untranslatable *hesed*, is an active compassion which presupposes a heart touched by the very compassions, the *rahamim*, of the Lord. And so, very quickly, with Jeremias and many of the psalms, this *hesed* in which everything is summed up is seen to be, not a human sentiment in some way natural to man, which a good upbringing would be enough to produce, but the essential characteristic of the heart of

[21] 1 Kings 8. 14–30.
[22] Cf. Num. 9. 15ff. and 1 Kings 8. 10–12.
[23] Ezech. 11. 16. Cf. chapters 8–11. See L. Bouyer, *op. cit.*, pp. 91ff.
[24] Cf. Lev. 16, and Heb. 9.
[25] Exod. 20.
[26] Osee 6. 6, quoted in Matt. 9. 13.

God which only his grace (for which *hesed* is still the first name) can communicate to the heart of man.[27]

This is why the moralization of sin—however accentuated it may appear in the last prophets and later in all the prayers of the ritual of expiations, beginning with the innumerable penitential psalms—never "laicizes" this ritual. Certainly this ritual, all ritual, in Israel, tended more and more to become spiritualized. Nothing is more characteristic than the sacrifice of praise: after having been a special form of sacrifice, accompanied by praise, it tended to become the "sacrifice" constituted by praise itself. But this does not mean the transformation of religion into mere morality. It is much more a deepening of the religious sense with regard to the whole moral life, having its corollary not in a religion without rites, but in a religion in which the rites become transparent for man's meeting with God, itself becoming an increasingly "mystical" encounter.

We should understand this to mean that the personality of the God of Israel (together with his overwhelming, all-conquering, wholly transcendent majesty) made itself felt as increasingly present, more and more immediately perceived in all things, to the degree that this transformation was brought about. Its term was not a religion without prayers and without rites, but a religion in which prayers and rites were permeated with the sense of the nearness of God together with his elevation. The Israelite is a man who lives, who tends to live, constantly in the sight of God. His perpetual reflex act is to cry with Isaias: "Woe is me, for I am a man of unclean lips and I live among a people with unclean lips, and yet my eyes have seen the Lord." But this reflex is accompanied by the continually renewed certainty expressed in the vision of the seraph taking the burning coal from the altar and saying: "This has purified your lips."[28]

The purity of heart towards which the requirements of religion thus tend is not a mere interior rectitude; it is the disposition to encounter God: God manifested in the history of his people, which is also the history of each person, God manifested as intervening in us in a mysterious way to carry out at the same time both his promises and his demands.

This is the ultimate meaning of that victory, ceaselessly renewed, which God wins for his own, the victory celebrated by the Purim—of that presence, ceaselessly restored in spite of all the infidelities

[27] Cf. Osee 11. 8 (with the correction suggested by Kittel of *nihumai* into *rahamai*) and Jer. 31. 1–3; also Psalms 5. 8; 35. 6; 47. 10.
[28] Is. 6. 5–7.

of Israel (which could abandon its God although God could never abandon it), which was celebrated in the Dedication.

Jewish Piety

Can we go further and set out more precisely, in the particulars of its practices and the actual perspectives of its faith, the piety of Israel at the moment when Christ was to appear?

Such a study is made very difficult both by the later development of Judaism once it had rejected Christianity, and by anti-Jewish Christian polemics. Later Judaism condemned or denied everything in the Judaism contemporary with the beginnings of Christianity which seemed to be related to Christianity or even capable of leading to it. The polemics of Christians tended more and more to present a caricature of ancient Jewish piety, making Christianity seem opposed to it to such an extent that how it proceeded from it could no longer be perceived.

However, the more new discoveries are made concerning the Judaism contemporary with the Gospel, the more we are struck by all that is common to both. Our manuals continue to erect a too easy contrast between the Pharisees—pious, but with a completely rigidified piety—together with the conservative but irreligious Sadducees, and the "rabble who do not know the law",[29] as if only the latter, among Jews who already had lost everything that made them Jews, had been capable of being touched by the preaching of Christianity. There is no doubt that this is an untenable position.

Not all the priests were so wrapped up in safeguarding the traditional institutions of Israel as to lose sight of its religious meaning. What is called the "Damascus Document"[30] gives evidence of the religious fervour, the eschatological expectation, of many priestly circles.

Nor were all the Pharisees prisoners of a dead legalism. This last supposition is bound up with a notion of the work of the scribes in general, and of the first-century rabbis in particular, which is a real caricature.

More generally, with the multiplication of documents concerning the priestly and rabbinical circles at that period, we can see more clearly how vastly over-simplified are the antitheses we have been accustomed to set up while ignoring a whole dynamic and complex mass.

[29] Cf. John 7. 49.

[30] G. Vermès, *Discovery in the Judean Desert*, New York, 1956, pp. 157ff.

The discoveries of Qumran[31] caused another class to be hastily added to an obviously inadequate classification. But the picture of the Essenes which, it was thought, could be reconstructed, using the mass of new material now available, and fitted into the already existing pattern of Sadducees, Pharisees, Herodians, Zealots, etc., ... has already fallen apart.[32]

What we must recognize, in fact, is that ancient Judaism was something much more rich, more varied in form and, above all, more flexible than we had imagined. Parties certainly existed and their positions tended to crystallize. But an intense fermentation of life and thought was none the less going on, with constant blendings which make it very difficult to attribute this or that document to one or another presumed class or party.

We are just beginning to discover the place taken by communities: the *Chaburoth*,[33] playing a rôle of widely diffused leavening and religious inspiration, a little like that of our religious orders, rather than constituting sects properly so called.

It was later, at the Talmudic period, that the legalism which had originated with the Pharisees, having definitely supplanted the priestly caste, railed against apocalyptic inspiration and against any immediate expectation of the Messiah tending to break with ordinary life. At that period also all the *haggadic* speculations guilty of having paved the way for Christianity, as well as the effort of "Wisdom" opening out the intellectual horizons of paganism[34] to the vision of devout Jews, became suspect or were condemned outright by the masters of *halakah*, the casuistic interpretation of the law. At the same time, all mystical search for, all actual experience of, a divine presence seemed to be extinguished. And yet all this, remaining latent in the Jewish soul, subtly reappears in the periodic resurgences of Cabbalistic gnosis or in the fervour, so often renewed, of groups of *chasidim*.[35]

[31] With the book of Vermès mentioned in the preceding note, compare Millar Burrows, *Dead Sea Scrolls*, Viking Press, New York, 1955.

[32] Compare J. Daniélou, *The Dead Sea Scrolls and Primitive Christianity*, Helicon Press, Baltimore, 1958, or A. Dupont-Sommer, *Les écrits esséniens découverts près de la mer Morte*, Paris, 1959, with the critical remarks of H. E. Del Medico, *L'Énigme des manuscrits de la mer Morte*, Paris, 1957, especially pp. 79ff.

[33] Even if the term is not attested until a later period, it is certainly much more applicable to the groups we have just described than is the term "sects" ordinarily given to them—implying an *a priori* judgment that nothing can justify.

[34] See the still valid remarks of O. Cullmann (inspired by Friedländer) in his book *Le Problème littéraire et historique du roman pseudo-clémentin*, Paris, 1930, pp. 173ff., on the *minim* spoken of by the Talmud.

[35] On this point, see Gershom Sholem, *Major Trends in Jewish Mysticism*, rev. ed., New York, 1946, pp. 80ff.

The narrow vision of itself provided by a certain kind of Talmudic Judaism projected on the past has, consequently, completely deceived us about the Jewish origins of Christianity. Conversely, familiarity with what Jewish tradition today as in the Middle Ages has kept in living form can renew our understanding of this past.[36] This is what the recent discoveries have already verified and furnished with invaluable clarifications.

In the first place, however obvious may have been the tendencies towards ingrowing or even towards sclerosis in the Judaism of the first century which account for the relative unsuccessfulness of Christian preaching, it is a basic error to think of them as dominant. It is true that the Pharisees already tended to codify a casuistry in which the living inspiration of the Torah ran the risk of being rigidified and all creative prophetic inspiration stifled. The priests, for their part, were only too completely victims of a secularization of the ancient Jewish institutions correlative with their attainment of earthly security. And the Herodians, also more or less sincere "collaborators", saw only what was to their immediate interest—but this does not mean that they were necessarily insensible to all authentic spirituality (Herod himself was not).[37] As for their enemies, the Zealots, we must not forget that their Messianism—seemingly wholly of this earth—their racism and their violence had a supernatural background.[38]

But it is more important to realize that the rôle of the scribes was in no way limited—at this period or any other—to the task of strict conservation which we are always tempted to attribute to them. Still less was their horizon entirely bounded by a niggardly casuistry. The scribes of the first century, it should not be forgotten, were the heirs of the ancient "sages" of Israel. And not only had "Wisdom" always been a creative mode of thought, but, far from tending exclusively towards ritual legalism, it was this "Wisdom" which produced, by its own development, what is called apocalypticism.[39] What apocalypticism was like at the beginning of our era, what varied potentialities it included, contradictory perhaps but of a surging ardour—this is probably what we most need to ascertain in order to understand the final, immediately pre-Christian, Jewish spirituality. And it is on this that the recent discoveries have most

[36] Hence the interest of a work like that of L. Gillet, referred to above: *Communion in the Messiah*.

[37] Cf. what is told us in Mark 6. 20.

[38] On these parties, see the succinct analysis of Tricot in his chapter in *Introduction à la Bible*, referred to above.

[39] See Dom Hilaire Duesberg, *Les scribes inspirés*, 2 vols., Paris, 1938 and 1939, as well as the study of D. Deden, "Le 'mystère' paulinien", in *Ephemerides theologicae lovanienses* of 1936, vol. 13.

certainly helped to shed light. It is now certain that we cannot relegate apocalyptic literature to a marginal place in Judaism, as if it had concerned only heterodox circles. This literature seems rather to have expressed, under more or less popular forms, a current in Judaism which had an almost universal influence, crystallizing at least something of the best of Jewish spirituality.[40]

The Apocalypses and Eschatological Expectation

Under the pressure of the precarious circumstances in which Israel had continually lived ever since the Exile among the great powers that ruled the world one after the other, the meditation of the scribes, nourished on the tradition of the last prophets, could no longer confine its hope within the ordinary course of history. Following the book of Daniel, they were no longer tempted, as were the first sages in Israel, to acclimate any merely human wisdom as such. Not only did they now expect from a supernatural "revelation" (this is the meaning of the word "apocalypse") the final solution of the problems posed to those faithful to the Lord by the world and its ways. What is common to all their "apocalypses" is their content as well as their framework, however varied may be its images. All look forward to a historic catastrophe which will be a new divine intervention, not less wonderful than the first Passover or even Creation. And all await it as imminent.

The description St John gives of the present world as "wholly in the power of the Evil One",[41] is the conviction of all these writings, and they express it in equally clear terms. But all likewise believe, in proclaiming that God is to intervene, that he will at last put an end to the kingdom of Belial and substitute his own. All are completely convinced that this will not be accomplished without final catastrophes which will test the faith of the elect. But it was precisely in order to prepare the elect for these disasters, to console or strengthen them, that these apocalypses were written.[42]

It is not surprising that this vision of things was accompanied, as we have come to see more and more clearly, by the appearance of a current of asceticism, in contrast to the optimism of the old religion of Israel. If the present world is condemned, then the believer, far from expecting temporal success to be the seal, even if not the whole reality, of the divine blessings, will cut himself off from such success. If the axe has already been laid at the roots of the tree, according to the phrase of the Baptist, who could still be eager to establish himself in its branches?[43]

[40] See L. Bouyer, *op. cit.*, pp. 156ff. [41] 1 John 5. 19.
[42] See H. H. Rowley, *The Relevance of Apocalyptic*, 2nd ed., London, 1947.
[43] Matt. 3. 10 and Luke 3. 19.

These tendencies, along with the hope in a future life as opposed to the present life, appeared so novel, in Israel, that dualistic Gnosticism and Iranian influences were for a long time brought up to explain them. Actually, they simply went along with the apocalyptic view of things, and as this view is indisputably in the line of the last prophets, so is it also with them that these tendencies are connected.

In the old religion of the patriarchs, the rich were called blessed—a quite natural consequence of the belief in the basic goodness of the Creator and his creation. But Isaias had already said succinctly: "Woe to the rich." And even before him the first prophets had cast doubts on the equivocal blessing of Israel's establishment in Palestine: now changed into a sedentary agricultural people, the former nomads, who had been faithful to their Lord when they lived from day to day under the leadership only of their heavenly King, had put the Baalim of natural fruitfulness in the place of the God of heaven. And their visible kings, like those of the other nations, in taking the place of the invisible King, had institutionalized this infidelity. The great prophet of Jerusalem thus came harshly to identify infidelity with the desire to attain security here below, whether by wealth, by luxurious buildings, or by political manœuvrings undertaken in the name of realism.

Jeremias and Ezechiel went one step further. They proclaimed the man blessed by God to be, not the well-established proprietor or the victorious king, but the proscribed, the exile, the man who seems cursed by God as he is scorned by men. What more novel in Israel, in one sense, and yet none the less more faithful to the pure line of prophetic inspiration than the portrait of the ideal "Servant of God" presented in the second part of the book of Isaias: ". . . We thought him one humiliated, struck by God . . . but it was our sins with which he was laden."[44] In other words, Job, the man of sorrows, is not some extraordinary sinner, struck by a special punishment; not only is he the servant *par excellence*, the friend of God: but it is also possible that his apparent chastisement may be a mystery, the mystery of salvation for the people of God, nay even for all peoples. . . .

The Jewish Communities

A life apart from ordinary life, such we see already sketched out with the Pharisees, but also and still more clearly with the priestly community of Damascus or the one revealed to us by Qumran,

[44] Is. 53. 4–5. On all this, see L. Bouyer, *op. cit.*, pp. 124ff., and my contribution to the collective volume *La Pauvreté*, Paris, 1952, "L'appel du Christ à la Pauvreté".

too clearly belongs to this same line of development for there to be any further need to resort to hypothetical foreign influences to account for it. It was connected quite naturally with the idea of the "remnant" of Israel, hidden in the mass of Israel according to the flesh, but already singled out by God's glance and to be disengaged by trials: an idea eminently prophetic.[45] Its primary manifestations were voluntary fasting carried to a rigorous simplification of all existence and gathering in communities bound together by eschatological expectation. Constant prayer, a more or less immediate preparation for martyrdom in imitation of the great "masters of righteousness", and a renunciation of all settling down in this world, followed normally.

In this line, we need not be astonished to find voluntary celibacy—the acceptance (at first sight so un-Jewish) of dying without descendants—entering into the perspectives deliberately welcomed.[46] The "Kingdom of God" now expected was no longer to be realized through the peaceful triumph and assured prosperity of the just, but through the great tribulation which the just had been the first to sense as imminent.

Jews who had reached this point understood that the divine designs finally open out on "mysteries", secrets impenetrable to merely human wisdom and even to the speculations of pious men when these are based on the ready-made views of Job's friends. It is no wonder that such Jews considered themselves, perhaps sometimes a little too quickly, as those to whom God normally should reveal these "mysteries" hidden from all others, from Jews merely according to the flesh as well as from non-Jews.[47]

The result was the birth, within Judaism itself, of that "gnosis" to be so highly developed within Christianity as well as outside it.

Jewish Gnosis and its Origins

Contrary to what a completely factitious nineteenth-century theory still would have us believe, "gnosis" was in no way originally a "heretical" creation, only later more or less assimilated by

[45] On this idea of the "remnant", see the article of A. Lelièvre on this word, in *Vocabulaire biblique*, published by J.-J. von Allmen, Neuchâtel-Paris, 1954, pp. 250ff.

[46] What Pliny, Philo and Josephus tell us about the Essenes presupposes, or even explicitly states, that the majority practised celibacy. It is less clear in the case of the Qumran community (see the article by A. Tricot already referred to in *Introduction à la Bible*, vol. 2). Outside of what St Luke's Gospel of the Infancy tells us concerning the mentality of the "poor", there is no doubt that John the Baptist and, it would seem, St Paul, even before their adherence to Christ had vowed themselves to celibacy. And this was already true of the prophet Jeremias (16. 1–4). See also Vermès, *op. cit.*, p. 57–8.

[47] See Vermès, *op. cit.*, pp. 138ff.

orthodox thinking thanks to the efforts of the Alexandrian Christians of the third century. Jewish "gnosis" is a product *sui generis* of Judaism, the indubitable heir both of the great prophetic tradition of the eighth to the seventh centuries and of Israelite wisdom. Soon enough, no doubt, it experienced deformations and foreign contaminations. But these were themselves the tributaries of a Judaism most faithful to its own line of development—tributary in their basic concept as well as in certain of their most constant characteristics, beginning with a particular vocabulary. And the most legitimate heir of this primitive "gnosis" was to be another "gnosis" in Christianity, and one no less basically orthodox. The heretical "gnoses" were only as it were embroideries along the edge of this continuous line.[48]

This "gnosis" is rooted in the "knowledge" of God fully developed as to its reality by the last prophets, while the first "sages" had begun to systematize the theory of it.[49]

For the prophets, the "knowledge of God" had a much more definite intellectual content than certain critics would wish. It meant above all the knowledge, specifically Jewish, that God is one and that he is the only Lord. But, certainly, it meant that knowledge as taking possession of the whole being, and as doing so in the first place by obedience to God's commands. It meant also and still more that knowledge as expanded into an invincible confidence, not only in Israel's election, but in God's fidelity, his love—attentive, active, unwearying and unconquerable—for all and for each one in the holy community. It meant life in his presence, and life with him. It meant peace, in the Jewish sense, that is, an abundance of serene life drawn from its Source, in immediate contact with him.[50]

48 The article, "Gnosis", by Bultmann, in the *Theologisches Wörterbuch* of G. Kittel, in spite of its great wealth of information, is typical in its adoption of the ready-made notion of "gnosis" developed by historians of the nineteenth century with no concern for the texts. Yet R. P. Casey, as early as 1935, rightly observed that "gnosis", in the language of Christian antiquity (and we might also say of Jewish antiquity), never designated something heretical; on the contrary, as we shall see, the Fathers always congratulated themselves on possessing the true "gnosis" and refused to consider what the heretics called by the same name as anything other than a pseudo-gnosis ("The Study of Gnosticism", in the *Journal of Theological Studies*, XXXVI, pp. 45–60).

49 E. Baumann, "ידה und seine Derivate", in *Zeitschrift für alt-testamentliche Studien*, XVIII, 1908, pp. 22ff. and 110ff., has clearly shown how the knowledge that we have of God, for the Old Testament, depends on that which God has of us, and this includes our election. However, as Dom Dupont rightly observes in *Gnosis, la connaissance religieuse dans les Épitres de saint Paul*, Louvain–Paris, 1949, p. 76, note 1, in connection with the knowledge of which God is the subject, Baumann also too greatly minimizes the intellectual aspect.

50 André Neher, in *L'Essence du prophétisme*, Paris, 1955, pp. 101ff., certainly has some of the best pages that have ever been written on this subject (also pp. 255–6). He has rightly brought out how the biblical use of ידה to designate

This knowledge implies a personal effort. It is indeed the fruit of a whole life's effort. This does not alter the fact that it remains a grace, the grace above all others: the unique, indivisible experience which God reserves for his own.

This prophetic knowledge was to be continued in the wisdom of Israel. Here it became the principle and, above all, the soul of a practical discernment, of a distillation of individual and collective experience. After the exile and the collapse of the earthly hopes of Israel, it succeeded in so raising up this weight of warmed-over examples, of down-to-earth considerations, that wisdom became a supernatural discernment of God's designs: the acceptance—no longer scandalized, but illuminated and strengthened—of mysteries, of the mystery of divine Providence. At this point, the wisdom of man was absorbed in the Word of God. . . .[51]

With the scribes of the first century, therefore, "knowledge" had become chiefly the profound understanding of the Torah which would enable them, above all, to make a practical application of it to every detail of existence: the *halakah*.[52]

This knowledge was eminently a knowledge of the Scriptures. And, what is more, it was a decidedly traditional knowledge. Together with knowledge of the "written Torah", it meant knowledge of the "oral Torah", the sentences of the Fathers which completed and explained it by applying it. But it would be a complete mistake to conclude that, as a consequence, it must have been nothing more than a scribe's science, consisting wholly in memory and rationalization. The scribe himself consciously remained the heir of the prophets. Even while he pretended to no autonomous inspiration such as theirs, he was conscious of possessing a charism.[53] With the last authors of the Bible, and doubtless also—although to a lesser degree and, above all, with less security—with the authors of the apocalypses, this consciousness of inspiration went along with the use of what has been called the "anthological" style,[54] meaning an expression of what is most personal to the author in terms assimilated from earlier writers. Here there is no need to contrast charism with meditation on a text *ne varietur*, nor charism

---

sexual union marks the close connection between knowledge and union in Hebraic thought. But it is not so certain that the formulations of Amos 3. 2: "I have known but you alone", nor even that of Osee 13. 5: "You alone have I known", can be interpreted along the same lines (Bultmann himself, *op. cit.*, casts doubt on this interpretation of K. Cramer's).

[51] See the works of Duesberg and Deden mentioned above.

[52] See Dom Dupont, *op. cit.*, pp. 215ff.

[53] *Ibid.*, pp. 214ff. and 254ff.

[54] See Grelot, "The Formation of the Old Testament", Conclusion of vol. I, *Introduction à la Bible*.

with tradition: on the contrary, they are conceived as implying one another. It was in meditating on the Torah or the ancient prophets that the scribe felt himself inspired. His inspiration did not supplant the tradition with which he was nourished: it illuminated it.

Again, we need not be surprised that, alongside the *halakah* and its minute precepts that appear to us as mere casuistry, the scribe placed the *haggadah* and its creations, so free that they appear to us as fantasy.[55]

The *haggadah* was not a mere illustration of ancient accounts, giving them reality by putting them within our reach. The creative *midrash* which it composed of elements provided by tradition illuminated the future with lights borrowed from the past, but it always presupposed a constant outpouring of the Spirit on his people. Its most characteristic product at the period when Christianity was to be born was what we call messianism.[56]

Messianism is the chief creative formulation given by the apocalypses to the eschatological sense, carried to the frenzy of immediate imminence. Messianic hope, nourished by the whole history of faith, looked for the decisive divine intervention as now at hand, while some of the characteristics of this intervention already seemed to shine out through the letter of the ancient texts as also through the shell of contemporary events. And this was particularly true in connection with the providential personage whose appearance, generally speaking, was the centre of all hope.

The "Messiah" was to be the "anointed" of God; the "son of David" and at the same time the "son of God", which meant to begin with simply the adopted child of the divine power. Victorious like David and faithful as he, the Messiah would re-establish the royal house of Israel and thereby assure the triumph of the divine Kingdom itself. The Psalms of Solomon give us a popular description of all this. Providential, if not supernatural, characteristics are not lacking; but the picture remains that of an earthly king with a particularly marvellous destiny, even though, it is true, his coming was to be the sign of cosmic transformations. The book of Henoch, on the contrary, envisages a personage who is directly supernatural. Here the Elect, to whom is entrusted the judgment and triumph of God over all hostile powers, demonic and otherwise, is the same as the "Son of Man" of Daniel, whose name he

55 On these two ideas, see in Lauterbach, *Rabbinic Essays*, the chapter entitled "The Ethics of the Halakah", pp. 259ff., and in Marmorstein, *Studies in Jewish Theology*, Oxford, 1950, the chapters on "The Background of the Haggadah" and "The Imitation of God in the Haggadah", pp. 106ff.

56 Even though we cannot accept all his conclusions, the fine book of Sigmund Mowinckel, *He that Cometh*, Oxford, 1956, must be considered to have renewed the study of this problem.

also bears. While he is a "man", this man is wholly supernatural—in his origin, in his mission, and in the way in which he fulfils it.

To judge from later Jewish exegesis, it does not seem as though, before Jesus' preaching, the personality of the suffering servant of Isaias, 53, had generally imposed itself as another image (and still less as the decisive image) of the hoped-for Elect. But we can ask whether in Israel, at this time, there were not more presentiments of the possible application of this text to the Messiah than we are led to think by a later Jewish tradition crystallized in opposition to the Christian interpretation. For, in the book of Henoch, some relationships can be found already sketched out between the wholly supernatural "Son of Man" of Daniel and the humiliated Servant of Isaias.[57] Furthermore, some apocalyptic writings, like the *Ascension of Isaias* in which neither the earthly Messiah nor the "Son of Man" appears, contain the more or less explicit statement of a rôle for the suffering of the just in the events at the end of time.[58]

However, as has been noted, it is not ordinarily the term for "knowledge" (*dahat*, rendered as *gnosis* in the Greek translations) which was applied to speculations of this kind.[59] Only the name "apocalypse", or "revelation", is connected with them, as meaning something objectively given. The term "gnosis", on the contrary, was applied to the discernment of what was prescribed by the Torah rightly understood, that is according to the *halakah* and the interior attitude corresponding to the eschatological—and, more precisely, the messianic expectation.

"Knowledge", then, always meant entering into God's designs, adapting oneself to them, and not simply speculating about them. In the line of purest Judaism, it certainly implied a dualism or rather a duality. But this was in no way a metaphysical dualism, reflected in intellectual criteria dividing *a priori* what is good from what is bad with the purpose precisely of recognizing which is which, but without hoping to change bad into good. The dualism implied in Jewish "gnosis" is rather a *historical* dualism, resulting from the disobedience of certain created spirits, their rebellion and the judgment which God, directly or by his "anointed", is to bring down on them. Hence "gnosis" includes an essentially moral choice,

[57] On this point consult the concise investigation of William Manson, in Appendix C of his work *Jesus the Messiah*, London, 1943, p. 171.

[58] This is the underlying theme of the whole part of this work which is certainly anterior to Christianity, entitled *The Martyrdom of Isaias* (edited separately, in an English translation, by R. H. Charles, in vol. II of *The Apocrypha and Pseudepigrapha of the Old Testament in English*, Oxford, 1913, pp. 159–62).

[59] See Dom Dupont, *op. cit.*, pp. 199ff. This author always has a tendency somewhat to overdo the contrast. Cf. in the contrary sense the writings of Qumran referred to by J. Daniélou in *The Dead Sea Scrolls and Primitive Christianity*, p. 100.

retaining "the fear of the Lord" as its sole principle of judgment, just as did ancient Jewish wisdom. It is in this sense that we must understand the Jewish prayers, so characteristic of this period, which ask God himself to grant "gnosis"[60] as his supreme gift, or give thanks for having been given it.

But it would be going to the opposite extreme to take away from this "gnosis" every intellectual element or to deny that it had any. Like the Wisdom that preceded it, and the "knowledge of God" of the prophets, "gnosis" included very clear certitudes. A certain glimpse of the invisible, pregnant with the future in which it will become visible to all, constituted at once the presupposition and the fruit of this apocalyptic "gnosis". It was because the scribe knew that the world was not limited to what everyone could see of it, because he believed that he had some perception of what lay beyond it, that, when he meditated or composed an apocalypse, he was aware or made aware of those great deeds of God which were to be accomplished. And it was because he awaited them and prepared himself for them, that he believed himself better able than other men to discern these future deeds, as he meditated on the Scriptures in the school of the Fathers, in union with that faithful "remnant" which lived more intensely than the great mass of the people the religion of all Israel.

In this respect, there is no longer any reason to oppose the "futurism" essential to any apocalypse to the "here and now" inherent in all mysticism. In spite of the artificial antitheses conceived by certain modern historians in a far too *a priori* way, the religion of Israel has always included a mystical, contemplative element. There is no doubt that this element was intensified at the period we are speaking of. And this intensification is a final constituent element in that unique Jewish "gnosis" which we are attempting to describe.

Jewish Mysticism

The focus of true Jewish mysticism lies in the conviction—so peculiar, indeed, to the people of Israel—that the same God who is the God of heaven, the supremely transcendent God, is yet the God of his people. We must understand this as meaning not only that he is the God who concerns himself with the people whom he chose in the covenant, but also the God who lives with them, who makes himself their travelling-companion here below. The more decided the opposition to idolatry on the part of the prophets and

[60] G. Vermès, *Discovery in the Judean Desert*, p. 143, is one of the rare writers who has seen the importance of these prayers for an exact understanding of Jewish gnosis.

of the Judaism, unanimous on this point, which was their heir, the more clearly was maintained the conviction: God is "with us".[61]

The priestly tradition localized this presence in the holy of holies of the Temple, on the propitiatory, in the space between the Cherubim. With the refusal to materialize this presence in any idol went the insistence on its mysterious manifestation through the dark cloud from which radiated a shining glory. This is what the rabbis called the *Shekinah*, the Dwelling of God with his own, manifested first in the column of cloud and fire when the people went out from Egypt, then in the supernatural storm of Sinai. Descending on the tabernacle, still visibly, it inhabited the temple of Solomon. Then it was to appear no more to profane eyes. The notion became increasingly spiritualized. Did not Ezechiel see the Presence leaving the temple soiled by idols, to make itself the invisible companion of the exiles? And the rabbis came to say that where two or three meet together to meditate on the Torah, the *Shekinah* is in their midst.[62]

But this spiritualization did not mean evaporation. The reality of the Presence was never in doubt. That it might manifest itself was the hope of Israel: "O Thou that art enthroned between the Cherubim, appear!"[63] The hope of the most devout was to see it—as the angels see it and are blessed, not as the wicked see it and are consumed. The nostalgia of so many of the cultual psalms, of 41–42 and 83, as well as the ardent hope of the psalms of the kingdom, centres on these thoughts. If Moses was so great, was it not finally because he saw God on the mountain and spoke with him face to face, as a friend talks to his friend? In expressing the Christian hope: "To know God as we are known", St Paul only gives his own formulation, in the most Jewish terms possible, of the most Jewish of desires.[64]

This mysticism was in no way opposed—quite otherwise—to eschatological expectation. Their fusion crystallized, for Jewish meditation, in the figure of Moses and also in that of Elias. He too had seen the divine Glory of Horeb.[65] The renewed vision of this Glory snatched him from this world and transported him beyond its present limits.[66] Before him, Henoch himself, having "walked

[61] W. J. Phythian-Adams remains up to the present time the author who has best appreciated the importance of this theme in the piety of Ancient Israel: *The People and the Presence*, Oxford, 1942.

[62] See L. Bouyer, *The Meaning of Sacred Scripture*, pp. 98ff.

[63] Cf. Psalm 17. 11 and 2 Sam. 22. 11; Psalm 98. 1; Hab. 3. 2; and Dan. 3. 55 (these two latter texts according to the reading of the Septuagint).

[64] 1 Cor. 13. 12. See the commentary on this theme in the work of Dom Dupont, *Gnosis, etc.*, pp. 51ff.

[65] 1 Kings 19. 1ff. [66] 2 Kings 2. 1 to 15.

with God" here below, "was found no more, because God had taken him away".[67] (It was not for nothing that the author of one of the most popular apocalypses of the period we are dealing with placed his work under the auspices precisely of Henoch.)

For even when the *Shekinah* was represented as dwelling in the Temple, this was only an intermediate, a provisional Presence of the God of heaven whom no house made by the hands of man can contain. It was a condescension, in present history which must have an end, by which God prepared—or, rather, prepared his own—finally to transcend its limitations. For the *Shekinah*, as Ezechiel saw it, was not a static presence: it was carried by the flaming chariot of the Cherubim and the Ophanim, the *Merkabah*.[68] To see the *Shekinah* is, therefore, to be prepared to be carried away by the *Merkabah*, which can never be tied down to earth....[69] Whither? no mans knows: towards the unknown, towards the inaccessible light in which God dwells, towards that city of God which the *Syriac Apocalypse of Baruch* had already described in its own terms as not the earthly Jerusalem, but another Jerusalem, wholly of heaven, one with the initial paradise which the Messiah will bring back, or, much better, into which he will reintroduce us....[70]

In return, this expectation of the blessed catastrophe to come was in no way opposed to its being individually anticipated by those who, far from fearing it, went out to the desert as if to meet it. Already, to the degree of their preparation, their fidelity to the Torah, their prayer nourished by meditating on God's great deeds in the past, they believed that they might receive at least some rays heralding the coming of the *Shekinah*, drink some drops of the water of life which God will lavish on his chosen ones.

The terms which we have just used recall the formulation of one of the psalms:

> In your light, we shall see light,
> with you is the source of life.[71]

But, above all, they call up the mysticism of St John. The documents found at Qumran assure us of the completely Jewish and traditional character of meditation on these two connected themes of the divine light and life promised to the believer.[72] And the Odes of Solomon obviously witness to a line of contemplative piety that was simply to develop from the best of Jewish spirituality in the purest and intensest fire of the New Testament.[73]

[67] Gen. 5. 24. [68] Ezech. 1.

[69] On this theme in Jewish mysticism, see G. Sholem, *Major Trends in Jewish Mysticism*, pp. 40ff.

[70] 4. 2–7. [71] Psalm 35. 10. [72] See J. Daniélou, *op. cit.*

[73] See J. Daniélou, *Théologie du judéo-christianisme*, Paris, 1958, pp. 40ff.

The Berakah

It is quite certain that the Judaism we have just described had already overflowed, before Christ's coming, the old framework of Jewish religious life. It sketches the outlines of the nascent Christian religious life.

The great mass of Jews, doubtless, remained attached to the sacrificial worship of the Temple. But Jewish piety, more or less consciously, sought and found other means of spiritual nourishment and other modes of liturgical expression.

The origin of the worship of the synagogue was explained for a long time as being simply a substitute for the Temple liturgy, necessitated by the Babylonian exile. But it seems that services of readings and prayers were in fact known to the Jews before exile. The Temple worship, furthermore, certainly included, from early times if not always, singing psalms to accompany the sacrifices. And, far from simply opposing the prophet to the priest, as did the historians of the nineteenth century, contemporary historians see the origin both of prophecy and of the very idea of the Torah in the *Toroth*, the more or less detailed oracles given by the priests themselves on the occasion of ritual celebrations.[74]

What remains indisputable is the increasing polarization of Israelite piety, from the time of the exile on, towards the worship of the synagogue, that is chiefly towards the meditative reading of the Bible and a prayer nourished by that reading. What was to characterize Jewish piety henceforth was, let us repeat, the religion of the Bible, but with the qualifications we have already made. We must not think that, in the context of the new synagogal ritual in which the reading of the Bible—even private reading—was located, the word absorbed the rite properly so called. It was rather that a new kind of rite was developed in closest contact with the word, the divine word proclaimed: the word prayed. Nothing is more typical of this than the *berakah*, the blessing-thanksgiving.

We have pointed out the change of meaning, very obvious throughout the psalms, which came about little by little in the use of the expression "sacrifice of thanksgiving" or "of praise". First this referred to a particular type of sacrifice which accompanied (or was accompanied by) a prayer expressing gratitude to God for some outstanding favour. Very quickly, perhaps even from the outset, the psalm chanted on this occasion was considered an integral part of the sacrifice. And soon the "sacrifice of praise" or "thanks-

[74] See J. Pedersen, "The Role played by inspired persons among the Israelites and the Arabs", in *Studies in Old Testament Prophecy presented to T. H. Robinson*, Edinburgh, 1950.

giving" came to designate the psalm itself: this is what was called the "sacrifice of the lips".[75]

In the same sense, one of the essential characteristics of synagogal piety was what we might equally well call the spiritualization of the sacrificial rite or the ritualization of all existence. For here less than ever does the spiritualization of the religious institutions of Israel mean any emptying out of their religious content, but rather, its permeating the whole of life. This is what tended to produce the *berakah*.[76] Its purpose was to make every action of the devout Israelite a sacred, a truly liturgical action. To this end, it had him take and express in connection with everything an interior attitude of grateful faith in the creative Word, source of all good. "Blessed be Thou, O Lord our God, King of eternity, Thou who hast . . ."— here follows the mention of the divine action expressed in biblical terms, recognized, that is, as basic to the action to be carried out. Thereby, what the faithful Jew was about to do was blessed and at the same time and inseparably he caused the glory of it to ascend to God. The *berakah* as a whole thus includes a true consecratory blessing and a thanksgiving. Or, better, everything is consecrated by thanksgiving, according to the typical phrase of St Paul in the First Epistle to Timothy: "Every creature of God is good, and nothing is to be rejected when it is taken with thanksgiving, since it is consecrated by the word of God, and by prayer."[77]

The last words happily define the spirituality proper to the *berakah*. Born of the Word of God, it is first of all an act of faith in God the Creator and Saviour, whose presence and redeeming action are discovered by faith to be shining through all things and every event. But this act of faith is already a prayer: a prayer in which we give ourselves up to the divine goodness in abandoning ourselves to the will of God made known through his word. We can say, consequently, that in the *berakah* is summed up the whole content of "gnosis" as we have described it, or again that the purest Jewish gnosis is its central object.

[75] In a text like verse 13 of Psalm 55 the reference would still seem to be to the ritual action prescribed in Lev. 7. 12–15, or 22. 29. But in Psalm 49. 14, the "sacrifice of praise" is clearly contrasted with victims. It is in the prophet Osee, however, that we see "the fruit of the lips" (according to the most probable reading) presented as the object of the sacrifice (14. 1), a theme taken up in the Epistle to the Hebrews (13. 15).

[76] On this subject, D. Hedegard, *Seder R. Amram Gaon*, pp. xxiiiff. and 139ff., must be consulted. See also A. Lukyn Williams, *Tractate Berakoth*, London, 1921. The recent article of Audet, "Esquisse historique du genre littéraire de la 'Bénédiction' juive et de l'"Eucharistie' chrétienne" in the *Revue biblique* of July 3, 1958, pp. 371ff., contains useful remarks, but is based on a narrow systematization with *a priori* assumptions of a deceptive clarity which force the texts more than they explain them.

[77] 1 Tim. 4. 4–5.

This is clearly indicated in the great daily *berakah* which constitutes the "Prayer" *par excellence*: the *Tephillah* of the Eighteen Blessings. The core of it is in this plea: "Instruct us, O Lord our God, in the knowledge (*dahat*) of Your ways and circumcise our heart that we may fear You."

It should be noted, however, that this sacralization of the whole of life permeated with "knowledge" found a new ritual focus which apparently tended to supplant the ancient sacrifices. And this was the common meal, the meal of the Jewish family assembled for the sabbath or a solemn feast, and still more the community meal of those *Chaburoth* the importance of which Qumran has revealed to us.

Among all the acts of the day, as is clearly shown by the treatise on the *Berakoth* of the *Mishnah* with the abundant commentary of the *Tosefta*, none lends itself more readily than the meal to this consecration by the word of God and prayer mentioned by the Apostle. Here, above all, man is led daily to recognize that his life is God's gift and that it cannot be faithfully lived except in thanksgiving.

But for the Israelite who ate the fruits of the holy land, this primary truth took on a new meaning. What he ate was blessed by him as being the fruit of the saving act by which God had freed him from the godless slavery of Egypt and taken him into the holy Kingdom of his love. And this new meaning, properly Paschal, was enhanced when the community of the faithful assembled, the devout "remnant", separated by their faith and hope from the "godless who have no hope". Their meal of communion became a real anticipation of the messianic banquet in which God would finally gather all his own into his Kingdom, together with Abraham, Isaac and Jacob. Then, after a succession of ritual blessings over all the dishes, over all the actions of this banquet, beginning with the breaking of the bread solemnly carried out by the person presiding, the great blessing of the final cup synthesized this whole pre-Christian Jewish spirituality which we can already call eucharistic. The evening light had been blessed, the incense, blessed in turn, had been burned; having washed his hands, the celebrant invited all present to give thanks:

> Let us give thanks to the Lord our God.
> This is fitting and right.

There followed a magnificent prayer, still used in the Jewish liturgy today, in which we already find the outline of the Christian anaphoras.[78]

[78] The most ancient known form of this prayer is to be found in the work of David Hedegard already mentioned, pp. 146ff.

It recalls creation and the first redemption by the Passover. Then the thanksgiving centres on the food provided by the promised land and on the knowledge of God that accompanies it. Whence follows the express consecration of the community to its God, and, with this self-abandonment in obedient faith to his designs, the final plea that he may carry out in the imminent eschatological future what he inaugurated in his great works of the past.

The Qumran texts, and what Philo and Josephus tell us about the Essenes, clearly bring out the fact that, for the most devout even of the Jewish priests, this ritual meal had come to take the place reserved of old for the Temple sacrifices.[79]

Palestinian Judaism and the Gospel

Certain readers may think that we have idealized this sketch; others, more precisely, that we have christianized it. Yet it is made up only of elements taken from what we know through Jewish tradition itself and commented on as this tradition itself comments on them. It is true that what we have described is not simply any kind of Jewish piety, but the piety of those Jews whom St Luke describes as waiting for the consolation of Israel. Undoubtedly, we have gathered together and brought out everything which, in the Judaism of the first century, was related to the Christianity to be born. But Christianity was born precisely from the convergence of all these elements. To say this is not to ignore its creative newness, but to recognize the providential preparations granted by God. The piety we have just described was that of Palestinian Jews such as those who became the first converts of Jesus. Above all, it is what could have been the piety of John the Baptist. It is what explains to us on the human level how the *Magnificat,* after the *Fiat mihi secundum verbum tuum,* could have flowered on the lips of Mary.

Hellenistic Judaism

We still need to ask ourselves what special place the Judaism not of Palestine but of the diaspora might have occupied in the prehistory of Christian spirituality.

An *a priori* theory still exists, inherited from the nineteenth century, of a basic opposition between the Judaism of Palestine, remaining Hebrew in thought as in language, and the Judaism of the diaspora and especially of Alexandria, become more or less completely hellenized. This picture of things, the product of an Hegelian scheme of history, is so familiar to modern historians that they no longer have the courage to rid themselves of it. Yet it does not hold

[79] See the texts and commentary in G. Vermès, *op. cit.*, pp. 38ff and 54ff.

up in face of the facts. St Paul is, as it were, the living refutation of this theory: "a Hebrew and son of a Hebrew", a Pharisee, a disciple of Gamaliel . . . and yet a Jew of the Roman city of Tarsus, speaking Greek as his mother-tongue, widely instructed in Stoic philosophy and morality, with no discernible trace of any conflict between these two aspects of his personality. But we have many other proofs of the concord and even of the constant communication that existed between these two parts of Judaism even up to the fall of Jerusalem. The Jews of Palestine never seem to have seriously suspected the supposed "hellenization" of their Greek-speaking colleagues, nor were these in the least conscious of being in any way cut off from their roots.

In fact, far from the spiritual assimilation which has been attributed to them, the "Hellenistic" Jews of Alexandria and elsewhere give witness of an astonishing fidelity to the most distinctive features of Jewish spirituality. And, what is more, everything concurs to indicate that it was they who "judaized"—and this to an unsuspected degree—a considerable part of Hellenism.[80]

The Greek version of the Bible, the work of the Alexandrian community, by clothing the Bible in Greek enabled it to retain its whole influence over Jews far from Jerusalem.[81] This Greek version, moreover, was also the instrument of a proselytism with a widely diffused and incalculable influence. The attempt is still stubbornly made to present first Hermetism and then Neo-Platonism as the chief means whereby Greek thought and religious characteristics penetrated first into Judaism and then into Christianity. But it is high time to consider at least the patent historical fact that Neo-Platonism, as to the greater part of its original elements and, doubtless to an even greater extent, mystical Hermetism were primarily products of this Jewish influence.

The last biblical writings, which come to us precisely through the Greek of the Septuagint—some of them (like the book called that of the Wisdom of Solomon) having been originally written in Greek —witness vigorously to this assimilating power of transplanted Judaism. With the hellenizing of its language, of its art, and even to some degree of its philosophical language, the book of Wisdom remains in its essence typically Jewish, in unfailing continuity with the whole Old Testament.[82]

[80] There is no good over-all study of Greek-speaking Judaism. Lacking this, the chapter devoted to Alexandrian Judaism by Jules Lebreton in the first volume of his *Histoire du dogme de la Trinité*, Paris, 1917, may still be read with profit.

[81] See *Introduction à la Bible*, vol. I, Gen. Int., sec. II, ch. I B (by H. Cazelles and P. Grelot).

[82] *Ibid.*, the chap. by A. Lefèvre on the Deuterocanonical Books.

Philo

Philo's is the personality—although it is the most commonly travestied—which best reveals the hellenized Judaism that was actually much more nearly a judaizing Hellenism. We could not devote to him the complete study he deserves without unduly lengthening this introductory chapter. But we need to consider his thought at some length, both because of his clearly representative character and because of the later influence which he exercised.[83]

This Jew of a great Alexandrian family, the courageous defender of his people in the Hellenistic Roman city, was almost the exact contemporary of Christ. He is persistently presented as a Greek philosopher, vaguely eclectic, who, at the most, clothed in biblical images, by the fallacious means of allegory, a thought foreign to Judaism except for a few biblical ideas also transformed into philosophic concepts. It would be difficult to make up a more completely mistaken picture, although it is true that Philo himself did a great deal to create this impression. But the same impression is continually being created by brilliant Jews who assimilate to the most astonishing extent the language, the culture and the superficial customs of widely varying civilizations, but, beneath all this, manage to preserve, with truly extraordinary fidelity, not only their faith, but their customs, their religious conception—so different from that of any other people—of the whole of life.

Philo, doubtless, spoke Greek as his mother tongue (it is not certain that he was ignorant of Hebrew in spite of all the confident statements to the contrary, but it is certain that no Semitic language could have been more to him than a dead or foreign tongue). He had a specialist's knowledge of the most diverse Greek philosophers (not only through the epitomized handbooks so abundant at his time and particularly in his city of Alexandria, but also through wide first-hand reading). And he aspired to join their ranks, to have his own thought examined and accepted by everyone concerned with these philosophies.

His position on the intellectual plane was in complete accord with his political status: in this Hellenistic city, Jews were at home, not as second-class citizens, but on the same level with everyone else. But no more than he would admit, for all this, that Jews should modify the religious practices essential to their way of life, did he think they should change their beliefs. Quite the contrary, he was

83 A complete bibliography may be found in the excellent work by J. Daniélou, *Philon d'Alexandrie*. The works of Philo are available in the editions of Cohn-Wendland, Berlin, 1896–1930, and of F. H. Colson and G. H. Whitaker, London–Cambridge (Mass.), 1928–52.

clearly convinced that he would triumphantly answer all the unsolved questions in Greek thought by the verities of the Bible. If he was not afraid to be found openly receptive to the most diverse elements of Stoic and Platonic thought, this was because he was so completely convinced that the partial truths discovered by these philosophies must all find their place in revealed truth. He did not even believe, in fact, that they had been able to discover anything substantial except by ways more or less directly derived from Jewish revelation.

While he concerned himself eagerly with problems of physics, of metaphysics and, above all, of ethics, he remained a Jewish exegete of the Bible, and an exegete with immediately missionary preoccupations. His universalism was not that of an eclectic ready to hail everything indifferently and to admit everything pell-mell: it was that of an apostle, intelligent but in no way a syncretist. Eager to win his fellow citizens to his faith, he was ready to make all kinds of adaptations but he refused any compromises.

Above all, he was a spiritual thinker, and as such, astonishingly close to the spiritual Palestinian Jews we have just described, both as to the bases of his doctrine and as to his practice. Like them, he searched the Scriptures primarily to draw out precepts for living. The concern of the *halakah* was his first concern also:[84] how does the Bible teach us to live? And with him as with the Jews of Palestine, what seems at first sight to be leading merely towards casuistry or—at best—towards a co-ordinated system of religious ethics, was actuated by an inspiration undeniably mystical. If there is one point on which he differed from Palestinian Judaism, it is that with him apocalyptic curiosity gave place to the first attempt to make a systematic study of mysticism. Doubtless in doing so he seems at first to have done away with eschatological expectation. But the profound desire for personal encounter with God which animated this expectation, far from being dimmed, in him opens out into full consciousness.

It is perhaps here that Philo's originality, formerly ignored, shines out both in relation to Greek philosophy and to Palestinian Judaism: the conscious search for God by the individual person replacing in his thought the simply moral or intellectual search of ancient Hellenism as well as the expectation of the coming of God, in history more than in the individual soul, so characteristic of the Judaism of Jerusalem.

[84] This is what R. Cadiou has brought out in the Introduction to his edition and translation of "The Migration of Abraham" ("Sources chrétiennes," No. 47) Paris, 1957, pp. 9ff.

Philo and Rabbinicism

We must be no less on guard against ignoring everything directly connecting Philo with the rabbis of Palestine. His insistence on the divine transcendence, including even the tendency to avoid the divine names, and the very special way in which he explains this transcendence under deceptively Greek clothing, remains not only Jewish but a direct tributary of rabbinicism. His "logos", his "powers", may borrow all possible literary disguises from the Stoicism or the Platonism of the period. There is no need to try to reconcile these contradictory elements. They are merely incidental trappings, very much in the style of the haggidic commentary only transposed into a Greek mode of expression, which clothed the speculations of the Hebrew-speaking rabbis on the *Memra* and the angels. Only thus can be explained the non-separation from God and the non-confusion with him of that whole world of intermediaries, as well as their no less disconcerting ability to be distinguished from one another indefinitely without ever becoming opposed or even isolated.

The most curious thing is that Philo himself continually tells us that here is the primary substratum of his thought. But modern commentators are so determined to make him a Greek philosopher and not a Jewish theologian that they do not even take the trouble to listen to him on this point, and so they persist in looking for impossible solutions to an imaginary problem. This being so, when he speaks in the style of a hierophant and presents his mystical piety in the language of the mysteries, we must guard against the complete misunderstanding into which Goodenough has fallen.[85] Philo never had the slightest idea of a mystery-religion set up by an ultra-hellenized Judaism with himself as its proponent. According to all the data provided by other sources and by his texts themselves—when one does not try to read into them by force something quite other than what they say—it is quite clear that such "Jewish mysteries" never existed, either at Alexandria or anywhere else.

Philo, quite simply, following Plato and many others, habitually used the poetic terminology of the Greek mysteries in speaking of any truth that was difficult to grasp (he does so even when he is dealing prosaically with the very obscure considerations of Stoic physics). But he uses this terminology in particular to say to the Alexandrian Greeks who surrounded him what St Paul was to say to the Greeks of Athens: the "unknown God" whom you have

[85] *By Light Light, The Mystic Gospel of Hellenic Judaism*, New Haven, 1935.

sought without finding, I will bring you to him. For Philo, in other words, "the great mysteries", the only "initiation" worthy of the name and of the aura with which it was surrounded were the highest religious experience he knew of. And this experience was wholly Jewish. It was the experience of Moses. Only he, on Sinai, had actually known it in its fullness. But towards this insurpassable and probably inaccessible paradigm the whole religious experience which was the proper possession of Israel was oriented and directed.[86]

Philo's "Theory"

This experience, in fact, presupposes the absolute transcendence of God. If it was given the name *theoria*, this in no way meant the kind of intellectual experience for which Aristotle or Plato used this term: the simple vision, global and intuitive, of the ideas towards which discursive thought leads.[87] On the contrary, in the most express fashion, Philo's *Theoria* presupposes the cessation of all experiences of this kind.[88] Neither does it mean entering into a region beyond the ordinary modes of human knowing to which a man might attain by his own efforts: it is the supreme gift of God.[89] *Theoria*, in Philo's sense, is the communication of a divine *pneuma* which, in spite of all the expressions taken from the Stoics, is in no way a deity immanent to the world or one in which the world is immersed. On the contrary, it is a *pneuma* itself transcendent, which in some way takes the place, in us, of our own spirit, our *nous*.[90]

Nor can any effort to purify merely the understanding lead us towards such an experience or, better, prepare us for it. What is needed is that moral purification, the work of piety above all, which God himself carries out in his own, as is shown in all the biblical

[86] It is to W. Völker that credit is due for having brought out the fact that Philo is a spiritual writer, and basically Jewish in his inspiration: *Fortschritt und Vollendung bei Philo von Alexandrien*, Leipzig, 1938.

[87] Yet Philo was well aware of an inferior contemplation: of the cosmos (*De spec. leg.*, III, 1–2; vol. V of the Cohn-Wendland ed., p. 129), or of the powers (which seems to describe the same experience: *op. cit.*, I, 332; *ibid.*, p. 69). This can also be found in the Alexandrian Fathers and in Evagrius.

[88] Cf. *De Abrahamo*, 122; IV, p. 24. This idea of the simplification necessary to see God, of the going beyond all multiplicity which alone can unite us with him, is found again both in Plotinus and in Christian writers such as Evagrius.

[89] *Leg. alleg.*, I, 38; I, pp. 59–60.

[90] *Quis rer. div. her.*, 264–5; III, p. 51. This text is at the origin of the very notion of ecstasy. Many mystics, both Christian and non-Christian, have used its terminology, and it is not always easy to see the exact meaning that they give to it. Also, Philo himself speaks of ecstasy as a "sober intoxication", another expression which was to be much used. (*De opif. mundi*, 71; I, p. 19.)

accounts.[91] Only by this road can we arrive at gnosis, which is essentially the knowledge of God as he is in himself.[92] This is why it is the royal road, for it leads to an encounter with the King.[93]. Its term is a second birth, a birth from the divine Word, making us children of the Logos.[94] It divinizes us in the sense that it makes us beings truly akin to God; none the less he does not cease to be unique, nor does man cease to be man and created by him.[95]

All this—still without using the word, which only came into use much later and in a Christian setting—constituted the first fully explicit, fully defined "mysticism". It was made explicit and defined in Greek terms. But, in this process, as has hitherto been too seldom noticed, this mysticism fashioned its own vocabulary. And it is certainly remarkable that it uses Greek terms already provided with a religious meaning, such as "mystic", only in a purely metaphorical sense. By contrast, all the substantial ideas on which it is based and with which it is constructed are biblical.

Philo's synthesis, doubtless, was his own. And it came to have an astonishing success outside of Israel. What is "mystical" about Plotinus was taken from Philo almost as such. What is similar in the Hermetic writings can hardly be explained by any other source. Thus it was Philo who more or less impregnated Alexandrian Hellenism with Jewish religiousness. To derive Philonian mysticism

[91] *De Cherub.*, 42; I, p. 178. For Philo, Moses is the model of this purification effected in us by God himself. It might be thought that the supreme experience to which it leads, as Philo conceived it, has been fully realized, in his opinion, only in Moses. See *De sacr. Ab. et C.*, 8; I, p. 201. Cf. *De gigant.*, 54; II, p. 52, and *De plant.*, 26–27; *ibid.*, pp. 129–30.

[92] *Quod Deus sit. immut.*, 143; II, p. 82.

[93] *Ibid.*, 160, p. 86.

[94] *De Conf. ling.*, 146; II, p. 247; they become *paidas logou.* The idea of the second birth is introduced in *Quaest. et sol. in Exod.*, II, 46–47.

[95] Strictly speaking, Philo does not speak of "divinization" or "deification". It is the Greek Fathers who introduced these expressions. He himself speaks of *ektheiazein* (*Leg. alleg.*, III, 44; I, p. 115) or of *epitheiasmos* (*De spec. leg.*, III, 1–2; V, p. 129). The first expression signifies rather "to transport to the level of the gods" and the second, "divine inspiration". Philo explains himself again in the *Quaest. et sol. in Exod.* by saying that the soul is "transformed into a divine being, to the point of becoming related to God and truly divine" (II, 29). We are borrowing this translation from Jules Gros, *La Divinisation du chrétien d'après les Pères Grecs*, Paris, 1938, p. 92, whose exposition is complete and faithful, except that he accepts without criticism the thesis of Pascher (*'Η βασιλικη 'οδος, der Koenigsweg zum Widergeburt und Vergöttung bei Philo von Alexandria*, Paderborn, 1931), according to which the mysticism of Philo is wholly borrowed from some Hellenistic mysticism . . . something which, oddly enough, it is impossible to find the slightest trace of except in authors much later than Philo who were certainly acquainted with him!

Furthermore, on the fact that this transformation does not prevent man's remaining a man (*De somn.*, II, 233; III, p. 279) while God remains unique, and that this name can be applied to other beings only by catachresis, Philo is also as categorical as possible (*ibid.*, I, 229, p. 235). Thus nothing in his mysticism actually transgresses the tenets of Judaism.

from Hellenism necessitates a complete reversal of the most securely established chronological data, as well as the conclusions of any at all searching analysis of the idea in question. Such a derivation explains Philo backwards by means of later and obviously syncretist Hellenism which certainly owes to him any "mystical" characteristics it may have. Before Philo, we seek in vain for anything like this in Hellenism, and it is to his Jewish piety that he owes all the constituents of his mysticism.

Philo and Allegory

One last trait distinctive of Philo and of his later influence on Christian spirituality is the eminently allegorical character of his exegesis. The word "mystical" was first, in fact, attached precisely to this type of exegesis, and it was from this primary technical sense that it came to acquire its specifically spiritual meaning.

Allegory, in the widest sense, was, of course, a method current throughout the entire philosophical and religious literature of the period. It might even be considered a particularly decadent device, at once taking the traditional content out of Hellenism and giving a stamp of artificiality to its last revivals. There is no doubt that Philo was encouraged to make such an extensive use of allegory by the mentality of the Greek culture in which he lived, and that the use of it led him into many factitious developments. But this has nothing to do with the question of where he first found the source of his method, still less, the very original biblical exegeses which he drew from it.

For Philo's allegory, in what is most specific to it, is biblical by virtue not only of the material it deals with, but also of the spiritual themes inspiring it. To this extent, it owes much more to the *midrash* of Palestinian Judaism than to any Neo-Pythagorean or Stoic type of allegory. One of the commonest forms of the *midrash*, in fact, is the explication of the historic events of the biblical past made so as to draw from it a transposition and spiritual application to contemporary events. Moreover, the figures and accounts which Philo thus "allegorizes" are precisely the customary objects of the *midrash*: the patriarchs and Moses, just as the spiritual line of thought that he draws from them is the lesson of the *midrash*, that is, progress in the "knowledge" of God. In this respect, his treatises on the Pentateuch are in the direct lineage of the sayings of the Fathers, as these are found in the Wisdom of Solomon.[96]

[96] See Daniélou, *op. cit.*, pp. 102ff. E. Stein has brought out (*Die allegorische Exegese des Philo von Alexandria*) the fact that, with Philo, the use of an allegorism oriented toward mysticism can only come from Judaism itself. He stops short at the idea of a hypothetical influence on him of those Therapeutes

It is undeniable, however, that, in his exegesis as in his spirituality, Philo is marked by his familiarity with philosophico-religious Hellenism. Yet it would be an exaggeration to say that he lost sight of the sense of history and reduced it to a veiled presentation of eternal and unchangeable essences. It would be more exact to say that he individualizes and "psychologizes" sacred history to the limit. He tends to make it merely an expanded paradigm of the history of the religious soul, as he conceived it. The sense of the *ephapax*, the saving event accomplished once for all by God on which all individual destinies depend for their concrete solution, tends to escape him. This lack and the weakening in him, if not the disappearance, of the eschatological sense so striking in Palestinian Judaism, are closely bound up with one another. Origen, who owed so much to him, firmly corrected him on these two points.

Alexandrian Judaism and the Christian Mission

The fact remains that, through Philo in particular, Alexandrian or, more generally "hellenized" Judaism, played a rôle perhaps no less important in the development of Christian spirituality than the Judaism of Palestine. If the latter prepared the very genesis of its primary elements, the former furnished the ready instrument for their systematization as well as their diffusion. St Paul, reuniting in himself these two complementary aspects of Judaism even though he either did not know Philo or did not take him into account, was thus fully prepared to be at once the first theologian and the first great missionary of Christian spirituality.

---

which he describes in the *De vita contemplativa*. Whatever may be the truth about this possible relationship, it seems certain to us that the Alexandrian tradition in which Philo is included, even if he did not himself inaugurate it, proceeds in a direct line from the Palestinian tradition. Among the same lines, see the observations of Cadiou in the introduction to his edition of the *De migratione*, pp. 9–11.

II

THE TEACHING AND THE INFLUENCE OF JESUS

It is quite certain that the soul of Christian spirituality lies in the absolutely unique influence of Jesus' words and of his personality, exercised first on his immediate disciples. But the very profundity of this influence seems to elude all efforts to encompass in any limited historical sketch the immediate words and impact of Christ. Bérulle, who produced such massive works, turned his pungent irony against himself in recalling that Jesus never wrote anything except on the sand and (he adds) we do not know what this was!

Jesus in History and in Faith

There is no cause for surprise, consequently, if the same thing has happened in the case of Jesus as happened previously with regard to the wholly human personality of a similar oral teacher like Socrates. Not only is the wealth of testimony embarrassing by reason of its inevitable diversity, but the force of the creative impulse, which Jesus—far more even than Socrates—communicated to the personalities that he formed, does not easily permit us to rediscover the original form of his teaching. With a master who is merely a professor, the students retain his formulations with no difficulty (often this is all they retain). But with an awakener like Socrates, his auditors do not know just how to transmit the letter of what he says, so many resonances has it aroused in their own minds. And when men were aware of having heard the very Word of God made flesh, they could neither hope to communicate its immediate impact by mere individual quotations nor to exhaust its fullness by any carefully wrought synthesis. This is certainly why the Church has neither chosen between the four images of Jesus and his teaching provided by the four evangelists, nor tried to substitute a made-up concordance.[1] Their differences, what we might

[1] Tatian's *Diatessaron* never had more than a local success for a certain length of time.

even be tempted to call their divergences, are no less necessary than their profound agreement in bringing out the unique reality of the Saviour's life and teaching. The living tradition of the Church, continually nourishing itself on the evangelists, will never finish the inventory of their riches.

Must we then despair of grasping the primary impact, the tenor and the original accents of the living message of Jesus, which is at the historical origin of all Christian spirituality? The *Formgeschichte* (Form-criticism) School has made us aware of the presumption of nineteenth-century attempts to provide, starting from the Gospel narratives, a "biography" of Jesus similar to the biographies of men who are simply men. It has taken away the naïvely rationalist hope of substituting a "Jesus of history" for the "Jesus of faith" presented to us in the Gospel documents.[2] This salutary modesty to which recent biblical criticism has led the historian, however, should not end in making us think that the Jesus of faith, even though he is indeed historical, must escape all apprehension by our merely human science. A recognition of the ultimately impenetrable mystery of his divine personality should not lead us to any such scepticism.

True, we cannot always arrive with certitude at the original form of his words (what sure criterion would allow us to determine the original formulation of the Beatitudes, for example?). Above all, we must not deceive ourselves as to the opportunities that might ever be given us of entering into his psychology. But certainly there are some fundamental characteristics of what he taught to the ears, of how he appeared to the eyes of his first disciples which we can recover through their later testimony. True enough, this testimony cannot be separated from the vision of faith wherein the Church finally understood in a supernatural way what could not be understood in any other—not that she in any way pretends to enclose him even in this vision. But this testimony bears, as it were in filigree, the sufficiently discernible trace of the elements of fact, the primitive elements, on which it was constructed. The evangelists did not write to enable us to make up a history in the modern sense of the word, but to communicate their faith to us, the faith of the Church. Yet this faith is too closely bound up with completely objective history not to allow us to rediscover at least the essential

[2] At the beginnings of the Formgeschichte school, O. Cullmann outlined its potentialities and their consequences in an article which will always be worth reading: "Les récentes études sur la formation de la tradition évangelique", in *Revue d'Histoire et de Philosophie religieuses*, V (Strasbourg–Paris, 1925), pp. 459ff. and 564ff. For an up-to-date evaluation, see the collective volume *La Formation des Évangiles*, Desclée de Brouwer, Paris, 1957.

lines of that history's shape. And these are the very lines that sketch out the mystery of faith.[3]

Let us add that, as modern criticism has dissuaded us from looking in the synoptic Gospels for a "historic Jesus" more easily distinguishable from the "Jesus of faith" in them than in St John, it has also in a singular way brought the invaluable witness of St John closer, in time and space, to the initial evangelic event. Neither the late date nor the origin foreign to the original context of the Gospel which used to be assigned to him are now tenable. In him as much as in the Synoptics, although in another way, we hear once more the echo of the first impressions made by Jesus on his hearers and witnesses.

Jesus and John the Baptist

One of the essential elements given us by the fourth Gospel, perhaps better than the others, for the historical understanding of Jesus is the intimate connection between the first public manifestations of Jesus and the activity of John the Baptist. The unique rôle of the latter at the origins of Christianity is a fact that the tradition of the Church, especially liturgical tradition, has preserved for a long time, above all in the East. But it must be admitted that nineteenth-century historians misunderstood it. Today nobody disputes the fact that the birth of Christianity cannot be understood except in strict correlation with the movement created by John the Baptist. More definitely, the first key to the teaching and work of Jesus is provided by the fact that he himself wished to begin by appearing as a disciple of John's and as continuing his work. It was later that things were reversed and John became the mere Precursor, and that, according to the phrase which the fourth Gospel attributes to him, Jesus "increased" while he himself "decreased".[4]

John represents the purest expression of those features of the Judaism contemporary with Jesus which bring us so close to Him that they already seem to reflect something of his presence. With John, the eschatological expectation became a final presentiment, leading at last to the certainty: the King stands at the door.[5] He is here. The sense of the precariousness of the "present age", consequently, reached its highest intensity. The practical consequence immediately followed: John himself not only permanently led the

[3] On this point, see the remarkable study by Harald Riesenfeld which largely dominated the congress on the four gospels held at Oxford in 1957: "The Gospel Tradition and its Beginnings", in *Studia evangelica*, Berlin, 1959.

[4] This has been well brought out by Maurice Goguel, *Au seuil de l'Évangile, Jean-Baptiste*, Paris, 1928.

[5] On the Baptist, see Matt. 3, 11. 2–9 and 14. 1–2; Mark 1. 1–15; 6. 14–29; Luke 1, 3. 1–22; 7. 18–34; 9. 7–9; John 1. 1–42; 3. 22–36.

life of abstinence and consecration of a Nazarean,[6] but went out into the desert, and drew the crowds after him. A new exodus was inaugurated, for a new encounter with God. But John was not only an ascetic who pursued to its limits the logic of an eschatological hope, sure of soon changing into vision. He was a new prophet, and early showed himself to be *the* prophet above all others.

In the Judaism of the time, with a spirituality seeming at first sight to be mainly composed of accumulated traditions, inspirations of the past, gathered together and ruminated upon, he caused a new inspiration to burst forth, one of incredible boldness. Like an Elias, he was not afraid to accost the great ones of the world and to pronounce the judgments of God upon them. Like an Isaias, his eyes saw the future that God has in reserve. But he did not see it from afar, and the events contained in it were not simply any kind of events somehow connected with the great divine designs. John saw a prophetic future on the point of becoming the present, and what he saw was the ultimate future, the supreme event, the coming of God in his final Kingdom. Paradoxically, he effaced himself before him whose herald he was but at the same time, unlike Moses, he promised no other prophet after himself: he is *the other* expected prophet, the one after whom there will be no other except him who abolishes all prophecy in accomplishing it for ever.

Metanoia

While the personal asceticism of the Baptist is striking—anchoritism, nakedness, extreme frugality—so is the moderation of his demands on others. We should obviously expect, with a mixture of disquiet and fascination, that he would drive the world to the desert. He merely drew it to the desert, which is something quite different. And on those who came to him he imposed no obligation other than that of strict justice. The soldier could remain a soldier, the tax-collector could even remain a tax-collector: the Judge who was to appear would not require a changed state of life, but a change of heart. Each person must decide the price he must pay so that his *metanoia* will be effective. But it is this change that matters, and not one or another means of attaining it or fostering it. The Kingdom and, still more, the King who stands already at the door, together with the *metanoia* which must be the echo in hearts and lives of the certitude of this coming—the whole message of the Baptist is contained herein.

The meaning and the content of *metanoia* are drawn from the idea of the Kingdom already prepared by the apocalypses; John

[6] Cf. Num. 6. 1–21.

limited himself to summing it up in a stroke of fire. As things are, in the world as it is conducted, God does not reign. It is His enemy who is the ruler. The coming of the divine Kingdom must, therefore, necessarily mean a break, a conflict with no hope of compromise. To prepare oneself for it, one must not hesitate in the face of any separation that may be required. But it is not the separation, the violent rupture, that matters by itself. And in any case, whether one wishes it or not, whether one anticipates it or awaits it, nothing will escape from it. God will bring it about for all men in his hour—that is, immediately. Separation is only the necessary condition of what does matter: a new heart, translating itself into a change of "way" (a "conversion" in the proper sense): ceasing to do evil, at last doing good or, more precisely, justice. Here John had nothing to add to Isaias. It is not by chance that all the witnesses agree on his predilection for that prophet. John illuminates the focal points of Isaias' preaching: the divine holiness as requiring justice, faith which is at the same time obedience.

This aspect of bluntness is certainly the most obvious one in his astonishing personality. But, let us repeat, the moderation of what he prescribed for those who trusted him is no less noteworthy. Certainly, mercy was not in the foreground of his teaching. He was visibly disconcerted, troubled, when he saw Jesus allowing himself to be contradicted. This divine long-suffering at first seemed to him to be in conflict with the imminence of the judgments he had been driven to proclaim. Yet, when Jesus recalled the word of Osee: "It is mercy that I desire and not sacrifice", his word is a direct echo of John's (if we may believe St Luke, who was undoubtedly well informed, as we shall see later): "Let him who has two tunics give one to him who has none, and let him who has food do the same."[7]

Just as with this compelling invitation to mercy, illuminating the justice in the foreground of the Baptist's teaching, so his positive announcement of the supernaturally creative character of divine grace (another aspect of *hesed*, let us recall) echoes in advance, in the piercing note characteristic of him, the very Gospel of Jesus: "Do not go about saying: we have Abraham for our father, for I tell you that God can draw children for Abraham from these stones."[8]

This phrase is perhaps the most unusual of all those attributed to the Baptist, as it is certainly the most untouched in its original crudity. A whole world is summed up in it, with that lapidary quality which seems to have been more marked with John than

[7] Luke 3. 11. [8] Luke 3. 8.

with any other prophet: the unfathomable depth that *metanoia* must reach to be real; the fact that the Judge himself is he who alone, unquestionably, can enable men to fulfil his requirements; the certainty (making ready for the widest universalism) that there is nothing that he cannot accomplish, however obscure his designs still may be. In a word, it is not only the judgment, in the narrow sense of the word, that the Baptist awaited, but the event that was to be the most creative and the most exalting, as much as and still more than the most terrible. Everything is possible, everything can be hoped for: but this is why we must, instantly, give up everything to God. . . .

John was so sure of this event, to him so close at hand that it was as it were already present, that the question was asked: was he the Messiah? He denied it, and, in his integrity which we are tempted to describe as carried to extremes, he also denied that he was the prophet, the expected Elias. He wished to be only the reed that bows under the gust of the Spirit, the voice that cries out in the desert. . . . But Jesus only apparently contradicted him, and certainly expressed the intimate conviction of John himself by affirming that Elias, in him, had already come, that prophecy had been completed in attaining its object. What proves this is the baptism John administered.

The Jews, let us note—the Gospel alludes to this—were familiar at that time with all kinds of baptisms, that is, purifying ablutions. But it is quite clear that John's baptism was something different. His baptism was in a direct line with his scandalous words about the children of Abraham: it was the equivalent of the baptism of proselytes—by which Gentiles were introduced into the people of God. . . . But it was to the Jews themselves that he gave it! He could not have stated more clearly that belonging to the true people of God presupposes a radical transformation which the Israelite needs as much as the non-Israelite.

On a number of these points, to begin with the last, John was not so violently original as he seems at first sight. He took up the ideas and practices more or less common in the *chaburoth* that we are coming to know better and better. It may even be that he often only proclaimed what the Essenes, in particular, practised and believed on their own account.[9] But he did not limit himself to replacing a prudent, discreet form of propaganda with preaching like a trumpet-call, addressed to everyone. He blew to red or even to white heat an inspiration which until then, it would seem, had not completely found itself.

[9] See the suggestions of J. Daniélou in *The Dead Sea Scrolls and Primitive Christianity*.

The Disciples of John and of Jesus

The synoptic Gospels all shed the same light on the meeting between Jesus and John, while the fourth Gospel casts a pattern of lights and shadows which allows us to divine much more than is actually stated. The most diverse historical witnesses, up to the late sect of the Mandeans, corroborate this impression.

John certainly led his contemporaries towards Jesus: the first disciples of Jesus, as the fourth Gospel expressly states, had first been disciples of John. And also there is no doubt that John himself had expressed his faith in Jesus, even if that faith had to go through dramatic trials at the time when John was in prison, pursued by Herod's resentment. But the transition from one to the other was not brought about as easily as one might think from a superficial reading of the texts.

The Gospel of St John allows us to suppose what later witnesses leave in no doubt: there was a prolonged conflict between the disciples of the Baptist on the question whether Jesus was or was not greater than he. Jesus' phrase, generally misunderstood: "I tell you that there is no one greater among those born of women, but the lesser one in the kingdom of God is greater," has no meaning except in reference to this conflict. "Lesser one" is not a superlative designating "the littlest" of the believers in contrast to John: a supposition in contradiction both with the part of the phrase that precedes it and with the clear statement of the evangelists that John believed in Jesus and so was not strange to the Kingdom. This "lesser one" is a comparative that can designate none other than Jesus himself, as many of John's disciples considered him.[10]

The conflict among these disciples is as it were the echo or the concrete manifestation of the conflict that divided John against himself. But what must be emphasized is that the turmoil that Jesus plunged him in did not contradict the supernatural clarity of his adherence to him; it was rather its inevitable consequence. Long before all others, more clearly than anyone else, John had realized in connection with Jesus what he himself first expressed in intentionally sybylline terms: "The Kingdom of God is in your midst"[11] (that is, in his person). But it was precisely this fact, seen so clearly, that made it more difficult for John than for anyone else to accept the obscure ways of humiliation, of "kenosis" which Jesus had followed from the time of his meeting with John, instead of the sudden revelation of splendour that John expected.

In this regard, the suspicion of certain modern critics that the fourth Gospel overstressed the categorical statement of the Baptist:

[10] Matt. 11. 11 and Luke 7. 28.

[11] Luke 17. 21.

"I am not worthy to loose the string of his sandals,"[12] in order to rally some tardy disciples of John's to Jesus, is not tenable. This statement is too fully in accord with John's hesitation, reported by the Synoptics, when Jesus presented himself for his baptism. And this last episode is itself too completely in conformity with what we know of his interior agony a little later, an agony that cannot be doubted, to leave room for any uncertainty. John's difficulty in understanding that the "Judge" could take the place of those to be judged, in receiving baptism, is as comprehensible as the will of Jesus to do so is undeniable.

From the outset, Jesus made his own everything John had said, he followed in his footsteps; but he bore in his person the unforeseeable. This is what explains the real crisis of John in his prison: not that he had ceased to believe, that he did not really believe that the Kingdom was present in Jesus and that Jesus was its King: it was on the contrary because he believed it so literally that he could not reconcile it with the attitude he saw Jesus persisting in.

The Gospel of the Kingdom

Jesus' first preaching was the Gospel (the good news) of the Kingdom, or better, of the Reign of God. The Sermon on the Mount in Matthew,[13] the sermon in the plain of Luke,[14] may include some summarizing and systematizing for purposes of presentation (varying from one to the other). But whatever may have been the date and the primitive form of many of the elements thus gathered together, there is no doubt that the theme which unites them was that of the first preaching of Jesus. It was, in fact, quite simply the theme of John's preaching: the Reign of God is to be established, invisibly it is already inaugurated.

What is immediately proper to Jesus, on the other hand, is the content he explicitly gives to the "Reign". Here again, however, what Matthew and Luke have him say is too closely related to the elements we have found in John's preaching for us to doubt that here we actually touch the substance of Jesus' first public words. But the deepening, the expansion of the ideas that he took over from his predecessor is instantly striking. For him also, the Reign of God meant the coming of justice, in the sense of the prophets, but how greatly enriched! For does not this justice include, or, better, is it not the realization of what can no longer be called simply *hesed*, for it is already the Christian *agape* in all its creative originality? The Reign, in fact, is revealed as the re-creating inter-

[12] Mark 1. 7; Luke 3. 16; John 1. 27; Acts 13. 25. Cf. Matt. 3. 11.
[13] Matt. 5–7. [14] Luke 6. 17–49.

vention of God: from stones he will not only draw out "children of Abraham" but sons for himself. Whence the conclusion replacing the "Be holy as I am holy" of Leviticus: "Be perfect as your heavenly Father is perfect."

It would seem that there we have, in the linking of these few points, the whole primal proclamation of the Gospel which was simply to be developed later on.

The Gospel of the Poor

"Blessed are the poor." These first words of the discourse in Luke and in Matthew, explain, while carrying to the limit, the astonishing parabola described by Jewish spirituality through the prophets up to John the Baptist. The final word of Jesus in John, "My kingdom is not of this world",[15] adds nothing to this firsı Beatitude. The "poor man" in Israelite piety had become the equivalent of "the faithful".[16] Here we see him already possessed of the divine blessing, since the Kingdom is already present.

But what follows goes even further: it does not bless merely the faith which abandons everything for the Kingdom. It blesses the faith which expresses itself, while becoming perfectly obedient, in the gift of self. The poverty which is blessed is not merely any kind of trusting poverty, but the poverty which results from a total generosity. It is the poverty which reproduces the generosity of God himself, which does not give because we have been given to, nor in order to receive in return: which gives for the sake of giving. "Love your enemies, pray for those who persecute you, thus you will be the sons of your Father who is in heaven, for he makes his sun rise on the wicked and on the good, and rain fall on the just and on the unjust. . . ."

The more we reflect on the extreme simplicity of this initial sermon, especially when reduced to what are most certainly its primitive elements, the more we are struck with all that is already included in it. At first it seems to be presenting merely an ideal of perfect life. Next we see that it conceals a new law, but a law that transcends all law in love. Then we discover, as it were overlaid on what it says of man, an ideal of God that from the outset is completely new. Finally, we discern the essential which is not stated: the necessary link between this revelation concerning God and this call to man. The event presupposed, the event which will make the Kingdom an actuality, which will inaugurate the reign, is a radical change in the relationship, not so much of man with God, as of God with man.

[15] John 18. 36.
[16] See A. Causse, *Les pauvres d'Israël*, Strasbourg, 1932.

Let us make this point clearer: it is the key to the whole sermon. If we lose sight of it or do not grasp it, everything becomes matter for misunderstanding. The most fundamental error of the evangelical exegesis of liberal Protestantism, illustrated naïvely by Jülicher's book on the parables, consists in believing that the preaching of the Kingdom of Jesus is a succession of statements flowing merely from superior common sense. Harnack, who saw clearly that Jesus' preaching of the Kingdom is intermingled with the proclamation of the divine Fatherhood, is less thoroughly mistaken; but he is mistaken none the less in reducing this proclamation to that of the infinite dignity of the human soul!

The preaching of Jesus proclaims no general and a-temporal truth of this kind. It proclaims, certainly, the divine fatherhood, but not in the least as something which happens of itself and which needs only to be recognized; it proclaims it, on the contrary, as the unheard-of event which makes one reality with the coming of the Reign.

The Divine Fatherhood

The "good news" that Jesus brings is no simple statement that God is Father. It is that now for us, for every man, there is a radically new possibility, an unhoped-for grace: the possibility, the grace of being made a child of God. The phrase of St John's First Epistle: "See with what love God has loved us: so that we are called the children of God and we actually are such," represents the final realization of the sense of the Gospel message.[17] It is as it were the last word of Christian meditation on the Gospel fact. But it is the essence of this same fact, in its whole first presentation, which is thus disengaged.

The teaching of the Sermon on the Mount, in other words, has nothing of that generous utopianism, that candid idealism, which the eighteenth and nineteenth centuries believed they found in it. Jesus did not propose any simple recipe for bringing about a better world, a recipe which would imply a naïve misunderstanding of the human heart as it is. He announced an unheard-of possibility, a truly "new creation", as St Paul says.[18] And this consists in replacing man's heart of stone with a real heart of flesh, the metamorphosis in which Ezechiel placed his hope of the new and eternal covenant promised by Jeremias. For it is completely arbitrary to take the Sermon on the Mount out of its context in the vain hope of finding some a-temporal teaching. The context is still that of John the Baptist: a catastrophe coming suddenly and from on high to break

[17] 1 John 3. 1. [18] Gal. 6. 15.

up the order of things, an intervention of the Creator in his creation, sweeping away from his path everything which opposes his will.... "He holds his flail in his hand and he will cleanse his threshing-floor; he will gather his grain in the granary; but he will burn the chaff with unquenchable fire...."[19] Not only did Jesus never say anything opposed to this view of things; he adhered to it as closely as possible. The Gospel of the Beatitudes does not deny it; it is superimposed on it. Here again, the writings of St John very clearly give the only valid interpretation of the primary facts: the revelation of *agape* in no way contradicts that of the judgment; it fulfils it.

Nor does it fulfil the judgment simply because the introduction of the divine *agape* into this world automatically brings about a sorting-out by its being accepted or refused. It fulfils it chiefly because the "judgment", in Jewish mentality, is not so much the sorting-out itself as the authoritative act by which the sovereign power intervenes and reveals itself.

In this regard, the immediate and inseparable context of the Sermon on the Mount is the sermon in the synagogue at Nazareth, where Jesus read Isaias:

> The Spirit of the Lord is upon me,
> because he has consecrated me by anointing;
> he has sent me to carry the good news to the poor,
> to announce deliverance to the captives
> and return of sight to the blind,
> to give back liberty to the oppressed,
> to proclaim the Lord's year of grace.

Jesus rolled up the scroll, gave it back, sat in the "seat of Moses" and said: "Today this passage of Scripture is fulfilled in your ears...."[20]

In his preaching of the judgment, John could only describe the gaping abyss opened out in the world by the divine intervention. But Jesus reveals the full meaning of this terrible chasm; it is the revelation of God as Father.

This is not to say that the fatherhood of God was ignored in the Old Testament. Faith in the covenant had assured Israel that it collectively possessed the privilege of divine adoption claimed by Semitic kings. Prophetic insight, while deepening the meaning of this fatherhood, had insisted on its entirely gratuitous character. In return, it had reserved it to the "remnant", the little group of the just and faithful, the "poor", in God's eyes the only true Israel.[21]

[19] Matt. 3. 12 and Luke 3. 17. [20] Luke 4. 16–21.
[21] See Osee 11. 1–11; Jer. 31. 9; Is. 63. 15–16 and 64. 7. Cf. Deut. 32. 20 and Wis. 2. 13 to 3. 12.

And now Jesus seems, at one stroke, to open out this privilege, not only to all Israel, but all men without distinction. Is this to say that he contradicts the previous progress of revelation, and replaces it with a universalism, or rather by a kind of indifferentism, where neither the choice nor the grace of God have any further place?

Here is the core of the possible misunderstanding. What Jesus proclaims, on the contrary, is a choice more disconcerting in its sovereign freedom than anything that had been foreseen, together with an outpouring of grace of an unimaginable prodigality. Not that in his eyes the evil in this world is a mere illusion, or a momentary setback which a better view of things will suffice to overcome. What he proclaims is that God has entered as the all-powerful King into his kingdom that had forgotten him. And now he reveals himself in a way quite different from anything that had been imagined. Men indeed recognized him as Creator, but they no longer knew his creative power. Now he is again at work, and his revelation baffles all expectations.

The Saving Intervention

Here we have two co-ordinated themes connected more with what Jesus did than with his preaching, but putting the latter in its proper light. That these themes belong, furthermore, to a primitive historical bedrock—in no way the product of Christian reflection but, on the contrary, one of the primary elements on which it would be exercised—is shown by the place given them in the account of Mark. They might be said, in fact, to constitute its foundation. The first of these themes is the warfare of Jesus against the demonic powers, the second the sovereignty over the Sabbath, proclaimed by action. These two themes unite in the most extraordinary and most undeniable of Jesus' actions: his solemn forgiving of sins.

By his exorcisms and his miracles of healing, that is, Jesus declared himself from the outset of his ministry to be the "stronger one" come into the world to dislodge "the strong one" already established here and to take away his weapons. Herod's phrase marvellously translates the common impression: "the Powers" act in him.[22] The divine activity (commonly attributed to angelic interventions) was revealed in Jesus' victorious conflict with the various manifestations of evil in this world.

But what constituted an outright declaration on the part of Jesus that it was actually this activity which was visibly manifested in him, was the very positive way in which he violated the sabbath. He did not merely say that "the sabbath was made for man and

[22] Matt. 14. 2 and Mark 6. 14.

not man for the sabbath".[23] While he thus brought out the truth that creation, with the sabbath following it, centered on man, was oriented towards man as its end, he also established in the clearest possible way the fact that, in his person, God was again taking up, repairing and perfecting the interrupted work of creation. This is the intended meaning of his cures worked on the sabbath day, and nobody among the Jews mistook it. The creative power that belongs to God alone was manifesting itself anew, in the very existence of Jesus.

The public forgiving of sins, sealed by miracles, brings together these two themes of war against the forces of evil and manifestation of the creative power of God. And it witnesses to the fact that the divine power not only acts through Jesus: it is his own, he disposes of it in its most divine aspect.

The phrase of Jesus about the doctor who does not go to the healthy but to the sick[24] decisively confirms the meaning which he seems to have attached to his mission from the outset. He did not come to reveal to itself a humanity which had been ignorant of its own possibilities of goodness. He came to heal and renew, with authority, with the creative power that belongs to God alone, a humanity enslaved, sick, sinful. This is why the Sermon on the Mount is not the charter of a more or less utopian ideal of mankind. It is the promise of a new humanity, produced by a wholly new intervention of God in which he would reveal himself in a light itself wholly new.

The activity of Jesus against the demonic powers, as recorded in the Gospel accounts, can in no way be reduced to a more or less adventitious element of folklore. The evangelists were so aware of its importance that they made it the whole context of Jesus' work. The account of the temptation, at the beginning of the first three Gospels, is certainly an intentional parallel to the account of the fall at the beginning of Genesis. As human history began with man's fall at the demon's instigation, so the history of Jesus begins with the same confrontation. But this time, it is victorious.[25]

Yet the fact that this implies the very conscious use of a catechetical device in no way indicates that the evangelists imposed on the events the veneer of a later interpretation. Quite the contrary, if there is one element of the Gospel context which seems somehow predetermined, it is this one. For it is precisely the context which the apocalypses had prepared for the Church. Here again it is obvious that this dualism (in the sense in which, as we

[23] Mark 21. 27.
[24] Matt. 9. 12; Mark 2. 17; Luke 5. 31.
[25] Matt. 4. 1–11; Mark 1. 12–13; Luke 4. 1–13.

have shown, the word is to be understood here), this view of a universe irremediably divided between fidelity to God and a rebellion going far beyond the merely human order was not a secondary element in the Judaism contemporary with Christ, but one of its basic convictions. And that Jesus himself endorsed it as such and formally made it His own is a fact as capital as it is undeniable.

The description of his activity as essentially anti-demonic inspired his parables about the strong and the stronger man, about the king who must bring his rebellious subjects to reason in order to enter into his kingdom, about the Kingdom that suffers violence.[26] Only the most unjustifiable *a priori* reasoning can authorize us to cast any doubt on the fully historical authenticity of these words, or to minimize their importance.

Jesus' coming into this world, consequently, at once appeared to his disciples, according to his own activity and his own words, as a very characteristic divine intervention—the intervention of a sovereign power asserting itself against a subordinate and rebellious power. In this conflict, the rebel power appears as a force of slavery and oppression. The sovereign power is revealed, on the contrary, as supremely liberating. Here we sense, ready to be sounded, the traditional themes of the paschal liturgy. The God who appears in the life of Christ is the saving God, the God who sets free, the God who effectively leads to the promised land.

But the miracles of healing, and especially the healings carried out on the sabbath day, take us much further than this. Here it appears that what God cares about in his creation, is man, and especially suffering man. It is for his sake that he once again takes creation in hand, so to say. And here he reveals himself with a tenderness, an understanding, a mercy, as near at hand as it is powerful. For man, for fallen man, beaten to the ground, God shows himself so loving that he breaks what seems to be his most sacred ordinances. The God whom the sabbath honours himself violates the sabbath, and he does so for the sake of man, sinful man. No bounds, then, can be assigned to his love, to his *hesed*, not even the limits that he himself had most solemnly established.

Yet all this only leads up to the supreme revelation. Not only does this goodness, this divine compassion, not ignore anything of the terrible curse weighing on man as on the whole universe. Not only does his love reach even to the evil that is in man and, by its sacred touch, suffice to heal him. But this love ignores none of the evil that makes one body with man, that vitiates his most intimate spiritual being: sin. The power which acts in Jesus confronts even

[26] Matt. 12. 29; Mark 3. 27; Luke 11. 21–22; Luke 19. 11–27; Matt. 11. 12.

sin, even the enmity with God which has become as it were a part of ourselves. It reveals the fire of the divine holiness that consumes iniquity. But it consumes the sin while sparing the sinner. It demands of him only the faith that abandons itself, that gives itself up to the marvellous Word: "Your sins are forgiven you...." If Jesus heals the sick at the same time as he absolves the sinner, it is to manifest the miracle, by its nature invisible, which is more marvellous, more creative even than the creation of a world: the effective regeneration of man, of his conscience, of his "heart"....

It is all this that gives its seal to the teaching concerning the divine fatherhood. This is what makes it not a sentimental dream, but a creative promise. Henceforth it is possible for man to be a child of God. He is not being mocked by being told: "Be perfect as your heavenly Father is perfect." For, in Jesus, this divine fatherhood is not manifested as perfection inaccessible to our imperfection. It is manifested in him, quite the contrary, as confronting and removing all barriers, one by one, surmounting all distances, taking on itself all opposition. In Jesus, this divine "perfection" which is the perfection of the creative gift of self, of the love that gives, that gives freely, that gives itself totally even to losing itself and finds herein its joy, its beatitude—this perfection is put within our reach. It appears in him as understanding man and his wretchedness, as suffering with him, as condescending to him. It appears in him as manifested in man.

Here, indeed, is a final and capital element in Jesus' preaching and especially in the radiation of his personality: the perfect sonship to which he calls us, which he promises us as the supreme grace, the "good news"—in him we see it consciously realized.

The Son

However positive was the preaching by Christ of a universal divine fatherhood, we cannot fail to be struck, even in a superficial reading of St Matthew or St Luke, by the fact that he speaks of his own sonship in an entirely different tone. God is "his" Father in an obviously unique sense. Particularly in reference to the judgment is this indicated. In the conclusion of the Sermon on the Mount according to St Matthew, it appears that Jesus will not undergo the judgment but will pronounce it. And this distinction is made clear in the fact that he admits a man to his Kingdom or excludes him from it, not according to whether he has called Jesus "Lord, Lord," but according to whether or not he has done "the will of my Father who is in heaven".[27]

[27] Matt. 7. 21.

In precisely the same context of ideas, but with a very characteristic inversion, this time putting the emphasis on relationship with himself, he says further on: "Whoever will confess me (that is to say, acknowledge me as master) before men, I will confess him (that is, recognize him as my disciple) before *my* Father who is in heaven."[28]

St Luke does not give these striking texts, but he too witnesses to Jesus' use of the expression "*my* Father", always in the same context of the judgment, when he ascribes these words to him:[29] "As my Father has bequeathed me the kingdom so I bequeath it to you" (this in reference to the Apostles). Luke testifies, moreover, to his familiarity with Jesus' habit of using this expression (2. 49; 24. 49, are especially significant).

Mark at first sight seems less familiar with this use. But he has texts that show him more aware than anyone else of the unique character of Jesus' sonship. In two passages where we should least expect it, for these are circumstances in which Jesus seems especially humiliated—when he attributes to the "Father" alone the knowledge of the day of judgment, and when he prays that he may be spared from death—Mark has him call himself "The Son" with no other explanation or call God "Father" in a sense that seems equally exclusive.[30]

It is also remarkable that, in the Synoptics, Jesus always calls God simply "Father" when he prays, while he invites his disciples to pray saying "Our Father". Does it not seem as if he himself avoided the plural? The Father is his in a sense that belongs to no one else. And the wholly new use made by the three Synoptics of the expression "Son of God" for Jesus himself is connected with this conviction of his unique Sonship.

In Mark, as early as the account of the baptism in which the voice from heaven (a *bath qol*,[31] a typically Jewish conception) resounds, God calls Jesus "My well-beloved Son",[32] that is, "only son," in the habitual sense of this expression among the Jews.

This is the more remarkable in that, while the expression "Son of God" had a directly messianic sense in Israel (corresponding to the general idea of a divinely adopted Messiah) it had no ontological meaning at all; it did not refer to any quality of nature.[33] However paradoxical it may seem at first sight, it seems evident that Jesus led his disciples towards the idea of such a meaning, not

[28] Matt. 10. 32. [29] Luke 22. 29. [30] Mark 13. 32 and 14. 36.
[31] See L. Gillet, *Communion in the Messiah*, pp. 224–5.
[32] Mark 1. 11.
[33] On all the biblical titles given to Jesus, see Vincent Taylor, *The Names of Jesus*, London, 1953, and, for their history in Israel, Mowinckel, *He that Cometh*.

so much by designating himself as "Son of God" as by applying to himself the title "Son of Man". Here again, in fact, it was particularly in the context of the judgment and of the rôle that he himself would take in it that we see him speaking of "my Father". But, in the apocalyptic terminology, inspired by Daniel 7, it is precisely the "Son of Man" who is the supernatural man (coming on the clouds of heaven) to carry out the judgment in God's name. By calling himself "Son of Man" in this context, therefore, Jesus is not insisting so much on his humanity—quite evident to his auditors—as on his hidden supernaturalness. By speaking of *his* Father, and in designating himself as *the* Son, he led them to think that this supernatural character was a far deeper reality than any prophet had led them to expect. With these ways of speaking, his attitude with regard to the sabbath, and his exercise of the power of forgiving sins all shedding light on one another, they should have resulted in already elevating the meaning of the term "Son of God" as applied to him.

But it seems undeniable that Jesus himself used, if not publicly at least within the circle of his disciples, fully explicit statements concerning the unique relationship with the Father that he entertained, making him *the* Son and the Father *his* Father in an absolutely unique way.

We are accustomed to considering such sayings as one of the most typical characteristics of the Gospel of St John. But we must not forget that nothing in the fourth Gospel is so clear, so formal on this point as a sentence in St Matthew, found as to its essence again in St Luke. Its presence in these two places is so surprising to the eyes of a minimizing criticism that Harnack called it "the Johannine meteor in the Synoptics". For it presupposes the idea of divine sonship as completely developed and, still more, stamps it with that emphasis on the reciprocal intimacy of Father and Son which seems so characteristic of the most mysterious words of Jesus in St. John's Gospel.

> I thank you, Father, Lord of heaven and earth, because you have hidden these things from the wise and learned and revealed them to the simple (literally, to children). Yes, Father, such has been your good pleasure. Everything has been given to me by my Father; and no one knows who the Son is but the Father, or who the Father is but the Son and he to whom the Son wills to reveal him.

This is Luke's (16. 21–22) version of this text, in a form which seems very primitive. Matthew (11. 25–27), besides additions external to this central core, substitutes "recognizes the Son" or "the

Father" (*epiginoskei*) for "knows who the Son is" or "who the Father is" (*ginoskei tis estin*).

The most noteworthy element in this text is not so much the statement that the "gnosis" of the Father belongs wholly to the Son, as that the Son is known only by the Father himself. The supernatural character of this sonship, hidden from the sight of men, could not be more clearly stated. Again, in the pure line of the Judaic "knowledge of God", "gnosis" here is a living intimacy and, more precisely, a loving reciprocity. Finally, as the "gnosis" of the Father is proper to the Son, as "everything" has been given him by the Father, it it he who is the author of the true and final "apocalypse", the perfect revelation: that of the Father as Father.

The efforts that have been made to wrest these texts from their place in the Synoptics are completely unsuccessful. Nothing more Jewish (more Hebraic, even) can be imagined, in this "*berakah*" for "gnosis", than the construction "have hidden from the wise and learned and revealed to the simple..." Consequently, far from being a fragment from St John gone astray in the Synoptics, this text witnesses to the fact that the many sayings of Jesus on the fullness of his sonship quoted by St John, and the very way in which he developed this theme, are in no way a creation of the last Evangelist. In the intimate circle of his disciples (Matthew and Luke are clear on this point also), Jesus certainly went further than the implications of his public teaching and activity touching his own person, however clear these may have been. In the exact line to which John the Evangelist devotes himself by preference, Jesus showed himself to be the Son of God in a unique way; he developed this sonship in the sense of an intimacy of "knowledge" in the most Jewish meaning of the word, as being at the same time community of life. And, by the same token, he showed himself explicitly as being the source of our own filiation and of the "knowledge" into which it is to flower.

Jesus and his Messiahship

Can we take one last step and define how Jesus himself described this work of "revelation" and of "handing on" which was to be his? On this point again, not only the formal witness, but the surest indications are given us by the Synoptics.[34]

They show us Jesus as very reticent, up to the last days of his earthly career, about giving himself or even accepting the title of Messiah. What they allow us to see of the popular conceptions of the Messiah, thought of as a new David winning easy victories, is

[34] See William Manson, *Jesus the Messiah*, pp. 41ff.

corroborated by the contemporary Jewish literature, in particular the Psalms of Solomon. Instead, according to these evangelists, Jesus seems to have designated himself, first implicitly (in statements made in the third person) and then explicitly, as the Son of Man. We have already mentioned how the allusion to Daniel 7, and to the vast echoing of that text in all apocalyptic literature, had given very definite overtones to this term. The "Son of Man" was the heavenly "man" sent by God from on high to be the agent of his ultimate designs, in the last times. But very quickly Jesus added another register, which at first sight seemed to be in complete discord with the foregoing. And the evangelists do not hide from us the fact that his auditors felt this and said so.

After Peter's confession (acknowledging precisely the messiahship of Jesus, but, indubitably, with the vaguely carnal idea of it we have just recalled), Mark shows us Jesus as "beginning to teach them that the Son of Man must suffer many things, that he would be rejected by the ancients, the chief priests and the scribes, that he would be put to death and that he would rise again after three days".[35] We remember the scandalized response of Peter. Later on, Jesus said still more formally: "The Son of Man is come not to be served but to serve, and to give his life as a ransom for the multitude."[36]

This last text left, and could have left, no room for hesitation in the disciples' minds. The allusions to chapter 53 of Isaias here become express quotations. Jesus gave them to understand as explicitly as possible that the wholly supernatural "Son of Man" (to whom the judgment, the victory over the forces of evil, the Reign of God are entrusted) is one with the Servant, humiliated and rejected, whose innocent sufferings and death are the redemption of sinners.

The most independent criticism has come little by little, constrained by the evidence, to recognize the fact that this paradoxical juxtaposition of the two images cannot be attributed to later revisions, but rather belongs to the original tenor of Jesus' words. In consequence, it is certain that it was he himself who interpreted his life, and more especially his death, along the lines of Isaias 53.

Later Judaism was so fully aware of how Christian exegesis of the Old Testament turned on this application of the "Servant Songs", that it came to deny them any "messianic" interpretation.[37] But what remains to us of ancient Palestinian Judaism confirms the fact that the most profound of the apocalyptic writers saw in the

[35] Mark 8. 31 (cf. 9. 31). [36] Mark 10. 45.

[37] See, for example, the Targum of *Isaias* which has been published by F. Stenning, *The Targum of Isaiah*, Oxford, 1949, pp. 178ff.

sufferings of the Servant a sign of the last times. The book of Henoch even seems to attempt, still awkwardly, to fuse the radiant figure of the Son of Man and the humiliated figure of the Servant. But a combination of the two, as perfect as it is natural, remains one of the newest creations of the New Testament, and it impossible to attribute it to anyone other than Jesus himself. Not only do the oldest evangelical traditions attribute it to him, but the unanimity of the most diverse later Christologies in establishing themselves on this basis cannot be explained in any other way.

Here we have the key to Jesus' attitude which was lacking even to the Baptist but which, once given, opens out all the mysteries of his teaching and his life.

Let us note that, however different they may be, the two prophetic images of the Son of Man and of the Servant have one point in common, and this point is certainly one of the foci of all Jesus' teaching. We mean to say that both these images imply a strict solidarity between the providential personality who is to realize the designs of God and the humanity which is the object of them. The "Son of Man" of Daniel comes on the clouds of heaven, in contrast to ordinary mankind of the earth earthly. But he none the less appears as a human figure, however elevated he may be above the common run of men. Conversely, even though the Servant seems to be the scum of mankind, abandoned, rejected by all, he is revealed as the man who has carried the sins of all men, whose wounds bring healing to all men. Jesus is presented as a new model of humanity, of the humanity which is the child of God, and at the same time as the author of the mysterious transformation which allows humanity to become in us what it is in him. How will he communicate to us this sonship which is the very promise of the Gospel and which he realizes in himself in an incomparable, unique way? Because he has taken on himself the weight of our sins in his voluntary humiliation, because his death redeems us from them.

The meaning both of the "poverty" that alone makes us agreeable to God and of the *hesed* of the last prophets that becomes the *agape* of the Gospel is at once clarified. And at the basis of everything, the mysterious divine fatherhood is illuminated in the providential death of the Well-Beloved. It is to the total "poverty" of faith that blessedness is promised, because blessedness means carrying the yoke of the "Messiah", the "easy yoke and light burden" which is none the less the cross of the Servant. Jesus' phrase about the cross that we must carry after him, as he himself took it up voluntarily, is certainly a theme which he not only suggested but formulated.

This "folly" of the cross, as St Paul was not afraid to call it,[38] is only the counterpart of a revelation of the divine love so great that *agape* is seen to transcend *hesed* as well as to fulfil it. In himself as in his relations with his creature, God appears with a grandeur of generosity, a holiness of love, surpassing anything man could conceive of. And so it is not astonishing that man should find himself taken up into an abyss of self-abandonment beyond reason. Here, indeed, is that loss of self, that being swept up by God in the wake of the *Merkabah*, which the rabbis hoped for and feared! And, at the same time, what new light radiates from the cloud in which Christ was enveloped and the *bath-qol* resounded: "This is my beloved Son in whom I have set all my affection!"[39] The glory of God becomes more precisely the glory of the *Father*, without for all that being any less mysterious.

Holiness and Humanity

One last quality is revealed, in all four of the Gospels, which without doubt echoes the first impressions made by Jesus on the group of his own. This is the paradoxical union in him of the most inaccessible holiness with a humanity which, on the contrary, is completely accessible.

On the one hand, it appears that nothing he did, nothing he said ever allowed anyone who had known him to suspect the least presence of sin in him. The phrase quoted by St John: "Which of you will convince me of sin?"[40] simply voices the extraordinary feeling communicated by the Synoptics: that of an unbounded humility, but one from which the consciousness of personal sin is totally absent.

The transcendence of this "man" who spoke and lived in our midst accommodated itself to participation in all our weaknesses, when they were not moral weaknesses—a participation no less extraordinary than his holiness, nay even the most extraordinary characteristic of this holiness, in itself not only exceptional but unique.

The fourth Gospel is often presented as if it was distinguished from the three others by its insistence on the divinity of Jesus. It would be more exact to say that it is distinguished by its insistence on the contrast between that divinity and the whole reality of his humanity. No one has described for us as has St John the physical weariness, the suffering, the compassion, the tenderness, even the emotion of Jesus.

[38] 1 Cor. 1. 18. [39] Matt. 17. 5 and Mark 9. 7. [40] John 8. 16.

If Jesus disconcerted the Baptist by his merciful humility, he must have disconcerted the disciples of the Precursor still more by the humanity enveloping his far more rigorous demands. The Baptist, when questioned, left the soldiers to their discipline, the tax-collectors to their tax-collecting, and required of them only justice. Jesus said: "If anyone does not hate everything that he has and even his own life, he cannot be my disciple."[41] But while John was the roughest of ascetics, a radical anchorite, Jesus lived among men and even among sinners. He did not fast; he was not an ascetic....[42] He himself seems to have emphasized the fact that future events, together with faithfulness to his doctrine and to himself, could lead men much farther along the way of detachment than the most rigorous forms of asceticism....[43] But the fact remains that, in the Gospel of the divine Fatherhood which is at the same time the Gospel of the *agape*, Jesus positively prevents asceticism, even carried as far as the voluntary acceptance of death, from falling into any condemnation of creation and of life.

His last word here below was to present his disciples with the broken bread, the shared chalice, as the symbols and more than the symbols of his sacrificial death. But it was in the exultant Eucharist for the "glory" of God given to men and poured out on all flesh that he "sanctified" himself for his own so as to "sanctify" them in the truth[44] (St John the Evangelist, here again, certainly gives us the faithful echo of that unique Supper with infinite prolongations).

The Judgment and the Spirit

When he thus departed from this world, what were the perspectives which he left with his disciples? Like John, like the apocalyptic writers, he left them looking forward to an immediate future of tribulations and catastrophes. But this future was no longer illuminated only by the hope of the final restoration in favour of the elect. Like his own sufferings, the suffering of his own would become a "trial": in St Luke, Jesus says to Peter: "Simon, Simon, Satan has been allowed to sift you like wheat, but I have prayed for you so that your faith will not fail."[45] What is called the "Synoptic apocalypse" (Matt. 24. 4–36; Mark 13. 5–37; Luke 21. 8–36), treating *en bloc* the sufferings of the persecution of the Church, of the end of Jerusalem, of the end of the world, centres all this on the perseverance of the elect, the condition of their salvation.

The constellation of sayings on the Kingdom that gravitates around this text is ordered on two axes. Some (the parables of the

[41] Luke 14. 26.
[42] Matt. 11. 17 and Luke 7. 34.
[43] Matt. 9. 15; Mark 2. 20; Luke 5. 35.
[44] John 17. 19.
[45] Luke 22. 31–32.

ten virgins) are dominated by the imminence of the coming in glory of the Son of Man, the necessity of living at each moment in readiness to meet him, with the correlative mistrust of the visible signs which men rely on to install themselves in this world and to postpone as long as possible any thought of the "eon" which is coming. The other sayings are, on the contrary (we might be tempted to say), permeated with the assurance that the Kingdom is in us and that it grows there without anyone's knowing of it (the grain of mustard seed, the sowing). What grows, more precisely, is the reception of the Gospel word in souls, that word in which the Kingdom is already present, as it is in Christ (the Sower). Whence that parable of the judgment (so full of prophetic reminiscences, cf. particularly Psalm 49) which discloses to us the presence of the Judge, then visible, today hidden in our neighbour, that neighbour which is every man. But we cannot go to meet him in our neighbour unless, in a certain way, we already have him in us: here is sketched out the teaching on the Spirit which the experience of the primitive Church would so greatly develop.

For the Baptist, the Spirit was but one with the fire of judgment: He was also the storm-wind coming to separate the chaff from the grain, according to the image taken up by Jesus at the approach of his death. But, in Jesus driving out demons, the divine Spirit also appears as Saviour before appearing as Judge.[46] And when Jesus sent his apostles to be exposed to the same hostility as himself, he promised them that the Spirit would be in them to speak in their stead.[47] Luke lets us glimpse what John would develop at length: a universal promise of the outpouring of this Spirit: "Will not the Father give the Spirit to those who ask for it?"[48]

[46] Matt. 12. 28.
[47] Matt. 10. 30; Luke 12. 12; cf. Mark 13. 11.
[48] Luke 11. 13.

III

THE PRIMITIVE CHURCH AND ST PAUL

THE preaching of the primitive Church was dominated by a twofold conviction bound up with a stupendous experience: the Christ given up to death has risen again: entered into the divine glory, he has sent the Spirit on his own.

The Primitive Preaching

However carefully composed (and even, perhaps, intentionally rewritten[1]) the Acts of the Apostles may have been, they none the less retain discourses of an obviously archaic quality. These discourses betray the embarrassment of the first Christians in the face of their experience and the complete overturn produced in all their ideas. This fact makes them the best witnesses possible to a fact so difficult to assimilate. Not only were the disciples sure that Jesus had come back to life, but from the outset his resurrection was recognized as a victory, as the liberation of his own from the power of evil: their salvation. Retrospectively, the resurrection illuminates his death and all that had gone before it. Above all, in the gift of the Spirit, it gives, besides a new understanding of everything, a wholly new life.

The first preaching of the days following Pentecost contains all this in summary form. But as yet it had no proper terms in which to express itself; it was not too clear what new vision of life and the world would recompose around the risen Jesus. St Paul, more than anyone else, may be considered the creator of Christian theology: of a formulated and unified expression of faith in the Risen Christ, of the experience of the Spirit. But his creative originality has too frequently caused scholars to ignore what he owed to the primitive Church in the very essence of what he was able to think out and express in so personal a way.

Peter's first discourse in the Acts on the day of Pentecost, with its

[1] See *Introduction à la Bible*, vol. II, pt. II, sec. 1, on the Acts (by L. Cerfaux).

lengthy quotation from Joel, begins by showing that the eschatological times have arrived, together with the new covenant announced by the last prophets and characterized by the communication of the Spirit to all the faithful. And this is the effect of the Resurrection. Or, more precisely, the Resurrection testifies, on the one hand, that Jesus' death forms part of the saving designs of God and, on the other hand, that these have been carried out and that Jesus fulfils the messianic promises. The key of the discourse is the phrase: "God has raised up this Jesus; we are all witnesses of it, And now, exalted by God's right hand, he has received from the Father the Holy Spirit, object of the promise, and has poured it out. This is what you see and hear."[2]

The Resurrection, in other words, is already seen not simply as making up for the cross, but as its fruit, and the principle of the effusion of the Spirit, from Jesus into all mankind. This is how we enter into the last times; this is how the messianic hope finds its realization in the new covenant. The covenant is not directly mentioned, but the text from Joel recalls it as directly, in its own way echoing Jeremias 31, as does the fiery manifestation of the Spirit, reminiscent of Sinai (we should not forget that Pentecost celebrated this memory[3]).

Peter's second discourse,[4] after the healing of the paralytic in the temple, takes up the theme of the providential character of Christ's death, witnessed by the prophets (recalling the words of Jesus pointing to Isaias 53 and the analogous texts). It introduces the new theme of the power of faith in his name (v. 16). And this same theme is taken up and developed in the third discourse before the Sanhedrin: "There is no other name under heaven given to men whereby we must be saved."[5]

The second discourse is, on the other hand, the first Christian text in which the idea of the two comings of Christ appears in full clarity. The last times are already here; with Christ's death and resurrection the supreme eschatological event has already taken place; but we await his return for the *apokatastasis*, the restoration of all things. The time in between is seen as the period for preaching the Gospel and for the *metanoia* which should result from it.[6]

These discourses, once again, are exceptionally interesting by reason of their archaic features, assuring us that the primitive form of Christian preaching has been respected. What proves this is not

[2] Acts 2. 32–63. On these first discourses in the Acts, see J. Schmitt, *Jésus ressuscité dans la prédication apostolique*, Paris, 1949.

[3] See Dom Thierry Maertens, *Le souffle et l'Esprit de Dieu*, Paris, 1959, particularly pp. 69ff.

[4] Acts 3. 12–16. [5] Acts 4. 12. [6] Acts 3. 19–21.

so much the supposition that the mass of Jews would be converted, but rather the expressions, so awkward, so inadequate to our way of thinking, designating Christ: "This man that God has accredited among you by the miracles, prodigies and signs that he wrought in your midst";[7] "His servant, Jesus, whom you gave up to death. . .".[8]

No less primitive is what the Acts tell us about life in the first Christian community. Community of goods is taken for granted, as in the most fervent *Chaburoth*.[9] But this is now described in the light of the Gospel *agape*: "The multitude of believers had but one heart and one soul." The three Jewish times of prayer were retained, at the third, the sixth and the ninth hours,[10] but the celebration of the eucharistic banquet[11] created a new focus of individual and collective piety which soon came completely to supplant that of the Temple. Let us not forget that the Gospel tradition, especially St Luke and St John, correlates the apparitions of the Risen Lord to the nascent Church with the *fractio panis*.[12] St John even testifies to a tradition, different from that of the Acts, according to which the first outpouring of the Spirit took place before Pentecost after a meal, like his promise at the end of the Last Supper.[13]

It was this complex whole, as yet unorganized but already basically coherent, which St Paul received from the embryonic Church.

St Paul's Personality

The nineteenth century was given to trying to describe St Paul's personality in a "historical" and "psychological" way.[14] There is much pseudo-scientific fantasy in these reconstructions, notwithstanding the relative abundance of extremely personal characteristics scattered throughout his Epistles and the various biographical data provided by himself and by the Acts. The fact is that we have some fairly detailed information about various episodes in St Paul's life, but remain completely ignorant about almost all the rest of it. The chronologies of his Epistles, made out to within a year (if not a month) by the majority of his modern commentators, are nothing but castles of conjectures, composed of probabilities; they seem to stand up only because it is impossible to prove or disprove them, lacking a single well-dated document. Furthermore, three or four

[7] Acts 2. 22. [8] Acts 3. 13 (cf. v. 26). [9] Acts 4. 32.
[10] Acts 2. 42, 46; 3. 1. [11] Acts 2. 42–46.
[12] Cf. Luke 24. 30–31; John 21. 9–14.
[13] John 14. 15ff. and 20. 22.
[14] See A. Schweitzer, *Geschichte der Paulinischen Forschung von der Reformation bis auf die Gegenwart*, Tübingen, 1933.

completely different systems are in existence, each as plausible or improbable as the others. The maps of the "missionary journeys of St Paul", never missing from Protestant Bibles, are equally uncertain, except for the small part of the outline provided by the passages in the Acts where the redactor speaks as an eye-witness.

All that we can state with certainty is limited to what St Paul himself tells us in a few lines of the Epistle to the Galatians.[15] He was a Jew of the tribe of Benjamin; a Hebrew, son of a Hebrew (that is to say, speaking the Hebrew language); born at Tarsus in Cilicia; a pupil of Gamaliel's in Jerusalem; and, on the other hand, a Roman citizen, speaking a very fluent if inelegant Greek; sufficiently acquainted with Hellenic thought and especially with Stoic moralism (the work, furthermore, of his compatriots of Cilicia); a Pharisee none the less, at least in tendency, nourished on rabbinical speculations. In virtue of all these accumulated contrasts, Paul must have been neither a "Palestinian" nor a "Hellenic" Jew in the sense defined by our modern textbooks, but a type doubtless far more common than the pure ones presented by imaginative historians. That, along with all this, he was "an ugly little Jew" as Renan wished him to be, is a conjecture that might possibly be drawn from some chance juxtaposition of ideas in his interminable and chaotic sentences, but is actually based on nothing but fantasy. All that we know is that, in their conceit, the Corinthians did not think him imposing or a good speaker in comparison with the fluent Apollo who was perhaps also the handsomer man.[16]

What the "Angel of Satan", the "sting in his flesh",[17] may have been—mentioned to correspondents who knew so well what he meant that he did not need to go into details—we shall never discover. We do not know anything about it, in spite of the flood of hypotheses ranging from neurosis to eye-trouble, in accordance with a variety of interpretations, all equally redolent of pedantic absurdity.

What we do see very clearly, however, is what betrays itself in almost every page of his Epistles and particularly in a marvellous passage of the Second Epistle to the Corinthians (which we owe to the incomparable folly of these same Corinthians)[18] and in some other passages almost as beautiful and equally aroused by the human stupidity which he seems to have suffered from as only a genius can: that is, his excessive sensibility, tempered by flashes of sarcastic humour, hiding or revealing a heart of truly magnanimous generosity. Choleric, authoritarian and yet argumentative, but

[15] Gal. 1. 2–2. 14. Cf. 2 Cor. 11.21–12. 10.
[16] Cf. Acts 18. 24; 1 Cor. 3. 4ff.; 2 Cor. 10. 10.
[17] 1 Cor. 12. 7. [18] 2 Cor. 11. 21–12. 10.

with a profound common sense and an exceptional power of intuition, absolute in his judgment and yet capable of a compassion going as far as tenderness, uninterested in anything that did not have a religious aspect and yet amazingly human—St Paul is a figure of the Jewish and Christian spiritual man whom one needs to become familiar with. Frequently he has been judged in contradictory ways—taxed with fanaticism or with intemperate dogmatism, seen sometimes as a man obsessed and sometimes as a heartless dialectician. But these fantasies vanish when we familiarize ourselves with his writings. Here we find, always vividly alive, one of the least conventional but most appealing saintly personalities of all history. But none of this gives us the key to his religious thought.[19]

St Paul's Sources

This key has been sought far and wide, even in regions the mere mention of which would have horrified St Paul himself, such as the mystery religions (which he must never have known) and their theology (which never existed). The simplest method is to go back and find this key in his own statements, so categorical and so fully corroborated by the many accounts in the Acts, accounts diffuse to the point of being somewhat embarrassing.

> "You have certainly heard tell of my former way of acting in Judaism, of the savage persecution I led against the Church of God and ravages that I caused it, and of my progress in Judaism, where I surpassed many compatriots of my own age as a fierce partisan of the traditions of my fathers. But . . . he who from my mother's womb set me apart and called me by his grace deigned to reveal his Son in me so that I might announce him to the pagans . . .[20]

The First Epistle to the Corinthians clarifies what this "revelation" was: an apparition of the risen Christ.[21] This is the episode on the road to Damascus, recounted in the Acts in three different places: 9. 1–19; 22. 5–16; 26. 10–18, with a wealth of details not always easy to put together, but a constant insistence on the essential: from a passionately anti-Christian Jew, Saul became the Apostle Paul, following on his vision of the living and glorious Christ.

[19] From the lengthy bibliography given in all the textbooks on the New Testament, it is enough to mention, from the viewpoint of the present book: A. Schweitzer, *Die Mystik des Apostels Paulus*, Tübingen, 1930, and the series of works by L. Cerfaux: *The Church in the Theology of St. Paul*, Herder, New York, 1959; *Christ in the theology of St. Paul*, 1959; *Le chrétien dans la théologie de saint Paul*, Paris, 1959.

[20] Gal. 1. 13–16.

[21] 1 Cor. 15. 8.

In fact, the conviction of Jesus' resurrection, with all that it signifies, clearly seems to be the principal focus of Paulinian teaching. And on this point it is impossible to see any difference between St Paul and the primitive Church. For him as for the apostles of Jerusalem, Christian faith is primarily faith in the resurrection of Jesus. And this faith, for him as for them, implies the certainty that it was Jesus' death that led to his resurrection: the resurrection puts his death in its proper light, in conformity with the Scriptures, particularly, that is, with Isaias' texts on the Servant.

What is peculiar to St Paul is the way in which he drew out the consequences of the resurrection, expressing them primarily in a series of contrasts or oppositions: between the "flesh" and the "Spirit"; the "law" and "grace"; the "present age", and the "age to come"; "the suffering of the present time and the glory which is to be revealed"; but, above all, between Adam and Christ and, more generally, between the old humanity, born of the earth, and the new humanity, issue of the resurrection. Behind these so typically Pauline oppositions, it should be noted, we shall find the eschatological context of the Gospel of Christ in its whole primary expression and then the bond established by the preaching at Jerusalem between Christ's resurrection and the outpouring of the Spirit.

The Two Adams

The most characteristic of these oppositions is the one which he was led to make by his own experience—between the old humanity and the new, united to the risen Christ. Two capital passages of the Epistle to the Romans[22] and of the First Epistle to the Corinthians[23] set out this contrast in the schema of the two Adams, principles of two humanities, the one condemned, the other justified. Numerous allusions to the "new man" in place of the "old man", to the "interior man" who is renewed while the "exterior man" is destroyed, and, certainly, another important passage in which the same opposition, though not stated, is glimpsed behind the text giving its difficulties their only possible solution—these indications, and others as well, give us reason to believe that this schema is really the matrix, as it were, of Paulinian spirituality.

Some modern scholars who have clearly observed this fact have tried to contest its originality. It is true that Philo gives us a whole play of speculations on the two Adams (re-appearing in Christian tradition with Gregory of Nyssa's idea of man and in later Jewish

[22] Ch. 5. [23] Ch. 15.

tradition with the figure of Adam Kadmon,[24] the original man, microcosm and centre of the cosmos). It is quite possible that St Paul was acquainted with these speculations. But the statements in the First Epistle to the Corinthians which lead us to think so also show that his conception is so different as to make it, in many respects, the exact contrary of Philo's.

All these rabbinical speculations, as well as the Babylonian (Gayomart, the mythological hero) or Iranian concepts which have been adduced as the source of St Paul's thought[25] are concerned with a myth designed to explain creation and the fall. The two Adams, or, more precisely, the two men here are primitive man, quasi divine, and actual man, fallen so low. With St Paul, on the contrary, it is the original man, it is Adam, who is the fallen man. And, as he brings out, it is only later that there appears, in the person of Jesus, the spiritual man, the heavenly man. For the myth of creation is substituted a history of salvation with exactly the reverse polarization. Attention is no longer concentrated on the first fall which led from a primal man to a degraded man, but on the free and gratuitous gift thanks to which fallen man is raised up at the end of time by the generous condescension of the "heavenly" man: "When the fullness of time had come, God sent his Son, born of woman, born under the law, to redeem those who were under the law, so that we might receive sonship."[26]

The first appearance of this theme contrasts specifically the sinful act and its destructive influence with the saving act and its limitless saving import. In this text of the Epistle to the Romans, St Paul draws the parallel between the actions of the two "men" rather than their personalities. He begins by announcing a comparison: "As by one man sin came into the world, and by sin, death, and so death was transmitted to all men, for all have sinned . . ."—but he loses his train of thought in a side issue. When he again takes up the thread of his main idea, it is no longer under the form of an analogy, but of a contrast:

> But it was not the same way with the fall as with grace (*charisma*); for, if the multitude (*hoi polloi*) died, much more has the grace (*charis*) of God and (his) giving (*dorea*), in the grace of the one man, Jesus Christ, been abundant for the multitude. And the gift (*dorema*) has not been like the fault of that one man who (first) sinned; the crime of one man called forth condemnation, but grace (*charisma*) called forth the justification of multiplied sins.

[24] The texts of Philo are *Leg. alleg.*, I. 31 and *De op. mundi*, 134; for Gregory of Nyssa, see his treatise on the creation of man, P.G., XLIV, 188ff. For Jewish speculations on Adam Kadmon, see G. Sholem, *Major Trends in Jewish Mysticism*, pp. 215, 265–7, 279, 400.

[25] See Kraeling, *Anthropos and Son of Man*, 1927.

[26] Gal. 4. 4–5.

Indeed if, by the sin of one man, death has reigned through the one man, much more will those who receive the abundance of grace and the giving of justice reign in life by the one Jesus Christ. Thus, then, as the sin of one man elicited condemnation for all men, equally the justice (*dikaiomatos*) of one man has elicited the justification of life for all men. For, just as by the disobedience of a single man the multitude of men were established as sinners, so, by the obedience of one man, the multitude has been established as just. As for the law, it intervened so that sin might abound; but where sin has abounded, grace (*charis*) has abounded the more, so much that, as sin has reigned in death, equally grace reigns through justice (*dikaiosune*) for eternal life, through Jesus Christ our Lord.[27]

How many insoluble problems have been raised in connection with this passage, in the desire to make it answer questions that the Apostle did not raise! Too rare, on the contrary, have been attempts to see exactly what his problem was and the solution he gives to it.

For St Paul, the act of the first man ("of Adam, type of him who was to come" v. 14) had essentially been one of disobedience, drawing down upon him death, drawing all other men after him into sin[28] and, consequently, into death. But this sinister fruitfulness of the first sin in sin and death is surpassed by the fruitfulness in justice and life revealed in the obedience of Jesus. On the one hand, a unique sin entails many sins and many deaths. On the other hand, a unique grace, which is also a unique obedience, justifies from numberless sins and calls forth a superabundance of justice and life for the multitude. The disobedience of Adam causes death to reign over men. The obedience of Christ causes men to reign in life.

In the text we have just read, what this "obedience" of Jesus concretely consisted in is not stated. But the lines that precede it leave no doubt: "Having been enemies, we have been reconciled with God by the death of his Son" (v. 10). The "obedience" of Christ, the "obedience" which more than compensates for the effects of Adam's disobedience, procuring justice and life for those whom disobedience has drawn into sin and death, making them reign in life when death had reigned over them, is precisely Jesus' death.

It seems undeniable that we find, here again, the direct influence of Isaias 53: in this death which is obedience and which, undergone by the just man, elicits the justification of sinners. We are, therefore, still following the line of the first apostolic preaching, itself guided by the Lord's own words, as to the meaning of his death.

27 Rom. 5. 15–21.

28 Whether or not they sinned in the same way as Adam—that is, against an explicit law—matters little. This is what is meant by the parenthesis we have omitted.

Sin and death

Where St Paul shows his originality is, first, in his conception of sin and death, then in that of grace, but especially in his whole synthesis of the two economies, starting from their respective principles, Adam and Christ.

Jesus does not seem explicitly to have taught anything about the economy of the present world other than what was taught by the apocalypses: it is a condemned economy, verging on its catastrophic end, because God does not reign therein. St Paul seems to have been the first to define more clearly what is decayed about "the present age". He does so in connection with man. Still more, it is within man—the pious man as well as the impious, the Jew as well as the Greek—that the mark of the demon's rule is evident to his eyes. The whole chapter 7 of the same Epistle to the Romans sheds light on the already remarkable implications of chapter 5. "Sin" is not an abstraction: "moral evil" as we call it. It is a truly evil power: "the law of the members" as St Paul says, which we all find within us, opposed to the "law of God", even when we give our interior assent to the latter. This power has extended its empire over the whole of mankind, starting from the first man, like a mysterious contagion. But we have the impression that it is something quite different from a kind of illness or deficiency: in each of us, sin takes the shape of a personal opposition for which we are personally responsible; but, at the same time, it seems to be in us all the multiform stamp as it were of a refusal not only all-inclusive, but unique.

So, too, for the attendant, or the shadow, of sin: death—death is certainly an individual, concrete event that will come upon each one of us. But it also is a kind of power that reigns in favour of sin over us all, being so closely bound up with sin as to seem like another face, the secret face now finally unmasked, of the same enemy.

Our original relationship with sin and death is described by St Paul, in the sixth chapter of the same Epistle to the Romans, as our having been slaves of sin, and as such devoted to death (v. 16), death being "the wage of sin" (v. 23).

Conversely, in the death of Christ our enslavement to sin is destroyed, provided that we are united with Christ and, more particularly, with his death, by means of baptism. This is the whole theme of chapter 6.[29]

So it is that Christ, in his death on the Cross, reveals and brings us "grace".

[29] Cf. vv. 2, 6, 7, 10.

Grace

What is "grace" for St Paul? We might say that it is every manifestation of that divine generosity by which Jesus had defined, as it were, the "perfection" of the heavenly Father. But it is more particularly that exceptional, unique manifestation: the appearance of Jesus, himself, his Cross. In chapter 5 of the Epistle to the Romans, the word *charis* repeatedly recurs. It gravitates around the Cross, explained as the manifestation of what is absolutely incomparable in God's love:

> Someone might conceivably be found ready to die for a just man; for a good man, yes, perhaps someone would go so far as to die, *but it is in this that God has manifested his love for us*: that Christ died for us *while we were still sinners.*[30]

This gratuity, this unheard of bounty—more than unmerited, beyond all hope—of the divine love, this is what grace is to St Paul. And it is Christ's Cross that supremely manifests this fulfilment, this supreme exaltation, of *hesed* in *agape.*

It follows that if Christ is contrasted with Adam as the obedient Servant to the rebellious sinner, he is opposed to him still more profoundly: by a contrast both of nature and of origin, as the "heavenly Man" to the "earthly man". It is in this new form that the theme of the two Adams reappears in the first Epistle to the Corinthians, chapter 15.

The Heavenly Man

St Paul has just insisted at length on the reality of Christ's resurrection, principle and pledge of our own. Then he sketches out the parallel, simply taking up again the motif of the Epistle to the Romans:

> Since death (came) through a man, through a man also the resurrection from the dead: for just as all died in Adam, so also all will be vivified in Christ.[31]

He then comes up against the objection: does the resurrection mean that we are to return to life with a body such as we have at present, weighed down with the pains and limitations of our present existence? No, he says:

> If there is an animal (*physike*) body, there is also a spiritual (*pneumatikos*). Thus it is written: "the first Adam was made as a living soul", but the last Adam as a vivifying spirit. Yet the spiritual was not the first, but the animal; then the spiritual. The

[30] 5. 7 and 8.

[31] 1 Cor. 15. 21–22.

> first man (was) of the earth, made of dust; the second man (is) of heaven. Like him who was made of dust are those made from him: like the heavenly man (*epouranios*), so those of heaven; and as we have borne the image of him who was made of dust, we shall also bear the image of the heavenly man. What I mean, brothers, is that flesh and blood cannot inherit the kingdom of God, nor can corruption inherit incorruptibility . . . For what is corruptible must be clothed with incorruptibility, and what is mortal with immortality. . . .[32]

Here we find everything that is included in "grace" in St Paul's sense of the word. It is not only an amazing condescension, the saving *act* of a limitless generosity: it is the gift of a new life, of a new *being*. This gift is made to us because Christ is "heavenly" because he has appeared in his resurrection as "life-giving Spirit", and has thus become for us a second Adam, the principle of a total renewal. This renewal will be completed by the resurrection, causing us to bear the image of Christ as we have borne that of Adam. Thus what is corruptible in us will be "clothed" with incorruptibility, what is mortal in us with immortality.

This image of clothing, applied to the resurrection, is a favourite one with St Paul; we find it again in the Second Epistle to the Corinthians:

> So long as we are in this tent [the transitory tent, *skene*, of our present body] we groan, weighed down as we are, because we desire, not to be naked, but rather to be reclothed [literally: clothed from above] so that what is mortal may be absorbed by life.[33]

The verses that precede, using the imagery of the First Epistle, explain that it is "from heaven" that we await this "clothing", so that we shall not be found naked.

In this last explanation, we find an allusion to the account of Genesis: Adam becoming conscious of his nakedness after he had sinned.[34] After the resurrection, man will no longer be in this state in which his sin has placed him, reduced to animality: the mortal in him will be as it were absorbed in life, because what is earthly will be absorbed in what is heavenly. And this will be brought about because the humanity that we have received from Adam will be as it were "clothed from above" with the new, "spiritual", "heavenly", humanity which is that of the risen Christ.

Nor should we imagine that this was only an object of hope for St Paul. He uses this image of "clothing" again, in connection with us and Christ, not to describe a future but rather a past reality

[32] 1 Cor. 15. 45–53. [33] 2 Cor. 5. 4. [34] Gen. 3. 7.

extended into the present, a present which already contains the future in embryo. For, in the Epistle to the Romans, the first passage concerning Adam and Christ, which we have already studied, leads directly to a development about baptism centred in this statement:

> All you who were baptized in Christ were baptized in his death: we were, indeed, buried by baptism with him in death, in order that as Christ was raised from the dead by the glory of the Father, so we also might walk in newness of life.[35]

And a parallel passage of the Epistle to the Galatians gives this still more precise formula: "All you who have been baptized in Christ, have been clothed with Christ."[36]

It follows that, when Christ's death extends its effects in us by baptism, it is already preparing the same effect of resurrection in us that it had in him. We may go so far as to say that, in a sense, we are already risen with Christ, inasmuch as baptism has united us to Christ dead and risen again. This is what the Epistle to the Ephesians says explicitly: "God has raised us up together and caused us together to sit in the heavenly places (*sunekathisen*) in Christ Jesus."[37]

This already real possession of the new being, the new life of the risen Christ, resulting from baptism, is obviously an object of faith, not yet visible. In a sense, however real it may be, it remains future:

> It is in hope that we have been saved (says the Epistle to the Romans), but hope that is seen is no longer hope; how can what is still seen still be hoped for? But if we hope for what we do not see, we await it by patience. . . .[38]

What, none the less, causes faith to have a content here and now, hope not to be completely unfulfilled even in the present, is the reality of the Spirit.

The Spirit

The passage we have just quoted from the Epistle to the Romans comes in the middle of an extensive development on the Spirit communicated to Christians in the Church. The following verse tells us:

> It is under these conditions that the Spirit comes to aid our weakness, for we do not know even how to pray as we should, but the Spirit intercedes for us with inexpressible sighs. . . .[39]

[35] Rom. 6. 3–4. [36] Gal. 3. 26. [37] Eph. 2. 6.
[38] Rom. 8. 24–25. [39] Rom. 7. 26.

This reality of the Spirit communicated to us is, for St Paul, what makes the resurrection of Christ, in a certain way, already present not only *for* us but *in* us. For it is the Spirit that manifests the mysterious inclusion of ourselves in Christ presupposed by the theme of the second Adam and expressed directly by the formula "in Christ Jesus", already encountered.[40] And it is the Spirit, present in us as in Christ, who witnesses to our divine sonship as he witnesses to Christ's.

Some scholars have denied that any possibility of mysticism—any ideal of union with God, of immediate knowledge of God—existed for St Paul. Others have held, with Albert Schweitzer, that St Paul's mysticism was completely eschatological, having no reality except in the future. St Paul's mysticism is certainly eschatological in the sense that it is wholly oriented towards a fulfilment which the resurrection alone can give it. But, in the life of the Spirit, there is a real anticipation of the life of the resurrection inaugurated by baptism and grasped by faith. To this extent, there is a Paulinian mysticism *for here and now*, which can equally well be called the mysticism of the Spirit or of the resurrection. It might be said that the whole purpose of chapter 8 of the Epistle to the Romans is to describe it:

> But now, there is no longer any condemnation for those who are in Christ Jesus, because in Christ Jesus the law of the Spirit of life has set you free from the law of sin and death. For what was impossible to the law, inasmuch as it was impotent because of the flesh, [here comes a very characteristic anacolouthon] . . . God has condemned sin in the flesh by sending his own Son in a flesh of sin, [as a sacrifice] for sin, so that the justice [*dikaioma*] of the law might be fulfilled in us who do not walk according to the flesh but according to the Spirit.
>
> Those who live according to the flesh are concerned with what is carnal; those who live according to the Spirit with what is spiritual. For the concern [*phronema*] of the flesh, is death, but the concern of the Spirit is life and peace; for the concern of the flesh is enmity with God, for it is not subject to the law of God; indeed it cannot be so; those who are in the flesh cannot please God.
>
> But you—you are not in the flesh but in the Spirit, if only the Spirit of God dwells in you. But if anyone does not have the Spirit of Christ, he is not Christ's. But if Christ is in you, the body is dead by reason of sin, but the Spirit is life by reason of justice [*dikaiosune*]. But if the Spirit of him who raised Jesus from among the dead dwells in you, then he who raised Jesus from

[40] See the celebrated study of Deissmann, *Die neutestamentliche Formel "in Christo Jesu"*, Marburg, 1892.

among the dead will vivify your mortal bodies also by the Spirit who dwells in you.[41]

Without intending to exhaust the richness of this text, let us emphasize how positive it is as to the actuality of the gift of the Spirit and of its effects manifested here and now. What follows, in fact, is an exhortation to co-operate with this gift for a whole transformation of our moral and religious life.

And we should particularly notice the close relationship established between this gift of the Spirit and the resurrection. The Spirit is "the Spirit of him who has raised Jesus from among the dead". "The Spirit of him who has raised Jesus from among the dead will vivify your mortal bodies."

On the other hand, this Spirit who is, therefore, that of the Father, is also described as the "Spirit of Christ". The dwelling of the Spirit in us (vv. 9 and 11) makes but one with the indwelling of Jesus himself (v. 10).

Christ in us

The gift of the Spirit thus appears as the substance of that life which St Paul describes as a life of "Christ in us" or as our life "in Christ Jesus", although he seems to prefer the latter formula. Our relationship with Christ, actualized by the gift of the Spirit and having its principle in baptism, is thus seen as a real entering of us into Christ, of his Spirit into us. This is how Christ has become for the sons of Adam as it were a second or, better, a final Adam—not that they are to be born of him by being separated from him, as they were born of Adam, but rather that they are to find themselves again in him, in such a way that it will be he himself who lives in them.

In fact, all these expressions are characteristic of St Paul. To the Ephesians, he says that we must grow according to the grace of Christ:

> until we all meet one another in the unity of faith and of the knowledge (*epignoseos*) of the Son of God in a single perfect Man, in the measure of the perfect age of Christ.[42]

In the Epistle to the Philippians, he sums up his own hope in the formula: "to be found in him".[43] To the Galatians, he says:

> I live, but it is no longer I who live, it is Christ who lives in me, and if I live now in the flesh, it is in the faith of the Son of God that I live.[44]

[41] Rom. 8. 1–11.
[42] Eph. 4. 13.
[43] Phil. 3. 9.
[44] Gal. 2. 20.

To the Romans:

> Consider yourselves as dead to sin but living to God in Christ Jesus.[45]

And, finally, he says again to the Philippians:

> "For me to live is Christ."[46]

And so, again using the image of clothing, he exhorts the Colossians to "cause your members that are upon the earth"—meaning the wicked inclinations of the flesh—"to die, having stripped off the old man with his works and put on the new, who is renewed in knowledge (*eis epignosin*) to the image of him who created him".[47] And while this imagery by itself might suggest something merely external, the complementary image of engrafting corrects this impression. We find this image, again in connection with baptism, in the sixth chapter of the Epistle to the Romans:

> If, indeed, we have become as it were one single plant with him [*symphytoi*] by assimilation to his death, we shall be one also for his resurrection. We know that our old man has been crucified with him, so that the body of sin is annihilated, in such a way that we are no longer slaves of sin, for he who is dead has been justified from sin. But if we are dead with Christ, we believe that we shall also live with him, etc. . . .[48]

The Body of Christ

One other vital image, that of the body and the head, definitively expresses our relationship with Christ, in the Spirit.

The question of the divine gifts of the Spirit and of their unity, in and for us all, is what immediately calls forth this image, in two chapters, one from the Epistle to the Romans and the other from the First to the Corinthians:

> For just as we have many members in one single body, and all the members do not have the same function, so we, who are many, are all one single body in Christ and members one of another. . . .[49]
>
> Just as the body is one, even though it has many members, and all the members of the body, though many, are one single body, so it is with Christ. For all of us have been baptized in the one Spirit to [form] one single body.[50]

In this same Epistle to the Corinthians, when St Paul reflects on the Eucharist as causing us to participate in the very body of the

[45] Rom. 6. 11. [46] Phil. 1. 21. [47] Col. 3. 9–10, cf. Eph. 4. 22–24.
[48] Rom. 6. 5ff. [49] Rom. 12. 4–5. [50] 1 Cor. 12. 12–13.

dead and risen Christ, the image of the body becomes more than merely an image:

> The bread that we break, is it not communion in the body of Christ? Because there is but one bread, we though many, become one single body; for we all partake of the one bread.[51]

This "body", that we become by communion in the "body" of Christ, goes beyond the image: it is the reality, mysterious above all others, of the life "in Christ Jesus" which is also the life of the Spirit in us. In the later Epistles "the body of Christ" appears as the proper designation of the Church, considered as "the fullness of him who completes himself fully in all",[52] and, reciprocally, Christ is called "the head of his body, which is the Church."[53]

Our Adoption

And finally, the Spirit that we have received from the risen Christ, or rather "in him", testifies that this assimilation to the risen Christ makes us sons, just as his own resurrection, by making him "lifegiving Spirit" had testified to his sonship.

The Epistle to the Romans proclaims this from its very first words:

> Jesus Christ has been established as Son of God with power according to the Spirit of holiness by his resurrection from the dead.[54]

And about ourselves, a little later:

> All those who are led by the Spirit of God are sons of God. For you have not received a spirit of slavery to be still in fear, but you have received the Spirit of sonship, in which we cry out: *Abba*, that is, Father! The Spirit himself testifies to our spirit that we are children of God; and if we are children, we are also heirs: heirs of God, co-heirs with Christ, if only we suffer with him so as also to be glorified with him.[55]

The inheritance that we share with him, through the Spirit, is evidently sonship itself.

It is to be noted that the Epistle to the Galatians presents a detailed verbal parallel to this text of Romans, proof of how important this train of thought was to St Paul. Here, however, instead of starting from the Spirit to arrive at the idea of sonship, the thought of our sonship leads to the idea of the gift of the Spirit:

> ... God sent his own Son, born of a woman, born under the law, ... so that we might receive sonship. And since you are

[51] 1 Cor. 10. 16–17. [52] Eph. 1. 23. [53] Eph. 1. 22; cf. Col. 1. 18.
[54] Rom. 1. 4. [55] Rom. 8. 14–17.

> sons, God has sent the Spirit of his Son into our hearts, crying: *Abba*, that is, Father! so that you are no longer a slave but a son, and if you are a son, an heir of God.[56]

Now, we can retrace the whole chain. The first Adam had begotten us in sin, for death—in slavery that is to say; *in* the final Adam we are begotten, on the contrary, "for the freedom of the glory of God's children".[57] For he is "the heavenly man", "life-giving Spirit". He is "established" as such by his resurrection, inasmuch as at his resurrection his divine sonship shone out to our eyes. We ourselves by baptism are made one single being with him in assimilation to his death, in view of his resurrection. The Spirit within us is the living witness of this assimilation and, therefore, of this communicated sonship. And it is nourished by the Eucharist so that we form in all truth "the body of Christ".

This sonship is developed by the life of faith, or rather "life in faith".[58] The soul of this life is found in the gifts of the Spirit, of which the most eminent is *agape*,[59] "the love of God poured out in our hearts by the Spirit who has been given us".[60] In the Spirit and the divine *agape* of which he is the source in our hearts, therefore, we live a new life here and now, a life of progressive assimilation to the risen Christ. The Second Epistle to the Corinthians describes this life in terms which define, as it were, the mysticism of the Spirit already mentioned. These are introduced when the apostle brings up, in order to contrast, the economy of the letter, that is, of the exterior law, and that of the Spirit:

> The Lord is Spirit, and where the Spirit of the Lord is there is freedom. We all, then, with face unveiled (in contrast to Moses and to the people of the old law), reflecting the glory of the Lord as in a mirror, are transformed into his image, from glory to glory, as by the Lord who is Spirit.[61]

This transformation, as the apostle explains again a little later in reference to the "interior man", is developed to the extent to which the "exterior man" is given up to death:

> Even if our exterior man is destroyed, our interior man is renewed from day to day. For the light tribulation of a moment produces for us, in an incomparable way, an eternal weight of glory.[62]

This "interior man", like the "new man", is obviously always "the final Adam", "the heavenly man" to whom we are assimilated "in Christ" by the Spirit.

[56] Gal. 4. 4–7. [57] Rom. 8. 21. [58] Cf. Gal. 2. 20, quoted above.
[59] Cf. 1 Cor. 13. [60] Rom. 5.5.
[61] 2 Cor. 3. 17–18. [62] 2 Cor. 41. 6–17; cf. Eph. 3. 16.

This, clearly, is the major theme of St Paul's thought, and around it is constructed the great text that expresses both his theology of salvation and his whole spirituality—the exhortation in the Epistle to the Philippians:

> Have in you the same mind that was in Christ Jesus, he who, being himself the divine image [in contrast to Adam, merely made *according to* this image], did not think of snatching at equality with God [in contrast to Adam whom the devil had successfully incited thereto]. But he annihilated himself, taking the image of a slave, made to the likeness of man [all this brings out how Jesus' appearance on earth was the exact counterpart of that of Adam, made to the image and likeness of God]. Being found in the condition of a man, he humbled himself, becoming obedient even to death—death on the cross [while the life of Adam had been marked by disobedience, a disobedience stimulated by his lust for the divine life]. This is why God has sovereignly exalted him, and given him the name which is above every name, so that at the name of Jesus every knee should bend—in the heavens and on earth and under the earth—and every tongue confess that Jesus Christ is Lord, to the glory of God the Father.[63]

The Heavenly Adam and the Son of Man

This vision of faith commands, as we have said, the great contrasts in which the whole spirituality of St Paul is set out: especially those of flesh and Spirit, law and grace. But before studying these more closely, we need to find the source, and so the exact import, of this central religious intuition of Paulinian Christianity. We have already mentioned the efforts that have been made to find Hellenistic and even Iranian origins both in Philo and in St Paul for the schema of the two Adams. But, to repeat, St Paul manifests his complete independence with regard to the myth to which Philo testifies. Whatever the origin of the latter's thought on this point, that of St Paul so little proceeds from Philo's that it seems to be its deliberate counterpart.

What should have struck the reader, on the contrary, after our previous study of Jesus' most certainly authentic teaching concerning himself, is St Paul's profound fidelity to this teaching. For what is the "heavenly Man" whom he awaits for the judgment of the universal resurrection, but the "Son of Man"?[64] St Paul's paradoxical juxtaposition of the supernatural characteristics of this "heavenly Man" with the humiliation and painful obedience of the

[63] Phil. 2. 7–11.

[64] See the study of Jean Héring, "Kyrios Anthropos", in the *Revue d'Histoire et de Philosophie religieuses*, Strasbourg, May–Oct. 1936, pp. 196–209.

Servant corresponds feature by feature with the fusion into one of these two apparently opposed figures: the Son of Man and the Servant—the fusion first made by Jesus himself with such creative audacity.

St Paul's Christology, then, is seen to be completely biblical, or, better, to be simply a systematizing—but one evidencing genius—of the definition of himself that Jesus had drawn from the Bible. And St Paul even faithfully reflects the way in which the teaching of Jesus brought out the idea of divine sonship in such startling relief—even though it is here that St Paul indubitably shows the greatest creative originality. In his thought, as in what we know most certainly about the teaching and the behaviour of Jesus, it appears both that Jesus is by nature "Son of God" in a unique sense and that we are all called to become sons of God, but by the grace of graces.

What Paul adds is the explicit connection between these two statements: the Son has taken on himself our condition and state as slaves in order to communicate his Sonship to us. Yet this explanation, Paulinian as it is, arises from the soteriology already implicit in the use Jesus had made of the sufferings of the Servant in order to explain his Cross.

The same origin must certainly be assigned to the Paulinian teaching, however personal it also may be, on the "Body of Christ which is the Church". This teaching exists in embryo in the image of the Servant, who is an individual, and who yet makes but one with the whole of the final Israel, just as the Son of Man in Daniel is already identified with "the people of the saints of the Most High".[65] Let us add that here again, the apostle's meditation was directed towards its final conclusions by such sayings of Jesus as this: "What you have done to the least of my brethren, you have done to me."[66]

St Paul and the Mysteries

All this being so, what are we to think of the attempts made by certain modern scholars to explain the significance which St Paul gives to the death of Christ, and his mysticism of incorporation into Christ, by his having been influenced by the Greek mystery religions of that period?[67]

These same explanations raise—let us remark at the outset—

[65] Dan. 8. 18. Cf. on these preparations of the New Testament in the Old, J. de Fraine, S.J., *Adam et son lignage*, Louvain, 1959.

[66] Matt. 20. 15.

[67] See especially, A. Loisy, *Les Mystères païens et le Mystère chrétien*, 2nd ed., Paris, 1930, pp. 223ff.

more problems than they pretend to solve. They begin by gratuitously endowing the rites (which we know very little about) of the mystery religions with an imaginary content borrowed from the Christian sacraments. For there is nothing in the texts allowing us to think that the mysteries ever conveyed the idea of a God dying voluntarily in order to save his worshippers (in any sense akin to the Christian meaning). These texts simply recall the catastrophe of gods fallen in spite of themselves, who were themselves the first to need salvation. And the worshippers' association with this salvation, through the mystery, never seems to have signified anything more or better than a special protection—nothing analogous with the new life, the ethical as well as ontological transformation, in which Paulinian "sonship" is realized. Just as salvation by Jesus' death is explained, in St Paul, by elements that are exclusively Jewish and drawn from the most primitive Christianity, so it is to this same source that we must look for the origin of his sacraments and of the meaning that he gave to them.

In actual fact, nobody has ever seriously held that St Paul knew of any baptism or Eucharist other than those of the Church. But the attempt has been made to see an innovation in the particular way whereby he relates them to the saving death of Jesus, as well as in his clear statement of the Real Presence in the eucharistic species.

The Eucharist

To begin with this second sacrament, it is noteworthy that, on the contrary, St Paul stressed the fact that he has received this interpretation of the Eucharist as a tradition coming from the Lord. And it is clear that, far from taking refuge thereby in any esoteric source, he is appealing to the tradition of the Church in Jerusalem. What proves this is the fact that, although he was exposed to such lively attacks on the part of Jewish and Judaizing Christians, he never seems to have been the object of any such criticism on this point.

Furthermore, no ancient witness to the Christian Eucharist is so thoroughly "Jewish" as that of the properly Paulinian tradition. Not only does St Paul keep the traditional Jewish term "cup of blessing" for the eucharistic cup, but also the Gospel account of the Last Supper in Luke, the most Paulinian of the evangelists, is, as we shall see later on, incomprehensible to anyone who does not locate it in the context of the Jewish liturgy.

Cullmann has demonstrated the series of misunderstandings underlying Lietzmann's theory of a Paulinian Eucharist centred on the

Supper and the death of Jesus in contrast to a primitive Eucharist which would have been a pure thanksgiving, illuminated simply by the memory of Jesus' presence with his own during the meals of his earthly life. The primitive Eucharist and the Paulinian Eucharist are both illuminated primarily by the manifestations of the risen Christ in the first eucharistic gatherings. And it is from these that light is cast on the Last Supper before the Passion.[68] Here as elsewhere, St Paul does nothing more than work out the implications of the beliefs of the primitive Church, recalling, after the resurrection, the words of Jesus that had preceded his death.

As for the idea of the eucharistic presence defined by the contrast of the body with the blood, it corresponds to categories so purely Jewish that it is impossible to seek an origin for it other than this same testimony of the Church of Jerusalem to Jesus' own words and acts.

Baptism

And, finally, as to St Paul's interpretation of baptism—might we not say that it projects, as it were, on to the baptism of the faithful a saying which the evangelists attributed to Jesus, one which it is supremely unlikely that they could have invented: "Can you receive the baptism with which I am to be baptized?"[69]—a transparent allusion to his death.

More generally, it must be admitted that Paulinian mysticism has a completely Jewish context. In the Second Epistle to the Corinthians, we found this mysticism expressed in terms of a seeing, or rather of a reflecting, that transforms and assimilates us to the image reflected. Efforts have been made to connect these terms with what is called Hellenic mysticism, particularly the kind believed to be found in the Hermetic writings. But, in actual fact, the context situates us in a purely Jewish world of thought. Here, with Sinai and the luminous cloud in which the Fathers were "baptized", we find the context of the mysticism of the *Shekinah*—and we have already mentioned how completely *sui generis* to Judaism this mysticism is. As to the supposition that an ontological assimilation of the worshipper to his God, a "divinization" (*theosis*) as it would be called later on, wherever it appears in religious thought betrays a Hellenistic influence—we shall see in the proper place what is to be thought of this notion.

Paulinian mysticism, the mysticism of the resurrection and of the Spirit, with its sacramental context, its completely biblical and

[68] Cf. H. Lietzmann, *Messe und Herrenmahl*, 1926, and O. Cullmann, *La signification de la Sainte-Cène dans le christianisme primitif*, Strasbourg, 1936.
[69] Mark 10. 38; cf. Luke 12. 50.

Jewish modes of expression, was the product of an experience (and of a reflection on that experience) undoubtedly personal to the highest degree. But this experience found its home, as it were, in the experience of the Church on the morning of the resurrection. And the interpretation of both the one and the other was constructed with elements of purely Jewish thought, under the single but capital influence of the words of Jesus treasured by the community of his disciples.

Let us see now the practical spiritual orientations, and especially the asceticism, that were to be dictated by this mysticism. Here come in the two great oppositions: flesh-Spirit, law-grace. These immediately depend on the opposition of the two Adams and the two humanities derived from them. And they are set in the wider context of the oppositions typical not only of primitive Christianity but of all the apocalyptic Jewish circles. This means that no more immediate or more serious mistake can be made than to identify St Paul's opposition of flesh to Spirit with the Greek body-soul dualism.

The Flesh and the Spirit

"The flesh", according to St Paul, is not the body as opposed to the soul, for the simple reason that the Spirit to which the flesh is opposed is not in the least the human soul but the "Spirit of God", the "Spirit of Christ". It might be said, then, that the "flesh" is what the whole man becomes, soul as well as body, when he does not have this divine "Spirit". The word "flesh" seems to have been chosen precisely to signify that it is not the living body which St Paul has in mind, but rather the being deprived of that breath of life without which he is nothing more than a corpse.

St Paul, furthermore, is not concerned with the specifically Greek dichotomy between the soul and the body. Faithful to the realism of Jewish thought, he always thinks of man as a whole: for him, the body does not imply so much the materiality of human life as opposed to its spirituality, as it does the organic unity of that life, indissolubly material and spiritual.

This is why eternal life, salvation made perfect, is for him in no way a deliverance from the body, but the resurrection of the body. Is not man's body called to become a member of Christ, a temple of the Spirit? And the prescriptions that he lays down for Christians regarding their sexual life, far from implying any condemnation of the body, expressly presuppose its necessary association with the life of the Spirit.

The Spirit, on the other hand, is obviously transcendental: it is, once again, the Spirit of God, the Spirit of the risen Christ—in other words the vital breath of God's own life. But, as the effect of Christ's resurrection and our union with him by faith and baptism, this Spirit is to animate, to permeate, to assimilate our whole life, the very depths of our being. So "the Spirit", for St Paul, comes to mean this whole new life which we are called to live.

The flesh, on the contrary, is a human life not vivified by this divine Spirit. This life is not only destined for death; it is nothing more than a death already in process.

While it is most important to keep all this in mind and not to confuse the Paulinian duality of the "flesh" and the "Spirit" with any kind of Greek and, still less, Manichean dualism, we must not conclude that the flesh has nothing in common with our corporal nature. Proof to the contrary are the cases—even though relatively rare—where St Paul uses the word "body" in a sense at least akin to that which he ordinarily reserves for the word "flesh". So he says: "Unhappy that I am! Who will deliver me from this body of death?"[70] Or, again, he speaks of "oppressing my body and reducing it to slavery, for fear that after having preached to others, I myself will be disqualified."[71] But his most revealing expression in this regard is in the eighth chapter of the Epistle to the Romans, where he says: "If Christ is in you, even though the body be already dead by reason of sin, the spirit is life by reason of justice." And he adds at once: "And if the Spirit of him who has raised Jesus Christ from among the dead lives in you, he who has raised Christ from the dead will also give life to your mortal bodies by his Spirit who dwells in you."[72]

We should note that, in this last text, the same word *pneuma* designates in turn the spirit of man destined to be immediately vivified by the Spirit of God (here the same as "the interior man" of whom the Apostle speaks elsewhere) and the Spirit himself. Conversely, here the body is the same as the "external man which is corrupted."[73] In other words, the flesh is not the body, but it is what man becomes when his created spirit no longer submits itself to the divine Spirit and, in consequence, no longer imposes a "spiritual" life on the body: by its own disobedience it has given free rein to the physical appetites of that body, and so become their slave.

When we have thoroughly familiarized ourselves with these ideas, then we are in a position to grasp the precise import of the exhortations in the Epistle to the Romans or the Epistle to the Galatians:

> Those who live according to the flesh are concerned with what is carnal; those who live according to the Spirit with what is

[70] Rom. 7. 24.
[71] 1 Cor. 9. 27.
[72] Rom. 8. 10–11.
[73] 2 Cor. 4. 16.

> spiritual. For the concern of the flesh [*to gar phronema tes sarkos*] is death, but the concern of the Spirit is life and peace; for the concern of the flesh is enmity with God for it is not subject to the law of God; indeed it cannot be so; those who are in the flesh cannot please God. But you—you are not in the flesh but in the Spirit, if only the Spirit of God dwells in you. But if anyone does not have the Spirit of Christ, he is not Christ's. . . .[74]

The beautiful passage follows, quoted earlier, on the Spirit dwelling in us and transforming even our mortal bodies. Then comes this conclusion:

> Thus, my brothers, we are no longer debtors to the flesh, to have to live according to the flesh. For if you live according to the flesh you will die. But if, by the Spirit, you cause the works of the body to die, you shall live.[75]

The Epistle to the Galatians explains the same teaching in concrete detail.

> Walk in the Spirit and you will not carry out the desire of the flesh. For the flesh sets its desire against the Spirit and the Spirit against the flesh; they are opposed to one another, in such a way that you do not do what you will; but if you are led by the Spirit. you are no longer under the law of the flesh. Now the works of the flesh are obvious: fornication, impurity, debauchery; idolatry and sorcery; quarrels, discord, jealousy, fits of anger, disputes, dissensions, divisions, jealousies, orgies, carousing and the like—and I warn you, as I have done already, that those who commit such sins will not inherit the Kingdom of God. But the fruit of the Spirit is charity, joy, peace, patience, kindness, goodness, fidelity, gentleness, self-control: against such things, there is no law. And those who belong to Christ Jesus have crucified the flesh, with its passions and desires.[76]

The Law and Grace

This last text takes us from the opposition between the flesh and the Spirit to that between the law and the Spirit, or, as St Paul prefers to say, between the law and grace. This opposition is perhaps even more delicate to grasp exactly than the preceding one, with which it is closely bound up. The same two Epistles, to the Romans and to the Galatians, particularly develop both themes, the Apostle declaring in the first, "You are no longer under the law, but under grace"[77] (4. 14), and in the second: "If you are led by the Spirit, you are no longer under the law".[78]

But what is the law? The word, as St Paul uses it, takes on a

[74] Rom. 8. 5–9.
[75] 5. 12 and 13.
[76] Gal. 5. 16–24.
[77] Rom. 4. 14.
[78] Gal. 5. 18.

series of meanings with an increasingly wider scope, ranging from the Ten Commandments to the whole of the Old Covenant. But he is usually referring to the legislation of the Pentateuch (the law of Moses, cf. 1 Cor. 9. 9), understood according to the Pharisees' interpretation as being a sacred code prescribing how to behave under all circumstances. In this sense, a man is "justified", by the fact that he carries out "the works of the law". But against this point of view—which was his before his conversion and which remained that of the judaizing Christians with whom he had to contend all during his career—Paul now declares:

> Through [*ex*] the works of the law, no man would be justified in God's sight, for, by the law [what was brought about was] consciousness [*epignosis*] of sin.[79]

The Epistle to the Galatians develops this idea further and immediately provides the Christian counterpart:

> Man is not justified by [*ex*] the works of the law, but only through [*dia*] the faith of Christ Jesus, and so we have believed in Christ Jesus, in order to be justified through [*ek*] faith in Christ and not by the works of the law, for, by the works of the law, no one is justified."[80]

In these two texts, we perceive the same allusion to Psalm 142. 2 ("no man"—literally, no flesh—"is justified in his sight").

In these two epistles, the counterpart of justification by the law is justification by faith. This last point is developed more fully in the Epistle to the Galatians, but it is formally stated in the Epistle to the Romans.[81] The two epistles illustrate the contrast between the two kinds of justification by invoking the example of Abraham: Gen. 15. 6—"Abraham believed in God and this was counted to him as justice"—recurs at the heart of substantially identical arguments in Romans 4. 3 and Galatians 3. 6.

The Epistle to the Romans shows us clearly how, in the mind of the Apostle, the opposition between "justification by the works of the law," and "justification by faith" results from the opposition between "the law," and "grace". The basic economy of the relations between God and man does not rest on (fulfilling) "the law," but on the "promise of God," given to Abraham first and then later to all believers who, as such, are the true sons of Abraham.[82] It is in this sense that justification is:

> by [*ex*] faith, to be according to grace, in order that the promise might be valid for all Abraham's posterity, not only for [the

[79] Rom. 3. 20. [80] Gal. 2. 16.

[81] Cf. Rom. 3. 22: "The justice of God by faith in Jesus Christ."

[82] Cf. Rom. 4, particularly 16–25.

posterity] which comes from the law, but for that which comes from the faith of Abraham. For he is the father of us all, as it is written (Gen. 17. 5): I have appointed you to be the father of many races—inasmuch as he believed in the God who brings the dead to life and who summons what does not exist as if it existed—; he (Abraham), who believed, hoping against hope, that he would become the father of many races, according to what had been said to him: such will be your posterity. . . .[83]

All this means that man does not become just from fulfilling the law by his own efforts to carry out its prescriptions, but from the grace of God:

"being justified freely [*dorean*] by his grace, through the redemption which is in Christ Jesus, whom God appointed in advance [*proetheto*] as a propitiation [or a propitiatory] by faith in his blood, for the manifestation of the justice [of God], in the non-imputation of previous sins, in the patience of God in view of manifesting His justice at the present time—manifesting, that is, that he himself is just and that he justifies him who has the faith of Jesus."[84]

This text is extremely condensed and it is not easy to give an exact explanation of every detail. Yet it defines very clearly the way in which grace is opposed to the law, by explaining everything that for this purpose is to be included in the term "grace". The law could not justify man unless he could fulfil it. But, in fact, it only brought out his incapacity to do so. In this regard, the startling "justice" of God is manifested in the gift of his Son, and particularly in his death, as constituting the supreme propitiation; whence pardon for the past together with, for the present, the justice communicated by God to the man who believes in the wholly gratuitous grace given him by God in the Cross of Jesus.

Does not belief in the Cross mean belief in the God who brings the dead back to life and who will, therefore, also justify the unjust by communicating his own justice to them in Christ?[85]

For this justification of the sinner by grace, by faith in Jesus crucified, is not a mere external, simply juridical, imputation of the justice of God in Jesus Christ. On the contrary, it is the principle of our transformation by the Spirit. St Paul says that "receiving the abundance of grace and of the gift of justice [we shall reign] in life through the one Jesus Christ",[86] explaining that, "Where sin had abounded, grace has abounded the more, so much that, as sin has reigned in death, equally grace reigns through justice for eternal life, through Jesus Christ our Lord."[87]

[83] Rom. 4. 16–18.
[84] Rom. 3. 24–26.
[85] Cf. Rom. 4.
[86] Rom. 5. 17.
[87] Rom. 5. 21.

And what follows clearly indicates what this means very concretely in the Christian life:

> What, then, are we to say? That we should remain in sin so that grace may abound? No, never! We have died to sin; how should we still live in it? Or do you not know that we all who have been baptized in Christ Jesus, were baptized in his death? We were, then, buried with him in death by baptism in order that, as Christ was raised from the dead by the glory of the Father, so we also should walk in a new life (*en kainoteti zoes*).
>
> For if we have become one single plant with him (*symphytoi*) by the likeness of his death, we shall be one with him in his resurrection. For we know that our old man has been crucified with him, so that the body of sin might be destroyed, in order that we should no longer be in slavery to sin: for he who is dead has been justified with regard to sin. But if we are dead with Christ, we believe that we shall also live with him, knowing that Christ, once risen from the dead, dies now no more; death has no further power over him. For, as he died, he died to sin once for all; but, as he lives, he lives to God. In the same way, consider yourselves dead to sin but alive to God in Christ Jesus.
>
> Therefore, let sin no longer reign in your mortal body so that you obey its desires; no longer give over your members to sin as the instruments of injustice, but present yourself to God as living men raised from the dead, and your members as the instruments of justice for God; for sin no longer rules over you; you are no longer under the law but under grace."[88]

This text sheds a definitive light on the preceding ones. Death comes from sin, but once death has been undergone, there is no more sin. Thus those who, by baptism and faith, have died with Christ are as it were dead to sin. But by faith in him who raises up the dead and at the same time justifies the unjust, they can "walk in a new life", they can give themselves up to justice as formerly they were given up to sin. This is what it means "to live under grace and not under the law".

These ideas are developed in the diptych of chapters 7 and 8. Chapter 7 describes for us the man who is "under the law": according to the "interior man" he delights in the law of God (v. 22), but he sees in his members another law, which wars even against the law of his understanding and makes him the prisoner of the law of sin in his members (v. 23). Whence the cry: "Unhappy man that I am, who will deliver me from this body of death?" (v. 24), and the immediate answer: "Thanks be to God, through Jesus Christ our Lord!" (v. 25).

[88] Rom. 6. 1–14.

The whole of chapter 8 then shows us how the law of the Spirit of life in Jesus Christ has delivered us from the law of sin and death (v. 2):

> For what was impossible to the law, inasmuch as it was impotent because of the flesh . . . God has condemned sin in the flesh, by sending his own Son in a flesh of sin and [as a sacrifice] for sin, so that the justice [*dikaioma*] of the law might be fulfilled in us who do not walk according to the flesh but according to the Spirit" (vv. 4 and 5).

Now we can understand, on the one hand, why the Apostle seems to identify "being in the flesh" with "being under the law".[89] The gift of the law by itself could only reveal the tragic power of sin in carnal man:

> We know that the law is spiritual, but I am carnal, sold to sin. What I do, I do not understand. For what I will is not what I carry out; I do what I hate . . . For I know that there lives in me, that is, in my flesh, nothing good: for to will the good is within my reach, but to accomplish it is not."[90]

It is in this sense that the law was given only to manifest sin,[91] that the law carries out God's wrath,[92] that the law came so that sin would abound,[93] and that now we are as though we no longer existed in relation to the law.[94] In fact, according to this line of thought, grace supplants the law, those who are led by the Spirit are no longer under the law.

On the other hand, we can now understand also how, without any contradiction, St Paul equally well says "that the goal of the law is Christ",[95] explaining in the Epistle to the Galatians that the law was like a pedagogue leading us to Christ.[96]

In the same way, he can say that "those who are led by the Spirit are no longer under the law[97] and almost immediately afterwards, add that "the law is not against such men".[98] For as the Epistle to the Romans says: "He who loves his neighbour has fulfilled the law . . . the whole law is summed up in love (*agape*)."[99] Again, the Epistle to the Galatians states: "For the whole law is fulfilled in one word: thou shalt love thy neighbour as thyself",[100] and again: "Bear one another's burdens, and so you shall fulfil the law of Christ."[101] And the whole fifth chapter of the Epistle to the Romans culminates in the statement: "The love of God is poured out in our hearts by the Holy Spirit who has been given to us."[102]

89 Cf. Rom. 8. 5–6.
90 Rom. 7. 14–19 and all that follows.
91 Rom. 3. 20.
92 Rom. 4. 15.
93 Rom. 5. 20.
94 Rom. 7. 6.
95 Rom. 10. 4.
96 Gal. 3. 24.
97 Gal. 5. 18.
98 Gal. 5. 23.
99 Rom. 13. 18.
100 Gal. 5. 14.
101 Gal. 6. 2.
102 5. 5.

The opposition of grace, of the Spirit, to the law, therefore, is resolved in a transcending of the law which is not abolition but fulfilment: because grace is the supreme gift of the divine love, because the Spirit is the gift enabling us to love as God loves.

If we are "justified by faith" and not "by the works of the law", the spirituality that results is not in the least indifferent to ethics, it is rather ethics renewed by the gift of the Spirit, the gift of the divine love accessible only to the faith "of Christ", that is, faith in the God who brings the dead to life and who justifies the wicked.

Paulinian Asceticism

This ethics of charity in faith—the practical applications of which St Paul does not fail to set out in detail at the end of each of his epistles—involves an asceticism. The fact that everything in the Christian life is the product of a pure gift of God in no way excludes human effort and one very systematically carried out; on the contrary, it makes such effort possible. The Epistle to the Philippians gives us the perfect formulation of this paradox—as liberating as it is exigent: "Work at your salvation with fear and trembling, for it is God who works in you both the willing and the doing according to his good pleasure."[103]

To say even more: what the "law of Christ", the "law of the Spirit" requires is precisely liberation with regard to the "law of the members", a deliverance which gives us up completely to God, to his *agape*. Whence the very special dialectic between slavery and freedom in St Paul's thought. We were slaves of sin, of death, of the enemy "powers".[104] Christ has freed us from all this.[105] But, the Apostle tells us: "Having been delivered from sin, you have become slaves with regard to justice . . . with regard to God."[106] On his own part, the Apostle continually proclaims himself the "slave of Christ",[107] or better, he says of himself, "through Christ, your slave".[108] Does he not invite all his disciples to make themselves: "through charity, slaves of one another"?[109] Christ himself, even though he was in the very image of God, took the likeness of a slave for our sake.[110] And it was by doing so that he was brought to the supreme lordship.[111]

And so our liberation, our exaltation in the divine sonship, through the Spirit, presuppose a voluntary subjection. Conversely, it is by this subjection that we become truly free, truly sons, because

103 Phil. 2. 12.
104 Cf. Gal. 4 and Rom. 7.
105 Rom. 6. 18; 8. 2; cf. Gal. 5. 1.
106 Rom. 6. 18–22.
107 Rom. 1. 1; Gal. 2. 10; Phil. 1. 1.
108 2 Cor. 4. 5.
109 Gal. 5. 13.
110 Phil. 2. 7.
111 Phil. 2. 11.

truly given up to the Spirit in love. Whence the formula already quoted "I oppress my body and reduce it to slavery, for fear that having preached to others I should myself be disqualified."[112]

This comes as the conclusion of a line of thought comparing the Christian life to the severe training undertaken by athletes eager to carry off a prize in the stadium:

> Do you not know that those who run in the stadium all run the race, though only one carries off the prize? Run, then, to win. But every athlete exercises restraint in all things [*panta egkrateuetai*]; they do it to win a wreath that fades, but we for an unfading one. I myself run, but not at random; I struggle, but not as someone who beats the air. I oppress my body, etc.[113]

The following chapter, recalling how the Hebrews sinned in the desert by giving in to their lusts, explains more fully the application of this image.

It is from this comparison of the Christian life to an athlete's training that we get the term "asceticism": taken from the Greek term for athletic exercise.

The central verse of this same chapter (10), as has been noted, explicitly relates ascetic training to the eschatological opposition between the present age and the age to come. What should urge us to asceticism is that for us "the end of time" has already come.[114]

It is this consideration which, in chapter 7 of the same Epistle, dictates the Apostle's teaching about marriage and voluntary continence. There is no question of condemning or depreciating marriage;—in the Epistle to the Ephesians, chapter 5, St. Paul declares that marriage is, and should be, in its whole reality, the very image of the union between Christ and his Church.

> But what I say, brothers, is that the time is short [literally, limited]. While it lasts, let those who have wives be as if they had not; those who weep as if they did not weep, those who buy as if they did not own, those who use this world as if they did not use it, for the order of this world is passing away. What I wish, is for you all to be free of anxiety. He who is not married cares about the things of the Lord: how to please the Lord. But he who is married is anxious about the world: how to please his wife. . . . What I say then is for your good, and not to impose a burden on you. . . .[115]

It would be a complete mistake to think that the Apostle gave this advice only in view of an imminent parousia. It is certainly essential to his vision to expect the parousia at any moment. But,

112 1 Cor. 9. 27.
113 1 Cor. 9. 24–27.
114 10. 11.
115 1 Cor. 7. 29–35.

while we must "use this world as if not using it," and the most radical kinds of abstinence, therefore, are recommended to the Christian, this is in order that his heart may not be attached to anything, from the moment when he "died to sin and lives to God in Jesus Christ".[116] From then on, indeed, as the Epistle to the Colossians says, "You are dead, and your life is hidden with Christ in God . . ." And so he exhorts: "If you are risen with Christ, seek the things that are above, where Christ is seated at the right hand of God; delight in the things that are above, not in those that are on the earth."[117]

Thus the dialectic of slavery and freedom is transposed into a dialectic of death and life, of death to the present world, of anticipated entrance into the world of the resurrection.

It is between these worlds, where baptism and faith place us, that there reverberates the final word of St Paul's ethics and asceticism:

> Everything is permitted to me, but everything is not fitting; everything is allowed me, but everything does not edify. Let each one seek not his own self-interest, but that of his neighbour. . . .[118]

Has he not just said: "Am I not free? . . ." But "being free with regard to all, I have made myself the slave of all."[119] This freedom is the freedom of faith, of grace, of the spirit. This slavery is the slavery of love.

The Mystery

The centre around which St Paul's whole spirituality is ordered is what he calls "the mystery". He defines it in the Epistle to the Colossians as: "Christ in you, hope of glory."[120] Once again, St Paul's mystery has nothing but the term in common with the pagan mysteries. As is indicated in the First Epistle to the Corinthians, where the term first makes its appearance, it is related to the Jewish wisdom and apocalyptic writings.[121] For "the mystery" is the great secret of God's royal plan for the world and for man in particular, the secret that the angels were not able to discover, which has been revealed to all in Jesus Christ. And Jesus is at once the revealer and the content of "the mystery." For the mystery is his Cross: foolishness for the Greeks, scandal for the Jews, but the supreme revelation of divine wisdom. And it is his Cross seen as the final fulfilment of the Scriptures that opens out

[116] Rom. 6. 12. [117] Col. 3. 1–4. [118] 1 Cor. 10. 23.
[119] 1 Cor. 9. 1–19. [120] Col. 1. 27.
[121] Cf. the whole of 1 Cor. 2, and the commentary given by Deden in the work mentioned above, p. 12.

its whole meaning—his Cross in the perspectives of his resurrection and of the new humanity, the new people, who will be born of it. In the Epistles to the Colossians and to the Ephesians, therefore, the mystery is Christ as accomplishing the reconciliation,[122] the recapitulation of all things[123] in himself, in the body of his flesh and, finally, in that body of the Church in which he realizes himself in his fullness.

[122] Col. 1. 20ff.

[123] Eph. 1. 9ff., and 3. 3ff.

IV

THE SYNOPTIC GOSPELS

The Synoptics and St John

As we have already said, the exegesis of the nineteenth century made much too rigid a contrast between the Synoptics and the Johannine Gospel. St John certainly contributes many more elements even to a strictly historical knowledge of Jesus than was formerly believed. And, conversely, the Synoptics give evidence, just as he does, of an ecclesiastical development. Far from being mere rudimentary biographies interspersed with collections of Jesus' sayings, these Gospels already testify, by their choice and presentation of words and deeds, to a process of ordered reflection. In particular, again like St John, they express formed spiritualities. The image of Jesus which they communicate to us reflects, with each one of them, a particular spiritual experience. And in each case, this experience, at least as to its conscious formulation, was posterior to St Paul's incomparable effort of religious thought and can be said to show traces of it.

Matthew presents an expression of the Gospel directly related to Jewish spirituality as we have described it and, doubtless, laid out according to the context of the Jewish liturgy. Mark, on the contrary, reflects the spiritual problem of the mission to the pagans, but a mission which, while certainly not unaware of St Paul, continued to be related directly to the primitive preaching of the Church of Jerusalem, and perhaps of Peter himself. Luke, for his part, is the Paulinian evangelist above all others, but a disciple of Paul who was much more completely hellenized than the Apostle himself (the author of this gospel was certainly Greek); yet this does not prevent his concerning himself with some of the most primitive expressions of the Gospel message. St John, then, comes to bring together, in a synthesis so happy that it seems completely spontaneous, on the one hand the Christian experience most directly drawn from intimacy with Jesus and no less directly related to the Judaism most open to the Gospel, and, on the other, the already ripened experience of the life of the Church, in an expression of faith so distilled that it immediately attains universality. It is along these lines that we shall study these four books here.

Our particular purpose in this study dispenses us from entering into the extraordinarily tangled discussions to which the synoptic problem has given rise. As everyone knows, a sufficiently large consensus of opinion seemed to have been reached, before the last war, as to the genealogy of the three writings. On the presumably primitive account of Mark, Matthew had grafted the hypothetical collection of the *logia*, the words of Jesus. Luke had rewritten the same work in his own way and style, and added certain materials of his own.

Today we may well ask ourselves whether this consensus of the exegetes (which still left room for many different shades of opinion . . . even for chasms!) is not beginning to break up. The "primitive" and independent character of Matthew has been re-established with sufficiently impressive arguments. Above all, the hypothetical picture of the *logia* has been undergoing so many contradictory transformations that certain scholars wonder whether it does not merely create additional complications. . . .[1] Without ignoring these discussions, we may keep them in the background of our study and, above all, avoid pretending to give any definitive solution. For we propose here to consider each Gospel, not as a source or a product of the others, but as a complete work in itself, and to consider it in the proper originality of its structure and the tendencies it reveals.

Matthew and the Torah

From this point of view, even if the literary dependence of Matthew with regard to Mark is to be maintained, it seems impossible to deny that he betrays at the least the persistence of an earlier spiritual atmosphere: that of a Christianity, a Church, still completely Jewish in their categories of thought and life.

The particular vision of the Gospel which Matthew offers us seems thus marked in its very structure. As was observed some time ago, this is ordered around five great discourses attributed to Jesus, corresponding respectively to chapters 5–7, 10, 12, 13 and 14–15. After each of these discourses the beginning of a new section is announced by the same stereotyped formula: "And it came about, when Jesus had finished this discourse. . . ."[2] Furthermore, each of these five discourses is preceded by a narrative section more or less clearly ordered to the discourse following it. With the Passion as a

[1] On the present state of research, see, together with the discussion of Harald Riesenfeld already quoted (p. 37, n. 3), the remarkable recent study by X. Léon-Dufour on the Synoptic Gospels in *Introduction à la Bible* (vol. II, pt I).

[2] 7. 28; 11. 1; 13. 53; 19. 1; 26. 1.

conclusion and the Gospel of the Infancy as an introduction, seven clearly distinct parts are thus indicated.

Even at first sight, the continual relationship brought out between the sayings and doings of Jesus on the one hand, and the events of the Old Covenant or the words of the prophets on the other, give the impression of a Torah, a new law, and one prepared for by the old. A deeper examination of the general organization of the Gospel offers the most astonishing confirmation of this view. Matthew seems, indeed, intentionally to have arranged the seven parts of his book in such a way as to make them a new Torah, corresponding point by point with the old.[3]

The prologue is explicitly the "book of the *Genesis* of Jesus Christ, son of David, son of Abraham".[4] It gives us the generation of the Messiah and events connected with his infancy, and so corresponds precisely to the idea of the *Toledoth* of Genesis and to the kind of pre-history of the people of God which it constitutes.

Still more striking is the way in which the second part of the Gospel corresponds to the book of Exodus. Concerned with the preaching of John the Baptist in the desert, then with Jesus' own stay in the desert (where he conquered the temptations which had beset the Hebrew people there: note the correspondence between the forty days and forty years), this section is completed by the Beatitudes and the Sermon on the Mount: the new Decalogue and the new code of the Covenant, constantly referring to the old: "You have heard that it was said to the ancients . . . but I say to you. . . ."

The section which begins with chapter 8, dominated by the formation and choice of the Apostles, is completed by the second discourse, prescribing their function. Is this not as it were a new Leviticus?

The fourth section leading towards the third discourse, that of the parables, is wholly dominated by the idea of the Kingdom, its extension, the conditions to be fulfilled to enter into possession of it. Is this not as it were another book of Numbers?

The fifth part opens with the announcement of the Passion, the transfiguration on the mount (where Moses appears with Elias) and a discussion on the identity of the "prophet" who is to come. Then comes the fourth discourse, on the humility and charity which are to inspire the disciples in their mutual relationships. Allusions to Deuteronomy, even formal quotations, constantly recur.[5]

[3] Cf. A. Farrer, "On dispensing with Q", in *Studies on the Gospel, Essays in memory of R. H. Lightfoot*, edited by D. E. Nineham, Oxford, 1955, especially pp. 75ff.

[4] 1. 1.

[5] Cf. Deut. 18, and Matt. 17. 5; Deut. 17. 14–20 and Matt. 17. 25 and what follows: Deut. 17. 2–13 and Matt. 18. 15–20; and still further, Deut. 5–6 and Matt. 19. 16–30.

The sixth part forming the transition to the account of the Passion, ends with the eschatological discourse: the ruin of Jerusalem is the necessary prelude to the coming of the Kingdom and is itself connected with the Passion of the Messiah. Beginning with the crossing of the Jordan[6] and marked by a stay at Jericho, this section certainly seems to invite us to see Jesus as a new Josue (the two names are the same in Hebrew) who will lead us into the promised land. But here the whole prophetic history of ancient Israel is condensed: the fall of Jericho is replaced by the fall of Jerusalem, on which the Kingdom is to be built up.

After this, the account of the Passion appears quite naturally as the supreme fulfilment of the prophecies.

Certain contemporary exegetes especially familiar with Jewish religious thought and life believe that this parallelism goes even deeper. The way in which Matthew connects Old Testament texts with the deeds and actions of Christ as well as his words—a way which is sometimes so illuminating, and also sometimes rather disconcerting—seems to these scholars to have been guided by more than the general notion of the parallelism between the old law and the new. They believe that it also indicates the author's concern to unfold the Gospel according to the pattern of biblical readings in the Jewish liturgical year. Thus the Gospel of Matthew would appear as designed for insertion into a Judeo-Christian synagogal liturgy, keeping the ancient ritual intact. After the traditional *perakim* of the Pentateuch and the *haphtaroth* of the prophets, would come the evangelical pericopes, their arrangement having been worked out by Matthew for this purpose. More than one text cited in connection with some Gospel episode, in a way we find unexpected, may well be simply an echo of this arrangement—which by its nature would necessarily involve some artifice.[7]

The use of such procedures is certainly in conformity with the obviously rabbinical mentality of Matthew. And, in this regard, this mentality is in continuity with that of the last prophets, who, at the period of the exile, used for contemporary events the images and formulations sacred to the Exodus and, in general, to the ancient history of Israel, in the first strata of the prophetic tradition.

Allegory and Paulinism

Here we find, in perfect harmony with the exegeses of St Paul, the first Christian applications of the allegorical method. A work

[6] 19. 1.

[7] See the commentary on St Matthew by P. Levertoff, in the *New S.P.C.K. Commentary*. Cf. R. G. Finch, *The Synagogue Lectionary and the New Testament*, London, 1939, pp. 71ff.

such as St Matthew's Gospel shows that this method—whatever we may think of certain ways of using it—was in no way introduced into the exegesis of the Church as if by violence at the period of the great Alexandrians, and Origen in particular. It is not even enough to admit that these later writers simply applied in their turn a method already used by the rabbis. We can go further and say that in the New Testament writers—heirs of the last prophets in this regard—allegory is already present and interior to the development of their religious thought. A writer like the author of the first Gospel enables us to put a finger as it were on how primitive Christology, for instance, was determined by transferring to Jesus all the traditional themes of messianism. And the same thing is true when we consider the redemptive work of the Cross in relation to what might be called Jewish Paschal spirituality, or the Church in relation to the Jewish *qahal*.

Here St Paul's influence seems to be no less marked than this fidelity to the spiritual, and even the liturgical context of a still intact Judaism. No evangelist is more radical than Matthew in declaring that the new covenant transcends the old simply because it fulfils it. Precisely because his Christianity adheres so closely to Judaism, he is persuaded that the whole truth of Judaism has henceforth passed into the Gospel and can no longer, as it were, subsist of itself. Hence the imprecations of chapter 23 against the Scribes and Pharisees, reminding us of the traditional reproaches made by the prophets against the leaders of the people. To suppose, as does Matthew, that the Christian Church is only the ancient *qahal* renewed, is in fact to say that the *qahal* no longer exists except in the Church. Hence the astonishing boldness which puts the fall of Jerusalem, in relation to the entrance into the Kingdom, in place of the fall of Jericho, in relation to the settlement in the promised land.

This combination, paradoxical in appearance only, of a literal fidelity to Jewish tradition together with an acute sense of the creative newness of the Gospel, is the constant note of Matthew's spirituality. We shall find it in each of the five great discourses into which he has systematically divided Jesus' teaching.

The Sermon on the Mount

The "Sermon on the Mount",[8] once again, is presented as the counterpart of the Decalogue and the Code of the Covenant. It opens with the Beatitudes, thus making the equivalent of the Decalogue a text as unlike a code of legislation as can be imagined.

[8] Ch. 5–7.

It would be impossible to indicate more effectively what is meant by that liberty with regard to the law which is so central to St Paul's point of view.

Instead of any constraint, even that of the highest moralism, here are promises, radiant promises of joy, but what new demands this change implies! This is the "law of liberty"; but, as what immediately follows in the sermon states explicitly, far from abolishing the old law, it fulfils it. This fulfilment is so complete that it discards, like an outgrown shell, what had prepared for it. The spiritual poverty, the mercy, the desire for that justice which is one with holiness, the *hesed* towards our brothers answering to that of God towards us, the purity of heart which opens out to the true "knowledge of God" and, finally, the work of "peace" inseparable from the acceptance of affliction—all this is simply the ideal towards which tended the piety of the *anawim,* the poor of the Lord, in contemporary Judaism. But thus brought together in a whole, spontaneously upsurging, no longer to be confined by any bounds, all this replaces the essentially negative commandment. The "law of the Spirit", supplants the "law written on tables of stone", as it subjugates the "law of the members".

The first part of the sermon that follows then takes up the Commandments, one after the other—against murder, adultery and lust, perjury.... In each case, the uprooting of the evil tendency within us is substituted for merely abstaining from the exterior act. And the conclusion states expressly that it is positive love—and what a love, that pardons, that gives and gives everything without concerning itself as to whether it is merited or not—that is now the only law. Still, it is from the old law that the formula is taken: "Thou shalt love thy neighbour as thyself." But, drawn from the whole and placed in an entirely new context, it takes on an entirely new meaning.

After the commandments of the Decalogue, the three essential practices of Jewish piety: almsgiving, prayer, fasting, are reviewed in the same light—the light of the Beatitudes. Following a theme already familiar to the last sapiential writings,[9] these three practices are praised as creating, for him who is faithful to them, wealth in heaven as opposed to the frailty of earthly treasures. But for this to be true, almsgiving, prayer and fasting must not be merely external acts, objects of self-glory or even of self-centred complacency. They must become, on the contrary, a living and so an interior adherence to the "Father", to his creative generosity.

The interiority of the true spiritual life, here developed even more insistently than in connection with the commandments, is

[9] Cf. Tob. 12. 6 and what follows.

not—and this should be noted—praised for itself, in the name of some kind of spiritualism. It is dominated by faith, by the thought of "the Father who sees in secret". It is the relationship of intimacy with him which is the spring of the interior life. This is also why "treasure in heaven" is not any kind of "spiritual wealth" as opposed to "material riches". As is indicated in the development that follows concerning Providence, this treasure is the infinite love, the all-powerful love of the Father, or, more precisely, it is our adaptation by faith to the generosity of this love: thus it carries us along in its current, and, at the same time, transports us beyond the narrow necessities of this world.

In this self-abandonment to the Father's love, the spiritual life must never become unrealistic in becoming supremely interior. On the contrary, the whole conclusion of the Sermon on the Mount emphasizes its realism and the materiality of the realizations of the Spirit. Trustful abandonment to Providence does not mean any negligence with regard to our needs; it is the best way to make sure that they will be cared for. And, conversely, the faith in the heavenly Father which is not translated into act, into a whole transformation of even the exterior aspects of our life starting from the interior, will be judged as not existing. He who believes himself to be justified by such a faith has done nothing but build on sand. Faith in the heavenly Father, faith in his love, if it is real, must change everything on earth, must carry out his will on earth as in heaven.

This code of the New Covenant has as its *leitmotif*: "Be perfect as your heavenly Father is perfect" just as that of Leviticus was: "Be holy as I am holy." The perfection meant here is the fullness of creative love: it is justice and also *hesed*, supreme mercy permeating the divine holiness with humanity, but also sanctifying the humanity that has entered into the secret of the Father.

Here again, we must see that this fullness is not to be approached without choices, and so without decisive renunciations. There are two ways we must inevitably choose between: the easy way of consent to the pull of the world; the hard and rocky road of the re-ascent to God, against that pull. To commit ourselves effectively to this ascent, we must be ready to leave everything behind on the way. This is the road of measureless wealth, but it is first of all the way of total poverty. The "heavenly treasure" is "poverty of spirit", and "poverty of spirit" is not playing at poverty; it is the most real poverty possible, or it is nothing.

The supreme model of prayer, the "Our Father", shows us the dynamic flow of the spirituality we have outlined step by step. Just as the revelation of the Torah was dominated by the previous revelation of the sacred Name, so with the practice of the new law. The Name which is henceforth to be sanctified is that of the Father. This presupposes that his will be done and not ours, that his reign comes, doing away with all rival rule. It is only on the basis of these unconditional petitions that prayer can ask anything for ourselves: for bread day after day—that is, a life organized not in independence of God, but in a constant and willed dependence on him, for the pardon of past sins preparing for the final victory over the Evil One, the Enemy. And prayer to the Father must also include the commitment to conduct ourselves as his sons, which means, first of all, as brothers, moved by the same love that moves him. . . .

The New Leviticus

After prolonged and deepened contacts between Jesus and the little group of the first disciples, particularly those led by Peter, Jesus made his decisive choice of the Twelve and addressed a second discourse to them.[10] Here we find once more the close union of Judaism and of what might be called the Paulinism of Matthew. Again it is to the Jews alone, in principle, that the Apostles are to address themselves, even though their number (that of the twelve tribes) is enough to indicate that they are to be, within Israel, the principle of a new Israel. But the conviction of Jesus is obvious that their mission, like his own, will provoke a radical break. What this discourse promises them, in fact, is the closest possible association with Jesus in his activity and even his supernatural powers, but also, as a consequence, in persecution.

This discourse is remarkable also because we find here at least in embryo an idea which St John was to develop systematically: the mission of the Apostles, like that of Jesus, not only prepares for the judgment, it also inaugurates it. But it is still the "good news" of salvation that they are to bring. And so, judgment and salvation are not so much two different messianic activities as the two different effects of the same activity.

This discourse leads to a twofold conclusion. On the one hand, it carries to an extreme the requirements of voluntary separation and death latent in the Sermon on the Mount. This is what might be called apostolic asceticism: no one can engage in the work of Jesus without having renounced everything. On the other hand, it reaffirms the solidarity, even the identification, of Jesus with his own: "Whoever receives you, receives me, and whoever receives me, receives him who sent me. . . . Whoever gives even a cup of

[10] Ch. 10.

cold water to one of these little ones because he is my disciple, in truth I tell you, he will not lose his reward."[11]

Here we touch the root of the idea of an "apostolate", and it is a Jewish root. The "Apostles" are the "envoys" (this is what the word means) of Jesus, as Jesus is the "envoy" of the Father. To "receive the Apostles" and "to receive" Jesus is the same thing, just as to "receive" Jesus and "to receive" the Father. This teaching is simply the application of a true mystical realism to one of the best-known formulas of the *halakah,* according to which the "*shaliach*" or "apostolos" of a person is his other self.

The Mystery of the Kingdom

Then we enter on a section dominated by the "mystery of the Kingdom of God", to take a term used by Matthew himself. This "mystery", evidently, is the supreme secret of apocalyptic wisdom, defined, for example, in Daniel, 2: the secret of God's design for human history, a secret which baffles the speculations of human wisdom, but which God discloses to whom He pleases. It is also and above all the secret which plays such a great part in the psalms of Qumran, the secret of the divine choice and of the works of God which only the poor of the Lord, those set apart for his Kingdom, can know. But it immediately appears that the secret, or the mystery, is that of Christ himself.

Here is where John the Baptist hesitates and Jesus confirms his faith by enlightening it. The eschatological signs truly are fulfilled in his person, even though his activity causes amazement, appearing as that of an unexpected Saviour rather than of the expected Judge. John is the greatest of those who are born of woman, as was probably often said by his disciples. But this does not preclude the fact that he whom these disciples still considered the lesser (Jesus himself) is greater than John in the Kingdom of heaven. "The littlest in the Kingdom of heaven is greater than he", the current translation, is, as we have said, a flagrant misinterpretation. *Mikroteros* is a comparative, which can only designate a single individual, not a superlative capable of an indefinite application.[12] Jesus confirms the supreme greatness of John, but proclaims a unique, a paradoxical greatness, surpassing John's which is still on the human plane.

Jesus' great declaration concerning himself and his relationship with the Father, which we have already commented on, follows quite naturally in this context. And the sequel confirms this declaration by showing, through Jesus' systematic violations of the sabbath,

[11] Verses 40 and 42. [12] 11. 11.

that he is taking up and completing the divine work with an authority properly divine.

Thereupon the mystery of his person is at once concealed and disclosed by the evangelist's expressly claiming for him the character of the Servant, as described in the second part of Isaias. This brings us back to the opposition aroused by Jesus. At the beginning of this section, Jesus had emphasized this opposition on the part of men, execrating the towns along the lake which had not received him. Now he reveals that the conflict is not simply one between himself and men, but between him and Satan. This is brought out in the central parable of the strong man who is to be ousted from his fortress so that "the stronger" may be installed there as master (does not this section more or less explicitly parallel the book of Numbers, which sets up the pattern of this installation by eviction?). Hence the theme of the judgment which will be effected, for men, on the basis of their having welcomed or rejected the "good news." Equally, what Jesus says about himself will find its justification in the sign of Jonas, as Jesus calls it, that is, his death and resurrection.

The Parables

Then comes the third discourse, that of the parables about the Kingdom and the conditions under which we enter into it.[13] The first of this series of parables, that of the sower, provides the evangelist with the opportunity to develop at length what we might call his theology of parables. Again he borrows a text of Isaias.[14] This teaching in parables corresponds to the mystery of election, of grace. The parables bring the light of faith to those whom grace touches, whom God has chosen. But those who are insensible to the divine advances are confirmed in their rejections by the obscurity of the parables. Thus, more clearly than ever, "the Gospel" inaugurates the judgment.

Then comes the detailed explanation of the first parable, that of the sower, treating it, as we know, according to strictly allegorical method, giving a special meaning to each concrete detail.

Many modern exegetes, with astonishing pedantry, deal in a very cavalier way with this explanation.[15] On the one hand, they do not like to see the New Testament, so soon and in one of the most Jewish of its authors, formally setting up this systematic method of explanation, since the vain attempt is still being made to call this

[13] Ch. 13. [14] Is. 6. 9–10; cf. Matt. 13. 10–17.

[15] This is true of the exegete whose influence has dominated the discussion of this question for a long time: A. Jülicher, *Die Gleichnisreden Jesu*, Tübingen, 1899.

method a purely Greek one and to maintain that the third-century Alexandrians introduced it into the Church as if by force. On the other hand, these exegetes maintain that the oriental *mashal* is a vivid story, only the general sense of which is meant to be transposed, details being introduced only to clothe or give life to the central or global image.

This is a characteristic example of those doctrinaire schematizations in which the *Formgeschichte* school has particularly indulged—here too faithfully following the example of the exegetes of the nineteenth century. What should be said instead is that the *mashal* is the most versatile form of enigmatic exposition imaginable. It is quite true that one ruling idea, and only one, is to be grasped beneath each parable or group of parables. But when this ruling idea itself implies a multiplicity of aspects all essential to it, the parable may quite well be allegorical as well. In the present case, the parable of the sower seeks to illustrate the idea underlying everything that precedes it: the different attitudes taken by men with regard to the Word of salvation are enough to judge them. Here it is quite normal that the details of the parable should show allegorically how men in fact do take different attitudes towards the same Word.

There is no doubt that one meaning is to be found in the series of parables making up the discourse we are studying: from that of the sower to that of the net, going through those of the wheat and the tares, the grain of mustard-seed, the leaven, the treasure and the pearl. This is not to deny that each parable is meant to bring out a different aspect. But all certainly are designed to explain what we might call the entrance into the Kingdom, the gaining of the Kingdom.

In general, modern commentators tend instead to say that this series is concerned with the development of the Kingdom itself. But this interpretation, which is often given by those exegetes who are most suspicious of allegory, remains in an odd way tributary to the allegorical mentality. It might be said to be marked by the two defects which so often afflict this mentality: attention to the materiality of the image at the expense of the intention which it serves, and the factitious application of categories foreign to the writer's thought. Thus the notion that these parables are designed to describe the immanent development of the Kingdom is entirely derived from the vegetative images in the parables of the sower, the mustard-seed and the tares. It obviously has nothing to do with the leaven, still less with the pearl, the treasure in the field, or the net. Moreover, it is a gross error to see under these images of plants the idea of continual growth by immanent evolution. It was only in modern times that such an idea took shape and was connected with vegetative life. For the ancients, on the contrary (as St Paul clearly shows in the fifteenth chapter of 1 Corinthians, and St John in the celebrated formula about the grain of wheat that must die), there was no real continuity between the seed and the plant: the seed had to die, to decompose and disappear, for the plant to take its place. Conversely, the seed was supposed to contain a minute but perfect image, integrally preformed, of the future tree.

Thus reflecting on these vegetative images, cannot, unless by a basic misinterpretation, lead us to the developmental theology of the Kingdom we are accustomed to. Moreover, it is not the materiality of an image taken by itself, in a completely arbitrary way, that gives us the key to this series of parables as a whole. This key must rather be found in their juxtaposition which produces a focus or axis of convergence.

This whole discourse is concerned with the welcome given to the Word, to the Gospel of the Kingdom (or rather of the Reign). We do not enter into this Reign, we do not share in it, simply because we have heard the Word. Among all those who hear it, this Word produces a very varied and very complex set of reactions. Some who seem at first to have gained the Kingdom are finally excluded (parable of the net). Some cause the Word to fructify speedily, but their fruit withers of itself (parable of the sower). Others, whose growth seems to come from the Word, in reality owe nothing to it and tend rather to stifle it (the tares). All in all, the development, if there is any, is quite equivocal. The birds who come to perch on the tree obviously have no share in it. The leaven lightens the whole mass—but of what? The parables of the treasure and of the pearl come expressly to show us that the Word of the Kingdom is only truly acquired by the man who has sacrificed everything for it.

What is in question, then, is not the internal law of the reign of God. This remains obviously wholly transcendent, something man has no power over. The question is rather that of the entrance of man into this reign (not only as a subject, but as a co-heir of the King, because the question is that of becoming a son of the heavenly Father). And for this, once again, it is not enough to have heard the Word: we must have put it into practice and, to this end, have staked our all on it. If, in this world, we have not consented to lose everything for the Kingdom, in the other world we shall, quite simply, lose everything.

The Ecclesiastical Discourse

It is perhaps difficult to find a dominating idea in the section, made up of miracles and discussions, which paves the way for the discourse following.[16] But the same note of finality is dominant here as in Deuteronomy. Christ's passion is again announced, and this time quite clearly. On the mountain, he appears transfigured between Moses and Elias. The confession of Peter is sealed by the promises concerning the Church, the new *qahal* of God's people. The multiplications of the loaves are so many preludes, as it were, to the messianic banquet. At the same time the renewal of the law is proclaimed explicitly, interiorizing it, substituting for a verbal or ritualistic piety one that engages the whole of life, and for a merely ceremonial purity the purity of the heart.

The following discourse, accurately named "ecclesiastical",[17] is instigated by a quarrel among the disciples about precedence. Jesus answers by making the child the model for his disciples, humility true greatness in the new people of God. For what follows shows that this people is essentially the community of grace—that is, of forgiveness: whence the central place of the parable about the lost sheep. This presupposes mutual forgiveness as the internal law of the new community. Thus it is, once again, that its members can pray with a single heart, sure of being heard, provided that they forgive one another as God has forgiven them. The conclusion is provided by the parable of the unforgiving creditor: how can we live in God's forgiveness unless we forgive one another?

What follows,[18] made up of events and sayings of Jesus, prolongs this atmosphere of Deuteronomy, of a religious law humanized and interiorized, but now positively detaching man from the earth. Here comes the teaching on marriage, brought back to the fullness and purity of its primitive institution, and followed by the praise of the renunciation of sexual delights and earthly riches. It is to integral detachment, accompanying a childlike trust in the heavenly Father, that is promised the greatest reward.

The New Josue

The parable of the workers sent into the vineyard at different times of day emphasizes the fact that everything about this reward remains a grace. What follows recalls again that to have a share in the ministry of the Son of Man is equivalent to participating in his Passion. Then comes the capital affirmation of the paradoxical identity of the Son of Man, the supernatural judge and king, and the humiliated Servant. The journey to Jericho and Jesus' healing of the two blind men directly prepares us for the entrance into Jerusalem.[19] The cleansing of the Temple, the parables of the sterile

[16] Chs. 14 to 17.
[17] Ch. 18.
[18] Ch. 19.
[19] Ch. 20.

fig-tree, of the two sons (one of whom first said no to his father, but then did his will, while the other, having said yes, did nothing), of the vine-tenders, all lead to radical declarations about the final establishment of the Reign of God in and by the overthrow of what had already seemed to realize it.[20]

The parable of the wedding feast, with its appendix about the guests who neglected to put on a festive garment, once more describes the indifference of those first called and the presumption of some of those who succeed them. The tribute due to Caesar delimits, while it consecrates, our duties towards the present life. The discussion on the resurrection categorically affirms that eternal life can none the less have nothing in common with the present life.

It might be said that Jesus definitively loosed the bonds with the present world in regard to himself, when, having formulated the unique commandment of love, he let it be understood that he was greater than David: the very one whom David had called his Lord.[21]

Let us merely emphasize the meaning of Jesus' summary of the law, as it stands out after the preceding teachings. Once again, we find here the highest degree of fidelity to Jewish tradition together with the highest degree of creative innovation. Jesus simply brings together a verse from Deuteronomy recited every day in the *Shema*: "Thou shalt love the Lord thy God with thy whole heart, with thy whole soul and with thy whole thought"[22] and a verse from Leviticus: "Thou shalt love thy neighbour as thyself."[23] But, thus selected and placed together, these two commands obviously take on a meaning without any precedent other than Jesus' own teaching of the Gospel of the Kingdom, in its most creative aspect. The question is not simply that of closely connecting the love of God with love of neighbour, nor in any way that of reducing the love of God to some kind of love of men. It is that of showing that we cannot love God, as he is and as Jesus reveals him, without loving our neighbour, and that true love of neighbour is brotherly love of a unique kind, flowing from the incomparable fatherly love that God has revealed to us all.

Next, a brief imprecatory discourse[24] forms an exact counterpart to the first section of the Sermon on the Mount, ending symmetrically with seven maledictions, to correspond to the eight beatitudes. For what is execrated here is the narrow attachment to the letter of the law that stifles its spirit, that exteriorizes the whole commandment in its material or negative prescription, and that canonizes the temporary institution, thus barring the way to the eschatological coming.

[20] Ch. 21.
[21] Ch. 22.
[22] Deut. 6. 5.
[23] Lev. 19. 18.
[24] Ch. 23.

In sight of Jerusalem and the Temple buildings, the last and apocalyptic discourse[25] proclaims that the reign of God will be inaugurated in the new and supreme overthrow of the holy people, the destruction of the holy city, the profanation of the Temple. But these events which are to strike down the people of God in its preparatory stage will not be spared the new, final people. Even in the last times, now close at hand, to be inaugurated with what will take place at Jerusalem in a few days, it must always be through tribulation, apparent defeat, the Cross, that the Kingdom is attained.

The Genesis and Passion of Jesus

In this brief look at the Gospel "according to Matthew", we have left aside the first and the seventh books. This is because the framework that they provide is a final example more significant than all the others, of that Judaism, at once intact and completely transfigured, so characteristic of the first Gospel.

The book "of the genesis of Jesus, son of David, son of Abraham" is written as explicitly as possible to establish the fact that Jesus is the expected Messiah. Born of a Virgin, by the power of the Holy Spirit, in the family of David, he is the realization of the prophecy of Isaias. The Magi bring him that homage of the nations which was to be an integral part of the messianic triumph. He is the personification of the adopted people of God in the Pasch which rescued it from Egypt; he is the supreme "Nazarean": that is, one consecrated. . . .[26]

In the face of all this, the account of the Passion, if we read it attentively, almost seems to say that Jesus *is not* the Messiah. This account is centred on the dramatic dialogue between Jesus and the high priest.[27] If we bring together the different versions of this major episode given by the different evangelists, it is easy to see that they are in basic agreement, but that they differ about the particular words exchanged. The reason for this difference, it seems, is Jesus' use, here even more than elsewhere, of that parabolic way of speaking which Matthew alone appears still to have understood in a completely primitive, that is to say Jewish, way. It is significant, therefore, that he did not hesitate, contrary to the other evangelists, to give us an apparently disconcerting formulation of Jesus' words. This formulation must, in fact, have soon seemed so scandalous that we cannot be surprised to find the other evangelists substituting glosses. These certainly preserved the profound meaning, but doubtless by sacrificing the letter of what was said. Matthew, on the contrary, had no fear of retaining this letter, for it fitted in perfectly with his general view.

[25] Ch. 24–25. [26] Chs. 1 and 2. [27] 26. 57–68.

In brief, the difference is this: all the evangelists agree substantially in reporting the adjuration of the high priest: "Are you the Christ, the Son of God?" But, while the other three have Jesus' answer "Yes" to this question, Matthew does not hesitate to have him answer "No". For, in Matthew, Jesus' exact words are: "It is you who say it (a polite way, for a Jew, of saying, No). But I tell you this, henceforth you will see the Son of Man seated at the right hand of the Power and coming on the clouds of heaven" (25. 64). The high priest then tears his garments, as in the other gospels, crying out, "He has blasphemed!"

In the other gospels, which give us the impression precisely that Jesus has accepted the messianic dignity, there is nothing, according to Jewish ideas, to constitute a blasphemy. Theudas, Judas the Galilean, and later Bar-Khokeba, gave themselves out as the Messiah. They were treated as impostors, but it never occurred to anyone to find their pretensions blasphemous. Nor should the title "Son of God", which the high priest, in Matthew's account, adds to the title of Christ (or Messiah), lead us astray: as we have already said, this traditional appellation then meant merely the elect or the adopted of God. To claim it for oneself meant nothing blasphemous.

But Jesus' formal quotation of Daniel (7. 13) by which he designated himself as the Son of Man—that is, a heavenly man, preeminently supernatural—even if equally an imposture, was one which included blasphemy, making Jesus—a man like other men in the eyes of the Jews—if not God himself, at least the direct manifestation of his power.[28]

We can readily understand that Matthew, while not hesitating to give Jesus' exact words denying that he was the Messiah in order to state that he was the Son of Man, was none the less persuaded that Jesus was indeed the Messiah and wished to be recognized as such—*but in a sense other than that in which this title was understood by Jews like the high priest*. This is the classic method of the prophets; unhesitatingly to deny something that they maintained elsewhere, doing so in order to state it in a sense free of the equivocal implications it had taken on in ordinary use.

Jesus is the Messiah, and he is not the Messiah. He is *not* the Messiah in the sense of a king merely of this earth, another David who would simply restore his reign. He *is* the Messiah in that he is the Son of man of Daniel, wholly supernatural. And again, he made this declaration only at the moment when he was to be given up to the Cross, that is, when it was to be revealed that the Son

[28] On this whole exegetical problem, one too often neglected, see the fine study of Jean Héring, *Le Royaume de Dieu et sa venue*, new ed., Neuchâtel-Paris, 1959, pp. 111ff.

of man, according to his earlier statement, had come not to be served, but to serve and to give his life as a ransom.

The messiahship of Jesus consists in his supernatural sonship, which causes the Kingdom that he brings to be truly "the Kingdom of heaven", as Matthew always calls it, faithful to the Jewish paraphrase. And he brings this Kingdom about by realizing the mysterious image of the Servant in Isaias, saving men, gathering together the new *qahal* to which even the pagans will be invited, and doing so by his death.

Thus the final knot is tied: the Cross of the Messiah explains the Cross proposed to the disciples, his sonship the mystery of their adoption in the grace of the Father.

Mark and the Gospel of Peter

The tradition attributing the first Gospel, or at least a first version of it still in Aramean, to Matthew (*alias* Levi), the publican, is contradicted by nothing in the book as we have it. And that attributing the second to Mark as, while in Rome, making use of Peter's oral teaching to compose his work, seems to be verified by the writing that bears Mark's name.

Not only do at least certain episodes abound in picturesque details indicating an eye-witness, but also the importance given in Mark's Gospel to events that directly concern Peter, from the healing of his mother-in-law to his denial, would seem to confirm the fact of such an origin. It has even been pointed out that certain odd turns of expression, as when the evangelist says "they", to mean "those who were with Simon", can be explained by his simply having rendered in the third person the accounts in which Simon Peter said "we".[29]

But the clearest evidence is the fact that this Gospel seems to correspond very closely to the position of Peter on the apostolic missions, as this, according to the convincing demonstration of Oscar Cullmann, can be deduced from other New Testament texts—substantially agreeing with Paul on what the mission to the pagans should be, but without his systematic elaboration of the problem.[30] Let us not forget that Mark belonged, through his mother, to the circle of the first disciples although he was of a younger generation, and that he was, for a time at least, St Paul's co-worker.[31] He seems, then, the obvious link between Peter's mission and certain of the very general characteristics of Paul's "Gospel".

[29] See the Introduction by J. Huby to the Gospel of Mark in the *Bible de Jérusalem*.

[30] Oscar Cullmann, *Saint Pierre, disciple, apôtre, martyr*, Neuchâtel-Paris, 1952, pp. 43ff.

[31] Acts 12. 12 and 25; 15. 37–39.

Mark's book is, in fact, a presentation of the Gospel at first sight apparently shorn as completely as possible of everything in Judaism which would have remained a sealed book to the majority of non-Jewish Christians. But as soon as the elements composing it are more deeply examined, nothing is found that could not have sprung from a very simple Judaism such as might have been that of a Galilean fisherman, transfigured by immediate contact with Jesus.

Matthew seems to have been primarily interested in presenting Jesus' teaching as completely as he could, arranged in function of its Jewish context both of thought and of living piety. But Mark sets down only a few of Jesus' essential statements and concentrates on Jesus himself—what he is: "the Son of God"; what he did: bring about the Reign of God. Yet for him, unlike St Paul, it is not meditation on the death and resurrection of Christ alone (or almost alone) that leads him to this Gospel concerning Christ (*evangelium de Christo*). It is meditating rather on what Jesus said and did during his whole public life that leads to Mark's Gospel of the Passion-glorification, and it remains here as it would have in the case of Peter, permeated with many concrete details.

None the less, it would be a mistake to believe, as the nineteenth century did too hastily, that Mark intended to provide a *history* of Jesus, meaning by this a biography in any sense related to the modern meaning of the term. What is true, as Gunther Dehn has well put it, is that Mark meant to group together various revealing historical events about Jesus: a collection, certainly coherent, of deeds and sayings, in which the coherence is neither that of some psychology, nor even a strict chronology, but rather the concordant impression of a series of memories illuminated after the fact by faith in the resurrection.[32]

It is in this sense that, as modern criticism seems to have established, it remains likely that Mark, following Peter, provided the basic outline for the three first gospels in the form in which they have come down to us. Our Gospel of Matthew, in the Greek form which is the only one we possess, certainly seems to depend on Mark for the general line of the account. But Matthew uses Mark primarily in a material way—as providing the framework for the systematic teaching he wishes to transmit. Thus on the foundation of Mark's outline, Matthew developed his own, as we have seen, beneath which the features of Mark's, though still recognizable, are considerably blurred. We must, then, go to Mark himself to see these features standing out in their proper clarity.

[32] Gunther Dehn, *Le Fils de Dieu*, Paris, 1936, p. 11.

The Gospel of the Son of God

As we know, St John wrote in conclusion to his Gospel: "This has been written so that you may believe that Jesus is the Son of God. . . ."[33] If it is true that St Mark is the author of the oldest written Gospel that has come down to us as such—as the majority of modern scholars now believe—the fact must then be recognized that this first Gospel proposed as its aim exactly the aim later stated by the fourth and last. The first words in Mark are: "The beginning of the Gospel (or the good news) about Jesus, Son of God."

More remarkable still is the fact that Mark's entire Gospel presents this divine sonship of Jesus in precisely the same general context as that in which John himself develops it: that of a conflict with a series of adversaries all dominated by an invisible power: the demonic kingdom.

With John, doubtless, even more than with St Paul, the idea of the divine sonship has been deepened by meditation. With Mark, we are tempted to believe at first sight that this is still an idea as rudimentary as it must have been with the centurion—and Mark is the only evangelist to quote his exclamation: "Indeed this man was son of God!"[34] But this impression is misleading: actually certain texts in Mark make the assimilation of "Son of God" to God as close as does St John. On the other hand, it is quite true to say that Mark leads us to this height from the starting-point of a presentation immediately comprehensible to non-Jews of that Greek-dominated period as well as to Jews: Jesus is the Son of God because "the powers", as Herod was to say,[35] act in him—meaning that in him a supernatural world has broken into our world.

Presented in this way, the sonship of Jesus is still within the primitive context of the apocalypses: of the Reign of God which is to be substituted for the reign of Belial. Yet this presentation was as meaningful to the non-Jew as to the Jew. For the Hellenistic world was living under a cloudy but overwhelming impression of powers of slavery and death oppressing the world of men. Its instinctive religious sense was dominated by the search for the "Saviour" who would bring deliverance—deliverance from fate, from death or at least from Hades, and from a vague moral wretchedness if not from sin. . . . It is by showing how clearly Jesus is this "Saviour", more ardently desired than clearly conceived, that Mark establishes that he is "Son of God" and that he is so in a sense going infinitely beyond and transcending both the banal meaning of the expression as the pagans understood it, and the

[33] John 20. 31. [34] Mark 15. 39. [35] Mark 6. 14.

meaning, already more forceful, which it could have taken on with the Jews.

Jesus and the Demons

From one end to the other of St Mark's Gospel, Jesus is seen in conflict with the "demons" who cause falsehood, sin, suffering and death to reign over the world. His death is to be a victory over these demons, and, at the same time, victory for those who believe in him.

This theme is stated at the outset. As he receives John's baptism, Jesus is proclaimed Son of God by the divine theophany (note the character of a very primitive if implicit Judaism, in the expression: "the heavens were rent", taken from Isaias, and of the *bath qol*, the voice that sounded from heaven). At once the Spirit who had descended on him, literally, "cast him into the desert". There he was tempted by Satan and conquered him. This victory of the Spirit of God in Jesus over the evil spirit might be said to be the whole theme of this Gospel and of St Mark's particular witness to the sonship of Jesus.

The second and third chapters are filled with a series of conflicts in which, from the very beginning of his preaching, Jesus became engaged: first with the Scribes, over the healing of the paralytic (we should note at once how the evangelist formally implies that Jesus, in making this cure, claimed divine authority for himself: he forgave the sick man's sins—something which the Scribes protested that God alone could do). In the same way, the meal with Levi provoked the opposition of other Scribes (this time, Pharisees). His attitude on fasting earned him the hostility of John's disciples. That of the Pharisees sprang up afresh after the episode of the wheat plucked on a Sabbath day and reached its height after the healing of the man with the withered hand: from that moment on, the Pharisees allied themselves with the Herodians to destroy Jesus.

The choice of the Twelve gives the opportunity for a reminder of the initial theme: "He appointed twelve of them, to be with him and to be sent to preach and to cast out demons." Immediately after, we see his near kindred declaring him out of his mind, and the Scribes of Jerusalem taunting him with carrying out his miracles only by the power of Beelzebub. To this Jesus answers by the passage about the house divided against itself, and the strong man whose weapons are taken away by a stronger man who then drives him out. We have already found this statement in Matthew, but it is in Mark that it takes on its whole meaning as the basic explanation of Jesus' work, in accord with this evangelist's entire presentation.

The Reign of God and Faith

Mark, as we know, has nothing equivalent to the Sermon on the Mount: since he was not addressing himself to Jews, he was not directly concerned with defining the attitude of Jesus in relation to the Torah. He does give us a series of parables on the Kingdom, more or less corresponding to those in Matthew; but here the accent might be said to be on the transcendence of the Kingdom: it is not men who do anything—it is like the harvest that grows of itself. Without developing the theory of parables to the extent that Matthew does, Mark is in substantial agreement with him[36] (Mark, too, quotes Isaias 4. 9–10). The "Mystery" of the kingdom is a matter of faith; it can be presented only in an enigmatic way; those who believe alone can penetrate these obscurities. Everything that follows goes on to show how little is faith natural to man.

When Jesus calms the storm, the disciples feel nothing but terror, not true faith, at the divine manifestation shown in Jesus. The same thing is true—and with much greater justification—of the Gerasenes after the episode of the healing of the possessed man. The crowd surrounding Jairus and his dead daughter simply mock Jesus, who nevertheless restores the child to life.[37] At Nazareth, his own town, he is not taken seriously. It is at this moment that the Twelve are sent out on their mission, and their task: to preach *metanoia*, conversion—or, better, change of heart—is specified, with the further mention of devils cast out and sick persons healed.[38]

The great miracles, like the multiplications of loaves, and the discussions on interior religion as opposed to the uncleanness inherent in sinful man, all lead up to Peter's confession, to the announcements of the Passion, and to the Transfiguration. At this point, we find once more the teaching on the detachment needed to follow Jesus, and the "service" which should characterize the activity of his disciples as it does his own.[39]

The Passion, introduced by the same eschatological discourse as in St Matthew, concludes this teaching. It seems clear that, in all the evangelists, the account of the Passion follows a traditional and probably liturgical pattern which they hardly modify at all. The contribution proper to each is the light in which the account is set out. Mark's is certainly the simplest, but for this reason the lines of apostolic thinking stand out in all the more striking relief.

Man is the prisoner of the powers of evil which exhaust all their resources in an absurd conflict with him who comes as man's saviour. And man is given a share in his triumph by *metanoia*,

[36] Mark 4. 1–33. [37] Ch. 5. [38] Ch. 6, especially vv. 12–13.
[39] What follows up to the end of ch. 10.

change of heart, leading from fear to faith in this Son of God who is Jesus. In this respect, Mark has kept intact the expression "Son of Man" on the mouth of Jesus as designating himself, and, up to the decisive moment of the Cross, he represents him as avoiding the character of Messiah. Jesus accepts it only when this acceptance can no longer mean anything other than the victory of the divine power in the heavenly "Son of Man", in and through the voluntary humiliation of the Servant . . .

The Gospel of Luke

In spite of its general parallelism with Matthew and Mark, Luke's work, it might be maintained, is much less like those of his two predecessors than is that of St John. The third Gospel, like the book of the Acts which is its sequel, gives evidence of being a notable effort to bring the "Gospel" into the literary genre of Greek history; it also constitutes a work with a clearly marked individual character. However, neither the one nor the other characteristic is more than indicated: the matter with which Luke was dealing proved too rebellious truly to take on the form he tried to give it; his personal intervention remains limited to the exterior and, more precisely, to the arrangement of his materials. In spite of some characteristic omissions and—when he cannot resign himself to leaving out some detail that interests while it embarrasses him—the quite obvious traces of whitewash, what is most Greek about Luke: the care for first-hand detail, must have led him to an unexpected result. For it is he who brings us certain of the most primitive elements of the Gospel message almost as such, even to their expression.

A physician, St Paul's companion (he seems to have composed the Acts from a kind of travel diary left as such),[40] certainly Greek and perhaps from Antioch, Luke is cultivated, sensitive, artistic, possessing feelings of delicacy foreign to the other New Testament writers. He is divided between a respect for first-hand documents or testimony and a taste for order, for a pleasing harmony which could easily have become rather superficial. His composition is a highly polished inlay with obviously tailored joinings, not always successfully concealing the artificiality of certain juxtapositions. We feel that he took great pleasure in using elements taken from tradition, oral or already written down, which others had left aside but which he had to find a place for: the parable of the prodigal son and that of the good Samaritan, episodes such as that of forgiving the sinful woman, the good thief, the disciples at Emmaus.

[40] Cf. Acts 16. 10–17; 20. 5–21. 18; 27. 1–28. 16.

Conversely, everything that shocks or might shock his audience—the stupidity or the baseness of the disciples, the "too" lively evidences of Jesus' human sensitivity, and anything indicating violence in word or deed—is passed over in silence, or, if this is impossible, minimized, and also everything that raises problems, such as any ignorance or appearance of ignorance in Jesus. Luke is always "edifying", always pleasing: it is hard to tell what springs from a caution already ecclesiastical and what proceeds more simply from a refined aesthetic sense in which a taste for shades of expression often weakens the sense of contrasts.

All this, at first attractive, runs the risk of cloying us when we examine it more closely: certain juxtapositions of Jesus' sayings, connected not by a theme but a mere word, verge on pious misconstruction. None the less, behind Luke's so Greek humanity lies a singular sense of mercy which is very Jewish in its origins and most purely Christian in its developments.

In spite of all his minor rearrangements of detail, no great originality can be found in his over-all plan. Apart from the accounts of the Infancy, he confines himself to two great interpolations introduced into Mark's outline. The first is the equivalent, but much more concise, of St Matthew's sermon on the mount.[41] The second, in the loosely knit framework of the ascent to Jerusalem, groups together, in little units interspersed with accounts, the greater part of the other teachings, some also found in St Matthew and some proper to Luke himself.[42]

Luke's true originality, quite apart from the characteristics of his personal psychology reflected in his work already mentioned, lies elsewhere. It consists in the persistence of certain great themes: poverty, prayer, and the gift of the Spirit. Everything is dominated by the vision of the merciful love revealed to us in Christ and the Holy Spirit—the love which, we must repeat, transfigures Luke's characteristically Greek humanity, his *philanthropia*.

The fact is that this Greek was not only the companion and, doubtless, the intimate friend of St Paul; he tried, as he says in his prologue to Theophilus, to familiarize himself with the environment in which Christ had lived and expressed himself. He made use of documents. But he also impregnated himself with what might be called the most primitive Christian spirituality, still closely related to the spirituality of Jewish apocalyptic circles. His claim to have gained direct knowledge of the environment of Mary and the Baptist, in the accounts of the Infancy, is impressively confirmed by the fact that he, a foreigner, managed to become so thoroughly

[41] 6. 20–8. 3. [42] 9.51–17.14.

formed in the spirituality of that environment. His account of the Supper (with the mention of the first cup and of the words of Jesus connected with it) show the extent to which he was familiar with Jewish piety. Thus Luke succeeded precisely in grasping an aspect of Jesus' teaching apparent only to those who, to use his own expression, "were waiting for the consolation of Israel".[43]

Poverty

This is what accounts, first of all, for what has been called his "Ebionism". For him, the voluntary poverty of the *anawin*, the devout Jews who had staked everything on the imminent realization of the messianic hope, remains the basic condition for admittance to the kingdom of God. In spite of his distaste for violent expressions, Luke has preserved the Beatitudes in the rugged form which even Matthew had found too brutal. Not only does Jesus, according to Luke, bless the poor without any other explanation, but he couples four of the beatitudes, beginning with those which sum up all the others, with four contrasting maledictions, the first being the categorical: "Unhappy the rich. . . ." Again, Luke is the only evangelist to report, without any softening, Jesus' statement: "Sell all that you possess and give it in alms",[44] and, going still further: "Whoever among you does not renounce everything that he possesses cannot be my disciple."[45] It is quite understandable that his delicacy should balk at the saying, retained by Matthew, about voluntary eunuchs,[46] but he makes up for it by placing the wife, not only once but twice, among the good things which must be abandoned by the perfect disciple . . .[47]

This insistence on poverty and on its necessary material reality is so striking that it has even been said (Goguel) that the kingdom of God, as Luke frequently presents it, must automatically bring about the exact contrary of things as they are in the "present age".

Prayer

But this poverty, for Luke as for the Jews of Qumran or, still better, the Virgin Mary, the old Simeon and the prophetess Anna, is the support of a total, absolute faith in the word of God. This faith finds its supreme expression in continual prayer, always along the lines of the purest and most exigent Palestinian Judaism of the

[43] There is no study of the literary characteristics of Luke so thorough as that of M. Osty in his introduction to this Gospel in the *Bible de Jérusalem*. On the account of the Supper in Luke, see my *Liturgical Piety* (Notre Dame, 1954, pp. 122ff.).

[44] 12. 33.

[45] 14. 33.

[46] Matt. 19. 12.

[47] Mark 14. 26 and 18. 29.

first century. Luke brings out that fact that urgent prayer, unwearied prayer, is based on an unconquerable certitude that God's heart is nothing but mercy: witness the parable of the friend who does not hesitate to go and find his friend in the middle of night, even though that friend and his family are all asleep, to ask him for an urgently needed favour, and finally to receive it. . . .[48] And the still more astonishing parable of the unjust judge, whom the obstinacy of the widow succeeds in conquering,[49] a paradoxical statement of the fact that prayer can accomplish everything.

But, still more remarkable than the positive teachings placed in Jesus' mouth, is Luke's insistence on the prayer exemplified by Jesus himself. No evangelist except St John has so often shown us Jesus at prayer: Luke stresses the fact that Jesus prayed at his baptism;[50] that he withdrew into the desert from time to time during his preaching in order to pray;[51] that he spent the night in prayer before choosing the Twelve,[52] and also before the Transfiguration.[53]

What is more, Luke continually punctuates his account with mentions of the thanksgiving evoked by Jesus' passing—in those who benefited from his miracles, in his hearers generally, and in his disciples in particular. It might be said that Luke's whole atmosphere is Eucharistic, or, more precisely, that the welcome given to the supreme divine word of the Gospel is, for him, supremely the Eucharist, the *berakah.* Especially notable in this regard are the hymns of Zachary, Mary, the Angels and Simeon in answer to the great initial proclamations of the Good News.

The Holy Spirit

With Luke, this sacred lyricism appears as the fruit of the Spirit, who has a place in his account unequalled in any of the others. As, in the Acts, he gives a lengthy account of the outpouring of the Spirit at the beginning of the Church, so in his Gospel also he continually shows us the Spirit at work in the manifestation of Jesus to the world, and he makes the Spirit the supreme gift of Christ, the riches of the poor, the reward of prayer.

The Spirit is continually intervening in his Gospel of the Infancy: the Angel promises that John will possess the Spirit,[54] that he will come down on Mary;[55] Elizabeth is filled with the Spirit at the Visitation[56] and Zachary at the birth of the Precursor,[57] and so is Simeon, the old man who welcomes Jesus in the Temple.[58] In a far more perfect way, Jesus is filled with the Spirit at his baptism.[59] It

[48] 11. 5–8. [49] 18. 1–8. [50] 3. 21.
[51] 5. 16. [52] 6. 12. [53] 9. 28.
[54] 1. 15. [55] 1. 35. [56] 1. 41.
[57] 1. 67. [58] 2. 25 and 27. [59] 4. 1.

is the Spirit who drives him first into the desert and then to men.[60] Jesus opens his mouth at Nazareth to quote Isaias 61. 1: "The Spirit of the Lord is upon me." At the supreme moment when he pronounces the great blessing for the intimate union of the Father and the Son (termed the Johannine meteor in the Synoptics), Jesus exults in the Spirit.[61] Even more characteristic, perhaps, is the statement which Luke puts in the mouth of the Saviour when he has him say that God will give the Holy Spirit to those who pray;[62] in a parallel text, Matthew merely says "good things".[63] And, lastly, the final promise of Jesus before leaving his own is that he will send them the Spirit.[64]

Mary

The last characteristic of St Luke which must be mentioned is the place which he was the first to give Mary in the Gospel. Not only does he speak of her at greater length than do the other evangelists. We might say that he incarnates in her the perfection of all those characteristics of Jewish piety which, in him, are transfigured in the light of Christ: total voluntary self-abandonment in faith, constant prayer and, more precisely, the exultant thanksgiving of a soul seized by the Spirit. The formula about her which he repeats twice is typical: "Mary kept all these things and went over them in her heart."[65]

Mary utters that capital phrase, so consonant with Jesus' own words about himself: "Here am I, the servant of the Lord; let it be done to me according to your word."[66] Elizabeth says to Mary: "You are blessed among women, and blessed is the fruit of your womb",[67] and then, "Blessed is she who has believed".[68] And the Angel had hailed her as she who above all had grace given her, the creature reconciled with God.[69] Not only does Luke emphasize the virginity in which she had become Mother, as Matthew had done already, but he lets it be understood that it was Mary's deliberate intention to remain virgin: "How can this be done, since I do not know man?"[70]

More generally, it is difficult to escape the impression that he wrote the whole Gospel of the Infancy, and of the Annunciation in particular, as a systematic counterpart to the account of original sin in Genesis. By her faith, Mary prepares for and anticipates in salvation as Eve, by her lack of faith, did with regard to sin. In each case, a dialogue between an angel and a woman precedes the

[60] *Ibid.* and 14.
[61] 10. 21.
[62] 11. 13.
[63] Matt. 7. 11.
[64] Luke 24. 59, cf. Acts 1. 4.
[65] Luke 1. 19 and 51.
[66] 1. 38.
[67] 1. 42.
[68] 1. 45.
[69] 1. 28.
[70] 1. 34.

decisive event, of which a man is to be the agent. The disobedience involved in the doubt and the desire of Eve has its parallel in the obedience in which Mary, believing and self-abandoning, commits herself to the Lord's will: the maid-servant of the Lord preparing the way for the Servant. Is not the *Magnificat* itself the sketch of the Beatitudes?

V

THE JOHANNINE WRITINGS

The Problem of the Johannine Writings

We have already mentioned how greatly the critical views on the Johannine writings have varied in the last fifty years. . . . At the beginning of this century it was taken for dogma that the Apocalypse could not possibly be by the same author as the other New Testament writings put under the name of St John. For it was assumed that John's Gospel and Epistles must be assigned to a date very late in the second century, and their composition located in a deeply hellenized environment. Today, on the contrary, the basically Semitic character of all the Johannine writings is obvious to everyone. The discovery of more and more ancient papyri, demonstrating that the fourth Gospel was in use together with the others from at least the first half of the second century, with the further discovery of a Gnostic Gospel going back to this same period and witnessing, by its obvious dependence, to the obviously still greater antiquity of the Gospel of John—all this began to break down the barrier of imaginary dates too hastily constructed. In addition, not only has the biblical context of the religious thought in this Gospel been clearly brought out, but the writings of Qumran have made evident its relationship to a Jewish spiritual current, properly Palestinian. A mysticism of light and life, an almost dualistic opposition between light and darkness—all this, to be found again in the Odes of Solomon, was already present in the psalms of Qumran before it became ordered, in the fourth Gospel, around the figure of Christ.[1]

Actually, Kittel's study of the Logos in the prologue of the fourth Gospel[2] should be enough to dissipate the illusion which has so long prevented modern scholars from recognizing St John the apostle as the author of this whole literature and, more particularly,

[1] See *The Fourth Gospel in recent Criticism and Interpretation*, by William Francis Howard, revised by C. K. Barrett, London, 1955.

[2] See his article on this word in the *Theologisches Wörterbuch zum Neuen Testament*.

of the Gospel which has borne his name as far back in history as we can go. It is precisely the theme of the Logos that has hypnotized scholars into seeing in John's Gospel a writing permeated with Greek religious philosophy. But this is a fundamental error. As with the themes of light and life, so St John's Logos is simply the final but completely homogeneous development of a biblical idea—that of the creating and saving Word. What is doubtless true, as Dodd has very delicately put it,[3] is that the author of the last Johannine writings had become sufficiently familiar with the general atmosphere of Hellenic circles to express a religious thought which remained substantially Semitic in terms which could make it immediately accessible to non-Jews.

In this regard, there remains, doubtless, a very noticeable difference in form between the Apocalypse and the Gospel. The language of the first is often simply Aramean transposed into a very crude Greek. That of the second, without being free of all Semitism, certainly indicates a habitual use of Greek by the redactor of the text as we now have it, and it is difficult to prove that the question is one merely of a translator. Above all, the composition of the Apocalypse remains wholly of the type peculiar to writings of this genre: the piling up of biblical images and echoes, the bewildering progression of thought by means of enclosing successive series, each time within the last term of the preceding series, etc.... Nothing could less resemble the regular progression—at once harmonious and very simply planned—of the fourth Gospel. It is for this literary reason that an exegete as prudent as Dodd still refuses to see the same writer behind two such different writings.

None the less, the extremely rigorous analyses of Dom Jacques Dupont[4] leave no room for doubt that the Gospel is built on precisely the same themes as the Apocalypse, combined in the same way, and that in the Apocalypse are interwoven all the biblical elements which are to be found, linked together in precisely the same way, throughout the whole of the Johannine literature.

If this is true, what are we to think of the difference in style and, above all, in language between the Apocalypse and the other writings traditionally attributed to St John? However undeniable this difference may be, it does not of itself preclude our finding but one author behind these writings, which seem so one in their profound thought. It is enough to assume that a considerable length of time must have intervened between the composition of the two

[3] C. H. Dodd, *The Interpretation of the Fourth Gospel*, Cambridge, 1953.
[4] Dom Jacques Dupont, *Esais sur la christologie de saint Jean*, Bruges, 1951.

writings—time enough for the young Palestinian, suddenly snatched from his native environment, to become familiar with another language and other habitual modes of expression. And it is precisely the tradition which attributes the authorship of all these writings to St John which also brings out his exceptionally long life and his finally settling in Ephesus, the great Eastern centre of Hellenism.

St John

But even if the return is now complete to a tradition too quickly misprized and for fallacious reasons, the mystery surrounding the Johannine writings is not dissipated. The more the spiritual personality of these writings seems clearly marked (in spite of the contrasts between the Apocalypse and the Gospel), the more the author effaces his historic self behind his work. In the case of St Paul, we are given information so direct and sometimes so picturesque that we are led to believe that we know everything material about him, whereas, in actual fact, we only know a few facts and distinctive characteristics. But St John so completely disappears in the very pure spiritual atmosphere he has created that the few details reported about him seem merely the projection of his spirituality. From the "Boanerges", the son of thunder[5] who wrote the Apocalypse after a first persecution, to the old man who had himself carried into Christian gatherings and could only say, "My little children love one another!",[6] we go from one pole of his work to the other; but we learn nothing thereby that is not already contained in this work itself and we certainly cannot find in it any of those individual idiosyncrasies which spring up everywhere in St Paul.

None the less, this apparent impersonality is not the impersonality of abstraction, any more than his symbolism—evident if not transparent throughout—is ignorance of history. A characteristic of John's Gospel (one too easily neglected, although it had already struck Renan), witnessing to the fact that its origins are far more primitive than they were once believed to be, is the concrete preciseness of certain typological or even psychological details: whether in connection with Jacob's well, the pool of Bethesda or the weariness of Jesus after a long journey. So the veiled figure that seems to stand motionless behind John's writings betrays a very lively sensitivity, unfailingly aroused by some detail no one else has observed. But his meditative reserve opens out in these memories

[5] Mark 3. 17.
[6] Cf. St Jerome, *In epist. ad Gal.*, III, c. 6.

depths in which the individual and the transitory give way to the permanent and the eternal.

The Apocalypse and the Martyrs

St John's Apocalypse[7] is dominated by the spiritual theme of "martyrdom", for which it provided this very term. For St John constantly uses this Greek word, meaning "witness", to designate the witness that Christians give to Christ by their death, the image of his own.[8]

The great problem for him, as for all the Jewish apocalyptic writers, is how to reconcile divine providence with the suffering and apparent defeat of the elect. And for him as for them, the solution lies in a revelation of God's designs, which proceed towards their accomplishment by ways that are mysterious, in the most proper sense of the term. As explained by St Paul and along the lines of the apocalypses, the "mystery" in the Christian sense is actually the secret of the ways of wisdom. In St John's Apocalypse—and here lies its originality—the solution is discovered in the glory promised to the "witnessing" of the martyrs, in the footsteps of the Lamb whom "they follow wherever he goes"; that is, in his triumph as well as in his death, and through death to triumph.[9]

The inaugural vision reveals the eternal glory of him who himself says to the seer: "I died, and now I am alive for evermore."[10] Thereafter everything in the book unfolds as it were on a twofold plane. On the earthly level of history and its temporal future, there is nothing but a succession of catastrophes in which the elect of God are ceaselessly put to trial. On the heavenly plane of eschatological eternity, these events flower in glory. It is not enough even to say that the sufferings of the elect will finally be rewarded. It is certainly the teaching of the book that, here and now, for faith, the "witnessing" given by their trials is glorious in itself. Reciprocally, their glory will eternally radiate from the marks of their sufferings. This is true of the Lamb who (chapter 5) appears in the radiance of "him who is seated on the throne", sharing the praises of which he is the eternal object. But, standing—that is, living—in this heavenly light, "the Lamb" remains none the less "him who was slain". Equally (chapter 7), the multitude clothed in white garments with palms in their hands are described as, "those who have come

[7] The commentary of E. Allo, published in 1933 in Lagrange's *Études Bibliques*, remains indispensable for research into the sources of the Apocalypse.

[8] Apoc. 1. 5; 2. 13; 3. 14; 11. 3; 17. 6, for "martyr"; 1. 2 and 9; 6. 9; 11. 7; 12. 11 and 17; 19. 10 and 20. 4, for "martyrdom"—the verb "to witness" taken in this particular sense, is found also in 1. 2; 22. 16, 18 and 20.

[9] Apoc. 7. 13–16; cf. 14. 1–5.

[10] 1. 18.

out of the great tribulation ... who have washed their robes in the blood of the Lamb."[11]

What is properly the glorification of the immolated Lamb, as of his witnesses, is their passing from the earthly plane to the heavenly, through mortal trial. In both the texts which have been quoted, death is presented as what has gained, for Christ and for his own, their access to God.

Light and Glory

From the fact of this accession, their glorification itself is, then, their immersion in the divine light, in that emerald rainbow radiating from the throne. It is quite certain that we find again here that conception of the divine glory, already so strongly emphasized in the ancient priestly documents, which compares it to a life-giving radiance. The world of God, the world in which the heavenly spirits live with him and in his immediate presence, is a shining world. Whether in connection with the heavenly sanctuary at the beginning of the book,[12] or the heavenly Jerusalem,[13] the Bride of the Lamb, at the end, this universe is described for us with a profusion of crystalline images: fiery crystal, precious stones, everything that can shine with this same supernatural light, is here accumulated. The most characteristic adjective used to describe the elect is *lampros*, meaning not only stainless white, but a bright radiance like that of the stars or the sun. Such is the linen with which the angels are clothed, such the *byssus* with which the wedding robe of the Bride is woven, such the river of living water, and even the morning star with which the Bridegroom identifies himself.[14]

Life and Light

This light, wherein every stain is abolished, is properly the radiance of the divine Presence, and as such it makes immortal. The image of the river of living water links up the theme of light with that of life. Again the appearance, all shining with light, of the "Son of man" proclaims him "the Living One".[15] And God himself, in his supernatural splendour, is praised by the spirits as "the One living for evermore".[16]

To the elect, in turn, the fruit of the tree of life is promised several times.[17] In the same way, they will receive the crown of

[11] Cf. 5. 6 and 22, with 7. 14.
[12] Ch. 4.
[13] 22. 1.
[14] 15. 6; 19. 8; 22. 1 and 16.
[15] 1. 18.
[16] 4. 9 and 10; *idem.*, 10. 6 and 15. 7.
[17] 11. 7; 22. 2, 14 and 19.

life,[18] doubtless woven of the leaves of that tree. And, equally, they are invited to drink at the spring of life,[19] of the water of life.[20]

Life and light inseparably characterize the resurrection both of Christ and of his own, just as life and light are the intrinsic characteristic of the Godhead. While this is a mysticism proper to the Apocalypse and one which is at the same time a theology in the most exact sense of the term, the formulation of both themes can be found in verse 10 of Psalm 35:

> In your light we shall see light,
> with you is the source of life . . .

While the divine glory and, consequently, the glorification of the elect thus appear as an ontological reality, it would nevertheless be a complete mistake to oppose its "physical" character to a "moral" idea. The glory of God is the radiance of his uncreated light, but it is also the living praise unceasingly given him by the creatures who live in his presence. And the glorification of these creatures is at once to reflect the radiant splendour of the divine presence and to glorify it by their praises. In the language of the Apocalypse, "to give glory" to God and to the Lamb[21] is to sing the hymns of thanksgiving permeating this book with a liturgical exultation. The sacred writer is so persuaded of this that he does not hesitate to use the words "blessing" (*eulogia*) and "glory" (*doxa*) as completely synonymous.[22]

What finally dominates his vision is the assurance that human history must flow into the glory of eternity. Better still, this history, in what is positive about it, proceeds wholly from God—is simply, if one may put it so, a ray of his glory. Nothing is more characteristic of this profound thought than the final appearance of the Bride of the Lamb, the heavenly Jerusalem. Quite obviously, it has been built up, through all human history, in the "immolated" history of the people of the saints. And yet when the heavenly city is at last revealed as the final glorious revelation of the Apocalypse, it appears as "coming down from heaven, from God. . . ."[23]

St John's Gospel

The Gospel of St John is at once seen to be different from the other three. It contains only a few facts, obviously chosen for their significance (the word "sign", furthermore, is dear to the evangelist, to designate Jesus' miracles, which for him put a seal as it were on his teaching: the healing of the paralytic at the pool of Bethesda

[18] 2. 10. [19] 7. 7; 21. 6. [20] 21. 6 and 22. 17.
[21] 4. 9 and 11; 5. 12 and 13; 7. 12; 11. 13; 14. 7; 19. 7, etc.
[22] Cf. 7. 12. [23] 21. 1.

following the teaching on the water of life;[24] the healing of the man born blind, the teaching on the light of the world,[25] etc.) . . . In return, it contains more numerous and more lengthy discourses of Jesus even than those in Matthew. Certain of these, like the ones just mentioned, are given publicly (for example, the great discourse on the bread of life[26]), but the majority are presented as private conversations with chosen disciples (this is particularly true of the long discourse after the Last Supper). Yet all have this in common: they are formally centred on the person of Jesus and his work. Because of this, they have no parallels in the Synoptic Gospels other than the great eucharistic text in Matthew and Luke which has been called, precisely for this reason, "the Johannine meteor".

It is noteworthy that, throughout these discourses and the dialogues interspersed through them, we find the fundamental theme of the Apocalypse: the entrance into glory through tribulation and, still more definitely, the immediately glorious character of tribulation accepted through faithfulness to God's will.

The Exaltation of Jesus

The evangelist's fondness for certain expressions with a twofold meaning has often been noted. The most striking example is the systematic use of the word "to lift up" (*airein*) throughout his account. First, in the conversation with Nicodemus, Jesus says: "And just as Moses lifted up the serpent in the desert, so the Son of man must be lifted up, in order that everyone who believes in him may have life everlasting."[27] The sentence immediately preceding speaks explicitly of going up to heaven. Yet the verse following is the famous text about God's loving the world so much as to give his only Son. . . . Is "to lift up", then, an allusion to the Ascension of Christ into the divine glory or to his passion on the Cross? Even here, it would seem, we must answer that the reference is twofold: to glory and to the Cross. . . .

An analogous phrase occurs in Jesus' great discussion with the crowds, in chapter 8: "When you have lifted up the Son of man, then you shall know what I am and that I do nothing of myself, but that I speak as the Father has taught me."[28] Here the formula "you have lifted up" can only mean the crucifixion, but the rest of the sentence implies the glorious manifestation which is the consequence of the crucifixion.

Finally, at the end of his last public declarations, Jesus says again: "And I, when I shall have been lifted up from the earth, will draw all men to myself."[29] Here the evangelist immediately

[24] Ch. 5. [25] Ch. 9. [26] Ch. 6.
[27] 3. 14–15. [28] 8. 28. [29] 12. 32.

explains: "He said this to signify what death he was to die."[30] But the whole context is that of the Judgment, of final victory over the "Prince of this world"....

The conversations introducing the Passion systematically develop the theology implied in these ways of speaking already so striking in themselves. Here the death of Christ is presented as being one with his glorification: "Father, the hour is come", Jesus says in giving himself up to the Cross, "...glorify me with the glory that I had with you before the world came to be ..."[31]

The Only Son of God

Yet if we wish to know the essential theme of the book in the eyes of its own author, we need only refer to its primitive conclusion: "These things have been written so that you may believe that Jesus is the Christ, the Son of God, and that in believing you may have life in his name."[32]

We cannot meditate too much on this verse. Here, better than anywhere else, we find what causes the disturbing ambiguity in St John. On the one hand, no formula can be imagined more strictly faithful to the very earliest expression of the Gospel about Jesus than this identification of the Messiahship with the divine sonship. As we have already noted, this formula is as fitting to the plan of St Mark as to that of the fourth evangelist. Yet there is no doubt that St John, even more than St Paul, brought to this term, "Son of God", some major clarifications which completely renew its meaning. Let us note none the less that these clarifications add nothing to the certitude, already so strong in St Mark, that to call Jesus "Son of God" is actually to attribute to him a divine character. But they explain in what sense the Son can be considered as clothed with the same divinity which none the less belongs to the Father alone.

On the other hand, in spite of these developments which make St John the supreme theologian of the divine sonship, he remains perhaps even closer than the Synoptics to the primitive use of the title of "Son of Man". With him, both in the Gospel and in the Apocalypse, this formula always refers immediately and only to the vision of Daniel 7. For John, "the Son of Man" is always the supernatural man, the man appearing in the divine glory to consummate the judgment. It seems, then, that with him there was no intermediate stage between the most archaic and the most developed Christology: between the eschatological "Son of Man" and the only Son of the Father.

[30] Verse 33. [31] Cf. the whole beginning of ch. 17. [32] 20. 31.

This adjective, "only" or, better, "unique" applied to Jesus' sonship is in fact the distinctive formula by which John characterizes it. It is undeniable, however, that he received this formula from the old accounts of Jesus' baptism, with their reference to Psalm 2, contenting himself with giving the equivalent Greek expression for the Hebraism: "well-beloved" Son. We must go further and say that with this formula, "the only Son", St John simply provides an expression for what the synoptics let us know of the attitude that was certainly Jesus' own with regard to the divine sonship: promising it to all, but claiming it in a transcendent sense for himself alone. John intentionally carries the logic of his formula to the point of reserving strictly to Jesus the title "Son" of God (contrary to St Paul's usage). In John's terminology, other men are always called only "children" (*tekna*) of God.

We might still ask if he himself was not aware of the danger that this new terminology might involve if the conclusion were drawn from it that our own sonship is not real. In his first Epistle, he says: "See what love God has given us: that we should be called children of God, and this we are."[33]

What is unique about the sonship of Jesus is the unique "knowledge" of the Father and of the Son, which defines this sonship for St John, just as in the famous text of Matthew and Luke that at one step attains St John's most highly developed formulations. In his prologue he says: "No one has ever seen God: but the only Son[34] has made him known to us."[35] Later on, in the simile of the Good Shepherd, Jesus draws the parallel: "I know mine and they know me as the Father knows me and I know the Father."[36] This recurs in the priestly prayer: "The world has not known you, but I know you, and they to whom you have sent me. . . ."[37]

This mutual knowing is then particularly defined as, or transposed into, a mutual presence: "You are in me, Father, and I am in you,"[38] Jesus having already said at the beginning of this last conversation with his disciples: "I am in the Father and the Father is in me."[39] Finally comes the last step: this mutual presence is a union, or rather a close unity of life: "That they may be one as we are one . . . that they may be one as you, Father, are in me and I am in you; that they also may be one in us."[40] This unity includes the common possession of all things: "Everything that is mine is yours, and what is yours is mine",[41] and, above all, the perfection of

[33] 1 John 3. 1.
[34] 1. 18. Or, according to another reading: "God the only Son."
[35] John 1. 18. [36] 10. 14 and 15. [37] 17. 25.
[38] 17. 21. [39] 14. 10; cf. 20.
[40] 17. 11 and 21; cf. 22–23. [41] 17. 10.

mutual love: "The Father loves the Son and has given everything into his hands . . ."[42] "the Father loves me because I give up my life . . .",[43] "I have kept my Father's commands and I remain in his love",[44] ". . . you have loved me, (Father), before the creation of the world."[45]

The Children of God

This mutual knowledge, it should be emphasized, being the inherence of the one in the other—union or rather unity in love—is simply the supreme flower of the biblical "knowledge of God" based on the knowledge that God has of us. But let us also note that the union *sui generis* which characterizes the unique sonship of Jesus is presented to us in the context of the union which he has willed to establish between us men, by his coming to us in order to transport us into his own union with the Father by his cross and his glorious ascension. We are called to know Jesus in order to know the Father, to be in Jesus and to have him in us as he is in the Father and the Father in him, so that we may be one in them, so that we may be consummated in unity—for the Son has loved us as the Father has loved him. "You have loved them as you have loved me . . .", Jesus says: "That the love with which you have loved me may be in them, and that I myself may be in them."[46] In a word: "He who has my commandments and who keeps them is he who loves me. And he who loves me will be loved by my Father, and I will love him and will manifest myself to him".[47]

This last text states clearly that, to St John, while the quality of being children of God is bound up with a whole mysticism and while it implies a physical, ontological regeneration, as we shall see, it none the less remains a reality which is fully ethical, completely faithful to the religious thought of the prophets.

St John's First Epistle tells us on the one hand:

> Well-beloved, we are now children of God, and what we shall be has not yet been disclosed. But we know that when he appears we shall be like him, because we shall see him as he is.[48]

Here, then, is the mystical line of thought, if we must call it that: a transformation on the ontological level, effected by a knowing, a transforming vision.

[42] 3. 35.
[43] 10. 17.
[44] 15. 10.
[45] 17. 24.
[46] 17. 26; cf. all the texts quoted above.
[47] 14. 21.
[48] 1 John 3. 2.

On the other hand, the moral line of thought immediately follows in the same Epistle:

> Whoever is born of God does not commit sin, because the seed (of God) remains in him; he cannot sin, because he is born of God. It is hereby that the children of God and the children of the devil are made manifest: he who does not carry out justice is not of God, nor he who does not love his brother . . .[49]

But before going further into the mystery of our sonship, we need to see more closely how it is offered us in Christ. In this connection, we must first examine St John's idea of the Word made flesh.

The Word made Flesh

As G. Kittel has clearly shown,[50] the Logos in the prologue of the fourth Gospel bears no relationship to that of Philo, still less to that of the Stoics. The question is not one of cosmological speculation, but of the history of salvation as Israel had always understood it. John's Logos, as is indicated at the outset by obvious allusions to the beginning of Genesis, is the creative and saving Word of the prophets. In order to understand what John meant to teach by means of this idea and these references, we need only recall what was said earlier about Jesus' deliberate violation of the sabbath, signifying that, in him, God himself was again taking up his work of creation, in order to repair and perfect it. This is precisely what John means to say when he declares that Jesus is the Word made flesh.

The whole Old Testament and all Jewish piety is suspended from the Word of God, from its all-powerful and salutary intervention, the salvation of his own. For the Apostles, the supreme Word is the Gospel, the good news of salvation proclaimed by Jesus. But very soon it became also the Word of which Jesus himself is the content: the Word of salvation, the Word of grace, the Word of the Cross which is the Word of reconciliation, Word of truth, Word of life and living Word.[51] Thus, even in the Acts of the Apostles, the "service of the Word", and the "witness given to Christ" are one and the same thing.

We should add that the *Memra* (word) of the Targums very often designates the divine presence, just as Word and Presence are connected in the Old Testament from its earliest strata. Here we have all that is needed to understand the sense in which John

[49] 1 John 3. 9 and 10.
[50] Cf. his article quoted above, p. 117, n. 2.
[51] See the references adduced by Kittel.

could say of Jesus: "And the Word was made flesh and dwelt (literally set up his tent, like the Presence of the *Shekinah*) in our midst."[52] In Jesus, God reveals himself perfectly in revealing his saving design. He carries out this design by giving himself, in that other himself which is his Son, come to us to establish between himself and us the same union that exists between his Father and himself. So the Word which is made flesh is described, from the first words of the prologue, as being the life and the light of men. In the Word is the life proper to God, the life which he communicated by creating through the Word, the life which the Word comes to restore. And this life is light: "Eternal life is to know You, the one true God, and him whom you have sent, Jesus Christ."[53]

The Light and the Darkness

But when the radiant and life-giving Word enters the world, it enters at the same time into conflict with the "darkness"—that is, as the rest of the Gospel shows, the powers of enmity which hold the world in slavery. "The light shone in the darkness, and the darkness could not stifle it."[54] Less explicitly, perhaps, than the Apocalypse, but as unmistakably, St John's Gospel is an account of this conflict, reaching its climax in the discussions of chapter 7. And the First Epistle sets out the opposition between "walking in the light", that is, in love, and "walking in the darkness", in the life of each faithful Christian.

This kind of dualism—or, more precisely, of dualism opposing light to darkness—has been attributed for a long time to the evangelist's supposed dependence on the currents of Iranean (?) gnosis permeating the Hellenism of his time. On the contrary, as the Qumran documents bring out, John's dualism is actually connected very closely with the Palestinian environment. The title of one of the Qumran writings could have been the title for all the writings of John: "The battle of the sons of light against the sons of darkness". The expression, "sons of light", so characteristic of St John, is equally characteristic of what has been called the "Community Rule", found in the Judean desert.[55] The same thing is true of still more exclusively Johannine expressions in the context of the New Testament, such as "the light of life",[56] "to walk in the darkness",[57] and the very typical phrase: "to do the truth".[58]

[52] John 1. 14.
[53] 17. 3.
[54] 1. 5; this translation, suggested by the Greek commentators, especially Origen, is certainly to be preferred.
[55] *Rule of the Community*, 1. 9 and 3. 4 (see the translation in G. Vermès, *op. cit.*, pp. 133ff.).
[56] Cf. John 8. 13 and Rule 3. 7.
[57] Cf. John 12. 35 and Rule 3. 21.
[58] Cf. John 3. 21 and Rule 1.

We have already mentioned how, within Judaism, these themes of light and life appear rooted as it were in the oldest foundations of the religion of Israel. With St John, after having defined his idea of the Word (we should remember that in the Apocalypse the Word appears as the faithful warrior, shining with fiery light, his vestments stained with blood, who brings about the reign of justice),[59] the themes of light and life come to dominate the whole first part of the Gospel. Here Jesus is identified first with the one and then with the other: "I am the light of the world,"[60] "I am the resurrection and the life."[61]

Life and Baptism

In the conversation with Nicodemus, life is shown as being given by the "new birth" of water and the Spirit, which is equally "birth from on high".[62] The reference to baptism is obvious. What follows shows that the evangelist here puts the earthly visible reality, water, in a mysterious relationship, through the Spirit, with the heavenly invisible reality, Christ's glorification, his descent that ends in a re-ascent. It is just here, in fact, that the first reference is introduced to the "exaltation" on the cross and in glory, already discussed.[63]

Chapter 4, bringing up again the image of living water, with the well (or better the spring) of Jacob, still further explains the life which will flow into man with the Spirit and the truth. This truth is obviously the definitive revelation of God in Christ, transcending and rendering obsolete all previous observances. The healing of the centurion's son follows immediately on the conversation with the Samaritan woman in which this theme has been developed. This whole first baptismal section ends with the healing of the paralytic at the pool of Bethesda.

Life and the Eucharist

In chapter 6, with the multiplication of the loaves and the declaration that Jesus is himself the bread of life, we go on to the Eucharist. "The flesh"—that is, mankind left to its own powers—"is useless", but the words of Jesus are "Spirit and life". Thus the flesh of Jesus, the flesh in which the Word was made flesh, the flesh "given for the life of the world", must be eaten in all reality, even though in a supremely mysterious way, so that we may have "life in us".[64]

[59] Apoc. 19. 13. [60] John 9. 5. [61] 11. 25.

[62] 3. 1–13. The evangelist is obviously playing on the two possible meanings of the same adverb.

[63] Verses 14ff. [64] Verse 63; cf. 54 and 57.

We should note in connection with the Eucharist, precisely as with baptism in chapter 3, first, the mention of the Spirit as giving his reality to what, without him, would be only "flesh" (material rite); second, the reminder of the Cross in the background and, still more, of the ascent into glory through the Cross; and, finally, the invitation to faith as alone capable of grasping the spiritual reality of the rite.

But here it is also stated that the union of the Son with the faithful is finally accomplished through the sacrament—the union, prepared by the incarnation, that causes us to participate in the union of the Son with the Father: "As the living Father has sent me and I live because of the Father, so he who eats me shall live because of me."[65]

But these two texts, furthermore, agree in stating that it is faith in the Son which is the ultimate condition of this life.[66]

Faith

The whole next section, with the theme of light again increasingly predominant following the theme of life, gives us a very clearly thought-out lesson on faith. And it is very interesting to see how this lesson rejoins the apparently crude catecheses of St Mark.

The unbelief, the incapacity to believe, not only of "the Jews"—that is the party of the Sanhedrin so quick to oppose Jesus, but also of the crowds and even of the disciples themselves, including the Twelve, is stressed by both the author who is perhaps the first of the evangelists and by the author whom everyone agrees in considering the last. St John, too, says as explicitly as possible that faith cannot come from man himself, but only from God's free gift.[67] For faith, as he conceived it, is seeing the invisible.

Here we must emphasize equally the verb and its object. For St John, faith is a seeing. Expressions such as "to see", "to contemplate" and their synonyms, with Christ or God himself as their object, are no less frequent with him than the term "to know".[68] Think of the extraordinary statement made by Jesus to Philip: "He who sees me, sees the Father who sent me."[69]

To see and to believe, however, are used in statements that seem contradictory: on the one hand, "the will of my Father is that anyone who sees the Son and believes in him has everlasting life";[70] on the other hand, "If you believe, you shall see the glory

[65] Verse 57. [66] Cf. 3. 36 and 6. 40 and 47.

[67] 6. 44 and 65; cf. 8. 43ff.; cf. especially 12. 39ff.

[68] In the work of Dodd, already mentioned, see the whole chapter on the knowledge of God.

[69] John 12. 45. [70] 6. 40.

of God".[71] Must we, then, see with the eyes of the flesh in order to believe, or on the contrary, believe in order to see? It seems clear that the alternative is a false one. It is because the invisible is made visible in Jesus and, in a certain way, it can now be seen with our eyes of flesh, that faith is possible. Faith none the less requires a supernatural gift, because it causes us to see, beyond the visible, what remains of itself invisible. But this does not mean that faith will not, finally, become a true seeing, as direct and immediate as sense-vision.

Yet it does presuppose a radical transformation of our whole being: "We shall be like him because we shall see him as he is".[72] This is the object of the supreme prayer of Jesus for his own: "Father, I will that those whom you have given me be with me where I am, so that they may see my glory, the glory that you have given me, because you have loved me before the creation of the world."[73]

Predestination

Faith, the seeing towards which it tends, the conflict of the light with the darkness—these themes lead us to the problem of predestination according to St John. The verse quoted above defines exactly the special conception that he had of it: from all eternity, the Father knows the Son and loves him; from all eternity also he "gives" to the Son those who believe in him. In St John's Gospel, the verb "to give" continually recurs in connection with everything concerning the salvation of men, the salvation entrusted to Christ. The extraordinary works of Christ for the salvation of the world are done only because they have been "given" him by the Father.[74] More generally, as regards salvation, *everything* has thus been "given" him.[75] However, if "authority has been given him over all flesh," it is "so that (he) may give eternal life to all those who have been given to (him)."[76] Faith is the result: "All that the Father gives me will come to me . . . and the will of the Father who has sent me, is that not even one should perish of all that he has given me, but that I should raise them all up on the last day. For it is the will of my Father that whoever sees the Son and believes in him shall have everlasting life; and I will raise him up on the last day."[77]

But, reciprocally, there is no faith except by this gift, a gift that is given to us today, but yet is one with the gift of ourselves eternally made by the Father to the Son: "No one can come to me if the Father who has sent me does not draw him . . .",[78] and "This is why

[71] 11. 40. [72] 1 John 3. 2. [73] John 17. 24.
[74] 3. 27; cf. v. 36 and 17. 4. [75] 3. 35 and 13. 3.
[76] 17. 2. [77] 6. 37–40. [78] 6. 44.

I have said to you that no one can come to me unless it has been granted him by the Father."[79]

Faith, then, makes its appearance when, the Word made flesh giving us "the words that you have given me and that I have given to them", these words are received by "those whom you have given to me".[80]

The World

These considerations present the other side as it were of St John's dualism—between the light and the darkness, between faith and unbelief. In particular, they explain his ambiguous words about the world: on the one hand, in the Gospel: "God so loved the world that he gave his only son, that everyone who believes in him may not perish, but have eternal life"[81]—on the other hand, in the First Epistle: "Do not love the world, nor what is in the world: anyone who loves the world does not have the Spirit of the Father in him . . ." with the explanation a little later: "The world is wholly in the power of the Evil One."[82]

It is Jesus' priestly prayer which gives the key to this apparent contradiction:

> I have made your name known to the men whom you have given me out of the world. They were yours and you gave them to me, and they have kept your word. It is for them that I pray: I do not pray for the world but for those whom you have given me, because they are yours. . . . I am no longer to be in the world, but they are in the world, and I am on my way to you. Holy Father, keep them in your name, those whom you have given me. . . . Now I am coming to you and I say this, while I am still in the world, so that they may have my joy fulfilled in them. I have given them your word and the world hates them, for they are not of the world, as I am not of the world. I do not ask you to take them out of the world, but to keep them from the Evil One. . . . As you have sent me into the world, so I send them into the world. . . . May they be one in us, that the world may believe that you have sent me. . . . May they be perfect in unity, so that the world may believe that you have sent me and that you have loved them as you have loved me. . . .[83]

All these statements become quite clear when they are brought together. "The world" is, certainly, creation which remains the object of God's love because it contains the elect, those whom he loves as he loves his Son, and whom he has given to the Son. But the world has fallen under the power of the Evil One, and the Son

[79] 6. 65.
[80] 17. 8 and 7.
[81] 3. 16.
[82] 1 John 2. 15 and 4. 17.
[83] John 17, *passim*.

is "given" precisely to disengage the elect from it. It is in this sense that Jesus has come not to judge (that is, to condemn) the world but to save it:[84] he is the Saviour of the world,[85] the bread that gives life to the world,[86] the light of the world.[87]

But, in another sense, this does not prevent Jesus from declaring that he has come into the world for a judgment (of condemnation),[88] that with his glorifying death the world is brought to judgment,[89] by the expulsion of the Prince of this world—henceforth, indeed, the world is already judged.[90]

The world is judged, in the condemnation of its present prince, the Evil One; it is saved, inasmuch as the elect in it are, precisely, "elect": that is, disengaged from the world by the choice of divine love: "You are no longer of the world, but I have chosen you" (*ego exelexamen umas ek tou kosmou*).[91]

Here, then, we find once more the most profound view of the Apocalypse: the whole history of salvation, within the history of the world, simply disengages what God has conceived, willed, loved and even realized by his decision alone, from all eternity.

The Judgment

In the last texts quoted, the seeming ambiguity of St John's notion of the world is seen to be resolved along with that of the judgment. Once again, Jesus has come not to judge the world but to save it. But he adds immediately: "He who believes (in me) is not judged;[92] he who does not believe has been judged already, because he has not believed in the name of the only Son of God. Here is what the judgment consists in: that the light has come into the world, and men have loved the darkness more than the light, because their works were evil. . . ."[93] In this sense, it can then be said without contradiction that "all judgment has been given to the Son" by the Father.[94] The judgment is brought about by the very salvation which delivers men from it: we are judged by whether we accept or reject the salvation brought by the Son to the world.

But salvation and judgment are carried out in the "departure" of the Son—that is, his death and glorification, and the "coming" of the Spirit.

The "Departure" of Christ and the "Coming" of the Spirit

The two are concomitant—the two aspects of the one decisive event. When Jesus speaks of the living waters that are to flow out

[84] 2. 17; cf. 12. 47 and 1 John 4. 9.
[85] John 4. 42 and 1 John 4. 14.
[86] 6. 33 and 51.
[87] 8. 12.
[88] 9. 39.
[89] 12. 31.
[90] 16. 11.
[91] 15. 19.
[92] Cf. v. 24.
[93] 3. 18ff.
[94] Verse 22.

of those who believe, the evangelist explains: "He spoke this of the Spirit which those who believed in him would receive; for the Spirit had not yet come, since Jesus had not yet been glorified."[95] Later on, it is Jesus himself who says: "It is good for you that I go, for, if I do not go, the Paraclete will not come to you. But if I go, I will send him to you."[96] What follows announces explicitly that this coming "will convince the world of judgment", for it will make it clear "that the Prince of this world has already been judged".[97]

Jesus' death and his ensuing glorification, therefore, are what enables him to "send the Spirit" to his own.

It is the Spirit that will give them the new birth at baptism, and "he who is born of the Spirit is spirit".[98] It is in the Spirit and the truth (undoubtedly the knowledge of God, in Christ himself, communicated by the Spirit) that we are to adore the Father.[99] It is the Spirit that vivifies the flesh of the Son of God so that it may be, in the Eucharist, the bread of life for those who believe.[100]

The Spirit comes, at the prayer of the glorified Christ, to dwell for ever in those who believe:

> The Spirit of truth, whom the world cannot receive, for it does not see him or know him: but you know him, because he lives with you and he will be in you.[101]

In Christ, the Spirit was near them here below: from his glory, Christ will send the Spirit within them:

> The Paraclete, the Holy Spirit whom the Father will send in my name, he will teach you all things and remind you of everything that I have said to you.[102]

For Jesus says again:

> There are still many things that I have to say to you but you could not bear them now. But when he comes who is the Spirit of truth, he will lead you into all the truth, for he will not speak of his own authority, but he will speak of everything that he hears; and he will announce to you the things that are to come. He will glorify me, for he will take what is mine and announce it to you.[103]

"We have a Paraclete with the Father, Jesus the just",[104] and the Spirit is "another Paraclete" whom the Father, or Jesus himself when he has arrived in the Father's presence, will send into us, because Jesus and the Spirit both play the same rôle of advocate and consoler, at once taking the client's part before the Judge and

[95] 7. 39.
[96] 16. 7.
[97] Verses 8–11.
[98] 3. 6.
[99] 4. 23–24.
[100] 6. 63ff.
[101] 14. 16–17.
[102] 14. 26.
[103] 16. 12–14.
[104] 1 John 2. 1.

strengthening him in preparation for the judgment (this is precisely the complex meaning of the word *parakletos*).

To carry out these promises, the Spirit will be communicated to the disciples by the glorified Christ.[105]

In St John's First Epistle, the witness rendered or not rendered to Christ is the principle whereby we are to discern the presence of the Spirit of God sent to us by Christ, or of the evil spirit who is in the world.[106] This witness is inseparable from the presence of love in us:

> If we love one another, God dwells in us, and his love is perfect in us. By this we know that we dwell in him and he in us, because he has given us his Spirit.[107]

Love

Thus the Spirit leads us to the goal of St John's spirituality, to love. The Spirit gives us this love together with knowledge, as he gives life together with light. "He who pretends to be in the light and who hates his brother is still in darkness; he who loves his brother is in the light . . ." says the First Epistle.[108] And it adds: "We know that we have gone from death to life because we love our brothers: he who does not love dwells in death."[109]

More than any other New Testament writer, St John consciously centres his presentation of the Christian message on love, *agape*. In his First Epistle, we might say that this theme becomes all-pervasive. And no other writer has so well laid out in detail the concrete demands of this love, while at the same time working out all the implications of what might be called its metaphysics.

The declaration in John 3.16 might be considered to be one pole of the highly unified spiritual universe into which St John introduces us: "God so loved the world that he gave his only Son, so that anyone who believes in him may not perish but may have eternal life." The counterpart of this statement—which, furthermore, gives it all its value, is then emphasized several times: the unique love which the Father has for the Son.

This love is described at the end of the same chapter: "The Father loves the Son, and has given everything into his hand."[110] The generosity of the Father's love for the Son involves (or is involved in) the generosity of the Son's love: "The Father loves me because I lay down my life",[111] and "As the Father loves me, so I have loved you".[112] This kind of contagion of love and its generosity, causing the beloved in turn to love as he is loved, is imbued as it

[105] John 20. 22.
[106] 4. 2; cf. 3. 24 and the whole of ch. 4.
[107] 1 John 4. 13–14.
[108] 1 John 2. 9–10.
[109] 1 John 2. 14.
[110] John 3. 35.
[111] 10. 17.
[112] 15. 9.

were with the primordial generosity of the original love, the Father's love: "You have loved them as you have loved me."[113]

The priestly prayer, in which we find this last formulation, brings out the eternity of the Father's love for the Son, and assigns, as the final motive for his incarnation and his Cross, the communication of this love to men: "That they may see my glory, the glory that you have given me because you have loved me before the creation of the world.... May the love with which you have loved me be in them and I myself be in them."[114]

It seems that this presence of Christ in his own is seen as the condition of this extension and communication of the Father's love. The simile of the vine, used after the Last Supper in a wholly eucharistic atmosphere, brings this out: "Live in me, and I in you.... Live in my love... as I live in his love (the Father's)."[115]

Communicated to the Son, the Father's love is not only extended to us by the Son: in the Son, already and finally, this love re-ascends to the Father. At the very moment of his arrest, Jesus points out the ultimate meaning of the Passion: "That the world may know that I love the Father."[116]

Communicated to us in the Son, this love in the same way re-ascends to the Son: "If God were your Father, you would love me",[117] Jesus said to the Jews. For our love for the Son and the Father's love for us appear as indissolubly bound up with one another: "He who loves me will be loved by my Father.... If anyone loves me, he will keep my word, and the Father will love him, and we shall come to him and make our dwelling with him."[118] This last phrase recalls the beautiful image of the Apocalypse: "I stand at the door and knock: if anyone hears my voice and opens the door to me, I will go in and dine with him, and he with me."[119]

In these last texts, the presence which was first introduced as the condition of love (see the simile of the vine) becomes its consequence. The fact is, it seems, that Christ must reach us by his incarnation, by the Eucharist that in some way extends the incarnation to us, in order to awaken this love in us. But this love opens out in us the presence of the divine life in its most intimate exchanges.

After the Supper, in giving himself up to the Passion, Christ realized the fullness of this communication of love. Here again, St John presents us with one of those characteristic formulations having two meanings that clarify each other: "Having loved his own who were in the world, he loved them *eis telos*," that is, both to

[113] 17. 23. [114] 17. 24 and 26. [115] 15. 4 and 9–10.
[116] 14. 31. [117] 8. 42.
[118] 5. 21 and 23. [119] 3. 20.

the end and to perfection.[120] It is then that he formulates and clarifies the commandment of love:

> I give you a new commandment: that you love one another as I have loved you. It is by this that all men will recognize that you are my disciples, if you love one another.[121]

Here we find an example of those completely Semitic formulations of St John's which seem logically contradictory while actually being complementary. He is obviously as positive as St Paul about the fact that, in the last analysis, there is no commandment other than that of love. But this does not prevent him from insisting, again and again, on the complementary fact that to love, so far as we are concerned, means carrying out the commandments.

Christ begins by stating this as applying to him before he asks it of his disciples: "Live in my love: if you keep my commandments, you will live in my love, as I have kept my Father's commandments and I live in his love."[122] For the love in question is no mere feeling: it must be translated into concrete, effective action. Here again it is clear that the "mystical" spirit of St John goes along with a strict realism. What is asked of us is clarified, as is the Father's "commandment" to Jesus himself, in the decisive phrase: "There is no greater love than this: that a man should lay down his life for those he loves."[123] This is evidently to be connected with the previous statement:

> The Father loves me because I lay down my life in order to take it up again. No one takes it away from me; I lay it down of my own accord. I have the power to lay it down, and I have the power to take it up again: this is the commandment that I have received from my Father.[124]

Here we rejoin St Paul's insistence on the Cross as manifesting the unique generosity of the divine *agape*, and the teaching of the Sermon on the Mount, that the divine sonship is manifested in total self-giving to the will of the Father, in the love of our brethren.

The Teaching of the First Epistle

The first Epistle develops this teaching on love in two different ways: clarifying still further its concrete realization in brotherly love amidst everyday actualities and, in a definitive way, raising the theory of it into a true theology of love.

Like the Gospel, this Epistle stresses the necessary identity between love and the keeping of the commandments.[125] It seems to be particularly concerned to show the absolutely practical character

[120] 13. 1.
[121] 13. 34–35.
[122] 15. 9–10; cf. 7. 29 and 14. 15.
[123] 15. 13.
[124] 10. 17–18.
[125] 1 John 2. 5; cf. 5. 3 and 2 John 6.

of these commandments: "The man who has resources in this world, and who, seeing his brother in need, shuts his heart to him—how can the love of God be in him?"[126] "If anyone says: I love God, and hates his brother, he is a liar; he who does not love his brother whom he does see cannot love God whom he does not see. And we have this commandment from him, that he who loves God loves his brother as well."[127] As we have already mentioned: "To walk in the light", "to have life" is, according to this Epistle, the same thing as "to love one's brother".

Here again, however, we must keep the complementary idea in mind. There is no love of God worthy of the name that can exist without the love of our brothers; but this does not mean that any kind of love for men can take the place of love of God. On the contrary, this love of men, so strongly inculcated, can only exist in us as a consequence of the authentic love of God. We cannot love God without loving our brothers, but, in order truly to love our brothers, we must first love God.

> Everyone who believes that Jesus is the Christ is born of God, and whoever loves him who has begotten him must love him who has been begotten by him [*that is, doubtless, both Christ and the regenerated*]. This is how we know that we love the children of God, because we love God and carry out his commandments, and his commandments are not burdensome, for everyone who is born of God has conquered the world, and this is the victory by which we have overcome the world: our faith.[128]

What follows recalls baptism and its relationship to Christ's death on the Cross.

The fact is that *agape* is wholly supernatural love:

> In this we have known love: because he laid down his life for us; we also are to lay down our life for our brothers. . . .[129] Love consists in this—not that we have loved God, but that he himself has loved us and has sent his Son to be the propitiation for our sins. Dearly beloved, if God has so loved us, so we should also love one another. No one has seen God; if we love one another, God dwells in us and his love is perfected in us.[130]

In a word: "Let us love, because he himself has first loved us."[131] Love, a love such as that shown us by the Cross, therefore, belongs to God alone. St John goes on to take the final step and to tell us that God is love:

> Brothers, let us love one another, for love is of God, and everyone who loves is born of God and knows God. He who does not

[126] 1 John 3. 17. [127] 4. 20–21. [128] 5. 1–4.
[129] 3. 16. [130] 4. 10–12. [131] 4. 19.

love has not known God, for God is love. In this has his love been shown to us, because God has sent his only Son into the world so that we might live through him. . . .[132]

And we have seen and we testify that the Father has sent the Son as the saviour of the world. If anyone confesses that Jesus is the Son of God, in him God dwells and he in God. And we have known the love that God has in us and we have believed in it. God is love, and he who lives in love lives in God, and God lives in him.[133]

The Unity of St John's Spirituality

The more we meditate on the writings of St John, the more their inner unity shines out, together with their amazing richness.

The realism of the strict ethical requirements of the prophets, the contemplative spirituality which had already developed a veritable mysticism of the divine presence in Israel, open out in an assimilation of the fact of Jesus dead and risen again, of his teaching, of the experience of an intimate unity with him here below. And all this is taken up into the current of the sacramental life of the Church—baptism and the Eucharist—and of its communal life—the realization of brotherly charity. Probably John had no more than the most superficial contacts with the spirituality of the Hellenism contemporary with him. But he expressed the reality of the primitive Christian experience in its original context in such a human and such a profound way that he gave to this experience, not only its most complete expression, but the expression most directly accessible to every man of his own time and of all times.

[132] 4. 7–9. [133] 4. 14–16.

VI

THE EPISTLE TO THE HEBREWS AND THE FIRST EPISTLE OF ST PETER

Jewish Liturgy and Christian Liturgy

THESE two last great texts of the New Testament, the Epistle to the Hebrews and the First Epistle of St Peter, should certainly be grouped together in our study. For they have this in common: they are the only writings in the New Testament that seem to have directly liturgical subjects. While the Epistle to the Hebrews is a meditation on the Jewish liturgy as finding its ultimate meaning in Christ, St Peter's First Epistle is without doubt the earliest meditation we have on the Christian liturgy. The focus of the first is the liturgy of Yom Kippur which becomes an allegory of Christ's death seen as a sacrifice or, rather, as *the* sacrifice. The second seems to be a homily on the Christian Pasch, that is, on Christ's resurrection interpreted according to the liturgical celebration in which it becomes the principle of Christian baptism.

Sacrificial Spirituality in the New Testament

The Epistle to the Hebrews is the only New Testament writing to present the death of Christ as a sacrifice in a systematic way. By reason of this, it constitutes the chief source of what might be called the sacrificial current in Christian spirituality as well as in theology. Not that ideas and, especially, images of sacrifice are absent from the other New Testament writings, but in these, it must be admitted, such ideas and images occupy only a marginal place. In any case, they are not developed systematically, nor, above all, are they given a definite liturgical orientation.

As we established earlier, the use of Isaias 53 to explain Jesus' death goes back to Jesus himself; and so it is to him also that the sacrificial expression of the Cross must be attributed. It is nevertheless true that, in the text of Isaias, sacrifice is expressly mentioned only in one verse:

If he has offered his life in sacrifice for sin [אָשָׁם]
He will see a long posterity,
He will prolong his days. . . .[1]

This text seems to be one of the first in the Old Testament to have paved the way for a transfer—already noticeable in the Judaism contemporary with the origins of Christianity—of the terminology of sacrifice to the whole spiritual life. We have mentioned this transfer in connection with the *berakah*. It can be found, it would seem, almost as such in St Paul. Thus he tells the Romans:

Present your bodies as a living and holy sacrifice (*thusian zosan, hagian*) pleasing to God, for this is your reasonable sacrifice (*logiken latreian*).[2]

This last expression has been connected with the *Testament of Levi*, where the angels are said to present to God "a rational and unbloody offering" (*logike kai anaimaktos prosphora*: 3. 6).

According to a more distinctly defined line of thought, St Paul applies these images particularly to the offerings of the faithful. So he says to the Philippians:

I have received, through the intermediary of Epaphroditus, what you have sent me, as a fragrant perfume, a fitting sacrifice, pleasing to God.[3]

These expressions are taken directly from Ezechiel,[4] where they are applied to the sacrifice presented by the priests for entering on their functions. Here also, it would seem, in the background of the Apostle's thought, is the memory of another text of Ezechiel,[5] which had made the transition from the idea of offerings to the idea that those who present them are themselves offered.

It is precisely this twofold sense: of making an offering and in so doing being oneself offered, that must underly the expressions in the Epistle to the Romans:

May I be the minister (*leitourgon*) of Jesus Christ to the pagans, discharging the sacred service (*hierourgounta*) of the Gospel so that the offering of the pagans may be acceptable, sanctified in the Holy Spirit.[6]

In this text, we should note again the allusions to Isaias 56 which foresees the pagans coming to take part in liturgical worship. But we should notice particularly the application of priestly terminology to the proclamation of the Gospel. This might be compared to the way in which the Apostle, in the Epistle to the Philippians, looks

[1] Verse 10. [2] Rom. 12. 1. [3] Phil. 4. 18.
[4] Ezech. 29. 18. [5] Ezech. 20. 40–41. [6] Rom. 15. 16.

forward to his eventual death for the sake of the Gospel as being a libation:

> If indeed I am to be poured out as a libation (*ei kai spendomai*) for the sacrifice and the service (*epi ten thusian kai leitourgian*) of your faith, I rejoice in it and I share my joy with you.[7]

Yet the only text in St Paul which directly applies sacrificial phraseology to the death of Christ is that of the Epistle to the Ephesians:

> He gave himself up for you as an offering and a sacrifice (*prosphoran kai thusian*) to God, as a fragrant perfume.[8]

It seems undeniable that, in expressing himself in this way, St Paul was thinking of the text of Psalm 39. 7–9.

> You took pleasure neither in sacrifice nor in offering,
> but you have opened my ears:
> You have desired neither holocaust nor sacrifice for sin;
> then I said: "Here am I, I am coming,
> in the scroll of the book I am spoken of.
> My God, I have delighted in doing your will
> your law is in the depths of my heart. . . ."

In other words, what the psalmist presents as *something other* than "sacrifice and offering" and as what God prefers to them, is now described by the very terminology proper to what this has replaced. This transfer is extremely important. It is found at the basis of the whole sacrificial vision of the Epistle to the Hebrews, even though too many commentators have neglected to note this fact.

We might be tempted to link up, with this unique text of St Paul's on the death of Christ as a sacrifice, another text found in the Epistle to the Romans. For the latter seems at first sight to lead directly into the sacrificial and, precisely, expiatory developments in the Epistle to the Hebrews:

> We are freely justified by his grace, by the redemption which is in Christ Jesus, whom God has predestined to be a propitiation by faith in his blood.[9]

This text certainly brings us close to the Epistle to the Hebrews with this mention of propitiation, but we should note that here the implicit image of sacrifice is not applied directly to Christ's death but rather to our faith in that death. Here, as elsewhere, the notion

[7] Phil. 2. 17. [8] Eph. 5. 2. [9] Rom. 3. 24–25.

by which St Paul explains the Cross is not that of sacrifice, but of redemption, that is, the ransoming of slaves.

It is, therefore, not to St Paul but to St John that we must look for the last stepping-stone to the concepts finally developed in the Epistle to the Hebrews. For he says:

> Jesus the just one . . . is the propitiation for our sins, and not only for ours, but for those of the whole world.[10]

And again:

> In this love consists, not that we have loved God, but that he has loved us, and that he has sent his Son as a propitiation for our sins.[11]

Here, at last, we have the direct application to the Cross itself, not only of ideas of sacrifice in general, but of the sacrifice of expiation.[12]

Paul and the Epistle to the Hebrews

This in no way precludes the Epistle to the Hebrews from deriving its basic inspiration from St Paul, as a very old tradition states, even though its style and actual composition must be attributed to a redactor other than the Apostle. This Epistle, in fact, represents exactly the same topic of allegorical explanation in relation to the feast of expiation, Yom Kippur, as that sanctioned by the Apostle in relation to the Pasch, in the First Epistle to the Corinthians.[13]

This allegorical form has led many critics to think of an Alexandrian editor—more precisely, a disciple of Philo's. But, as is sufficiently established by the two Epistles to the Corinthians, there is nothing particularly Alexandrian about the allegorization of the Old Testament, and still less can anything specifically Philonian be discovered in the Epistle to the Hebrews. The basic idea of the Epistle—that the liturgy of Jerusalem, and the previous cult of the Tabernacle, correspond on earth to a model in heaven—comes from the text of Exodus itself. Nor had the Palestinian *haggadah* waited for the Alexandrian Jews to draw inferences from this text. In fact, by its emphasis on the priesthood; by its allusions to Melchisedech and to the problem of Jesus' coming from the tribe of Juda even though he has a rôle that must be called priestly; and, above all, by the very principle it follows in its transfer of technically

[10] 1 John 2. 2. [11] 1 John 4. 10.

[12] We shall deal further on, in connection with 1 Peter, with St Paul's application of Paschal images to the death of Christ.

[13] 1 Cor. 10. 1ff.

liturgical ideas, the Epistle is directly connected with a priestly environment. The "Hebrews" to whom it was written were probably a priestly community like that of Qumran or of the Essenes, and whoever wrote it is obviously at home in their most characteristic forms of thought.[14]

Our Access to God through Christ

The great Christological and angelogical prologue places us at once in the context of these speculations. Here Jesus appears among the incorporeal spirits but as transcending them all, so that, through him, we are given direct access to God. This is the primary idea of the whole epistle, and the idea towards which the author very consciously and explicitly intends everything to lead. What he is concerned with in the sacrificial liturgy of the Old Testament and particularly in the liturgy of Expiation, is the idea of access to the divine presence. And, for him, the pre-eminence of Christ is defined by his having opened up to all men, once and for all, a means of access to the presence of God, and to his immediate presence, not a figurative but an entirely real one.

In order to lead us up to this presence, the Son of God had first to come down to us, to take on himself "flesh and blood", so as in it to annihilate the power of enmity which kept us from approaching God.

> Since the children (of a family) share the same flesh and blood, he too shared ours, so that through death he might destroy him who held the power of death, that is, the devil, and might deliver all those who through fear of death, were subject to servitude all their lives long.[15]

This beautiful text, as has been noted, is the New Testament passage most frequently quoted by the Fathers of the Church in explaining why Christ had to die.[16] Better than any other, it sums up the victorious struggle against the powers of evil in which, as St Paul (especially in his last Epistles), the Synoptics (especially St Mark) and St John all agree, is to be found the meaning of the Cross.

Yet the author of the Epistle does not go on to devote himself to this aspect. Not that it seems unimportant to him; on the contrary, it is absolutely essential to his vision, with the emphasis that

[14] See Jean Daniélou, *The Manuscripts of the Dead Sea and the Origins of Christianity*, pp. 111ff. Cf. the chapter by J. Cambier on the Epistle to the Hebrews in *Introduction à la Bible*, vol. II.

[15] Heb. 2. 14–16.

[16] G. Aulen, *Christus Victor*, Fr. trans., Paris, 1949, p. 109.

he places on the blood that must be shed to cleanse from sin.[17] But it is the other aspect of the reality that concerns him. To him, freedom from sin, from the devil and from death is not an end in itself. It is the indispensable prerequisite for mankind's access to the divine presence. This access itself is what he has most at heart. And, we might say, if there is anything purely Paulinian in this Epistle, it is certainly this very idea. A *leitmotif* phrase from the Epistle to the Ephesians might serve to summarize the Epistle to the Hebrews: "Through him (Christ) we have access to the Father."[18]

The Priesthood of Christ

The priestly theme is first introduced, immediately after the passage quoted above, expressly in this context. On the one hand, his likeness to us makes Jesus "a merciful high priest, and one in whom we can have confidence in what concerns God, in such a way that the sins of the people are expiated."[19] But on the other hand and above all, sharing ourselves in a "heavenly vocation", in him we have "the apostle and the high priest of our confession."[20] This means that, as high priest, it is he who represents us in God's presence and guarantees the validity of our claiming a truly heavenly destiny. The whole of the fourth chapter, consequently, dwells at length on the fact that we are now called to enter into the great Sabbath of God, promised to the fathers of the Hebrew people as the end of all labours, both of God and of men. And the conclusion is: "Having thus a high priest who has gone beyond the heavens, Jesus, the son of God, let us hold fast to what we profess."[21]

Priesthood, as the Epistle conceives it, is therefore essentially mediation. "Every high priest is taken from among men and appointed to represent men in the things of God."[22] And the priesthood of Jesus is wholly transcendent in relation to the levitical priesthood. His is a priesthood "according to the order of Melchisedech", the King of Salem, that is, of peace, whose very name means king of justice, to whom Abraham paid the tithe—proving *a fortiori* that the levitical priests, being descendants of Abraham, are inferior to him. Jesus does not need, as they do, ceaselessly to present new offerings for his own sins as well as for those of the people's. He has made his offering once for all, and it was the offering of himself.[23]

[17] Cf. 9. 22 and the whole context.
[18] Eph. 2. 18 and 3. 12.
[19] Heb. 2. 17.
[20] 3. 1.
[21] 4. 14.
[22] 5. 1; cf. 8. 6 and 9. 15.
[23] 7. 27.

The ancient offerings were continually renewed because they were only figurative, incapable of producing more than a ritual purity or more than a symbolic access to God.

> But Christ has come as high priest of the good things to come. Through a better and more perfect Tabernacle, not made by the hand of man, that is, not belonging to this creation, and not by the blood of goats and bullocks but by his own blood, he has entered once for all into the sanctuary, having won eternal redemption. For if the sprinkling of the blood of goats and bullocks and the ashes of a heifer can sanctify those who have been defiled, how much more will the blood of Christ, who by the eternal Spirit offered himself without stain to God, purify our conscience from dead works so that we may give worship to the living God. And so he is the mediator of a new covenant, according to which, now that his death has intervened for the redemption of transgressions committed under the first covenant, the elect may receive the promise of the eternal inheritance.[24]

All this is effected because Christ brings the reality which the old covenant only prefigured: he enters not into an earthly sanctuary made to the image of the heavenly one, but into the heavenly one itself, just as his blood washes away our sins, not in figure but in full reality.

> For Christ has entered, not into a sanctuary made by men's hands which is the image of the true sanctuary, but into heaven itself, now to appear before the face of God on our behalf—and not to offer himself again and again, as the high priest enters each year into the holy of holies with a blood not his own; if this were true, he would have had to suffer many times since the foundation of the world; but only once, towards the end of the ages has he appeared, to destroy sin by his sacrifice. And as all men must die once, after which comes the judgment, so Christ, having offered himself once to take away the sin of the multitude, will be seen without sin a second time by those who await him for their salvation.[25]

Here we are at the heart of the Epistle. Having developed the general idea, taken from the very words of Exodus,[26] that the earthly sanctuary and what is done there is only an image of the heavenly sanctuary, the author directly applies it to the expiatory liturgy of Yom Kippur. As the high priest, once a year, entered into the holy of holies to pour out the blood of the victim on the propitiatory, so Christ, once for all, entered into the sanctuary of the divine Presence itself, with his own blood that actually abolishes sin.

[24] 9. 11–15. [25] 9. 24–28. [26] Exod. 25. 40; cf. Heb. 8. 5.

The sense in which Christ is Priest and his death sacrificial can now be set out clearly. The Epistle is sometimes explained as if it provided a definition (or even a theology) of sacrifice according to the Old Testament, in order then to show how Jesus, in his death, fulfilled all this perfectly. Such an explanation borders on nonsense. Quite the opposite—the Epistle explains that "the law had a shadow of the good things to come, but not the image of their very realities."[27] It begins, therefore, using the verses of Psalm 39 to which we have seen St Paul referring, to bring out the fact that Jesus is not a priest in the old covenant nor did he offer any sacrifice in the sense of those included in that covenant.[28]

> For it is impossible that the blood of bulls and goats should take away sins. This is why he said, on coming into the world: You have desired neither sacrifice nor offering, but you have prepared a body for me; holocausts and sacrifices for sin have given you no pleasure. Then I said: "Here am I, at the head of the book it is written of me that I should do, O God, your will."[29]

As the author himself comments:

> First he says: You have desired neither sacrifices nor offerings, nor holocausts or sacrifices for sin, and you have taken no pleasure in them—and then he says: "Here am I, I come to do your will."[30]

The priesthood and the sacrifice of Christ, in other words, are nothing merely ritual and figurative: they are the carrying out of the divine will in the gift of self.

> In this will, we have been sanctified by the offering of the body of Christ once for all. Every priest has been appointed to serve daily and to offer again and again the same sacrifices which could never take away sins. But he, having offered once and for all one single sacrifice for sins, is seated at the right hand of God, henceforth waiting until his enemies are put under his feet. For by one single offering, he has once for all made perfect those whom he has sanctified.[31]

Here again, towards the end of the Epistle, we find the initial theme of struggle and victory over the enemy forces of sin, of the devil, of death. And again it is introduced to prepare for the final introduction of the theme of priestly mediation. As the author has already said a little earlier:

> There have been many priests because death prevented them from remaining, but he, because he lives for ever, has a priest-

[27] Heb. 10. 1. [28] Cf. 7. 13 and 8. 4. [29] 10. 4–7.
[30] Verse 8. [31] 10. 10–14.

hood that cannot pass away. This is why he can save even to the end those who approach God through him: he is always living to intercede in their behalf. Such is the high priest we needed: holy, innocent, incorruptible, separated from sinners, and raised high above the heavens . . .[32]

For it is beyond the heavens that we are to be taken up through his sacrifice by the way that he has opened to us.

The Holy Spirit testifies to this, for, having said: "This is the covenant which I will make with them after those days", the Lord says: "I will place my laws in their heart and I will write them in their understanding; and I will no longer remember their sins and their iniquities". Now, when these have been forgiven, there is no further need of offering for sin. Having then, brothers, free access to the sanctuary (*parresian eis ten eisodon tonagion*) in the blood of Jesus, the new and living way that he has inaugurated for us through the veil, that is, through his flesh, and a high priest set over the house of God, let us go forward with a sincere heart, in the fullness of faith, with hearts purified from all evil conscience and bodies washed in a pure water, and let us take possession without ever turning away from hope. . . .[33]

It might be said that, in this last text, we see the flowering of the particular spirituality of the Epistle to the Hebrews. We see also the extent to which it is bound up with the allegorical method, and how a certain renewed use of Jewish allegory is essential to Christianity.

The Priesthood of Christ and Allegory

To devout Jews, like the author and the intended audience of this Epistle, Christianity must appear definitive because it realizes what had only been prefigured in the old covenant. We go from the figure to reality, because we go at the same time from the earthly to heavenly and from the exterior to the interior. The old covenant, by its expiatory rites, could confer only a purity of convention, which would have had no substance at all if its rites had not themselves prefigured the Christian reality. The new covenant, on the contrary, according to the promise of Jeremias, is the law transferred from external practices to the intimate depth of the heart. But this is possible only because the ritual sacrifices have been transcended and replaced by that sacrifice with no analogue, wholly new and definitive, the sacrifice which is the death of Christ as the perfect accomplishment of God's will. Thereby the way is opened up for us to the divine Presence, to the immediate Presence of God welcoming us with Christ into his rest, his eternal sabbath.

[32] 7. 23-26.

[33] 10. 15-23.

Hope and Faith

Yet our salvation is still an object of hope. But, as the author of the Epistle says in his own words: "Faith is the substance of what is hoped for, the demonstration of the invisible,"[34] for our faith has Christ as its object and his death has already introduced him into the heavenly sanctuary, where he is "the author and the perfector (*archegon kai teleioten*) of faith, he who, for the sake of the joy that was offered him, endured the Cross, making light of its shame, and is seated at the right hand of God".[35]

Then, following the tradition of the sapiential eulogies, comes the magnificent praise of all the Fathers of God's people. What the Fathers all had in common was their complete abandonment of things present and visible for the sake of God's promise. Yet it is not they, but we, who have seen the fulfilment of this promise.[36]

> For we have not come near to the fire that can be touched and that consumes, to the cloud, the darkness, the tempest, the blare of the trumpet and the voice that spoke, such a voice that those who heard it implored that it would speak to them no more—for they could not bear the prescription: "If ever a beast touches the mountain, it shall be stoned"—and the apparition so terrifying that Moses said: "I am in fear and I tremble." You have come near to the mountain of Sion and to the city of the living God, to the heavenly Jerusalem, and the myriads of the Angels, to the festival gathering[37] and the Church of the first-born whose names are written in heaven, and to God the judge of all, and to the spirits of the just made perfect, and to Jesus, the mediator of the new covenant, whose blood poured out speaks more eloquently than that of Abel.[38]

These are the realities to which we are introduced by baptism and faith. It is through them that, having become one priestly people, we all have access to "an altar from which those who serve in the Tabernacle have no power to receive their food".[39]

The Eucharist

The allusion to the Eucharist here seems clear, although the word "altar" may not designate the Eucharistic table itself, but rather the Cross, or still more directly, the immolated but glorious body of Christ.

Yet this altar has been set up outside the earthly sanctuary, outside the holy city itself; the Jerusalem of this earth.[40] This fact

[34] 11. 1. [35] 12. 2. [36] 11; cf. the last verse.
[37] The festal assembly of the people of God.
[38] Heb. 12. 18–24. [39] 13. 10. [40] 13. 12.

invites us to separate ourselves, not only from the Jewish people, but from everything here below:

> Let us then go to meet him outside the city walls, bearing his shame, for here below we have no lasting city; we seek one which is to come. Through him, then, let us in everything offer to God a sacrifice of praise, that is, the fruit of lips that confess his name. And never forget to show kindness and to live in communion with one another: it is by such sacrifices that God is pleased.[41]

It might be said that these last words propose to us the whole concrete realization, here below, of that renewed sacrificial piety which the Epistle inculcates, while we await the heavenly consummation. The sacrifice of praise which, in all things, is to be offered to God through Christ, which is the fruit of lips that acknowledge him, might well be the Christian Eucharist itself. But it is the Eucharist seen in all its original richness, still in immediate contact with the Jewish Eucharist: exultant thanksgiving in faith for the great deeds of God and, at the same time, self-abandonment to his whole saving design, through the concrete realization of a "communion" in charity of which Christ and his Cross are as it were the soul. Thus, at the end of the Epistle, is found again the primary statement of St Paul that the whole Christian life is sacrifice, but in dependence on the unique truth of the inimitable sacrifice of expiation: the Cross of Christ which opens to us the gate of heaven, of the immediate presence of the Father.

Unforgivable Sin

We cannot leave this Epistle without saying something about a spiritual problem (to be encountered again in connection with the *Pastor* of Hermas), a problem which has been connected with certain of its formulations. Are there any unpardonable sins, any sins that can no longer be forgiven? For the Epistle says:

> For those among us who sin voluntarily after having received the knowledge of the truth, no sacrifice for sins remains: only the terrifying expectation of the judgment and the fury of the fire that is to destroy the rebellious. A man who disregards the law of Moses is put to death without pity on the evidence of two or three witnesses. What still worse punishment shall not be judged fitting for the man who has trodden under foot the Son of God and profaned the blood of the covenant in which he has been sanctified, and outraged the Spirit of kindness. . . .[42]

But the problem thus raised seems clearly to be a false one. What the author of the Epistle means to say in this passage is, once again,

[41] 13. 16. [42] 10. 26–29.

that the salvation brought by Christ is the final, definitive one, so that the man who turns away from it cannot expect to find any other.

The First Epistle of St Peter

The character of a liturgical homily, so marked in the Epistle to the Hebrews, is still more evident in St Peter's First Epistle. It seems that the greater part literally is a homily addressed to a group of neophytes, who must have been baptized on the feast which, in the whole Church and especially in Rome, remains the supreme baptismal feast: the Pasch, become the Pasch of the resurrection.[43] Thus it might be said that the spirituality of this Epistle and that of the Epistle to the Hebrews together constitute a real diptych: from the Jewish liturgy interpreted in a Christian sense, we go to the Christian liturgy woven of motifs taken from the Old Covenant but transfigured; we go from meditation on the death of Christ to meditation on his resurrection. In both the one and the other document, priestly themes remain in the foreground. St Peter's Epistle, in fact, explicitly develops what was implicit in the conclusion of the Epistle to the Hebrews: all the baptized are made, in Christ dead and risen again, a people of priests.

The interpretation of the death and resurrection of Christ as being our Pasch is found in St Paul: "Christ, our Pasch, has been offered in sacrifice...."[44] A corresponding phrase is found in St John, in the phrase of the Baptist: "See, there is the Lamb of God who takes away the sins of the world...."[45] The cult of the Lamb, so characteristic of the Apocalypse, seems to be directly referred to in 1 Peter 1. 18–20.

Efforts have been made to find other analogies between this Epistle and the Epistle to the Ephesians in particular. But the former exhibits analogies above all with Peter's discourses quoted in the Acts, and it is hard to say whether the other relationships which scholars have tried to discover are not rather due to the fact that it represents a typical example of a more or less stereotyped catechesis. All the New Testament writers necessarily made allusions to this catechesis, allusions which we are not always able to track down. We can say that in this Epistle it is given directly and in a somewhat developed form. Did not the author make into a letter, sent from Rome (the symbolic "Babylon" of v. 13) to the communities in Asia Minor, a homily patterned on a baptismal celebration, in the context of a paschal Eucharist?

[43] See F. L. Cross, *I. Peter, A Paschal Liturgy*, London, 1954.
[44] 1 Cor. 5. 7. [45] John 1. 29.

Baptismal Homily and Paschal Liturgy

The third to the twelfth verses of the first chapter form a kind of introductory hymn, in the form of a *berakah*. An exhortation follows, the first part of which, since it expressly invites its auditors to the profession of the Christian faith, must have led up to the baptism itself (after v. 21). Then we go from the future to the past: baptism would seem to have been conferred and the new Christians are being led to their first communion. A full theology of the definitive people of God as a priestly people is set out. Then (beginning with chapter 2, v. 11) the Paschal Eucharist seems to be concluded with a series of exhortations to carry into everyday life the new ways of living and acting proper to God's people, ways which are those of the dead and risen Christ himself. With the new doxology and AMEN of 4. 11, the liturgical homily properly so called seems to end. The last part of the Epistle draws from the homily a synthesis of Christian teaching applicable to its distant correspondents, so that they might understand the meaning of the trials overwhelming them—trials which may have motivated the putting-together and dispatch of the letter.

The use of a homily as a letter seems still more obvious here than in the case of the Epistle to the Hebrews—a procedure too natural to a preacher to cause us any surprise. In the present case, this fact affords us an inestimable benefit: here, still more directly than in the first part of St John's Gospel, we surprise on the wing, as it were, the thoughts and sentiments of the first Christians in their liturgical celebrations. Here we find not only the earliest form of baptismal and eucharistic catechesis, but also the earliest echo of a Christian Pasch.

The Pasch of the Resurrection, and Baptism

As often happens in St Paul's Epistles, the initial *berakah* flows imperceptibly into exhortation.

> Blessed be the God and Father of our Lord Jesus Christ, who in his abundant mercy has given us a new birth into a living hope by the resurrection of Jesus Christ from the dead, into an incorruptible inheritance, immaculate, unwithering, laid up in the heavens for you—you who are protected in the almighty power of God through faith, for the salvation to be revealed in the last times.
>
> Rejoice in him if you still have to suffer many trials for a little time, so that the testing of your faith, incomparably more precious than gold assayed in the fire, will be found praiseworthy, glorious and honourable in the revelation of Jesus Christ—him whom you love without having seen, in whom, not yet seeing but believing,

> you rejoice with an indescribable and glorious joy, winning the prize of faith, the salvation of your souls.
>
> This salvation is what the prophets sought and pondered on, those who prophesied about the grace which was destined for you, asking themselves for whom and for what age the spirit of Christ which was in them made his revelation to them, when he witnessed in advance to the sufferings that awaited Christ and to the glory that was to follow them. And they served that which has now been proclaimed to you by those who have brought you the Gospel, in the Holy Spirit sent from heaven: these things on which the Angels desire to look.[46]

While it is probable that this text refers primarily to the imminent baptism of a group of catechumens, it seems to invite them to see in the sacrament a real anticipation of the parousia. The "incorruptible, immaculate, unwithering inheritance" has been prepared for them in heaven by the divine *hesed*. Its content is the new life which has the resurrection of Christ as its principle. This is the proper object of all the prophecies. And it is towards the revelation, the anticipated communication of this life that the trials are leading to which the catechumens are submitted, just as the trials of all Christians (as the end of the Epistle goes on to say) lead towards the parousia. It is the catechumens who, in the first intention of the text, love Christ without having seen him and, believing without seeing, already rejoice with an indescribable joy at the thought of gaining the prize of their faith, salvation. But, in the transferred meaning of these formulations as used in the epistle, this is still more profoundly true, perhaps, of Christians tried by persecution, as the author's correspondents must have been, and consoled by the expectation of the parousia.

Then follows what would be called in later texts the *invitatio ad fontem*: the call to approach the baptismal font:

> You, then, having girded up the reins of your conscience, vigilant, fix your final hope in the grace that is conferred upon you in the revelation of Jesus Christ. Like obedient children, do not conform yourselves to the lusts of your former state of ignorance, but as he who has called you is holy, so become holy in all your behaviour, as it is written: "Be holy as I am holy". And since you call your Father him who judges each one according to his works, without regard for appearances, live in fear [of him] so long as you dwell [here below], knowing that you have been ransomed from your vain behaviour inherited from your fathers, not with anything corruptible nor with silver or gold, but by the precious blood of the Lamb without spot or

[46] 1 Peter 1. 3–12.

> blemish—Christ, predestined before the creation of the world and manifested in these last times for your sake. Through him you have believed in God who raised him from the dead and who gives him glory, and so your faith and your hope are in God.[47]

Here it appears more clearly than ever that baptism is the "revelation of Christ" to each individual before the coming of the parousia to all men. The grace of the parousia, in fact, is given here to those who receive baptism. Hence the necessity for the complete break between the life which they inherited from their fathers according to the flesh and the new life that they are to inherit from God. To them henceforth applies the exhortation given to Israel of old in Leviticus: "Be holy as I am holy."

We do not find here the transfer made by St Matthew: "Be perfect as your heavenly Father is perfect", but it is striking that here again the exhortation to holiness comes in direct connection with the announcement of the divine fatherhood. We should note how clearly this fatherhood with regard to men stands out as the supreme "Good News", bound up with the "ransom", the price of which was the blood of Christ.

Here returns, with greater clarity than in the introductory hymn, the juxtaposition of God's eternal predestination, of which Christ's death and resurrection obviously form the central object, and his anticipated "manifestation" to those who believe.

In these allusions, on the one hand to the divine Fatherhood and on the other to the faith of the auditors, we can see a twofold monition in preparation for the recitation of the Lord's Prayer and the Symbol of faith, immediately preceding the baptismal rite.

The Eucharist and the Priestly People

The section of the exhortation that follows is marked by a change of mood and tense: from the imperative to a series of verbs in the perfect indicative—while the baptized are invited to take part in the eucharistic banquet, they are also instructed at length on their new condition: they are entering into the construction of a holy temple built up on Christ as its cornerstone; they themselves constitute a people of priests.

> Having sanctified your souls in obedience to the truth until you have brotherly love without hypocrisy, love one another sincerely from the bottom of your hearts, now that you have been reborn not of a corruptible seed, but of an incorruptible: by the word of the living God that endures. For all flesh is as grass and all its glory like the flowering of grass: grass withers, its

[47] 1. 13–21.

flower falls, but the word of the Lord remains for ever, that is, the Word that has been proclaimed to you.

Rejecting, then, all malice and all deceit, jealousy and all false speaking, like new-born children desire the milk which is logical and without deceit so that you may grow in him for salvation, once you have tasted how good the Lord is.

Coming to him, the living stone rejected by men but chosen by God and precious, as living stones, build yourselves into a spiritual dwelling, to be a holy priesthood, to offer spiritual sacrifices pleasing to God through Jesus Christ, as it is written in Scripture: "See, I am setting up in Sion a cornerstone, choice and of great worth, and the man who believes in it will not be confounded." Honour is yours, because you believe; but for those who do not believe "the stone rejected by the builders has been made the cornerstone and also a stumbling block and a scandal", these stumble over the Word by not believing in it, as they were destined to do. But you are a chosen race, a royal priesthood, a holy nation, the people that he has acquired as his own so that you may proclaim the wonderful deeds of him who has called you out of darkness into his marvellous light, you who formerly were not a people, but who are now the people of God, you who had not obtained mercy, but now have obtained it.[48]

It would be difficult to emphasize too greatly the importance of the Word, according to this text. The Word, proclaimed to the catechumens, is what leads them to faith; the Word, in baptism, is the incorruptible seed of their regeneration. And the Word again, in the Eucharist, nourishes them as with a "logical" milk, that is one of which the profound reality is the "Logos". While, for the author of this text, the "Logos" did not have all the metaphysical clarity given it in the prologue of St John's Gospel, it seems certain that here too it designates Christ himself, not only as the object of the Gospel, but as a personal presence, in the preaching and in the sacraments of the Church.

The eucharistic food, while ensuring that the baptized would grow up in the Lord—whose goodness, now, they would soon have directly tasted—will make them all together one temple of God with him, a temple of which he is always the unique foundation. At the same time, in the Eucharist in which they all take part, they are the priests of this Temple, so the "philadelphia", the society of brotherly love to which baptism has introduced them, which is manifested and increased in the Eucharist, is the definitive people of God. The qualities of the priestly people, given to Israel of old according to Exodus,[49] belong to this new people still more

[48] 1. 22–2. 10.

[49] Exod. 19. 6 and 23. 22.

fully, just as they are, according to the phrase of Osee, supremely the people once called Lo-Ruchama and now called Ruchama.[50]

Let us note again the allusions to Psalms 33. 9: "Taste and see how good is the Lord", and 117. 22: "The stone rejected but chosen." The first seems to be one of the hymns most anciently and universally used for eucharistic communion; equally, the second seems always to have belonged to the Paschal liturgy.

The last part of this exhortation must have been addressed to the neophytes before they parted, after the sacred banquet, laying out for them the programme of the new life henceforth to be theirs.

> "Beloved, I urge you, as strangers and travellers, abstain from carnal lusts which war against the soul. Live good lives among your pagan neighbours, so that, while now they revile you as evil-doers, they may be initiated by your good works and glorify God on the day of his visitation. . . .[51]

In this connection, it is interesting to note the use of the word *epopteuontes* in this text, a word used technically in the pagan mysteries for the vision offered to initiates. The day was to come when Christians would themselves use this word for baptism, but we have not yet come to that period. The author of the Epistle still applies the word to the pagans, but it is the life of Christians which, as he sees it, is to constitute the pagans' "initiation", as it were, into Christianity.

Suffering with Christ

The end of the homily goes on to apply this general programme to the duties of all to the State, of slaves to their masters, of wives to their husbands and husbands to their wives. The dominant idea is the way in which Christians should witness to their faith by suffering for it when they must, as Christ suffered:

> Christ suffered for you, leaving you an example, so that you might walk in his footsteps.[52]

While the Christian horizon cannot as yet be said to be filled with the vision of martyrdom, in this Epistle martyrdom already occupies a place equal, quantitatively at least, to that of the parousia, from which it seems inseparable. It might be said that here baptism becomes the anticipation at once of martyrdom and of the parousia.

> Since Christ suffered in the flesh, you also should struggle in the same frame of mind, telling yourselves that he who has

[50] Osee 1. 6 and 9; cf. 2. 3 and 25.
[51] 1 Peter 2. 11–12.
[52] 2. 21ff.; cf. 3. 13–18.

suffered in the flesh has ceased to sin, so that during the time that remains to you to live in the flesh, you may live, not according to the lusts of men, but according to the will of God.[53]

And so comes the conclusion:

For all men, the end is now near. Be sober, then, and watch in prayer, having above all a sincere love one for another, for love covers a multitude of sins. Practise hospitality towards one another without complaining; let each of you, according to the gift that has been given him, render service to the others, as good stewards of the multiform grace of God. If anyone speaks, let it be the words of God. If anyone renders a service, let it be with the strength that God provides, that in all things God may be glorified through Jesus Christ: to him be glory and power for ever and ever. Amen.[54]

The Epistle concludes with a resumption of the theme explaining the Christian's sufferings—doubtless the reason why the homily was written and sent out in this form to Churches suffering trials. So the author has set out the enduring spiritual lesson of baptism and the Eucharist, celebrated at a period still very close to the Saviour's Passion and amidst the first difficulties that the world raised for the first Christians.

[53] 4. 1–2.

[54] 4. 7–11.

CONCLUSIONS CONCERNING THE NEW TESTAMENT:

THE EPISTLE OF ST JAMES, THE SECOND EPISTLE OF ST PETER, THE EPISTLE OF ST JUDE

The Epistle of St James

THE lengthy moral and spiritual exhortation concluding the First Epistle of St Peter has its parallel in the ending of all St Paul's Epistles. But there exists one New Testament writing in which such an exhortation takes up the whole letter: the Epistle of James, attributed to that James, the "brother of the Lord", who obviously played such a great rôle in the Church of Jerusalem, and who was perhaps the same person as the apostle James, son of Alpheus.[1] It might be said that with this Epistle we return, at the end of the composition of the New Testament, to its beginnings. For this writing seems so typically Jewish that occasionally it has been supposed that the single mention of the name Jesus in it outside the signature, at the beginning of chapter 2, must be a Christian interpolation in a purely Jewish text.

It should rather be said that this Epistle verifies what has continually been brought out in this book: the ready openness of the best of Jewish piety to the Gospel, in the first century.

Conversely, following Luther and more or less influenced by his distrust of this text which he called "an epistle of straw", older exegetes tried to see this Epistle as an anti-Paulinian reaction. This supposition, obviously, is connected with the fact that Paul and James both use the same examples, especially that of Abraham, in the one case in favour of salvation through faith, and in the other, apparently, of a salvation through good works.[2] But, to the majority of modern critics, it appears that this antithesis is a delusion. James speaks of showing faith through works, and thus, while he would obviously be embarrassed by the Lutheran interpretations given to St Paul, he in no way contradicts St Paul himself.

[1] See the chapter on the Epistle of St James, by J. Cantinat, in *Introduction à la Bible*, vol. II, pt. III, ch. I.

[2] Cf. Rom. 4 with James 4. 21–26.

Actually, nothing in the New Testament more closely resembles the closing exhortations of St Paul than this Epistle of St James. We may seriously doubt that James ever suspected the existence of the texts of St Paul which he is supposed to have been combating. The probability is that both used the same catechetical series of traditional examples, interpreting them in an equally free way, according to the custom observed again and again in the *haggadah*.[3]

Morality and Spirituality

Since our study has an immediately spiritual objective, we do not need to dwell at length on the importance in primitive Christian teaching—apostolic in the strictest sense of the word—of the catechesis on morals as such. The Epistle of James, which constitutes the most developed witness we possess in this regard, will aid us, as we conclude our study of the New Testament, to show how morality and spirituality here enhance one another.

It is the existence of this catechesis, which seems to have been particularly stereotyped in the categories of its ethical portion, that may explain certain analogies in St James with the First Epistle of Peter, for example. This catechesis is also what makes it very difficult to ascertain which of these Epistles is anterior to the other—notwithstanding the fine assurance with which so many exegetes dispose of these questions.

Trials and Poverty

James is connected, even more closely than St Luke, with the tradition of the "poor" in Israel. He remains rooted in it with every fibre. His whole Epistle, or at least by far the greater part of it, leads up to a eulogy and a practical definition of this poverty, as a moral and ascetical ideal having directly religious motivations.

Like Peter in his first Epistle, James is dominated by a concern to explain the trials assailing faithful Christians and above all, the behaviour and attitude in which these trials are to be accepted. Trial, for the Christian, is a reason for joy, precisely because it puts his faith to the test and reveals the love of God that should animate it.[4] It is in this regard that the rich man is at a disadvantage, as it were, in comparison to the poor man, and not the other round, and this is why the rich man should congratulate himself on being reduced to poverty.[5]

[3] Cf. the commentary of J. Chaine, Paris, 1927, pp. lxixff.
[4] James 1. 2. [5] 1. 10.

Not that trials, and particularly temptations (the Greek *peirasmos* does not distinguish between them) come from God.[6] Man alone causes them, by his lusts.[7] On the contrary, what comes from God is the gift of grace, the supreme gift of Wisdom extolled by the author, which is above all the discernment revealed precisely under trial.[8]

On the subject of this gift, St James gives this wonderful formulation, so close both to St John and St Paul, although this similarity is in all probability again to be explained by the common ground of the same catechetical theme, rather than by any influence of one or the other:

> All good giving and every perfect gift comes from on high, descending from the Father of lights, with whom there is no change nor shadow of alternation. According to his design, he has begotten us by the Word of truth, so that we might be the first-fruits, as it were, of his creation.[9]

This formula then leads to a whole passage on the Word received in such a way that it takes root in us and that we are among those who not only hear it, but also do it.[10]

This Word, which James describes as "the perfect law of liberty"[11]—in a way wonderfully characteristic of the true import of his Christian Phariseeism, as we might call it—asks of us, then, a faith which is manifested by works. The development of this central idea is preceded by a second and more detailed comparison between the rich and the poor, insisting again on the superiority of the poor man before God, and ending in an exaltation of brotherly *agape,* expressly indentified with the Jewish *hesed*.[12]

Faith and Works

Now comes the great passage on true faith as proved by works, in contrast to the dead faith that produces none. And here we find the same examples as those St Paul uses to illustrate faith as opposed to works not animated by faith—Abraham and also Rahab.[13]

All this is expressly situated in the apocalyptic context of waiting for the Kingdom, exactly as in the Sermon on the Mount. And what follows shows the vivid sense, possessed by a Judeo-Christian such as James, of the continuity between Wisdom and apocalypse.

A diatribe against verbal intemperance, particularly on the

[6] 1. 13. [7] 1. 14. [8] Cf. 1. 5.
[9] 1. 17–18. [10] 1. 19–26. [11] 1. 25.
[12] 2. 1–13. [13] 2. 14–26.

part of those who lightly undertake to teach others, leads to the praise of the true Wisdom which comes from on high (a gift of God, like the Word) and leads to peace.[14] Then comes a final lesson, in contrast, on the causes of trouble and division: especially the friendliness of the world, the enemy of God.[15] And then a final and still more violent denunciation of the rich, especially close to the tone of the Gospel sermon in St Luke's version.[16]

In the same atmosphere, the Epistle closes with a series of exhortations: again to patience, against vain speaking, on the power of prayer, finally on fraternal correction—this last point, doubtless, in implicit justification of what the writer has been doing.[17]

Wisdom and Apocalypse

The relationship of the Epistle to those Jewish circles most aware of the preaching of the Apocalypses is obvious. We might even ask whether its outline, seemingly lacking in order, was not patterned after that of the *Testaments of the Twelve Patriarchs*, which would explain the unusual salutation "to the twelve tribes that are in the dispersion".[18]

But this Epistle also indicates how, at this period, apocalyptic piety could go along with the most thoroughly rabbinical Judaism —the Judaism, that is, most concerned with the *halakah*, the concrete application of the law to every detail of daily existence. This Epistle demonstrates, above all, how the best of this sacred moralism, far from being opposed to the Gospel of the Kingdom, was ready to welcome all its requirements. The constant echo in the Epistle of the words of Christ reported by the Synoptics is the more striking in that it is never possible to discover a precise borrowing. We are led to think that the "brother of the Lord" and the evangelists drew independently from the same source; but the former must have been particularly familiar with that source in order to draw continual inspiration from it with so free an ease.

As a Christian and a Jew—and still more Christian, perhaps, for remaining so Jewish—James shows us better than any other author how the moralism of the Old Testament could live on and be carried still further in the New, without ever being opposed—quite the contrary—to a mysticism of the creative Word, of the wholly free and gracious Wisdom. But it is because of its asceticism of evangelical "poverty", in imminent expectation of the Kingdom, in perfect docility to God in the midst of the obscurities of faith, that this mysticism of the Word and of grace is able so completely

[14] Ch. 3. [15] Ch. 4. [16] 5. 1–6.
[17] 5. 7–18. [18] 1. 1.

to irradiate that "religion pure and undefiled" which consists "in the presence of the Father, in visiting orphans and widows in their affliction and in keeping oneself unspotted from the world".[19]

2 Peter and Jude

The Second Epistle of Peter and the Epistle of Jude both maintain (and bring back, if this were needed), at the end of the apostolic era, the eschatological expectation which henceforth would be more and more in danger of fading into the background.

The Epistle of Jude puts us on guard against the heretical gnoses which tended to substitute for this expectation of faith fantastic speculations in which faith dissolves.[20]

The Second Epistle of Peter stresses more particularly the fact that "in the Lord's sight one day is like a thousand years and a thousand years like one day".[21] And, to the mythological speculations of false gnostics, it opposes the mysticism which anticipates eschatology, the mysticism of which the transfiguration of Christ becomes as it were the symbol.

> For it was not by following any sophistical fables that we have brought you to know the power and the parousia of our Lord Jesus Christ, but after having been the eye-witnesses of His majesty. For he received honour and glory from God the Father when the Glory of majesty brought him these words: "This is my well-beloved Son, in him is my joy", and we heard that word, sent from heaven, when we were with him on the holy mountain.[22]

This statement can be considered as the final word of the New Testament. Taken with the other phrase: "That you may become partakers of the divine nature,"[23] this Epistle might be considered as setting up, if not the foundation, at least the starting points characteristic of the two great syntheses of Christian mysticism: that of the East, inspired by the light of Thabor, and that of the West, connected more closely with the essential divinization of human nature by grace.

Conclusions on the New Testament

With these last writings, we have come to the end of the New Testament, and an absolutely unique phase in the history of Christian spirituality has ended. Everything that is to follow must live on the elements that have been gathered together. Nothing

[19] 1. 27.
[20] *In Introduction à la Bible*, vol. II, pt. III, ch. III and IV.
[21] 2 Peter 3. 8.
[22] 2 Peter 1. 16–18.
[23] 1. 4.

more, strictly speaking, can be added to them. What can happen is only that, according to the historical circumstances in which the Christian Church will be called to live, one or another aspect of the apostolic teaching will unfold all its implications, according to the needs of the moment, the problems that life will set.

We have been led to distinguish historically the teaching of Jesus from that of the Apostles. But we must emphasize the fact that these two teachings were never considered to be separate entities but a single whole, in the constant view of the Church and of Christians. The Apostles, the various New Testament writers, never pretended to teach anything other than "the Gospel of Jesus", that is, the teachings of Jesus himself illuminated by his actions and illuminating them in return. The properly apostolic charism, in this regard, was understood by the Church not only to be an inspiration that sealed all the Apostles' teaching with divine authority, but an inspiration designed very precisely to transmit to successive generations the authentic and integral message of Jesus. Whatever may be the rôle of the redactional element, in which the culture and characteristics of the different writers are reflected, they intended simply to be witnesses; and it has always been the conviction of the Church that they were in fact faithful witnesses to Jesus. The historical study of their testimony has succeeded in convincing us that they interpreted the fact of Jesus at the school of Jesus. Even when St Paul, St Matthew or St John present the most highly developed and orderly syntheses, the elements thus ordered go back to Jesus, and the principles of their ordering are also certainly derived from him.

The written witness of the apostolic generation, however, cannot be separated from the living witness of the Church, the Church which the Apostles caused to live. It is within this life that the apostolic writings are to be understood, and they themselves, especially the later ones, reflect a Church already organized, as to its rites and as to their interpretation. Behind the writings of the Apostles, as behind the consciousness of the primitive Church, is their living catechesis. This consciousness of the primitive Church is extended without a break into the Church of the following generations, in particular through its liturgical tradition: the tradition of common prayer and common celebration. The works of the earliest Christian writers, whom we call the Fathers, therefore, not only offer us an interpretation of the apostolic teachings in direct historical continuity with the Apostles. They also extend the echo of that living tradition in which their teaching was rooted, just as in the New Testament writings. Thereby, however dependent they may be on these writings, the Fathers do not depend on them exclusively. Beyond the apostolic writings, they continue the global and direct testimony to the apostolic teaching which the Church constitutes by her life, by her institutions. This evidence accompanies the New Testament. In a sense, it precedes it as much as it follows from it. Or, better, the New Testament can be understood only as immersed in the living preaching of the Church, which continues the living preaching of the Apostles.

In consequence, as the Apostles are not mere imitative successors in relation to Christ, neither are the Fathers in relation to the Apostles. Just as the Apostles give us the Spirit of Christ, so the Fathers retain the Spirit of the Apostles. We shall find in the Fathers no mere commentary on the Apostles' teaching, but its direct echo continued.

PART TWO

The Fathers

VII

THE FIRST CHRISTIAN GENERATIONS

CHRISTIAN spirituality in the first generations after the apostolic era is very difficult to evaluate precisely. On the one hand, the documents that we have from this period are few in number and hardly more than occasional writings. Doubtless they allow us to make a certain number of inferences. But there are so many gaps in our knowledge that conjecture must necessarily play a great rôle in all attempts at reconstruction. On the other hand, in spite of the rapid expansion of Christianity during this period, the teachings of the Apostles were still a very present reality. Everyone could still have known, if not the Apostles themselves, at least those who had been close to them. Under these conditions, the importance of an oral tradition, still immediate and still giving life to the texts of the New Testament, makes the few original texts bequeathed to us from this period of quite secondary importance.

Problems of the Second Century

These considerations, ordinarily neglected, render factitious certain modern hypotheses that have too easily passed into axioms. Chief among these is the idea that, for some mysterious reason, the influence of St Paul's teaching suddenly evaporated. This basic tenet of the majority of Protestant historians (and of many Catholics impressed by their statements) has no solid foundation at all. It is entirely based on the combination of a worthless argument *e silentio* and a complex of ready-made notions. This last is what first needs to be disposed of.

By "Paulinian teaching", Protestant historians wish us to understand a doctrine of justification by faith which, in St Paul's own thought, never had either the all-inclusive position or, above all, the significance which they attribute to it. There is no need to be surprised at the fact that no trace of their view of things, which never took form before Luther, is to be found in the writers of the first Christian generations, granted that, in fact, it cannot be found in the New Testament either, unless by some optical illusion. But as for authentic Paulinian teachings—the saving victory of Christ, through his Cross, over the powers of death; the opposition between the new man, risen with Christ and the old man, dead in Adam; the mysticism of the Spirit—if none of this is to be found explained *ex professo* in the course of the first century after the Apostle's death, we can still find many proofs of the fact that these teachings always remained alive and vital. In one author at least (the only one who was led by circumstances to put down in writing something like a complete sketch of his vision of Christianity), St Ignatius of Antioch, these salient points are actually re-expressed with striking originality, and so are those which set out, as it were, the heart of Johannine teaching. And if methodical developments of these various themes are not more numerous, the reason is quite simply that the literature of that period, or what has come down to us of it, almost completely ignored all such systematizing.

Another prejudice of Protestant origin to which impartial historical criticism can lend no support is the existence of an imaginary opposition between a kind of charismatic life in the Church (presumably primitive) and an institutional one that progressively stifled it. Here again, we have a fantasy arbitrarily projected onto the reality. Far from supporting this notion, the more we succeed in rediscovering the reality, the more we find that the illusion vanishes. In the light of recent discoveries (Qumran, etc.,) the ecclesiastical forms which seemed, to the scholars of the last century, so highly developed that the authenticity of documents testifying to their existence from the end of the second century (Letters of St Ignatius) was often denied, now are revealed as being very closely patterned on the organization of Jewish pre-Christian communities.[1] In the primitive Church, generally speaking, we always find charisms and the hierarchy existing together. And there is not a single text or a single fact which presents us with any systematic opposition of the former to the latter or the other way around. Doubtless there existed as at Corinth, at this period with Clement just as formerly with St Paul, cases of conflict between *certain* charismatics and *certain* authorities, or between authorities themselves. But this in no way prevents the fact that, in the ordinary course of events, the experience of the charisms and the experience of the hierarchically organized life of the Church formed but one entity.

[1] See J. Daniélou, *The Dead Sea Scrolls and Primitive Christianity.*

One last opposition is more in accord with reality: the one already pointed out between a Judeo-Christianity and a hellenizing Christianity. But we have already indicated the extent to which this has been artificially hardened, from the interpretation of the New Testament, and how this interpretation is itself only the result of a too schematized view of Judaism. Furthermore, the majority of the documents we possess from the period under discussion could with good reason be placed in either category. In other words, these categories are somewhat artificial. In all these texts, indeed even those that are the most Semitic in thought and literary expression such as the *Odes of Solomon*, the original language is the common Greek. And those which are not only the most hellenized but the most westernized, such as the Epistle of Clement, are shot through with biblical elements just as the others are, and continue to interpret these elements in a fundamentally Jewish context of thought. This last opposition, or rather distinction, between Judeo-Christianity and Helleno-Christianity, must, therefore, be considerably modified if it is not to lose all meaning.

The Texts

This leads us to make a rapid inventory of the documents from this period which we have at our disposal. Obviously we should first take into account those called the Apostolic Fathers: The Shepherd of Hermas, The Epistle of Pseudo-Barnabas, the *Didache*, the Epistles of St Clement of Rome, of St Ignatius of Antioch and of St Polycarp of Smyrna, to which we might add the fragments of Papias and the anonymous Epistle of Diognetus.[2]

The first three of these writings, whatever the place and date of their composition may have been, remain completely immersed in a universe of thought still wholly Jewish in texture. The *Shepherd* might be considered to be an apocalypse occasioning a Christian *halakah* on penitence. The Epistle attributed to Barnabas is a *midrash* which simply extends the line of thought of the Epistle to the Hebrews in its interpretation of the Old Covenant. But it seems still freer than the latter of the Alexandrianism which scholars have tried to find in both the one and the other. The *Didache* now seems to be a Christian equivalent of the Community Rule of Qumran or the analogous Rule of the community of Damascus.

With the Epistle of Clement, doubtless, we begin to pass into a different context. Here the elements, so to say, are the same as with St Paul, but the perspective is reversed. The author is no longer a

[2] For a bibliography of editions and studies of these writers, we especially recommend J. Quasten, *Patrology*, vol. I, Newman Press, Westminster, Md., 1950.

Jew, "a Hebrew, son of a Hebrew" while still being a Roman citizen proud of his citizenship. He is a Roman nourished on the Bible and on interpretations of it handed on by Christians still wholly Jewish in formation. The situation of Ignatius and Polycarp, while less clear-cut, still seems analogous. These Asiatics are Greek in culture, and more or less Greek in race. But while they have some familiarity with the modes of Greek thought which seem more native to them than to a St John, they have hardly advanced any further than he did in the translation of a Christianity still profoundly Semitic in its ways of thinking.

Papias presents no personal interest. He is merely a conscientious but unintelligent collector of any memories of the sub-apostolic era that might still be recovered. The author of the Epistle to Diognetus, on the contrary, whether an Alexandrian or not, is as naturally Greek as is St Luke. He addresses himself to Greeks as to his brothers and he is quite at home in their way of speaking to one another. The rather disdainful way in which he puts the vanity of paganism on the same level as that of Jewish "superstitions" should, nevertheless, not deceive us. When he comes to express his Christianity, he does so as a man of the Bible and he appeals to no properly Greek ideas in order to present the Bible to Greeks.... None the less, it is quite true that he comes at a turning-point. After him, the apologists can present Christianity to us as the true philosophy. And at that time we shall need to ascertain the precise import of this undeniable mutation.

The authors, however valuable they may be, still do not make up a whole by themselves. To reconstitute the more or less complete cycle of a Christian's life at that time, with these writings as our starting-point, would require bringing in what we know (however little this may be) about the liturgical life of the Church of the period. And it would also mean reimmersing these writings in a vast popular literature, of a rather miscellaneous character, difficult to analyse, but very revealing.

This last element poses a problem. This burgeoning of works that lack genius and even depth, but that are by this very fact expressive of the tastes of the mass of Christians, presents disturbing tendencies. It is difficult to assign the exact part played by heterodoxy properly so-called and, quite simply, by pious foolishness. But there is no doubt that, whether with regard to asceticism or beliefs, positions here do not seem very settled. Throughout this flood on which float some pearls, the transition is imperceptible from pure Christianity to the heresies which we have become accustomed, since the nineteenth century, to call "gnostic". We gather the painful impression that Christianity would not have spread so quickly in these first generations, if it had not disintegrated a little everywhere. What are we to think?

The truth is, it seems to us, that Christianity was providentially born during an immense crisis. In this crisis, it was Judaism that first disintegrated, in the midst of a pagan world itself undergoing a change in which it is difficult to distinguish potential rebirths from undeniable decadence. Christianity appeared at the heart of a general ferment of Judaism, which undeniably prepared the way for it. But this ferment prepared the way also for something quite different: for that syncretism, welcoming on its own account all sorts of Semitic influences, which invaded Mediterranean Hellenism like a tidal wave coming from the East. Jewish gnosis was already being contaminated at the time when Christianity was born within it. It was inevitable that Christianity should begin to spread in all the currents and counter-currents arising between a Judaism that was disintegrating and a Hellenistic religiosity in which everything was intermingled and confused.

We must not see in this popular Christianity, therefore, only a dissolution of the apostolic faith. It was also and much more the saturation, by Christian influences penetrating more or less deeply, of the already existing currents of gnostic syncretism. As J. Daniélou has clearly shown in his study of Judeo-Christian theology,[3] we can discover throughout the gradations of more or less heterodox gnoses a group of common elements which do not present anything dubious but rather reflect the first expressions of the authentic Christian faith. Some concrete examples will help us to clarify this general view.

Eschatology: the Problem of Millenarianism

The primary and most serious problem of Christian spirituality at this period of birth and transition is, indubitably, the problem of eschatology. The various forms of millenarianism which it was to occasion show clearly that the strangeness of so many of the characteristics of sub-apostolic Christianity does not necessarily mean heresy. Indeed, nothing is more delicate than the necessary adjustment of Christian thought in this domain. It cannot, in fact, even be said that the perfect focussing has ever been attained. An unresolved tension seems inherent to the situation in which the Church will remain until the parousia.

Millenarianism,[4] born, it would seem, in Asiatic circles, among those "presbyters", those "ancients", themselves disciples of the

[3] *Théologie du Judéo-Christianisme*, Tournai, 1958.
[4] Daniélou, *op. cit.*, pp. 341ff.

Apostles, whose sayings Papias gathered together, not without frequently burying them under a heavy weight of interpretation, soon spread far more widely. Under very variegated forms, from the frank materialism of Cerinthus to the speculations—toned down in various ways—of St Irenaeus, of Methodius of Olympus and again of the young Augustine, it proceeds from a double source. The first, obviously, is the mention in the Apocalypse of St John[5] of the thousand-years reign inaugurated by the first resurrection, that of the just, which seems to be anterior to a final unleashing of the power of Satan before the universal resurrection and the last judgment which will destroy evil totally and for ever. The second is a more or less formal conformation of the pattern of the final history of the Church to that of the history of Christ at the end of his life on earth. The "millennium" seems to have been conceived according to the ambiguous conditions under which the Risen One appeared to his disciples before his ascension. In the same way, it was supposed, we are moving towards a situation in which, for the just, death will already be overcome, but the conditions of the present life continue to some extent. People will eat and drink, as did Christ with his own during those forty days. Later, when evil, unchained for one last time, has been completely vanquished, the just in turn will pass through a final transformation. After that, they will no longer be made of that flesh and blood which, as the Apostle says, cannot inherit the kingdom of heaven.

The success of such speculations is quite understandable, since they seem to reconcile all the texts of the New Testament and at the same time to realize literally the hopes formulated in the Old. But, in spite of these advantages, the definition of the intermediate state after the first resurrection and during the "millennium", found great difficulty in extricating itself from a childish materialism. Papias speaks of enormous grapes that are to vie for the honour of satiating the elect. Irenaeus carefully avoids such excesses, while still allowing an exuberance of nature that he had to work hard to restrain within reasonable limits. Others, like Methodius, are still more prudent but not without falling into oddities, imagining a sabbatical nature: radiant, but unfruitful. Some of these dreams lingered on, we should note, even in the Latin Middle Ages; can we not find some traces of it in the cosmos of the resurrection as this is represented in the supplement to the *Summa Theologica*? At the extreme, a Cerinthus scandalizes us by the unbridled sensualism of his pious imaginings.

We should take note of the fact that the narrow literalism and

[5] Apoc. 20. 2–7.

concordism which gave rise to all these more or less strange dreams are not only an inheritance from the crudest forms of Jewish messianism. We also have here a first effect of Bible reading by men to whom the exact sense of its literary genres no longer came easily. These were so different from the Greek genres to which these men were accustomed that it was only with difficulty that they could make the necessary distinctions between the images and the realities which these veiled. In this transition, the freedom and flexibility of the haggadic interpretations began to grow set and hardened, except when such interpretations were confused with a purely arbitrary symbolism lending itself too readily to undue spiritualization. Something of this second temptation already appears in the Epistle of Barnabas. It is certain that the Christian school of Alexandria yielded only too much (although less than has been attributed to it) to this same temptation. But in doing so, as we shall see, it was not the only one nor, perhaps, the most blameworthy.

Agreement was finally to be reached, but only after a two good centuries of effort, on a concept of the final resurrection having a respect for its mystery sufficient to hold firmly to the two ends of the chain: the universal effect of the redemption on the cosmos and on man in particular, saving his body as well as his soul; and the necessary spiritualization of the body in that state which we can only hope for, but not pretend to depict. But to arrive at this concept, new discussions were to be required—those aroused by the attempt of Origen, which was once more unsuccessful, but in the sense opposite to that of millenarianism. And, again, the presentation of Christian teaching on this point will never completely escape from many hesitations, whatever the agreement to be slowly attained concerning all the elements of the problem that must be respected.

Contrary to the rather childish curiosity of the milleniarists and their vain efforts to define precisely the distinction between the first resurrection and the final victory of good over evil, an exegesis of the Apocalypse was worked out which perhaps over-simplifies things a little. This exegesis is the one expressed by St Augustine at second hand, but which he did not invent. It sees the first resurrection as simply the spiritual resurrection of baptism, the "millennium" being nothing other than the age of the Church preceding the parousia and the eternal kingdom.

At first sight, the adoption of these new conceptions would seem to mean that one part of eschatology is put off into an uncertain future, while the other part disappears as if by some sleight-of-hand or is presented as already realized. This is what Loisy said: "The

Kingdom of God was expected, and it was the Church that came." But this presentation, especially at the period we are now studying, also greatly over-simplifies things.

The truth is rather that the sense, so strong in the New Testament, of our having already entered into the eschatological times with the Passion and Glorification of Christ was retained. But for the Church this does not so much mean that eschatology is already realized as that it is, under a certain aspect, anticipated. The tension between the present and the future was in no way relaxed in consequence. Nor did this future cease to appear as imminent, although the futility of trying to calculate the length of the time of waiting was more clearly understood.

We should rather say that the realization grew clearer of the Christian life as being situated in a paradoxical intermediate state. In the risen Christ, we know that the Church has already gained everything that she is to possess after the last times, as Christ already possesses it. And we are persuaded that the Church in which we already live, as it is already constituted, is to the eyes of faith no other Church than the eternal Church we are awaiting. It was in the development of this certainty that the experience of the Spirit was extended, and at the same time stabilized, from the apostolic period to the one following it.

Charisms and Gnosis

It is not only the *Didache* that witnesses to the fact that "charisms", more or less extraordinary, more or less analogous to those of Pentecost, and especially prophecy and visions, did not disappear. A part of the popular literature we have mentioned leads us even to suspect that these phenomena were so fascinating as often to become degenerate. But other texts, much more respectable in nature, notably the best-attested Acts of the Martyrs, indicate the persistence of these charisms under forms that seem similar to those of the charisms indicated, for example, in the life of St Paul, as related in the second part of the Acts of the Apostles.

Because of the obvious *naïveté* of its author, the *Shepherd* of Hermas is a particularly convincing example of the simplicity with which "inspiration", vision and prophecy continued to form a living whole. But the Epistle called that of Barnabas shows us how the importance of the charism of "gnosis" now stands out. There were, doubtless, many fluctuations in the way in which this charism was understood, and still more in the content assigned to it, and this fact was to arouse the first vigorous reactions of the Catholic Church to define heresy and precisely to distinguish orthodoxy from it. But this Epistle is in agreement with the Apostolic Fathers as a whole in locating the focus of gnosis in meditation on the Scriptures, at the school of the Apostles, centred on Christ and his Cross, and in considering it not as a mere intellectual effort but as a living grasp of the realities of salvation. For this reason, the character of being a gift of the Spirit as proper to true gnosis is maintained, while its necessary extension in *agape* is reaffirmed and emphasized. Clement's Epistle is particularly happy in its implicit working out of this connection. "Gnosis" causes us to recognize the wonderful harmony of the actions of God in history. It opens out to us the humility of those to whom God has been merciful and, as it were, the humility of his mercy itself. So it necessarily leads us, by the very paths of this humility in faith,[6] to a realization of charity in the Church.

The Primitive Liturgy: the Eucharist

This invites us, following the example of Clement himself, to examine the liturgical context of this life in the Church in which gnosis is acquired and charity exercised. We should note the fact that it is to Clement, apparently, that we owe the meaning which Christianity was to attach precisely to this word, "liturgy". Using it in the traditional Greek sense of the public service rendered by an individual to the community, Clement applies it for the first time to Christian worship. This takes place in one of those developments he delights in concerning the co-ordinated harmony (cosmic in the primary sense of the word) of the works of God and, particularly, of charity. The Corinthians are not to encroach upon one another's sacred functions. As Paul had already explained in the first letter he sent to the same Church, all charisms must be exercised in the awareness that they are co-ordinated manifestations of the same Spirit, for the building up of one Body, that of Christ, in charity. This vast meditation on the work of creation and redemption comes to its climax in these terms:

> Since these are things which are now quite clear to us who have gazed into the depths of the divine gnosis, we ought to do everything that the Master has prescribed for us to carry out at the appointed times. Now he has prescribed that we should discharge ourselves of offerings and liturgies, not at random and without order, but at set times and hours. He himself has determined by his sovereign decision at what places and by what ministers they are to be carried out, so that everything will be

[6] We shall take up this question in greater detail in connection with these same writers when we trace the development of gnosis throughout the whole patristic era.

> done in a holy way according to his good pleasure and be agreeable to his will. Those, then, who present their offerings at the appointed times are welcomed and blessed; for, in following the ordinances of the Master, they do not go astray. On the high priest, special liturgies have been conferred; for priests, special places have been marked off; to the levites fall their proper service; laymen are bound by the precepts particular to the laity.[7]

What follows shows the transference of all this to the new hierarchy established on the foundation of the apostolate. But what is most interesting for our purposes here is the conclusion of this passage:

> Brothers, let each of us, in his proper rank, give thanks to God (*eucharisteito*) with a good conscience, without transgressing the rules governing his own liturgy.[8]

For Clement, in other words, the supreme work of the assembled Church is the eucharistic prayer in which all participate, but each in his rank and according to his proper function.

Nothing is more revealing both of the newness of Christianity and also of its permanent root in the ground of Jewish spirituality than an examination of the eucharistic formulas left to us by the primitive Church as compared with those of Judaism. Here we find again the "benedictions" for all things so characteristic of the latter, which already brought all creation and the whole life of man into the orbit of thanksgiving. But the many "eucharists" are now definitely centred in the "Eucharist" of the bread and the cup, carried out in the assembly of the Church. And this fundamental "Eucharist" gathers all things into the Eucharist of Jesus: the Eucharist that he pronounced at the Last Supper and that we make our own to give thanks for his own gifts and especially for the Cross.

The great prayer ending Clement's Epistle gives us as it were a direct echo of Jesus' Eucharist, while it also recalls continually the Jewish *Tefilah* of the Eighteen Blessings:

> May the creator of the universe
> guard intact over the whole world
> the reckoned number of His elect
> through His beloved Servant (*paidos*), Jesus Christ.
> Through Him, we have been called from darkness to light,
> from ignorance to the knowledge of the glory of His Name.
>
> We hope in You,
> principle of all creation.

[7] *First Epistle of Clement of Rome to the Corinthians*, XL.
[8] *Ibid.*, XLI, 1.

You have opened the eyes of our hearts
so that they might know You,
You alone are the Most High in the highest,
the Holy One who rests among the holy.
You bring down the insolence of the proud,
You frustrate the plans of the nations,
You raise up the humble
and throw down the powerful;
You enrich and make poor,
You take away and give life.

The one Benefactor of spirits
and God of all flesh,
You examine the depths,
You survey the works of men.
Help in danger,
Saviour of those without hope,
Creator and Guardian of every spirit;
You multiply the peoples of the earth,
but, among them all, You have chosen those who love You,
through Jesus Christ, Your beloved Servant,
through Him, You have taught them, sanctified them,
honoured them. . . .[9]

As in the *Shemoneh-Esreh,* this blessing expands into an all-embracing intercession, finally taken up in the current of thanksgiving:

O You, who alone possess the power to realize these things
and to give us those that are better yet,
we confess You through the high priest
and protector of our souls, Jesus Christ:
through Him be glory and magnificence to You,
now, and for the generations of generations
and in the ages of ages. Amen.[10]

While we notice in this prayer, as in all analogous Christian prayer, the same concentration on gnosis as in the last Jewish prayers, we remark also how this gnosis is focused in the exultant contemplation of the mystery of Christ. It is placed as it were at the centre of our vision of God's whole work, and the victorious expansion of *agape* radiates from it.

Analogous remarks might be made about the eucharistic prayers of the *Didache*. These certainly bring us back to a usage still very close to the Jewish one. For, as in the latter, there is (cf. the Supper in Luke's Gospel) the individual blessing of the cup taken by each person at the beginning of the meal. The formula given is a discreet

[9] *Ibid.*, LIX, 2 and 3.

[10] *Ibid.*, LXI, 3.

christianization of the traditional Jewish formula (the Christian insert is italicized):

> We give you thanks, O our Father,
> for the holy vine of David Your servant:
> *You have made us know it through Jesus, Your Servant.*
> Glory to You for ever and ever.[11]

The Christian addition is an obvious allusion to the words of Jesus after the Supper, in St John: "I am the true vine. . . ."

For the breaking of the bread by the president of the assembly, at the beginning of the common eucharistic meal, there is the analogous:

> We give You thanks, O our Father,
> for the life and for the gnosis
> *that You have given us through Jesus your Servant.*
> Glory to You in the ages![12]

Then comes the following prayer, the greater part of which may well also have a Jewish antecedent:

> As this broken bread, once scattered over the mountains,
> was gathered into one,
> so gather Your Church together from the ends of the earth,
> in Your Kingdom.
> Yes, to You be glory and power
> *through Jesus Christ*, for ever and ever.[13]

Finally, at the end of the common meal, comes the great blessing over the cup of the celebrant. This also is still patterned on Jewish formulas (equivalents of which have always remained in use in the synagogue) with, each time, the properly Christian touch that completes them:

> We give you thanks, O holy Father,
> for Your Holy Name
> that You have caused to dwell in our hearts,
> for the gnosis, the faith, and the immortality,
> that You have granted us *through Jesus Your Servant*,
> Glory to You through the ages!
> You it was, O all-powerful Master,
> who created the universe, to the praise of your Name:
> You have given men food and drink
> that they may enjoy them
> and give You thanks.
> But You have favoured us
> with a spiritual food and drink
> and with eternal life *through your Servant.*

[11] *Didache*, IX. [12] *Ibid.* [13] *Ibid.*

We give You thanks above all
because You are mighty.
Glory to You in the ages!
Remember, Lord, to deliver your Church
from all evil, and to perfect it in Your love.
Gather together from the four winds
the Church that You have sanctified
in the Kingdom that you have prepared for it.
For to You is the power and the glory
for all ages!
May Your grace come and the world pass away!
Hosannah to the God of David!
If anyone is holy, let him come;
if he is not, let him do penance.
Marana, tha!
Amen.[14]

These formulas call for a very illuminating remark made by J. Daniélou, which is also applicable to the formulas of Clement. When we compare these texts with the first chapters of the *Acts* (as is suggested by the texts themselves in their striking use of *pais* to designate Jesus: at once the "Servant" of Isaias and the beloved "child"), it seems that the frequent mention of the divine Name here has a definite implication. To Christians, this Name which has been revealed is doubtless Jesus himself.[15] Not only is he, in their eyes, the Word of God *par excellence,* object of the definitive gnosis, but he is the living Word in Whom God reveals himself to us—that is, as Father—in the unique Well-Beloved become the brother of us all.

We have italicized the whole conclusion of the prayer, because it seems to us to be typically Christian, contrary to what immediately precedes it. *Hosannah to the God of David!* seems a deliberate correction of the Gospel formula: *Hosannah to the Son of David.* The correction would appear to have been inspired by Jesus' words, commenting on Psalm 109—that the Messiah is not so much David's Son as his Lord. The *God of David* hailed here would, then, be a cryptic confession of the divinity of Jesus.

After this, the call to repentance, as the prelude to communion, places us in the context of one of the most agonizing spiritual problems for the first Christian generations—the question of sins committed by Christians after baptism, which is the whole subject of the *Shepherd* of Hermas.

14 *Ibid.*, x. In the event of an originally Jewish text, "Church" would have been only the translation of "*qahal*" and "love" of "*hesed*".
15 *Op. cit.*, pp. 199ff.

A last point that strikes us in this conclusion is the expression of eschatological expectation:

Marana, tha! Lord, come!

Quoted by St Paul, translated at the end of the Apocalypse of St John, this formula, obviously addressed to Christ, clarifies, again in a specifically Christian sense, the hope previously expressed in terms common to all Jewish apocalyptic literature:

Let your grace come and this world pass away!

So we grasp how the liturgical celebration, the Eucharist over the bread and the cup, expresses this anticipation of eschatology, which is something quite different from doing away with true eschatology, as would be the case in an eschatology fulfilled. Doubtless, everything is given to Christians here and now in the eucharistic celebration. But the Presence still veiled, which is the object of faith, is what most potently nourishes and excites the hope of the Presence revealed. This theme is to be a constant one in eucharistic piety, from the expression of it which is the most ancient still available to us, up to the last lines of the *Adoro te*.

With these prayers of the *Didache*, where we feel that we have come upon the very transition from the last pre-Christian Jewish piety to the spirituality of the Church in its first upspringing, we should compare the collection of eucharistic prayers which fill the seventh book of the *Apostolic Constitutions*. This compilation as such is probably not anterior to the fourth century. But Wilhelm Bousset and, more recently, E. R. Goodenough have clearly shown that the seventh book is a collection of Jewish texts, again christianized by some inserts only.[16] And the eighth book, which contains a whole series of fundamentally Christian prayers, beginning with the greatest eucharistic anaphora which Christian antiquity has bequeathed to us, seems constantly to make use of Jewish formulas. This explains why the first part of this anaphora, up to the Sanctus, is hardly more than a repetition of the *berakah* for creation quoted in the previous book. In the same way, the prayer for the consecration of a bishop, a "eucharist" for the divine providence shown in the leading of his people, seems to enshrine a formula which might have served for the installation of Jewish "presbyters" or of a *mebaker* such as we find at the head of the Qumran communities.

In this way, we can follow the transition between a period in which the Church simply took up Jewish prayers with some additions which clarified *gnosis* in the sense of St Paul's "mystery", and

[16] Wilhelm Bousset, article quoted below (p. 237) and E. R. Goodenough, *By Light Light*, Yale Univ. Press, New Haven, 1935.

a second period, more properly creative, in which none the less reminiscences of the Jewish liturgy remain present throughout.

The Primitive Liturgy: Prayer and Word

Moreover, while the eucharistic Supper is clearly the focus of Christian worship and the spirituality nourished by it, there is no doubt that the assembly of the Christian Church begins with a synagogue-like gathering for readings and prayers. The universal arrangement of the most diverse Christian eucharistic liturgies testifies to the primitive character of this combination.

Just as, in the synagogues, the Bible readings gave a place to one or even several homiletic allocutions on the part of the rabbi or rabbis present, so the Christian assemblies included from the first, after the Gospel, very free and very varied forms of commentaries "inspired" in different ways. According to the Acts of the Apostles and the First Epistle to the Corinthians, we see how these might go from completely unforeseen charismatic manifestations to apostolic exhortations proclaimed with authority. And from what St Jerome, towards the end of the fourth century, describes as still customary in Palestine, we see how something of this procedure lingered on for a long time, all the priests present still being liable to be called on to give their interpretations before the bishop presiding at the synaxis gave his own.

The ancient Church saw the most carefully prepared exegeses of consecrated "doctors", no less than the kinds of witnessing which we would call the most "charismatic" in the sense of spontaneous, as various kinds of "charisms", but given to each for the good of all.

We should note, as ancient Syriac literature abundantly indicates, that for a long time, in the East at least, the "inspired" homily developed in forms hardly less lyric than didactic. Here we should see one of the origins, and perhaps the chief one, of Christian hymns. And here again, as Schirmann[17] has demonstrated, the continuity seems striking, even as to poetic form, from the *piyutim* of the synagogue to the hymns of Ephrem and even to the canons of the Byzantine choirmasters (themselves very frequently of Semitic origin, like Romanus Melodus).

And so the primitive homily, far from being a kind of religious lecture, appears as a preparation for the Eucharist itself, with which it presents striking analogies. This helps us to understand how the homiletic theology of antiquity tended to develop into

[17] Jefim Schirmann, "Hebrew Liturgical Poetry and Christian Hymnology", in *The Jewish Quarterly Review*, XLIV (1953), pp. 123ff.

doxology. In pieces as late as the *Te Deum*, we find this same continuity between confession of faith, hymn, and eucharistic anaphora.

The whole collection called the *Odes of Solomon*, very close to the *Hodayoth* of Qumran, appears to be a collection of commentaries on the great Johannine themes of light and life, in which exhortation is at once and inseparably didascalia and psalmody.

> As the sun is the joy
> of those who seek its day,
> so my joy is the Lord,
> for He is my sun.
> His rays have brought me back to life,
> His light has dispersed all darkness before
> my face (Ode XV).
> ... I have believed in the Christ of the Lord
> and it has been shown me that He is the Lord.
> He has shown me His sign
> He has led me in His light....[18]
>
> Drink at the waters of the living spring of the [Lord,
> for it is open to you.
> Come, all you who are thirsty,
> take the drink that quenches thirst.
> Rest near the spring of the Lord:
> it is lovely and pure, it calms the soul.
>
> Its waters are sweeter than honey,
> the harvest of bees is in no way comparable to it.
> for it springs from the lips of the Lord,
> it takes its name from the heart of the Lord.
>
> Eternal and invisible, it flows:
> before its appearance, no one had seen it.
> Happy those who have drunk of it
> and quenched their thirst![19]

Christian Gnosis

Texts such as these are more effective than any explanation in helping us to understand the nature of the gnosis brought by Christ, which appears as the privileged object of all "eucharists". As the Epistle of Pseudo-Barnabas shows with a thoroughness leading to some extremist over-simplifications, this gnosis consists in finding Christ, his work, the "way of justice" that he has opened out to us, behind the whole teaching of the Bible. But even more than in Judaism, this gnosis is not simply knowledge of the Scriptures, nor even the "discernment of spirits": it is trust in God, love of God, union with him, and all this henceforth realized "in Christ".

[18] Ode XXIX. [19] Ode XXX.

Ignatius of Antioch, by the intensity of his faith, while he awaited martyrdom, expressed in pure and burning terms this mysticism of primitive Christian gnosis. Speaking to lukewarm Christians, he says:

> Why, then, are we not all made wise (*phronínoi*) in receiving the gnosis of God, which is Jesus Christ? Why, then, do we perish foolishly, ignoring the grace which the Lord has sent us in truth?[20]

What follows shows that, for him, this "gnosis of God, which is Jesus Christ" is concentrated in the glorious Cross and, more generally, in what he calls "the three resounding mysteries": "the virginity of Mary, her childbirth, and the Lord's death", the saving virtue of which he develops at length.[21] But it is in his Epistle to the Romans that we find the explicit manifestation of the profound aspiration which we sense everywhere in his work, underlying both meditation and exhortation:

> My earthly love (*eros*) has been crucified and in me there is no more fire for material things (*pur philoülon*), but rather a living water that murmurs within me and says to me: "Come to the Father!" I no longer take pleasure in corruptible food nor in the joys of this life: what I desire is the bread of God, the bread that is the flesh of Jesus Christ, the son of David; and for drink I desire his blood, that is to say, incorruptible love (*agape*). . . .[22]

These various texts help us to locate Christian gnosis at the confluence, so to say, of its various tributaries. It is first and always the understanding of the Scriptures, but wholly illuminated and absorbed in Christ. In this regard, nothing is more expressive than this other phrase of Ignatius to the Philadelphians:

> . . . I heard it said by certain men: "I believe only in what I find in my records, that is, the Gospel", and when I said to them: "It is written!" they answered: "That is precisely the question." But my records are Jesus Christ; my inviolable records are His cross, His death, His resurrection, and the faith [that comes] through Him: it is in these that I desire, in your prayer, to be justified.[23]

But this "Christic" knowledge of Scripture tends of its own accord towards effective encounter in the sacrament of the Eucharist. This latter, however, as the preceding formula clearly points out, nourishes the desire for the eternal meeting to be brought about by martyrdom itself. The "bread of God" that

[20] Ignatius, *To the Ephesians*, XVII, 2.
[21] *Ibid.*, XIX.
[22] Ignatius, *To the Romans*, VII.
[23] Ignatius, *To the Philadelphians*.

Ignatius desires is all this: the eucharist, martyrdom, the eternal consummation, in "the incorruptible love" of union with God in Christ.

Cross of Glory

As gnosis is connected with the Scriptures, as it is their Christian assimilation, it then appears as having two poles: the Saviour's Cross, but the Cross including the resurrection and all its effects; the Church, but the Church as the body of Christ dead and risen again, "realizing himself fully in us", according to St Paul's phrase.

Ignatius again shows us the relationship between these two themes, or rather the natural prolongation of the one in the other, in a rather curious image used in his Epistle to the Ephesians:

> You are the stones of the Temple of the Father, prepared for the building of God the Father, raised to the heights by the machine of Jesus Christ, which is the Cross, using as your cable the Holy Spirit.[24]

Hence the search for "types" of the Cross throughout the whole Old Testament (a search of which the Epistle of Pseudo-Barnabas is a remarkable example, by reason both of a certain already quite perceptible artificiality and the undeniable fervour of a search certainly inspired by the Pauline teaching on the "mystery"). Hence also the vision of the Cross in the light of glory, and the spontaneous allegorizing of this vision in an effort to express its cosmic import.

Throughout these meditations, Christ's Cross is always associated with its effect in us and, still more, with our necessary association with it. Hence the contemplation of the Cross is prolonged in a meditation on baptism and a meditation on martyrdom.

And so Barnabas, in his search for "types" of the Cross, says: "Let us now find out whether the Lord took care to show in advance the water and the Cross. . . ." He finds a remarkable example in the phrase of Psalm 1 about the tree planted on the river-bank:

> Note how He has set the water and Cross in the same place. For this means to say: Happy are those who have gone down into the water, having put their hope in the Cross.[25]

We shall soon return to the themes of the Cross and martyrdom. But what must be emphasized as the background of all this, in the primitive Christian vision, is the fact the Cross is always contemplated in the light of the resurrection and the final triumph of Christ and his own. It is most significant that at this period the

[24] Ignatius, *To the Ephesians*, IX, 1.

[25] *Barnabas*, XI, 1 and 8.

"sign of the Son of man"[26] which is to appear in heaven to proclaim the Parousia is always interpreted as an appearance of the Cross. This is surely the meaning of *semeion expetaseos*, literally "the sign of the extension" spoken of in the *Didache*.[27] More explicitly, the *Apocalypse of Peter* has Christ say:

> As the lightning that flashes from the East to the West, so shall I come on the clouds of heaven, while my Cross will go before my face.[28]

The same thing is to be found in the *Epistle of the Apostles* and in the eighth book of the *Sibylline Oracles*.[29]

As to the way in which the Cross itself was to receive a cosmic interpretation, we see very clearly in a page of St Irenaeus how this theme is connected with St Paul's Epistle to the Ephesians. In fact, we find two echoes of it combined. The first is Ephesians 3. 18, on the "length, the breadth, the height, the depth of the knowledge of the love of Christ". The second is Ephesians 2. 14–16: "He has broken down the wall of separation, of enmity, in his flesh . . . in such a way as to reconcile the two (Jews and pagans) in one single body with God in Christ, killing enmity in himself." Here is Irenaeus' text:

> As we had lost [the Word] by wood, so it is by wood that He has once again manifested Himself to all, showing in Himself the length, the height, the depth and the breadth, and, as one of our predecessors has said, reuniting the two peoples in one single God by stretching out His hands: there are two hands, indeed, because the two peoples were scattered to the extremities of the earth, and there is one head because there is but one God.[30]

Irenaeus' mention of a "predecessor" shows that he is simply taking up a traditional theme. It is found again in many other places, for example in this invocation to the Cross in the *Martyrdom of Andrew*, from which so many expressions have passed into the liturgy of this saint, first in the East and then in the West:

> [O Cross], I know your mystery, for which you were set up. Indeed, you have been set up in the world to strengthen what is unstable. One part of you is elevated in the heavens, so as to designate the Word from on high; another part goes out to right and left, so as to put to flight the fearful power of the adversary

[26] Matt. 24. 30. [27] Ch. XVI.

[28] P. 209 of the translation of S. Grébaut, in *Revue de l'Orient chrétien*, V (1910).

[29] For the first of these texts see *Patrologia orientalis*, IX, 139. Cf. also Oracle 244 of the eighth book.

[30] *Adversus Haereses*, V, III; ed. W. W. Harvey (2 Vols., Cambridge, 1857 repr., 1929), III, p. 372.

and to gather the world together into one; and one part of you is planted in the earth, so that you may reunite the things that are on earth and in the depths with the things of heaven. O Cross, machine of salvation of the Most High! O Cross, trophy of the victory of Christ over His enemies! O Cross, planted in the earth and bearing your fruit in the heavens![31]

The Cross and the Church

These texts are enough to make us understand how completely, as has already been said, the theme of the Cross and the theme of the Church could be linked together in the meditation of the first Christians. Is this link not already explicit in St Paul, for whom the mystery is Christ on the Cross, while the revelation of the mystery is carried out in the Church?[32]

In the visions of the *Shepherd* of Hermas, the Church appears as an aged woman, because she was "created first, before all things . . . it is for her that the world was made".[33] This is to be understood (as what follows indicates) not of a pre-existence properly speaking, but of a predestination in God, as stated in the phrase of Ignatius of Antioch to the Ephesians[34] concerning the Church "predestined before the ages to be for ever". At the same time, according to Hermas again, the Church is like a tower founded on the water and built by angels. The woman whom he had seen before says to him:

> The tower that you see built up is I, the Church, I who appeared to you just now and previously. . . . The tower is built on the water because our life has been and will be saved by water. The tower has for foundation the word of the all-powerful and glorious Name, and for support the invisible power of the Master. . . .[35]

It is obvious that the water is that of baptism, just as the divine Name (here particularly) must be Christ himself. But in the background of the baptismal and Christological context, we perceive an element constant in primitive Christian gnosis: the outlines of an allegorical exegesis of creation, effected by the divine Word, beginning with the primordial waters. Thus, just as the Church is given to us as the end of creation, so the Cross appears as the new creation, restoring and perfecting the old.

All this finds its most complete expression in a text which the manuscripts present as a second epistle of Clement of Rome, but

[31] Ed. Lipsius-Bonnet, *Acta apostolorum apocrypha*, II, 1. Leipzig, 1898, pp. 54–5.

[32] See Eph. 3. 10 and 1 Cor. 1. 18–2. 8.

[33] *Vision*, II: 4, v. 1; cf. *Vision*, I: 1, v. 6.

[34] Prologue.

[35] *Vision*, III: 3, vv. 3–5.

which is in reality, according to Quasten, "the oldest Christian sermon that has come down to us"[36]:

> It is, then, brothers, in doing the will of God our Father that we belong to the first Church, the spiritual Church, which was created before the sun and the moon . . . the Church of life. For I do not think that you are ignorant that the living Church is the body of Christ. In fact, Scripture says: "God made man [he made them], man and woman." The man is Christ; the woman is the Church. And the Bible and the Apostles say that the Church is not of the present age, but from on high (*anothen*). She existed, in fact, spiritually, like our Jesus, and she has been manifested at the end of time to save us.[37]

This text again deserves a long commentary. In the first place, it also witnesses to the fact that one of the fundamental elements of gnosis is meditation on the account of creation in Genesis, which ends in discovering the redemption, as in filigree. Here the creation of man and woman is revealed as a "type" of the union of Christ with the Church, his bride and his body, following out two themes prepared to be brought together by St Paul's Epistle to the Ephesians. It would seem that St Paul already refers to this interpretation of Genesis as to a traditional exegesis, when he says, in connection with what is said about marriage in Genesis: "This mystery is great, in relation to Christ and to the Church".[38]

It might be said that gnosis, in thus deepening the mystery of the Church and of the Cross, is defined as "gnosis of *agape*".

In fact, the Church, living by the Cross in the eucharistic celebration, appears throughout all these texts as being the realization in the world of the love of God which the Cross has manifested and communicated to us.[39]

The Church and Agape

It is in accordance with this vision that we must understand the insistence of Clement and Ignatius on the hierarchical order in the Church and on the necessity for respecting it, particularly in liturgical life. For the hierarchical order is conceived as the source, the manifestation and, finally, the guardian of this communication of the divine unity to man in *agape*. Nothing is more typical than the dedication of the Epistle of Ignatius to the Church of Rome as "the Church that presides at the *agape*". Clement as it were goes to meet St Paul's thought in using the Stoic vision of the harmony of

[36] *Op. cit.*, I, p. 64.
[37] *Second Epistle of Clement*, XIV, 1–2.
[38] Eph. 5. 38.
[39] For these last two paragraphs, we are particularly indebted to Daniélou, *op. cit.*, pp. 290ff.

the cosmos as an illustration of the theology of the Church as the Body of Christ. And Ignatius directly expresses the liturgical vision of the Church, common to both these writers, in his images of the choir and the lyre, which resound rather with Platonic echoes:

> ...You should have only one and the same thought as your bishop, as you already do. Your venerable presbyterium, truly worthy of God, is united to the bishop as cords to the lyre, and it is thus that from the perfect harmony of your thoughts and your charity a concert of praises arises to Jesus Christ. Let each of you enter into this choir: then, in the harmony of concord, you will take, by your very unity, the keynote of God, and you will all sing with one single voice, through the mouth of Jesus Christ, the praises of the Father who will hear you and, by your good works, will recognize you as the members of His Son. It is therefore to your advantage to keep yourself in irreproachable unity: it is thereby that you will enjoy a constant union with God Himself.[40]

The Christians of the first ages were immediately aware that the reality, under the weight of human sin, would constantly tend to fall from this ideal. It is against these schismatic tendencies that Ignatius continually insists on the unity in charity which should be the fruit of the Eucharist, as it is the safeguard of its authenticity:

> Take care, then, only to participate in one single Eucharist: for there is only one flesh of our Lord, one cup to unite us in His blood, one altar only; as there is only one bishop, surrounded with the presbyterium and the deacons, the associates of his ministry: in this way, you will do all things according to the will of God.[41]

The Two Ways, and Simplicity

The entrance into this choir, into this unanimity of love, thus has as its necessary counterpart a choice, a break with the world of sin where the *agape* of God is unknown or misunderstood. The theme of the two ways and the two "spirits" between which we must choose once for all, taken up from Jewish catecheses by the Sermon on the Mount, was to be faithfully preserved in ancient Christian catechesis. It fills the first part of the *Didache*; it recurs in the Epistle of Barnabas:

> There exist two ways of teaching and of acting: that of light and that of darkness; but there is a great difference between them. Over the one are set the angels of God, conductors of light, over the other the angels of Satan. God is the Lord since the beginning

[40] Ignatius, *To the Ephesians*, IV.
[41] Ignatius, *To the Philadelphians*, IV.

of the ages and for ever; Satan, the prince of the present time that favours impiety.[42]

The same Epistle expressly draws out from this, in the chapter that follows, the capital importance of *aplotes*, corresponding to the Hebrew *tam*: simple, integral. *Aplotes*, indeed, is opposed to the divided soul, to *dipsuchia*, the duplicity which tries (improperly and vainly) to avoid the choice between the two ways.[43]

This teaching is one of the most remarkable constants to be found in the most different apostolic Fathers. Clement tells us:

> [The Father] pours out His graces with sweetness and goodness on those who come to him with a simple heart (*aple dianoia*): having no duplicity (*me dipsuchomen*).[44]

The *Shepherd* for its part, continually puts us on guard against *dipsuchia*.[45] To this dividedness it opposes true faith together with *aplotes*, hence the gravity of sin after the definitive choice which baptism presupposes as already made.

The whole *Shepherd* is written, however, to proclaim the possibility of post-baptismal repentance. But this, precisely, has no meaning if it is not finally to destroy *dipsuchia*.

It is, then, precisely along the line already traced out by St Paul[46] that the primitive Church after him understood asceticism. Continence, *enkrateia*, in all its forms, has no other end than to prevent the soul from remaining divided. We can understand, then, why the theme of asceticism always appears as the counterpart to the theme of adhesion to Christ, and virginity as the perfection of union with him.

Encratism

The chief deviation to which the ascetic ideal of the first centuries was sometimes reduced in popular literature was an insistence on continence so fervent that it came rather to neglect its motivations. Then, under the influence of the pessimistic dualism of the period, marriage came to be condemned along with the whole of life in the flesh. This is what has been called encratism.[47]

But martyrdom, for the first Christian generations, was in any case the ideal instance of union with Christ in trial leading to perfect union with him in the life of charity. Any study of primitive spirituality must, then, finally converge in the experience and the theology of martyrdom.

[42] *Barnabas*, XVIII, 1–2. [43] Cf. XIX, 2 and 5. [44] *I Clement*, XXIII.

[45] Cf. especially *Mand.* IX; and also *Vis.* II, 2, v. 4; III, 3, v. 4; III, 4, v. 3; III, 7, v. 1; IV, i, v. 4; IV, 2, v. 6. [46] See 1 Cor. 7. 25ff.

[47] See the article on this word by G. Blond in the *Dictionnaire de Spiritualité*, fasc. XXVI–XXVIII, Paris, 1959, col. 628ff.

VIII

MARTYRDOM

THE importance of martyrdom in the spirituality of the early Church would be difficult to exaggerate. But it did not have this exceptional importance merely for the particular period when the majority of martyrdoms took place. After the elements of the New Testament, certainly no other factor has had more influence in constituting Christian spirituality. There is hardly need to add that the reality and the theology of martyrdom are already to be found in the New Testament. But there is hardly any other instance where we can so clearly see that doctrinal development at work which is bound up with the whole experience of the Church in the world.

It is not easy to evaluate the exact extent of the persecutions, materially speaking. We do not need to discuss here the problems that have been raised with regard to the number and the extension of the various waves of persecution during the first three centuries, even in connection with their immediate material effects on the life of the Church. Neither shall we examine the controversial question of the legal bases on which the persecutions were carried out. Yet we should make it clear that they affected the spirit of the Church even more by the continually imminent threat that they caused to weigh upon it than by the actual number, however large it may have been, of those directly touched by them. Only the persecution of Decius, in the middle of the third century, the more serious since it followed after a prolonged period of relative peace, seems to have been generally and really systematically pursued. But, up to the period of Constantine, the Church was an illegal, or at least unrecognized, association and to adhere to it always meant accepting the ban of ordinary society, a ban which might go as far as a direct threat to life and possessions. This was how martyrdom, or simply the possibility of it, during three centuries, came to crystallize in a new form the eschatological hope of Christians. Once again, few realities have had more importance or a more lasting importance than this in the development of Christian spirituality.[1]

The Literature of Martyrdom

There is an abundance of literature to inform us about everything connected with martyrdom in the first centuries. This literature is of different kinds, and the texts are of very unequal value. But it includes at least a solid core of first-hand documents which are among the most priceless in the history of spirituality.

A first category consists of accounts of martyrdoms. But here we need to distinguish three groups of very unequal interest.

The most ancient form is analogous to the account of the first martyrdom in the New Testament: the death of Stephen as reported in the Acts of the Apostles,[2] an account put together very shortly after the events took place, and one in which the recollections of eye-witnesses have been collected with a minimum of literary research. The oldest example of these *Martyria*, or *Passiones*, is the *Martyrdom of Polycarp* of Smyrna, composed almost immediately after the event (156). The closeness to the facts seems still more certain in the *Letter of the Churches of Vienne and Lyons to the Churches of Asia and Phrygia*, inserted by Eusebius in the first three chapters of his *Ecclesiastical History* (177 or 178). The *Passion of Perpetua and Felicitas* (they underwent martyrdom at Carthage on 7 March 202) is of still more immediate interest, from the fact that it contains the actual diary kept by one of the martyrs, Vibia Perpetua, with her personal reactions.

Very impressive also, but by reason of their extreme matter-of-factness, are the Acts of the martyrs properly so called. These documents are presented as simple verbal records of official judgments. The most ancient, certainly, is that of the *Acts of St Justin and his Companions* (the converted philosopher, whom we shall speak about later on), executed at Rome, probably in 165. The *Acts of the Martyrs of Scillium in Africa* (17 July, 180) belong to the same genre, as do the *Preconsular Acts of St Cyprian,* bishop of Carthage, martyred on 14 September 258.

As the title of this last document indicates, these Acts are presented as being copies of official archives. Whether this character is authentic or not is disputed by historians. Lietzmann, for example, thinks it is a question, if not of pastiches, at least of free reconstructions of official texts, since Christians would have had

[1] All the necessary bibliographical information will be found in *Patrology*, by J. Quasten, I, pp. 176ff.

[2] Acts 6. 8–8. 3.

difficulty in obtaining copies of the latter.[3] Yet in the examples just mentioned, there is no room for doubting that stenographic notes taken at the event itself must have been used and that, consequently, these documents must be considered first-hand in this sense.

But, as history went on, the more numerous became compositions that were inspired in a general way by these two preceding types, but with the rôle of literary fiction developed in proportion to the amount of time separating the composer from the events he claims to relate. This is indicated first of all in the more or less fictitious discourses put into the mouths of martyrs, such as the apology (very beautiful none the less) attributed to the martyr, Apollonius. With Acts such as those of St Cecilia or St Agnes, we find ourselves in the realm of popular edifying literature, sometimes verging on fairy-tales. It is unfortunate that these last productions found a place in liturgical books such as the Roman Breviary and Martyrology. Even when they retain some attested facts and touching expressions of popular piety, they cannot rival the more ancient great texts which directly open out to us the experience of the Church of the martyrs.

Other very valuable witnesses to this same experience, although more developed than the authentic accounts of martyrdoms, are given by the theological writings which martyrdom soon inspired. The first example, incomparable in many respects, is furnished by the Epistles of St Ignatius of Antioch. On his journey to Rome where martyrdom awaited him, he wrote one after the other to the Churches which had given him hospitality and, above all, to the Church of Rome to prevent anyone from intervening to have him escape his death-sentence. Particularly in this last text, we have the reflections which awaiting for martyrdom inspired in a bishop of the beginning of the second century (he suffered under Trajan, 98–117), a personality of exceptional spiritual and theological depth.

We should also include here the *Exhortations to Martyrdom* composed on different occasions by spiritual writers to afford the support of their religious thinking to Christians under trial. The most interesting are those of St Cyprian and of Origen, both of whom, moreover, were a little later to add example to teaching.

Nor should we neglect a treatise, containing doctrine already much less trustworthy, like the *Ad martyres* of Tertullian. Its very deviations reveal the dangers to which a spirituality as high and pure as that of martyrdom could be exposed, dangers which were not without effects later on.

[3] See H. Lietzmann, *History of the Early Church* (2 vols., Meridian, New York, 1961).

Jewish Precedents

Although martyrdom is so characteristic of primitive Christianity, we should not forget that it had precedents in Judaism.[4] The *Letter of the Churches of Vienne and Lyons* is fully aware of this since it says:

> As for the blessed Blandina, the last of all—the noble mother who had exhorted her children and sent them victoriously to the King, who had herself gone through all her children's battles—she then hastened to join them, rejoicing and exulting at her exodus, as if she had been called to a marriage-feast and not to be thrown to the beasts.[5]

The allusion is clearly to the mother of the seven brothers delivered to death under Antiochus for having refused to sacrifice to idols.[6] This text, like the account of the young Hebrews thrown into the furnace for an analogous reason,[7] is frequently connected, in the documents we are considering and, later, in the liturgy for the feasts of martyrs, with the "witnessing" of Christians to their faith.

Conversely, certain texts revealing the Jewish piety contemporary with the origins of Christianity present a sketch of themes which were to be developed in connection with Christian martyrdom. The fourth book of Macchabees already contains the idea that the death of a prophet is like the seal of perfection set to his life.[8] Here we find also the idea that God gives supernatural strength to those who suffer for faithfulness to his law,[9] and that this death leads them to incorruptibility.[10] This last point is equally emphasized by the *Martyrdom of Isaias,* which explains that the prophet put to death is absorbed in the vision of God and filled with the Holy Spirit.[11]

The Christian martyr, however, is distinguished not only by faith in Christ, but by the explicit connection of his death with Christ's. Here again, the *Letter* of the Christians of Lyons must be quoted. For here we find a reminder of Stephen's martyrdom, recalled precisely for the sake of this characteristic.[12] Still clearer are these statements :

> They loved to reserve the title of martyr to Christ, the "faithful and true martyr" (allusion to the phrase of the Apocalypse,

[4] See E. Lohmeyer, "Die Idee des Martyriums im Judentum und Urchristentum", in *Zeitschrift für systematische Theologie*, vol. V (1927, Gütersloh), pp. 232–49.

[5] Eusebius, *Eccles. Hist.*, V, I, § 55.

[6] 2 Mach. 7. 20ff.

[7] Dan. 3.

[8] 4 Macc. 7. 15.

[9] 6. 5–7.

[10] 9. 21–22.

[11] *Martyrdom of Isaias*, V, 7 and 14.

[12] Eusebius, *Eccles. Hist.*, V, II, § 5.

3. 14), the first-born from among the dead, the prince of the life of God.[13]

This quality is not only Christian, but "Christic", presupposing a special relationship with Christ, and this enables us to understand the rôle played by martyrdom in an undeniable development of eschatology.

Martyrdom and Eschatology

Théo Preiss, in a debatable but stimulating study of the Epistles of St Ignatius, emphasizes this fact and even greatly distorts it. While the Christians of the New Testament awaited the return of Christ in glory, in an eschatological vision that was at once transcendent and collective, Ignatius represents a real metamorphosis of eschatology on these two points. His concentration on the eucharistic sacrament and on martyrdom individualized and "immanentized" the eschatological vision. In other words, he puts it within human power to set in motion final spiritual realizations while also making these the objects of individual experience. The sacrament replaces the parousia, and the aspiration for martyrdom prepares the way for a substitution of the "Christian death" of the individual for the general resurrection.[14]

It is quite true that the Eucharist and martyrdom constitute two poles, and closely connected ones as we shall see, in the spirituality of St Ignatius. But it is a first deformation of his thought to attribute to him a conception of the sacrament by which man would have power over the presence of Christ, instead of depending in faith on his free and sovereign coming; and another deformation to believe that, in his thought, martyrdom was a substitute for the resurrection. Let us leave aside the sacramental problem for the moment, and see how Ignatius regarded the relationship of martyrdom to eschatology.

It is true that Ignatius speaks of "immortality" on different occasions. But this formula, borrowed from the current way of speaking, gives no evidence of any disappearance or obliteration in his thought of the Christian view of the "resurrection". Not only does he use this other term far more frequently than the word "immortality", but even when he uses the latter it is obvious that he is thinking in the sense proper to the other term. His Epistle to the Smyrniotes, indeed, states with unambiguous precision that Christian hope, as it is already realized in Christ, does not look

[13] *Ibid.*, § 3.

[14] Th. Preiss, "La Mystique de l'imitation du Christ et de l'unité chez Ignace d'Antioche", in *Revue d'Histoire et de Philosophie religieuses*, XVIII (1938), Strasbourg, pp. 197–241.

towards a natural immortality of the soul, but to the resurrection of the body. For him, the Docetists are unconsciously wishing themselves harm, for, in denying the reality of the flesh of Christ, they are destining themselves to a disincarnate immortality which, he does not hesitate to say, is worth no more than that of the demons.[15] The reality of the Passion and the reality of the Resurrection, these two go together and are equally essential.[16] Christian hope is fed with the certainty that "after his resurrection, Jesus ate and drank with his disciples like a corporeal being, even though spiritually united with the Father". Hence, indeed, it comes about that the believer accepts very real sufferings unhesitatingly, because he also expects, thanks to Christ, a resurrection which will be equally real.[17]

> As for myself, I know that I believe that, even after His resurrection, Jesus had a body. When He came near to Peter and His companions, what did He say? "Touch me, feel me, and see that I am not a bodiless spirit." Immediately they touched Him, and at this intimate contact with His flesh and His spirit, they believed: *hence their contempt for death and their victory over it.*[18]

The last words, that we have italicized, are decisive. The disciples did not expect from death as such an immortality of the soul disengaged from its bonds with the body. Quite the contrary, they expected, from Jesus' resurrection, a like victory over their own death.[19]

On the other hand, it is quite true that one of the most characteristic expressions of Ignatius is the word *epitugchano,* with a genitive complement which is usually "God" and once "Christ".[20] It seems that these phrases must be translated as "attain" or "gain"—sometimes simply as "arrive at". Must we for this reason suppose that Ignatius envisaged martyrdom as a great human deed which would enable him to conquer God or Christ in a great struggle? Do we have, consequently, in these expressions, the sign of a mysticism pretending to raise itself to God by human effort, and thus opposed to the essentially unmeritable grace of the parousia?

15 Ignatius, *To the Smyrniotes*, II.

16 *Ibid.*, III. 17 *Ibid.*, IV. 18 *Ibid.*, III.

19 Ignatius repeats this to the Magnesians, in terms with a beauty which becomes fully luminous in the light of the previous text. "Our life is risen like the sun, thanks to Him and His death: this mystery which certain persons deny is the very source of our faith and our patience, by which we can be found disciples of Jesus Christ, our only Master" (ch. IX).

20 We find *epituchein theou* in *Ephesians*, X, 1; XII, 2; *Magnesians*, XIV: 1; *Trallians*, 13, 3; *Romans*, I, 2; II, 1; IV, 1; IX, 2; *To Polycarp*, VII, 1. In *Romans*, V, 3, we have *ina Iesou Christou epituche*. We also find *eanper charitos epitucho* (I, 2), *epituko* used absolutely (*ibid.*, VIII, 3) and *ina en o klero eleethen epitucho* (*Philadelphians*, V, 1).

It would be difficult to make up more perfect nonsense. We should note first of all that the Greek expression, far from indicating the product of an effort, signifies on the contrary a happy encounter. The writings of St Paul always use it to mean the attaining of the divine promises, in the more or less immediate context of the idea of election.[21] It is remarkable, furthermore, that Ignatius himself uses the word once for "obtain grace" and once again for "gain the inheritance which is fallen to me by [God's] mercy".

This way of speaking—so interesting and certainly characteristic of Ignatius—can, therefore, in no way be opposed to a spirituality of grace expressing itself in a saving event. It signifies that martyrdom is itself conceived as included in the divine grace: its importance flows from the fact that it offers us a possibility, by assimilation to Christ dead and risen again, of attaining and, in a certain sense, of anticipating the eschatological event. But there is nothing here that goes beyond the content of the idea of martyrdom as already very clearly laid out in St John's Apocalypse. Concrete experience simply causes the teaching—which itself had no other purpose than to enlighten this experience—to be fully lived and "realized".

In fact, it is only in this sense that it can be said that martyrdom, according to Ignatius, individualizes and anticipates the Parousia of Christ and the resurrection of Christians. And we must still add that, in his thought, this last point is in strict continuity with the Johannine view according to which, as we have said, not only does the Cross produce the Glory that follows it, but the Glory is already in some way given in the Cross.

Our interpretation is verified in the connection, very frequently made by Ignatius, between this expression *epituchein theou* and the other expression, almost equally typical of this writer, *en Iesou Christo eurethenai*. We might say that this expression is doubly Paulinian: by the use (of biblical origin) of the verb in the sense of "to be known" (that is, "judged") by God, and by the phrase which is perhaps the most characteristic of Pauline mysticism. It follows obviously that "to attain God" is, for Ignatius, only the counterpart of the justification that God himself freely bestows upon us in Christ.

And so, a few lines before saying to the Ephesians that he hopes to "attain God" in the footsteps of St Paul, Ignatius tells us that the essential thing in his eyes is to "be found in Christ Jesus for eternal life".[22] And at the same time he recommends himself to their

[21] Cf. Rom. 11. 7 and Heb. 6. 15 or 11. 35.
[22] Ignatius, *To the Ephesians*, XI, 1.

prayers so as "to be found in the inheritance of the Christians of Ephesus".[23] For, he says to them again, "You are the road of those who are carried towards God by martyrdom."[24]

In the Epistle to the Romans we find an analogous combination. Ignatius has emphasized that he will never find another such opportunity to "attain God".[25] He therefore suggests to them a little further on:

> Be content to pray for strength for me, without and within, not only to speak but to will, so that I may not only be called a Christian but may be found such. For if I am found such, I may also be called such, and it is then that I shall be faithful, when I appear no more to the world.[26]

Further on, the same connection:

> Let me become the fodder of the beasts, by which I can attain God. I am the wheat of God and I am ground by the teeth of the beasts, so that I may be found the pure bread of Christ.[27]

And again, a few lines later:

> Pray to Christ for me, so that, by means [of the beasts] I may be found a sacrifice to God. . . .
>
> Let nothing visible or invisible prevent me from attaining Christ. Let the torments of the devil fall on me if only I attain Christ.[28]

The Desire for Martyrdom

All these clarifications are needed to avoid the danger of misunderstanding the desire for martyrdom expressed even more powerfully than elsewhere in the Epistle of St Ignatius to the Romans and running through the whole ancient literature of martyrdom.

> I am writing to all the Churches and am letting them know that I die for God willingly, at least if you do not prevent me. I adjure you: do not have any untempered good will towards me. Let me become the fodder of the beasts, by means of which I can attain to God. I am the wheat of God and I am ground by the teeth of the beasts to be found the pure bread of Christ. Rather, urge the beasts on so that they may be my tomb and that they may leave nothing of my body, so that in going to sleep I shall not be a care to anyone. Thus I shall be truly a disciple of Jesus Christ: when the world no longer sees my body. Beg Christ for me: so that, by their means, I shall be found a sacrifice to God. I do not

[23] *Ibid.*, 2.
[24] *Ibid.*, XII, 1.
[25] Ignatius, *To the Romans*, II,
[26] *Ibid.*, III, 2.
[27] *Ibid.*, IV, 1.
[28] *Ibid.*, IV, 2 and V, 3.

give you commands like Peter and Paul: they were Apostles, and I am only a man condemned to death; they were free; and I, up to the present moment, am a slave; but death will make me a freeman of Jesus Christ in whom I shall rise again free.

For the present, I am learning in my chains to desire nothing. From Syria to Rome, on land and on sea, by night and by day, already am I fighting against beasts, chained as I am to ten leopards—I mean the soldiers who are guarding me and who seem to be the more evil the more good is done them. Their harsh treatment serves me for a school in which I am formed every day.

But I am not justified for all that. Let me but be enjoyed by the beasts that have been prepared for me. I hope that they will be eager for me, and I will urge them on so that they will devour me promptly, not as they have done with certain persons that they were afraid of and did not touch. If indeed, by chance, they do not wish to devour me, I will even force them. Forgive me: I know what is best for me. Now it is that I begin to be a disciple. Let nothing, whether visible or invisible, by envy prevent me from attaining Jesus Christ. Fire and cross, the assaults of beasts, wounding, being torn to pieces, dislocation of bones, mutilations of my members, the breaking of all my body under the millstone—let the worst torments of the devil fall upon me, if only I attain Jesus Christ.

Nothing of the pleasures of the world or the kingdoms of this age will serve me. It is good for me to die for (*eis*) Christ Jesus rather than to reign over the ends of the earth. It is he whom I seek: he who died for us—he whom I desire: he who rose again for us. It is my birth that is approaching. Forgive me, brothers, do not keep me from living; do not wish me to die. He who desires to belong to God—do not deliver him to the world, do not seduce him by material things. Let me receive the pure light. When I shall be there, then shall I be a man. If anyone has God in him, let him understand what I desire and let him have pity on me, knowing what constrains me.

The prince of this world wishes to snatch me away and to corrupt the desires that I have for God. Let none of you who may be present as spectators come to help him. Rather help me, that is, help God. Do not speak of Jesus Christ while at the same time desiring the world. Let there be no room in you for envy. And even if I beg you when I am there, do not listen to me; listen rather to what I am writing you. For it is as alive that I am writing, and desiring to die. My desire (*eros*) has been crucified; in me there is no longer any ardour for what is material, but a living water that murmurs within me and says within me: "Come to the Father!" I no longer take any pleasure in a food of corruption and in the pleasures of this life: it is the bread of God that I desire which is the flesh of Jesus Christ of the race

> of David, and for drink, it is His blood that I desire, that is, incorruptible love (*agape*).[29]

It is easy to see how a reading of this text—one of the most beautiful and perhaps the richest in theology of all the texts available on martyrdom in the ancient Church—can raise the question we have already mentioned. Do these expressions of hostility to the world and, more precisely, to "matter" mean that we should see here some influence of Platonic spirituality, opposing matter to spirit, life in the body to the better life of a discarnate soul?

Placed in the proper context, these words certainly have no such meaning. We have already indicated and proved by decisive texts the extent to which such "spiritualism" not only would have been foreign to Ignatius' thought, but is formally condemned by his own clear statements. It must rather be said that he uses these terms here as St. Paul speaks of the "flesh" and St John of "the world". What compels him towards death is actually no condemnation, partial or complete, of creation. In the Epistle to the *Smyrniotes,* in the full current of the vigorous statements we have already quoted against the Docetism that refused any real incarnation, we find this positive statement which might be considered the key to our text:

> If it was in appearance only that our Lord carried out His various acts, it is also in appearance only that I am laden with chains. Then why am I vowed to death by fire, the sword, the beasts? But to be near the sword, is to be near to God, to be with the beasts is to be with God, provided that one suffers all this for the name of Jesus Christ. It is to associate myself with His passion that I endure everything, and it is He who gives me the strength for it, He who made himself perfectly man.[30]

Nothing could be more precise: it is not death itself that the martyr seeks in death, it is Jesus Christ. For it is when one dies for him that one becomes his true disciple, as Ignatius repeats.[31] Then one suffers *with him* in conformity with the exhortation of St Paul.

Martyrdom and the Imitation of Christ.

Moreover, martyrdom can be considered the supreme example of the imitation of Christ. This theme is expressly sounded by Ignatius in the letter to the *Magnesians*:

> It might be said that there are two kinds of coins, that of God and that of the world, and that each bears the image which

[29] *Ibid.*, IV–VII. [30] Ignatius, *To the Smyrniotes*, IV.
[31] *To the Ephesians*, III, 1 and *To the Magnesians*, IX, 2.

is proper to it; those who do not believe, that of the world, and those who believe in love (*en agape*), the image of God the Father by Jesus Christ. If we are not completely ready, through Him, to die in order to suffer like Him (literally: with His suffering), His life is not in us.[32]

As the *Epistle to the Ephesians* says more briefly:

> Let us rival one another in being imitators (*mimetai*) of the Lord, as to who will suffer more injustice, deprivation, contempt.[33]

After this, it is not at all surprising that St Polycarp, from the first words of his letter to the Philippians sent together with the collection of the letters of Ignatius, says that martyrs are "the imitations of the true *agape*,"[34] that is doubtless of *agape* as it was manifested in Jesus. This line of thought is carried on when, some years later, the *Martyrdom of Polycarp* himself was written, which contains these words:

> We adore (Christ) as the Son of God; we honour *the martyrs as Christ's disciples and imitators*. We love them because they deserve it, by reason of their incomparable love for their King and their Master.[35]

The same thing is found in the *Letters of the Churches of Vienne and Lyons,* which calls the martyrs "the emulators and imitators of Christ."[36]

Origen simply summarizes a whole tradition in saying that the martyrs are the "imitators of God and of Christ."

But the idea of imitating Christ does not exhaust what so vehemently impels Ignatius' Epistle to the Romans. The theme of imitation finds its meaning only in its fusion with the hope of "attaining Christ", of "being found in Christ".

It is now time to clarify the content of these expressions. The question is obviously that of a presence of Christ, still better of a presence of Christ in us (and of us in him) to be brought about by martyrdom.

We might say that this is the purpose of martyrdom. But, with Ignatius and the whole of the literature devoted to martyrdom, the same transfer is effected as when St John speaks of the death of Jesus. Not only is his glorification in the latter case—or, in the texts we are now analysing, the martyr's attaining the glorified

[32] Ignatius, *To the Magnesians*, v, 2.
[33] Ignatius, *To the Ephesians*, x, 3.
[34] *Letter of Polycarp*, I, 1.
[35] *Martyrdom of Polycarp*, XVII, 30 cf. I, 2.
[36] Eusebius, *Eccles. Hist.*, V, II, § 2.

Christ—to follow death, to be its consequence; it is already effected *in this death itself*.

Martyrdom and the Eucharist

In order to understand this, we need to consider a very remarkable fact already noted: the relationship and the kind of intentional confusion which Ignatius seems to bring about between what he says about martyrdom and what he says about the Eucharist.

The latter, according to him, is "a remedy of immortality, an antidote so that we may not die but live for ever in Christ Jesus".[37] In other words, it is a participation in the risen Christ, which assures us of ourselves rising again. But the Risen One whom we receive is he who suffered in his flesh, and whose suffering saved us through the *agape* that it manifested. And so Ignatius says to the Smyrniotes, who appear, as we have already said, to have been threatened with Docetism:

> [The heretics] abstain from the Eucharist and from prayer because they do not confess that the Eucharist is the flesh of our Saviour Jesus Christ, which endured the Passion for our sins and was raised up by the Father in His goodness. Those, therefore, who oppose themselves to the gift of God will die of their own disputes. They would do better to love (*agapan*) in order to rise again.[38]

It is indeed remarkable that Ignatius always goes on from the presence of the *Christus passus* in the Eucharist to charity:

> Take care to participate in one Eucharist only: there is only one flesh of Our Lord, only one cup to unite us in his blood, only one altar, as there is only one bishop, surrounded by the presbyterium and the deacons, the associates of his ministry; in this way, in all things you do the will of God.[39]

It is when we have just re-read these texts that the phrases already quoted from the Epistle to the Romans take on their full meaning:

> I am the wheat of God and I am ground by the teeth of the beasts, so as to be found the pure bread of Christ . . . I no longer take pleasure in a corruptible food or in the pleasures of this life: it is the bread of God that I desire, which is the flesh of Jesus Christ of the race of David, and, for drink, I desire His blood, that is, incorruptible love.[40]

[37] Ignatius, *To the Ephesians*.
[38] Ignatius, *To the Smyrniotes*, VII, 1.
[39] Ignatius, *To the Philadelphians*, IV.
[40] Cf. the whole text quoted above.

These last words, in the context in which they appear, mean that the Eucharist is as it were the proper nourishment of the martyr. It appears that we should go even further: it seems to Ignatius that the Eucharist gives his martyrdom its substance. Only thus can the first words be explained, in which it is the martyr himself who is to become the Eucharist.

Without in any way forcing the thought of Ignatius, we can explain it by saying that the Eucharist, in nourishing us with the risen Christ, associates us with his Passion and, very particularly, with the *agape* which is its soul; and reciprocally, martyrdom, as realizing in our lives the perfection of *agape*, gives its whole realism to the union with the *Christus passus* brought about by the Eucharist and finally reveals in us the presence of the risen Christ. In the Eucharist, he has given us the seed of what he is, he has set in motion in us the process that brought him to his risen life. In martyrdom, this process unfolds and this seed bears its fruit: in suffering with Christ, not only do we rise with Him, but we become in some way the Risen One.

In the Martyrdom of Polycarp, all these implications seem to become explicit. It is particularly illuminating to find those who are recounting the death of Ignatius' friend, the man who had devotedly gathered together Ignatius' letters, now reporting Polycarp's own death in these terms:

> Having raised his eyes to heaven, he said: "Lord God almighty, Father of Your well-beloved child (*paidos*), Jesus Christ, by whom we have received knowledge of You (*ten peri sou epignosin*), God of the Angels and of the powers and of all creation, and also of the race of the just who live in Your presence; I bless You because You have judged me worthy of this day and of this hour, so that I may be counted among the witness (*en arithmo ton marturon*) and may take part in the chalice of Your Christ for the resurrection of eternal life, of the soul and of the body, in the incorruptibility of the Holy Spirit. May I, among them, be received in Your presence today in a sacrifice rich and acceptable, O God without deceit and true. For this and for all things, I praise You, I bless You, I glorify You, through the eternal and heavenly high priest, Jesus Christ, through whom is to You, with Him, and the Holy Spirit, glory now and in the ages to come. Amen.
>
> When he had pronounced the *Amen* and finished his prayer, the executioners lit the fire. A great flame sprung up, and we saw a wonder—we to whom it was given to be witnesses of it—which we have retained so as to proclaim it to others. The fire formed as it were an arch and, like the sail of a ship filled with the wind, it surrounded the body of the martyr. And he himself in the midst appeared not like flesh being burned, but like bread in the oven,

like gold and silver tried in the furnace, and we breathed the perfume of it like the smoke of incense or some other precious aromatic perfume.[41]

It is obvious that the liturgical character of this death has been intentionally emphasized. The Bishop of Smyrna, in the prayer that he pronounced, in the whole atmosphere of his death, consecrated it as a final Eucharist. He himself here appears as the altar-bread.

We should compare with this account the many expressions in which Ignatius did not hesitate to speak of his death as a sacrifice offered for the Church. Does he not say to the *Romans*:

> I ask only one thing of you: to let me offer myself in libation to God while the Altar is all prepared.[42]

Still more formal are his statements to the *Ephesians*:

> I sacrifice myself (*agnizomai*) for you, Ephesians, the ever famous Church.[43]

And above all to the *Trallians*:

> My spirit (*pneuma*) sacrifices itself (*agnizetai*) for you, not only now, but when I shall attain God.[44]

But it is important to emphasize the fact that all these texts are to be interpreted not only in the sense that the martyr, in imitating Christ, in following after him by his power, offers himself also in sacrifice. They signify much more precisely that, in his death, the martyr reveals himself as forming but one being with Christ, dead and risen again. The central words of the great text to the *Romans* which we have quoted leave no doubt that here indeed is its most profound thought.

> It is good for me to die for Christ Jesus (this might be translated more exactly: *to die in such a way as to be in Christ Jesus*) rather than to reign over the ends of the earth. It is He whom I seek: He who died for us—He whom I desire: He who rose for us. It is my birth that is approaching. . . .[45]

The last words sketch out a theme which will be taken up in the liturgy of martyrs: their death is a birth and, for this reason, its anniversary is celebrated as their true *dies natalis*.

[41] *Martyrdom of Polycarp*, XIV and XV.
[42] Ignatius, *To the Romans*, II, 2.
[43] Ignatius, *To the Ephesians*, VII, 1.
[44] Ignatius, *To the Trallians*, XIII, 3; cf. *To the Romans*, IV, 2, quoted above. We should compare with these texts those in which Ignatius defines himself as *antipsuchon* to his correspondents (*To the Ephesians*, XXI, 1 and *To Polycarp*, II, 3; V, 6).
[45] Ignatius, *To the Romans*, VI, 1.

But what interests us more particularly here is the idea that in dying they are born to a life which is the very life of him who died and rose again: let us go further: when they die, it is henceforth he who lives in them.

The assimilation between the Eucharist and martyrdom must, therefore, be understood exactly. It does not mean that martyrdom would be an equivalent of the Eucharist. It means that what is given obscurely in the Eucharist reveals its reality in martyrdom: the presence in us of Christ dead and risen again.

The Presence of Christ in the Martyrs

There is no doubt, and the texts already quoted indicate this sufficiently clearly, that this presence of Christ in the martyr appears as an object of experience. The Christian writers were quite convinced that Christ revealed himself, conqueror of death in them as in himself, at the moment when they consummated their martyrdom. The martyr himself, naturally, was the immediate beneficiary of this revelation, but something of it might be communicated to those present. For this reason, martyrdom appeared as the greatest charismatic experience in the ancient Church.

There is first the certainty, so strongly expressed by the *Letter of Lyons* in connection with Blandina, that Christ gives to the weakest of martyrs a strength that is obviously supernatural:

> We had all been afraid for Blandina. Her mistress according to the flesh, who was part of the group of martyrs, an athlete of the faith, feared that the young girl would not be able frankly to affirm her profession as a Christian, so frail she was. But Blandina found herself filled with such strength that she ended by exhausting and wearying the executioners. These worked in relays from morning to evening, to torture her by every means: they had to avow themselves at the end of their resources. They were astonished that she still breathed, her body torn and wounded. They admitted that a single one of their tortures was enough to take away life; how much more such great tortures and so many of them. On the contrary, the Blessed, like a generous athlete, was renewed in her confession. For her, it was a comfort, a rest, a pause in suffering to say only: "I am a Christian: with us, nothing evil happens."[46]

The martyrdom of Carpus (probably condemned under Marcus Aurelius, at Pergama) does not speak only of a strength from on high: the martyr has a vision of the glory of Christ which sustains him at the supreme moment.

[46] Eusebius, *Eccles. Hist.*, V, I, §§ 181–9.

The nearest spectators saw that he smiled. Surprised, they asked him:

— Why are you smiling?

The Blessed answered:

—I have seen the glory of the Lord and I am in joy. You see me now set free, I no longer know your miseries.

A soldier piled the faggots. When he had kindled the fire, Carpus, the Saint, said:

—We are born of Eve as you are, she is our common mother: we have flesh like yours. But when we fix our eyes on the tribunal of truth, we are capable of suffering everything.[47]

But the text which is the most expressive, in its extreme simplicity, is certainly a celebrated passage from the *Passio Felicitatis et Perpetuae*. Felicitas in her prison gives birth to a child and cries out with pain:

> If you wail like that, one of the jailers said to her, what will you do when you are exposed to the beasts?
>
> — Now, she answered, it is I who suffer; *then, there will be Another in me who will suffer for me*, because it is for Him that I will be suffering then.[48]

In a more general way, this document is particularly rich in statements about the charisms with which the confessors of the faith were graced, not only at the final moment, but as soon as they began to suffer for Christ. To them, visions, prophecies, seem to be experiences to be taken for granted in their situation. *The Letter from Lyons* gives something of the same impression. Ignatius himself had already said to the Philadelphians:

> There are those who wished to deceive the man of flesh that I am, but the Spirit is not deceived, for He is of God. He knows, indeed, whence He comes and whither He goes, and He denounces what is hidden. When I was among you, I cried out, with a loud voice, the voice of God: "Adhere to the bishop, to the presbyterium, and to the deacons." Some among you supposed that I said this because I knew of the schism of certain persons. But He for whom (*en o*) I am bound is my witness: I knew nothing with a human and carnal knowledge. It was the Spirit who proclaimed it, in saying: "Do nothing without the bishop, guard your flesh as the temple of God; love unity, fly schisms: become imitators of Jesus Christ as He is the imitator of His Father."[49]

In Africa, such importance was given to the charisms of confessors (that is, those who were under arrest, waiting for martyrdom)

[47] *Acts of Carpus, Papylus and Agathonice.*

[48] Ed. R. Knopf, *Ausgewählte Martyrakten*, Tübingen, 1901, p. 53–5.

[49] Ignatius, *To the Philadelphians*, VII.

that a great part of the correspondence of St Cyprian with regard to them was to delimit the bounds of what they could do and to prevent them from encouraging, more or less consciously, a relaxation of ecclesiastical discipline.

These difficulties, and even the troubles caused by Montanus, did not prevent Andrew of Caesarea from stating again:

> It is the confession of the faith, otherwise called martyrdom, that gives the Spirit of prophecy.[50]

This constellation of the various charisms around martyrdom should not, however, cause us to forget that it is martyrdom itself which, in the texts we have just studied, appears as the supreme charism. It is such because, first of all, by it we "attain" Christ, we "attain" God, with all the mystical realism that these expressions have with Ignatius. It is the supreme charism also (and this is equally in conformity with the clearest tendencies of Ignatius' thought even though he does not say it as expressly) because it represents the perfection of charity.

Let us recall the phrase of Polycarp calling the martyrs the "imitators of the true *agape*". Clement of Alexandria is to say:

> We call martyrdom *teleiosis* [that is, at once "achievement" and "perfection"] not because man reaches the end (*telos*) of his life, here as elsewhere, but because here he produces a work of perfect love (*teleion*).[51]

Martyrdom and Baptism

With this twofold certainty (that martyrdom consummates union with Christ, that it is the supreme development of *agape*) is connected the idea of martyrdom as a baptism of blood. It takes two forms. The first concerns catechumens, that is, believers put to death for their faith before having received baptism. The Church did not hesitate to consider that their martyrdom was for them the equivalent of a baptism. The second concerns the baptized. For them, martyrdom was as it were a second baptism, renewing and definitively consummating the effects of the first.

Tertullian, in his *De Baptismo*, unites the two ideas in a formula very much in his own style: *Hic est baptismus qui lavacrum et non acceptum repraesentat, et perditum reddit*, which might be translated: "This is a baptism which takes the place of the baptism of water when it has not been received, and which restores it when it has been lost."[52]

[50] *Com. in Apoc.*, 57; P.G., CVI, 400 B.
[51] Clement of Alexandria, *Stromata*, IV, iv; Staehlin, II, p. 255.
[52] Tertullian, *De Baptismo*, XVI, 2.

He gives the reason for this in saying elsewhere:

> We can no longer rightly reproach the martyrs with anything since in their baptism (*lavacro*) they laid down life itself. Thus it is that love covers a multitude of sins, that love by which in loving God with all one's strength, that strength by which one struggles in martyrdom, and with all one's soul, that soul which one lays down for God, one becomes a martyr.[53]

After him, St Augustine makes a formal application of this reasoning even to those who have not received sacramental baptism.

> For all those, even if they have not received the bath of regeneration, who die to confess Christ, this confession merits the remission of sins, as would their ablution in the holy baptismal fountain. For He who said: If a man is not born of water and the Holy Spirit, he will not enter into the Kingdom of God, has exempted these persons in saying, no less absolutely: He who confesses me before men, I will confess him before My Father who is in heaven; and elsewhere: He who loses his life for my sake will find it.[54]

But it is Origen who has most boldly developed the theme of martyrdom, not only as a substitute for baptism for those who had not received the latter, but as a second baptism, more perfect than the first, for the baptized themselves.

> Only the baptism of blood makes us more pure than the baptism of water. It is not I who have the presumption to say this, but it is Scripture that affirms it, when the Lord says to His disciples: "I am to be baptized with a baptism that you know not of, and how am I pressed that it be carried out."[55] You see that He calls the outpouring of His blood a baptism. And if I do not deceive myself, this baptism is more powerful than the baptism of water. For there are very few indeed who, having received the latter, can keep it immaculate even to the end of their life. But he who has been baptized with the baptism of blood cannot sin henceforth. And if it were not temerarious to make such a statement, we might say that by the baptism of water past sins are purified but that, by the baptism of blood, future sins are themselves taken away. There sins are removed; here they are destroyed.[56]

This teaching, resumed in his *Exhortation to Martyrdom*,[57] is

[53] *Scorpiace*, VI; P.L., I, 158 A.
[54] St Augustine, *De Civitate Dei*, XIII, vii.
[55] Luke 12. 50.
[56] Origen, *In Judic. hom.*, VII, 2; ed. Baehrens, II, p. 57.
[57] Ch. xxx; ed. Koetschau, I, p. 26.

found expressed in almost the same terms by St Cyprian in his own *Exhortation*:

> As by divine permission, we have given a first baptism to believers, let us prepare them all for another, in explaining to them and teaching that here is a baptism which is greater as to grace, more sublime as to power, more valuable as to honour: a baptism in which it is the angels who baptize, a baptism in which God and His Christ exult, a baptism after which no one sins, a baptism which consummates the progress of our faith, a baptism which unites us with God as soon as we have left the world.[58] In the baptism of water, we receive the remission of sins; in the baptism of blood, the crown of virtues.[59]

Preparation for Martyrdom and Substitutes for it.

Origen and Cyprian have given us the purest examples of these *Exhortations to Martyrdom*—examples which, once again, they were to seal a little later, both dying for Christ. The highest theme of encouragement was to be defined by Origen in explaining that martyrdom is thanksgiving, the supreme Eucharist of the Christian, as in the martyrdom of Polycarp:

> The holy man, whose nobility desires to respond to the blessings that God has given him, seeks what he can do for the Lord in response to all that he has received. He finds nothing that can correspond to these blessings and be given to God by grateful man, other than the death of martyrdom. For there is written in Psalm 115 first an embarrassing question: "What shall I render to the Lord for all that He has given to me?" Then comes the response of the man who asks himself how to make return to the Lord for all that he has received: "I will take the chalice of salvation and call upon the name of the Lord." The chalice of salvation is a common name for martyrdom, as we find in the Gospel: when to those who wished to sit at the right and left hand of Jesus in His Kingdom desiring greater honour, the Lord said: "Can you drink the chalice that I am to drink?"[60] This chalice is martyrdom: this is evident from the words: "Father, if it be possible, may this chalice pass from me. None the less, not what I will, but what Thou wilt."[61] Thus we learn that he who has drunk this chalice that Jesus drank will sit, will reign, will judge, with the King of kings. Such is the chalice of

[58] There is perhaps an echo here of Tertullian's opinion that only martyrs would be admitted to eternal life immediately after death.

[59] Cyprian, *Ad Fortunatum, de exhortatione martyrii*, praef. IV; P.L., IV, 680 A.

[60] Matt. 20. 22.

[61] Matt. 26. 39.

> salvation; he who takes it calls upon the name of the Lord, and whoever calls upon the name of the Lord will be saved.[62]

This beautiful text gives us a final opportunity to observe the wholly positive character of the desire for martyrdom in the ancient Church. We see more clearly than ever that authentically Christian asceticism, as Lebreton has well said, is never a condemnation but a preference. It is not in the school of the orthodox martyrs, but by burying himself in a sectarian pessimism, that Tertullian could encourage the faithful to martyrdom by considerations as ambiguous as the following:

> When we recall the fact that the world is rather a prison, we realize that you yourselves (he says to the confessors) have rather escaped from prison than entered into it. The world is covered with much thicker darkness, blinding the spirit of men. The world carries much heavier chains, weighing down the spirits of men. The world breathes far more unbearable odours: the debauchery of men. Finally, the world includes a far greater number of criminals, I mean the whole human race. . . .[63]

This rhetoric springing from a wholly negative pessimism has a tone which is in complete contrast with all the orthodox literature of martyrdom. Yet this tone must be noted. For just as the charism of martyrdom presents many characteristics making it, as it were, the first, and perhaps the richest of the experiences from which the idea of the mystical experience was to be drawn, just as the idea of martyrdom as a second baptism prepared the way for that of monasticism as a second baptism, so the deviation that we see arising with Tertullian in connection with the interpretation of martyrdom will be found again in connection with the interpretation of monastic asceticism.

In fact, the continuity from martyrdom to monasticism, in Christian spirituality, is clear on all these points. And it is particularly evident in the *Exhortations to Martyrdom*.

In the same way as we have seen asceticism appearing in the New Testament as a preparation for the Parousia, for the "passage" of this world and for the "coming" of the other in Christ, so it can be said to have developed in the early Church particularly as a preparation for martyrdom. But, let us repeat, here we have not so much a displacement of perspectives as their maintenance throughout changing circumstances. Origen emphasized the fact that persecutions bring Christians to see the permanent necessity

[62] *Exhort. ad Mart.*, XXVIII, ed. Koetschau, I, p. 24. The last words are an allusion to Joel 2. 32.

[63] Tertullian, *Ad Martyres*, II; P.L., I, 695 B.

of living in the world as if not living in it.[64] Conversely, the more or less voluntary trials that precede martyrdom prepare us to leave this world by detaching us from it.[65] Tertullian's teaching on this point is along the same lines, and here beyond reproach.[66] Both the one writer and the other are led to make a comparison between martyrdom and athletic effort (*agon*), obviously derived from St Paul, the developments of which seem quite ready to be transferred from martyrdom to asceticism in general.[67]

From the times of the persecutions, indeed, the question arose whether there was not some possible substitute for martyrdom itself: whether there might not be some equivalents of martyrdom which would have the same value in the eyes of God. At the end of his *Exhortation*, Origen raises the question: what good is it for us to be prepared for martyrdom, if, in the end, martyrdom is not imposed on us? He does not hesitate to say that, if the preparation has been fervent enough, it could be a true unbloody martyrdom. The same teaching is often formulated by St Cyprian. But already Clement of Alexandria had not hesitated to say that everyone could make his death a martyrdom provided that he prepared for it with the fitting dispositions:

> If martyrdom consists in confessing God, every person who conducts himself with purity in the knowledge of God, who obeys the commandments, is a martyr in his life and in his words: in whatever way his soul is separated from the body, he will pour out his faith, in the manner of blood, all during his life and at the moment of his exodus. This is what the Lord says in the Gospel: "Whoever leaves his father, his mother, his brothers, etc. because of the Gospel and my name",[68] such a man is blessed because he realizes not only ordinary martyrdom but the gnostic martyrdom, in living and acting according to the rule of the Gospel, by love for the Lord. For gnosis is the knowledge of the Name and the understanding of the Gospel.[69]

64 Origen, *In Jerem. hom.*, IV, ed. Klostermann, p. 25.
65 Origen, *Exhort. ad Mart.*, XXXVII–XXXIX and XLI–XLIV; Koetschau, I, pp. 34ff. and 38ff.
66 Tertullian, *Ad Martyres*, III; P.L., 1; 697–8.
67 With the preceding text, compare Origen, *Exhort. ad Mart.*, XVIII, ed. Koetschau, I, p. 16.
68 Cf. Mark 10. 29.
69 Clement of Alexandria, *Stromata*, IV, iv, 15; ed. Staehlin, II, p. 255.

IX

THE PROBLEM OF GNOSIS: CHRISTIAN GNOSIS AND HELLENISM

THE text of Clement quoted at the conclusion of the previous chapter forms a transition from our study of martyrdom to that of gnosis. How the nineteenth century interpreted the presence of the theme of gnosis in orthodox Christian spirituality is well known. This theme would be foreign to Christianity as to authentic Judaism. The Alexandrians, and Clement in particular, must have taken it up from the syncretist "gnosticism" and dubiously acclimated in the Catholic Church. In itself, furthermore, the theme of gnosis arose from a first effort to conciliate Christianity, and more generally, the truths of the Bible, with Greek religious philosophy. This series of statements, repeated to satiety in all the manuals for the last hundred years, has met with protests left unanswered. But nobody has as yet dared seriously to question it. None the less, it needs to be analysed, for, in the light of the texts and of the most certain facts, it is nothing but a collection of errors and confusions.

Gnosis, as we have already said, was not originally a heterodox idea, either in Christianity or in Judaism. The Alexandrian Christians did not need to introduce it into orthodox Christianity, for the simple reason that it had always had an important place in it. Even with these Christians, even with Clement—the Christian theologian doubtless most infatuated with Greek philosophy—gnosis was never defined by the combination of Christianity and philosophy. As Clement says in the text we have just quoted: "Gnosis is the knowledge of the Name and the understanding of the Gospel", a definition which might have come from all the first generations of Christians and from the Christian groups that were most purely biblical and Jewish in their formation.

Christian Gnosis and Hellenism

The truth—and it is quite different—is that gnosis became a problem in the context of the meeting of Christianity with Hellenism, this last word being taken, furthermore, in the widest sense as meaning the syncretist culture of the regions around the Mediterranean where Greek was spoken, in the first centuries of our era. For it was under these conditions that those heresies made their appearance to which the nineteenth century applied the name "gnostic" to the point of making this name almost their exclusive prerogative. But this is a use contrary to the whole of Christian antiquity which, beginning with St Irenaeus, never saw in these speculations anything more than a "pseudo-gnosis", reserving true gnosis to the Catholic Church alone.

The development of gnosis in the Church of the first centuries leads us, then, to study the problem of the encounter between Christianity and Hellenism. But it is important first to dissipate the illusion that this problem is bound up with that of the origins of gnosis. It is only one element in the development of gnosis—an element at once troublesome and stimulating.

We have no intention of embracing here either the entire problem of the heresies called gnostic, still less the entire problem of the hellenization of Christianity. We shall study this last only in so far as it has a directly spiritual bearing. As for the former, we shall concern ourselves with it only to the extent to which orthodox gnosis was constrained to define itself in reference to the gnoses, or "pseudo-gnoses", that were in one way or another heretical.

Nevertheless, the first point to be emphasized is that the Hellenism contemporary with the beginnings of Christianity must be of immediate concern to us. For nothing is more remarkable than its increasingly spiritual orientation as it developed along its own lines.

Philosophy and Spirituality

When Christianity was born, the Greek philosophies were turning into religious philosophies. They tended to go on, as by an irresistible transition, from the search for truth to the search for salvation. Or, to put it another way, the "truth" that they were seeking at this period was precisely "salvation".

However surprising it may seem at first sight, this development is already notable in Epicureanism. But was this not a kind of atheism, at least in practice? This is true, but its search for *ataraxia*, "the absence of perturbation", as the ideal of the sage, betrays the deception hidden under this apparently irreligious attitude. Had not Epicurus already done away with the gods because he expected from them something other than the old Greek gods could give? His desire for a harmonious life, which he thought could be satisfied only by resignation, is indeed desire for a "salvation", a desire that simply measures the derision of powers that set themselves up as divine and urges that a "nature" which transcends them is more divine.[1] In any case, with his disciple Lucretius, these implications become explicit, if not as yet fully conscious. Concerning the deliverance that Democritean "science" means to him, the enthusiasm, paradoxical only in appearance, which the power of cosmic life aroused in this strange atheist betrays what a drama of redemption had in fact been undercut by enfranchisement from the gods:

Aeneadum genetrix, hominum divumque voluptas,
alma Venus! . . .

Later Stoicism was to cause the same spiritual aspiration to flow in an intellectual mould not so much opposed to the preceding as balancing it. This Stoicism was frankly to avow the religiousness sought equally in the negations of Epicureanism. The Stoics' "spirit", their *pneuma* of subtle fire animating the world which they proclaimed divine, is in reality no more "spiritual", in the sense in which we understand the word, than is the "nature" of Democritus.[2]

The willed tension of Stoic morality, on the other hand, does not suppose a more ascetic acquiescence in the real, the ordering of which escapes us, than does the *ataraxia* of Epicurus. Conversely, the smilingly heroic acceptance of inevitable suffering, on the part of the old man led into his falsely Sybaritic garden, is already, perhaps, no less religious than the *amor fati* which solved the problem of freedom for Epictetus, the slave, as that of the domination of self for Marcus Aurelius, the Emperor-philosopher.

But this torsion in a religious sense of all the philosophies of expiring Greek thought prepared this thought, at the moment when Christianity was born, for a final metamorphosis. It could seem so mystical, in the sense which the word was to take on in later Christian experience, that we have come, by an unconscious reversal of viewpoint, to see mysticism as already fully constituted outside this experience by what should appear to us rather as the last void that might be said to have been opened out in the human soul at the approach of what was to transcend it. We mean, obviously, Neo-Platonism.

1 Festugière has brought out the error of seeing Epicurus as an atheist (*Épicure et ses dieux*, Paris, 1946; especially pp. 71ff.). He had already observed the extent to which the authentic Epicurean ideal is close to the Buddhist nirvana (see *L'idéal religieux des Grecs et l'Évangile*, Paris, 1932, p. 65, n. 4). On the actual transformation of the Epicurean school into a Church, see F. Picavet, "Epicure fondateur d'une religion nouvelle", in *Revue d'Histoire des religions*, XLVIII (1893), pp. 315–44.

2 See G. Verbeke, *L'évolution de la doctrine du Pneuma du stoïcisme à saint Augustin*, Paris-Louvain, 1945.

The Origins of Neo-Platonism

The most recent studies lead us to ask ourselves whether Neo-Platonism does not rather deserve the name of Neo-Stoicism.[3] Panaetius of Rhodes developed a Platonizing line of thought in the framework of a Stoic cosmology. The humanity here defined as its own proper ideal is a victory of reason over animality and this reason itself relates us to the celestial world. However, the friend and counsellor of Scipio, the inspirer of the first books of Cicero's *De Officiis*, does not seem to have admitted a personal survival. The hopes of the *Dream of Scipio* do not seem to have been those of this merciless critic of the *Phaedo*.[4]

With his disciple, the Syrian Posidonius of Apamea, who came to live in Rhodes and was Cicero's master, the Stoic unity of the cosmos is maintained. There is no intellectual world opposed to the material world: the spirit itself is included in it. The whole universe, however, is unified in a vision having a religious vitalism: here Zeus is cosmic life in its transcendent unity—nature, power emanate from him and become diversified in all things without being broken up—the destiny, the whole of the energies individualized within nature.

But had he not already gone further? Certain scholars, following Norden in particular and his commentary on the sixth book of the *Aeneid*, believe that they can find in the eschatology of Virgil, as in the *Dream of Scipio* and even in Plutarch, common views all originating with Posidonius. They would make him the true founder of Neo-Platonism, even in its being a spirituality still more than a metaphysics. For he distinguished two regions in the soul and in the world: that of pure light, of heaven, to which the soul belonged by its origin and most intimate nature; and that of confusion and corruption, this sublunary world in which we are plunged by the passions of the body. Hence the ideal of reintegration, ascetical purification, according to which the soul would return to itself in disengaging itself from the world and reuniting itself to God.

Even if Posidonius did not actually formulate this conception so clearly, it is undeniable that it crystallized at his period from various elements which he had certainly blended: taken from ancient Stoicism, from a Platonism in which the most religious elements had been rediscovered and reassembled, without forgetting the Neo-Pythagorean currents then resurging, in an Eastern atmosphere not easy to reconstruct. For we not only find this same *Weltanschauung*

[3] See M. Spanneut, *Le stoïcisme des Pères*, Paris, 1957. Along these lines, very interesting observations are to be found in Edwyn Bevan, *Stoics and Sceptics*.

[4] See E. Bréhier, *Histoire de la Philosophie*, vol. I, pt. II, Paris, 1942 (4th ed.), pp. 394ff.

in the great texts just mentioned, but also in a Seneca, as well as in the pseudo-Aristotelian *De Mundo*. And it might well be that Philo, who expounds this world view in his *De opificio mundi*, took it directly from a lost commentary by Posidonius on Plato's *Timaeus*.[5]

It might be said that in the synthesis thus effected, the most diverse elements came to be united under the influence of an aspiration towards unity which remodelled these elements before bringing them together. Is not later Stoicism dominated by the search for a harmony between man and a world the nature of which is essentially "sympathetic", in the sense that all the elements in it respond to one another and live only in a symbiosis in which nothing exists in isolation? As for Plato, the reading that was given him at that time presupposed it as self-evident that the Idea of the Good, the Demiurge who makes the world according to his ideal model, and the Soul that holds it together, are all one and the same being: that unique God with many manifestations towards whom the religious syncretism of the period tended.

Neo-Pythagoreanism

It is precisely at this confluence of philosophy and religion that the Pythagorean traditions which then took on new life also came to play the part of a catalyst. Had they not already influenced Plato with regard to the most spiritual aspect of his teaching? The soul compared to the harmony of the strings of the lyre and for this reason declared immortal, since the golden numbers had a "reality" transcendent to that of the matter which yields to them—this comes from original Pythagoreanism. And the soul fallen into matter as into a tomb, the tomb of the body (*soma—sema*) but remembering a previous existence in which, divine, it lived with the gods—this is the Orphic myth which was so soon mingled to the point of fusion with teachings properly Pythagorean.[6]

At the period near to the beginnings of Christianity, a Nigidius Figulus, in the immediate circle of Cicero, shows us how these beliefs revived with the asceticism they implied and the theurgic practices—that of divining in particular—which caused him to be treated as a magician and a "mathematicus". A basilica, with frescoes depicting an allegory not easy to decipher, was discovered not long ago near the Great Gate. It might well have been the sanctuary in which a fraternal group—we do not quite dare to say

[5] See Bréhier, *op. cit.*, pp. 401ff. and also Bevan, *Stoics and Sceptics*.

[6] On all that, see the whole first part of the book by Jerome Carcopino, *De Pythagore aux Apôtres*, Paris, 1956.

a true sect—of this theosophy hesitating between philosophical revery and true religion[7] gathered together for conversations and, maybe, some ritual meals. But above all, with Posidonius and many others, it was the aspirations it betrayed, the hopes it so poetically expressed, that animated the eclecticism in which Stoicism, revived Platonism, and many other ingredients besides, were intermingled in the most religious philosophy ever known to pagan antiquity.

It would be difficult to say for how many souls such a philosophy must have served in turn as an involuntary propedeutic for Christianity, as its possible rival, and, finally, as the valuable instrument for many formulations that were concerned even more directly with spirituality than with dogma.[8]

St Justin,[9] the martyr, is the first avowed example of this kind of intellectual and religious adventure.

St Justin

A Syrian like Posidonius (he was born at Flavia Neapolis, the ancient Sichem, towards the end of the second century), he himself tells us about his search:

> Wishing myself also to enter into the company of one of the philosophers, I entrusted myself to the teaching of a Stoic. But having passed some time with him, since I had made no progress in the knowledge of God (for he himself did not know Him, and he denied that this knowledge was necessary), I left him. I went on to another, who professed to be a Peripatetic, an acute mind, to hear him. But after this man allowed me to converse with him for some days, he proposed that I should fix his fees, for fear that our relationships would be fruitless. Thereupon I left him in turn, no longer considering him to be a philosopher. But as I felt myself continually eager to hear something extraordinary and properly philosophical, I addressed myself to a celebrated Pythagorean, who made much of possessing a superior wisdom.
>
> But when I asked him to admit me among his familiar students, he asked me: "Are you versed in music, astronomy and geometry? Or do you indeed imagine that you can acquire any knowledge that leads to beatitude without first learning these things and causing your soul to pass from sensible to intelligible

[7] See the book of J. Carcopino, *La basilique pythagoricienne de la Porte Majeure*, Paris, 1944 (7th ed.). A portrait of Nigidius Figulus will be found on pp. 196ff.

[8] On all this, see G. Bardy, *La conversion au christianisme durant les premiers siècles*, Paris, 1949, especially pp. 46ff.

[9] For a complete bibliography, see J. Quasten, *Patrology*, I, pp. 198ff. In Migne, P.G., VI.

things, so that it will be disposed for the contemplation of virtue and the Sovereign Good?" He then greatly praised these sciences to me and, having said again how necessary they were, he dismissed me when I said that I was ignorant of them. I was the more troubled and discouraged at this because I thought that he knew something. But, considering all the time that it would take me to go through these sciences, it did not seem possible to me to wait so long. It seemed better to address myself to the Platonists, who were held in great esteem. I therefore joined myself to one of them with a great reputation who quite recently had settled in my country. I spent my whole time with him and I made progress every day. Thinking of the incorporeal realities ravished me; the contemplation of the ideas gave wings to my spirit, so much so that in a short time I thought myself to be a sage and I foolishly imagined that I was soon going to see God. It was with this idea that there came to me a great desire to have peace, and I retired to a solitude, in a remote place, a little village on the seashore. When I went there, an imposing old man, whose features spoke kindness, followed me at some distance. . . .

Justin turned around, at first irritated at not being left in solitude, then they engaged in conversation on what he had come to seek. The old man heard Justin's profession of Platonic faith, but vigorously criticized the idea of an immortality of the soul that would be natural to it in virtue of an innate relationship with the divine. To this he opposed the dogma of a creative God, on whom our whole life depends. To the discouragement that first took hold of Justin at hearing him take the Platonic arguments to pieces, he replied:

Many centuries before all these men who call themselves philosophers, there were others, blessed, just, loved by God, who spoke from the divine Spirit and proclaimed what we see accomplished today. They are called the prophets. They alone knew and announced the truth to men. . . . Their writings are always here, and the reader can profit from them to the greatest possible extent in learning what is concerned with the beginnings and the end, and everything that it is important for the philosopher to know who gives them his faith. For they used no demonstrations, being witnesses of the truth, too worthy of faith to need all that . . . As for you, pray that the door of the light may be opened to you: for these things are not accessible to all, but only to those to whom God and His Christ grant an understanding of them.[10]

In fact it was the reading of the Bible and prayer that led Justin to the Christian faith. But when he had fully adhered to it, far from abandoning his life as a philosopher, he considered that

[10] Justin, *Dialogue with Trypho*, 2 and 7; P.G., VI, 478 and 492.

he had found, as the old man had said to him, the true philosophy. Wearing the pallium, that is, the poor cloak which the Cynics, those popular philosophers more or less permeated with Stoicism, had made into a uniform, Justin in turn offered to dispute with all comers. First adopting the wandering life of his early masters, he later established himself, under Antoninus the Just, in Rome, and opened there a school of philosophy in which Christianity was proposed as the true philosophy. Tatian, the other great Syrian apologist, was his disciple at this school. But he also found an impassioned opponent in the person of the Cynic, Crescens, who may well have been the instigator of the denunciation that earned martyrdom for Justin, as well as for six of his companions and disciples.

The ironical remarks made by Justin about his various teachers, in the preceding account, should not deceive us. Justin was one of those converts who perhaps do not fully appreciate what has preceded their conversion until after they have been converted. But then he appraised how much unconscious preparation for the truths which he went on to discover had existed in the speculations which had only imperfectly satisfied him so long as he was held up in them. Still better, he discovered here unsuspected resources, not only the better to express but, perhaps, the better to understand his Christianity itself.

This is what takes shape in his theory of the *Logos spermatikos*. For, in his mind, the union was established between the Word made flesh of St John and the Stoic Logos, that subtle fire animating the whole universe, which had then come to be confused with all the Platonic Ideas and, in addition, had already been compared by Philo to the creative Word of the Bible. All the philosophers, in discovering something of the Logos, had simply shown that he himself had placed in them some seed of his own truth in creating them. Moreover, they had doubtless benefited, in more or less obscure ways, from some echo of its preparatory revelation to Moses and the prophets. But these fragments could not come together, still less reach the one totality of the living knowledge of the true Logos, except in its proper personal communication: in the Incarnation, in the Son of God made man, Jesus:

> All the right principles which the philosophers and law-givers have discovered and expressed, they owe to what of the Logos they have partially found and contemplated. It is because they did not know the whole Logos, who is Christ, that they often contradict themselves. . . . But everything that they taught that is good belongs to us Christians. For, according to God, we adore and love the Logos, born of the unbegotten and ineffable God,

> since He was made man for us, so as to heal us of our ills by sharing in them. Some writers have been able to see the truth indistinctly, thanks to a seed of the Logos that had been deposited in them. But it is one thing to possess a seed and a likeness proportioned to our faculties, and another thing to possess the very object, the participation in, and the imitation of whom both proceed from the grace that comes from Him.[11]

This optimism, so ready to welcome every partial truth, is, as we can see, in no way opposed to an extremely acute sense of the transcendence of Christianity, of what is unique and supra-rational in the redeeming incarnation. As a result, we should see in Justin not so much a hellenization of Christianity as the christianizing of Hellenism. By this we mean that his use of the terminology and even of the essential notions of the Hellenic philosophy of his times signifies a re-fashioning of these ideas before applying them to biblical truths as much as, and even more than, an accommodation of Christianity to the framework of Greek thought. The consideration, wholly biblical in its foundation, of the divine creative and saving event, and particularly of the event of the redeeming incarnation, draws to itself and reorganizes in function of itself everything that Justin brought with him in the way of elements taken from his successive philosophic allegiances.

We should go further and observe that Justin is typical of the philosophers of his time in his disposition to let himself be taught by "sacred words", that is, any revelation that is proposed as such.[12] He is the exemplar of those in whom this disposition was to open up a philosophy already religious in intention to invasion by the religion of the Bible. But how many of these philosophers, without going so far as to reach Justin's complete adherence to Christianity, were not more or less influenced by these wholly new ideas, Jewish or Christian, which Clement was soon to call "the barbarian philosophy"? His statement that the old Greek philosophers must have been taught, more or less directly, by Moses and the prophets is open to discussion. It may be that there is more in this idea than might appear, if only we apply it to the prehistory of Neo-Platonism in which it should be located. We shall soon see the motives which lead us to think that there is good reason to accept his statement about Neo-Platonism itself.

The "Logical Sacrifice"

It seems to us, however, that, even more than his speculations about the Logos, the developments he gave to the idea of the

[11] Justin, *Second Apology*, 10 and 13; P.G., VI, 460 C and 465 C to 468 A.
[12] In particular, see Festugière, *La révélation d'Hermès Trismégiste*, I, Paris, 1944, pp. 309ff.

logike thusia, the "reasonable sacrifice" confirm the fact that the Christian philosophy which he was the first to propagate was saturated with the Bible.

In his *Apologies* to the emperors, we see him taking up the philosophical arguments, which Seneca had summed up shortly before, for rejecting the ritual sacrifices and substituting for them the adoring contemplation in which we give ourselves up to the divine will.

> We are in no way ungodly men because we honour the Author of all things, not by victims and libations, which, as we know, give Him no pleasure, but by prayers and thanksgivings for the blessings received from Him. We think, indeed, that the only way of honouring Him worthily is not to consume with fire what He has given us, but to turn it to our service and to that of the poor, in expressing to Him our thanks by words and hymns: for His having given us life and health, for all things remaining in their proper state, for the seasons succeeding one another as they should, while He has allowed us to hope and to ask Him for immortality.[13]

But it is enough to turn to the *Dialogue with Trypho* to see that, with Justin, this philosophical expression of the spiritualization of sacrifice recaptures very accurately the eucharistic piety of later Judaism, as we have described it. Here is what Justin says to the Jews and has them say:

> God rejects your sacrifices, offered by your priests when He says: "I will not accept victims from your hands, for from the rising of the sun to its setting My Name has been celebrated among the nations, while you have profaned it." It is true that you answer by saying that the victims of the Israelites are no longer offered in Jerusalem, and that it was of these that God was weary. But you say that it is the prayers of the dispersed of His people which God says are acceptable to Him, and that it is these that He here calls sacrifices. I quite agree that prayers and thanksgivings are the only perfect sacrifices acceptable to God, provided that they are presented to Him by men who are worthy to do so. . . .[14]

But it was not the ancient Israel that could realize the ideal sacrifice towards which it tended, any more than the pagan philosophers could effectively know the "logical" religion the coming of which they obscurely sensed. It is for the Church, in her celebration of the Eucharist for the death and resurrection of the

[13] *First Apology*, 13; P.G., VI, 345 B.
[14] *Dialogue with Trypho*, 117, P.G., VI, 746 BC.

Lord, to carry out what had been prepared in Judaism and sought after in the best of the ancient religious philosophies. In fact, Justin adds immediately after the lines we have just quoted:

> But the only sacrifices that it is fitting to carry out—it is the Christians to whom it has been granted to carry them out, when, through two forms of nourishment, the one solid and the other liquid, they are reminded of what the Son of God suffered for them.[15]

The truth is, as he said a little earlier in commenting on the vision of the prophet Zachary, concerning the renovation of the priesthood prefigured by the new vestments of the high priest:

> All of us who are called by the name of Jesus Christ, as being one man in God, the creator of all things, by the name of this first-born Son, stripped of our ragged clothing, that is to say, our sins, and inflamed by the Word (*Logos*) of our calling, we are made the true pontiffs of God, as God Himself testifies by saying that in all places the pure and pleasing sacrifices of the nations will be offered to Him. But God receives victims only from His priests. From which it results that it is the *sacrifices of this name that Jesus Christ has handed on*, that is to say, the Eucharist of the bread and the cup, in whatever place anywhere on earth that Christians carry it out, that God accepts, witnessing that they are pleasing to Him.[16]

Behind all these texts the presence should be noted of a passage from Malachias which makes its appearance in Christian eucharistic writing with the *Didache*:[17]

> My will is no longer in you, says the Lord, and I will not accept the sacrifices of your hands. This is why, from the rising of the sun to its setting, my name will be (or is) glorified among the nations: in every place a sacrifice will be (or is) offered in my Name, a pure offering, for my Name is great among the nations, while you have profaned it.

We should notice here again, in Justin as in the writers who are the most completely Judaeo-Christian, the assimilating of the divine "name" to Jesus. And so we observe that his theology of the Lord, even when it is the most completely clothed in Hellenism, remains profoundly Jewish at heart, just as his notion of the "logical" sacrifice, however interiorized and rationalized it may be, remains Jewish and Christian: concentrated in the Eucharist of Jesus understood still in its most primitive sense.

15 *Ibid.*, 746 D.
16 *Ibid.*, 116–17; col. 745 AB. Cf. 41, col. 564–5.
17 Ch. 15. The text quoted is Mal. 1. 11.

Deformations of Christianity by Hellenism

However, this did not prevent the welcome so generously given to Greek thought concerning the Logos from giving a certain slant to the expressions and religious argumentation of Justin. The same thing is true of the other apologists, and the consequences were to make themselves felt two centuries later, in Arianism.

For in Hellenism the notion of the Logos first took form in a cosmological context, not a soteriological one. Above all, it gave an account of the immanence of the divine in the world. The result was that the existence of the Logos seemed to be bound up with that of the world, and this dependence actually became such that the Logos tended to appear, as with Philo himself, as being a *deuteros theos* in relation to the transcendent God: a being divine in a sense, but not God purely and simply. Behind this gliding of one idea into another and the rupture it was preparing, we see outlined the temptation which was to be that of all Christian "humanisms": that of a natural spirituality which the redemption would do nothing but restore and perfect, to the detriment of the divine transcendence and of grace.

What was only a temptation, and succeeded in producing only some superficial deviations in Justin and the other apologists, came to reveal itself in the various form of heretical gnosis as the first heresy and the most fundamental misunderstanding of the very essence of Christianity.

In these heretical gnoses, we might say, the element of ancient spirituality which was the least tractable to the Gospel strove to correct the Gospel in order to reduce it by force to a framework that it could shatter.

We have seen how, since Plato, Hellenic spirituality already rested on views at once dualistic and intellectualistic. At that time, dualism came from the East by way of Pythagorean or Orphic traditions: a radical opposition between a world that is fundamentally good, nay even divine, that of the "spirit", and another world, essentially imperfect, if not evil, that of "matter", with which any connivance of the "spirit" could only be a fall, the very origin of evil. Greek intellectualism thought to find salvation simply by the effective recognition of this primordial fact.

At the period we are now studying, new influences from the East revived in Hellenism the features of this scheme of things already familiar from ancient times.

Heretical Gnosticism

With Simon Magus, it would seem, these influences were decidedly at work to transform Jewish gnosis in a fundamentally anti-biblical sense.[18] Among a whole group of Alexandrians: Basilides, Valentinus, Carpocrates, and of Syrians like Bardesanes, or Asiatics like Marcion, these influences came in turn to deform Christian gnosis. In the middle or towards the end of the second century, efforts were multiplied in the centre where missionary Christianity was organized; that is, Rome, to swing the whole preaching of the Church over to the same sense. But neither the unction and the intellectual brilliance of a Valentinus, nor the seductive simplification of all problems by Marcion succeeded in winning the day. With the first, as in the majority of the heretical systems of this period to which the name of Gnostics is usually and mistakenly reserved, spirituality was enveloped in one of those cosmogonies with many hierarchies of intermediaries, systems which at that time seemed to have entranced both Greek and Jewish thought. Eons or angels descended in endless cascades from a pleroma in which everything is divine, towards a foreign matter in which everything is mired and becomes degenerate. To this fall, which is one with creation itself, is opposed the mission of the Logos, more or less strictly identified with the man Jesus. But since salvation is nothing but the recovery of an eon fallen into matter, the incarnation could be only apparent. It must lead, in fact, to a salvation which is not a redemption of the whole of man, but a disengagement in man of what has never ceased to be immortal "spirit", that is to say, an escape from the bonds of the body and the world. The coming of the Logos brings salvation only in setting in motion the gnostic illumination by which his own could recognize themselves in him.

With Marcion, the laborious chains of eons and their odyssey disappear. But the basic pattern is still clearer. For the two principles: the divine "spirit" and the increated and irredeemable "matter", two gods are substituted or superimposed. The demiurge, creator of all things and the God of the Old Testament, is only an inferior deity, in which evil together with being in this world finds its origin. The Saviour God delivers us from this: that is to say, the cross of the Saviour only frees our soul along with his own from the chains of the body.

Behind all these systems, we are tempted to see the same myth: the one we have already pointed out in Philo's explanation of the two Adams. Here primitive man is a man who is only "spirit" and who, for this reason, is divine. The second man is historical man, corporal man, man in this world, that is to say, fallen man. Salvation, for him, consists in the knowledge of his own original mystery, which of itself opens the gates of his prison. The Christ

[18] See H. Leisegang, *Gnosis*, French trans., Paris, 1951, pp. 48ff.

of the Gospels is only introduced into this scheme as the manifestation of the archetypal man who is to reawaken in us the memory of our own kinship with him, a kinship which has never and can never be lost. He is not truly incarnate, since His salvation is not that of saving the world but simply of saving us from it, or, better, of arousing us to deliver ourselves from it in awakening in our soul a gnosis which is simply the true knowledge of ourselves.[19]

Christian Reactions to the Heretical Gnoses

Justin was the first to oppose to these "false gnoses" the true gnosis which is that of the mystery of Christ, of his incarnation and his Cross, liberating because re-creative. But his works on this subject have been lost, and it is St Irenaeus who remains the great witness of the Church's rejection of the heretical "pseudo-gnosis" and its refutation by her doctors.[20]

We might be tempted to see in Justin and Irenaeus the two first conspicuous examples of two tendencies which between them have divided men's minds all through Christian history. In Justin, we see the tendency towards generous openness to foreign ideas; with Irenaeus, insistence on the tradition proper to the Church, distrust (if not absence of interest) with regard to thoughts that come from outside. . . . Certainly such a view of things would not be wholly erroneous. But we need to add to it certain strong qualifications. We should not forget, first of all, that Justin's writings against heretics have been lost and that, if we possessed them, they might lead us very strongly to modify the first impression of welcome given by his famous texts on the Logos. And neither should we forget that these same texts are not free of bitter criticism and biting irony with regard to the schools of philosophy which he had frequented. In the same way, the urbanity of the *Dialogue with Trypho* and the effective sympathy he maintains with Jewish traditions in no way prevents him from expressing himself very forthrightly as to the unbelief of the Jews and the vanity of their practices when they do not lead to Christ.

19 Our knowledge of heretical gnosticism has just been enriched and renewed by a series of discoveries of ancient texts. See Doresse, *Les livres secrets des gnostiques égyptiens*, Paris, 1958 (English trans., *The Secret Books of the Egyptian Gnostics*, London), and F. L. Cross, *The Jung Codex*, London, 1955. It should be noted that G. Quispel, reacting against the views of Bousset, Reitzenstein and, more recently, Bultmann, refuses to see the myth of the primordial Man as a product of Babylon or Iran. On the contrary it was Jewish speculations, he thinks, that were at the origin of the most diverse forms of this myth. Cf. "Der gnostiche Anthropos und die Jüdische Tradition", in *Eranos Jahrbuch*, XXII (1953), pp. 195–234.

20 See F. M. M. Sagnard, *La Gnose valentinienne et le témoignage de saint Irenée*, Paris, 1947.

Conversely, if St Irenaeus has no sympathy for the "pseudo-gnostics", we should not forget that what he reproaches them for above all is their pessimism with regard to creation, with regard to man as he came from the hands of God.

What more positive formulation of Christian humanism could be found than his: *"gloria Dei, vivens homo"* (*Adversus Haereses,* Bk. IV, ch. xxxiv, p. 7; ed. Harvey, Vol. II, p. 219)? And let us not forget that, according to him, the reason why God became man in order to save man is that the redemption had to be carried out *secundum suadelam,* in such a way that neither the honour nor the freedom of man were violated by it. In the same way, his so exclusively "ecclesiastical" horizon in no way prevents him from showing a moving sympathy for the barbarian populations who welcomed Christ. He impatiently does away with the speculations of Hellenistic philosophy, but simply because he sees that they actually formed a screen preventing the authentic Gospel from shining out.

St Irenaeus

We know that Irenaeus, like Justin, was an Easterner, coming from Asia Minor (where he must have been born around the year 130). But, in his case, the circumstances that led him to the West are not known. What is certain is that he was a Christian from his childhood, as is witnessed by the very moving memories that he brings up in his letter to the Roman priest Florinus, tempted by the teaching of Valentinus:

> These opinions, Florinus, to speak moderately, are not those of sound teaching; these opinions are not in accord with the Church, and they impel those who believe in them into the greatest ungodliness. Even the heretics who are outside the Church have never indicated opinions like this: these opinions were not transmitted to you by the old men who preceded us, those who were familiar with the apostles. For I used to see you, near Polycarp, when I was still a child in Asia Minor, and you were a star at the imperial court and eager to have Polycarp have a good opinion of you. Indeed, I remember the events of those days better than what has happened since, for what we learn as children grows with the soul and makes one thing with it. So I can describe the place where the blessed Polycarp used to sit and speak, how he came in and went out, his way of living, his physical aspect, his public conversations, how he spoke about his relationship with John and the others who had seen the Lord, how he remembered their words and the things that he had heard them say about the Lord, his miracles and his teaching, how Polycarp had received all this from eye-witnesses of the life of the

> Logos and reported it in accordance with the Scriptures. At that time also, by the Lord's mercy, I heard those things eagerly and I noted them down, not on paper, but in my heart. And always, by the grace of God, I have faithfully pondered them, and I can testify before God that if that blessed and apostolic old man had heard anything (such as you have been saying), he would have cried out and, stopping his ears, as he used to do, he would have said: "O good God, what times have you kept me to live in, that I must submit to this!" and he would have fled from the place where he had heard it, whether he was sitting or standing. . . .[21]

This very concrete and living text, which was a special joy to Newman, calls up all the aspects of Irenaeus' personality: his fidelity —not only respectful but enthusiastic—to the tradition of the Church, along with his warm humanity.

The Church and the Safeguard of the True Faith.

As was already apparent with Ignatius of Antioch, in the dramatic test of the faith constituted by the first great heresy, recourse to the Church, to its somehow intangible continuity with apostolic Christianity through the chain of its bishops, was to become an element increasingly emphasized as being at the foundation of all authentic Christian spirituality.

To the esoteric teachings of the heretics, pretending to found their fantastic gnoses on secret traditions going back nearer and nearer to the Apostles, Irenaeus was the first formally to oppose the public tradition, verifiable by anyone, connecting the Church with the apostles, from bishop to bishop.

> Indeed, the tradition of the apostles is clear to the whole world, it is possible to observe it in every Church, for those who wish to see the truth. We are prepared to enumerate those who were set up as bishops over the Church by the apostles, and their successors down to ourselves. And they taught nothing nor knew of anything like the ravings of these [heretics]. Indeed, if the apostles had known any hidden mysteries (*recondita mysteria*) which they taught to the perfect apart and in secret, it would have been above all to those to whom they entrusted the Churches themselves that they would have transmitted such things. . . .[22]

Then follows the celebrated passage about the supreme succession and tradition, those of the Roman Church.

Even if this recourse to the traditional authority of the hierarchical Church in order to discriminate the true faith from heretical

[21] Quoted in Eusebius, *Eccles. Hist.*, V, xx, §§ 4–7 (Bardy, pp. 61–3).
[22] *Adversus Haereses*, II, III; ed. Harvey, II, pp. 8–9.

corruptions came to be defined in a quasi-juridical way in opposition to these corruptions, nevertheless it always presupposed, with Irenaeus as with Ignatius of Antioch, a conception of the Church centred on the experience of the Spirit and *agape*. No one has been better able than Irenaeus to perceive and to express the unbreakable unity of the Church in traditional continuity with Christ through the bishops and Apostles, and of the Church as the dwelling-place of the Spirit.

> We keep our faith, received by the Church and continually renewed by the Spirit of God, as a deposit of great value, kept in a good vase, which renews the vase itself. For this is the gift of God entrusted to the Church, as breathing to creatures [at the time of creation], in such a way that all the members, in receiving it, are vivified. In it has been bestowed the communication of Christ, that is, the Holy Spirit, pledge of incorruptibility and confirmation of our faith, the stairway of our ascent to God. In the Church, as it is said, God has appointed apostles, prophets, teachers, and every other operation of the Spirit, in which none of those men participate who do not agree (*qui non concurrunt*) with the Church, but deprive themselves of life by a wicked opinion and an activity still worse. Indeed, where the Church is, there is the Spirit of God; and where the Spirit of God is, there is the Church and every grace, the Spirit being the truth. This is why those who do not participate therein do not receive the food of life from the maternal bosom, nor draw from the pure spring that proceeds from the body of Christ, but they dig themselves cracked cisterns in ditches in the earth, and they drink putrid water in the mud, flying from the Church that would guide them, rejecting the Spirit that would instruct them.[23]

What appears to Irenaeus as the essence of this faith of the Church, as opposed to the false gnoses, is what he calls, following the Epistle of St Paul to the Ephesians, "the recapitulation".

The Recapitulation

As he understands it, this word designates at once the taking up of the whole erring history of mankind into the saving "economy" of Christ, and the salvation and reconciliation of all things in Him. The "recapitulation", therefore, is at once opposed to the two errors stating that the God Who is the Father of Christ is not the creator of all things, visible and invisible, corporeal and spiritual, while the Word is incarnate in appearance only. As Irenaeus says first in the third book of his *Adversus Haereses*:

> When the Son of God was incarnated and became man, He recapitulated in Himself the long history (*expositionem*) of men,

[23] *Ibid.*, III, xxxviii, 1; Harvey, II, pp. 131–2.

bringing us salvation in a universal way (*in compendio—syntomos*), in such a way that what we lost in Adam: existence to the image and likeness of God, we regained in Jesus Christ.[24]

And, as he explains in Book V, this recapitulation of all history itself implies a recapitulation of all things in their Author:

> What the man who had perished had been, this the Logos became for our salvation, realizing in Himself what was necessary for communion with Him and for gaining salvation in Him. For the Lord, taking the slime of the earth, had fashioned man from it, and it was for him that everything was ordered in the coming of the Lord. He, therefore, also had flesh and blood and not another [flesh], but he recapitulated that very flesh that the Father had fashioned in the beginning, seeking what had been lost. And this is why the Apostle, in his Epistle to the Colossians, says: . . . You have been reconciled in the body of his flesh,[25] that is to say that the just flesh has reconciled the flesh which was captive to sin and has brought it into friendship with God.[26]

Hence, for Irenaeus as for Ignatius, the importance and the meaning of the Eucharist:

> Since we are His members, while still being nourished by His creation. . . . He has consecrated the chalice of this creation as His blood, from which our own body grows. Every time, then, that the chalice [that we have] mixed and the bread [that we have] made receive the word of God and the Eucharist becomes the body of Christ, the substance of our flesh grows from it and is strengthened by it. . . . How, then, can the heretics say that the flesh cannot receive the gift of God which is eternal life—that flesh which is nourished with the body and the blood of the Lord and which is a member [of His body] . . .? [27]

More profoundly, by this assimilation to Christ, who first made himself like us, St Irenaeus sees us as assimilated in him to God, participating in the very life of the Trinity.

> Our Lord, in these last times, recapitulating all things in Himself, has come to us, not as He could have but as we could see Him. For Himself, indeed, He could have come in His incorruptible glory, but then we could in no way have endured the grandeur of that glory. Because of this, the perfect bread of the Father gave Himself to us as milk, as He was in His presence (*parousia*) as man, so that being nourished as it were at the breast of His flesh and becoming accustomed by this form of

[24] Ch. xix, 1; Harvey, II, p. 95.
[25] Col. 1. 22.
[26] *Adv. Haer.*, V, xiv, 2; Harvey, v. II, pp. 361–2.
[27] *Ibid.*, ii, 2; Harvey, II, pp. 319–21.

nourishment to eat and drink of the Logos of God, we could receive that bread of immortality which is the Spirit of the Father.[28]

A text of the *Demonstratio praedicationis apostolicae,* referring not to the Eucharist but to baptism, goes still more deeply into this relationship between our recapitulation in Christ and what Dionysius of Rome, a little later, extending Irenaeus' own line of thought, was to call the recapitulation in the Father:

> When we are regenerated by the baptism that is given us in the name of the three Persons, we are enriched in this second birth by the good things that are in God the Father, by means of His Son and of the Holy Spirit. For all those who carry within them the Spirit of God are led to the Logos, that is to say, the Son, and the Son takes them and offers them to His Father, and the Father communicates incorruptibility to them. And so it is that, without the Spirit, we cannot see the Logos of God; and without the Son, we cannot attain the Father, since the gnosis of the Father is the Son, and the gnosis of the Son of God is obtained by means of the Holy Spirit; but it is the Son who by His office distributes the Spirit, according to the good pleasure of the Father, to those whom the Father wills and as the Father wills.[29]

In a word, according to the formula that the *Adversus Haereses* attributes to the "Ancients", the presbyters:

> By the Spirit, they ascend to the Son, and by the Son to the Father, and the Son finally returns His work to the Father, as the Apostle says.[30]

Vision of God and Life in God

We should note, in the above text from the *Demonstratio,* the use of the expression "to see the Logos of God". For St Irenaeus not only made his own the special expressions of Johannine mysticism, but assimilated them in a very personal way, as this other beautiful text indicates:

> In His wonderful greatness and glory, "no man can see God and live",[31] for the Father is incomprehensible; but in His love and His humanity, and because He can do all things, He has granted even this to those who love Him: to see God, as the prophets foretold it. For "what is impossible to men is possible to God".[32] Of himself, indeed, man cannot see God. But He,

[28] *Ibid.*, IV, vi; Harvey, II, pp. 292–3.
[29] Ch. vii. Cf. Ignatius, *To the Ephesians*, xvii, 2, on "the gnosis of God, which is Jesus Christ".
[30] *Adv. Haer.*, V, xxxvi; Harvey, II, p. 429.
[31] Exodus 33. 20.
[32] Luke 18. 27.

when He wills it, is seen by men, by those He wills, when He wills it and how He wills it. For God has power to do anything: seen in a prophetic way through the Spirit, He is seen, through the Son, adoptively, and He will be seen paternally in the Kingdom of heaven—the Spirit preparing man for the Son of God, the Son leading him to the Father, and the Father giving him incorruptibility for eternal life, which comes to each one from the fact that he sees God.[33]

In the same spirit of Johannine mysticism, Irenaeus has us go on from the vision of God to the divine life that is communicated:

> Just as those who see the light are in the light and share in its splendour, so those who see God are in God, participating in His splendour. But the splendour gives them life: thus they participate in life, those who see God. And it is because of this that He who is incomprehensible and intangible and invisible gives Himself to be seen, to be understood, to be grasped, so as to give life to those who grasp and see Him by faith. For, just as His greatness is unfathomable, so His goodness is ineffable, the goodness by which, being seen, He gives life to those who see Him. Since to live without life is impossible, the possibility (*huparxis*) of life comes from participation in God, and participation in God is to know Him and to enjoy His goodness. Thus men see God in such a way that they live, made immortal by the sight and truly attaining God.[34]

The texts just quoted are enough to show the extent to which Irenaeus—in his conception of Christianity and particularly in his spirituality—was faithful to the teachings of the New Testament. And these texts also show that the development of these teachings does not necessarily require combining them, in whatever way this be understood, with a thought foreign to the original Christian tradition. All that is necessary is to meditate on them at the heart of the living experience of the Christian in the Church.

Salvation through the Incarnation and Salvation through the Cross

Certain modern scholars, however, have contested this interpretation of Irenaeus' work. Harnack tried to find in him the first great representative among the Fathers of what he calls a "physical" or "mechanical" notion of the Redemption. We should understand this to mean the idea that the redemption was brought about, not by the death of Christ, but by the fact of the Incarnation alone. In consequence, the redemption would not be conceived, in the biblical way, as a victory over sin, but as a victory over death,

[33] *Adv. Haer.*, V, XXIV; Harvey, II, p. 216.
[34] *Ibid.*, 6; Harvey, II, pp. 216–17.

that is to say as a "divinization" more or less analogous to the apotheoses dreamed of by paganism.

Behind all this, in fact, would be floating typically Greek ideas, such as a notion which, we are told, is Platonic concerning the unity of human "nature"—a unity such that the incarnation of the Logos would automatically involve the divinization of all humanity (whence the expressions, "physical" or "mechanical" applied to the theory of the redemption thus laid out).[35]

In the same line of thought, Seeberg sees in Irenaeus the typical representative of that theology of the first centuries in which so many modern historians believe that they have discovered an almost total eclipse of St Paul's teaching on the Cross.[36] Even Bonwetsch, such a perceptive analyst of Irenaeus' thought on so many delicate points, reproaches him for the very secondary place and rôle he gives to the death of Christ.[37]

These interpretations already appear odd, to say the least, when we read Irenaeus' work as a whole, without allowing ourselves to be hypnotized by some expressions interpreted *a priori*. But there is worse to come. Other modern scholars, calling themselves Catholics, have appeared to take up this opposition and make it rebound to Irenaeus' glory. Both in the modernizing school of Anglo-Catholicism following Charles Gore and among some compromising disciples of Teilhard de Chardin, Irenaeus has been hailed as a theologian for whom sin and its reparation had only a secondary importance. In return, the Incarnation, as he conceived it, would be simply the consecration of the process of evolution, thanks to which God, in the total Christ, as they say, would appear at the term of this process.

It is difficult to imagine more complete nonsense, produced by the deplorable method of interpreting a writer according to some isolated texts, and these read only in the light given by the associations of ideas which certain formulations arouse in the readers' minds—but in minds completely strange to the historical and literary context from which these formulations have been excerpted.

The whole of the last-given interpretation, in fact, hinges on the page in which Irenaeus answers the question: why was the Incarnation brought about so late in history? His answer amounts to saying that God actually produced it at the moment when history was ripe for it—the Logos who was to become incarnate having, up to that time, throughout the Old Testament, been educating mankind through their experience of sin and its effects. This idea

[35] A. von Harnack, *Dogmengeschichte*, I (4th ed.), p. 613.
[36] Seeberg, *Lehrbuch der Dogmengeschichte*, I (2nd ed.), p. 330.
[37] N. Bonwetsch, *Die Theologie des Irenäus*, p. 113.

of a continuous and progressive maturation of history, under the impulse of the Logos and tending towards the incarnation, is removed by the commentators of whom we have been speaking from its coordinates in Irenaeus' thought: the history of sin on the one hand, the fact of the Old Testament on the other. And once this one idea has been referred unduly to the whole of human history, neglecting therein all consideration of an original fall, the "recapitulation" of Irenaeus is given up defenceless to the final sleight-of-hand which transforms it into a plain and simple identification of all history with a "machine for making gods".

All this ignores the fact that Irenaeus himself asks the question: "Why did the Logos become flesh?" and answers it, not once but repeatedly, in terms which are completely concordant and of a clarity that would be blinding if only the reader took the trouble to read them. The whole twelfth chapter of the third book of the *Adversus Haereses* is devoted to answering this question, and the answer is finally condensed by Irenaeus in the formula: "To destroy sin, to do away with death and to bring man to life".[38]

And the whole chapter explains at length that this could only be accomplished by the mortal struggle of the Cross, by which Christ substituted his obedience for the disobedience of Adam. Nothing could be more Paulinian; and all the great Paulinian references to the Cross can actually be found grouped together in this magnificent chapter.

A little further on, again combining the reference from the Epistle to the Romans to the two "Men" with that of the "strong man" of the Synoptics, he says:

> Man was created by God so that he might have life. If now, having lost life, wounded by the serpent, he could not return to life, but was to be finally abandoned to death, then God would be conquered and the malice of the serpent would have overcome His will. But since God is at once invincible and magnanimous, He has shown His magnanimity in correcting man and in putting all men to the test, as we have said. Yet, by the second Adam, He has bound the strong man and destroyed his arms, and He has done away with death, bringing life to man who had been subject to death. For Adam had become the possession of the devil and the devil held him in his power, having perversely deceived him in subjecting him to death when he had offered him immortality. Indeed, in promising them that they would be like gods, which was not in his power, he brought about death in them. This is why he who made man captive was himself made captive by God, and

[38] *Adv. Haer.*, III, XIX, 6; Harvey, II, p. 103.

man whom he had captured found himself freed from the slavery of condemnation.[39]

In other words, as Irenaeus says again in his *Demonstratio*:

The Logos of God was made flesh . . . to destroy death and to give life to man, for we were in the chains of sin and destined to be born through the state of sin and to fall under [the empire of] death.[40]

These texts need no commentary. They bring out what is already clear from the texts we have quoted on the "recapitulation". This is in no way an assumption by God of human history in general, but a new beginning and a complete reversal, in the history of the Cross, of the history of Adam's sin. The death from which we have been delivered, according to Irenaeus, is so little opposed to sin that it includes it as an essential element, according to the correct expression of Bonwetsch.[41] Life, for Irenaeus as for St John, is always life with God, in holiness and justice. And, finally, the idea of a redemption by the incarnation, as opposed to the redemption by the Cross has so little foothold in his thought that the incarnation, for him, has no other meaning than to make the obedience of the Cross possible.

What is true, for example, and what Brunner,[42] in his vigorous refutation of the theses of Harnack and Seeberg, has too greatly neglected, is that, with Irenaeus, the Cross is never separated either from everything that prepared for it in the earthly life of the Saviour and in the whole of sacred history, and still less from what follows: the Resurrection, the Ascension and the Glorification of all believing mankind following its Head. This is what is clearly brought out in the great study which Gustaf Aulen has devoted to Irenaeus at the core of his *Christus Victor*.[43]

To all this should be added the fact that Irenaeus, far from including any automatism in his view of the redemption, has brought out (perhaps more emphatically than any other theologian) the fact that the Cross of Jesus can have no effect so far as we are concerned if we are not determined to take up our Cross and follow him.

He Himself whom Peter had recognized as the Christ, He who had called Peter blessed because the Father had revealed to him the Son of the living God, He also said that He had to suffer much and to be crucified. And then He reprimanded Peter, who thought that He was the Christ but understood this

39 *Ibid.*, XXXII, 2; Harvey, II, p. 125.
40 Ch. XXXVII.
41 Bonwetsch, *op. cit.*, p. 80.
42 E. Brunner, *Der Mittler*, p. 229.
43 Pp. 34ff.

> in a human way and was opposed to His Passion, and He said to His disciples: "If anyone wishes to come after me, let him renounce himself, let him take up his cross and follow me. For he who wishes to save his life will lose it and he who loses it for my sake will find it." These words, obviously, Christ said as being the Saviour of those who would be given up to death because of their confession and thus would lose their life.... He will save, therefore, both those who suffer persecution and those who are scourged and put to death for Him, and not by another cross, but by the passion that He Himself was the first to undergo and His disciples afterwards.... Indeed, He Himself promised to confess before His Father those who would confess His name before men, and to deny those who denied it, and to confound those who would confound this confession. But, even so, certain men have gone to such extreme audacity as to despise the martyrs, to insult those who let themselves be killed for confessing the Lord, who endure all that the Lord predicted and so strive to follow the way of the Lord's passion, exposing themselves thus to martyrdom and being counted by us in the number of the martyrs. For, when their blood will be required of them and they obtain glory, then all those who have not honoured their martyrdom will be confounded by Christ.[44]

This beautiful text is worthy to serve as the final word of the writer who appears in history as the messenger sent to Rome by the future martyrs of Lyons and who, most probably, ended his own episcopal ministry by martyrdom.

Heretical Gnosis and Orthodox Gnosis

The last clarifications we have been led to furnish concerning Irenaeus' spirituality put us in a position clearly to define his attitude in the face of the heretics' gnosis. This attitude is frequently presented as a mere total rejection with no modifications. But this is a vastly over-simplified view. As we have already said—and we shall return to the subject at length in a moment—Irenaeus did not reject all gnosis along with the heretical gnostics. Quite the contrary, what he reproaches them with is that they are false gnostics; they have substituted a "pseudo-gnosis" for the true one. And again, this gnosis, as he conceived and practised it, was not simply alien to the preoccupations of the gnostics he was combating. These were themselves still tributaries of the most traditional and orthodox Jewish gnosis in concentrating their thinking on the problem of evil and redemption. We must go even further, and deny categorically that every solution of this problem implying a certain

[44] *Adv. Haer.*, III, xix, 4; Harvey, II, pp. 98–9.

dualism, in whatever way this be understood, must be the product of influences strange to the thought of the Bible, in Judaism or Christianity.

In a sense, orthodox gnosis is as dualistic as is heterodox gnosis. What opposes the one to the other is that the first envisages a historical dualism where the second tends to find a metaphysical dualism.

The gnosis of Irenaeus, like that of St Paul, of St John and, before them, of the most purely Jewish apocalyptic writers, firmly believes in one only God, creator of all things and alone capable of being their Saviour.

But all these writers precisely take creation so seriously that they completely respect the freedom of created wills and the mystery of their interplay in the Creator's hands (those hands which Irenaeus often speaks of and which are for him the Son and the Spirit). To orthodox gnosis, therefore, redemption does not mean a simple deliverance of pure spirits imprisoned by an original error in a body and a world that are themselves irredeemable. Redemption is a conflict, a victory won in a great battle by the Creator who comes to fight with and in His fallen creature against the powers of hatred which this creature's disobedience had itself unloosed. Thus everything is to be saved, matter as well as spirit, of the human creature who makes his own the divine battle and victory. But the spirit itself will be lost which persists to the end in that original fault, which was not simply a mistake but a rebellion. When this truth has been clearly perceived, a truth which Irenaeus' work against heretical gnosticism brings out in unshadowed light, it may perhaps be easier to discern the fundamental error of certain modern attempts to "demythize" primitive Christianity.

Pagan Myths and Christian Faith

Bultmann is certainly correct when he emphasizes the fact that there were certain presuppositions common to heretical gnosis and to the vision of human life and the world (which we should not hesitate also to call a "gnosis") in the Christianity of the Fathers and the New Testament, as well as in Judaism. But Bultmann fails to make the necessary distinctions when he rejects the introduction into the world of a transcendent Saviour as a gnostic theme common to biblical and Christian writings on the one hand, and to heretical (or pre-Christian) religious thought on the other.[45] For the idea which is the most specifically biblical

[45] R. Bultmann, *Kerygma and Myth* (Harper, New York, 1961).

and Christian is that which forms the *leitmotif* of Irenaeus' polemic against pseudo-gnosis: the Creator is *also* the Redeemer; he who made the world has also taken hold of it again, by the incarnation in all its reality, in order to re-create it, to destroy sin, death and the power of death in it and to bring back into it life in holiness.

And Bultmann is also not aware that what he wants to retain, after the "demythization" of the ancient Christian formulations, is nothing other than the a-temporal affirmation underlying all the gnoses which are really foreign to the divine Word of the Bible and the Gospel: a "salvation" which every human "spirit" can grasp in the awakened consciousness of its eternal bond with the divinity, so setting itself free from its false bond with the "world" of bodies. In such a view, the existence of Christ has no importance in itself, but only by reason of the meaning with which it is clothed for us by a "kerygma", in itself detachable from all history. But this view, far from being what distinguishes the Gospel from a gnosis which owes nothing to it, is precisely the error which a theology as basically evangelical as that of Irenaeus had to denounce in the "gnostics" who had understood nothing of the true "gnosis", the one which comes wholly from the Word of God, not the Logos of the philosophers, but of the Logos made flesh.[46]

46 This observation was formulated for the first time, so far as we know, by Jacques-Albert Cuttat in "The Religious Encounter of East and West," article published in *Thought*, vol. 33 (1958–1959), Fordham, pp. 493ff.

X

THE DEVELOPMENT AND CONTINUITY OF GNOSIS FROM ITS ORIGINS TO SAINT IRENAEUS

HAVING come so far in our study, we are now in a position to describe and analyse the development of orthodox gnosis during the first two centuries. We have already pointed out more than once the importance of this idea and the reality to which it refers in ancient Christian literature. It should be noted that as far back as 1915 Wilhelm Bousset drew attention to the need for research along this line.[1] But up to the present time, his suggestions have had little effect. The originality of orthodox gnosis and the central place that it occupies in the whole of primitive spirituality is still too generally ignored. And this is because the prejudice still exists—one refuted, however, by simply reading the texts—that the word *gnosis,* in its technical meaning, must have been a heretical term. The Alexandrian Fathers, Clement in particular, in striving to give it a meaning that would be acceptable to orthodoxy, would have been the first to seek to have it recognized as having rights of citizenship in the Church. But, in doing so, they would have been engaged in a hazardous enterprise, destined to failure.

The least that can be said, however, is that Christian writers, as has already been abundantly indicated, had in no way waited for Clement in order to use *gnosis,* in a very well-defined sense, without any shadow of hesitation. And far from having the least consciousness, in doing this, of borrowing something from heresy, it is clear that they believed themselves to be following the most traditional line of thought. An objective examination of the facts and the texts leads, it seems to us, to finding these writers entirely correct on this point.

[1] W. Bousset, "Eine jüdische Gebetsammlung im VII. Buch der Apostolischen Konstitutionen", in *Nachrichten von der königlichen Gesellschaft der Wissenschaften zu Göttingen*, 1915, fasc. 3, pp. 468–79.

St Paul's Gnosis

There is no doubt that the principal source of all orthodox Christian gnosis is the writings of St Paul. The recent study of Dom Jacques Dupont, *Gnosis, la connaissance religieuse dans les épitres de saint Paul,*[2] has shed much light on this question by its very thorough analyses. Any further study must use these as its starting-point, even though they need to be corrected and, above all, completed on several points.

The first thing that Dom Dupont seems to have established beyond question is that the meaning, certainly already very precise, which St Paul gives to the word *gnosis* (as well as *epignosis*) owes nothing to Greek philosophy. The latter, particularly up to the time of St Paul, never gave this term either any special importance or, still less, any technical meaning. In Greek philosophy, the technical term designating a developed kind of knowledge was not *gnosis* but *episteme*. The idea of knowing, in so far as it was expressed by terms related to *gnosko,* had no references other than to the famous Delphic precept: *gnothi sauton*, "Know thyself". This in no way directs us towards religious gnosis, but only towards reflexive self-knowledge.[3]

In return, it is true that certain terms connected with *gnosis* by St Paul retain a shade of meaning given them by Stoicism. This is the case particularly with the term *pleroma* and the meaning, at once cosmological and religious, which it had acquired. Here it should be noted again that the question is one of a very popular Stoicism which had passed into the mentality of the people in the form of a certain atmosphere of cosmic piety, without implying any definite notion.[4]

As to what is called today, without looking at it too closely, "pagan mysticism", meaning by this the mysteries of the oriental religions invading Roman paganism, the close-knit discussion to which Dom Dupont has submitted the hypotheses of Norden on the origins of gnostic terminology lead to two chief conclusions. The first is that *gnosis* and the terms related to it, only took on their religious tinge in later Hellenism and acquired a very particular technical meaning in an Alexandrian environment to begin with.[5] But the first writer in whose work this meaning shows itself is Philo, a little before St Paul, a century before Plutarch and his *De Iside et Osiride,* and two centuries before the Hermetic writings. Now, the analysis of Philo's texts leads to the conclusion—the second of Dom Dupont's—that in Philo himself *gnosis* never takes

[2] Louvain–Paris, 1949.
[3] *Op. cit.*, p. 530.
[4] *Op. cit.*, p. 471.
[5] *Op. cit.*, p. 365.

on this definite meaning except in direct dependence on a biblical text concerned with the "knowledge of God" which he has been led to comment on.[6]

Thus, even in later Hellenism, or more precisely, in religious Alexandrianism, *gnosis* does not seem to have taken on a special meaning except as the effect of the Greek Bible.

This is precisely what St Paul indicates, for his part. His "gnosis", as lexicographical analysis shows, owes nothing (and for good reason) to the old Greek philosophy, since St Paul never knew anything about this philosophy. Still less can his use of the word be made to depend on the more or less "mystical" religiousness of later Hellenism. In St Paul, the influence of the Bible is direct, and the context in which the term appears remains basically Jewish.

In fact, the first content of St Paul's gnosis is the "knowledge of God" in the most ancient and traditional sense of the term. The formulation of the First Epistle to the Corinthians, on knowing God as we have been known, is typical. It is primarily a question of a religion of trusting intimacy and obedience into which the faith of the prophets has opened out naturally.[7] In a narrower sense, the Apostle uses the word as did the rabbis, the teachers of the law, at the same period: gnosis, in this sense, would be the judicial and casuistic knowledge of what the law allows or forbids man to do. For it appears that the Corinthians, among their charismatic gifts, were especially distinguished for having received from the Spirit the gift of discernment.[8]

But the usage that St Paul then makes of the word extends its meaning. Gnosis, for him, is not simply an inspired *halakah,* but an apocalyptic kind of knowledge: the knowledge not only of what man should do or avoid in order to stay in God's ways, but also of these ways themselves in all their perspectives. As early as in the Epistles to the Corinthians and still more broadly in the Epistles of the captivity, gnosis is an apprehension of the secrets of God concerning the world and man, and uniquely the great secret: the "mystery" of Christ and His Cross, which recapitulates all history, reconciles all creation with its creator.[9]

Paulinian Gnosis and Jewish Gnosis

Nevertheless, as it seems to us, Dom Dupont gives only an artificial explanation of this extension from the narrowly rabbinical sense of the word to this last sense. According to him, the pivot

[6] *Op. cit.*, pp. 361ff.
[7] *Op. cit.*, pp. 87–8.
[8] *Op. cit.*, pp. 212ff.
[9] *Op. cit.*, pp. 528 and 540.

by which we go from the one meaning to the other would be simply the fact that gnosis, strictly nomodidascalic in contemporary Jewish terminology and in the use made of the term by the Corinthians, none the less appeared to them as a "charism", a gift of the Spirit. To St Paul himself, on the other hand, every gift of the Spirit was bound up with eschatology, with a charismatic anticipation of the final realities. And this accounts for the change-over in meaning, which would be entirely due to St Paul himself, from casuistry to the contemplation of the "mystery" of Jesus.

This subtle explanation seems to be as far-fetched as it is futile. For Dom Jacques Dupont here ignores the fact that the Jewish literature contemporary with the beginnings of Christianity, far from restricting gnosis to rabbinical casuistry alone, already included in it the knowledge of the "mysteries", that is, of apocalyptic secrets: the secrets of God's designs which he himself reveals to whom he will. It is not true that *gnosis*, as Dom Dupont states, has no precise literary affiliations in Judaism except with nomodidascalia, and not equally directly with "apocalypse" and the "mysteries". To become convinced of the contrary, it is enough to refer to chapter 2 of the book of Daniel. D. Deden, in his masterly study of the Paulinian mystery, has shown that here are to be found all the sources of St. Paul's apocalyptic vocabulary and of the "mystery" in particular, precisely as it appears in the First Epistle to the Corinthians. And, in this chapter, we read in verses 29 and 30 of the Septuagint version:

> . . . He who reveals the mysteries (*anakalupton mysteria*) has revealed (*edelose*) to you what is to happen. And this mystery has been revealed to me, not by reason of the wisdom which is in me above all men, but rather to reveal (*delothenai*) it to the king; what you had in your heart was shown to me in gnosis.[10]

This basic text, then, includes the direct connection between "gnosis" and "apocalypse", the explicit application of *gnosis* (and related terms) to the discernment of eschatological mysteries. It is remarkable, furthermore, that all this appears from the outset in the context of a distinction between acquired "wisdom" and an infused "knowledge". What is true (as we noted above) is, that in this text, the understanding of mysteries does not belong to gnosis under an aspect of pure speculation. It remains related to that discernment of hearts, and so of the ways that man must follow, which itself

[10] It should be noted that the version of Theodotion is still more remarkable, for it gives at the beginning: *o apokalupton mysteria egnorisen soi* and further on it again uses *gnorisai* instead of *delothenai*, with the final: *ina tous dialogismous tes kardias sou gnos*.

unquestionably proceeds from the "knowledge of God" of the prophets.

In the New Testament, the synoptic Gospels give us two examples of the use of *gnosis* which show the same orientations.

The first comes in connection with parables and their eschatological meaning which goes unperceived by the crowd. St Matthew has Jesus say these words to his disciples: "To you, it is given to know the mysteries of the Kingdom of heaven; to the others this is not given."[11] Is it not remarkable that here we find *gnonai* linked with *mysteria*, and again in connection with knowing the final realities by anticipation?

But the second text is no less remarkable. We have already commented on it at length: this is the famous *logion* of Matthew 11. 27 and Luke 10. 22 on the "knowledge" of the Son by the Father and by those to whom he has been pleased to "reveal" him.

These texts, too neglected by Dom Dupont, suffice to persuade us that *gnosis* must have already acquired in Judaism a technical meaning applicable not only to the teaching of the law, but equally to the understanding of the divine secrets concerning the supreme events. Furthermore, these texts indicate sufficiently that the Corinthians, in making "gnosis" a charism, had precedents for doing so with which St Paul must have been as familiar as they.

The texts of Qumran, which Dom Dupont did not use, confirm all this in a decisive way. In the *Midrash of Habbakuk*, gnosis is "the knowledge of the mystery", that is, very precisely, of the arrival of the last times.[12] The Rule of Qumran speaks of the "mysteries of gnosis"[13] and tells us that the "true gnosis" is only to be given to those who "choose the way".[14] They alone are to be instructed in "the marvellous and true mysteries".[15]

In these same texts, we should notice both the connection maintained between the apocalyptic gnosis and the "way" to be discerned and chosen, and the charismatic character of this gnosis. It has its source in God himself,[16] it is a "wisdom hidden from men, a gnosis and a thought [hidden] from the sons of men"[17]; it is God "who opens the heart of his servant to this gnosis."[18]

We see once more how thoroughly we are justified in maintaining that the Judaism contemporary with the beginnings of Christianity knew nothing of the cleavage between rabbinical circles and apocalyptic circles, or the opposition between tradition and inspiration,

[11] Matt. 13. 11; cf. Luke 8. 10.
[12] *Midrash of Habbakuk*, VII, 1–8.
[13] *Community Rule*, IV, 6.
[14] *Ibid.*, IX, 17; cf. X, 24.
[15] *Ibid.*, IX, 18.
[16] *Ibid.*, XI, 3.
[17] *Ibid.*, XI, 61.
[18] *Ibid.*, XI, 15–16 (translation of all these texts in Vermès, *op. cit.*, pp. 138ff.).

which so many modern historians obstinately insist on, in spite of the texts.

And at the same time the meaning of St Paul's gnosis is clarified in that Jewish context which is proper to it. It was from Jewish tradition that St Paul received the idea of a *gnosis* which was already specified as being not only a knowledge of the Scriptures channelled along casuistic and legalistic lines, but also an understanding of the secrets of God concerning ultimate ends. As we see in the Jewish apocalypses, whether in fourth Esdras or the book of Henoch, this "gnosis of the mysteries" could already develop the cosmological preoccupations which also are not absent from the Epistles of the Captivity. But even here, this gnosis remains moved by the practical concern to find the "way" of salvation, a concern derived naturally from the *gnosis theou*, the "knowledge of God" of the prophets, through the meditation of the Sages of Israel. In any case, whether it leans towards practical discernment, eschatological hope, or even religious cosmology, Jewish gnosis as imbibed by St. Paul remains at once nourished by Scripture: as knowledge of the Law, in the most extensive meaning the word had with the Jews—and yet a "charism", that is, a gift of the Spirit. And, finally, even in Judaism, this gnosis is directed precisely towards the problem of evil—or, better, that of the fall and its reparation. It is with good reason that recent writers, notably Daniélou,[19] believe that behind a whole series of Christian texts of the early centuries can be seen a body of already traditional Jewish exegesis of the first chapters of Genesis.

With St Paul himself, the "gnosis of the mystery" becomes gnosis of Christ and especially of his Cross, but the Cross seen in all the perspectives of the reconciliation of Colossians, or the recapitulation of Ephesians. For him, the "mystery" is now the key to the Scriptures and, at the same time, the key to the whole history of the world, found in the "revelation" of the great secret of divine wisdom, which is "Jesus Christ and Jesus Christ crucified". And so, in the third chapter of Ephesians, St Paul finally comes to explain what he calls "the understanding (*sunesin*) of the mystery of Christ" as our entering into the reconciliating design of God which recapitulates all human history in the Cross of Jesus and reconciles all things in his body which is the Church. This whole vision of faith is present to his mind as to that of his audience when he hopes that they will:

> be strengthened by the Spirit of God as to the interior man, in such a way that Christ will dwell by faith in your hearts, being

[19] J. Daniélou, *Théologie du Judéo-christianisme*, pp. 101ff.

> rooted and founded in *agape*, so that you may understand with all the saints the length, the width, the height and the depth: to know (*gnonai*) the *agape* of Christ that surpasses *gnosis*, in such a way that you may be fully perfect in all the fullness (*pleroma*) of God.[20]

This text gathers together all the elements which must concur for a definition of Christian gnosis, as being an unexpected development of Jewish gnosis, but of it alone, and not of the heretical ones.

As a gift of the Spirit, gnosis presupposes the new man, that interior man who is the product of a true indwelling of the risen Christ in us. It proceeds from the very faith which welcomes that presence and is nourished by the *agape*, the love with which God loves us and which is at the same time the final object and the primary source of our faith. It is intimate knowledge of, and participation in that love which might be called what is most divine in God. Being knowledge of *agape*, as communicated by God to us through Christ, this knowledge surpasses all knowledge, in the human sense of the word, to lose itself in a fullness which is the fullness of God himself.

St John and Gnosis

As we have already said, St John takes as his point of departure these supreme heights of St Paul's thought.

Neither the word gnosis nor its synonym *epignosis*, particularly dear to St Paul, is to be found even once in any of the Johannine writings. But no New Testament author presents such an abundant use of *gignosko*: "to know". And here, more than ever, St John is characterized both by his primitivism and his unique profundity. For him, "to know" almost always has God (or Christ) as object. On the one hand, it presupposes the conformation of the whole of life to the divine and properly Christian "commandments", that is the commandment of love with all its concrete requirements, the love which consists in "giving one's life for those whom one loves". But, on the other hand, gnosis is inseparable not only from love but also from consummated unity. And so, in us also it tends towards that unique reciprocal knowledge in which, as already stated in the great *logion* of Matthew and Luke, the intimacy, the incomparable unity of the Father and the Son, is affirmed. Never does gnosis take on more mystical qualities, in the sense of being a saving knowledge of God, in a love that assimilates us to him as perfectly as possible.

[20] Eph. 3. 16–19.

And so we see how Christian gnosis was born in Jewish gnosis and of it, and how it is distinguished from it.[21]

The Originality of Christian Gnosis

In the ferment of Judaism on the brink of the first century—a ferment which recent discoveries enable us to understand more and more clearly—a certain new "knowledge" of God in the Scriptures began to open out. The precise concern to perceive the path, the "way" of salvation, oriented it towards the *aion mellon*, the age that was to come, in which God would reign. And so it separated its adepts even now from the *aion outos*, the present age which God was coming to judge and condemn. This "knowledge" was a more or less ascetical kind of casuistry. But it was at the same time a speculation on the cosmic and moral genesis of evil and, above all, an eschatological vision, just as *halakah* and *haggadah*, juridical and historico-metaphysical commentary, were mingled together in the traditional science of the rabbis. The first Christians, participating in this search in the context of Judaism, were distinguished from their brothers by the fact that they made Christ and his "mystery" the key to this "gnosis", while they also attributed to the same Christ the outpouring of the Spirit necessary to attain "true gnosis". Does not St Paul tell us that the Spirit alone fathoms "the depths of God" (*ta bathe tou theou*)?[22]

However, where the Christian revelation was in no way accepted, Jewish gnosis very quickly degenerated. It became more and more submerged in a dualistic asceticism, in phantasmagorical speculations and visions, under the waves of influences from the East which, at this period, came to flood Hellenistic paganism as well as Judaism. Or else it shrank and hardened into a legalism more and more turned back on itself. On the one hand, according to the expression of St John's Apocalypse, this meant *ta bathea tou satana*, "the depths of Satan".[23] And on the other, was the reaction of the rabbis of the Talmud, who included in their condemnation, under the name of *minim*, both the Christian Jews and those who had simply given in to the syncretism of the period. Hence also the very remarkable fact that the earliest Christian heresiologists designated the Judaizing gnostic sects by the same words as those applied to the first Christians themselves: Nazoraioi or Ebionites (that is, "poor") . . .[24]

In this way, as Friedländer foresaw with startling perspicacity in

[21] See above, pp. 15ff. and pp. 51–2.
[22] 1 Cor. 2. 10.
[23] Apoc. 2. 24.
[24] See O. Cullmann, *Le problème littéraire et historique du roman pseudo-clémentin*, pp. 173ff.

1898, we can discern how both the "gnosis" of the Church and heretical "gnosis" have their roots intertwined in the same soil of Jewish "gnosis", born in a restless Judaism, apt for creative transformations and also for mortal contaminations.[25]

This is verified, in the early Church, by the development of orthodox gnosis in the face of the accelerated degeneration of the syncretist gnoses. For these developments can be understood only when we see them as being the continuation and growth within Christianity, according to the example given by St Paul and St John, of this entire complex—increasingly richer and more unified —of Jewish gnosis being made Christian.

The Apostolic Fathers

In three of the Apostolic Fathers, the few incidental mentions of *gnosis* are sufficiently rich in exact echoes to assure us how much the gnosis of St Paul and St John, with all its fundamental harmonies, remained a living reality to the sub-apostolic generations. But in two other writers among these Fathers, we already find a development as original in its details as it remains basically faithful to New Testament tradition.

A word should be said first of all about the *Didache*, the *Shepherd* and St Ignatius of Antioch. We have already quoted and commented on the prayer of the *Didache* (IX, 3) which begins with these words:

> We give You thanks, O our Father, for the life and the gnosis that You have made us know (*egnorisas*) through Jesus Your Servant.

Life and gnosis are brought together in the same way in X, 2, which we also studied earlier:

> We give You thanks, O holy Father, for Your holy Name that You have made to dwell in our hearts, for the gnosis, the faith and the immortality that You have made us know through Jesus Your Servant.

Against the traditionally Jewish background of the knowledge of God which is life in him, it is remarkable that *gnosis* appears in these texts as being the primordial gift which Christ brings us.

But the third passage of the *Didache* in which gnosis is mentioned places us still more directly in the immediate context—as restored to it by Dom Dupont—of the First Epistle to the Corinthians. For here we read that the proper task of Christian didascalia

25 M. Friedländer, *Der vorchristliche jüdische Gnostizismus*. See also, the same author, *Die religiösen Bewegungen innerhalb des Judentums im Zeitalter Jesu*, Berlin, 1905.

is to increase in the Church "justice and gnosis of the Lord": *eis prostheinai dikaiosunen kai gnosin kuriou.*[26] Here, therefore, gnosis is connected with "justice", that is, in the pregnant sense familiar to Israel, the complete practice of a life of fidelity to God. But it is interesting that in the Church "justice" remains the object of a didascalia received from Judaism and renewed in Christ.

That this didascalia is always presented as being a deepened understanding of the Scriptures is not formally stated here. But it is highly probable, especially when we compare this text with a very curious one from Hermas.

In the second vision of his *Shepherd*,[27] the Ancient One, who is the Church, first gives Hermas an undecipherable writing; then she gives him the key to it. Naturally, it is concerned with penance, which is Hermas' great preoccupation: "The gnosis of the writing was revealed to me" (*apekalupathe moi e gnosis tes graphes*). Nothing tells us expressly that the writing in question is a biblical text. But it is interesting to observe the spontaneity with which Hermas uses *gnosis* to designate the interpretation of an obscure text in the sense of the gifts made by Christ to the Church. This is the more remarkable in that the common Greek speech of the time knew nothing, it seems, of a meaning of *gnosis* applied to the interpretation of an enigmatic text.

Our third author will give us the most compact formula of any that we have met so far in the first Fathers. And we cannot imagine anything closer to the heart of St Paul's thought on this subject. Ignatius of Antioch writes to the Ephesians:

> Why do we not all become wise (*phronimoi*) in receiving the gnosis of God, which is Jesus Christ?[28]

In this phrase, Jesus no longer appears simply as the object or even the source of the divine "gnosis": he is identified with it. As Camelot has brought out in his recent edition of Ignatius, the context greatly enhances this formula. It seems to follow from it that "gnosis" is essentially the knowledge of the great saving acts accomplished by Christ, and that this knowledge gives immortality. We shall find these themes associated again in many later developments. But it is important to see them proclaimed in such an early writer and one whose whole thought remains so close to the New Testament.

But with two other writers among the Apostolic Fathers, we find much more than the sparse reflections gleaned so far, however suggestive these may be. Both the one writer and the other present

[26] *Didache*, XI, 1.
[27] Ch. II, 1.
[28] Ignatius, *To the Ephesians*, XVII, 2.

us with a matured and almost methodical teaching on gnosis. This remains in strict continuity with St Paul. Nevertheless, it also presents certain very remarkable characteristics of the "gnosis" familiar to later writers—the very characteristics which have made these writers suspect of having been highly contaminated by heretical "gnoses". But any "gnosis" foreign to the Church is not so much as mentioned, whether by way of blame or praise, by the two writers we are now to study. On the other hand, it is very instructive to observe their complete unity of views in everything concerning gnosis, while in everything else they seem to be connected with two completely different traditions. These writers are St Clement of Rome and Pseudo-Barnabas.

St Clement of Rome

In his Epistle to the Corinthians, "gnosis" appears on three different occasions. The first is in the introduction, which seems like a pastiche of St Paul's introductions to his Epistles. Before Clement openly corrects his correspondents, he begins by giving thanks for all the heavenly gifts that he can find among them. He is going to reprimand them for their disorders, but first he congratulates them for the abundance and diversity of their charisms. He enumerates four of these in particular. The first two may be mentioned merely as a matter of convention: faith and piety (*eusebia*). The third is more clearly appropriate, since it is *philoxenia,* hospitality, the location of Corinth as a cross-roads of the Mediterranean world being well known. The last (should we say, the climax?) of these charisms is "perfect and certain knowledge", *ten teleian kai asphalen gnosin.*[29] Nothing in the immediate context permits us to define this *gnosis*. Yet it is well to keep the qualifying adjectives in mind, for we shall come across them again.

But the second text not only helps to define "gnosis" but also gives it as it were its dimensions and its dynamism. Clement has just explained that Christ is the high priest of our offerings and the support of our weakness. Then he adds:

> Through Him, we hold our gaze fixed toward the heights of heaven, through Him, we reflect as in a mirror (*en oprizometha*) His faultless and sublime face; through Him, the eyes of our heart are opened; through Him, our powerless and darkened understanding (*dianoia*) flowers again, turned toward His light; through Him, the Master has willed that we should taste the immortal "gnosis" (*tes athanatou gnoseos emas geusasthai*).[30]

We should note that, in Ignatius, "gnosis" has already appeared in a context of immortality. Now it is gnosis itself which is described

[29] *I Clement*, I, 2.

[30] *Ibid.*, XXXVI, 2.

as immortal. But what is most striking about this text is its centring of the ideas of light and contemplation, associated with this immortality, on the idea of "gnosis". All this is very significant, for these are the characteristics which have caused "gnosis" to appear as a specific product of what is called Hellenistic "mysticism", characteristics which scholars like to believe foreign to the Bible and primitive Christianity. None the less it is quite clear that here we are very close to St Paul, whose very terms are recalled with all the biblical resonances included in them. And, furthermore, if there is anything which is marked with moderation, traditionalism, the intentional absence of originality—all the most distinctive characteristics of the ancient Roman Church—it is this letter of Clement's.

However, while this text once more puts "gnosis" in close relationship with Christ, while it brings out as does no other its not only inspired but contemplative character, it does not shed very much light on its proper content. This is what is brought out in the third text we are to examine. After a lengthy quotation from Job intended to show the nothingness of human wisdom, Clement goes on to tell us:

> This being clear to us, and our gaze having plunged into the depths of "gnosis", we must do everything in the order appointed by the Master and at the appointed times.[31]

This gaze plunged into the depths of "gnosis" certainly sends us back to the exegesis of Job, illuminated by Christ, which has just been given us. We can be the more certain of this since the expression *egkekuphotes eis ta bathe tes theias gnoseos* recalls three other texts in which Clement uses the rather rare word *egkupto*, always to designate the profound understanding of the Scriptures. We have seen, on the other hand, how this expression *bathe* seems to be proper to the vocabulary of *gnosis* since the New Testament.

But it is not less interesting to notice what follows. It might be said that this is Clement's central idea, the reason for his writing the whole letter: that is, the ideal order which ought to reign in the Church and especially in what we must already call the "liturgy", since the term here makes the first appearance which orients it in the direction of its technical Christian meaning. The possession of "gnosis", that is the contemplative vision of God's saving design —the design which is realized in Christ and understood in the twofold light of the Scriptures and of the enlightenment which gives an understanding of them—then leads to carrying out the sacred order which God has willed for his Church. This is to be done according to the basic idea which Clement now unfolds.

[31] *Ibid.*, XL, 1.

> Let each of you, brothers, give thanks to God (*eucharisteito*) in his proper rank, remaining in a good conscience, not transgressing the canon of his function (*leitourgias*) as it has been appointed for him, in holiness (*en semnoteti*).[32]

At this point, we have the impression not so much of an enlargement as of a flowering of the "gnosis" we have seen outlined in St Paul. Always centred on Christ, always charismatic, always connected with Scripture (being the highest form of understanding it), here we see gnosis become a divine vision that makes immortal, from whence flows the order willed by God, not only for the life of individual Christians, but for the communal and sacral life of the Church. It is as though all the composite features of St. Paul's "gnosis" have finally fused together in the bright light of this contemplation.

The Epistle of Barnabas

What is still, in Clement, only the resultant of some extremely pregnant but extremely sober expressions, becomes the object of numerous and concordant texts in the Epistle attributed to Barnabas. It is true that this epistle poses a preliminary problem. Was not Pseudo-Barnabas more or less infected with heretical "gnosis" and its dualism, radically opposed to the Old and New Testaments? How then, can he be called in to witness to the orthodox use of the word "gnosis"?

No more decisive answer can be given to this question, it seems to us, than the one which emerges from his "gnostic" texts themselves, when these are aligned with the texts we have already examined in authors whose orthodoxy cannot be questioned.

With Barnabas as with Clement, gnosis appears in the preamble.[33] He explains that he is writing to confirm Christians in the faith, and the whole letter is strongly polemic. We know very little about the adversaries he is combating, but his warning against fables and wearisome searchings, his distrust with regard to pretended charisms, his insistence on the practice of a virtuous Christian life, are so many characteristics which lead us to believe that he was opposed precisely to those whom he is stubbornly said to resemble. According to the whole context of this first mention of the word, the "perfect gnosis" (notice this adjective already used by Clement) seems clearly to be the accompaniment and support of a fully developed Christian life, because it rests on a solid and balanced faith which avoids all aberrations.

In the second text in which gnosis is mentioned, it is again in

[32] *Ibid.*, XLI, 1.

[33] *Barnabas*, I, 5.

connection with the whole Christian life, but with a greater insistence on the intellectual elements which this life includes.[34] Barnabas gathers together everything that could "aid faith": fear, patience, long-suffering, self-mastery. When we have all these gifts, he says, then wisdom (*sophia*), science (*episteme*) and *gnosis* all flourish happily together (*syneuphrainontai*).

Then we find an interesting definition of the "just man". It is "he who, having the *gnosis* of the way of justice", actually takes this way.[35] Here we find once more the language of "gnosis" in its source in nomodidascalic Judaism. This is not fortuitous in our author, as we shall see more clearly when we come to our last quotations: "gnosis", in the obviously very definite sense in which Barnabas takes it, remains systematically placed in relationship to the discernment of the "way of justice".

Then we come to a whole series of texts in which *gnosis* designates a Christian interpretation of the Old Testament. After a flow of quotations from the Bible, the author tells us first: "Learn what gnosis says." And the answer is: "Hope in Him who will be manifested to you in the flesh, Jesus."[36] "Gnosis", then, consists in discovering the true sense of the Old Testament, the sense which is given in Christ or, better, which he himself constitutes.

The text which follows, although more curious, has a very similar use of the term.[37] We are told that three hundred and eighteen persons of the household of Abraham were circumcized. The *gnosis* of this text is a symbol of Christ and his Cross which Barnabas says he has discovered in the number mentioned. Equally, the *gnosis* becomes the (allegorical or moral) explication of the foods forbidden by the Mosaic law.[38] Further on, we find once more an expression already familiar to us: *to teleion tes gnoseos*, "the perfection of gnosis", and here again it is to a Christian explanation given in connection with Abraham, the father in faith of the uncircumcized nations, that the phrase is applied.[39]

It has sometimes been supposed that the final texts of Barnabas on "gnosis" formed part of a collection added on to the first part of the work, because here *gnosis* seems to take on a purely ethical meaning. This supposition ignores a third of the texts already mentioned, which find in this last part of the work parallels that are merely more explicit. In chapter XVIII, v. 1, *gnosis* is related to *didache*, while the theme of the two ways is also brought in. Here we should recall the fact that this same theme is one of the chief themes in the *Didache of the Twelve Apostles*. Along the same

[34] *Ibid.*, II, 2–3. [35] *Ibid.*, V, 4. [36] *Ibid.*, VI, 9.
[37] *Ibid.*, IX, 8. [38] *Ibid.*, X, 10. [39] *Ibid.*, XIII, 7.

lines, in chapter XXI, v. 5, "gnosis" is called *gnosis ton dikaiomaton*: "gnosis of justifications", after we have been told at the beginning of chapter XIX that it has been given to us so that we may "walk in the way of light".

If we bring together all these instances, it is self-evident that we are still very close to St Paul and, more particularly, to the Jewish context of the First Epistle to the Corinthians, while the developments observed in Clement do not leave their presence unknown.

For Barnabas, in fact, "gnosis" remains in contact with *didache*, that is, with the teaching of "didascalia" which consists above all in a moral explication of Scripture. But this explication is henceforth oriented basically in reference to Christ and his work, and especially to the Cross.

The abundance of Old Testament resonances which this "knowledge" continues to evoke are very characteristic: "gnosis" is connected with fear (I, 7) with the "way of justice" (V. 4) with the commandments (called *dogmata*, IX, 7; *entolai*, IV, 11 and VI, 1; *dikaiomata kyriou*, (VI, 1 and X, 2). But no less characteristic is the fact that gnosis is a divine gift coming from Christ (IX, 8; cf. XIV, 5). It is related to the promises fulfilled in him (V, 7). And, Barnabas says, when we hope in him, we are recreated from foundation to roof to become a temple of God (XVI, 8–10; cf. IV, 11).

Finally, we should note the relationship established throughout the Epistle between "gnosis" and the Christian's effort towards spiritual progress. The preamble speaks of struggle for an authentic faith. But there is question also of the effort needed to realize to the greatest degree the *agape* which occupies a great place in this letter (cf. IV, 9) in which Barnabas tells us that he does not pretend to speak as a master of didascalia, but as is fitting for one who loves (*hos prepei agaponti*). It is not a question (cf. again I, 17) of discovering new truths, but of advancing in the fear of God, always to be understood in the wide sense of the prophets. We might describe Barnabas' "gnosis" by saying that its whole purpose is to cause us "to feel the goodness of the Father" (*aisthanesthai . . . ten gnomen tes agathosunes tou patros emon*).[40] Here we see the fusion of the various aspects: that of the loving knowledge of the loving Father and that of the penetration of the Scriptures, the purpose remaining always our progress in that "knowledge of God" in which the prophets had summed up the whole of religion.

After this, there is no need to expatiate on how Barnabas remains faithful to orthodoxy. If it is true that he seems to speak to chosen disciples, it is not any special doctrines that distinguish them, but,

[40] *Ibid.*, II, 9.

quite simply, uncommon fervour. As to the connection with the heretical gnostics which scholars have tried to deduce from his undeniable anti-Semitism, this rests on a confusion which is a flagrant contradiction. The extremist "simplicism" of certain exegeses, in which he condemns the Jews because they took literally the sacrificial prescriptions of the Old Testament, does not come from his radically opposing the Old Testament and the New, but, quite the contrary, from his too thoroughly identifying them. What Barnabas ignored was not the continuity of the two Testaments, but the difference between them. He had, therefore, nothing in common with the heretical "gnostics": we rather might say that his own "gnosis" made him, in this sense, the supreme anti-gnostic.

The Traditional Character of Gnosis in St Justin

In Justin we find quite a number of texts in which the term *gnosis* appears. But if he is preparing the way for a profound transformation of orthodox "gnosis" by bringing together for the first time the elements of Greek philosophy and the traditional content of this gnosis, it is no less noteworthy that this still has no effect whatever on the conception of it. In his *Dialogue with Trypho*, he speaks of the "grace of knowing" the Scriptures in their true sense, that is, discovering Christ in them.[41] But it should be emphasized that, according to him, the Christian sense of the Scriptures is their only true sense, which the gross and carnal Jews did not grasp. The texts furthermore, were figurative and intentionally obscure to prevent the unworthy from understanding them.[42]

The extent to which this position agrees with the one said to be shocking in the Epistle of Barnabas has not been sufficiently pointed out. According to Justin, it is only in the Church that the gift of the Spirit is conferred thanks to which Scripture yields its authentic meaning. But if we have this gnosis, he says elsewhere, the gnosis which was in the prophets (who thus belonged to the Church much more truly than to the Synagogue), then everything has enduring value.[43]

St Irenaeus and the Synthesis of Orthodox Gnosis

We must go on to Irenaeus in order to discover all the riches of the teaching, which we can now call traditional, concerning orthodox "gnosis". This statement may prove disconcerting, since we have become so accustomed to seeing this writer as the supreme champion against all kinds of "gnostics". But an attentive examination

[41] § 30; P.G., VI, 537C.
[42] See, for example, *Dialogue with Trypho*, 92; P.G., VI, 693ff.
[43] *Ibid.*, 113; col. 733C.

of his texts allows us to observe what R. P. Casey seems to have been the only one among modern historians to notice: never once does Irenaeus, any more than any other of the early Fathers, use the term "gnosis" or "gnostic" in an unfavourable sense. Never does he reproach Valentinus, Basilides, Carpocrates, or any other with being a "gnostic". He reproaches them with *not* being gnostics in spite of their pretensions to this title. What he is tracking down, in fact, is what he himself, according to the first Epistle to Timothy,[44] calls "pretended gnosis" (*pseudonumos gnosis*). The title of his great work, as should not be forgotten, is *Five books of exposition and refutation of pretended gnosis*. Far from testifying against the existence of a "gnosis" worthy of the name, such a title would seem to presuppose it. And this is precisely what is verified by a study of the work itself.

The first text which should be examined is a commentary on the beginning of 1 Corinthians 8: "Gnosis inflates, charity edifies". Here is Irenaeus' explanation:

> Paul is not attacking the true gnosis of God, unless he is accusing himself, but he knew that there were certain persons who, under pretext of gnosis, were lacking in the love of God.[45]

The rest of the text[46] shows what distinguishes "pretended gnosis," as Irenaeus sees it. It claims to find in Scripture a knowledge which is foreign to it. In consequence, it is not the mere abundance of scriptural quotations nor the eagerness with which they are paraded that testifies to true "gnosis". It is the fact that it does not claim to find in Scripture the solutions of problems other than those which Scripture itself intends to solve. Faithful to the Spirit of Scripture, we should not try to find in it what God has not seen fit to reveal:

> Let us not be embarrassed because God has reserved for Himself things that are beyond us.[47]

This capital idea, explained and deepened, is found again in another passage in which Irenaeus, again after opposing a false conception, goes on to re-establish the one which seems to him to be fully acceptable.[48] The heretics distinguished from the body of the faithful certain "psychic" or "spiritual" persons, and reserved to the

[44] 1 Tim. 6. 20.

[45] *Adversus Haereses*, II, XXXIX; ed. Harvey, I, p. 345. Even though here we have only the Latin text, with *scientia*, there is no doubt that the Greek had *gnosis*, since it is this word which is in the text of St Paul being commented on.

[46] Ch. XL; *ibid.*, pp. 347–8.

[47] *Adv. Haer.*, II, XLII, § 3; Harvey, I, p. 355.

[48] *Ibid.*, I, IV; Harvey, I, pp. 94–7. On this text, see the commentaries of Damien van den Eynde, *Les Normes de l'enseignement chrétien dans la littérature patristique des trois premiers siècles*, Louvain–Paris, 1933, p. 135.

latter a special teaching which a difference of nature made them alone capable of assimilating. For Irenaeus, on the contrary, all believers are capable of receiving the gifts of the Spirit. But he recognizes it as a fact that all do not advance equally in perfection, and so there are inequal degrees in their knowledge (here he uses *eidenai* and not *gnonai*). However, the difference does not consist in the "spiritual" persons' discovery of another God, but in the fact that they are capable of making a greater effort to read the Scriptures and to penetrate them. And so they succeed in incorporating everything that is found in the Scriptures into the great central truths of the faith, into what Irenaeus calls the "hypothesis of the faith".

To grasp all that Irenaeus includes in this last expression, we must go back to the explanation he gives of it elsewhere.[49] To the man who is incorporated into the true tradition of the Prophets, the Lord and the Apostles, what is to be sought and found in Scripture is not left to chance or to the whims of each individual. To the heretical "gnosis", the verses of the Scriptures are like so many pieces for a mosaic which an artificial virtuosity manipulates in such a way as to produce the incongruous image of a dog or a fox. For the faithful Christian, the "hypothesis of the faith" enables him to rediscover the true image of the King which is in fact pictured by the mosaic, because he carries this image within himself. As Irenaeus says a little further on:

> He who has received his baptism and who keeps inflexibly to the canon of the truth, will recognize (*epignosetai*) the names and the phrases which come in the Scriptures, but he will not recognize the blasphemous ordering (*hypothesis*) [of the heretics]. For if he has knowledge of the gems [in the mosaic], he will not accept the fox in place of the image of the king. On the contrary, putting back in its proper place each of the words which are spoken to him and harmonizing them with the body of the truth, he will despoil their work [of its imposed form] and denounce its unreality (*anupostaton*).[50]

In other words, true "gnosis" consists in laying hold of the proper and organic unity of the divine word in Christ, and not in playing with the texts in order to fashion fantastic conceptions. Under these circumstances, the following are the themes it studies, thereby in no way dissipating the "mystery" but, to the degree that it progresses, giving itself up to an increasingly adoring contemplation of this mystery:

> It exercises itself above all on what is said in parables in such

[49] *Adv. Haer.* I, I, § 15; Harvey, I, pp. 67–8.
[50] *Ibid.*, I, I, § 20; Harvey, I, pp. 88–9.

a way as to incorporate it into the "hypothesis of the faith" (*oikeiou te tes pisteos hypothesei*); it exposes God's way of acting, His economy with regard to mankind. It illuminates the patience of God in the apostasy of the Angels and the disobedience of men; it proclaims why one and the same God made some beings temporal and others eternal, some earthly and others heavenly. It understands why, being invisible, he none the less appeared to the prophets, and not under one form only, but under various forms. It points out why several covenants were concluded with man and it teaches what characterizes each one. It fathoms the reasons why God enclosed all [men] in unbelief so as to have mercy on all. It gives thanks for the Logos of God becoming flesh and undergoing the Passion. It proclaims why the Parousia of the Son of God takes place at the end of the ages, which amounts to saying that the origin appears at the end. It unveils the end and the things to come, to the extent that they are set down in the Scriptures. It is not silent as to the reasons why the nations who had not been known [by God] have been made by Him coheirs, concorporal, coparticipants with the saints. It proclaims that this mortal flesh will be clothed with immortality, this corruptible being with incorruptibility. It publishes the fact that "Not my people" has come to be called "My People", and the "Unloved" the "Well-Beloved", so that "more numerous are the children of the sterile woman than of her who had a husband". Indeed, it was for all this and for everything like this that the Apostle cried out: "O the depth of the richness, the wisdom and the knowledge of God (*gnoseos theou*); how deep are His judgments and how unfathomable His ways!"[51]

In other words, what is slowly opened out to the "spiritual man" by progress in "gnosis", and to the extent and degree that he becomes "spiritual", is how Christ is the key to the whole history of salvation, to the whole history of the world, and how this then finds its solution in the knowledge of the great mystery of the creative and redemptive *agape*.

In another place, Irenaeus comes back to the rôle and the place of the true spiritual man (*discipulus spiritualis vere recipiens spiritum Dei*). It might be said that it is the person who has put himself into the dispositions necessary to penetrate the Scriptures, developing one and the same effort to progress in *agape* by inserting himself more and more fully into the living tradition of the Church. For such a man, Irenaeus tells us, "all things harmonize: *omnia ei constant*, for he has the "true gnosis", which is indistinguishable from the apostolic *didache* fully assimilated.[52]

[51] *Ibid.*, I, IV; Harvey, I, pp. 95–7. The final quotation is Rom. 11. 33.
[52] *Adv. Haer.*, IV, LIII; Harvey, II, pp. 261–3.

XI

THE SCHOOL OF ALEXANDRIA: CLEMENT

No historian is tempted to neglect the importance of the Christian School of Alexandria, particularly of Clement and Origen. But it was only a few years ago that this importance began to be recognized as being at least as great in the field of spirituality as in that of theology. The work of Völker was a positive revelation to many students of patrology who apparently had not suspected that Origen[1] is above all a spiritual writer, and that this is no less true of Clement.[2] It has also become apparent that the chief sources of what we might call erudite monastic spirituality, beginning with the Cappadocians, and then Evagrius Ponticus, are to be found in Origen. As a consequence, he is indisputably above all others the Father of Christian mysticism as it came to be defined from the fourth to the fifth centuries.

Yet all this takes on its true value only when the Christian School of Alexandria is located in its exact place in the intellectual and spiritual development of its time. But there is still much uncertainty of opinion in this regard; above all, far too many ready-made ideas are still prevalent, ideas increasingly denied by the facts and the texts. It is important, then, to bring about, or at least to indicate, certain rectifications before going any further.

What was the "School of Alexandria"?

The first necessity is to ascertain precisely what "the School of Alexandria" means. How many historians still take it for granted without a shadow of doubt that we are dealing with a well-defined institution, with Pantaenus, Clement and Origen succeeding each other in regular succession as its head! G. Bardy, in a study that has been given too little attention, has brought

[1] Walther Völker, *Das Volkommenheitsideal des Origenes*, Tübingen, 1931.
[2] Walther Völker, *Der wahre Gnostiker nach Clemens Alexandrinus*, Berlin-Leipzig, 1952.

out how much illusion there is in this view of things.[3] Philip Sidetes was first responsible for it, and everyone after him seems to have been satisfied with his interpretation, without being aware that it rests on nothing substantial and that a whole series of precise and well-established particulars contradicts it.

All that we know for certain is that around the year 180, Pantaenus, a Christian teacher, taught at Alexandria; a little later, Clement also taught there, and seems to have been influenced by his predecessor, although we do not know precisely how. But nothing authorizes us to think that the "School" of Clement, if it was a school properly so-called, had any continuity with the "School" of Pantaenus other than the purely mental one of this influence itself. What is more, nothing allows us to be certain that either the teaching of Pantaenus or that of Clement had any official connection with the Church (it has even been disputed that Clement was ever a priest; this seems, however, to be going too far).

The link between Clement and Origen is no less vague. Bardy casts doubt not only on Origen's "succeeding" Clement in any position, but on his ever having been Clement's disciple. The letter of Alexander of Jerusalem to Origen does seem to testify to this last detail, but this is the most that can be said.

It is true that Eusebius seems to be explicit on all these points.[4] But, when we read him attentively, we perceive that he is only piling up conjectures, projecting into the past the situation existing in his own times, led by his concern to show the regularity of succession everywhere in the Church.

Actually, it is not before 212–15 that we can begin to speak of the Christian School of Alexandria as an institution and an official or semi-official institution in the Church. Here again, we need to see exactly what took place at that time. The persecution of Septimus Severus drove the catechists out of the city. Origen was only eighteen years old. But he belonged to a well-known Christian family and was already famous as a "grammarian", that is, an expert in literary studies. The bishop, Demetrius, knowing the courageous ardour of his faith, began to use him, it seems, as a provisional catechist. Then, later, he entrusted this post to him in a definitive way.

But the appointment of Origen soon began to attract an influx

[3] G. Bardy, "Aux Origines de l'École d'Alexandrie", in *Recherches de science religieuse*, XXVII (1937), pp. 65–90.

[4] Eusebius, *Eccles. Hist.*, V, x and xi; VI, ii, iii, iv, vi, viii, xiv, xv, xvi, xviii, xix, xxi, xxiii, xxiv, xxv, xxvi, xxvii, xxviii, xxx, xxxi, xxxii, xxxiii, xxxvi, xxxvii, xxxviii, xxxix.

of cultured disciples. What up to that time, therefore, had been a catechetical school like that of any other Church, that is, one in which sailors were as much at home as converts from philosophy or from Valentinian Gnosticism, came to be transformed. Origen began, however, by devoting himself to this common and, by the nature of things, elementary catechesis, and did so wholeheartedly. As long as the persecution lasted, he made the school a preparation for martyrdom as well as for baptism. But, when things calmed down, this catechesis tended to be extended, in his hands, into a kind of catechism of perseverance for intellectuals.

Origen was so well aware of this that he brought in a collaborator, his disciple Heraclas, whom he soon entrusted with the baptismal preparation. Then the spontaneous tendency of the master could be given free rein, and his teaching became more and more a very personal kind of initiation into the true sacred science that he went on to build up.

It did not take a very long time for this new orientation given to the catechetical school to disturb first a certain number of the more or less routine-minded faithful, and then the bishop himself. There were complaints of novelties taught by Origen. The faith of the simple faithful could no longer be found in the problems that were discussed. Even more than the publication of the *Commentary on St John,* that of the *First Principles* (*De principiis*) must have been a real scandal. The consultations which important personages, even bishops, such as those of Palestine, wanted to hold with him, did nothing to calm these rancours—quite the contrary. At the time of a first journey to Jerusalem, Origen was summoned by Demetrius to come back and resume his functions. Fifteen years later, in 230, a second journey to the same place led the local bishops to give him the priesthood, and, in spite of their intention of thereby smoothing away difficulties, this constituted the final rupture. Condemned by an Alexandrian synod with the sentence confirmed by Rome, deposed, completely replaced by Heraclas, Origen had to become an exile in Caesarea.

There he entered on a final period, paradoxically much more "ecclesiastical", much nearer to the problems of the common faith, his priesthood aiding this development. However, the "didascalia" of Alexandria became once more what it had never officially ceased to be: a simple catechetical school like any other. This is not precisely what we are accustomed to think of as the "School of Alexandria".

To summarize; a tradition of Christian philosophical studies was created little by little, by the private teaching of Pantaenus and, later, of Clement. It was in this atmosphere that was formed the young Christian avid for spiritual perfection that was Origen at the time of Severus' persecution. Then came his appointment to head the catechetical school. Up to this time, the intellectual current we are dealing with had had nothing to do with this school, but now it was introduced into it. At this time, then, the "School of Alexandria" took the form of an outgrowth of the regular catechetical school. Accepted at first, though not without some uneasiness being soon manifested, and later only barely tolerated, it was finally and rather harshly cut off from this school. Then its influence—without being abolished in Alexandria—spread to many other places, beginning with Palestine.

As a consequence of all this, the term "School of Alexandria" is hardly more than a historical fiction, allowing us to group together a succession of religious thinkers—what they have in common, moreover, being not so easy to define precisely. But in any case we are not to see behind them any fixed and continuous institution.

The Origins of Neo-Platonism

Another problem raised in connection with the so-called "School" is that of its relations with Hellenistic philosophy and, more particularly, with the birth of Neo-Platonism. The fact is that the two developed more or less concurrently in the same city, and we cannot avoid the problem posed by the contemporaneous development, in the same place, of the last pagan school of religious philosophy and the first school of Christian philosophy to produce more than the formulation of an ideal and some sketch of a programme. Actually, the scholars of the nineteenth and of the first years of the twentieth century seem to have seen no problem here at all. According to them, Alexandrian Christianity and the great succession of Greek Fathers following it only indicate, step by step, the stages of a progressive hellenization of Christian thought and spirituality, patterned on the same stages in the development of Neo-Platonism. The influence of the latter was total in a unique sense, and this is revealed in the succession of Christian teachers who more or less passively reflect the succession of pagan teachers coming a very little earlier.

How anyone could attribute such strange passivity to thinkers as original and personal as Clement and, above all, Origen—to say nothing of their successors, can only be explained by the unjustifiable prejudice that we have already denounced more than once. It had to be shown at any cost that any thinking, in Christianity and also in Judaism, must necessarily be a foreign importation.

Since the faith of simple people, the faith of the Church, supposedly includes no intellectual elements or at most only some "ferments" of thought themselves of a very meagre intellectuality, every Christian thinker, as such, must automatically find himself depending on non-Christian thought. Once we abandon this prejudice, which nothing justifies and everything contradicts, the factitious schema in which it inevitably ends can no longer be imposed on a body of facts and texts to which it too clearly does not pertain.

But the fact still remains that the last Hellenistic philosophy and the Christian culture developed together with it at Alexandria manifest a symbiosis in which it is very difficult, however desirable, to seek to define the interchanges of influences and stimulations.

From this point of view, it might be of interest to examine briefly a recent theory of very brilliant if rather fragile construction, which tends completely to reverse the views still too often retained —the equal fragility of which we have just emphasized once again.[5] We are speaking of the hypothesis constructed by E. Elorduy for the purpose of deciphering the enigma posed by the writings of the Areopagite, which we shall consider later on.[6] If we can believe it, Pseudo-Dionysius would actually be no other than the common teacher of the young Plotinus and the young Origen, that is, Ammonius Saccas. The latter would not be a Christian gone over to philosophy by apostatizing, as according to the testimony of Porphyrius which has never been seriously criticized. On the contrary, he would have transformed a Greek philosophy into what is called Neo-Platonism—a philosophy here again an heir of Stoicism still more than of Platonism—under the direct influence of the Christian faith. In this way, the Neo-Platonism of Plotinus and his disciples, far from being a capital source for the thought of the Greek Fathers, would be merely a "laicized" form, so to say, of a philosophy directly Christian in inspiration. It would not be the Christian Alexandrians and their successors who bear the vestigial traces of the last Greek thought, but the latter that would have been moulded according to Alexandrian Christianity, starting with one of its most original thinkers. Pseudo-Dionysius would be, not the last link in a Hellenizing tradition beginning with Clement and Origen, but, in the person of Ammonius, the master of the latter and also the master of the supposed founder of the Neo-Platonic school.

[5] See, for example, E. Bréhier, *op. cit.*

[6] E. Elorduy, "Es Ammonius Sakkas el Seudo Areopagita?" in *Estudios eclesiasticos*, XVIII (1944), pp. 501–47; "Ammonio Sakkas. La legenda de sa apostasia", in *Pensamiento*, III (1947), pp. 5–27. See also, by the same author, in the first review cited, the same vol., "Estoicismo y cristianismo", pp. 375–411.

This new theory seems obviously unacceptable, in its complete form—the identification of Pseudo-Dionysius with Ammonius Saccas apparently being a wholly gratuitous hypothesis. But apart from this kernel of improbability, we must recognize the fact that Elorduy has brought together too many elements, commonly ignored but of indisputable importance, for his theses to be simply discarded.

Without speaking of Stoic elements and their predominance in the unique entity obstinately called Neo-Platonism, it is quite certain that Elorduy has succeeded in firmly establishing a fact which a large number of writers—for example, Cadiou in his beautiful book on the *Jeunesse d'Origène*[7]—have at least suspected: the apostasy of Ammonius Saccas is a pure legend. The biblical and Christian character of his idea of the transcendence and the unity of the divine life leaves no room for doubt. Whatever characteristics of the God of Plotinus approximate these, therefore, come from the very same source, and the least that can be said is that, consequently, the Christians who drew from the Plotinian tradition, in order to formulate their spirituality, to a great extent did no more than take back what belonged to them by right.

These considerations lead us to see the problem more comprehensively and from a higher viewpoint. The immense and rather confused intellectual vitality of Alexandria, especially with regard to everything touching on the interior life, is a complex of which we are as yet far from having analysed the components. At the period we are dealing with, it was manifested in the redaction of the *Corpus hermeticum,* before producing either the fully-formed Neo-Platonism of Plotinus or the religious thought of the Christian teachers already mentioned. It will be worth our while to pause for an instant over this collection of writings to which the name of "Hermetica" has been given.

Hermetism

The character of these writings is very composite.[8] They include the greatest diversity of topics, from astrology or magic to real spirituality. In this, they well reflect the cosmopolitanism and the syncretism of the immense intellectual as well as commercial emporium that Alexandria had become since the Ptolemys. What

[7] Paris, 1936, pp. 184ff.

[8] See, with the edition and translation Nock-Festugière, *Hermès Trismégiste,* six vols., Paris, 1945, 1954 and 1956, the commentary provided for these texts by the other four volumes of Festugière, *La révelation d'Hermès Trismégiste,* Paris, 1944, 1953, 1954.

might be called religious Hermetism is developed in only two of the eighteen treatises of the *Corpus*: the first, the famous *Poimandres,* and the thirteenth. We can find a faithful echo of it, it seems, in the other fragments gathered together by Stobeus, as well as in a treatise, not Greek like all the preceding, but Latin: the *Asclepius,* falsely attributed to Apuleius.

This whole collection is presented as the product of a revelation (a *hieros logos*) of *Poimandres,* the "Shepherd of men", who is "the understanding of the absolute power", or again, in the thirteenth treatise, of Hermes Trismegistus to his son, Tot, on "palingenesis". The opposition between the intelligible world and the physical world, which must be stripped off in order to attain the first one, comes from the Platonic tradition. The primitive *nous*, "life and light", bringing forth another *nous*, which goes on first to create fire and *pneuma* and then the seven *archontes* whose administration of the sensible world constitutes *heimarmene* (destiny), presents an interplay of Stoic elements in a context of thought which is biblical or Jewish as to its original source, just as it was with Philo. The central myth of "salvation", through the "*gnosis theou*", of the primitive, heavenly, spiritual man who has fallen into matter and who reascends to God by disengaging himself from the sensible, is indubitably the same myth we have already found in Philo. But here, while the biblical vocabulary has kept something of its personal warmth in the proposed encounter of man with God, it still appears to be submerged in the current of a foreign thought, in which the fall is confused with creation, and salvation with a pure and simple reabsorption into God.

This thought is a variety of that same Hellenistic mixture the chief components of which we have already discussed, to which is added a particularly strong dose of semitizing orientalism, with a significance which seems, however, to be mainly literary. The local colour of Tot and of Hermes Trismegistus should not too greatly deceive us. In any case, the dependence either on Philo himself or, more generally, on a type of Jewish thought expressing itself, like Philo's, in a language and contexts of thought accessible to "Hellenes", seems to be beyond dispute. This dependence bears very precisely on the most religious element of the Hermetic "gnosis" and is indicated by its whole vocabulary of revelation and of knowledge as bringing about likeness. And this is true even when a more or less superficial layer of Platonism hellenizes its expression, confusing the knowledge that produces likeness (a basically biblical idea) with likeness as a necessary condition of knowledge (a Greek idea).

What Hermetism seems to owe to Philonism, and so to the

Bible and to Judaism, Neo-Platonism, we can now hardly doubt, owes to Christianity, through Ammonius Saccas, perhaps a generation later.

Pantaenus

But it must be admitted, before arriving at this conclusion, we should like to know more about this mysterious Pantaenus who is always presented as the first Christian thinker of Alexandria. Unfortunately, we are still in the most complete ignorance on this point, and the conjectures that have been made up, sometimes very ingeniously, to raise a corner of the veil, remain completely gratuitous. We have Clement's celebrated passage about the last of his teachers, the man who doubtless led him to Christianity:

> The last that I met, but the first in power, I discovered in Egypt where he was hidden.... He was a true Sicilian bee; he gathered flowers in the field of the prophets and the apostles and brought forth in the souls of his hearers a pure honey of gnosis.[9]

But is it certain that he means Pantaenus rather than some other teacher? Who can give us any assurance?

With still greater reason we cannot look at the *Epistle to Diognetus* for the spiritual features of this great unknown: what basis can be found for attributing to an author, who is nothing but a name to us, a book the anonymity of which is so well guarded?[10]

We must resign ourselves to the fact that it is only with Clement that the School of Alexandria begins to take shape for us. Furthermore, this shape is at once so clear and its characteristics so seductive that they have been transferred too blithely to Clement's "successor" without sufficiently taking account of the extent of the differences that distinguish the two writers.

Clement

Taking up Clement's first work, the *Protrepticus*, at its first page, we are struck by the strangeness of the tone, in relation to all the Christian literature we have met with so far:

> The assembly of the Greeks at Delphi applauded the death of the dragon, while Eunome sang the epitaph of the reptile;

[9] *I Stromata*, I, 12; cf. Eusebius, *Eccles. Hist.* V, XI, 4.

[10] The identification proposed (very prudently, moreover) by M. Marrou, reminds us a little of the attribution to Elpenor by Giraudoux's Ulysses of these two verses: "Ma vie a son secret, mon âme a son mystère . . ." and: "Qu'est-ce que tout cela qui n'est pas éternel?" See vol. XXXIII of "Sources chrétiennes", Paris, 1951, p. 266.

> the serpent's hymn or its threnody? I cannot say. But it was a concert and Eunome played to the hour of the dogstar. Behind the leaves, on the hills, the cicadas sang, burning in the sun. They certainly did not sing for the dead dragon, Python, but for the most wise god, on a mode of their own far better than the airs of Eunome! A string of Locrian is broken; a cicada flies up on the bridge of the cithera, and chirps away on the instrument as if on a branch. . . .[11]

This satisfaction in recounting the old legends, before giving a philosophico-mystical commentary on them, breathes a native Hellenism not previously encountered in any Christian writer. Already we can see Clement proposing himself as the hierophant of new mysteries, the soul of which may be Christian, but the body and something of the spirit wholly Greek.

Yet we should not let ourselves be deceived by a truncated quotation. However willingly Clement lent himself to his own performance, first of all he is no hierophant but rather, and particularly in this *Protrepticus*, a kind of fashionable lecturer. (We should not forget that this is what most authors amounted to at this period, even philosophers like Seneca.) His audience, as he himself tells us, was in great part made up of persons of leisure with intellectual pretensions, curious young men, blasé rhetoricians, mingled with exquisites of rather too great refinement and showily dressed women. All this charmed circle knew, moreover, that they were listening to a man of subtle mystification. A moment after winding up, in a lower key, his recollections of the ancient legends, he goes on to say to his audience out of the blue:

> How, then, can you believe these empty legends and suppose that music could tame savage beasts? While the shining face of truth, alone perhaps, seems to you made up and wins only looks of mistrust?[12]

This is a common procedure with him. Having set out with the greatest poetic feeling (and an erudition that seems at least second hand) all that can be said about the mystery religions, he changes his mind (or pretends to change his mind) in the same way, and says what amounts to "But all this, in the final analysis, is nothing but a collection of nasty stories! . . ."

In other words (and this has been too seldom pointed out), in Clement's Hellenism there is a great deal of acting, while the

[11] Clement of Alexandria, *Protrepticus*, Clement's works are given in Migne: P.G., VIII and IX. O. Staehlin has provided a critical edition in the Corpus of Berlin. See J. Quasten, *Patrology*, II, pp. 7ff. for a complete bibliography.
[12] *Ibid.*

undeniable personal satisfaction that he takes in it himself is a romantic pleasure: an antiquarian's dream, in no way duped by what he amuses himself with before lulling others with it. For this quality—even if it is true, as Epiphanes states, that Athens was Clement's birthplace—Alexandria certainly deserved to become his home. In his erudition, in his untiring curiosity, he is above all a delighted collector.

But just as the polite and refined superficiality of his audience hid, or could hide, a sincere spiritual search, so, behind this urbanity of Clement's which is scarcely its own dupe, there is a serious Christian whom we must beware of misunderstanding. His intellectualism has been greatly exaggerated. Certainly, everything that he writes is steeped in intellectuality, is sometimes even a little overripe with a decadent intellectuality. But the moral concern remains dominant throughout, and it is a very spiritual aspiration which always gives, explicitly or not, the meaning of this moralism.

It is taken for granted that his whole work, and particularly the *Stromata,* those "carpets" that he composed around hundreds of reminiscences and quotations, is dominated by the ideal of the "true gnostic". But, as our preceding chapters have sufficiently indicated, it is entirely chimerical to presume that he himself introduced this theme into orthodox Christian spirituality, borrowing it from heretical gnosis. On the contrary, he did nothing but take up the theme from Catholic tradition, and it cannot even be said that the new notes he introduced into it proceed specifically from heretical gnosis.

The Ideal of the Gnostic

It is enough to read the definition of gnosis which he gives in the second book of the *Stromata* to realize that it simply sums up all that we ourselves have been gathering together of the tradition of the first centuries, precisely at the time when it appeared.

> Here are the notes that characterize our gnostic: first, contemplation; then the fulfilling of the precepts; finally the instruction of good men. When these qualities are encountered in a man, he is a perfect gnostic. But if one of them is missing, then his gnosis is crippled.[13]

Let us take up the elements of this gnosis one by one. We recall the fact that "didascalia", more precisely the teaching of the "way" to be followed, is the primitive locus of Christian gnosis, where

[13] *II Stromata,* 10, 46.

it was born of Jewish gnosis. "The fulfilling of the precepts" is St John's very formula in which the "knowledge of God" of the prophets is taken at its source at the very moment of becoming fully Christian. Finally, the *theoria*, on which everything depends, is that view of the divine plan as a whole in Scripture and in history which St Paul identifies with true Wisdom, and which St Irenaeus, as we have seen, makes the exclusive privilege of Catholic tradition.

In fact, Völker has well brought out that, while Clement's gnosis is animated by the basic concern for regulating one's life, it is above all a knowledge of the Scriptures in which everything is illuminated in function of Christ, in the light of the tradition of the Church. Here are some of the essential texts, collected and very perspicaciously commented on by Völker.

"Gnosis", the sixth book of the *Stromata* tells us, "is the principle and author (*demiourgos*) of every action conformed to the Logos (*logike*)".[14] Transposing this wholly biblical idea into Stoic terms, in the manner both of St Paul and Philo, the fourth book defines it as an "energy" which is the "purification of the *hegemonikon* of the soul", that is, of its power of judging and choosing.[15]

As such, gnosis is seen by Clement as the gift of God: the gift of Christ above all. We find it far less than it finds us.[16] Baptism makes it possible to us, by making God knowable to us from the fact that the eyes of our soul are purified.[17] In the *Protrepticus*, the Logos cries out: "Freely (*charizomai*) I give you the Word, the knowledge of God, I give you [this] freely, in perfection, in myself."[18] "The grace of gnosis" indeed "comes from the Father by the Son."[19]

However, Clement explains, it is by reading the Scriptures to us himself and enlightening them by his own word that Christ gives us gnosis.[20]

We must, therefore, read the Scriptures in tradition, which, for him, is not so much a reality external to the Scriptures as their natural presentation by the Church: "What is in harmony with the inspired words being transmitted to us through the blessed apostles and didascales" who have transmitted these words themselves.[21] Indeed, the Scriptures remain a dead letter if we have not

[14] *VI Shomata*, 69, 2; ed. Staehlin, II, p. 466, 2.
[15] *IV Stromata*, 39, 2; Staehlin, II, p. 265, 27ff.
[16] *I Stromata*, 32, 4; Staehlin, II, p. 21, 21ff.
[17] *Paedagogus*, I, 28, 1; Staehlin, I, p. 106, 22ff.
[18] *Prot.*, 120, 3; Staehlin, I, p. 85, 4ff.
[19] *V Stromata*, 71, 5; Staehlin, II, p. 374ff.
[20] *IV Stromata*, 134, 4; Staehlin, II, p. 308, 1ff.; *VII Stromata*, 95, 3; Staehlin, III, p. 66, 23.
[21] *VII Stromata*, 103, 5; Staehlin, III, p. 73, 4ff.

what he calls "the ecclesiastical canon" to read them with. This means a living rule of interpretation which he has admirably defined as: "The symphony of the law and the prophets in the covenant which has been transmitted to us by the apparition (*parousia*) of the Lord."[22]

All this coincides in every detail with the description of gnosis given us by the most orthodox authors, particularly St Irenaeus.

The first originality and the first difficulty raised by Clement's texts lies in some wordings which seem to make gnosis the object of a special and apparently secret tradition in the Church. Let us, then, look at these texts, which have been collected by Fr Camelot, O.P.[23]

The most important is found at the beginning of the first book of the *Stromata,* where Clement enumerates his teachers (not in a very clear way: here among others is the famous phrase about the Sicilian bee which has been applied to Pantaenus). This is how he concludes:

> The Lord has consented to share the divine mysteries and this holy light with those who can understand. And so, it is not to a great number that He has revealed what is not for the great number, but to some to whom He knew that these teachings would be fitting: those who were capable of receiving them and of allowing themselves to be formed by them. For the inexpressible secrets like God Himself are entrusted to the word and not to writing. And if someone objects that it is written: "There is nothing hidden which shall not be brought to light, and nothing veiled which is not to be revealed", let him know from us that the Lord has announced by this *logion* that the secret will be illuminated for him who hears in secret, and what is veiled like the truth will be shown to him who is capable of receiving under the veil what is transmitted, and what is hidden from the crowd will be visible to some. If not, why do all men not know the truth? And why is justice not loved, unless justice is not for all? But the mysteries are transmitted mystically (*mystikos*) as they are in the mouth of him who speaks and of him who listens, or, rather, not in his voice, but in his spirit.[24]

Further on in the same book, he says again:

> Since tradition (*paradosis*) is in no way common or vulgar, at least for him who senses the grandeur of the word, the wisdom must be hidden which was expressed in the mystery

[22] *VI Stromata*, 125, 3; Staehlin, II, p. 495, 6ff.

[23] In his work, *Foi et Gnose, introduction à l'étude de la connaissance mystique chez Clément d'Alexandrie*, Paris, 1945, pp. 90–4.

[24] *I Stromata*, 1, 13; Staehlin, II, pp. 9–10.

[an allusion to 1 Cor. 2. 7], that which the Son of God taught, to purify our tongue and our ears, not to throw pearls before swine. "What I have said in your ears," Christ said, "preach from the housetops": He invites us to receive the hidden traditions of true gnosis, explained in a superior and eminent way and, as we have heard them whispered in our ears, to transmit them to him who should receive them, but not to give out to all, without distinction, what was said to them in parables.[25]

In Book VI he sums it all up by saying simply:

Gnosis has been transmitted to a small number since the apostles, by a succession of teachers, and without writing.[26]

Must we really see in these declarations, as Camelot admits following Lebreton, the proclamation of an esoteric tradition, opposed to the common tradition of the Church, as there certainly did exist occult traditions referred to by heretical gnostics, such as Valentinus? In his fine book *La Vie spirituelle d'après les Pères des trois premiers siècles,*[27] Bardy had already written: "It would be prudent not to lean too heavily on these formulas." For as Völker rightly remarks,[28] the content of these apparently esoteric traditions seems to be exactly the same as that of the "ecclesiastical canon": that is, the allegorical interpretation traditional in Christian exegesis.

Here again, we believe, we should perceive first of all—while taking care not to exaggerate its importance—a mere literary device, commonplace throughout the whole of Greek antiquity. Already used by Philo, in the same city of Alexandria, in connection with exegeses of this type, this device consists in using a "mystic" way of speaking for any explanation of abstruse matters, whatever they may be. These formulas should not put us on the wrong track: they signify merely that we are dealing with kinds of knowledge which require special study, not within the reach of the first comer, and needing both competent masters and disciples capable of learning from such masters. In the present case, if we re-read the preceding sentences without any preconceived ideas, it would be difficult to find in them anything other than a statement, in the amphigouric language which that period delighted in, of the fact that few men, even among Christians, take the trouble seriously to deepen their faith and to put themselves, for this purpose, to study with the teachers who are never lacking in the Church.

25 *I Stromata*, 12, 55–6; Staehlin, II, pp. 35–6.
26 *VI Stromata*, 7, 61; Staehlin, II, p. 462.
27 Paris, 1934, p. 98.
28 *Der wahre Gnostiker*, pp. 363–4.

If we still doubt that Clement means to say simply this, we have only to refer to a text in the *Eclogae propheticae* which is perfectly clear as to his basic thought:

> As the sea belongs to all, but one man swims in it, another trades, another fishes; and as the earth is common to all, but one travels over it, another cultivates it, another goes hunting, and still another works mines and another builds, so, when we read the Scripture, one draws from it [simply] faith, another inspires his conduct by it, and still another draws from it [complete] religion thanks to gnosis.[29]

Gnosis and Philosophy

When this unreal problem of esotericism has been removed, the real originality of Clement's gnosis can be examined. This is his idea that Greek philosophy, or more exactly the encyclopedic knowledge of the period, constitutes as it were a propaedeutic which is, if not necessary, at least very useful for Christian gnosis. This is what he says on this subject in the sixth book of the *Stromata*:

> Those who exercise themselves in gnosis borrow from each discipline what is useful for the truth: the gnostic seeks in music the proportion of the harmonics; in arithmetic, he notes the ascending and descending progression of the numbers, the relationships of one to another, and the way in which the majority of things depend on a proportion in the numbers; in geometry, he contemplates matter itself; he accustoms himself to think of a continuous space and an unchangeable substance, different from that of bodies; astronomy raises him above the earth; it raises him by the mind even to heaven; it draws him into the movement of the stars; it makes him speak continually of divine things, the harmony of beings with regard to one another; it was by this study that Abraham was awakened and raised to the knowledge of the Creator. The gnostic also profits from dialectics, where he finds the division of genus and species, where he learns to distinguish beings until he arrives at things simple and primary.
>
> The crowd, like children frightened by masks, fear the philosophy of the Greeks, afraid that it will carry them off. But if faith, not to say gnosis, is so weak in them as to be destroyed by specious appearances, let it be so, since they avow by this that they do not have the truth. For, it is said, the truth is invincible, only false opinion is overthrown.... But the gnostic pursues the truth by distinguishing what is general from what is particular. For the cause of every error or false opinion is not

[29] *Eclogae propheticae*, 28; Staehlin, III, pp. 145–6.

to be able to distinguish wherein things resemble one another and wherein they differ. If we do not carefully follow arguments starting with definitions, we mingle what is general and what is particular and inevitably fall into the most inextricable confusion. The distinction of names and of things in the Scriptures themselves brings a great light to souls; for it is necessary to pay attention to words that have several senses, and to seek to find out what they really mean; this is how right discernment is arrived at.

All the same, what serves no useful purpose must be avoided, what takes up time in a fruitless way. The science of the gnostic is for him an exercise preparatory to the exact possession of the truth to the extent that this is possible, and for the refutation of sophistical discourses which hinder the progress of the truth. He will, therefore, neglect nothing of what belongs to the encyclopedic studies (*ta egkuklia*) and to Greek philosophy, but he will not study them as essential; he will regard them, although necessary, as secondary and accessory. What the fomenters of heresy use to deceive, the gnostic will use for good.[30]

We need to clarify precisely what this text is saying. However useful to gnosis, in Clement's eyes, the contributions of philosophy and, more generally, of Greek culture may be, for all that they do not constitute gnosis, and are not even part of it, properly speaking. On the contrary, the error of the false gnoses, he believes as did Irenaeus, is precisely to wish to construct gnosis from the starting point of human philosophies, and not from the Scriptures understood according to the "ecclesiastical canon". Wherein, then, lies the usefulness of these studies? It is twofold. On the one hand, they preserve the formulations of Scripture from a naïve usage which would be nothing but a continual misinterpretation and, at the same time, they serve to refute error, which is a false interpretation. Here properly is the use of dialectics. But, further, it leads, by the deepened contemplation of creation, to the contemplation of the revealed truth.

This last theme should be emphasized. It is certainly central with Clement, as Newman clearly saw. For Clement, the physical world is symbolic in its very essence, and it is this which prepares us to understand the symbolism of the Scriptures, surely a capital element of gnosis in so far as it is connected with the allegorical interpretation of the Scriptures. Here we need to clarify the sense in which he understands this symbolism, for it is in the pure Jewish tradition. For Clement, the contemplation of the physical world itself is to lead us to discover its spiritual—meaning by this,

[30] *VI Stromata*, 10, 80–3; Staehlin, II, pp. 471ff. Cf. further on, 90–3; Staehlin, II, pp. 477–8.

personal—character. For a primary element in gnosis is angelology: the perception that this world, which may seem inanimate, is merely the covering and the translation of spiritual existences.

Völker has very rightly emphasized this point and its persistence in Jewish and Christian tradition. Gnosis causes us to attain, behind sensible things, not only to intellectual realities, as in Platonism, but, quite precisely, to spiritual beings. And it is in having us discover the angels behind the cosmos by associating us with them that it prepares us, like them, to see Christ behind the whole of sacred history.[31] To this extent gnosis sees "behind the world the intelligible realities and, beyond these realities themselves, more spiritual ones".[32] And so "gnostic souls, going in turn beyond each company (*politeia*) of the [angelic] orders, attain the higher places themselves".[33]

Gnosis and Mysticism

This leads us towards a summit of gnosis which seems decidedly mystical, if this word is given the meaning of a divine vision transforming man into the image of what he sees. The gnostic is called to "know God": *gignoskein,*[34] or *epignonai,*[35] to "see God",[36] to "possess" him: *chorein.*[37]

Clement develops these themes by having recourse to philosophic expressions of *theoria* and *episteme,* as well as to the mystery images of *epopteia,* as in this text of the second book of the *Stromata* where he says that "to know God is the greatest "*theoria*", that which is of the initiate" (*epoptike*), the "science of being itself" (*to onti episteme*).[38] But this language should not deceive us: all these developments gravitate around Paulinian and Johannine texts concerning the *gnosis theou* and *gnonai theon.*

Völker also quite rightly brings out the fact that these expressions, in Clement, are not to be interpreted on an intellectual level, but rather in function of his teaching on prayer.

In texts close to those just quoted, prayer is always "conversation" (*homilia*) with God.[39] Culminating in thanksgiving for gnosis itself,[40]

[31] Cf. *IV Stromata,* 153, 4; Staehlin, II, p. 317, 15ff.
[32] *VI Stromata,* 68; Staehlin, II, p. 465, 35ff.
[33] *VII Stromata,* 13, 1; Staehlin, III, p. 10, 6ff.
[34] *II Stromata,* 47, 4; Staehlin, II, p. 138, 12; *III Stromata,* 101, 2; Staehlin, II, p. 242, 25; *VII Stromata,* 47, 3; Staehlin, III, p. 35, 19.
[35] *Paedagogus,* I, 25, 1; Staehlin, I, p. 105, 2; *ibid.,* I, 53, 3; p. 122, 5; *ibid.,* II, 14, 6; p. 164, 16.
[36] *VII Stromata,* 68, 4; Staehlin, III, p. 49, 17.
[37] *Prot.,* 106, 3 and 113, 3; Staehlin, I, p. 76, 12 and p. 80, 5. Cf. *VII Stromata,* 8, 6; Staehlin, III, p. 8, 6.
[38] *II Stromata,* 47, 4; Staehlin, II, p. 138, 11ff.
[39] *VII Stromata,* 39, 6; Staehlin, II, p. 30 (see also all that follows).
[40] *VII Stromata,* 31, 7 and 35, 3; Staehlin, III, pp. 23, 26 and 27, 18.

it tends to become interior prayer,[41] silent prayer,[42] constant prayer which makes but one with the whole of life.[43]

It is to the extent that the gnostic attains this state that he becomes the equal of the Angels.[44]

But precisely what content is to be given to these expressions? Does Clement intend to speak of what we understand today by the term "mystical experience"? We must certainly not force terms the significance of which was defined only very progressively in tradition. But the best way of grasping exactly what Clement means to say is again to see how he himself defines the progress of gnosis in function of the whole Christian experience and, in particular, to try to locate gnosis in relation to the development of faith and *agape*.

At first sight, Clement seems to express himself on this subject in contradictory terms. In the fourth book of the *Stromata*, he tells us that "gnosis is raised on the foundation of the sacred triad: faith, hope and charity"[45] while in the sixth book he writes that "gnosis becomes firmly founded through charity".[46] Actually there is no real contradiction.

Gnosis is a development of the Christian consciousness which is at the heart of the development of the Christian life as a whole. But it can equally well be said that gnosis is nourished on the assimilation of the truths of the faith by the practice of charity, and that charity is perfected by gnosis (*teleiotai te gnosei*), according to a very similar formula of Clement of Rome.[47] For "agape is engendered by gnosis",[48] while it is "its quality of loving (*eraston*) which leads to the contemplation of God (*heautou theorian*) him who gives himself wholly to this contemplation by the love of gnosis (*te tes gnoseos agape*)".[49]

The supreme state is one in which we know the God of love by the fact that we love as he loves: "God is love and He is knowable (*gnostos*) to those who love Him.... We must enter into His intimacy by the divine *agape* so that we can contemplate the like by the like."[50]

Clement is the first author to characterize this state as

41 *VII Stromata*, 36, 5; Staehlin, III, p. 28, 23.
42 *VII Stromata*, 39, 6; Staehlin, III, p. 27, 27.
43 *VI Stromata*, 102, 1; Staehlin, II, p. 483, 6; *VII Stromata*, 35, 6; Staehlin, III, p. 27, 27.
44 *VII Stromata*, 57, 5; Staehlin, III, p. 42, 10.
45 *IV Stromata*, 7, 54; Staehlin, II, p. 273.
46 *VI Stromata*, 9, 78; Staehlin, II, p. 470.
47 *II Stromata*, 9, 45; Staehlin, II, p. 136. Cf. *I Clement*, I, 2.
48 *VII Stromata*, 59, 4; Staehlin, III, p. 43, 17.
49 *VII Stromata*, 10, 3; Staehlin, III, p. 9, 9ff.
50 *V Stromata*, 1, 12; Staehlin, II, p. 334.

"deification", using the word *theopoiein* (which in classic Greek sometimes means apotheosis; more frequently, the fabrication of idols) in a spiritual sense completely without precedent, which was to become current in the Alexandrian tradition. He says in his *Protrepticus*.[51]

"The Logos of God was made man so that you might learn how man can become God", and, a little further on: "By His heavenly teaching. He deifies man (*theopoion anthropon*)".[52] The sense in which he intends this is explained along the New Testament lines of our real adoption in and by the Son: "Those who know [the Son], He calls sons and gods."[53]

Apatheia

Still in connection with the summit of the gnostic life, of assimilation to God, Clement introduces into Christian language the term *apatheia*. Starting with the Cappadocians and Evagrius Ponticus, this term will be taken up by the spirituality of erudite monasticism where it will play a great rôle. But it will also provide a pretext for later anti-Origenist attacks, a pretext taken up by modern scholars for accusing Christian Alexandrianism of inhumanity and the paganization of traditional spirituality. This is actually a twofold misinterpretation. Even with the Stoics, *apatheia* is in no way an inhuman insensibility, but a state in which the sage has succeeded in freeing himself from exterior influences by being able to dominate them. With Clement himself, the explanations that he gives of his use of the term are still more precise: he means a domination acquired, by the grace to which our liberty yields itself, over everything in us which is opposed to the radiance of charity. Far from the *apatheia* of the gnostic rendering him insensible to Christian *agape*, therefore, it is actually only its triumphant radiation:

> If the gnostic does not have desire, some people say, he can no longer eagerly strive towards the resembling of perfect men. If, then, all intimacy with the good is realized in virtue of a tendency, how, they say, can he who tends towards the good remain "apathetic"?
>
> But these men do not understand, it seems, the divine character of love. For love is no longer a tendency of him who loves: it is a loving intimacy, which establishes the gnostic in the unity of faith, without his having any further need of time nor of space. Already established by love in the good things that he will possess, having anticipated hope by gnosis, he no longer tends

[51] *Prot.*, i, 9; Staehlin, I, p. 9. [52] *Prot.*, xi; Staehlin, I, p. 81.
[53] *VI Stromata*, 16, 146; Staehlin, II, p. 507.

towards anything, having everything that he could tend towards. He remains, then, in the one unchanging attitude, loving in gnostic fashion, and he does not have to desire to be made like beauty, for he possesses beauty by love. What need is there now of courage (*tharsous*) or of desire (*epithumias*) for this man who has gained loving intimacy with the God who is passionless and who is himself inscribed among his friends by love? For us, the perfect gnostic must be removed from any passion of the soul. For gnosis achieves exercise, exercise then gives habit or accustoming, and this calming (*katastasis*) ends in *apatheia* . . .[54]

This text shows very clearly the two closely connected characteristics of the *apatheia* of the gnostic: it is a calming of all the disordered tendencies of our fallen nature by their perfect submission to charity fully possessed; by this very fact it ends in a stable condition which is as it were a foretaste of eternity.

On the first point, Clement has no difficulty in showing that what is positive in our most diverse tendencies finds its transcendent fulfilment through charity and so, where it reigns, everything else is surpassed. However this in no ways means for him any extinction of the human, but rather its unification in a fullness in which everything is taken up and transfigured which is worthy of being so.

He always loves God towards whom alone he is wholly turned, and, because of this, he hates none of God's creatures. He desires nothing, for nothing is lacking for his assimilation to Him who is good and beautiful. He loves nothing and no one with an ordinary love, but he holds his creator dear through creatures; he is not exposed to desire or appetite, he lacks none of the goods of the soul, being already united by love to the Friend to whom he belongs according to his free choice and coming nearer and nearer to Him by the habit of ascesis, being happy in the possession of His good things, he cannot be unlike the Master in *apatheia*.[55]

On the second point: the establishment of the perfect gnostic in a permanent state of joy and peace, Clement justifies himself against the objections that are made against the existence of such a state on earth by showing how the gnostic is such only by attaining the great objects of divine truth: now they have for him a reality in comparison with which everything else fades away, hence his joyful and unalterable peace.[56]

It follows that we must not see in this state any artificial and chimerical Quietism, but a progressive absorption in the truth which is love. What finally proves this is the active and realistic generosity

[54] *VI Stromata*, 9, 73–4; Staehlin, II, p. 468.
[55] *VI Stromata*, 9, 71–2; Staehlin, II, pp. 467–8.
[56] *Ibid.*

of the gnostic. For he is no false spiritualist: he honours the body and the world, recognizing in them the work of God.[57] And so he loves his brothers with a charity that embraces the needs of the body and those of the soul, even though it naturally culminates in the communication of gnosis.[58] But this communication, like the gnosis which is its object, is an affair of life more than of words:

> The gnostic who has acquired the habit of doing good, acts well rather than speaks well; he asks to suffer together with the sins of his brothers; he prays for the confession and conversion of his neighbours, he desires to have his dearest friends share his own proper goods—and such are all his friends. Thus causing the seeds deposited in him to grow, according to the agriculture ordained by the Lord, he remains without sin; he is master of himself and he lives by the spirit with his compeers in the choirs of the saints even though he is still kept on the earth. Such a man, who acts and speaks thus day and night according to the commandments of the Lord, arrives at perfect joy, not only at dawn when he arises, and in the middle of the day, but also when he walks about, when he goes to rest, when he dresses and undresses. He instructs his son if a son is born to him; he cannot separate himself from the commandment and from hope; he always gives thanks to God, as do the living Beings which glorify the Lord in the allegory of Isaias;[59] he is patient under all adversity: "The Lord," he says, "has given, the Lord has taken away".[60] Such a man was Job who accepted the loss of external goods and even that of bodily health, because of his love for the Lord. "He was", says Scripture, "just, holy, removed from all wrongdoing."[61] Holiness here signifies justice with regard to God according to all the divine dispositions, and it is for having known this justice that he was gnostic.[62]

It must be admitted, in pausing at this last page, that Clement has the art of engaging us effortlessly in a long and unexpected voyage. The agreeable humanist, a little talkative and diffuse, who first captured a public, doubtless more curious than fervent, by the delightful grace of his explanations, led it insensibly towards the heights of a pure and exacting spirituality. There is no doubt that his work, particularly his description of the ideal gnostic, more directly than any other opened the way for the spirituality which was soon to be called mystical. On this point, Fénelon was certainly not deceived, even if it is true that to some extent he forced Clement's expressions.

[57] *IV Stromata*, 26, 163–4; Staehlin, II, p. 320.
[58] *VII Stromata*, 1, 3; 9, 52–4; Staehlin, III, pp. 4, 38–40, 49–50.
[59] Isaias 6. 2. [60] Job 1. 21. [61] Job 1. 1.
[62] *VII Stromata* 12, 80; Staehlin, III, p. 57.

XII

THE SCHOOL OF ALEXANDRIA (CONCLUSION): ORIGEN

After Clement, Origen gives an abrupt impression of a shift both in tone and in mentality. Intellectually, to begin with, here is an extremely rigorous mind, very firmly attached to the elucidation of major problems, coming after an insatiable reader in whom there was more openness to everything than eagerness to get to the bottom of anything. But spiritually above all, with Origen, the love of God, of Christ, is of a vehemence that contrasts strikingly with Clement's aspiration, so facilely serene. As we go from one to the other, the Cross of Jesus, grasped with something of that spiritual passion characteristic of St Paul, comes back into the foreground.

But before going on from Clement to Origen, as is the usual procedure, we need to try to clarify, as far as this is possible, what the latter must have received from Ammonius Saccas, who remained his master far more than Clement.

Ammonius Saccas

Some time before the work of Elorduy, Cadiou had already patiently demonstrated that Hierocles, as we know him from the compilation of Photius, gives a testimony perfectly concordant with that of bishop Nemesius of Emesa on Ammonius' teaching, followed by Origen as well as Plotinus.[1] And there is no doubt that this teaching is at the basis of some of the most striking features of Origen's thought when he opposes pagan cosmologies.

After a whole series of Hellenistic thinkers on whom a biblical influence undoubtedly was exercised, but still without breaking up the original framework, Ammonius Saccas appears as the first to cause the biblical teaching on God and his creation radically to prevail. He was, in fact, born of Christian parents. Raising himself to philosophy, as did others, from the humblest manual labour (he

[1] R. Cadiou, *La jeunesse d'Origène*, Paris, 1936, pp. 186ff.

had been a stevedore at the port of Alexandria, hence his nickname of Saccas), teaching officially at the Museum established by Ptolemy, he does not seem in any way to have denied his Christianity in order to become a philosopher, as Porphyrius makes out in his *Life of Plotinus*.[2] Quite the contrary, what we know with the greatest certainty about his teaching either is of very orthodox Christian inspiration, or else, in areas where the doctrine of the Church had not yet been defined, no definition having as yet been sought out, it does not indicate any more of a departure from orthodoxy than is to be found in his disciple, Origen.

Three major points result from this teaching. The first is that Ammonius not only gives as the origin of the world the will of a transcendent God alone, but also, breaking with the old idea of Hellenism which had still survived even where the idea of creation was most closely approximated, he rejected any idea of a pre-existing matter. While matter has a native disposition to receive the forms imposed on it, this is because it comes from the divine will alone as do these forms themselves.[3]

After this, the world appears to him as being a wholly personal universe, in which he distinguishes pure spirits (*theoi*), angels placed in relationship to the material cosmos, and man in whom the spirit is as it were integrated with the cosmos.[4]

The result, finally, is an anthropology which already corrects Plato by Aristotle. Man in no way appears as a pure spirit fallen into a body naturally hostile to it. Quite the contrary, he is a spirit whose native condition is to be in a body and for whom this constitutes his proper test.[5]

For, just as creation is an act of the pure free will of God, the appearance of created spirits in their various ranks sets a test for them in which it is their will alone, their free will called into existence by that of God, which will determine their sin or their holiness. They do not sin because they are in matter, any more than those who are detached from it are impeccable. They sin or not simply according to whether or not they realize, each in his own place and in a wholly fraternal co-ordination, the design of the divine Wisdom for all things and each thing.

Here, for the first time in Greek philosophy, the cosmological pessimism of Pythagoras or Plato, identifying or tending to identify matter and evil, and Stoic fatalism, identifying providence with an implacable destiny, the very negation of all liberty, are both over-

[2] Porphyrius, *Vita Plotini*, 3.

[3] See Elorduy, *Es Ammonius Sakkas el Seudo-Areopagita?* pp. 513–14, and see Cadiou, *op. cit.*, pp. 190–1.

[4] *Ibid.*, pp. 191–8.

[5] *Ibid.*, pp. 198–203.

come. When these elements which can be considered as certain in the teaching of Ammonius are compared with certain characteristics of that of Origen and with that of Plotinus, several observations are thrust upon us. They bring out the extent to which Plotinus, like Origen, depends on Ammonius.

The first is that Origen is so greatly dominated by the fundamental place, entirely biblical and Christian, given in the teaching of Ammonius to the liberty of creatures as well as of the creator, that he goes beyond the mark. He will not admit, as we see particularly in his *De Principiis*, the original and enduring stability of the created universe as Ammonius conceived it, going from pure spirits to man through the angels who rule the cosmos. For him, every created spirit is destined to be as perfect an image of its creator as possible, and so to arrive at the height of detachment with regard to matter. If all are not in fact at this height, it is because all do not use their freedom equally well. Thus the different degrees of being are only a reflection of the different degrees of the fidelity (or infidelity) of created freedoms in relation to the creative freedom.

Again, for Origen, these inequalities are only provisory. The universe, as we see it, is neither the primitive universe nor the definitive universe. It is now in an intermediate state between the original fall and the *apocatastasis*, the final reintegration which is the whole purpose of the redemption. When this has produced all its effects, the redeemed spirits will find themselves in the blessed equality of a spirituality as pure as is possible to created being (to Origen, this always presupposes a certain corporeity, however spiritualized this may be).[6]

This view of things, with Origen, is connected with his personal thesis, so particularly exposed to the protests of more conservative theologians, according to which souls on the way to reintegration are submitted to a transmigration, or rather a series of transmigrations, corresponding to the successive degrees of their progress. The idea of such a metensomatosis (rather than metampsychosis, since it does not admit the possibility of going from man to animal or plant, nor the other way round) is found in Ammonius. With him, it seems to be directly connected with the same vision of history as pedagogical. But it is also connected with the difficulty of combining Aristotle with Plato: the substantial spirituality of the soul, and its native union with a particular body.

In this regard, it is undeniable that Plotinus inaugurates the solution to the problem which is logically the most coherent, in

[6] See R. Cadiou, *Introduction au système d'Origène*, Paris, 1932, pp. 32ff.

getting rid of these residues of mythology and simply affirming the cosmic unity of the soul. But it is in the line of the problems inherited with the synthesis of Ammonius that such a solution, however original it may be, is also located.

Origen

The young Origen,[7] in whom the thought of Ammonius would reveal to itself certain of the most profound Christian intuitions that it bore within it, was born of Christian parents, and even particularly fervent ones, if we may deduce this from the precocious ardour of his faith. Under the persecution of Severus (202), when his father, Leonidas, was sentenced, his mother had to resort to the stratagem of hiding his garments so that the fifteen-year-old Origen would renounce the idea of running to the tribunal and denouncing himself as a Christian. He made up for it by addressing to his father, whose martyrdom was imminent, a letter which has justifiably been seen as a first sketch of the *Exhortation to Martyrdom* which would later be one of his best works. This father, whom an ancient historian shows us as respectfully kissing the heart of his sleeping son, was not deceived in him.

But the intellectual activity and precocity of Origen were no greater than the youthful enthusiasm of his faith. When their possessions were confiscated, he gained a living for his family by teaching, in spite of his youth. He was only just eighteen when Demetrius called him—something almost beyond belief—to take charge of the catechetical school, in the circumstances and with the results we have already mentioned.

From this moment, as Eusebius insists, he won his auditors even more by the heroic witness that his whole life gave to his faith than by his exceptional brilliance.

> As was his word, it was said, so was his conduct, and as his conduct, so his word. Thereby above all, through the divine power that sustained him, he led thousands of people to emulate him....

His thirst for martyrdom, indeed, sprang from a fervour translated into extremely rigorous asceticism:

> He devoted himself, Eusebius continues, to the most philosophic life possible, as much by the exercise of fasting as by a strict measure of time for sleep, and he made a habit of sleeping

[7] For a complete bibliography, see J. Quasten, *Patrology*, II, pp. 40ff. Origen's work, given in Migne, P.G., XI–XVII, is the subject of a critical edition now being published in the Corpus of Berlin by different authors (we shall indicate the particular editor in each case). The Lommatsch edition is still useful for the works not edited by Berlin.

not on a couch but directly on the ground. He thought he should observe with special attention the words of the Lord about not having two garments, not using sandals, and also about not wasting one's time in taking thought for the future.[8]

It was during these first years, when we can well believe that the violence of his asceticism, like his devouring intellectuality, proceeded from a passionate temperament, that he came to take literally the saying in St Matthew about those who make themselves eunuchs for the Kingdom of God. Here is a first example of those exaggerations which were to put him involuntarily in conflict with the Church, not by reason of any infidelity whatsoever, but because of the kind of childish *naïveté* with which this astonishing precursor, this theologian and spiritual thinker "without father or mother", would to the end rush out on hitherto unexplored paths of intellectual and spiritual adventure.

However wide, even universal, his scientific and philosophic interests still were at this period, he came very quickly to concentrate on holy Scripture and on that scholarly, informed meditation on it which, in his hands, was to become theology as we know it; that is, sacred doctrine methodically set out with all the resources of profane thought. It is only at Caesarea, from 231 on, after the dramatic crisis which we have related, that, having become a priest, he was to combine an activity, religious in its object but profoundly intellectual in its methods, with a great deal of preaching in a much more popular style. The spirituality which is here expressed directly and with relative simplicity had no less been the soul of all his work since the beginning.

We might say that Origen created many of the most permanent literary forms of Christian thought and that he contributed more than anyone else to fix in their forms or to direct the development of those he did not create.

With his *De Principiis,* in which he examines the basic principles of the Christian concept of the world as he sees it, he created the theological treatise. In his *Contra Celsum,* however constrained by the insistence of his friend Ambrose to use a form that did not appeal to him, he gave a model refutation of an adversary of the faith, so detailed and so patient that from this refutation alone we can reconstruct the original work almost in its entirety.

But, above all, he produced lasting models for all the types of work and studies which have Holy Scripture as their object: from the establishment of the critical text, whether in the original or in its versions, with the *Hexapla*, to the great commentaries on St

[8] *Eccles. Hist.*, VI, III, §§ 7–10.

Matthew, St John, the Epistle to the Romans, or the Canticle of Canticles, going through the detailed studies on one or another particularly difficult passage to the Homilies which, on the contrary, make directly available to the faithful the spiritual fruit of scientific research.

Finally, in the same line of spiritual application of religious thinking, he presented the two first great treatises on a major spiritual problem: on Prayer and on Martyrdom.

It is regrettable that almost all his correspondence is lost to us. But the little that we possess and everything that the ancients tell us about it assure us that it constituted, after the Epistles of St Paul, the first and greatest example that Christian antiquity has preserved for us of what we would call a "direction" at once and inseparably intellectual and spiritual.

We have already recalled how, under the persecution of Decius, around 250, the fervour that had animated all this work and found its most direct expression in the *Exhortation to Martyrdom* received its seal. Put to prolonged torture, he died soon after the trial.

It is curious that the nineteenth century retained above all, and sometimes exclusively, the intellectual aspect of this life and this labour. The work of Völker, *Das Vollkommenheitsideal bei Origenes*, was needed to make us realize that this life and labour all bear the mark of the spiritual man far more than that of the theologian as we understand the term and whose type he contributed more than anyone else to create.

The Bible and the Cross

The fact is that .his personality and this work are so fascinating only because they express to the maximum degree the conjunction of an intellectual search, served by the greatest abilities, and a spiritual sense that could find its way nowhere but in the Cross. If there is a Christian humanism in which the substantive has in no way devoured the adjective, it is with this transcendent intellectual, whose intelligence is so human, so concrete, but who remains above all a seeker for God, and who has recognized him from the outset in Christ, in the crucified Christ, whose imprint is stamped on his whole life.

Once again, it is here that the differences between him and Clement shine out much more clearly than the resemblances. However Alexandrian he too may have been, by his information, his universal openness to all currents of thought, Origen is in no way a curiosity-seeker, charmed with the beautiful ideas and images that he collects. He is a man passionately seeking total truth, seeking it everywhere, but with an unequivocal severity towards all those recesses of Greek thought in which this search had bogged down as it were intentionally. And his Christian gnosis, far from ever surprising us as does Clement's by a serenity that we suspect of having been too easily acquired, rather disquiets us by its refusal of any halt in a quest of God, an imitation or better a pursuit of Christ carrying his Cross, in which we never seem to have finished with the detachments needed in order that finally God may be truly "all in all".

The greatest difference between the two gnoses is that Clement's so easily turns back on itself, in order to understand itself, to describe itself, and perhaps to savour itself. Origen's, on the contrary, hardly describes itself at all and, above all, never does so except fragmentarily, wholly taken up as it is with its one unique object: the mystery of Christ, contemplated in the Scriptures.[9] It was in this way, probably, that Origen exercised the deepest and most enduring influence on all later Christian spirituality.

Of course, Christians had not waited for Origen to realize that they had in the Bible the supreme and, in one sense, the unique source of their whole spiritual life, for everything that the Church can give them finds in the Bible its first expression, directly inspired by God. But in the history of the Church hitherto there had been no other example of an intellectual activity, so powerful and so resourceful, wholly devoted to "fathoming the Scriptures", nor, above all, of a spiritual perception so directly magnetized by what is as it were the heart of the Scriptures according to St. Paul: the mystery of Christ, the mystery of his Cross.

In this regard, we need carefully to distinguish a twofold aspect in the contribution of Origen to the meditation of the Bible traditional in the Church. He came to it with all the resources and, inevitably, with something of the dead weight of the culture of his time. As he himself called it in his letter to Gregory the Wonderworker, he "carried away the treasures of Egypt" to devote them to the worship of the Lord. But also, and it is this which is still too little appreciated, beyond anyone else he regained and expressed, in that meditation which was wholly his own, the soul of the most traditional meditation of the Scriptures, Jewish as well as Christian.

From Hellenism, and particularly from Alexandrian Hellenism, he brought to the study of the Bible above all the resources of philology. We might say that not only Christian antiquity, but the whole of the Middle Ages lived on the treasures accumulated by Origen. St Jerome expanded them a little, but perhaps less than might appear, in the direction of Hebraic culture. St Ambrose was

[9] On this theme and its centrality in Origen's work, see Hans Urs von Balthasar, *Parole et Mystère chez Origène*, Paris, 1957.

the first to make them available to the West; St Augustine classified them and exploited them in a systematic way, but without renewing their basis and even diminishing it a little. We have to wait for the great humanists of the Renaissance, such as Erasmus, following Lorenzo Valla, to find in this field as fresh and as extensive a return to the sources. And, again, this return to the sources was directly inspired by a study and admiration of Origen.

Origen's Allegory and Gnosis

However, it is in the philosophy which is superimposed on this philology that the dead weight we have mentioned makes its appearance. The sempiternal accusation levelled at Origen, of having introduced allegorical exegesis into the Church, is an absurdity. It presupposes an almost total ignorance of ancient Christian exegesis and of the Jewish exegesis from which it proceeded (rabbinical exegesis as much as and even more than that of Philo). But it is true that the methods which Origen used to develop allegorical exegesis, and which have much in common with those of Philo, include, like the latter, some measure of artifice. This artifice is connected, without any doubt, in the mentality of Origen as in that of Philo, with popularized Platonic cosmology. The idea that the visible world is an image, and is of concern only as being an image, of the invisible realities, has a central importance here. We should note that Origen, after Philo, made a great deal of the fact that strikingly analogous lines of thought are to be observed in what is most Hebraic in Jewish thought: the statement in Exodus that Moses made the tabernacle, and all the objects used in worship, according to an ideal model that the Lord had shown him on the mountain. Hence this conclusion, perhaps a little precipitate:

> It is certain that these mysteries have been known and completely grasped by the man who was ravished to the third heaven and who, finding himself in heaven, has seen the true Jerusalem, the city of God, who has also seen Mount Sion, in whatever place it is found, who has also seen Hebron and all the cities that Scripture shows us scattered here and there; and not only has he seen all this, but he has grasped in spirit the reasons for all this.... And so, we who believe that here are things divine and mysterious, let us make ourselves, by our actions, by our merits, worthy of these secrets, capable of understanding them, so that, when we have worthily understood them, we may attain them in the heavenly heritage.[10]

[10] *In Jesu Nave Hom.*, 23, 4; P.G., XII, 938D. Lebreton, in vol. II of Fliche and Martin's *Histoire de l'Église*, Paris, 1955, p. 276, connects precisely this text with the curious declarations of the *De Principiis* (II, x, 5–7) as to what we shall discover in heaven.

This text helps us to see the twofold potential deformation which such an infusion of Platonism could introduce into Christian exegesis and spirituality. First, the spiritual world here becomes a simple duplicate of the sensible world, exaggeratedly parallel in all its details and, in return, completely foreign in its substance. The consequence is that history is in danger of evaporating into pure symbols of unchangeable realities: neither here below nor "in heaven" could it be said that anything happens. Earthly events are only the shadows cast by unchanging spiritual realities.[11]

Actually, this is only a danger into which Origen was sometimes drawn by the bent of the intellectual equipment he was using. But the critics make a singular mistake in seeing in his exegesis only these miscarriages and in judging his methods by devoting themselves preferably to the times when they turn in a vacuum.

Once again, in his exegesis and in what is most decidedly allegorical about it, there is also something quite different. This is what supports, as it were, those great intuitions, so directly biblical and Christian, that electrified Origen in the teaching of Ammonius, in which, doubtless for the first time, they became completely explicit. Hence his own very severe criticism—as we must incessantly repeat—of that Greek thought which was closed in on itself, however shrewd he may have been in his positive appreciation of the particular resources it could offer for the formulation of a Christian thought. For Origen, better than anyone else, appreciated the decisive importance, for a Christian view of the world, of the supreme biblical revelation: that the world is the setting and, as it were, the stake in a drama in which the mysterious interweaving of two free wills is being worked out, one of which proceeds from the other but is no less free for all that: the will of God, the will of spiritual creatures. And so, however anxious he is always to go on from the simple anecdotal detail of biblical "histories" to the permanent reality of the "Spirit", he runs no risk of profoundly misunderstanding the fact that the Spirit reaches us at the very heart of history.[12]

To this extent, his allegorical exegesis or, more precisely, his "spiritual" exegesis in the sense in which he understood this term, does not cause history to evaporate into an idea. On the contrary, it makes us grasp in past history and achieve in our own history the coming of the Spirit, thanks to the incarnate Word. Oriented thus, allegorical exegesis becomes as it were the discovery, in

[11] See Daniélou, *Origène*, Paris, 1948, pp. 175ff., and especially 195.

[12] On this whole question of allegorical exegesis in Origen, the masterly work of H. de Lubac, *Histoire et Esprit, L'intelligence de l'Écriture d'après Origène*, provides clarifications that might well be considered definitive (Paris, 1950).

Scripture itself, of the law according to which, as the Word condescends to the world and to man, the Spirit comes to penetrate and transfigure them. And this law, or rather this mystery of history, which is the great mystery of God's Wisdom spoken of by St Paul, came to appear to Origen as the law of the cross.

To him, the Cross is neither a mere a-temporal symbol nor an isolated event, fallen from heaven into our history but never really belonging to it. The Cross is what is sought in the preparatory revelation of the Old Testament, what is found, or rather given, in the definitive revelation of the Gospel, but which is only to be fully assimilated in the total experience of the Church. Within this experience, each individual experience is inserted as an integrating part of the eschatological realization of the whole body of Christ.[13]

All this is properly the mystery of the Word, as he conceived it, the Logos making but one with the Son of God, but only becoming accessible to us in his historical incarnation, from whom are inseparable all those human words of the Old and the New Testaments, in which and by which the eternal Word has come near to us and has saved us. The historical events of the Old Testament, and the original revelation which cannot be detached from them, find, therefore, their focal truth, in some way—the truth they prepared for and sketched out, but which in return, alone fully illuminates them—only in the event, the supreme revelation of the Cross of Jesus. And again, if this Cross is to be understood, to have, in those who have understood it, the fullness of the realization towards which it tends of itself, it must become the cross of the Church, which is realized in the cross that we all carry, each on his own account, following after Jesus. In this way the literal sense flowers properly speaking into the mystical sense, related to Christ and to the Church, as the body is revealed only in the soul. Yet the mystical sense itself finds its spiritual realization in the moral sense, by which the Christian makes his own the profound reality which the faith has as it were traced out under his eyes.[14]

[13] See the texts collected and commented on by H. Urs von Balthasar, *op. cit.*

[14] This definition and this distinction of the mystical sense and of the moral sense is formulated with particular clarity by de Lubac, *op. cit.*, pp. 139ff. He shows very clearly that Origen sometimes contents himself with a moral sense, more or less inspired by Philo, and in any case having nothing specifically Christian and then adding the mystical sense as the properly Christian sense by which the Old Testament leads to the New. Elsewhere—and it is here that he shows himself at the same time most happily traditional—it is from this mystical sense, referred to Christ and the Church, that he draws a moral sense, which can then be called "spiritual" in the full meaning of the term.

Here we meet once again the distinction, so often misinterpreted, which Origen held to so strongly and which is as it were the hinge of his whole concept of gnosis: between "simple faith" and "supreme faith": *psile pistis* and *kurios pisteuein*:[15]

Is this a question of two faiths properly speaking, distinct and having different objects, so that we would have to go on from common Christian belief to some esoteric ideas, reserved for a few persons? Those who have believed this, in connection with Origen as with Clement, on the basis of current ways of speaking too literally interpreted, have still less excuse with him than with his predecessor. For Origen has too clearly explained to us himself what he means by a distinction of this nature for us still to be able to interpret it wrongly. It is clarified particularly, in the same Commentary on John in which the preceding formula is found and a few pages away from it, by the distinction between believing simply "in the name of Jesus" (*eis to onoma autou*) and believing "in Him" (*eis auton*).[16] This amounts to saying that there is absolutely no question of a distinction between faiths having a different object, but rather between different stages of one and the same faith in us. In the former, the object remains in some way exterior to us, it is only a word to us; now we are incorporated into it, the Spirit has placed its whole reality within us. This goes along with the distinction that he makes elsewhere between Christ "with us" and Christ "in us". Faith becomes gnosis as this transition is brought about.

The development of gnosis, according to Origen, follows the stages marked out by Clement: the discovery of the meaning of the visible world as the revelation of a universe of persons placed in existence by the supreme Person of the Father. And this is the prelude to the discovery of the meaning of the Scriptures as the revelation of the Father sending us his Word who is his Son to bring us back, from the unlikeness into which sin has made us fall, to the likeness to which the cross alone can restore us.[17] In certain respects, this gnosis, with Origen, not only forges as it were a propedeutic for itself in the preparatory exercises of philosophical reflection, but it is itself organized into an intellectual system by the theology, thought out and built up, which is at once its support and its product.

Yet here is not its true reality. This remains eminently spiritual, whatever may be the intellectuality with which it is clarified and

[15] *Comm. in Jo.*, x, 43; ed. Preuschen, p. 221, 13ff. and 23ff.

[16] *Ibid.*, x, 44; p. 223, 5ff.; cf. the exact observations of Marguerite Hart, *Origène et la fonction révélatrice du Verbe incarné*, Paris, 1958, pp. 264ff.

[17] Cf. Völker, *op. cit.*, pp. 91ff.

sometimes overcharged. And it might be said that this basic spirituality which remains the property of the Christian gnosis of Alexandria, however intellectualized it may ever seem to be, is characterized in distinction from Clement both by an asceticism of the Cross and by a mysticism of the Logos.

Origen's Asceticism

On this asceticism and its close connection with this mysticism, the chief text on which Völker has rightly concentrated the attention which it merits but which no other modern scholar has given it, is that of the *27th Homily on Numbers*. Here we touch on the connection between Origen's spirituality and exegesis and Philo's, and, in the latter, on what he has that is drawn from the deepest Jewish spirituality.

The soul must progressively uproot itself from the world in which it is buried, in forgetfulness of God, by the *pathe*, the egoistic desires that have ruled it.

In this process of detachment, it must recognize not only that it must strip itself of what weighs it down and draws it along with a wholly material weight, but also that it has to struggle against the perverse spiritual powers who work in a positive way, by playing on its desires, to turn it away from God.

This detachment and this struggle are carried out only by an imitation, which is also a participation, in the life of Christ.

These are the three great ideas at the basis of this Homily and of all Origen's asceticism.

The imitation-participation in the life of Christ is announced from the outset as the theme in some sense underlying the whole of our ascetical and mystical life. For the stages which it is to go through, sketched out by the stages of the wandering in the desert treated in this Homily, make but one thing with the stages by which the Word, in becoming incarnate, first descended to us, and then, in returning to the Father, ascends again to Him:

> The sons of Israel were in Egypt, in the works of king Pharaoh, given up to straw and brick, until the moment when groaning they cried to the Lord and when, to hear their laments, He sent them His word through Moses and had them come out of Egypt. When we also were in Egypt, I mean in the errors of this world and the darkness of ignorance, when we were working at the works of the Devil, in the midst of concupiscences and carnal pleasures, the Lord had pity on our distress, and He sent the Logos, His only Son, to snatch us from ignorance and error and lead us to the light of His divine law. . . .

Moses expressed himself exactly when he said: "The sons of Israel will go up with their Strength."[18] What is their Strength, if not Christ, who is the "Strength of God"? He who goes up, goes up with Him who has come down to us, and he tries to arrive at the place whence He came down, for He did not come down from necessity but from kindness, so as to fulfil the word: "He who has come down is the same who has again gone up."[19]

This descent and reascent of the Logos, finding its fulfilment in us in the ascetic life, comes to detach us from this world in which sin has as it were ensnared us and bring us back to God.

"Moses wrote their stages and their stations because of the word of the Lord."[20] He wrote these things, therefore, "because of the word of the Lord", so that, in reading them, we might see how many stages, stations, await us in the journey towards the Kingdom, so that we might prepare ourselves for this route, so that at the sight of the road that we must travel we should not allow ourselves to waste away in idleness and inaction for the duration of our life, so that we should not be delayed by the vanities of this world, so that we should not take pleasure in all the delights of seeing or hearing, or touching, or smelling or tasting, so that the days would not fly by in this way, so that time would not go on without our hastening to cover the distance of the journey to be made, so that we should not fail on the way, so that we should not undergo the fate of those who could not arrive at the goal, whose "members fell in the desert".[21] We are on a journey, we came into this world only to go from strength to strength, and not to remain on the earth by love of earthly objects, like him who said: "I will destroy my barns and build bigger ones . . . and I will say to my soul: My soul, you have much grain laid up for many years . . . eat, drink and enjoy yourself."[22] Ah, may the Lord not say to us as to that man: "You fool, this night they will take away your soul." He does not say, "this day", but "this night": that man is struck down by night as were "the first-born of the Egyptians", because he loved the world and shared the life "of the princes of this world of darkness".[23] Now this world is called darkness and night, because of those who live in ignorance and do not receive the light of the truth. These do not start from Ramasses and do not go to Succoth.[24]

[18] Num. 33. 1; the explication which immediately follows is an implicit quotation of 1 Cor. 1. 24.

[19] *Hom. 27 on Numbers*, 2–3. The last phrase is a quotation of Eph. 4. 10.

[20] Num. 33. 2. [21] Heb. 3. 17. [22] Luke 12. 18–20.

[23] Eph. 6. 14. [24] *Ibid.*, 8, pp. 527–8.

We should note that this allegorization of the exodus is directly connected with the theme of the wandering of the patriarchs and their descendants, as developed in the Epistle to the Hebrews. More precisely, the insistence on the fact that the return journey to God will not end in entering into his rest (cf. the next paragraph in the same Homily) unless we renounce earthly lusts, comes from the allegorization of the same theme in the Second Epistle to the Corinthians, where St Paul himself is certainly tributary to more ancient Jewish sources.

The Warfare against the Demons

The last words in our quotation, however, already bring up, behind the necessary detachments and breaking-away, the struggle against the demons and their captivity from which we have to escape. Further on, in fact, the Homily explains how the conversion that the divine Logos accomplishes in us is the vengeance on the gods of Egypt mentioned in Exodus at the time when the Hebrews escaped:

> It seems to me that vengeance is carried out on the demons when a man, drawn by their seductions to the worship of idols but converted by the Logos of the Lord, renders Him the worship that is due Him; by the very fact of this conversion, a vengeance is carried on on the seducer. In the same way, if a man drawn into fornication by the demons is converted to a good life, loves chastity and weeps for his errors, the very tears of his repentance are a searing burn for the demon and so vengeance is taken on the author of seduction. In the same way, again, if someone turns from pride to humility, from luxury to moderation, on all these occasions, he scourges and torments the demons who have led him into these errors. To what torments are they not a prey, do you think, when they see someone, following the Word of the Lord, "selling all his goods, giving them to the poor . . . taking up his cross and following Christ"? But what goes beyond all other torments and punishments for them is to see someone applying himself to the Word of God, and deepening by an ardent study the gnosis of the divine law and the mysteries of the Scriptures. . . .[25]

The theme of the struggle against the demons is equally central in Origen's view of Christian asceticism and his view of the redemption. It illuminates the cross of the Christian and the cross of Christ, or rather does so by this Cross itself.

[25] *Ibid.*, pp. 530–1. On this and the following texts, cf. S. Bettencourt, *Doctrina ascetica Origenis*, Vatican City, 1945.

Here is what he says again about the spiritual combat in the 14th and 15th Homilies *In Jesu Nave*:

> You see the multitude of the hosts of the adverse powers and the wicked demons that are aroused against Jesus and the army of Israel. All these demons, before the coming of our Lord and Saviour, possessed the souls of men in complete tranquillity and security: they reigned over their minds and over their bodies. But when the kindness and mercy of God our Saviour appeared on earth and taught us to live lovingly and holily in this world, separated from all contagion of sin,[26] in such a way that each soul regains its liberty and the image of God to which it was created in the beginning, then the battles and combats begin on the part of these wicked spirits who up till then owned men's souls. If the first demons are conquered, then others much more numerous arise and join them, conspiring for evil, for they always flee away from good. If they are conquered a second time, other still more wicked powers arise a third time; and the more the people of God increase, the more this people grows and is multiplied, the more also the demons assemble in still greater numbers to fight against it.[27]

This struggle of the ascetic against the forces of the devil as Origen sees it, we should note, like that of Christ himself, does not concern him alone but the whole body of Christ:

> So long as the enemy powers who work sin in us do not come on, so long as they do not tempt us to evil, do not arouse us to combat, they cannot be put to death and destroyed. This is why we say that God authorizes and, even more, that He excites the adverse powers in some way to come out against us, so that we may be victorious over them and that they themselves may be put to death. . . .
>
> . . . And I think that all the saints, in fighting against these spirits of evil, in dominating them, in overcoming each of them, diminish the army of the demons and in some way destroy a great number of them. For example, if someone triumphs by a chaste and pure life over the spirit of fornication, it is no longer possible for that spirit which has been conquered by this saint again to attack another man; but, like those spirits who asked Jesus not to be precipitated into the abyss—which the Lord momentarily allowed through a personal provision—so it would seem natural that all the wicked spirits who are conquered by the saints are thrown into the abyss or into the exterior darkness or into the place that is fitting for them, by Christ, the just judge and ruler of this conflict in the life of men: it is for this reason that, since a great number of demons

26 An allusion to Titus 2. 12.

27 *In Jesu Nave Hom.*, 14; ed. Baehrens, II, pp. 376–7.

have already been conquered, the pagans can come to the faith, which would not be possible if all their legions still subsisted in their original integrity.[28]

This vision of the ascetical combat is dependent on the completely Pauline vision that Origen always gives of Christ's Cross as his triumph over the rebel powers. Thus he writes in another of the *Homilies on Josue*:

> The son of God was visibly crucified on the Cross, but invisibly, on the same Cross, it was the devil who was crucified with his principalities and his powers. Does this not appear true to you if I bring you the witness of Paul: "He has despoiled the principalities and the powers and given them up boldly to be a spectacle, triumphing over them by the Cross?[29] There are, then, two aspects to the cross of the Lord: the one is that which made St Peter say that Christ crucified has left us an example,[30] and the other that according to which this cross was the trophy of his victory over the devil, by which He was at once crucified and glorified.[31]

This same text from Colossians, which comes back on Origen's lips or under his pen every time he mentions the cross of Jesus, is applied equally to the cross of the Christian. For is not this cross, in his vision, always the cross of Jesus?

> Each of those who are crucified with Christ despoils the principalities and the powers and gives them up to be a spectacle, triumphing over them on the cross, or rather, Christ effects this in them.[32]

The descriptions of this spiritual combat which Origen multiplies witness to the same use of the resources of Stoic psychology which St Paul was the first to exemplify. Once again, these descriptions also are touched by more than a trace of the Neo-Pythagorean or Platonizing idealism of the period (and its pessimism with regard to this world). But the basis of it is the restoration of the freedom of man in the freedom of God which is at the centre of all the metaphysics of Origen as of Ammonius Saccas, and is so essentially Christian. At the time of the Pelagian controversies, his insistence on this aspect of things caused Origen to be suspected or accused of having reduced grace to the rôle of a simple aid to human freedom. Actually, if the practical and ascetical point of view which is his in these questions always causes him to start with

28 *In Jesu Nave Hom.*, 15, 5 and 6; Baehrens, II, pp. 389–90.
29 Col. 2. 14–15. 30 1 Peter 2. 21.
31 *In Jesu Nave Hom.*, 8, 3; Baehrens, II, p. 338.
32 *Comm. in Matt.*, xii, 25; ed. Klostermann, I, pp. 126–7.

the liberty of man which is in some way to regenerate itself, grace, in very clear texts, appears to him not only as coordinated with this effort, but as anterior to it, both logically and chronologically.

The Mysticism of the Logos

But the primordial rôle of grace appears most evidently not in the ascetical but in the mystical aspect of the ascent of the soul. The *27th Homily on Numbers,* to which we must always return, mentions on various occasions the "visions" bestowed on the soul that progresses in the ascetical way. It seems that Origen distinguishes two kinds. The first are characteristic of the initial stages and incite us to spiritual effort. They nourish hope while its realization is still far off:

> We begin indeed to observe, to perceive hope, to come and measure the height of our progress; and we grow little by little, being more nourished by hope than wearied by our efforts. This pause, or this station, is "facing Magdalum". For Magdalum is translated as magnificence. With the ascent to this observatory and the magnificence of future things under our eyes, the soul, as we have said, is restored and nourished by great hopes. For it is still on the way, and not settled in perfection.[33]

A little further on, Origen is more precise about these visions that accompany the spiritual ascent itself. But he emphasizes their possible ambiguity. In the struggle against the demon powers, visions can just as well be the deceiving work of the devils as a divine gift. Hence the importance of the gift of discernment of spirits. We should note that here we find again one of the themes inherited from Jewish spirituality by primitive Christian spirituality. But here we discover perhaps the first example of its application to what are called today mystical phenomena.

> They left the Red Sea and camped in the desert of Sin. Sin is translated: bush or temptation. Here is when the hope of true goods begins to smile on you. But whence comes the hope of true goods? It was in a bush that the Lord appeared and answered Moses, and this was the first apparition of the Lord to the sons of Israel. But it is not without reason that Sin is also translated temptation. Sometimes the angel of iniquity "transforms himself into an angel of light".[34] And so we must mistrust ourselves and take precautions to discern gnostically the nature of the vision, as did Josue, son of Nave, when he had a vision: knowing that it hid a temptation, he immediately asked the being that appeared to him: "Are you one of ours

[33] *Hom. 27 on Numbers*, 9; ed. Mehat, p. 535.
[34] 2 Cor. 11. 4.

or of our enemies?"[35] So, then, the soul which in its progress has come to the point of having the discernment of visions thereby proves that it is "spiritual" in "discerning all things".[36] This is why, among spiritual gifts, the "discernment of spirits" is mentioned as a gift of the Holy Spirit.[37]

But the visions of the perfect are quite different from these preparatory visions which remain equivocal:

> Then "we arrive at Rathma" or "Pharam". Rathma is glossed: consummate vision; Pharam, visible face. Why does the soul not grow to the point that, insensible to the sorrows of the flesh, it has consummate visions, it understands the perfect meaning of things, it knows with more fullness and depth the reasons for the incarnation of the Logos of God and the forms that clothe the economy of this mystery?[38]

Doubtless we must not try to clarify too greatly what these various "visions" are. We are on more certain ground in emphasizing that they have their place in a spiritual progress in which already Origen saw the moving force, so to say, of the continuous ascension of the soul as being a providential alternation of "refreshments" that encourage it and "tribulations" or "bitternesses" that exercise it:

> "They departed from the bitter waters and camped at Helim. Helim is a place where there are twelve springs of water and seventy-two palm trees." See, after the bitterness and difficulties of temptations, what delightful places welcome you. You would not have arrived at the palm-trees, if you had not endured the bitter trials; you would not have arrived at the sweetness of the springs, if you had not overcome sadness and difficulties. Not that this is the end of the journey and the achievement of everything, but God, who rules the economy of souls, places along the very course of the journey, in the intervals of work, refreshments thanks to which the soul, reanimated and refreshed, comes back ready to confront the rest of the work.[39]

If, then, these visions along the road nourish hope, it seems that the "consummate visions" correspond to what St Paul calls "the understanding of the mystery": an interiorized comprehension of the Scriptures causing us to attain the very heart of the design of God as it is realized in Christ. Exegetes of these texts have tended to intellectualize them in an exaggerated way, as if the fully developed "gnosis" which they describe was nothing but

[35] Josue 5. 13. [36] 1 Cor. 2. 15.
[37] *Hom. 27 on Numbers*, 11; ed. Mehat, p. 540. The last words allude to 1 Cor. 12. 10.
[38] *Ibid.*, 12; pp. 543–4. [39] *Ibid.*, 11; pp. 537–8.

theological speculation. It is first of all an illumination: the "perfect" are "illuminated by God with the illumination of gnosis".[40] The Logos gives them a wine that causes them "to escape (*existon*) from human things, to be carried away and drunk with a drunkenness not unreasonable but divine."[41] Finally, the same commentary on John which gives us this formula explains how *ginoskein* is to be understood in the Johannine sense, as a fusion and a union: *to ginoskein anti tou anakekrasthai kai henosthai*.[42]

All this leads to the developing of Origen's gnosis into a true mysticism of the Logos, as we have said. This is formulated by two complementary series of images, both of which will be of great importance throughout all later spiritual tradition.

The first is that of the growth of the Logos in the soul. The second is that of the marriage of the Logos and the soul, inside of the union of Christ and the Church. The first theme is developed in connection with Luke 2. 52: "Jesus grew in stature and grace". The second fills the *Commentary on the Canticle of Canticles*.

In a passage from the Prologue to this latter commentary[43] as well as in a page of the *14th Homily on Jeremias*,[44] we find Origen interpreting the verse of Luke on the growth of Christ as the growth of the Logos in us, by means of progress in the virtues and—inseparable from this—the expansion of gnosis. This theme should be compared, as Völker has done,[45] with the developments of the *Commentary on St John* concerning the transition from the presence of Christ "with us" to his presence "in us".[46]

But it is chiefly the theme of the marriage of the Logos with the soul that serves to express what might be called Origen's mysticism, thus determining, in a whole tradition of spiritual commentaries on the Canticle, one of the principal veins of later mysticism. We should note that this theme is, for Origen, something quite other than an occasional development into which he was led solely by the study of Solomon's Canticle. On the contrary, this study gathers together a series of themes related to the idea to be found more or less throughout the whole of his work. Whether he is speaking of the beauty of the soul, the Bride, and that of the Logos, the Bridegroom (who is Truth), of their marriage and their spiritual union, of its fruitfulness, or of the impossibility here below of remaining always on the heights of this union (hence the alternations

40 Ps. I, XI, 382; Lommatsch.
41 *Comm. in Jo.*, I, 30; Preuschen, p. 37, 15ff.
42 *Comm. in Jo.*, XIV, 4; Preuschen, p. 303, 2; cf. p. 320, 17ff.
43 *Comm. in Cant.*, prologue; ed. Baehrens, p. 85, 14ff.
44 *In Jer., Hom.*, 14, 10; ed. Klostermann, p. 114, 29ff.
45 *Op. cit.*, p. 99.
46 *Comm. in Jo.*, X, 10; Preuschen, p. 17, 29ff.

of dryness and interior joy, connected with the flights of the Logos who goes away only to deepen the soul's desire, to wound it and burn it in his love), or finally, of the entire absorption of the soul in longing for her Beloved: all these themes, developed in the commentary on the Canticle, as Völker has clearly shown, have characteristic echoes throughout the whole of Origen's work.[47]

There is no doubt that the growth of the Logos in the soul, his marriage with it, for Origen, are already charged with the mystical content which, during the following generations, will be brought out with increasing clarity: these themes refer, that is, to a true spiritual experience in which the soul is directly conscious, under the action of the Spirit, of the union effected between her and the Logos. However, there is no longer any doubt that the locus of this experience, from beginning to end, remains a more and more intimate, more and more personal assimilation of the profound sense of the Scriptures. This is why the bridal mysticism of the Soul and the Logos is always inserted as it were within the theology of the marriage of Christ and the Church. The *Commentary* does nothing, in this regard, except interiorize and individualize what the *Homilies on the Canticle* develop on the Christological and ecclesiological level.

And so we read, in the first of these Homilies:

> Understand that the Bridegroom is Christ, and the Church that Bride without spot or wrinkle of whom it is written that Christ will present her to Himself all glorious, without spot or wrinkle or anything of the kind, but holy and immaculate. As to those who, while still being of the faithful, are not such to this degree but seem to have in a certain measure obtained salvation, observe that these are the believing souls who are presented as young maidens beside the Bride. By the men who are with the Bridegroom, understand in return the Angels and those who have arrived at the stature of the perfect man. See, then, in my opinion, four different orders: the one Bridegroom and the one Bride, the two choirs which sing together, the Bride singing with the maidens and the Bridegroom with His companions.[48]

And the *Commentary* says:

> This Scripture speaks of that love with which the blessed soul burns and is enflamed for the Logos of God, and she sings this epithalamium by the Spirit, through whom the Church is united and joined to her heavenly Bridegroom, Christ, desiring to unite (*misceri*) with Him through the Logos, to conceive of Him and to be saved in this chaste bringing forth of her children, when

[47] *Op. cit.*, pp. 104–9.
[48] *In Cant. Hom.* I, 1; ed. Baehrens, pp. 28–9.

> they live in faith and holiness, having been conceived in the sobriety of the seed of the Word and sent into the world and engendered either by the immaculate Church, or by the soul, seeking nothing corporal or material, but burning with the one love of the Word of God.[49]

So it is again that the same transition, from the mere hearing of the voice of Christ to the vision of his face (which is the passage from the Old Testament to the New) is also the progress of the soul in the knowledge of the Logos, by a deeper and deeper perception of the truths of Scripture.[50]

In the whole of actual life, the Logos is already present for the faithful soul, but he is also always still to come, and to this extent still absent:

> Thus, sometimes the Bridegroom is present and He teaches, sometimes we say He is absent, and we desire Him, both the one and the other are fitting both to the Church and to the fervent (*studiosa*) soul. Indeed, when He allows the Church to suffer persecutions and tribulations, He seems to be absent from her; and when again she progresses in peace and flourishes in faith and good works, she understands that He is present with her. And so it is for the soul; when she is seeking a meaning and desires to recognize things obscure and hidden, so long as she cannot do so, the Logos of God is undoubtedly absent from her. But when what she is seeking comes to mind and appears to her, who can doubt that the Logos of God is there, when He enlightens her understanding and gives her the light of gnosis? And again we feel that He has left us and then returned through everything that is opened or closed to our perceptions. And we will endure this until we become such that not only He revisits us frequently, but that He deigns to dwell with us. . . .[51]

After this, it is easy to see that the problem which Völker raised: whether Origen's mysticism includes ecstasy, in whatever way this be understood, is a false problem. His mysticism means a going beyond the simple external view of things and of Scripture itself, to enter into the most mysterious realities which the world and that new world which is the divine Word, at the heart of the created world, are to open out to the "gnostic". But this going beyond and this entrance are the most profound experience of a faith to which "the love of God poured out in our hearts by the Holy Spirit" has as it were given substance. This, as Origen conceived it, could not be reduced to any particular psychological experience.

49 *Com. in Cant.*, prologue; *ibid.*, p. 74.
50 *Com. in Cant.*, III; *ibid.*, pp. 201–6.
51 *Ibid.*, pp. 202–3.

Like Clement, Origen contrasts his "gnostic", "pneumatic" or even "perfect" Christian with the ordinary Christian. But with the dynamism that characterizes his whole spirituality, we should not be surprised to find that he emphasizes the relativity of this "perfection". Apparently "impeccable", if he is compared with ordinary men, before God the "gnostic" is the humblest of men and the most conscious of his weakness. And, in any case, here below spiritual progress can have no end. The *17th Homily of Numbers* formally states that here "gnosis" always remains the infinite pursuit of an infinite object, a quest essentially unachievable.

> ... For those who labour at Wisdom and gnosis, as there is no end to their efforts—for where will be the limit of the Wisdom of God?—the more we approach it, the more depths we discover; the more we examine it, the more we understand its ineffable and incomprehensible character; for the Wisdom of God is incomprehensible and inestimable—for those, I say, who advance along the route of the Wisdom of God, Balaam does not praise their houses, for they have not arrived at the end of the journey, but he admires the tents with which they always uproot themselves and always make progress; and the more progress they make, the more the route of the progress to be made lengthens out and tends to the infinite. Such is the reason why, considering in spirit their progress, he calls them tents of Israel.
>
> In truth, whoever makes some progress in gnosis and has acquired some experience in this domain knows this well: hardly arrived at some speculation, at some knowledge of the spiritual mysteries, the soul sojourns there as in a tent; but after having explored other regions, going on from these first discoveries, and having accomplished other kinds of intellectual progress, folding its tents in some way, it tends higher and there establishes the dwelling of its spirit, fixed in the stability of the senses [of Scripture]. But again, departing from there, it discovers other spiritual senses, which appear after the first; and so it is that always "tending towards what is ahead",[52] the soul seems to advance like the nomads with their tents. The moment never comes when the soul, encircled with the fire of gnosis, can give herself time and rest; she is always again flung forward from the good towards the better, and from this better towards still higher sublimities.[53]

It follows that the *apatheia*, which characterizes the gnostic of Origen like that of Clement, has a different coloration with Origen. He emphasizes the fact that *agape* overflows it. Not only is

52 Phil. 3. 14.
53 *Hom. 17 on Numbers*, 4; ed. Mehat, pp. 347-9.

apatheia a gift of God: "a purity of soul that proceeds from his grace",[54] not only do we remain *apathes* "only in the hands of God",[55] but *apatheia* is in itself inferior to "blessing", that is the expansion of the *agape* of the gnostic towards his brothers, in active charity.[56] In the final analysis, everything takes on its true meaning for the gnostic only in the entire ordination of his life to the glory of God.

Mysticism of the Logos and Mysticism of God

The mysticism of the Logos that we have examined expands, in fact, into a mysticism of God. If we took literally a text from the *De principiis*,[57] we might think that two quite distinct stages were meant, as if we were to go from one object of contemplation to another, from one personal relationship to another. For this text contrasts those who come to understand God inasmuch as he is Wisdom with those who arrive at being capable of God simply and solely in such a way that he is "all in all". A text of the Commentary on St John follows the same line of thought, telling us that "we cannot arrive in the Father's presence without previously having been raised by ascending to the divinity of the Son, by which we can be led as by the hand to the beatitude of the Father."[58]

In reality, this mysticism of God is not meant to replace a mysticism of the Logos, which would then be only preparatory. It is simply the explication of everything implied in the mysticism of the Logos himself, who is essentially the revealer of the Father. Here we need to recall Origen's trinitarian theology. The dynamism of the Trinity is necessarily reflected in the dynamism of the gnostic experience. Wholly referred to the Father, as he is the expression of him, the Logos leads us to him, to the vision of "the face of the Father who is in heaven",[59] simply by the deepening of the knowledge we are granted of the Logos himself. And, just as the flesh of the Logos does not vanish from our awareness when we discover in it the revelation of the Logos who has become flesh, neither does the knowledge of the Logos disappear in the knowledge of the Father: we must rather say that it is consummated in it.

In this state, our spirit "is divinized in what it contemplates".[60] As

[54] Ps. 17, XII, 63, Lommatsch.
[55] *Frag. hom. in Jer.* 30, ed. Baehrens, p. 214, 18ff.
[56] *Ibid.*
[57] *De Principiis*, III, 6, 9; ed. Koetschau, p. 290, 20ff.
[58] *Com. in Jo.*, I, 27; Preuschen, p. 35, 4ff.
[59] Ps. 26, XII, 112, Lommatsch.
[60] *Com. in Jo.*, XXXII, 27; Preuschen, p. 472, 30.

Origen says to Celsus, "it is raised to friendship with God and to communion with Him"[61] by a "participation in the divinity".[62]

Here it is Origen's Christology that enlightens us as to what he means. Christ, indeed, is the model of our perfection, so that in him the soul is united to the divinity, not only to the point of *koinonia*, but even of *henosis*, as a fire unites with another fire so completely that now there is only one fire.[63]

As Völker again has brought out, the *Treatise on Prayer* has us follow the line of the phases of this mystical development through the phases of prayer itself: *deesis*, asking for goods that are spiritual but still limited; *proseuke*, in which we abandon ourselves to pure intercourse with God; and *doxologia*, in which we are wholly absorbed in his glorification. With Origen as with Clement, as vocal prayer is interiorized and purified, it goes beyond itself into the prayer of silence, characterizing the state of union with God in a liberation from the body. Then prayer becomes vision, but it is a vision in love, and so it flowers into *enteuxis*, that is, intercession for our brothers.[64]

Origen's insistence, in this treatise, on the fact that prayer must always ascend to the Father through the Son, and never stop at the latter,[65] must be understood in the same way as we have explained the opening out of the mysticism of the Logos into a mysticism of God. In both cases, and for the same reason, there is no question of relegating Christ to a secondary rank, as if his divinity was not fully recognized. It is simply a matter of adapting our participation in the life of the Trinity to the dynamism of this life, which causes everything to reascend to the Father through the Son in the Spirit, as everything proceeds from the Father in the inverse order.

Martyrdom remains for Origen, as we said above, the perfection of that "knowledge" of God of which the divine Word is the source, the knowledge developed only in prayer that penetrates and transforms the whole of life, at the price of a crucifying asceticism. Here is revealed, in fact, how profoundly the Cross characterizes Origen's mysticism itself. With him, there is not first an ascesis of imitation of Christ, then a mysticism of the Logos, and finally a mysticism of God. It must rather be said that the believer, in participating in the cross of Jesus, passing on to gnosis, consummates his union with the Logos, which union itself is perfected in "God all in all".

61 *Contra Celsum*, III, 28; ed. Koetschau, p. 226, 17.
62 *Ibid.*, 37; p. 234, 2ff.
63 Cf. *De Principiis*, II, 6, 3, and *Contra Celsum*, VI, 47.
64 XIV, 2; Koetschau, p. 331.
65 XV, 1; *ibid.*, p. 333.

This again is verified in the portrait that Origen has drawn for us, alongside that of the martyr: the portrait of the doctor, who, having penetrated the sense of the Scriptures, opens it out to others. It is his own portrait that he has drawn here without seeming to be aware of it. We cannot do better than use, as the conclusion to this study, the summary given of this portrait by Hans Urs von Balthasar.

> The Church alone conserves Scripture intact and understands it, since she has the Spirit who dictated it. In her, "Jesus seeks instruments through whom He may teach". The doctors are therefore truly "the lips of Christ", the "psalter of Christ", and her teaching, the temple of the Word. In this temple is renewed every day the miracle of the multiplication of the loaves—of the Bread of souls distributed through the hands of apostles: "So long as the loaves remain whole, nobody restores his strength, nobody is satisfied, and we do not see the loaves themselves multiplied.... Not unless these loaves have been broken into morsels by the disciples, that is to say, unless the letter has been turned over and over and broken up, is its meaning made available to all."
>
> And there remain twelve baskets, not of fragments and débris, but of accumulated riches. For each word resembles a grain of wheat that dies and is reborn as a heavy sheaf; it is mysteriously identical with the blood of Christ poured out and fructifying souls. But these riches are only the explication of the infinite concrete Unity of the Logos, in whom are hidden all the treasures of wisdom and knowledge, they are only the always more pressing invitation to raise ourselves towards that Unity.
>
> The Unity of the Word of which the one Catholic Church is the guardian—it is to the Church that Origen adheres with all his strength, after her that he wishes to be named, it is her tradition that he wishes to understand. What is called his allegorism is, in his thought, nothing other than the development of Christian dogma by the doctors of the Church, a teaching which itself is Scripture in act.[66]

Plotinus

As we leave Alexandria and Origen, it might be well to draw the parallel between his mysticism and that which was developed at the same period by another disciple of the same master, Ammonius—that is, Plotinus. Once again, Plotinus, like Origen, remains marked by certain of the great biblical statements about God for which Ammonius gained rights of citizenship in philosophic thought. As transcendent, one, pure of all confusion with the created as

[66] *Op. cit.*, pp. 57–8.

possible, the God of Plotinus still *creates*. He who is "the first living One" cannot rest in himself, as if he were jealous of himself or impotent, he who is the power of all things... but something in some way must come from Him".[67] And so the *nous*, Intelligence and the Intelligible, proceeds from the One, as his child (*paida*), a "second God"; then from the *nous*, the immaterial soul that animates all things.

The diversity of these things, however, comes wholly from matter, which, by a return to the old Greek conception, cannot itself owe anything to God. Hence evil, which is not really distinct, in its source at any rate, from finite, multiple existence.

Individual souls, fallen and broken up by their fall into matter, will not, therefore, regain their "homeland", the divine soul, except through a conversion (*epistrophe*).

This begins through purification, by which the soul separates itself from the body, becoming wholly impassible, pure of all the sensible *pathe*. Then it is ready for the flight towards the One: pure intellectuality regained, which constitutes its "resemblance to God". This is consummated in union, *henosis*, necessarily ecstatic, since it rescues it from all distinct existence in rescuing it from all multiplicity. "Pure resemblance of God placed in the presence of God, for then there is nothing to separate them—in virtue of the principle that incorporeal beings are only separated by their differences and are united as they resemble one another—it is as it were absorbed by the One, submerged and lost in the infinite immensity of his presence."[68]

It is remarkable to see how much this last Greek thought, entirely absorbed in spirituality, owes to biblical and Christian inspiration. However solicitous Plotinus may be to remain Platonic in his expression of the Good "diffusive of itself", his God, who is the One, but who is the Father; who gives being, first of all to a divine "child" who is by his essence Intelligence and the Intelligible, and then to a multitude of living things vivified by and gathered together in a single divine soul—is this not as it were a shadow of the trinitarian God of the New Testament? In return, it is a pre-existing matter alone that calls forth the appearance of distinct existences, while the processions from this God are all necessary. Moreover, if the purification of man and his union with God are described as the work of liberty, this is only, it seems, for the reason that by definition it escapes from the necessity of the material world. And it only escapes from this necessity to be

[67] *Enneades*, IV, VII, 9; lines 14–15 and V, IV, 1, lines 34–8.
[68] R. Arnou, *Le Désir de Dieu dans la Philosophie de Plotin*, Paris, 1921, p. 145.

reabsorbed into the divine existence, which itself is not fully such except in the supreme stage of the indistinction of the One.

Here, therefore, just as in Hermetism, in spite of the admirable impulse of this spirituality and the purity of the vision underlying it, and even though Hellenism here seems to receive the greatest measure of biblical and Christian inspiration that it could admit without breaking apart, creation and fall are still but one, as are, equally, conversion and annihilation of distinct being. The God who is pure Spirit, the living God, could be assimilated into Greek thought, but not the personal God whose Love arouses, seeks, finds again, and freely restores the persons whose liberty flowers in his own.

XIII

THE ORIGINS OF MONASTICISM

We have just been speaking of Plotinus' spirituality, which he himself defines as "a flight of the alone to the Alone": *monos pros monon.* Shortly after his time and Origen's, a movement characterized both by flight and by solitude was born in Christianity—monasticism. It is not surprising, therefore, that scholars have tried to find the origin of this movement in a spirituality of Neo-Platonic inspiration.... But, once again, the documents and the best established facts do not allow us to accept this hypothesis drawn from mere analogies of language: nothing is more purely Christian than the antecedents of monasticism, and nothing more purely evangelical than its primary motivations.[1]

The Pre-history of Monasticism

Today we may even seriously ask ourselves whether Christian monasticism had not already had a pre-history in Judaism. However prudent we may be in the hypothetical reconstruction of the community at Qumran, we must recognize the fact that it constituted, in a Judaism concentrated on the expectation of the Messiah, a group having a common effort in the ascetical life as its reason for existence.[2] It is not certain, true enough, that there ever was a "monastery" at Qumran, but it is certain that the documents found there testify to the existence of a society of Jews separated from the mass of the people, not so much by particular beliefs, as by a particular effort to lead together a more fervent life in the observance of the law and the expectation of the Kingdom of God.

That primitive Christianity was largely recruited from among such circles is proved by the many features it has in common with them, whether with regard to spirituality, liturgical life or ecclesiastical organization. In consequence, we need not be surprised if

[1] A detailed study of the different modern theories attempting to account for the appearance of monasticism is to be found in my work: *La Vie de saint Antoine, essai sur la spiritualité du monachisme primitif,* Saint-Wandrille, 1950.

[2] See G. Vermès, *Discovery in the Judean Desert,* pp. 36ff.

the community at Jerusalem, grouped around the apostles, presents so many quasi-monastic characteristics that it can be maintained, as a theme traditional up to the end of the Middle Ages, that the monastic life is only the continuation of the "apostolic life" in the Church. We should understand this last term, in the sense given to it by all antiquity, as being not primarily a life of missionary activities, but, according to the text of the Acts, a life in which Christians persevere together in prayer, in community of goods, in the breaking of bread . . .[3] It is on solid grounds that a student of monastic origins like Dom Germain Morin upheld his apparent paradox: it is not so much the monastic life which was a novelty at the end of the third century and the beginning of the fourth, but rather the life of adaptation to the world led by the mass of Christians at the time when the persecutions ceased. The monks actually did nothing but preserve intact, in the midst of altered circumstances, the ideal of the Christian life of early days.[4]

And there is another continuous chain from the apostles to the solitaries and then to the cenobites, whose ideal, less novel than it seems, spread so quickly from the Egyptian deserts at the end of the third century. This chain is constituted by the men and women who lived in continence, ascetics and virgins, who never ceased to be held in honour in the ancient Church.[5]

As we have already said, the esteem of the first Christian generations for virginity consecrated to Christ was so high that a popular literature could go so far as to extol it in terms implying a real depreciation of marriage. But we should in no way conclude from this that the ideal of virginity, so ancient in the Church, is in any way connected with the dualistic theses of heretical gnosticism. Once again, in the Gospel and in St Paul, both exalting the positive Christian value of marriage, virginity also finds its first and fundamental justification: as an effort to realize immediately and totally the reality of which marriage offers an image and a partial realization; the union of Christ and the Church, of the Word of God and humanity redeemed from sin by the cross of Jesus.

These themes run through all the Christian literature of the first three centuries, in St Cyprian as in Tertullian, in Methodius of Olympus[6] as in Origen, in spite of everything that distinguishes,

[3] Acts 2. 42. On the traditional meaning of the expression "the apostolic life", see Dom Jean Leclercq, *The Perfect Life* (Liturgical Press, 1961).

[4] Dom Germain Morin, *L'idéal monastique et la vie chrétienne des premiers jours*, 3rd ed., Paris, 1921.

[5] See Hugo Koch, *Quellen zur Geschichte der Askese und des Mönchtums in der alten Kirche*, Tübingen, 1931, pp. 23–76.

[6] See in particular his *Banquet of the Virgins*, in which the eulogy of virginity is systematically developed, in intentional opposition to the spirituality of the

and often contrasts, their types of spirituality. And, very soon also, it was clearly apparent that so fundamental a renunciation of the life of this world as that implied in voluntary virginity must be completed and sustained by all sorts of other renunciations. It is, then, around this new centre—the importance it had taken on being very characteristic of the New Testament in relation to the Old—that the whole ancient ideal of the *anawim* was perpetuated.

However, as very recent research indicates, the practice of virginity consecrated to Christ did not emerge from the domain of private piety and become the object of a vow, of a profession and public consecration before the Church, until the period when monasticism in general came to be organized.[7]

Martyrdom and Anchoritism

What were the immediate origins of monasticism?

As we have already brought out, a work such as Origen's *Exhortation to Martyrdom* shows us the transition as it were in the making from the ideal of martyrdom as prepared for by asceticism to the ideal of asceticism as the equivalent of martyrdom. Monasticism, however, is not simply asceticism, but an asceticism having a life separated from the world, apart from the world, as its most salient characteristic. Even this had its immediate preparation in the last persecutions. What St Gregory Nazianzen tells us of the life of St Basil's grandparents, at the time of the persecution of Maximinus, is very revealing.[8] Persecutions could cause faithful Christians to retire to the desert and there freely lead a life of the most precarious kind. A world become, on the contrary, too friendly to Christianity but without much alteration in its ways and its spirit—might not such a world, by a quite natural development, lead them to take the same road, so as to find once more, along with austerity, the detachment and the fervour they had known and could no longer know in a life suddenly become too easy?

It was not by chance that anchoritism, the retreat to the desert, spread so suddenly just as the State made its peace with the Church. There is certainly a very close connection between these two contemporaneous historical facts. When a world in which Christians as

---

eros in Plato's *Banquet*. Translated into French by Jacques Farges (Paris, 1932), this curious work is commented on by the same author in his thesis, *Les idées morales et religieuses de Méthode d'Olympe*, Paris, 1929.

[7] All the documents have been submitted to a very clear analysis by René Metz in the first part of his work on *La consécration des vierges dans l'Église romaine*, Paris, 1955, pp. 41ff.

[8] *Orat. XLIII*; P.G., XXXVI, 501.

such were separated and proscribed was succeeded by a world in which they came to be in honour, but a world whose spirit had hardly changed for all that, the best Christians, by instinct, would freely choose the state of proscription no longer imposed on them by circumstances. In a world which no longer treated them as enemies, they would feel obliged to live as enemies of the world: they sensed too well that, without this, they would soon become its slaves.

The reaction was so natural that it seems more and more to have been spontaneously the same in more than one place at the same time.

Antiquity believed that monasticism, having been born in Egypt, was diffused everywhere from there. Modern research has caused the idea to be dropped, as a later legend, that Syrian monasticism preceded Egyptian.[9] Actually, it seems, monasticism appeared in both countries at almost the same time and quite independently. But there is no need, in order to explain this, to go and look among the recluses of Serapis for an example, which actually affords no true analogy to what it is supposed to clarify. It was the Gospel alone, heard and taken literally by simple souls in Egypt and in quite different places as well, that caused anchoritism to arise in the general conditions we have described. The *Life of St Antony* by St Athanasius presents us with a good Egyptian Christian *fellah* who heard the words read in church: "If you wish to be perfect, go, sell all you have: give it to the poor, then come and follow me: you will have treasure in heaven."[10] To become the father of all monks, he needed no more than to decide to practise these words to the letter.

The Oldest Monastic Texts

This leads us to make an inventory of the texts we have at our disposal in order to be present, by way of first hand documents, at the birth of monasticism. There are three principal ones, to which are added the valuable subsequent collections that reflect a teaching not developed until later, but enshrine facts and testimonies which are certainly primitive. We mean, in the first place, the *Vita Antonii* just mentioned and the oldest of the *Lives of Pachomius*, as given to us in its original Coptic by Mgr Th. Lefort,[11] to which must be added the collections of the *Apophthegms of the Fathers*

[9] See Jerome Labourt, *Le christianisme dans l'Empire perse sous la dynastie sassanide*, Paris, 1904, Stanislas Schiwietz, "Das Mönchtum in Syrien und Mesopotamien und das Aszetentum in Persien", in *Das morgenländische Mönchtum*, Vienna, III (1938), pp. 400ff., and above all A. Vööbus, *History of Asceticism in the Syrian Orient*, vol. II, Louvain, 1960.

[10] Athanasius, *Vita Antonii*, 2; P.G., XXVI, 841 C.

[11] Th. Lefort, *Vies coptes de saint Pachôme et de ses premiers successeurs*, Louvain, 1943.

which give us the very words of the Fathers of the monastic life.[12] All this is illuminated by the anecdotes and other sayings gathered in abundance in collections such as the *Historia Lausaca* of Palladius or Cassian's *Conferences.*[13] But these last two texts, however valuable they may be, already bear the marks of a later systematization: here we can follow the transition from a primitive, popular monasticism, wholly evangelical and entirely ignorant of philosophical problems or influences, to the erudite monasticism which was to be its heir, that of Evagrius Ponticus in particular.

The *Life of St Antony* is of unparalleled interest in our study. For it is the oldest monastic biography we possess.[14] Its immediate success was considerable: no other work, certainly, has done more to propagate the monastic life. The anecdote told by Augustine in his *Confessions* is well known, about two young men entering by chance into the cell of a solitary near Treves, finding the *Vita*, reading through it, and deciding then and there to embrace this kind of life. Even if the historical value of the *Vita* were little or nothing, which is assuredly not the case, its historical importance would remain; even if the person of Antony had never existed before the portrait made of him, the type provided by this portrait would none the less have produced innumerable exemplars. As St Gregory Nazianzen already remarked, the *Vita* gives us the *charakter*, that is, the imprint, the mould, of the primitive monastic life.[15]

[12] Three collections of Apophthegms are in existence. The first, an alphabetic one, has been preserved for us in Greek (P.G., LXV, 71–440). The two others, in which the sentences are classified according to virtues or vices, only exist in translations: Latin for the second (P.L., LXXIII, 855–1022; cf. the collection edited by Dom Wilmart in the *Revue bénédictine*, 1922, pp. 185–98), and the third (P.L., LXXIII, 1025–66); Syriac for the second alone (Wallis Budge has provided an English translation of this Syriac one in *The Paradise of the Holy Fathers*, London, 1907). Wilhelm Bousset has tried to trace the history of this collection: *Apophtegmata, Texte Ueberlieferung und Charakter des Apophtegmata Patrum*, Tübingen, 1923. See also Jean-Claude Guy, "Remarks on the Apophtegmata Patrum", in *Recherches de science religieuse*, XLII (1955), Paris, pp. 252–7. Selections are to be found in *The Wisdom of the Desert*, by Thomas Merton (New Directions, New York, 1960; London, 1961); *The Desert Fathers*, by Helen Waddell (paperback); *Stories of the Early Fathers*, tr. by Ernest Budge, Oxford, 1934; *A Treasury of Early Christianity*, ed. by Anne Fremantle (Mentor book, paper, New Am. Lib. of World Literature, New York); and *Spiritual Writers of the Early Church*, F. Cayré (20th Cent. Encyc. of Cath.), Hawthorn, New York, English edn. entitled *The First Spiritual Writers* (Faith and Fact Books), Burns & Oates, London.

[13] Bibliographical references will be given further on, in connection with each of the writers.

[14] Many English translations are available, including one in the volume *Monastic Life* of the *Formation of Christendom* series (London), G. Garitte is preparing a critical edition on the text of the *Vita*, but its prodigious diffusion means that an immense amount of work is required to complete this task. See H. Dörries, *Die Vita Antonii als Geschichtsquelle*, Göttingen, 1949.

[15] *Oratio in laudem Athanasii*, P.G., XXXV, 1088 A.

The Life of St Antony

Born around 251, entered on the monastic life about his twentieth year, Antony would have died at an age of a hundred and five years. These dates bound precisely the period of the first expansion of the ideal expressed in the *Vita*. This ideal is what we wish to bring out.

Its first pages, in which the author explains his plan, strike a note characteristic of early monasticism, as yet unorganized. This is the kind of athletic competitiveness to which the ascetics devoted themselves, causing some to learn from others and all to rival each other in zeal. It might be said that we have here the antecedent as it were of the religious novitiate, in this spontaneous desire to imitate the heroes of the monastic life, to put oneself to school with them in a spirit of holy competition. With this was very closely allied the idea that the monastic life is essentially progressive.[16] Later on, the canonists would tend to see it only as a state of life, defined once for all by the vows. But at this stage, the vows were still unknown and the monastic life seemed, on the contrary, to be a commitment to detachments and correlative ascents which were to have no end here below.

Reitzenstein has brought out the dynamism inherent in the *Vita*:[17] its particular purpose is to show us, after the transition from the ordinary life to the cenobitic life, the passing on from this in turn to more and more complete anchoritism, until this anchoritism itself flowers in spiritual paternity. There is nothing static about this ideal; on the contrary everything tends continually to go beyond what has already been achieved.

We have already mentioned the purely evangelical character of Antony's vocation. A peasant in easy circumstances, who had been left by the premature death of his parents with the care of their affairs and the responsibility for bringing up a young sister, he felt paralysed in the spiritual life by all these cares. He dreamed longingly of the life of the apostles who had left everything to follow Christ, of the community in Jerusalem where no one owned anything in order to lead the interior life free and unencumbered. It was under these circumstances that he heard the reading of the Gospel urging total detachment. He hesitated no longer: once having arranged for his sister's future, he disposed of all his possessions. Living apart in a hut near his own village, after taking counsel with another "spiritual", he applied himself to a life described for us as one of self-scrutiny and discipline. This already

[16] *Vita Antonii*, 3; P.G., XXXVI, 844.

[17] R. Reitzenstein, "Das Athanasius Werk über des Leben des Antonius", in *Sitzungberichte der Heidelberger Akad. d. Wiss.*, 1914, pp. 11 and ff.

announces a theme which will stand out with growing clarity in the course of the book. In ordinary life, a man is as it were led along blindfold by his passions and by everything that flatters them in the world. The basis of asceticism is, therefore, a liberation necessary to awaken a consciousness of self which will be truly human and Christian. And this in turn will be at the basis of a recasting of the whole of existence, which is henceforth to accord with this renewed consciousness of self.[18]

But what were the occupations of the new monk? We note that at this stage he had not completely abandoned the common life, in the sense of life in the midst of his human brothers. He lived on the outskirts of his village a life which, materially speaking, was simply that of the poorest of its inhabitants, whereas up to that time he had doubtless been among the most comfortably off. The monk is first of all a poor man, a really poor man and, as such, a labourer, a manual labourer. This fact, this conviction is at the basis of the whole primitive monastic ideal. Work, work which brings sweat to the brow, is the primary form of asceticism, the necessary basis for all the others. And the *Vita* makes it very clear that, now that Antony had simplified his life, reduced his own needs to the minimum, the work that ensured his subsistence from day to day allowed him at the same time to give a great deal in charity. All this is typical both of the realism and of the evangelism of this spirituality. True, the monk is a monk because he is separated from the world; but it is from its joys and comforts that he is separated, not from the tasks of his brothers and from his responsibility in their regard; quite the contrary. The love of God that would soon drive Antony into solitude is in no way the desire for a lazy, aesthetic, egoistic kind of contemplation: it is the most realistic kind of Christian charity.

However, throughout his life of labour itself, the monk applies himself to a new task which is properly his own: prayer, a prayer which tends to become constant. And this prayer is not any kind of prayer: it is expressly told us that it is a prayer nourished by reading, obviously the reading of holy Scripture.

It is on the basis of these essential occupations that the virtues and practices which came to characterize this first period of Antony's life are sketched out. He had not lost contact with men, and the author, let us repeat, intends to describe this phase as the model of the cenobitic life, that is, a life in which ascetic exercise is pursued in detachment but not yet in complete solitude. It is most remarkable to see the humanity, the equilibrium that

[18] *Vita*, 2; col. 841.

characterize it. The pursuit of amiability (*to charien*) towards men goes along with assiduity in prayer. The exercise of patience, which is in the background of both kinds of effort, is as it were the necessary counterpart of a flowering of charity.[19]

All this is supported by a collection of practices which Antony drew from the example of the other ascetics whom he visited and from whom he learned with docility. These practices all have as their purpose that awakening, that vigilance we have mentioned, for which the flight from comfort, from accommodation to the world, is only the necessary condition. First, there are night vigils, filled with meditative reading of the divine word. Then comes constancy in the trials of all kinds which make up the existence of a monk—by definition, a poor man, voluntarily humiliated. Among these stand out fastings and *chamoeonia*, that is, the practice of sleeping directly on the ground, by which the monk, according to St Paul's phrase, treats his body roughly so as to keep it under control.

Thus the first efforts of the novice monk are directed towards a new equilibrium in his life. However, the author emphasizes, this equilibrium is not a goal, but a first stage in the spiritual ascent. Up to this point, the crucial point has not yet been revealed to the monk: that of the necessary struggle against the demon. For he does not reveal himself to the novice, as the whole of ancient monasticism tells us, and the sign that a man is emerging from the noviciate is precisely the discovery of him. All the same, from the outset, it is important that asceticism appears for what it is: a work of faith, in which the monk does not imagine that he himself can be the artisan of his own holiness, but simply gives himself up to the demands of Christ's word, to be in a position to trust in his promises. The struggle against the demon, the necessity of which will soon disclose itself, can thus be recognized as the work of Christ in us before being our own work. Very characteristic is the emphasis placed on this necessary correlation between asceticism as motivated by faith, nourished by faith, and the transition to open warfare against Satan. From the first interior conflicts on their meaning is shown us in St Paul's phrase: *It is not I* [*who fight*], *but the grace of God that is in me.*[20]

The devil first reveals himself indirectly, under his usual masks of the world and the flesh. Antony feels himself seized with regrets at what he had left behind. What he had done seemed mad. Had he not been positively culpable in entrusting his sister's upbringing to others (a group of virgins), instead of continuing to be responsible

[19] *Vita*, 3–4; col. 844–5.

[20] Gal. 2. 20. Quoted in *Vita*, 7; col. 852.

for it himself? And, after these specious thoughts, then the flesh reawakens, and temptations which seemed to have been overcome now obsess him with a force and insistence never known before. Throughout all this, his arms are faith and constant prayer, aiding him to maintain without relaxation the hard discipline to which he had submitted himself. The demon, gaining nothing from this interior revolt which he had aroused in Antony's soul, now reveals himself as having been behind the temptations that seemed entirely natural. But the terror of such a revelation has no more success than the snares of the world and the flesh. Antony merely answers him with the words of the psalm: "The Lord is my help, I look down on my enemies."[21] The biography ends the account of this first passage of arms with these words: "Such was Antony's first victory over the devil. But it was rather, for Antony, the success of the Lord, who *has condemned sin in the flesh, so that the justice of the law might be fulfilled in us, who walk, not according to the flesh, but according to the Spirit.*"[22]

And, while the author emphasizes how Antony redoubled his austerities in his first spiritual combat, he emphasizes also that he encouraged himself by meditating on the saying of the Apostle: *When I am weak, then am I strong.*[23] Important also is the statement that Antony never settled down in assurance of victory, but only in the certainty that victory could be renewed in him from the constant presence of the Lord.

> He himself did not remember the time gone by but, day after day, as if he were beginning his asceticism again, he strove rather to go forward, repeating continually the word of St. Paul: *Forgetting what is behind me, and tending with all my strength to what is ahead, I run straight to the goal.*[24] He remembered also the word of Elias: *The Lord lives, in whose presence I stand today.*[25] He noted that in saying: *today* Elias did not reckon time that had passed. And so, as if he was always at the beginning, every day he strove to be in the state in which we must appear before God: pure of heart and ready to obey His will and no other.[26]

The Desert and the Devil

It was at this point that Antony went on to anchoritism, withdrawal into solitude. This was done in two stages. To begin with, he withdrew to tombs which were not a great distance from the

[21] Ps. 117. 7. Quoted in *Vita*, 6; col. 849.
[22] *Vita*, 7; col. 853 A. The quotation is from Rom. 8. 4.
[23] 2 Cor. 12. 10. Quoted in the *Vita*, 7; col. 853 A.
[24] Phil. 3. 14. [25] 1 Kings 18. 15. [26] *Vita*, 7; col. 853 B.

village, a devoted friend bringing him a little bread. Then, when he was sufficiently hardened, he fled resolutely to the desert and spent twenty years in an old ruined fort in which he barricaded himself.[27] It is most significant that this transition was made at the moment when the necessity for carrying on his asceticism as a struggle against the demon fully dawned in his consciousness.

For, as Karl Heussi has fully proved in his book *Der Ursprung des Mönchtums*, in primitive monasticism in general, the retreat to the desert in no way expressed any simple desire for tranquillity, for leisure for extended contemplation in the sense of Greek philosophy. If the monk buried himself in the desert, it was with the intention of fighting against the devil, and for the reason that solitude seemed to be his usual dwelling-place.[28] On this point, the *Vita* is particularly transparent. When the devil saw Antony's decision, he tried all kinds of devices to stop him. When Antony, in spite of everything, had shut himself up in his fort, the curiosity-seekers who came to find out what they could believed they heard the raging demons crying out, "Go away from us! What are you doing in the desert? You will not endure our conspiracy."[29]

Obviously, this idea is what seems to us most fantastic in the *Vita*, and the strangeness of this or that account of the demons' doings which we encounter only brings this out the more. But we must resign ourselves to it, for, once again, it is found everywhere in the *Apophthegms of the Fathers*, and we shall understand nothing of the meaning of primitive anchoritism if we do not first attempt to understand what gave it meaning for the anchorites themselves.

The Gospel origin of this idea must first be emphasized. The three Synoptics show us Jesus, when he was about to enter on the decisive phase of his life after the baptism given him by John, driven into the desert by the divine Spirit there to meet the devil and undergo his temptations.[30] It is in order to imitate Jesus in this focal episode in his life that the monk buries himself in the desert.

Behind these Gospel accounts just as behind our oldest monastic texts, we need to perceive the concept which comes to light, a concept clarified for us by the Judaism contemporary with the origins of Christianity. Here the world appears, let us recall, as fallen into the power of the spirit of evil. Man himself had arisen as a possible saviour of creation, but he had been tempted and conquered by the demon. In solitude, however, the demon rules

27 *Vita*, 8; col. 853 C.
28 Karl Heussi, *Der Ursprung des Mönchtums*, Tübingen, 1936, p. 111.
29 *Vita*, 13; col. 861.
30 Matt. 4. 1–15; Mark 1. 12–13; Luke 4. 1–10.

directly, without anything to screen his presence. In the same way, he haunts tombs, because there death has definitively, it seems, assured his victory over man. To dwell in tombs, to retire into the desert is, then, deliberately to affront him in order to struggle with him face to face and, according to the word of the Gospel, to dislodge the "strong man" from his fortress, by the power of the "stronger man", so as to take away his arms and reduce him to impotence.

If all this, in spite of its undeniably biblical and evangelical content, still seems to us to be mere mythology, it might be well to bring out the profound psychological realities underneath these appearances, and the meaning that they give to them. The ascetics of whom we are speaking, following the sacred authors and certainly Christ himself, recognized this fact: solitude alone allows man to discover, and so to face, all the obscure forces that he bears within himself. The man who does not know how to be alone, does not know either (and secretly does not wish to know) what conflicts there are in the depths of his heart, conflicts which he feels that he is incapable of untangling, even of touching. Solitude is a terrible trial, for it serves to crack open and burst apart the shell of our superficial securities. It opens out to us the unknown abyss that we all carry within us. And, as the tradition that we are examining affirms, solitude discloses the fact that these abysses are haunted: it is not only the depths of our own soul, unknown to us, that we discover, but the obscure powers that are as it were lurking there, whose slaves we must inevitably remain so long as we are not aware of them. In truth, this awareness would destroy us, if it were not illuminated by the light of faith. Only Christ can open out to us with impunity "the mystery of iniquity", because he alone, *in* us today as *for* us in the past, can confront it successfully.

Seen in this light, which is their own, the strange devilries described by ancient monasticism should neither disconcert us nor deceive us. They are simply the translation made by the popular imagination of a truth of faith, which is certainly one of the most profound truths of the Gospel.

Antony's first essay at solitude, in the tombs, was the occasion of a trial the interpretation of which is also very enlightening, opening a vein with immense prolongations in Christian spiritual tradition. For he went through a trial by darkness, in the course of which he had the impression of being abandoned by God to the evil powers. He persevered, but in the most naked faith. At the end of the trial, a luminous vision of Christ consoled him. But he could not refrain from this complaint, "Where were you? Why did you not appear at the beginning and end my pains?" But a voice answered him: "I was there, Antony, I was waiting to see you fighting . . ."[31]

Do we not find here again, in a much simpler form, the theme already worked out in Origen's *Commentary on the Canticle*, according to which alternations of drynesses and illuminations constitute as it were a rhythm of trials and strengthenings inherent in spiritual progress?

Return to the World

The twenty years, profoundly mysterious, that Antony passed in the most complete seclusion in the depths of the desert, came to be wholly taken up with this hand-to-hand combat with the spirit of evil. At the end of this time, some friends who burned to imitate him broke down his door. He let them do it, and here is how he appeared to them:

> Antony came out, as one initiated into the mysteries in the secret of the temple and inspired by a divine breath. Then, for the first time, those who had come saw him. They were lost in wonder: his aspect had remained the same; he was neither fat from lack of physical exercise nor emaciated by his fastings and struggle against the demons, but just as they had known him before his withdrawal. Spiritually pure, he was neither shrunken with regret nor swollen with pleasure; in him, neither laughter nor sadness; the multitude did not trouble him, having so many people greeting him gave him no excessive joy: always equal to himself, governed by reason, natural.[32]

This description of the anchorite emerging from his solitude is remarkable in many respects. The bearing, wholly literary, of the allusions in ancient Jewish or Christian literature to mysteries and initiations has already been sufficiently explained so that the reader will not be led to make any mistake about what is said on this subject.

There is no question of likening Antony's seclusion to that of the recluses in the temple of Serapis, as if he owed anything at all to their example:[33] it is clearly only a rhetorical formula to tell us that he had entered into the most profound Christian experience. This is defined by a double character: the consummate anchorite is now wholly penetrated, wholly possessed by the Spirit of God, who has driven out of him once and for all the spirit of evil and his illusions. The immediate consequence of this is that Antony no

[31] *Vita*, 10; col. 850. [32] *Vita*, 14; col. 864 C.

[33] On the attempts that have been made to connect the first Egyptian monks with the recluses in the temple of Serapis, see my *Vie de saint Antoine*, p. 50.

longer clings to his solitude: it had not been an end in itself for him; it was this victory in him of the one Spirit over the other that had made him seek it. Now that the victory is won, that the divine Spirit has taken possession of him, he returns to the world voluntarily, or rather, he lets the world rejoin him. Henceforth the perfect charismatic, the complete monk, does not need to fear the world. According to the phrase of St. John, he who is in him is stronger than he who is in the world.[34] Men can no longer tempt him, separate him from God. On the contrary, it is he who now finds himself in a position to guide them, to lead them to God. Here anchoritism reveals how little it is a way of escaping from charity. On the contrary, it is simply the means of effectively gaining integral charity. Anchoritism did not make Antony a contemplative unconcerned with the fate of his brothers: it made him a spiritual father beyond all others.

> Through him, the account continues, the Lord healed many persons suffering in their bodies, and purified others of demons. Antony had received from God the grace of consoling the afflicted, of reconciling men at odds with one another. He told them to esteem nothing in the world more than the love of Christ. In exhorting them to the remembrance of future goods and of the love for us to which God witnessed who did not spare His only Son but delivered Him up for us, he persuaded many people to embrace the solitary life, and it was in this way that the desert was peopled with monks, with men who had renounced all their goods and inscribed their names in the city of heaven.[35]

After this, we must once again mention the two characteristics attributed to this veritable recasting of Antony's humanity, purified and pacified by the spiritual combat: it is presented to us as "governed by reason" (literally, "logical") and "natural".

The first term presupposes the identification between the Word of God and true reason: it is in the man whom Christ has taken possession of, entirely dominated, that reason conformed to its divine archetype is really restored. Otherwise it is only a false appearance, a deceiving wisdom that does not go beyond the surface of things. In the same way, it is in the man whom the divine Spirit has permeated without meeting any obstacles that human nature finds itself again as God had willed it to be. This in no way means that the monastic life would dispense with grace. Quite the contrary, as we have seen: wholly based on faith, wholly consistent with faith, it is simply as integral as possible a giving up of self to grace. In return, however painful may be the operations of divine grace

[34] 1 John 4. 4.

[35] *Vita*, 14; col. 864 D.

in us, it in no way tends to a mutilation, but to a healing, a restoration of human nature. The finished ascetic is the only truly developed man, because it is in God, through the cross of Christ, that he has found his development.

This state, although the word does not appear here, clearly corresponds to that of the "gnostic", the "perfect", the "spiritual man" of Clement and, above all, of Origen. We should note again the means whereby the spiritual fatherhood is carried out, which with our monks as with their predecessors, the great Alexandrian spiritual writers, is inseparable from Christian perfection. Two things manifest it and realize it with Antony, and are found again in the whole collection of the *Apophthegms*: the word of witness, exhortation, illumination, and power over physical things whether for healing or freeing from diabolic possession. *Rema kai dunamis*, these two charisms of the "spiritual man" are also, quite obviously, a direct transposition from the Gospel, of what the crowds came to seek from the Saviour.

At this point, the *Vita* pauses to present Antony's teaching, in a kind of fictitious discourse which doubtless gathers together and amalgamates a number of its hero's sayings.[36]

We can distinguish three main parts. The first is a eulogy of the monastic life considered as the only true life. As a counterpart, we find the profound observation that the monk only renounces what every man must renounce, sooner or later, whether he wants to or not. But in the freedom of the monk's renunciation is found the secret of its fruitfulness: privations that are merely painful and sterile when simply endured, reveal themselves as lifegiving when freely accepted in the perspectives of faith.

The monastic life, furthermore, is nothing other than a life wholly pursued in the presence of God, and, because of this, continually in progress.

Finally, the place occupied by the demons and their illusions, far from signifying any subjection to them, manifests their nothingness before God. Wholly powerful over man so long as they hide themselves, they are forced by the ascetic to unmask themselves only so that they may be destroyed by the power of faith.

These last themes introduce the rules for the discernment of spirits. The divine Spirit and the angelic spirits who serve him produce peace, but an active peace that opens the soul to spiritual desires. The wicked spirit, on the contrary, casts the soul into perturbation, discouragement, and that *acedia* which makes everything distasteful and the things of God of no interest. Above all, it

[36] *Vita*, 16ff.; col. 865ff.

seems, the wicked spirit attaches us to the visions that he procures, while heavenly visions always impel us ahead in that quest for God which has no end here below.

After this, Antony's life went on, in the midst of the disciples who came to him in the desert, broken by descents into Alexandria whether to give witness in favour of the true faith against heretics, or to offer himself to eventual martyrdom, in a return of the fire of persecution.[37]

At the end, Antony once more sought solitude. And now it was to let himself be absorbed in intercourse with God, before the death that he sensed to be near at hand.[38]

It might be said that this invaluable document has gathered together all the elements of primitive monastic life in a spontaneous synthesis. This is so true that there is no one of its paragraphs which could not be illustrated by a sheaf of apophthegms. Conversely, having done this, we discover that there is nothing in the very varied collections of these apophthegms which could not be inserted somewhere in the *Vita Antonii*.

Monasticism and Christianity

Throughout this whole literature, there are certain constants which we need to emphasize all the more because the later development of monasticism did not take place without obscuring them to some degree. The first is that the primitive monk in no way appeared to be a kind of specialist, his vocation was not a particular vocation, considered by himself or by others as more or less exceptional. The monk was simply a Christian, and, more precisely, a devout layman, who limited himself to taking the most radical means to make his Christianity integral. In his asceticism, he proposed no other end but to be saved. Arsenius, a man of the world but a deeply religious one, heard a voice saying to him: "Fly from men and you will be saved."[39] All his life, the monk asked for no other teaching from his elders than the means of attaining this: "Tell me, I pray you, how I can be saved".[40]

It follows as something quite natural to the monks themselves that their ideal models were not necessarily professional monks, if we dare say this, but could equally well be laypeople living in the world, if they actually practised there the detachment that gives one up wholly to charity. A common theme of the *Apophthegms* is that of the good monk who desires to know who is the most edifying monk in the country and has a vision referring him to

[37] *Vita*, 44ff.; col. 908ff.
[38] *Vita*, 49ff.; col. 913ff.
[39] *Apophthegmata Patrum, Arsenius*, 1; P.G., LXV, 87.
[40] *Ibid., Hierax*, 1; col. 231 and *Macarius Alexandrinus*, 23 and 24; col. 272.

someone who is not a monk at all. The *Historia Monachorum* makes such accounts the matter of the last conversations of Paphnutius with his disciples, from which he himself draws this conclusion:

> ... that we must not despise anyone in this world, whether they are engaged in the management of fields, or in barter or in commerce, because there is no condition in this life in which souls faithful to God are not met with, who in secret carry out the actions that please Him. This makes us see that it is not so much the profession that each one embraces, or what seems the most perfect in his manner of life, which is agreeable in His eyes, but sincerity and the disposition of the spirit joined to good works.[41]

Under these conditions, the first monks were in no way inclined to see their asceticism as an end in itself. Cassian sums up admirably what is insinuated or inculcated in many ways by the *Apophthegms* when he writes:

> Our fastings, our vigils, meditation on Scripture, poverty and the privation of all things are not perfection, but the instruments for acquiring it.[42]

This asceticism, furthermore, particularly in Egyptian monasticism, remains a mere exercise of liberation, of disengagement from the bonds of the flesh and the world. It was to allow the spirit to awaken, to be fully receptive to the divine Word, completely ready to follow Christ at the first suggestion. True enough, the ascetic practices of these religious men were rough and painful, and the monks knew it well. But as much as they insist on the necessity for bearing manfully all the trials that constitute asceticism, to the same degree are they free from all "dolorism". One must suffer to be a monk, but the suffering did not interest them; their thought never stopped at it. What they wished was to die to themselves, to their "old man", so that the "new man" who is Christ himself would be free in them. And so they did not hesitate to condemn too rigorous austerities whenever, instead of freeing the spirit, they came to weigh it down. Cassian, once again, finds the formula summarizing a whole tradition: "Excessive fasting brings about the same evil as gluttony."[43]

In Syria, spectacular austerities soon appeared, as R. Draguet says,[44] which were unknown in Egypt: stylites who lived on columns, iron chains, burial alive, or solitaries who exposed them-

41 *Historia monachorum in Egypto*, 16; P.L., XXI, 391.

42 *Conferences*, I, 7.

43 *Conferences*, II, 16.

44 R. Draguet, *Les Pères du désert*, Paris, 1949, p. xliii.

selves unprotected to the elements. But, here again, it was not suffering that was sought for: it was endurance, indifference to everything that is not essential, in that spirit of athletic competition which could, certainly, easily degenerate (and all ancient literature is vividly aware of it, stigmatizing in a good-humoured way the ascetics who play to the gallery), but which generally remained a very bracing incentive to generosity and spiritual virility.

Furthermore, we must not deceive ourselves, permeated as we are with a false spiritualism, vaguely Cartesian, which presents us with a wholly spiritual asceticism as the ideal. The materiality of monastic asceticism, without which there would have been no monasticism, is an integral part of that "reasonable" character which these ancient masters never ceased to emphasize. Let us say quite simply that it is the direct fruit of their spiritual good sense: they knew that man is inseparably body and soul, and they did not deceive themselves about the possibility of reforming the soul without going by way of the body. With no illusions concerning the "world" or the "flesh" in the biblical sense of the word, these ascetics had no contempt either for creation or for the body. It was precisely, we might say, because they did not misprise the latter that they knew how necessary it is to master it in order to free the soul. The picture that is given us of Antony as he emerged from his solitude is in no way that of an ascetic emaciated by an asceticism that is its own end: it is that of a man calmed, brought into equilibrium, in whom everything human has become as it were transparent to the Spirit, docile to his influence. Only, neither he nor others like him shared our illusions about the ease with which one can arrive at this state! The basic place in asceticism given to work, a work that was effective, simple and not too absorbing for the spirit, but real work and work well done, is the best guarantee of the realism of this asceticism. A monk who has to work primarily to gain his very simplified livelihood and to facilitate the practice of charity, and not merely to kill time, runs no great risk of losing himself in fantasies.

And what was the prayer of these monks? It was a prayer which was, which tended to become constant. But it was not any kind of prayer: it was essentially the continual "meditation" on Scripture, meaning its rumination. In his hours of prayer, and in particular during the great night-vigil, the monk interspersed copious readings from the different books of the Bible with psalmody and brief prayers which helped him to assimilate the readings and the chants. But, throughout the whole of his day, he did not cease to recall the sacred words, which he learned by heart as far as possible, beginning with the Psalter. Thus as Lucius says in opposing one of the "enlightened" who were soon to appear, wishing to suppress work in favour of perpetual prayer:

> I will show you that it is in staying at my work that I do not stop praying. I am there, seated with God; and when I set my little leaves to soak and when I weave rope from them, I say: "Have mercy on me, O God, in the greatness of Your goodness, and wipe away my sins in the multitude of Your mercies."[45] Now, is this not praying?[46]

Austerity, work, contemplative prayer which is simply a meditation, that is a constant assimilation, of the divine Word—such a life, if it is to be well led, requires, precisely, the guidance of a proved leader. Thereby, we might say, anchoritism escapes in two ways from the danger of an isolation which would be as little Christian as human. On the one hand, the anchorite novice cannot profitably bury himself in solitude if he is not guided by the experience and counsels of an elder. And, on the other hand, the fruit of anchoritism is precisely spiritual paternity. Once again, one does not go into solitude for solitude's sake, but so that the Spirit of God in us will oust the evil spirit from his hiding places and supplant him. But when the Spirit has entirely taken hold of a solitary, he becomes the father of all.

Cassian, again, sums up the whole tradition of the desert in making discretion, that is, the gift of discerning the path God wills for us, a gift essential to the solitary but one which is not acquired except in docility to proved masters. Here are the words he puts on the lips of the Abbot Moses:

> True discretion is only acquired by a true humility. And the first proof of this true humility is fidelity in leaving the discernment of all our actions, and even of all our thoughts, to the wisdom of our superiors, to give up following our own light in order to follow theirs in all things and not to distinguish good from evil except by the rules they have given us. This way of acting not only teaches the young solitary to walk straight in the true path of discretion, but it defends him even from all the artifices and all the ambushes of his enemy. For a man can never be seduced when he follows in his conduct, not the rules of his particular judgment, but the examples of the elders; and the whole skill of so subtle an enemy can never overcome the simplicity and the ignorance of the man who is never embarrassed to disclose all the thoughts that come to him and who, far from keeping them to himself in a dangerous and criminal silence,

[45] Ps. 50. 3.

[46] *Apophthegmata Patrum, Lucius*; P.G., LXV, 253; cf. Cassian, *Institutiones*, II, 15.

exposes them to the judgment of superiors and then rejects them, or accepts them, according to their advice.[47]

In the beginning, however, the superior, or more precisely, the "abbot", that is, the spiritual father, was not a personage endowed with an official function: he was simply the perfected spiritual man. The anchorite whose anchoritism had been fruitful, so to say, made no difficulties about allowing other men to join him and consented willingly to communicate to them everything he had received in solitude. The "abbots", whose sayings and the examples that illustrate them are collected in the *Apophthegms*, were precisely this.[48]

Pachomius and Cenobitism

In this regard, Pachomius was to pave the way for a development which transformed monasticism from top to bottom by institutionalizing it. At the term of this development, reached, furthermore, only in the West, the "abbot"—even though the great necessity, or at least the desirability, of selecting for this function an eminently spiritual man was maintained—became essentially an official personage, a superior in the canonical sense of the word. It was around this development of the very idea of the abbot that the transition was made from pure anchoritism (complete solitude) or mitigated anchoritism (solitaries grouped around a "spiritual father") to cenobitism as later ages were to know it. It should be emphasized, however, that the cenobitism of Pachomius never completely succeeded in supplanting the ancient type of monasticism except in the West, and quite slowly. In the East, the two conceptions went on living side by side, and the second never actually succeeded in doing away with the first.

The *Life of Pachomius* brings out very clearly the circumstances which called for this development. Unlike Antony, Pachomius was a convert. Called up for military service, he was touched by the charity of the Christians at Thebes towards the recruits and he promised himself that, if he escaped from conscription, like them he would devote himself to the service of others. Released at Antinous, he stopped at the Christian village of Chenoboskion where he received baptism, about the year 307. He made his apprenticeship in the anchoretic life with a neighbouring hermit, Palemon. At the end of some seven years, he believed that he heard a voice reminding him of his vow to put himself at the

47 *Conferences*, II, 10.

48 See Irénée Hausherr, "Direction spirituelle en Orient autrefois", vol. 144 of *Orientalia christiana analecta*, Rome, 1955, pp. 39ff.

service of others. The application that he then made of this was to build with his own hands a little enclosure containing buildings where he could gather together some companions.

For it had very soon become apparent that primitive monasticism, under the form of complete freedom, brought with it material difficulties, many risks, and finally a considerable falling-off. However simplified material life might be, when pursued individually it could become so difficult that the spiritual effort of the monk ran the risk of being more encumbered than liberated by this simplification. As a result, but above all (especially when we consider the considerable vogue that anchoritism immediately had among the ordinary people of Egypt) because lacking regulation: an authority imposed on all, monasticism risked losing itself in fantasy, in illusions, and degenerating from the very fact of its own development.

So Pachomius, it seems, starting simply with the intention of facilitating the material organization of the life of his future disciples, came to impose on them a detailed rule, to organize them into a community, under the undisputed authority of a superior. Here is what we are told about his first essay:

> When he saw the brothers gathering around him, he set for them the following rule: each would take care of himself and would occupy himself with work on his own account, but they would have a common purse for everything relating to material needs, food for example, or again, the entertainment of the guests who came to visit them—for they ate together; they would give over to him the care of what they had to dispose of, and this freely and willingly, trusting him to watch over all their needs, it being understood that he was their trusted agent in matters of business and their father according to God.[49]

All this, however, led only to a disappointing result. Pachomius' recruits, seeing only the material advantages of his system, treated him like a domestic servant and not as their head.

> Seeing his humility and his condescension, they treated him haughtily and with complete lack of ceremony, and, on all occasions, if he had to take a decision for the regulation of some of their affairs, they contradicted him to his face and insulted him, saying that they would not obey him. But he, far from doing the same to them, endured them with great patience: "They will see," he said, "my patience and my sorrow, and they will come back to God; they will do penance and they will fear God."[50]

[49] French trans. from R. Draguet, *op. cit.*, p. 91.

[50] *Ibid.*, p. 92.

But this hope proved deceptive and, after four or five years of patience, Pachomius, having passed the night in prayer, decided on a radical change in his methods. He would compel his companions henceforth either to accept a set rule, the first point being obedience to his authority, or else they would go away:

> ...Now, when you are called to the synaxis (that is, common prayer), you will all come and you will not act in my regard as you have been doing.... In the same way, when you are called to eat, you will come together, without acting as you have done all the time; and if you have some business to carry out related to our common needs, you will all come together, and not be careless about it as you have been up to this time. If now you are disposed to disobey the instructions that I have given you, go wherever you please!—*the earth is the Lord's with all that is in it*,[51] and if you wish to go somewhere else, do so as you will, for, so far as I am concerned, I will not keep you any longer unless you conform to all the instructions that I have given you.[52]

The monks began by making fun of this unexpected language. But this time the gentle Pachomius had become hard, and realizing that he would never get anywhere with these undisciplined men, he seized the bar of the gate for a cudgel and pushed them outside. After this,

> by a providential disposition of God, there came to him three men: Pseutaesius, Souros and Psoios, who told him of their desire to become monks in his company and to serve Christ. He asked them if they were capable of separating themselves from their parents and following the Saviour and he tested them; when he was satisfied that their dispositions were good, he gave them the monastic habit and welcomed them into his company with sentiments of joy and love of God. As for them, once they had entered into the holy congregation, they devoted themselves to great exercises and many kinds of asceticism.[53]

In his goodness, Pachomius continued, during the whole length of their novitiate, to take charge of all responsibilities and the heaviest of the material tasks. But he developed an exact rule to which he submitted them. Recruits grew in number and, when they reached a hundred, he built a church for the Office, although they continued to go to the village church for the eucharistic liturgy. Even when this came to be celebrated in the monastic church, it was the village clergy who celebrated it. For Pachomius held to a completely lay idea of monasticism, the idea common to the *Apophthegms*, fearing jealousy and vainglory for monks promoted

[51] Ps. 23. 1. [52] Draguet, *op. cit.*, p. 96. [53] *Ibid.*, p. 98.

to the priesthood. Conversely, when priests came and asked to be monks, he admitted them only if they accepted the same life as the rest.

He divided his monks into houses, each containing brothers who carried on the same trade for the good of the community: weavers, makers of matting, tailors, carpenters, fullers, shoemakers, bakers, cooks, gardeners and cultivators, herdsmen, infirmarians, etc.... each house had its superior, aided by a second in command, but all remaining subject to his supreme authority.

The prayer in common included three meetings daily in the various houses, in the morning, at midday and in the evening, taken up with the reciting of psalms. There was a supplementary prayer before going to bed, and the night was broken by the synaxis of the vigil, where Scripture was read at length, interspersed with psalms and prayers.

The costume of the monks remained the same as the anchorites': a linen tunic, a hood to cover the head and a cloak of goatskin. The diet, though very frugal (nothing cooked and no meat), was less severe than the anchorites' since it included not one but two meals a day (except on Wednesdays and Fridays). Again, the sick in the infirmary were explicitly to be treated more gently. On entering the monastery, the monk disposed of his goods. He could no longer possess anything as his own. His chastity was protected by the regulations of a strict prudence. But the great novelty consisted in the absolute obedience to the superior now required. This was at once the basis of the common life as instituted by Pachomius, and the great virtue of the monk, by which he renounced his own will. It was further inculcated and safeguarded by a whole series of graduated sanctions, proportioned to the infractions, going from a reprimand to dismissal, including fasting on bread and water, conditional excommunication and blows with a cane. In looking at this arsenal of weapons against disobedience, we should forget neither the very popular character of the recruitment nor the extreme forbearance with which Pachomius actually administered it.[54]

Once the monastery at Tabennisi was developed, Pachomius' sister, Mary, asked him to set up and organize a monastery nearby for nuns, which he did.[55]

All this clearly represents a considerable mutation in monasticism. First, and this is perhaps the most important aspect, it was

[54] On all this, see the rest of the *Life of Pachomius* (in Draguet, *op. cit.*, pp. 98 and ff.) and Armand Boon and Th. Lefort, *Pachomiana latina*, Louvain, 1932 (containing the essential texts of the Rule of Pachomius which have been preserved for us).

[55] *Life of Pachomius*, V; in Draguet, *op. cit.*, p. 101.

institutionalized: it became a hierarchical organization with definite laws. The taking of the habit accompanied by a formal promise of obedience (the origin of the religious vows to be formulated later on) made the monk a figure apart, the member of a social category more and more strictly defined by external laws rather than by a wholly personal aspiration towards the integral Christian life. Obedience now dominated the whole of life; materially, because it ruled all its details, spiritually, because it became the basis of all asceticism. Actually, obedience and, more particularly, the ideal of an obedience as humble, as complete, nay even as blind as possible, was already to be found in the *Apophthegms* of anchoretic origin. But this was obedience towards a spiritual master, towards the Elder whom the monk had freely selected. It now became obedience to a superior officially recognized as the head of a community and, at the same time, obedience to a whole collection of codified regulations. From this fact, obedience came to take on a double character not found hitherto, which was to become the source of long-lasting ambiguities.

Under a certain aspect, obedience remains a spiritual ordeal and, once again, even becomes the basic ordeal of the monastic life. As such, its finality is wholly interior, having as its direct object the spiritual good of the person who obeys. But, at the same time, obedience now is the condition *sine qua non* of harmonious community life: it is what assures good order and cooperation among all the members. Between these two aspects, obviously, a latent tension exists. And this tension was to increase as, on the one hand, religious institutions developed and weighed more heavily on the individual, and as, on the other hand, the religious individual himself, refined by spirituality, became more vividly aware of the uniqueness of his personal problems. This tension was to be resolved, in the West, only in the modern era, as the canonical legislation of the Church became oriented more and more decidedly towards a distinction and even a radical separation between the superior of the community as such and the spiritual director.

Eremitism and Cenobitism

It is interesting to observe the reactions of Egyptian monasticism generally towards all these innovations. On the one hand, the success of Pachomius' cenobitism was striking; it had found the ideal means of escaping from the anarchy that threatened to engulf anchoritism and, above all perhaps, of providing for all aspirants to the monastic life a methodical and strict formation, a trial and a period of adjustment to their vocation. This is expressed, for example, in this apophthegm of St Syncleticus:

> All those who live, as do we, in a monastery, should esteem obedience more than continence, because continence can lead to vanity, while obedience is always accompanied by humility.[56]

On the other hand, it seems that a great number of monks persisted in thinking that monasticism attains its full flowering only in the solitary life. Two motivations can be distinguished, more or less clearly expressed, behind this feeling.

The first is an obscure reaction but one which, none the less, was never to cease making itself felt through all monastic history, especially in the East. We might formulate it by saying that monasticism belongs to the order of charisms, of spiritual liberty, and therefore it seems contrary to its profound and original nature to enclose it in any legislation, any organization, however well thought-out these may be. Not only, so to say, does the habit not make the monk, neither does the rule, nor material obedience to a superior, nor any practices that may be laid down, but only the interior life to which all practices are ordered, the life which no practice, however well ordered, can produce of itself. The true monk is not and never will be the man who has succeeded in conforming his conduct to a framework, however ideal: he is the "spiritual man" above all, and the "spiritual man" who is judge of everything and who cannot be judged by any exterior criterion.[57]

The second objection against a monasticism reduced to organized cenobitism is that it is essential for the monk to leave everything for God alone. His insertion, his adaptation, even his perfect incorporation into the best social framework imaginable cannot define him. The work of the monk is not only a work to which solitude is essential, it is also a work that the monk alone can accomplish. His brothers, and life in common with them, can help him, can put him on the right path; but it is up to him alone, in intercourse with God alone, to arrive or not at his goal.

Behind the definition and the consolidation of monasticism into a stable state, through Pachomius' cenobitism, the primitive feeling, so strongly expressed in the *Vita Antonii*, would persist: that the monk is someone who can never halt, never settle down anywhere. This is the theme of journeying as did Abraham, the theme which Origen, after Philo, had developed so forcefully. But being most certainly part of the common Christian catechesis, it took on a

[56] Draguet, *op. cit.*, p. 223.

[57] This "spiritual" character of Eastern monasticism had already been brought out by Karl Holl, *Enthusiasmus und Bussgewalt in griechischen Mönchtum*, 1898.

renewed urgency in monasticism. Cassian echoes it in the Third Conference.[58]

> The tradition of our Fathers and the authority of Scripture teaches us that there are three kinds of renouncements which each of us must work to carry out with all his strength. The first is to reject all the pleasures and all the riches of this world. The second is to renounce ourselves, our vices, our wicked habits, and all the unruly affections of the spirit and of the flesh; and the third is to withdraw our heart from all things present and visible and apply it only to the eternal and invisible. God teaches us to make these three renouncements all at once by what He said to Abraham first of all. "Go out!" he told him, "from your country, from your kindred, from the house of your father; that is, leave the goods of this world and all the riches of the earth. Go out from your ordinary life and from the wicked and vicious inclinations which, attaching themselves to us by our birth and the corruption of flesh and blood, are as it were naturalized and become one thing with ourselves. Go out from the house of your father, that is, lose the memory of all the things of this world and of everything that presents itself to your eyes. . . ."
>
> . . . We shall then arrive at this third renouncement when our spirit, no longer weighed down by the contagion of this animal and earthly body, but purified from the affections of the earth, is raised to heaven by continual meditation on divine things, and is so taken up with the contemplation of the eternal truth that it forgets that it is still enclosed in fragile flesh and, ravished in God, it will find itself so absorbed in His presence that it has no longer ears to hear or eyes to see and it cannot even be struck by the greatest and most perceptible objects.[59]

The persistence of such a conception explains why, in spite of the success of Pachomius' cenobitism, even in Egypt anchoritism continued to develop alongside it. A little later, towards the end of the fourth century, another founder and legislator, Shenute, was to organize another cenobitical colony near Atripe in which the rigour of the rule and of obedience went far beyond what had been known in the Pachomian community. It was he who took the last step towards the monastic vows by being the first to require from his monks a written promise of obedience. In return, this reinforced cenobitism was recognized as a way and not an end: as the apprenticeship, and a particularly exacting one, for anchoritism. With Shenute, when the cenobites were fully formed, they were allowed to withdraw,

[58] On this theme in ancient monasticism, see H. von Campenhausen, *Die asketische Heimatslösigkeit im altchristlichen und früh mittelalterlischen Mönchtum*, Tübingen, 1930.

[59] *Conferences*, III, 6.

whether temporarily or permanently, to the mountain grottos and live in complete solitude.[60]

In concluding this chapter, it might be well to give our readers an idea of the expansion of monasticism in the different forms it was to take up to the end of the fourth century.[61]

The First Expansion of Monasticism

Antony's disciples constituted one of the first centres at Pispir, in the lower valley of the Nile, from the first years of the century on. A little later, around the Abbot Ammon, a second anchoretic colony, which was to become very numerous and famed throughout the entire world, was formed in the desert of Nitria, on an arid plateau about fifty miles south-west of Alexandria. Some miles to the south-west of this colony was built up an annex, the Cells, reserved for those who were considered ripe for complete solitude. Finally, around 330, Macarius the Elder founded a particularly secluded anchoretic colony still further to the south, more than fifty miles from Nitria, in the desert of Scete. While Nitria, relatively accessible, was capable of being permeated by Greek influences, and, thanks to the residence of Evagrius Ponticus, became towards the end of the century one of the first centres of erudite monasticism, Scete remained for a long time a faithful witness to primitive Coptic monasticism, and so essentially popular in character.

While Lower Egypt remained the homeland of anchoritism, it was in Upper Egypt and, more precisely, in the Thebaid, that Pachomius propagated his organized cenobitism. Tabennesi was its first centre, which swarmed to Pbow (some two miles to the west). Then other groups added themselves to his community, or rather, we should say, his congregation: Chenoboscium where he himself was converted, then Tmousopis, Tsi, Tsimine. At the request of the Bishop of Akhmin, still another foundation was made there, and a last one, Phnoum, near Esuch. Pachomius died in 346, carried off by an epidemic which ravaged the religious, especially at Pbow.

Some miles away from Akhmin, near the end of the reign of Constantine, Bgoul founded the neighbouring community of Antripos, where his nephew Shenute, towards the end of the century, introduced his reform of Pachomian cenobitism.

So much for Egypt. But already in Syria, as we have said, monasticism had appeared, at the same time, or almost the same time, as in Egypt, and, despite ancient legends, quite independently. This

[60] See Dom Patrice Cousin, *Précis d'Histoire monastique*, Paris, 1958, pp. 55ff.

[61] References to the sources for, and an analysis of the most recent works on all that follows will be found in the very valuable work of Dom Patrice referred to in the preceding note.

remained almost completely anchoretic. However, the region being still pagan in great part, the monks soon carried on a considerable missionary activity and many of them were promoted to the priesthood or the episcopate.

The oldest name mentioned by Sozomen is that of Aones, established in the neighbourhood of Carrhae at the beginning of the fourth century, and, a generation later, that of Julian Saba, in the mountains of Edessa, and his disciple James of Edessa. At the same time, more to the east, we find another James, who became the Bishop of Nisibis and the master of St Ephrem, who, having retired in the mountains of the Nisibia, where he led the ascetic life, after the capture of the village by the Persians (363) went to Edessa to found his celebrated school.

In the Sassanide kingdom itself, it is towards the year 340 that we find the activity of Aphraates, whose ascetic conferences are addressed to both men and women solitaries. Later on, having become a monk under the name of James, Aphraates was to be the superior and bishop of a Christian monastic centre, Mar Mattei, in Adiabene.

In the mountains of Antioch of Cyrene, in the desert of Chalcis, the monks were so numerous at the end of the century as to transform into hermitages the fortified posts of the *limes romanus*.

We have already mentioned the peculiarities of the asceticism in these various related countries. The most celebrated was the stylitism illustrated by St Simeon (389–459), at some distance to the north-west of Antioch. He remained for thirty-seven years on his pillar, and around him were organized a monastery and a whole series of charitable works.

On the origins of Palestinian monasticism, we have abundant information in the lives of Paul and Hilarion by St Jerome; but it must be admitted that these documents are highly suspect, and that the existence of the personages whom he extols is not even very certain.

What we know more about, for this period and in this region, are the two groups of Latin monasteries: that of the two Melanias and of Rufinus of Jerusalem; that of Paula and then of Eustochium at Bethlehem, the latter under the immediate influence of St Jerome. Even the monasteries who drew their recruits from the locality itself were, in this country flooded with strangers on pilgrimage, frequently the work of such pilgrims: such was the laura of St Euthymius (Armenian), between Bethany and Jericho; the coenobium of his disciple Theoctistus (in the gorge of the waddy of Dabor); or, later, in the fifth century, the great laura founded near the Cedron, south-west of Jerusalem, by the Cappadocian, St Saba. Here again, the anchoretic life was much more important than the cenobitic. It took the modified form of the laura: a group of solitaries who gather every Saturday and Sunday for services and spiritual reunions around a master, in a vast grotto or some central buildings.

Towards the middle of the fourth century, a personage whose doctrines have been much disputed, the austere ascetic Eustathius, who was bishop of Sebaste, propagated monasticism in Asia Minor.[62] He inspired St Basil, and thus unknowingly prepared the way for a new transformation of monasticism, by which, from an essentially popular and evangelical movement, it was to become a school of learned spirituality, wholly permeated with the heritage of Alexandria and, above all, of Origen.

[62] On this personage who remains quite mysterious, see David Amand, *L'ascèse monastique de saint Basile*, Maredsous, 1948, pp. 52ff.

XIV

ERUDITE MONASTICISM: THE CAPPADOCIANS

ALTHOUGH born in Egypt, not far from Alexandria, where Clement and Origen had just contributed such original developments to Christian spirituality, primitive monasticism seems to owe nothing to these thinkers. Completely popular as to its native soil, completely evangelical as to its primary motivations, it was in no way an intellectual movement in its beginnings. And these beginnings were made in the context of a Church still foreign to the "Greek" world, and because it wished to remain so.

Yet only two or three generations at the most had gone by before monasticism had provided itself with a theological teaching, the elements of which appeared as if all prepared in the spirituality of Origen. This conjunction did not come about in Egypt itself, however. It had to be made by way of Cappadocia. It was here that monasticism, originally the spirituality of very simple Christians, became erudite in becoming Origenist. But it was an Origenism that had been rethought and rectified as well as broadened, thanks to the Cappadocians (SS. Basil, Gregory Nazianzen and Gregory of Nyssa) which furnished monasticism with a well-worked-out theory accompanying an organization also methodically thought out and no longer simply empirical as was that of Pachomian cenobitism.

To understand how such a change could take place, we must begin by familiarizing ourselves with a new type of intellectual Christian, a type of which these three men were distinguished representatives, with personal shades of difference which it is important clearly to distinguish.

The Cappadocians

In the first place, the Cappadocians were not only thinkers, men of culture, nor even humanists like Clement, enamoured of the old myths. These were men of learning, and also men of the world. It must be added, obviously, that the learning with which they were so profoundly imbued was that of their time: a culture in which philosophy, after mingling with spirituality, had been absorbed in a rhetoric in the mid-stream of an archaizing renaissance. At Alexandria in the third century, all types of thought, all the myths, had flowed together in a religious eclecticism. At Caesarea in the fourth century and still more at Athens—where these men went to complete their formation as the sons of great families destined for important affairs, the law-court above all—the art of the rhetor had become (or again become) supreme. (We say, "again become", for in many respects it was only a new form of sophistry, merely more brilliant and with more intermingled elements than the ancient one.)[1]

We are inclined today to be unjust to rhetoric in general and to the rhetoric of that period in particular. Without doubt, it characterized a period when culture tended more to immortalize a whole past than to renew itself. But our authors came just in time to offer it what it had lacked: new themes, new subjects, that were to give an unexpected content to a formalism whose virtuosity was exhausting itself in vacuity. And, however strange the statement may appear at first sight, the predominance given to the word by the profane culture of the end of the fourth century, was marvellously adapted to clothing a thought wholly nourished by the divine Word.[2] In fact, we misunderstand the intention at least (and much more than the intention) of the art of a Libanios if we see it as nothing but hollow verbalism. The rhetor at this period, by the perfect mastery which he believed himself to have attained of a language, of a literary heritage, of a complete experience of the word, was conscious of wielding a sovereign power over the minds of men by which, he flattered himself, he could remake the world to his liking. Such a conception, nourishing ambitions that might be thought beyond reason, none the less prepared minds to welcome a divine Word, exactly as Origen had conceived it for his part: as a new creation, interior to the first, and leading it back to the original divine design, precisely by being introduced into the hearts of men and there remaking them according to the will of God.

Another element is no less essential for understanding the spirituality of the Cappadocians: the Arian crisis which was

[1] For a fine study of the environment and the literary formation of the Cappadocians, see A. Puech, *Histoire de la littérature grecque chrétienne*, III, Paris, 1930, pp. 235ff. On Libanios in particular, cf. A. J. Festugière, *Antioche païenne et chrétienne*, Paris, 1959.

[2] See what Puech has to say (*op. cit.*, p. 338) about the connection made by Gregory Nazianzen himself between the divine Logos and the "logoi" of the rhetoricians.

surmounted thanks to them and, above all, the kind of virulent rationalism which the Arianism they triumphed over had taken on in becoming "anomean" with Eunomius. As we know, Eunomius pretended that the divine essence was definable by innascibility and, as such, was fully knowable by human reason. And so he categorically refused divinity to the Son. If the dangers of a theology of the Logos too strictly dependent on the notions of Greek philosophy had already been revealed with Arius, here it was the whole of Greek rationalism which positively refused to accept the Christian mystery. What was the more remarkable with the Cappadocians, even the two Gregories, however speculative, was that, without turning in the least toward irrationalism, they replaced this mystery at the heart of their theological conceptions.[3] But it is in their spirituality that we can best appreciate how profound is their perception of the transcendence of the Christian God, in the very fact that he is the living God in a sense which the Greeks had not even a notion of.

Among the three great Cappadocians, Basil is the man of action, Gregory Nazianzen the poet, Gregory of Nyssa the religious philosopher; but all three are above all spiritual men and theologians in whom the most refined intellectual life was very early put wholly at the service of the faith.

Basil and his brother, Gregory of Nyssa, with their elder sister Macrina and their younger brother Peter (who died as archbishop of Sebaste) belonged to a Christian family of long standing and among the most notable in Cappadocia. Their paternal grandmother, Macrina the Elder, had been converted by St Gregory Thaumaturgus, the most famous of Origen's students. Their mother, Emmelia, was another example of the Christian matron, as was Nonna, the mother of Gregory Nazianzen. Born about 330, Basil soon decided on the career of rhetor and lawyer which had been that of his father. First brought up by his father, he went through the schools of Caesarea, of Constantinople, and finally of Athens. It was at Caesarea that he must have come to know Gregory Nazianzen, the son of the bishop of that city (who had come later to Christianity and the bishopric after having belonged to the sect of the Hypsistarians). After Caesarea, their paths diverged for some time, Gregory going to Alexandria while Basil departed for Constantinople. But Basil rejoined his new friend at Athens. These were years of common intellectual enthusiasm, but already dominated by religious aspirations directed from the outset

[3] Vl. Lossky makes some excellent remarks on this point in his *Essai sur la Théologie mystique de l'Église d'Orient*, Paris, 1944, pp. 31–2.

towards the monastic life. When they had completed their studies, however, they both taught rhetoric for some time, Gregory at Athens, Basil in his own country.

Macrina the younger, meanwhile, had already withdrawn into the solitude of Annesi, above the valley of the Iris, on a property belonging to the family, to lead the monastic life. Her influence, during these years, was combined with that of the bishop of Sebaste, Eustathius, who had introduced monastic asceticism into Cappadocia, to decide Basil to put into practice his plans for the religious life. Towards this end, he began by undertaking a journey methodically planned to gain information about the great centres of monastic life in Egypt, in Syria, and in Mesopotamia. On his return, he gave his goods to the poor, and also settled in the valley of Iris. Remembering their former intimacy, he summoned Gregory, now returned from Greece, to join him. The latter, about 360 it seems, did in fact come for a visit. This visit was taken up with the composing, done together by the two friends, of the *Philocalia,* an anthology of Origen's texts on spirituality and, more particularly, the reading of the Bible.[4]

One or two years later, however, Gregory was a priest with his father, the Bishop of Nazianzen. Basil, for his part, about the same time, was ordained by Eusebius, the Bishop of Caesarea. In 370, he was elected to replace him and, the following year, he forced Gregory, who previously had accepted the priesthood only with difficulty, to let himself be consecrated Bishop of Sasima. In the same year, the other Gregory, Basil's brother (five years younger it seems) was consecrated Bishop of Nyssa. He also had formerly shared their solitude at Annesi, after the same career as rhetor which they had followed, and, in his case, marriage as well.

Basil's episcopate represented, in the nine years he still had to live, the perfect example of a mind practical as well as speculative, and even more practical than speculative, put at the service of pastoral zeal. It might be said that he came to the relief of Athanasius of Alexandria in the struggle against Arianism. He was the first to put in perfect focus and to cause to prevail the precise positions, prepared by Basil of Ancyra, thanks to which the faith of Nicea was maintained while avoiding any trace of Sabellianism, that is, of personal confusion between the Father and the Son. In the face of the Arianizing Emperor Constans, he defended these positions with a fearlessness that assured their success, just as he explained them untiringly to the Latin West.

[4] On this period in the friendship of Basil and Gregory, see Stanislas Giet, *Sasimes, une méprise de saint Basile*, Paris, 1941, pp. 37ff.

At the same time, he organized the monastic life and what we now call social work in his diocese with an activity and a decisiveness astonishing in such a puny intellectual, worn down with the stomach trouble which prematurely carried him off.

It was to make sure of having auxiliaries in his ecclesiastical policy that he gave the episcopate to his friend and to his brother, in spite of the impassioned repugnance of the former (who never set foot in the miserable little market-town which should have been his episcopal city) and the mediocre practical abilities of the latter.

Gregory Nazianzen, having gone back to solitude after his forced consecration, emerged only to aid his ageing father until after Basil's death. Then, he was seen taking up the struggle in his stead, even at Constantinople where, with the cathedral in the hands of the Arians, he proclaimed the orthodox faith in his little basilica of the Anastasis. The Council of Constantinople of 380–81 saw his victory and that of Gregory of Nyssa, for the faith of Nicea. He was even enthroned as bishop of the capital. But, disgusted with its intrigues, he took flight again into solitude. Later, he administered for some time the diocese of Nazianzen when his father died and provided it with a successor. He then retired for good to the neighbouring village of Arianzen where he had been born and where he died in 389 or 390.

The other Gregory, for his part, who was to end his days in Nyssa towards 395, was occupied above all with intellectual activity and increasingly concerned with clarifying the problems posed by monastic spirituality.

Basil and Monasticism

The spiritual, and more properly monastic, work of Basil was above all a work of legislation.[5] But the precise rules that are his gift to the monastic life reflect a maturely thought-out conception of this life. These rules are extant in two collections. The first, *Regulae fusius tractatae,* gathers together thirty-five spiritual conversations discussing the principles of monastic asceticism. The second, *Regulae brevius tractatae,* includes three hundred and thirteen answers to detailed questions, abundantly indicating that

[5] See P. Humbertclaude, *La doctrine ascétique de saint Basile de Césarée*, Paris, 1932. Stanislas Giet is to be credited with having shown clearly that the monastic teaching of St Basil is clarified by being replaced in the general context of his whole eminently social idea of Christianity: *Les idées et l'action sociale de saint Basile*, Paris, 1941, pp. 183ff. More recently, David Amand has devoted an exhaustive study to the ascetic teaching of Basil, starting from a profound examination of its sources: *L'ascèse monastique de saint Basile*, Maredsous, 1948, and better still, Dom J. Gribomont, in *Théologie de la vie monastique*, Paris, 1961, pp. 99ff.

this is in no way a fictitious composition, but clearly a casuistic collection inspired by problems encountered in his own experience.[6]

The basic idea dominating these works as a whole is not only a categorical preference for the cenobitic life, but a condemnation of the anchoretic life on principle. Once again, it would be well to clarify exactly what kind of cenobitic life is in question, for it is no longer the type that had been organized by Pachomius.

On the motivations for the monastic life, it is to be noted that Basil draws on the purely evangelical themes of primitive monasticism. The monk is simply a Christian who wishes to take the most effective means to obtain his salvation. Here is how, in Letter 223, he explains his own vocation:

> As for myself, I had given much time to vanity.... One day, waking up as from a deep sleep, I opened my eyes to the wonderful light of the evangelical truth...; weeping bitterly for my miserable life, I prayed that a rule of conduct would be given me to enter into the ways of piety. Above all, I took care to rectify somewhat my way of living which long familiarity with the wicked had disordered. I had read the Gospel and noted that the great means of attaining perfection was to sell one's possessions, to share them with our brothers who are in want, and to disengage oneself completely from the cares of this life without keeping any attachment of soul to the good things of this earth, and I hoped to find some brother who had chosen this way, with him to succeed in crossing the surging floods of this short life.[7]

In fact, Basil never envisaged this life sanctified by renouncement, by detachment, as a strictly solitary life, but always as a life in common:

> Who does not know, indeed, that man is a gentle and sociable being, and not solitary or savage? Nothing is as proper to our nature as to enter one another's society, to have need of one another, and to love the man who is of our race. After having given us these seeds which He has cast into our hearts, the Lord came to claim their fruits and He said: "I give you a new commandment: to love one another."[8] The Lord, wishing to arouse our souls to observe this commandment, did not require of His disciples either unheard of prodigies or miracles (even

[6] P.G., XXI, 620–1428. On the problems concerned with a critical edition, see Dom J. Gribomont, *Histoire du texte des Ascétiques de saint Basile*, Louvain, 1953. Outside of the *Rules*, the authenticity of which no one doubts, agreement is far from being reached on what is to be retained among the other ascetic writings that have been attributed to St Basil.

[7] *Epist. 223*, 2; P.G., XXXI, 337 BC.

[8] John 13. 34.

though He gave them, in the Holy Spirit, the power to do such things); but... what did He say to them? "All will know that you are My disciples by the love that you have for one another."[9]

Everywhere He unites these precepts to such an extent that He refers to Himself the good deeds of which our neighbour is the object. "For I was hungry, and you gave me to eat..." and He adds: "Everything that you did to the least of my brethren, you did to Me."[10] And so, by means of the first precept, it is possible to observe the second, and by the second to go back to the first: in loving the Lord, to love also the neighbour, for "He who loves me," says the Lord, "will keep my commandments", and, "My commandment is that you love one another as I have loved you."[11]

Further on he says even more rigorously:

As the foot has its own ability but lacks others, so that, without the assistance of the other members, it does not find in itself the power to subsist nor help to procure what is lacking to it, so, in the solitary life, what we have is without usefulness and we are without aid in what is lacking to us: for God, our creator, has decided that we should have need of one another, so that, as it is written,[12] we should be united with one another.[13]

After this, in the same rule, he adds more:

See! The Lord, in the excess of His condescension, was not content to teach us His doctrine, but in order to give us a clear, an obvious example of His humility, in the perfection of His love, He washed and dried with a towel the feet of His disciples ... But whose feet will you wash? Whom will you care for? How will you put yourself in the last place, if you live alone with yourself?

And this other word that it is pleasing and good for brothers to live together,[14] how can this be verified in solitude? A community of brothers is, then, a stadium in which athletes are exercised, a good road towards progress, a continual training, a constant concern for the commandments of God: its end is the glory of God according to the commandment of our Lord,[15] but it also preserves the example of the saints of whom the Acts of the Apostles tell us:[16] "All the believers were gathered together and they had all their possessions in common", or again, "The multitude of the faithful had but one heart and one soul: there was no one who kept for himself anything that he possessed, but everything was in common."[17]

[9] John 13. 35. [10] Matt. 15. 35–40.

[11] *Regulae fusius tractatae*, 3, §§ 1 and 2; P.G., XXX, 340 C. The two quotations at the end are John 14. 15 and 15. 12.

[12] Eccles. 12. 20 (?)

[13] *Regulae fusius tractatae*, 7, § 1; *ibid.*, col. 345 D.

[14] Ps. 132. 1. [15] Matt. 5. 16. [16] Acts 2. 44 and 4. 32.

[17] *Regulae fusius tractatae*, 7, § 4; *ibid.*, col. 347 E.

These statements are so categorical that it is not surprising to find, in the *Regulae brevius tractatae,* that a monk who asks if a man who has been formed by the common life may not then withdraw to the desert, receives as his answer :"This is nothing but a mark of self-will and remains foreign to those who honour God."[18]

Such excluding of everything except cenobitism on principle is certainly dominated by a view of the Gospel which we might be tempted to describe as literalist were it not so obviously enlightened by Paulinian and Johannine conceptions of charity. We should note that it remains quite in the line of the gnosis of Clement or Origen, who did not conceive the gnostic life as being formed otherwise than in the common life and as sharing with others all the spiritual riches that it might acquire. For it is not less true that behind the wholly evangelical Christianity of Basil we find, in perfect harmony with it and illuminated by it, a very Greek kind of humanism. The preliminary considerations on the basically social nature of man paraphrase Aristotle[19] and are completely impregnated with the Hellenic sense of human life as life in a City. We should emphasize this initial remark, for it can be made again and again in connection with the most varied works of the Cappadocians. On the one hand, they are stricter than any of their predecessors among hellenizing Christians in their fidelity to the Word of God—hence their clear-eyed criticism of the Greek conceptions which cannot be assimilated by Christianity. On the other hand, it was a humanism truly lived, not detached ideas only, which they brought back from Greece to incorporate into their so essentially Christian spirituality.

However, while Basil tends to eliminate as an error or a deviation the primitive type of monasticism which had no cenobitical organization or finally refused to be enclosed within it, in return his cenobitism is a new kind. The first point distinguishing it in relation to Pachomius' is that Basil's cenobitic society is to remain small. This seems to result from two considerations. The first is that community life should protect the recollection of its members as completely as would pure solitude. And the other is that the relationships of the superior with his monks and, in general, of each monk with the others, should remain personal.[20]

Another feature, perhaps, has no less importance: the integration of this monasticism into the Church. A text of Gregory Nazianzen's, at first sight seeming a little obscure, enlightens us as to the process

[18] *Regulae brevius tractatae*, 74; P.G., XXX, 441 C.
[19] *Politics*, III, 4.
[20] See Giet, *op. cit.*, p. 200.

of reflection by which Basil reached this conclusion.[21] It seems that before his time Cappadocia had known either monasteries built in far-off solitudes, or ascetics living in the world and there devoting themselves to different charitable or apostolic tasks (they were called *migades*: that is, mingled with the world). Basil came practically to abolish the distinction, in arranging the life of his monasteries in such a way that silence, recollection, even times of actual solitude were arranged for, while still closely associating these monasteries with all the works of the Church to which his episcopate was to contribute such a great development. Ready to welcome all the guests who presented themselves, the Basilian monastery included an orphanage and schools in which children were brought up for the monastic life or even prepared for life in the world. The monks took part in all the social works of the Church, whose focus they became and they constituted as it were a select stock for ordinations to the various ecclesiastical ministries.

Very revealing is the answer given, in the 277th brief rule, to the question on the *tamieion* where the Lord prescribes that he who prays should "go into his room".[22]

> The circumstances under which this command was given indicate its bearing: it is addressed to people tormented by the desire to be pleasing to men. If anyone suffers from this passion, then, he is right to withdraw in prayer and to live in solitude until he can accustom himself no longer to attend to the praises of men, but to look at God alone.
>
> However, when anyone, by the grace of God, is purified from this passion, it is no longer necessary that he hide what is beautiful.
>
> This is what the Lord teaches us when He says: "A city cannot be hidden if it is built on a mountain-top, and one does not light a lamp to put it under a basket, but on a candlestick, so that it will give light to all who are in the house. Let your light so shine before men, that they may see your good works and glorify your Father who is in heaven."[23]

Presupposing complete poverty for the individual monk, although expressly allowing property to the community, the Basilian monastery was austere.

> The athlete may be recognized by his well-developed muscles, the colour of his skin, and the Christian shows by the emaciation

[21] This text of *Orat. XLIII* and a discussion of it will be found in Giet, *op. cit.*, pp. 185ff.

[22] Matt. 6. 16.

[23] *Regulae brevius tractatae*, 277; P.G., XXX, 513 G. The final quotation is from Matthew 5. 14–16.

of his body and the pallor that flourishes on *enkrateia* that he is truly an athlete running in the path of Christ's commandments.[24]

For while Basil, like the two other Cappadocians, shared the Greek admiration for the cosmos, he was altogether of his time also in seeing, with Plato, the body as a stranger to the soul, and even, with Plotinus, as a heavy weight encumbering it, the source of the impurities that corrupt it. *Enkrateia,* the renouncement of sensual pleasures and, more generally, of all the attachments that come from the body such as family ties, is, therefore, at the centre of asceticism. It allows freedom to flower—the freedom to carry out all the commandments of Christ formulated in Scripture, which are the only final rule of monasticism.

On the base of this weakening of the life of the senses, a new life, ruled by the will of God alone, is to be organized.

Work and the hours of the divine office, by now almost completely developed according to the plan that they have preserved to our times, took up practically the whole of the monastic day. Everything tended towards charity through obedience. This was regulated by the authority of an all-powerful superior, although he might call for the assistance of other officials (Basil expressly rejected every tendency to introduce democracy into the government of his communities). Stanislas Giet has rightly brought out the fact that this obedience is justified, in the Rules, not so much by the immediate good of the individual who submits himself as by the harmony it assures to the life of the community. The authority exercised, furthermore, as well as the obedience given, is justified by this end.[25] What is sanctifying, then, in the cenobitic life as thus conceived is adaptation to the life of the community as such. And this appears, in the final analysis, as the supreme means as well as the purpose of monastic asceticism.

It would be difficult to imagine a more radical change in any institution than that effected by Basil within monasticism. As he wished it to be, it is almost the exact opposite of what it had been to begin with. From an essentially solitary effort towards liberation, it became, quite the contrary, an essentially communitarian institution. It is in integrating himself into an ideal society that the individual is to be formed for a spiritual life, the very concept of which is social. Separation from the common life of men remains the only common characteristic. But Basil's separation tends to replace one society by another and no longer in any way to engage

[24] *Regulae fusius tractatae*, 17, § 2; P.G., XXX, 361 A.
[25] Giet, *op. cit.*, pp. 200–3.

the monk in a spiritual adventure that is solitary by its very essence, whatever its later reverberations may be.

Our manuals repeat unwearyingly that the Basilian ideal was imposed on the whole monastic Orient. There are few statements taken over by one author from another that are quite so untrue. Actually, the Basilian ideal was only imposed generally in the West and, moreover, under the mitigated form of the rule of St Benedict, which we shall speak of further on. The monastic life of the East, on the contrary, has never ceased to tend, even through cenobitism, towards anchoritism.[26]

What is true is that Basil's practical regulations, very moderate as a whole, inspired St Theodore, in the ninth century at Constantinople, in his organization of the famous monastery of Stoudios. From there, they passed to the holy mountain of Athos,[27] and then, with St Theodosius of Petchersk, to the monasteries of Kiev and Russia. But always, in the Basilian framework as well as outside it, the ancient monastic ideal of the early days has been maintained in the East. In Russia in the fifteenth century, the effort of St Joseph of Volokolamsk integrally to impose the ideal of Basil together with its material organization met with the unconquerable resistance of St Nilus Sorsky.[28]

Behind this apparently anarchic persistence of primitive monasticism there is, and we should not deceive ourselves about it, the basically interior and charismatic character of the monastic ideal, a character which the Orient has never become resigned to giving up. But, even at the time and alongside Basil, under different forms, his brother and his friend had recovered this ideal in the very framework of the institutions created by the Mentor who had apparently subjugated them.

The Personality of Gregory Nazianzen

It is curious that Basil, doubtless the most rigorously social Christian in the whole history of the Church, should have had for his very intimate friend Gregory Nazianzen, the most irreducibly individualistic. When we read through St Gregory's correspondence, his poems above all, and even his homilies, we cannot help being struck by the personal touch that he puts on everything. Of an exquisite sensibility, almost in the pathological sense of the term,

[26] The recently published work of Theoklitos Dionysiatous, *Between Heaven and Earth* (in Greek), Athens, 1956, in which is presented the best of contemporary Athonite spirituality, is the most convincing witness to this fact. See the long account given by Rev. André Louf, O.C.S.O., in *Istina*, 1959, no. 1, pp. 9ff.

[27] See Dom Patrice Cousin, *op. cit.*, pp. 88ff.

[28] See the studies on these great figures of Russian monasticism by Ivan Kologrivof, *Essai sur la sainteté en Russie*, Bruges, 1953.

he was one of those beings avid for sympathy, for friendship, but who can find, if not happiness, at least a tolerable condition, only in solitude. There, opening out their hearts for themselves, they can find peace if they find God. There is no doubt that Gregory was an incorrigible romantic. He does not possess the grand tone of Augustine, but his voice—more familiar, more simply human—has a resonance that often affects us even more deeply.[29]

When we read the half-ironic, half-bitter letter that he sent to Basil after his stay in the monastery at Annesi,[30] we might gain the impression that he was one of those men for whom monasticism can have only false attractions: that of a solitude where one can finally be wholly one's own rather than God's own. This judgment would be superficial and unjust. It is enough to read his poems on virginity to understand how profound a sense he had of the detachments necessary to be wholly God's. But it could certainly not be expected of such a man that he would seek perfection by applying himself to becoming no more than a well-adjusted cog in a harmonious but rigid mechanism.

In return, and Basil must certainly have known it, it was not for the sake of polishing himself, of turning himself over and over in the manner of Montaigne, that he sought solitude. It was to give himself up to "gnostic" meditation on the word of God, in the sense of Clement and, above all, of Origen; it was to become truly the disciple, the friend, the living member of the Christ whom he called with such enthusiasm "my Christ"![31] Basil who, for his part, never doubted that the final purpose of monasticism, even in the way in which he understood it, was to give oneself up to the divine Word in this same way,[32] was well aware of what he was doing when he summoned Gregory to join him, at Annesi, first of all, and in having him compile the *Philocalia* of Origen. Such a man, in spite of everything about him that was congenitally opposed to Basil's conceptions, was better able than anyone else to provide them with the supplement of soul that such delicately adjusted mechanisms required in order not to rotate in a void.

More than Basil, whose asceticism retains such a reflection of the

[29] It is surprising that hardly any recent studies can be cited on this exceptional personality (see, however, E. Fleury, *Saint Grégoire de Nazianze et son temps*, Paris, 1928, re-edited in 1950), and J. Plagnieux, *Gregoire de Nazianze théologien*, Paris, 1951). Works in P.G., XXXVI-XXXVIII. In fact, so rare are the modern scholars who have taken the trouble even to open the volume of his poems, in which the essence of his spirituality is to be found, that nobody is as yet aware of all the ideas systematized by Gregory of Nyssa which actually originated with his namesake.

[30] *Epist.*, 4; P.G., XXXVIII, 24ff.

[31] Cf. *Orat.*, XXVII, 4; P.G., XXXVI, 285.

[32] Cf. *Epist.* 2, to Gregory; P.G., XXXII, 2224ff. A translation and commentary is given in David Amand, *op. cit.*, pp. 86ff.

encratism of Eustathius of Sebaste that he could see in marriage and Christian life in the world nothing more than a concession to human weakness,[33] Gregory was sensitive to the positive values of a life woven around family ties. But he distinguished the more clearly the value proper to consecrated virginity and the way in which it contains in embryo all the separations of monasticism.

The Monastic Vocation according to Gregory Nazianzen

For Gregory as for the whole of primitive monasticism, it is only the desire for complete fidelity to Christ, for a decisive break with everything that could separate us from him, that explains the monastic vocation. This is what he says of his own:

> Seeing how the cause and the effect are one thing
> Anger and the murder that proceeds from it,
> The disposition to blaspheme and the false oath,
> In refusing ourselves to that without which evil
> Would not exist, we flee evil itself.
> Hence, for me, the pricelessness of the choir of virgins
> Imitating the angels' discarnate life
> To unite themselves to God and to Him alone.
> In this state, everything urges us towards another life
> And we desire to be carried away when we are
> Detached from the bonds and the laws of marriage,
> From which Christ, born of a virgin Mother,
> Has withdrawn me, making me virgin by new laws.
> For, come into this life in these bonds,
> Forced to know as transient what is transitory,
> As corrupted what is corruption, to discover something better
> Than the visible and the uncertain,
> In joy I lead back to God His image
> By a life free and detached from all bonds,
> Without leaving here any vestige of my skin
> That life might swell up in its turn like one more goatskin;
> With all my being I move wholly towards God,
> With many companions in harmony with me
> Seeing only the life that we hope for.[34]

It is most interesting to note that these verses come at the culminating point of a great poem *On Virtue, arete*, which is doubtless the most complete expression of the Cappadocian humanism. Werner Jaeger has shown that this idea of *arete* is central in Greek humanism and that the development of the latter is centred on the

[33] See the minute analysis of Basilian *enkrateia* to which David Amand has devoted himself. On Basil's view of marriage, see Giet, *op. cit.*, pp. 42ff.
[34] *On Virtue*, tenth poem of Section II, vv. 885–909; P.G., XXXVII, 744–6.

development that the idea of *arete* itself was called to undergo.[35] But in Gregory's vision, the epic of *arete* in humanism was nothing but a fumbling search for the life conformed to reason, the life given to man in biblical revelation alone, and finding its development only in monasticism. Thus it was Abraham's going out of Ur, Moses' ascent of the mountain, Elias' being taken up, the Baptist's witnessing that showed the way to what the most virtuous of the Greek sages tended towards. The Christian life in its perfection, that is, the monastic life, alone realizes it.

It follows that Gregory would consecrate and systematize the usage then becoming customary of calling the ascetic Christian life the "philosophic life". We have already seen St Justin presenting Christianity as the true philosophy. Clement opposes "barbarous philosophy" to the pretentions, unjustified in his eyes, of Hellenistic philosophy. For him, the true philosophy is at once and inseparably Christian teaching and living. With the historian, Eusebius of Caesarea, already, however, the philosopher is not any Christian, but only the monk.[36] For Gregory, the life of the monks is "philosophy in works" *di ergon philosophia*.[37] In fact, in the funeral oration for his brother Caesarius, he defines the meaning of *philosophein* as "to harmonize oneself with the life above", that of the Angels and of God himself.[38]

In another poem, which is an exhortation to virgins, he equally emphasizes how the domination of the instincts by reason is in conformity with the profound nature of man, but can find in Christian asceticism alone all its meaning and all its resources.

If nature does not dominate the flesh
As the divine image divinizes me, what more have I than the beasts wholly subject to the motions of the flesh?
Although, then, nature is untamed, with the majority of men,
We know none the less that a superior order can conquer it.
As for me, whose body is like that of all men,
The cross has dominated it in rescuing me from the world,
To which, of myself, I had attached my heavy flesh.
Indeed, I desire to die with Christ so as to rise with Him,
Bearing everything that He bore: the Word, the body, the nails, the resurrection.[39]

35 See his great work, *Paideia*, vol. I, Oxford, 1946, pp. 3ff.

36 G. Bardy, "'Philosophie' et 'philosophe' dans le vocabulaire chrétien des premiers siècles", in *Revue d'Ascétique et de Mystique*, XXV (1949), Toulouse, pp. 106ff.

37 *Orat.*, VI; P.G., XXXV, 721. Cf. *Orat.* XXV, *In laudem Heronis philosophi*; *ibid.*, col. 1198ff.

38 *In laudem Caesarii*; P.G., XXXV, *Orat.* VII, col. 765 B.

39 Poem II, Section II, vv. 560–7; P.G., XXXVII, 622–3.

For, as the great poem on *arete* explains again:

When the enemy, having struggled with Christ,
Withdrew, vanquished by a nobler flesh
Which had taken nothing for forty days and forty nights,
So that he had still more shame for his vain temptation,
The law of voluntary affliction was introduced. . . .[40]

Thereby the monks succeed the martyrs,

. . . increasing
The holy and new mystery of Christ
From whom we have received the name with which we are named.[41]

Hence this cry from the heart:

For me, Christ is the reward for everything,
And I carry the poverty of His cross as richness.[42]

Marriage and Virginity

And so we see how he locates virginity with regard to marriage, the building up of the earthly city with the exclusive search for the heavenly city, according to his other great poem in praise of virginity:

As a painter, tracing out images on a picture,
Begins with light and dark strokes
To sketch his subject, and then, later on,
Completes the representation by putting in the colours,
So virginity, that in every age belonged to Christ,
Appeared first in a few persons only, hidden in the shadows,
So long as the law reigned under dark colours,
And its hidden splendour was seen by only a small number.
But when Christ, of a chaste Virgin Mother,
Free from all bond, like to God, without stain, appeared,
(For He had to be born without a marriage and without a father),
He sanctified women by repulsing Eve, the harsh mother,
And defied carnal laws, by the Gospel preaching,
The spirit succeeding to the flesh and grace entering in,
Then virginity shone out to the eyes of mortal men,
Freed from this world and freeing the weak world,
Surpassing marriage and the ties of life
As the soul surpasses the flesh;
As the wide heavens, the earth; as the life that remains for the blessed
That which passes; and as God is beyond man.

[40] Poem X, Section II, vv. 636–40; *ibid.*, col. 726.
[41] *Ibid.*, vv. 701–2; col. 730–1. [42] *Ibid.*, vv. 464–6; col. 714.

Then, around the resplendent King stands the immaculate and heavenly choir,
Which from the earth hastens towards divinization,
Bearing Christ, honouring the Cross, despising the world,
Dead to earthly things, attentive to heavenly;
Lights of the world, clear mirrors of the light,
Those who contemplate God, belong to Him and possess Him.
. . . Those to whom marriage and the ties of life are dear,
[say]: We follow the law established by the Son of the eternal Father
When He united the first Adam to the woman drawn from his side,
So that man may be born of man as his fruit, and, throughout the generations,
Even though he be mortal, man may dwell in his descendants as the grain in the wheat;
In carrying out this law and union of love,
We aid one another mutually and, born of the earth,
We follow the primitive law of the earth which is also the law of God,
. . . See then, what wisely chosen marriage brings to men:
Who, then, has taught wisdom, penetrated the depths,
Sounded what is on the earth, in the sea, under the heaven,
Who, then, has given laws to cities and, before these laws,
Who established the cities? Who discovered the arts,
Who has filled the forum, the houses, the gymnasiums,
The army for fighting, the tables for feasting,
Who has gathered together the choirs singing in the temples,
Who has put down the fierceness of primitive life, cultivated the earth,
Crossed the seas? Who, then, has reunited in one what was separated,
But marriage? And there is yet more:
We are one another's hand, ear, foot,
By the blessing of marriage that redoubles our strength,
Rejoicing our friends, desolating our enemies.
Cares shared sweeten trials,
Common joys are still happier
And accord makes riches more precious,
Nay, it is more precious than riches for those who do not possess them.
Marriage is the key of moderation of the desires,
The seal of unbreakable friendship,
. . . The unique drink from a fountain enclosed that those outside do not taste;
It does not spread outside nor draw from without.
Those who are united in the flesh make but one soul
And they raise a like spire of their piety by their mutual love.

For marriage does not remove from God
But brings all the closer to Him because it is God Himself who urges us to it . . .

How does virginity answer:

I leave to others what makes up the reward of this life.
But for me
There is only one law, one thought: that, filled with divine love,
I depart from this earth towards the God who reigns in heaven, the author of light.
. . . Carrying out the law of the king of all things, to Him alone
Am I bound in love, and I have abandoned all earthly love,
This law established by the Son born of the eternal Father,
He who is born of a Father who knows no ties, incorruptible from the incorruptible,
When at the beginning He put Adam in paradise, also with no ties.
. . . Giving his love to one only, he comes nearer and nearer to Christ,
He who loves Him who loves him, sees Him who sees him
And goes to meet Him who comes to him . . .[43]

The Mysticism of Gregory Nazianzen

The mystical aspiration, that gives meaning to consecrated virginity and to the solitude in which it tends to bury us, has been still better expressed by Gregory in the discourse in which he attempted to justify the flight following on his half-forced ordination:

To me, nothing seems preferable to the state of the man who, closing his senses to exterior impressions, escaping from the flesh and the world, re-entering into himself, retaining no further contact with any human things except when necessity absolutely requires it, conversing with himself and with God, lives beyond visible things and carries within himself the divine images, always pure, untouched by any admixture with the fugitive forms of this earth; become truly and becoming every day more truly the spotless mirror of the divinity and of divine things, receiving their light in his light, their resplendent brightness in his more feeble brightness, in his hopes gathering already the fruit of the future life, living in the commerce of the Angels, still on this earth and yet outside it, carried even into the higher regions by the Spirit. If there is one of you who is possessed by this love, he knows what I am trying to say to you and he will pardon my weakness.[44]

[43] Poem I, Section II, vv. 189–562; *ibid.*, col. 537–55.
[44] *Orat.*, II, 7; P.G., XXXV, 413 C ff.

This beautiful text, however, does not explicitly reveal the wholly Christian character of the mysticism which, as we have already seen in the poetic texts, underlies Gregory's asceticism. But, in fact, if there is anything that his meditation on Scripture at the school of Origen has brought out, it is precisely the Christian and even "Christic" character of this divinization which, following the Alexandrians, he makes the very purpose of his whole spirituality. On this point his whole homilies are wonderfully clear. For him, all Christianity is to cause us to live the divine life in Christ, as Christ made our human life his own in his flesh. More precisely still, taking up the theme that had become central in the theology of St Athanasius, that God was made man in Jesus Christ so that man might be divinized, he conceives this process as being realized by an extension that is to be made to us of that divinizing transfiguration of human existence accomplished in the life of Christ. The heart of his meditation on the Gospel might be said to be the "mystery" in the Pauline sense of the word: the mystery of Christ in us, of which Gregory says very forcefully: it is "the new mystery that concerns me":

> I must be buried with Christ, rise with Him, inherit heaven with Him, become son of God, become God. . . . This is what is the great mystery for us, this is what God incarnate is for us, become poor for us. He has come to raise up the flesh, to save His image, to remake man. He has come to make us perfectly one in Christ, in the Christ who has come perfectly into us, to put within us all that He is. There is no longer man nor woman, barbarian nor Scythian, slave nor free man,[45] characteristics of the flesh; there is now only the divine image that we all bear within us, according to which we have been created, which must be formed in us and impressed on us, so strongly that it will suffice to make us known.[46]

In this association established by the incarnation between Christ and us, Gregory very clearly distinguishes a twofold aspect: on the one hand, in condescending to all our miseries, Christ makes it possible for us to participate in his own divine life. This is the theme he develops in his discourses on Christmas or Epiphany:

> He has taken the form of a slave to give us liberty, He has come down to raise us up, He was tried so that we might conquer, He was despised to glorify us, He died so as to save us, He went up to heaven to raise us out of sin.[47]

[45] Col. 3. 11.
[46] *Orat.*, VII, *In laudem Caesarii*, 23; P.G., XXXV, 785.
[47] *Orat.*, I, 5; P.G., XXXV, 400.

From this, he concludes that we must give ourselves to Christ unreservedly. This is the whole meaning of asceticism as he conceives it:

> We should then give all, offer everything to Him who gave Himself as redeemer of our sins. And we can give nothing as good as ourselves, if we really understand the mystery.[48]

It is in this sense that his poem *On Virtue* presents the ascetic life as the supreme form of sacrifice.[49] In this perspective, the relationship between Christ and ourselves appears in a new aspect: no longer that of a contrast between the incarnation of the Word and our divinization in him, but of an imitation of his cross which is actually a participation. This is the theme of his sermons on Easter. Taking up all those compounds with *syn* forged by St Paul and multiplying them as Paul did, he says:

> Be crucified with Christ, be put to death with Him, be buried with Him so as to rise with Him, be glorified with Him and reign with Him.[50]

It is truly Christ himself who effects this mystery in us and who, at the end of time, will accomplish it:

> He carried me wholly in Himself, with my miseries, to consume in Him what is wicked as fire consumes wax, as the sun absorbs the vapours of the earth, and to have me share in all His goods by uniting me with Himself. . . . [Finally], we shall no longer be many (*polla*) as we are now by reason of the passions that divide us, we who do not possess God in our souls or who barely possess Him. Then, we shall all be deiform (*theoeideis*) because we shall possess in ourselves God whole and entire and God alone. Such is the perfection to which we are tending.[51]

The explicit condition of all this is that God, in Christ, has made His own everything that properly belongs to humanity. Hence the importance in Gregory's eyes of doing away with the error of Apollinarius of Laodicea who removed from the humanity of Christ any *nous*, any merely human intelligence, making out that the Logos took its place. On the contrary, Gregory protests:

> Because of our guilty flesh, Christ had need of flesh; because of our soul, He had to have a soul; and so, because of our *nous*, it was necessary for Him to have a *nous* also. Was it not actually our *nous* that sinned in Adam, even before the body? . . . It has

48 *Ibid.*
49 Verses 642–7; P.G., XXXVII, 726–7.
50 *Orat.*, XXXVIII, 18; P.G., XXXVI, 332–3.
51 *Orat.*, XXX, 6; P.G., XXXVI, 109 and 112.

therefore more need of salvation than the rest. Now what needed to be saved was assumed. And so the *nous* was assumed.[52]

But how does Gregory represent this divinization? According to him as according to the Alexandrine tradition synthesized by St Athanasius, it is the fruit of the incarnation, but it is actually realized when, by our association with the cross of the Saviour, we share in his glorification.

If the ascetical effort is the condition of this divinization, it remains supremely the work of the Spirit. The whole conclusion of the last of the theological Orations[53] develops this idea that the Spirit is he who divinizes us, and this is the reason why he must be God himself living in us.

On the other hand, the second of these Orations tells us, in eternity we shall know God as we have been known by him when our *nous* and our reason are united to him to whom they belong (*to oikeio*) and the image is raised to the archetype towards which it is now tending.[54] But, as things are now, none of the patriarchs or prophets has contemplated the divine essence, no more than did St Paul in his ecstasy.[55] The admixture of the senses that enters into all our present knowledge explains why Solomon, the supreme sage and contemplative, has as the goal of Wisdom the discovery that she is always fleeing from us.[56]

These reservations should be compared with the allegorical commentary, presented at the beginning of the same Oration, on the contemplation of Moses on the mountain. In the shadow of the rock, which was the Word incarnate, he could see God only from behind (*ta opisthia*), this vision of God "from behind" signifying the knowledge, not of his essence, but of what he manifests of himself to us in his works.[57] For, as Gregory is not afraid to say, unhesitatingly correcting Plato's formulation in the *Timaeus*,[58] it is not only true that we cannot express the knowledge that we can have of God, but also that his essence remains finally unknowable, either to those men who are raised the highest and have become friends of God, or even "to the superior and intelligible natures which, as being quite close to Him and illuminated with His whole light, none the less see perhaps something of it, but not all, more perfectly and clearly than we do, and some more than others, according to the analogy of their orders".[59]

[52] *Epist.* 101, to Cledonius; P.G., XXXVII, 185.
[53] *Orat.*, XXXI, §§ 29–31; P.G., XXXVII, 165ff.
[54] *Orat.*, XXII, § 17; P.G., XXXVI, 48 C.
[55] *Ibid.*, §§ 18–20; col. 49–53.
[56] *Ibid.*, § 22; col. 53 B.
[57] *Ibid.*, § 3, col. 29.
[58] *Timeus*, 28 C.
[59] *Orat.*, XXVII, § 4; col. 32.

Here we can leave Gregory Nazianzen. He has given us as it were the interior of that monastic ideal the contours of which Basil had so forcefully delineated. But the point where Gregory's speculation stopped is the one from which would be launched that of the other Gregory, Bishop of Nyssa.

Gregory of Nyssa

Gregory Nazianzen had expressed his hesitation in the face of the monastic vocation under the forms it had taken up to that time. In order to follow it, must he, could he sacrifice the searchings of the intellect and their apostolic fruit?

Gregory of Nyssa did not limit himself to realizing in act, as did his namesake, the union of a life of monastic asceticism and an intellectual and apostolic one: he built up a whole system of Christian thought which would be the justification of the monastic life and provide it with a mysticism made expressly for its needs. We must say even more: it was Gregory of Nyssa who prepared within monasticism a final development of Alexandrian gnosis which would lead it towards what the following periods would call, precisely, mysticism.[60]

It is beginning to be recognized that Gregory of Nyssa was one of the most powerful and most original thinkers ever known in the history of the Church. He was also one of the spiritual writers who most deeply influenced the spirituality of Eastern monasticism. His discovery by the West brought about one of the most active ferments in the meditation of the spiritual writers of our high Middle Ages or of the twelfth century. The importance of this influence, even

[60] Attention has been drawn to the unequalled importance of Gregory of Nyssa as a spiritual writer as well as a theologian by Hans Urs von Balthasar, in his book: *Présence et pensée, Essai sur la philosophie religieuse de Grégoire de Nysse*, Paris, 1942. A little later, Jean Daniélou devoted himself more particularly to showing the Christian originality of Gregory's spirituality by distinguishing it from its Greek sources: *Platonisme et théologie mystique, Essai sur la doctrine spirituelle de saint Grégoire de Nysse*, Paris, 1944 (2nd ed., 1954). But in the meantime our appreciation of the influence exercised by the spiritual work of St Gregory of Nyssa in the monastic circles of antiquity has been renewed by the research undertaken by Werner Jaeger for his edition of Gregory's ascetical works. The result was first the publication of the volume, *Gregorii Nysseni Opera vol. VIII*, 1; *Gregorii Nysseni Opera ascetica* edited by Werner Jaeger, Johannes P. Cavernos, Virginia Woods Callahan, Leiden, 1952. (Prof. Jaeger died at the age of seventy-three in October 1961, with eight volumes of the edition of Gregory's works published or in press; the work is to be completed by his associates.) Jaeger himself drew the conclusions of an important discovery to which his research had led, in *Two Rediscovered Works of Ancient Christian Literature: Gregory of Nyssa and Macarius*, Leiden, 1954. Finally, in 1955, Walther Völker, carrying on his series of studies on the development of Christian spirituality in the line of the School of Alexandria, gave us his *Gregor von Nyssa als Mystiker*, Wiesbaden. Gregory's Works in P.G., XLIV–XLVI.

where it was immediately exercised, nevertheless was only recognized a short time ago. For this to come about was needed Werner Jaeger's discovery of the integral text of his *De Instituto christiano* and the subsequent demonstration that the writings of Pseudo-Macarius, far from having influenced this treatise, were in many respects nothing but a popularization in monastic circles of Gregory's own teaching.[61]

At almost the same time, the influence of Gregory was recognized, not only on Evagrius, but on the whole Syrian School. It was by this last shift, perhaps, that he appeared as the precursor and doubtless the chief inspirer of the unknown who is still concealed for us under the mask of the Areopagite.[62]

If the originality of Gregory of Nyssa's thought has for so long remained unknown or misunderstood, this is certainly due to the quality of his philosophic culture. In an age of handbooks and chrestomathies, he was one of the rare writers of whom we can be sure that he had read the ancients integrally and had completely assimilated them. But this assimilation is precisely of such a quality that he finds no difficulty in dominating the immense mass of ideas and formulations that he possesses, in order to use it and submit it to the expression of his own thought. Yet even Jaeger finally came to be absorbed in the admixture of terminological or notional elements that Gregory might have taken from Platonism and from Stoicism. But he always remained aware of the very personal way in which Gregory utilized all this.

The basis of Gregory's thought, in fact, remains Christian and biblical, at the school of Origen, whom he understood perhaps better than anyone else, but used with the sovereign freedom which is always his. A spontaneously metaphysical mind, in which keenness of existential perception was allied with vigour of methodical reflection, he had, nevertheless, little sympathy for a thought that was set out dialectically, in the manner of Aristotle. The struggle against Eunomius, and the apparent strictness, so deeply fallacious, of his *a priori* deductions about the divine realities, contributed more than a little to strengthen Gregory in his repugnance which was to become instinctive. On the contrary, in the manner of Plato and doubtless of Socrates, his thought spontaneously weds itself to the complexity of a concrete problem by means of analyses that reunite and complete one another in order to envelop the whole reality, even though they do not flatter themselves that they will exhaust it by any premature unification. Very much in the spirit of

[61] W. Jaeger, *Two Rediscovered Works*, etc.
[62] See further on, pp. 369ff.

Plato also is his tendency to take up again, for further deepening, a particular problem raised for the first time at the heart of a more general problem. The "retraction", in this very special sense, is continual in his work.

The outline followed by this retractation is particularly noticeable in his spiritual writings, but is perceptible throughout. In general, his thought goes through three successive stages. At the starting point comes the biblical, Christian intuition, grasped in a text or a theme that he draws from tradition, Philo or Origen often being his guides. Then comes the compact and very personal expression of this intuition in the philosophic language that is his own, and here we must be on guard against too quickly interpreting its terms as we might if we found them in Plato, in later Stoicism, or even in Plotinus. And, finally, this thought is unfolded by a return to the Bible in which the connections, not only with a single isolated text, but with the whole current of tradition are indicated and justified.

One last feature characteristic of his time has been brought out very happily by Fr Daniélou:[63] we must never forget that the context of his most personal meditations always remains liturgical. It is within baptismal and eucharistic perspectives that his thoughts develop and that his spirituality is to be understood. His *Catechetical Discourse*, the most compact and vital synthesis to be found in patristic Christianity, manifests this admirably. It is in this book, clarified by the treatise on *The Creation of Man*, that we must look first for the characteristics of the very particular *Weltanschauung* on which his whole spirituality came to be built up.

The Frame of St Gregory's Thought

A superficial reading of these two works might cause us to believe that he simply transferred to Christianity Platonic dualism, a dualism of essences, opposing the soul to the body, intelligence to the sensible world. Actually he is, on the contrary, fully aware of the profoundly unified view of creation which is that of the Bible, with the most acute perception possible of a divine transcendence which is not in the least that of the "spirit" in general in relation to "matter", but that of the living God in relation to his creatures, whatever these may be. This transcendence, furthermore, in no way excludes immanence; quite the contrary. And here, as previously with St Paul, Stoic representations and expressions are very much at the service of a sense of the unity of the cosmos based on the very unity of God on whom everything depends. Conversely,

[63] *Platonisme et Théologie mystique*, pp. 27ff.

Platonic dualism lends its formulations to a Christian dualism, completely existential, in which it is not primarily matter that is metaphysically opposed to spirit, but sin that is opposed to the will of God.

For Gregory, in fact, reality, coming wholly from the Creator, is basically spiritual. The sensible world is not foreign to the intelligible world. It is rather what becomes a sector of that world as the drama of free wills is enacted in it. All the qualities of the sensible are intelligible, spiritual qualities. Its materiality is made up only of their consistence in a separate order. And this order, as we know it, does not exist apart from man. But man is as we see him today—animal, sexual, torn apart between the *pathe* (that is, the impressions of a sensibility that rules him) and the impotent aspiration of a spiritual being whose *pothos*, superior desire, continues to tend on high, towards God—because of sin.

This does not mean to say, according to Gregory, that, historically speaking, man has not always been like this. It means to say that he has appeared as such since the beginning because God created him by including in his creative fiat the sin which he knew created freedom would consent to, but with the means of repairing it. The animality of sinful man, in fact, allows him to subsist, by means of generation, in spite of his sin. But his true nature is still defined by the *eros* that always draws him towards the divine beauty, in spite of the *pathe* that keep him and isolate him in a world hardened and as it were coagulated around itself.[64] And so, as the *Catechetical Discourse* strongly expresses it, the redemption necessarily takes on the painful and mortal aspect of a breaking of the earthly vase, hardened in its counterfeit form, so that a new pliability may be given to it and it may be refashioned in its divine form.[65]

This is what is realized in the resurrection of Christ, in which corporeity itself triumphs over the *pathe* and becomes wholly spiritual, wholly absorbed, but not consumed for all that, in the Spirit. Baptism extends this reintegration to us and, in those whom chrism has made other Christs by the anointing of the Spirit, the Eucharist nourishes the body of Adamite humanity with this new humanity of Jesus Christ in which matter has become wholly porous to the very Spirit of God animating our spirit.[66]

It is in function of this basic view, in which Platonism and Stoicism and the whole more recent synthesis of Plotinus have

[64] See Gregory of Nyssa, *La création de l'homme* (Introduction and trans. by Jean Laplace, S.J., notes by Jean Daniélou, S.J., "Sources chrétiennes", vol. VI, Paris, 1943), particularly chapters XVI to XVIII, pp. 150ff. and, in the Introduction, pp. 48ff.

[65] Cf. von Balthasar, *op. cit.*, pp. 19ff.

[66] *Ibid.*, pp. 152ff.

been utilized but recast in the new Christian intuition, that Gregory's spirituality was to be built up and formulated.

The Biblical Commentaries

This development takes place in two series of works. The first is a succession of biblical commentaries, in the manner of Origen, commentaries, that is, in which exegesis seeks to disengage from "history" the "Spirit" who always has a perpetual actuality for us, because he animates not only a narrow sector of time but the entire history of the Church and of each person in her. These are the Homilies on the Psalms, on the Canticle of Canticles, and the *Life of Moses*. The different books of the Psalms, the vicissitudes of the nuptial drama undergone by the Bridegroom and Bride, become so many images (or, better, sketches) of the development of the spiritual life through which the Church, in us, must go towards its full development. The term is the life of the resurrection.

And we must not seek here, as has been done too often, so much for precisely defined stages as for the graph and above all the direction of a movement, an impulse, which is what counts above all in the eyes of the writer. This beautiful text from the *Eleventh Homily on the Canticle* is certainly central:

> The manifestation of God was made first to Moses through light; then He spoke with him in the cloud; finally, having become more perfect, Moses contemplated God in darkness. The passage from darkness to light is the first separation (*anachoresis*) from false and erroneous ideas about God. The more attentive understanding of divine things, leading the soul by invisible things to the invisible reality, is as it were a cloud that obscures everything sensible and accustoms the soul to the contemplation of what is hidden. Finally, the soul who has travelled by these ways towards the things that are on high, having left earthly things so far as this is possible to human nature, penetrates into the sanctuaries of the divine knowledge (*theognosia*) surrounded on all sides by the divine darkness.[67]

Too great an effort should not be made to discern in this text the scheme of the three ways of the spiritual life which became classic after Pseudo-Dionysius. At the most, it can be said that perhaps we find here an element of its prehistory, as in the division made by Origen between the teaching of *praktike theoria* in the Proverbs, of *physike theoria* in Ecclesiastes, and of *theologia* in the Canticle.[68] But besides the fact that we cannot, without distorting

[67] *Eleventh Homily on the Canticle*: P.G., XLIV, 1000 CD.

[68] See the Prologue of the *Comment. on the Cant.* Cf. Daniélou, *Platonisme et Théologie mystique*, p. 18.

the texts, make the succession of light, cloud and darkness with Gregory coincide with the three divisions of Origen, it is not even possible to adjust his own distinctions, as expressed here, to the five stages which he distinguishes elsewhere to correspond with the five books of the Psalter, still less, in spite of the number three, with the way in which he distinguishes, on his own account, at the beginning of the same Homilies on the Canticle, the childhood of the spiritual life which should be nourished by the Proverbs, its youth with Ecclesiastes, and its maturity with the Canticle.[69] We should note that Basil laid down the scheme of these three books in still another way: childhood, maturity, old age.[70]

In fact, it is not even certain that the cloud and the darkness, to limit ourselves to these two terms, are different realities. What Gregory says is that when the cloud has obscured superficial lights, then the believer can distinguish in the darkness of this cloud itself the deeper spiritual realities. As is shown clearly in all the Homilies on the Canticle and in the *Life of Moses*—itself entirely a retractation of the text of the Homilies we have just quoted, in which the theme recurring throughout and finally dominant is that of perpetually going beyond what has already been achieved—we have here, not so much stages in, as the permanent elements of a progress which can never end. Detachment (the separation induced by the sight of the true realities afforded us by revelation) obscures the vision which had previously engrossed us of a world in which we are immersed in the sensible. At the same time, in this obscuring, the divine realities shine with a new light. But this illumination, inasmuch as it still remains partial, must in its turn appear dark to us, so that we may go on to more light.

In this essentially dynamic perspective, the cloud and the darkness are at once and inseparably the obscurity in which we lose the knowledge of worldly realities and the obscurity which engulfs, one after another, the revelations of divine realities we believed ourselves to have, to the extent to which we penetrate these realities more perfectly, in understanding also more and more perfectly that we shall never exhaust them.

The Monastic Writings

It is this permanent pattern of the experience interior to all its stages which the second series of Gregory's spiritual works allows us to analyse more deeply. Here we are dealing with a group of works, directly concerned with monasticism, in which the primary

[69] *Homilies on the Canticle*; P.G., XLIV, 768 A.
[70] *In principium Proverborum*; P.G., XXXI, 412 C.

elements of spirituality are methodically examined. The first as to date is the *De virginitate* (doubtless written before Gregory was made bishop). It might be said that this is, as it were, the abstract side of a diptych completed by the concrete example of the *Life of Macrina*, Gregory's sister, and the inspirer of the monastic vocation of Basil himself.

For Gregory of Nyssa as for Gregory Nazianzen, virginity remains the key idea of the whole of Christian asceticism, in monasticism as before it. But, while its concrete realization implies monastic asceticism with all its consequences, the understanding of it leads us to the heart of Gregory's whole spiritual teaching.

For him, physical virginity is as it were the covering and the support of an interior virginity which results from the image of God according to which we are created. He describes this virginity and explains it by taking up the Plotinian formulas about the purification of the *nous*.[71] More generally, he applies to ascetical virginity the typically Neo-Platonic idea of the *syndesmos*, that is, the bond constituted by the mixed forms which cause two categories of distinct but contiguous beings to be united.[72] According to the conception which the Cappadocians were led to make of the Trinity itself, God the Father, in the procession of the Son and the Spirit, is the archetype of virginity, whose integrity is in no way, quite the contrary, opposed to the highest fecundity.[73] The recovery of the virginity of the soul by its attainment of *apatheia* (its liberation from the tyranny of its lusts which make it the slave of the *pathe*) thus causes it to attain perfection (*teleiosis*) in reuniting with God, its model.[74] And so we can already understand how the Homilies on the Canticle can express the final basis of this virginal mysticism in its images of marriage. Recovery of the virginity which the soul had lost and regaining the bond with the Father in the Son are but one thing.

The same basic idea is taken up again in another form in the letter addressed to Harmonius, usually entitled *De professione christiana*.[75] Here Gregory defines the meaning of the name of Christian as being an imitation of God as this is proposed to us in Christ, an imitation which, according to the Platonic formula, is an assimiliation to what God himself is.

The same question again, following the method described above, is taken up for a new and much more substantial treatment in *De*

[71] *De Virginitate*, V; P.G., XLVI, 348 D.
[72] See W. Jaeger, *Two Rediscovered Works*, etc., pp. 25ff.
[73] *De Virginitate*, II; P.G., XLVI, 322 C.
[74] *Ibid.*, col. 314.
[75] In Jaeger's ed., pp. 129–42. For a commentary, see Jaeger, *op. cit.*, p. 28.

perfectione. For since perfection is defined by our assimilation to Christ whose name we Christians bear, Gregory goes on to develop his whole Christology starting from a study of the names of Christ in the Scriptures. These names, according to him, show that Christ, in assimilating our humanity to the divine life, realizes that life according to virtue in which antiquity saw perfection. In him, then, we find not only the way towards perfection but the goal to which this way is to lead us.[76]

The final synthesis of the De Instituto

All these ideas are taken up once more in a work recently discovered in its integrity, the *De proposito secundum Deum,* or *De Instituto christiano* as it is alternatively called by Migne who knew it only in a mutilated form.[77]

The introduction to this treatise provides an excellent example of the dexterity with which Gregory of Nyssa uses Platonic concepts (and even a schema of harmonized concepts) to express a thought basically Christian. What he proposes, according to the Greek title is the *skopos kata theion* of the Christian life and, specifically, of the monastic life. The idea of *skopos,* of the end to be attained in life, is fundamental in Platonism (and doubtless also in the thought of Socrates). With it is connected the whole metaphysics of the *eros* in the *Banquet*: the *eros* urging the soul towards the end that gives meaning to its nature. Gregory, however, unlike a Platonist even though he takes up this whole chain of reasoning, does not go on simply to oppose the permanent nature of the soul to that of the body, but the state of corruption in which the soul finds itself as a consequence of sin, captive to the *pathe*, to the primitive state, or rather the ideal one, in which it reflects the will of God its creator.[78] Christian perfection consists in regaining this conformity. It is accessible to us thanks only to the "knowledge of the truth" that God has put within the reach of those who desire it.[79] This is the way of salvation.[80]

Here we recognize the terminology and the context of specifically Christian ideas that we have been following through tradition up to the Alexandrians. The *Life of Moses*, in the same way, shows us man as giving himself up to the *pathe* by neglecting *gnosis*, but freeing himself from their tyranny by regaining it.[81]

On many occasions, and here also, Gregory defines gnosis very

[76] Ed. Jaeger, pp. 143ff. See Jaeger, *op. cit*., pp. 29–30.
[77] Complete ed. in Jaeger, pp. 1–89. Migne gives the incomplete text in P.G., XLVI, 287–306.
[78] Ed. Jaeger, p. 40, 1–6. [79] *Ibid*., p. 41, 3ff. [80] *Ibid*., p. 41, 18.
[81] *Life of Moses*; P.G., XLIV, 348 B.

biblically and traditionally, as "the distinction between good and evil",[82] while connecting it with the Platonic *phronesis*. For we recall the fact that this is defined, at the end of the *Republic*,[83] as the capacity to judge and to choose between good and evil, and that Plato presents this as being the only science (*episteme*) worthy of being sought. This *gnosis*, causing us to distinguish the true good from the good that is only apparent, is therefore "knowledge of the realities"—the true realities: *gnosis ton onton*. It is, finally, the knowledge of God Himself, as the source of all good, who has set his image in the depth of the soul where we find it again when we separate ourselves from everything that has falsified this image in us.

Völker has no difficulty in showing that, for Gregory of Nyssa as for the Alexandrians, the only source of this *gnosis* is the word of God, received in the tradition of the Church.[84] However adroit Gregory may be in clothing his description of it with the best Platonic speculations, he is categorical, furthermore, on the fact that the philosophy of those outside, as he says, by itself remained always in the pains of childbirth, not succeeding in bringing forth its fruit to the world, even though it had advanced towards the understanding of Christianity.[85]

Again, it is not the application only of dialectics to Scripture that will draw from it the true *gnosis*, as Eunomius and his disciples imagined. The true *theoria,* the "contemplation of the mysteries" or the "mystical contemplation" of the secret of the Scriptures, as Gregory is never weary of repeating, belongs only to "those who fathom its depths by the Holy Spirit and who know how to speak in the Spirit of the divine mysteries."[86]

It is entirely in this sense that the *De Instituto christiano* goes on to develop its subject and its method, addressing itself explicitly to the communities of monks organized by St Basil:

> Since you possess this *gnosis* and you have given to your *eros* the direction that accords with the true nature of your soul, you have gathered together with zeal to imitate in your community, by your actions, the apostolic model. And now you desire that I should serve you as guide for the journey of your life and that I should show you the goal of this way of life and the will of God, with the path that leads to this goal. You desire also to know how those who follow this path are to lead their common life, how the superiors are to direct the philosophic[87] choir and

[82] Heb. 5. 14. [83] *Republic*, x, 618 bc. [84] *Op. cit.*, pp. 156ff.

[85] *Life of Moses*, P.G., XLIV, 329 B. and *Orat. in laudem Gregory Thaum.*; P.G., XLVI, 901 A.

[86] *Contra Eunom.*, III, I, 42; ed. Jaeger, I, II, p. 15, 22ff.

[87] The reader will remember already having found this expression in Gregory Nazianzen as designating monasteries.

what exercises [88] those who desire to climb the peak of the highest virtue must undertake in order to prepare their soul to become a worthy receptacle of the Holy Spirit.[89]

All these metaphors: of the journey (*poreia*), the ascent (*anabasis*), of the sheer peak of virtue, are borrowed from the most ancient Greek poets, as Jaeger rightly observes: from Hesiod, from Simonides and from Tyrteus.[90]

But, as is announced by the mention of the divine Spirit for whose coming everything is a preparation, what follows shows the wholly Christian sense in which Gregory interprets these metaphors.

Since, then, you ask for such an instruction, not only oral but also written, in such a way that you can retain it, and draw it later from the storehouse of memory, so to speak, for use in different circumstances, I shall try to correspond with your zeal and to speak as the grace of the Spirit leads me to speak, knowing well that the canon of your piety is firmly established on the basis of the true dogma of our faith—a deity who is one in His essence but in three hypostases—and taking account of your effort to mount towards the divine by a laborious journey. It is in this way that I am writing down for you these seeds of instruction, selecting them from among the fruits that the Holy Spirit has given me, but often also making use of the words of Scripture as a proof of what I say and to illuminate the interpretation that I give to them, for fear that I might seem to be abandoning the divine gifts received from on high and substituting for them the poor products of my own mind, or else to be setting out an ideal of piety in harmony with the doctrine of philosophers from outside and, swollen with vain pride, interpolate the Scriptures with it in my ignorance.[91]

These revealing lines bring out very clearly the path that we have described taken by Gregory's thought and expression. At the same time, they justify it against the critics who have already allowed themselves to be deceived by his dextrous handling of philosophic ideas, and so have ignored the essentially Christian basis of his thought. What follows leaves no doubt in this regard.

He who desires, therefore, to lead his body and his soul to God in accordance with the law of religion and to consecrate to Him a pure worship unstained by any bloody sacrifice [we have already found this theme in the other Gregory, and always in connection with the monastic life], must make the faith which the

88 The term *ponos* is taken from the Stoics.
89 *De Instituto christiano*, Jaeger, p. 41.
90 Jaeger, *Two Rediscovered Works*, etc., p. 52.
91 *De Inst. christ.*, Jaeger, p. 41.

> saints have taught in the Scriptures the guide of his life and he must give himself up to the pursuit of virtue (*arete*) by obeying this faith perfectly. He must free himself completely from the chains of earthly life and put away once for all any slavery to what is base and vain. By this and his life, he must become wholly God's possession, knowing well that he who has faith and purity of life has the power of Christ as well, and where there is the power of Christ there is also deliverance from the evil and the death that ravages our life.[92]

Baptism is the pledge of this work of the Spirit within us, the work which achieves, through our ascetic efforts, the realization of the virtue that befits our nature[93] and renders us impregnable, like a fortress, to the assaults of the enemy. And so the new being who is born in us at baptism will attain the whole stature of the mature age that his nature requires.[94] But, as "the knowledge of the truth" given by God in Christ alone can guide us towards this end, so, reciprocally, it is this growth and it alone that can develop in us the divine gnosis.[95]

This development, furthermore, can have no end in which we might take rest. On the contrary, the greatest obstacle to grace is the relaxation of the effort to make progress (*prokope,* another Stoic term) after the first signs of encouragement given us by this grace.[96]

The centre of the treatise is dominated by a development, which remains classic in the whole of the Christian East, of the "*synergy*" between the work of the Spirit in us and our own work, the work of the Spirit being simply a restoration of our own freedom. For:

> the perfect will of God is that the soul should take the form of piety, that soul which the grace of the Spirit causes to flower to supreme beauty by concurring (*syngenomene*) with the efforts (*ponois*) of the man who conforms himself to it. . . . For the body grows without us . . . but the measure and beauty of the soul in the renewal of its conception, which is given it by the grace of the Spirit through the zeal of him who receives it, depends on our disposition (*gnome*): to the degree that you develop your struggles for piety, to the same degree also the grandeur of your soul develops through these struggles and these efforts.[97]

We should note, that, in this text and others like it, Gregory takes the subjective viewpoint of the ascetic, inviting him to strive so that the Spirit may manifest himself in him. We find this same thing in all the writers of the following generation, and up to

[92] *Ibid.*, p. 43.
[93] Cf. above pp. 315–16.
[94] *De Inst. christ.*, Jaeger, pp. 44–5.
[95] *Ibid.*, p. 46.
[96] *Ibid.*, p. 60. Cf. p. 65.
[97] *Ibid.*, p. 46.

Cassian. Here, obviously, is the starting-point for Pelagianism, placing human effort before grace. But, for Gregory of Nyssa as for all those who followed him faithfully, we must never forget that the human effort of the ascetic is always seen as an effort in and on the basis of faith, and so undertaken and carried out by the strength of the Spirit whose manifestation is its goal.

Theognosia

The deepening of the gnosis to which all this leads is the *theognosia* in darkness brought out in the *Life of Moses.* Its formulation is so characteristic of Gregory of Nyssa that antiquity has attributed to him a treatise devoted to the explanation of this term, even though he certainly was not its author.[98] We must seek its meaning both from the *Life of Moses* and from the *Homilies on the Canticle.*

With Gregory, we might say, *theognosia* tends to become a particular psychological experience, of an ecstatic nature, in which the presence of God is apprehended, in a manner at once luminous and obscure, by the new spiritual senses which are developed or, perhaps, revived in the soul. All these terms, used with a precision hitherto unknown, can be gleaned from his work, particularly from the last two writings mentioned.

As for ecstasy first of all: the *De virginitate* had already spoken of going beyond oneself (*ekbas autos eauton*), of surpassing one's nature.[99] The *Life of Macrina* says that she had gone out of human nature.[100] The *Life of Moses* says that he "abandons everything that appears, not only what falls under the senses, but everything that the intelligence (*dianoia*) thinks it sees."[101] In the *Sixth Homily on the Canticle*, equally, the Bride is said "to abandon the senses", and, in the eleventh, "to abandon the things of this earth".[102] This might be compared with what Gregory tells us of St Paul, caught up to the third heaven and there receiving "the ineffable gnosis".[103]

Akin to this theme are those of "sober intoxication", taken from Philo, [104] and of the sleep of the senses, the condition of the awakening of the soul to the appearance (*emphaneia*) of God.[105]

A different but kindred theme must also be mentioned here: that of the quieting, the peacefulness (*hesychia*) in which we can be

[98] See Jaeger, *Two Rediscovered Works*, etc., p. 82.
[99] *De Virginitate*, x; ed. Jaeger, p. 290, 4.
[100] *Life of Macrina*, Jaeger, p. 390, 7.
[101] *Life of Moses*, II; P.G., XLIV, 376 D–377 A.
[102] *Sixth Homily on the Canticle*; P.G., XLIV, 892 D, and in the Eleventh col. 1000 D.
[103] *Contra Eunom.*, III, I, 16; ed. Jaeger, I, II, p. 7, 6ff.
[104] *Fifth and Eleventh Homilies on the Canticle*; P.G., XLIV, 873 D and 990 B.
[105] *Eleventh Homily on the Canticle, ibid.*, col. 993 AC.

"attentive to the contemplation of invisible things".[106] This theme, already familiar with Basil[107] and known also to Gregory Nazianzen,[108] will assume considerable importance later on.

The "sense of the presence" of God, on the other hand, is the very expression forged by Gregory of Nyssa to describe the experience of the Bride of the Canticle, who, he says,

> is surrounded with the divine night in which the Bridegroom comes near without showing Himself . . . but by giving the soul a certain sense of His presence (*aisthesin tina tes parousias*) while fleeing from clear knowledge (*katanoesin*).[109]

We might consider this "sense of his presence" as being the most intimate effect of the spiritual senses, first proposed by Origen, which, for Gregory, are developed concurrently with the extinction of the carnal senses.[110]

So, according to the *De Virginitate*,[111] the eyes of the soul see an "intelligible light" (*noeton*). We have already mentioned that, both according to the *Eleventh Homily on the Canticle* and the *Life of Moses* which this Homily directly echoes, this "light" can be paradoxically described as "darkness": it is, says the *Vita,* a "resplendent darkness" (*lampros gnophos*).[112]

> What is signified by Moses' entering into the darkness, and the vision he had of God therein? The present account seems, indeed, somewhat to contradict the theophany at the beginning.[113] Then it was in light and now it is in darkness that God appears. Do not think, however, that this is not in accordance with the normal succession of the spiritual realities we are considering. The text teaches us hereby that the religious gnosis (*tes eusebeias*) is light when it first begins to appear: for it is opposed to impiety which is darkness, and darkness is dissipated by the enjoyment of the light. But the more the spirit (*nous*) in its march forward has attained, by an application always greater and more perfect, to an understanding of what the knowledge (*katanoesis*) of realities is and approaches nearer to contemplation, the more it sees that the divine nature is invisible. Having left behind all appearances, not only those perceived by the senses but those that the intelligence believes it sees, it goes continually further within until it penetrates, by the effort of the understanding, to the

106 *Comm. on Psalm* 1. 7; P.G., XLIV, 456 C.

107 *Epist.* 9, 3; P.G., XXXII, 272 C; cf. *Epist.* 2, 2; col. 225 C and 228 A and *Epist.* 14, col. 277 B.

108 *Orat.*, XXVI, 7; P.G., XXXV, 1287 A.

109 *Eleventh Homily on the Canticle*; P.G., XLIV, 1001 B.

110 See Daniélou, *Platonisme et Théologie mystique*, pp. 238ff.

111 *De Virginitate*, v; ed. Jaeger, p. 277, 12.

112 *Life of Moses*; P.G., XLIV, 377 A.

113 The vision of the burning bush; Exod. 2.

invisible and unknowable, and there it sees God. The true knowledge (*eidesis*) of Him whom it seeks, indeed, and the true vision of Him consists in seeing that He is invisible, because Him whom it seeks transcends all knowledge, completely separated by His incomprehensibility as by a dark cloud. This is why John, the one raised so high, who entered into this shining darkness, says that "no one has ever seen God",[114] by this negation defining the gnosis of the divine essence as inaccessible not only to men but to every intellectual nature. When, therefore, Moses had progressed in gnosis, he declares that he sees God in darkness, that is to say that the divinity is essentially what transcends all gnosis and all comprehension.[115]

However, even though all these texts lead us decidedly towards mysticism conceived as an obscure experience, they should not be interpreted too strictly. No more than Gregory's ecstatic formulas allow themselves to be reduced to a psychological experience, is this vision in the resplendent darkness for him so much an experience located at a certain stage of spiritual development as it is one aspect of the whole of this development, even though this aspect certainly should predominate more and more.

Properly speaking, in fact, the discovery of God for Gregory comes about much less in any definable experience than in the necessity, more and more clearly perceived, of going beyond all experience. This is what he calls, alluding to St Paul's phrase:[116] "forgetting what is behind me and tending (*epekteinomenos*) towards what is ahead", "epectasy" (*epektasis*), in a revealing passage from the *Sixth Homily on the Canticle*:

Since the intelligible and immaterial is pure of all circumscription, it escapes from limitations, being bounded by nothing. But we must distinguish, on the one hand, the uncreated reality creative of beings, which is always what it is and, being always equal to itself, is superior to all growth and all diminution and cannot receive any good; and, on the other hand, the reality brought into existence by creation, always turned towards the first cause and conserved in the good by participation in what envelops it. In a sense, then, this latter is continually being created, growing by its augmentation in the good, in such a way that no limit can any longer be seen in it and its augmentation in the good cannot be circumscribed by any limit, and yet the actual good, even if it appears the greatest and most perfect possible, is never anything but the beginning of a superior good. Consequently, here also is verified the word of the apostle

114 John 1. 18.
115 *Life of Moses*; P.G., XLIV, 776 C–777 B.
116 Phil. 3. 11.

that by epectasy towards what is ahead, the things which had formerly appeared fall into oblivion. Indeed, the greater reality, manifesting itself as a superior good, draws to itself the dispositions of those who participate in it and forbids their looking back to the past, cutting off the memory of inferior goods by the enjoyment of higher goods.[117]

Presence of God, Search for God

Hans Urs von Balthasar has given an illuminating analysis, throughout the whole work of Gregory, of the exact bearing and precise meaning of the mysticism in which the vision of God "from behind", already treated by Gregory Nazianzen as characteristic of Moses, takes on the sense of a perpetual going beyond.[118]

At first sight, it would seem as though the experience were here purely negative. But what freights it with a positive content is, first of all, the fundamental conviction that the soul is created to the image of God, and that the progress of grace and of ascetic effort restores it to that image. More precisely still, it is the soul's most intimate nature to be, not a mere image, inert and as it were separated from its model, but rather a mirror in which the presence of God is revealed as the soul gives itself up to the divine advances.

Perhaps Gregory never seems so Neo-Platonic as when he is developing this theme. Like Plotinus, he speaks of a purification of the soul, which will restore it to its primitive state, take away the rust or the dirt, bring out from the marble the statue buried therein.[119]

But his thought is actually quite different. For him, there is no question of bringing out in the soul a divine quality which would be inherent to it and hidden only by exterior stains. The question is that of withdrawing the soul from sin in such a way that, grace having been given back to it, God will once more become present to it and will recreate his lost image, as the sun can again strike the mirror which had been cut off from it by some dark screen. His commentary on the fourth Beatitude, "Blessed are the pure of heart" is very clear on this point:

God has imprinted the image of the good things on His own nature on creation. But sin, in spreading out over the divine likeness, has caused this good to disappear, covering it with shameful garments. But if, by a life rightly led, you wash away

117 *Sixth Homily on the Canticle;* P.G., XLIV, 885 A–888 A. For a commentary see Daniélou, *Platonisme et Théologie mystique*, p. 317.

118 *Présence et Pensée*, pp. 67ff.

119 *Enneades*, I, vi, 9, with *De Virginitate*; P.G., XLIV, 372 AB. (See also *Comment. on the Psalms*, XI; P.G., XLIV, 544.)

> the mud that has been put on your heart, then godlike (*theoeides*) beauty will again shine out in you. And so it is that he who is pure of heart merits to be called blessed, since in looking at his own beauty, he sees in it its model. Just as he who looks at the sun in a mirror, even if he does not fix his eyes on the sky itself, nevertheless sees the sun in the mirror's brightness, so you also, even if your eyes could not bear the light, possess within yourselves what you desire, if you return to the grace of the image that was placed in you from the beginning.[120]

And this, in turn, leads us to a still more profound and higher aspect of the spiritual progress or ascent. In this going beyond, in this very flight, the soul that abandons itself to the attraction which the divine beauty exercises on the superior *eros*, reanimated in it by the Spirit, simply discovers the *agape* of God descending upon it. For the God towards whom the liberated soul is tending is not the infinity merely of indeterminacy, nor even merely a presence more intimate to the soul than it is to itself, but truly the upspringing, generous fountain: the living God who gives life. It is this fountain of *agape* that the *Eleventh Homily on the Canticle* has us contemplate,[121] a fountain which, by the incarnation, comes to spring up in us ourselves. A fountain sealed, this Homily tells us,

> by purity, so that it is reserved for its possessor and no strain of troubling thoughts can tarnish and wrinkle the transparent and ethereal surface of the water of the heart.... Here the Bride receives the highest praise. For while everywhere else Holy Scripture applies the image of living water to the life-giving nature, here it infallibly witnesses that the Bride is a fountain of living water.... Here is truly the height of the paradox. For while all other wells contain their water in repose, the Bride alone possesses it flowing within herself in such a way that she has at once the depth of the well and the perpetual motion of the river. Who can fittingly describe the wonder of the assimilation thus accomplished? Perhaps, indeed, there no longer remains anything to attain above herself: having been assimilated in everything to the primal Beauty, in every detail, she imitates the fountain in becoming the fountain, the Life in being life, the water in becoming water. Living is the word of God, living the soul that receives this word within her.[122]

These last texts invite us to go beyond any notion of experience or of knowledge, in whatever way these might be understood, to reach the final depth of Gregory's mysticism. For, in fact, it is in

[120] *Orat. on the Fifth Beatitude*; P.G., XLIV, 1272.
[121] *Eleventh Homily on the Canticle*; P.G., XLIV, 1000 AB.
[122] *Ninth Homily on the Canticle*; P.G., XLIV, 977 AD.

ontological and existential terms, and not simply in terms of knowing, that it must finally be formulated.

Love and Union

Knowledge flowers from union: the homily on Stephen tells us he was "raised to the knowledge (*katanoesin*) of God, being associated (*anakratheis*) to the grace of the Holy Spirit".[123] Gregory, in his *Sixth Homily on the Beatitudes,* explains that, for the Bible, "to know means the same thing as to possess",[124] and, a little further on, that "he who knows God possesses through this knowledge (*dia tou idein*) all the good things that actually exist".[125] Gnosis itself is defined, in the opusculum to Hieron on children who die prematurely, as "participation (*metousia*) in God."[126] This is what the *Sixth Homily on the Canticle* expresses in a similar way by saying that there is produced between the soul and God "a mutual compenetration, God coming into the soul and the soul being transported in God", or again that the soul becomes "susceptible of the divine indwelling".[127]

This mysticism of *agape*, of a love which is the substantial communication of God to the soul, in the perspectives of the trinitarian theology of the Cappadocians much more clearly than in the uncertain outlines of Origen's Trinity, remains from one end to the other a mysticism of Christ, while at the same time being a mysticism of God in the strictest sense. This is expressed in a text from the *Fourth Homily on the Canticle,* in other respects quite close in its tonality to Origen's mysticism and yet at the same time announcing some of the most sublime developments of Byzantine mysticism:

> The Bride praises the skilful archer who has so well directed his arrow towards her. For she says: "I am wounded with love." She shows thereby the nature of that arrow which is planted in the inmost depth of her heart. The archer is *agape*. That God is *agape* we have been taught by Holy Scripture—He who sends His chosen arrow, His only Son, towards those who are to be saved . . . so that it may introduce into him whom it pierces, together with the arrow, the archer Himself—as the Lord says: "I and the Father are one and we shall come and we shall dwell with him. . . ." O beautiful wound and happy blow by which Life penetrates within, by the cleaving of the arrow opening for itself as it were a door and a passage-way! For hardly does the soul

123 *Orat. on Stephen*; P.G., XLVI, 977 AD.
124 *Orat. on the Fifth Beatitude*: P.G., XLIV, 1265 A.
125 *Ibid.*, 1265 B.
126 *De inf.;* P.G., XLVI, 173 C. Cf. 173 B and D, 180 D.
127 *Sixth Homily on the Canticle*; P.G., XLIV, 889 D and 893 C.

feel itself struck by the arrow of love, when already its wound is transformed into nuptial joy.[128]

The goal of Gregorian mysticism is, therefore, the gathering together of the whole Church, of the whole of human nature restored to its original unity dismembered by sin, in Christ, the new and final Adam who, in coming down to us, transports us all together into the living unity of the trinitarian God, the God who is love:

> When perfect *agape* has excluded fear . . . or fear is changed into love, then everything that is saved will be one unity, by growing together with the one Good, and all will be, in one another, one in the perfect Dove. . . . In this way, encircled by the unity of the Holy Spirit as by the bond of peace . . . all will be one single body and one single spirit. . . . But it is better to take up the very words of the divine Gospel: "That all may be one, as You, Father, in me and I in You." . . . The bond of this unity is glory, and that this glory is the Holy Spirit anyone who is familiar with Scripture will be convinced when he reflects on the word of the Lord: "The glory that You have given me, I have given to them," for, in all truth, He gave them this same glory when He said: "Receive the Holy Spirit."[129]

Faithful to the same vision of the *agape* that finally dominates the mysticism of Gregory of Nyssa, the definitive exposition of his theory of asceticism, in the *De Instituto christiano*, ends for its part with a description of the cenobitic society as an organization for mutual service in the flowering of love.[130] And so, on the heights of their common biblical inspiration, St Gregory's contemplation rejoins and vivifies St Basil's ideal of a monasticism essentially communitarian.

[128] *Fourth Homily on the Canticle*; P.G., XLIV, 852.
[129] *Fifteenth Homily on the Canticle*; P.G., XIV, 1116 CD.
[130] *De Inst. christ.*, ed. Jaeger, pp. 66ff.

XV

ERUDITE MONASTICISM (CONCLUSION): PSEUDO-MACARIUS, EVAGRIUS PONTICUS

THE influence on monasticism of the Cappadocians, and very particularly of Gregory of Nyssa, appears more and more clearly as studies are multiplied on the spirituality of the end of the fourth century and the fifth. St Basil had effected an integration of monasticism with the life of the Church that we would be tempted to find only too successful, were it not for the dumb resistance offered to it by that whole part of previous tradition which it had refused to assimilate. His brother, who seems to us to have, in this domain particularly, developed and ordered many of Gregory Nazianzen's intuitions, to an even greater extent marked the most interior spirituality of monks with ineffaceable characteristics.

In this regard, a threefold posterity might be attributed to Gregory of Nyssa. In a first line, which seems to have been brought about by monks in direct relationship with the monasteries of Basil, perhaps in Syria,[1] his thought was methodically "popularized". In the body of the writings attributed to Macarius, the substance of Gregory's spiritual thought was made available to the least cultivated minds. In a different line, with Evagrius Ponticus, Gregory's influence, modifying horizontally, so to say, a monasticized Origenism, came to permeate the monastic circles of Egypt itself. Finally, doubtless in Syria first of all, what was on the contrary most personal and most ordered in this thought came to be the seed of a new development, no less original with regard to Gregory's thought than was his with regard to Origen's. We mean the Areopagitical writings: that series of works so puzzling in many respects, in which one of the most powerful intellectual and

[1] W. Jaeger, *Two Rediscovered Works, etc.*, pp. 227ff.

spiritual personalities in the history of the Church is revealed without betraying its identity.

The Problem of "Macarius"

Egyptian monasticism had two Macariuses: Macarius of Alexandria and Macarius called the Egyptian, or of Scete, for he was the chief monastic organizer of the desert of that name. A certain number of apophthegms of both, which may be authentic, have been preserved for us. But a whole literature has been attributed to the second, who was evidently a very great spiritual master (it was he who formed Evagrius himself to the monastic life). The most important part of this literature is made up of fifty Homilies which, in many cases, are actually rather conferences, in the sense in which Cassian uses the word: that is, spiritual conversations directed by the master to answer the questions of his disciples. These Homilies are characterized by a very distinctive style: of warm exhortation, overcharged with biblical echoes or quotations. By this style as well as by its themes, the *Great Letter* is closely connected with the Homilies. It might be considered as an introduction to the whole collection, for it sums it up and integrates the greater part of its themes.

The fortunes and misfortunes of the Macarian writings in recent research constitute a very revealing page on the ironic fecundity of scientific error in the criticism of texts and the establishment of lines of influence.[2] Only a few years ago, it had become apparently indisputable dogma that the Homilies constituted the source book, as it were, in the Euchite or Messalian sects—those disciples of Symeon of Mesopotamia who maintained, at the end of the fourth century, that the whole life of the monk should consist in permanent prayer. Dom Villecourt, by careful comparison of the *Great Letter* of Macarius with the *De Instituto christiano* attributed to St Gregory of Nyssa in the form that was then known, actually seemed to have established beyond any possible dispute the fact that the latter work depended on the *Letter*, and was therefore not by Gregory. The *Letter* itself, by its insistence on prayer above all, by its belief in the cohabitation of sin and grace within us, by its aspiration towards a quasi-sensible experience of the divine light, seemed to him a typical product of the Messalian school. And since the Homilies were obviously closely connected with the *Letter*, they were included in this judgment . . . without mentioning the Pseudo-Gregorian writing.[3]

[2] *Ibid.*, pp. 147ff.

[3] L. Villecourt, "La date et l'origine des 'Homélies spirituelles' attribuées à Macaire", in *Comptes rendus des séances de L'Academie des Inscriptions et Belles-Lettres*, 1920, pp. 29–53.

In the meantime, the research of Werner Jaeger and his collaborators on the critical edition of Gregory of Nyssa led them to the discovery of a complete manuscript of the *De Instituto christiano*, the one given in Migne only corresponding to a fairly late and incomplete paraphrase.[4] Then the whole complexion of the problem began to change. Since, H. Dörries on his part had brought to light an older and more complete form of the *Great Letter*, attributed to Macarius,[5] there is no longer any possible doubt, as Werner Jaeger has clearly established, about three points which reverse the whole previous construction:

1. The *De Instituto*, in its complete form, is obviously an authentic work of Gregory of Nyssa, in which he gave, in his old age, a most interesting retractation of his whole ascetic teaching and of certain elements of his mystical thought.

2. The *Great Letter*, also in its primitive and complete form, depends on the authentic *De Instituto*, far from the reverse, and the same thing is true of the fifty Homilies.

3. The kind of pan-Messalianism, which the historians of the last twenty years succeeded in finding in the most varied Greek spiritual writers of the fifth century and beyond, is now dissipated as being an optical illusion, the accidental cause of which has now disappeared. In fact, the Messalians did nothing but crystallize and exaggerate themes emanating from the more or less Basilian monastic circles of Syria or Mesopotamia directly influenced by Gregory of Nyssa. But these themes, which were to be taken up and carried along by the whole spiritual tradition of the Eastern Church up to modern Hesychasm, have absolutely nothing heretical about them. Quite the contrary, whatever may have been the new precision given them by the thought of Gregory or of certain of his disciples, they belong to the most ancient stock of Christian spirituality.

The Great Letter

The greater part of the *Letter* (about fifty printed pages out of seventy), follows the *De Instituto* of Gregory of Nyssa step by step.

[4] See above, p. 352.

[5] H. Dörries, of Göttingen, who was entrusted, for the editions of the Academy of Berlin, with preparing that of the Macarian writings has given the result of his research on the manuscript tradition of these works in *Texte und Untersuchungen z. Gesch. d. altchristlichen Lit.*, 4. Reihe, 10. Bd., 1. Heft, Leipzig, 1941. Here is to be found all the available information on the rediscovered text of the "Great Letter", pp. 144–57. It was with the agreement of Dörries that Jaeger, in an appendix to his volume, *Two Rediscovered Works, etc.*, published for the first time the authentic text of this "Letter", using photostats of the manuscript Vaticanus gr. 710 and of the manuscript Vaticanus gr. 694 (both from the twelfth–thirteenth centuries) taken by Dörries himself.

But it translates the latter's very difficult theological expressions into more available terms, while also substituting for the still imprecise monastic terminology of Gregory the formulations that had become canonical towards the end of the century.

It is interesting, however, to bring out what the author of the letter thought he ought to add to his very faithful presentation of Gregory's ideas. We find first a development on the cenobitic life, the humility in charity which it requires, in the light of the Paulinian teaching, already recalled by Gregory, on the body of Christ. All the members are to render one another mutual assistance, each one putting his particular talents at the service of the community, but in return having the certainty of benefiting, even participating in the charisms of the others. And from this is particularly deduced what ought to be the relations between the religious who are engaged in the material tasks necessary for the life of the community and those who, during the same hours, are free for prayer.

One needs to be only slightly familiar with any monastic community to recognize here one of the difficulties raised by religious at every period. The way in which the author deals with it is enough to refute any suspicion of Messalianism. However great his esteem for prayer, he formally refuses to choose between prayer and work, or to exalt one at the expense of the other.[6]

In the commentary he is led to make on the episode of Martha and Mary in St John's Gospel, he opens the long tradition finding here proof of the preference to be given to prayer, but in emphasizing just as strongly that this same text teaches us no less the necessity and dignity of work. He goes so far as immediately to add a reminder of Christ washing the feet of his disciples, in order to insist on the capital importance, not only of work in general, but of the service of the brethren in particular. All the same, he then mentions the phrase of the Acts, on the Apostles' decision that in spite of everything they should prefer "the service of the Word and of prayer" to the "service of tables".[7]

After this, the letter goes on to the objections of those opposed to the monastic life who say that its perfection cannot be realized. The monastic ideal, it says, is possible if, first of all, one has faith in the Scriptures; and, secondly, if one gives oneself generously up to the task of realizing what they prescribe; and if, in the third place, one does not lose sight of the purpose of this effort, which is *apatheia* and liberty in the service of God. However, it adds, all

[6] *Macarii epistula magna*, in Jaeger, *op. cit.*, pp. 281ff.
[7] *Ibid.*, pp. 288–9.

this is not really possible unless the monk does not trust in his own strength, but in that of God, basing what is his own effort on the word of God telling us that he is the One who raises even the dead. It is lack of faith, it says, invoking the Epistle to the Hebrews, which in the final analysis prevents so many from entering into that rest which is the goal of all our effort, the fruit of the work of the Spirit in us: the new creation of purity of heart.[8]

It is remarkable that this development of the letter, in spite of what is most original about it, in its treatment of the image of the body of Christ as in its exegesis of the Gospel of Martha and Mary, is still connected with two basic ideas of Gregory's text: on the one hand, the supereminent value of prayer and the need for giving it the first place in a monastic community;[9] on the other hand, the real possibility of man's realizing the monastic ideal in the concrete conditions in which God has placed him.[10]

The Homilies of "Macarius" and the Thought of Gregory of Nyssa

The same close connection with Gregory's thought is found again in the Homilies. In the first, the dominant idea is that the soul becomes light when the divine light comes within it. This idea is encountered in many places in Gregory and in the *De Instituto christiano* in particular.[11] But the author of these Homilies gives it such descriptive and enthusiastic developments that we are, here more than elsewhere, tempted to forget its source.

In commenting on Ezechiel's vision, he writes:

> The soul that has been deemed worthy by the Spirit to participate in His light and that has been illumined by the splendour of His ineffable glory, when He has prepared it to become the throne of His glory, becomes wholly light, wholly face, wholly eyes, and there remains no further part of itself that is not filled with the spiritual eyes of light. That is to say, it has nothing of darkness, but it is wholly light and spirit, wholly full of eyes, having now no back, but presenting its face on all sides, the ineffable beauty of the glory of the light of Christ having come into it and dwelling in it. Just as the sun is wholly like itself, having no other side, no inferiority, but is wholly resplendent with light, is wholly light and equally so in all its parts, or as, in the fire, the light of the fire is wholly like itself, having nothing primary or secondary, greater or smaller, so the soul, that has been fully illuminated by the ineffable beauty of the glory

[8] *Ibid.*, pp. 291ff.
[9] See *De Instituto christiano*, ed. Jaeger, pp. 66ff.
[10] *Ibid.*, pp. 42ff.
[11] Cf. Pseudo-Macarius *First Homily*; P.G., XXXIV, 349ff., and *De Inst. chris.*; Jaeger, pp. 48, 50, 51, 56, 83.

of the light of the face of Christ and filled with the Holy Spirit, worthy to become the dwelling and the temple of God, is wholly eye, wholly light, wholly face, wholly glory and wholly spirit, Christ in this way adorning it, carrying it, directing it, sustaining it and leading it and so illuminating it and decorating it with spiritual beauty.[12]

The *Second Homily* is no less Gregorian in the way in which it explains the liberation of the soul with regard to the *pathe*, a liberation which is to cause it to regain, thanks to divine aid, the primitive purity which consists in the conformity of the will of man with that of God.

The *Third Homily*, returning to the question of the different activities of monks in the same monastery, praying, reading, or working, is still closer, just as is the first and greater part of the *Letter*, to the *De Instituto*.

In the same way, the *Fortieth Homily*, for example, on the degrees that exist in virtue as in vice, in heaven and in hell, and on the progress which must be incessant, by an unceasing struggle —and the forty-first, on the continually progressive character of the spiritual life, which causes him who abounds in grace to recognize all the more clearly his sin and his estrangement from God—only develop, with the greatest fidelity to their source, although the greatest originality as to expression and applications, the themes central to, and everywhere present in Gregory.[13]

The originality of "Macarius", so evident as to form, is reduced as to content to a concentration on certain Gregorian themes taken separately and nourished with a whole tradition of monastic experience. It seems that here three poles can be distinguished, all to be found in Gregory but now standing out in a new light: the first is the mysticism of light, brought out most clearly in the text we have already quoted; the second is the insistence on prayer and, if possible, constant prayer; the third is the acceptance of the progressive character of the spiritual life, with all its consequences.

Mysticism of Light

On the first point, while "Macarius" is attached to formulas of light, he completely neglects the images of darkness accompanying them in Gregory. The particular fervour of his expression, on the other hand, gives his formulations a certain coloration of personal experience.

In a very interesting controversy, some years ago, Fr Daniélou

[12] *First Homily*, II; P.G., XXXIV, 451 AB (cf. XII, 461 C ff.).
[13] Cf. above p. 357.

differed from Prof. Völker on the question of which is the most mystical, in the sense of speaking from experience: Origen or Gregory of Nyssa. Fr Daniélou exalts Gregory in comparison with Origen, while Prof. Völker refuses to see any appreciable difference between the two from this point of view.[14] We must, obviously, begin by defining what is called a "mystical experience". If we include under this term what has been defined in accordance with the descriptions of writers of the sixteenth century or later, it is useless to try to find "mystical experience" in the spiritual writers of the third or fourth century. But it may be that with "Macarius", for instance, we can first notice an orientation towards an insistence on the personal, direct, character which the experience of the divine realities may take on. This will tend henceforth to be defined not only by its object but by certain particular psychological impressions of the subject.

So he writes, in the conclusion of the *First Homily*:

> If you become the throne of God and the heavenly charioteer is seated upon you, and your whole soul has become a spiritual eye and entirely light; if you are fed with the nourishment of the Spirit; if you have drunk of the water of life, and are clothed with the garments of the ineffable light; if your interior man has been established in the experience and the fullness (*en peira kai plerophoria*) of all these things, then in truth you are living the eternal life. But if you have no consciousness of all this in yourself (*synoidas seauto*), weep, be sad and groan, because you have not as yet entered fully into participation of the eternal and heavenly richness, and you have not received fully (*akmen*) the true life.[15]

Along the same lines, he says in the *Forty-ninth Homily*.

> If anyone, having renounced this world, has not recognized in fullness (*plerophoria*), in place of the old carnal communion, communion in what is heavenly; and if he does not possess, in place of the seeming joy of the world, the interior joy of the Spirit, the consolation of heavenly grace and divine satisfaction in contemplating (*epophthenai*) the glory of the Lord, as it is written; and to say it all, if he has not now acquired in his soul incorruptible joy in place of the joy that is only for a short time—then he is salt that has lost its savour.[16]

Yet we must still be very prudent in interpreting texts such as these. The light of which "Macarius" speaks so eloquently, like the

[14] Cf. Völker, *Gregor von Nyssa als Mystiker*, p. 211, in which he presents and discusses in a long note the positions taken by Daniélou in his book, *Platonisme et Théologie mystique*.
[15] *First Homily*, XII; P.G., XXXIV, 461 D.
[16] *Forty-ninth Homily*, I; *ibid.*, col. 812 D–813 A.

"spiritual senses" of Origen or Gregory, is indeed experienced by the soul as a reality, as the supreme reality. There is no doubt of this. What is less clear is the way in which we are to understand it. Later on, in the East, was to emerge the idea of a luminous vision of God making itself perceptible even to the eyes of the body. It would be very difficult to find a line of "Macarius" which is indisputably to be interpreted in this sense. It is not even perfectly certain that he understood this light as a particular impression of divine grace on the soul, rather than as an illumination of the whole interior life....

Constant Prayer

The second distinctive theme in the Homilies of "Macarius", as we have said, is their insistence on prayer as the chief activity of the monk, tending to absorb, or at least to saturate, all the others.

It is here perhaps that we have the key to the attribution of these texts to Macarius the Egyptian. According to the apophthegms of his that we possess the authenticity of which there is no room seriously to question, this seems to have been the most outstanding characteristic of the founder of Scete, together with insistence on complete humility and recollection, as well as insistence on a prayer that places us simply and wholly in the hands of God.

The Abbot Macarius was asked: How should one pray? The old man answered:

> "There is no need to lose oneself in speaking. It is enough to hold out one's hands and to say: Lord, as You know and will: have mercy. If the combat presses hard, say: To the rescue! God knows what is needful for you and will have pity on you."[17]

A Coptic cycle of apophthegms that has been published by Amélineau comes back continually to this invocation, adding to it the concentration on the name of Jesus. It is difficult to think that these texts are not connected with a local Egyptian tradition that we can consider as established, at least in its spirit:

> The Abbot Macarius the Great said: Be attentive to this name of Our Lord, Jesus Christ, in contrition of heart; when your lips are moving, draw it to yourself and do not lead it into your mind only to repeat it, but think of your invocation: "Our Lord Jesus, the Christ, have mercy on me", then, in repose you will see His divinity reposing on you. It will drive away the darkness of the passions that are within you, it will purify the interior man with the purification of Adam when he was in paradise—this blessed name that John the Evangelist called on,

[17] *Apophthegm* 16; P.G., XXXIV, 249.

saying: "light of the world", "sweetness that never satiates" and "true bread of life".[18]

One more text from the same source:

> The Abbot Evagrius said: Tormented by the thoughts and the passions of the body, I went to find the Abbot Macarius. I said to him: "My father, give me a word, that I may live by it." Then Macarius said to me: "Attach the rope of the anchor to the rock and, by God's grace, the ship will cross the diabolic waves of this deceptive sea and the tempest of the darkness of this vain world." I said to him: "What is the ship, what is the rope, what is the rock?" The Abbot Macarius said to me: "The boat is your heart: guard it. The rope is your spirit; attach it to our Lord Jesus Christ who is the rock that has power over all the diabolic waves and surges that the saints are contending with; for is it not easy to say with each breath: Our Lord Jesus, the Christ, have mercy on me; I bless You, my Lord Jesus, help me?"[19]

In these last texts, we find gathered together all the ideas concerning prayer which are included in our Homilies: guarding the heart, concentration on thoughts on Christ, the unceasing prayer of faith. In return, the express mention of the invocation of the name of Jesus in connection with all this is not found in the Homilies, while it was to become, in the Byzantine mysticism which constitutes their posterity, the focus of that fervent prayer which they so powerfully encouraged. However, other apophthegms, the date of which there is no doubt about, assure us that the first monks were very familiar with the constantly renewed invocation of the name of Jesus. It seems, therefore, that this whole block, which was to be as it were cut up and sculptured at will by enthusiastic readers of Pseudo-Macarius, may well go back to Macarius himself.

On the guard to be kept over the heart and prayer, here is perhaps the most characteristic text of the Homilies:

> Sin has the power and the impudence to enter into the heart. The apostle says: "I desire men to pray without anger and without evil thoughts." Now, it is from the heart that wicked thoughts emerge, according to the Gospel. When you come to prayer, then, inspect your heart and your spirit (*nous*), have the will to send your prayer pure to God and carefully examine whether there is any obstacle to this, whether your prayer is pure, whether your spirit is occupied with the Lord as is the worker with his work, the husband with his wife.[20]

[18] *Annales du Musée Guimet*, XXXV (1894), Paris, p. 160.

[19] *Ibid.*, 161. Jean Gouillard, *Petite Philocalie de la Prière du coeur*, Paris, 1953, has rightly brought out the importance of these two texts.

[20] *Fifteenth Homily*, XIII; P.G., XXXIV, 584 C.

Here we should note the connection established between pure prayer and the guard over the heart. This is an idea found in Evagrius, which he develops in a very personal way. In its primitive form, this also may go back to Macarius of Scete. As to the heart, it is quite evident that it remains in these texts conceived according to the biblical idea, that is, as the seat of moral decisions. This is what another passage of the same Homily brings out:

> Grace engraves the laws of the Spirit in the hearts of the sons of light. Therefore they should not draw their assurance only from the Scriptures of ink, for the grace of God also engraves the laws of the Spirit and the heavenly mysteries on the tables of the heart. For the heart commands and rules the whole body. And grace, once it has taken possession of the pastures of the heart, reigns over all our members and all our thought. For in the heart are the spirit (*nous*) and all the thoughts of the soul and its hope. Through it, grace passes into all the members of the body. Equally with those that are children of darkness: sin reigns over their heart and passes into all their members. . . .[21]

This text was to have an important place in the development of Byzantine hesychasm. It took its name from *hesychia*, and we have already seen the importance given to this by the Cappadocians—an importance which was to be reinforced, as it were, with Pseudo-Macarius. We have a first sketch of hesychasm in the following text, taken from the *Sixth Homily*:

> Those who approach the Lord should make their prayer in a state of quietness (*hesychia*), of peace and of great tranquillity (*katastasis*), without uneasy and confused cries, but by applying their attention to the Lord by the effort (*ponos*) of the heart and the soberness of their thoughts.[22]

In fact, here soberness (*nepsis*) appears, together with *hesychia*, as surrounding the "attending to the Lord" considered as the proper task of the heart.

In this context, prayer appears as the activity around which everything in the life of the monk is to be concentrated.

> Just as when the body is working at something, it applies itself, wholly engrossed, to its work, and all its members lend one another mutual aid—in the same way the soul should wholly and entirely strip itself for prayer and love of Christ, being no longer agitated and scattered by its thoughts, but attaching itself with its whole expectation to Christ. . . .[23]

[21] *Ibid.*, XX; col. 589 A.
[22] *Sixth Homily*, I; *ibid.*, col. 517 C; cf. III, col. 520 B.
[23] *Thirty-second Homily*, I; *ibid.*, col. 741 C.

> The summary of all good activity, the highest of our works, is perseverance in prayer. By it, we may each day acquire all the virtues by asking them from God. Prayer procures for those who are judged worthy of it communion in the holiness of God, in the energy of the Spirit, and the union (*synapheia*) of the whole awareness of the spirit (*tou nou diatheseos*) with the Lord in an ineffable love. He who, each day, forces himself to perseverance in prayer is consumed by the spiritual love of a divine *eros* and of a burning desire for God, and he receives the grace of sanctifying perfection.[24]

The Co-existence of Sin and Grace

After these two inseparable teachings, on ardent prayer and on the spiritual light that it causes us to contemplate, these Homilies, as we have said, again follow a Gregorian theme in continually insisting on the progressive character of the spiritual life. They introduce an innovation, however, in relation to Gregory, by proposing some initial attempts at outlining gradations in this progress.[25] But they show originality above all in dilating at length on one consequence of this progression which can never be finished; the co-existence in the same man of sin and grace, which must always exist here below.

It is this statement, repeated many times, of *simul peccator et justus*, which has alarmed modern commentators and convinced them of the Messalianism of our author. But it must be read with a little more attention than seems to have been given it. "Macarius" in no way considers this condition as being normal: for him, while grace always finds sin present ahead of it in the spiritual man, it never ceases to fight against it. The final word, as clear as could be desired, is given in the following text, precisely as the conclusion to the fiftieth and last of the Homilies:

> The soul has many members and a great depth, and once sin has entered therein, it takes possession of all these members and of the pastures of the heart. But, when a man sets himself to seeking it, grace comes to him[26] and occupies perhaps two members of the soul. But the inexperienced man, encouraged by grace, thinks that in coming it has taken possession of all the members of the soul and that sin has been uprooted. In fact, the greatest part is dominated by sin, and only one part by grace. It is deceived and it does not know it. Many things still remaining to be enlightened by the awareness (*diathesei*) of our self-consciousness, we have given briefly, as to wise men, a rudiment, so that in

[24] *Fortieth Homily*, II; *ibid.*, col. 764 B.
[25] Cf. in the *Twenty-sixth Homily*, chapters XVI and XVII; *ibid.*, col. 685.
[26] Note this typical phrase of the Gregorian "synergism".

> working and in fathoming the power of these words you may become still more wise in the Lord and may increase the simplicity (*aploteta*) of your heart in His grace and the power of His truth, if you apply yourselves in all security to your salvation and, delivered from all distraction and fraud of the adversary, you are judged worthy of being found standing upright and unconquered on the day of our Lord Jesus Christ.[27]

These last words leave no doubt as to the true import for Pseudo-Macarius of the theme of the coexistence of sin and grace in us. It simply continues an ancient theme, already traditional with the rabbis and taken up by primitive Christian catechesis: starting from the original *dipsychia*, the Christian should bend all his effort towards *aplotes tes kardias*, simplicity of heart, so as not to be judged and condemned by Christ.

Placed in its true context and given its normal clarification, the teaching of "Macarius" regains, with all its richness and depth, the assured balance which Eastern tradition has always recognized in it. At the same time, it keeps, by its aspiration: the quest for God, for Christ, which runs through it, as well as by the lyricism of the many texts in which this is set down, the perpetually vital attraction which made it popular. Through it, we might say, a reciprocal osmosis was effected between the riches of the collective experiences of very simple monasticism and the very active intellectual ferment of that great and almost unequalled spiritual thinker, Gregory of Nyssa.

Quite different, although scarcely less influential, is the synthesis of Evagrius Ponticus.

Evagrius Ponticus

Thirty years ago, this name was hardly mentioned in passing by historians of spirituality. The rather meagre body of his known works, moreover, did not seem to them to have been very extensively utilized. In fact, he was only mentioned as a name, linked with that of Origen in the arguments for or against the latter.

For, from the beginning of the fifth century, the name of Origen divided monasticism in two camps, up to the condemnation of Origenism at the time of the council called that "of the three chapters", a condemnation in which Evagrius was included.

But discoveries connected with Evagrius have been multiplying during the last decades. Not only has the attention that it deserves finally been given to the edition made available by Frankenberg in 1912 of the works of Evagrius preserved only in the Syriac tradition

[27] *Fiftieth Homily*, IV; P.G., XXXIV, 820 D–821 A.

(while proposing a bold reconstruction of their original Greek),[28] but we are now aware of the fact that others of his works, and still more important ones, have come down to us in the original, under the cover of a reassuring name: the *De malignis cogitationibus*, and above all the *De Oratione*. Their attribution to St Nilus allowed them to influence all the Byzantine Middle Ages, as has been demonstrated by I. Hausherr and M. Viller. The latter, in 1930, established the fact that St Maximus the Confessor, even though mentioning the name of Evagrius only as that of an abominable heretic, did not hesitate to borrow from him the kernel, or rather the heart, of his spiritual teaching.[29]

Four years later, Fr Hausherr, in establishing the authenticity of the attribution of the *De Oratione* (a point on which the Syrians had, furthermore, never been mistaken), at the same time brought out clearly the coherence of Evagrius' teaching. It appears as being the first complete system of Christian spirituality and, in any case, the system the precision of which must have so greatly appealed to a multitude of monastic masters that, even when the author had been condemned, his work and its radiation did not cease to assert themselves, if in strangely roundabout ways.[30]

No one today still doubts that Evagrius is one of the most important names in the history of spirituality, one of those that not only marked a decisive turning-point, but called forth a real spiritual mutation. This does not mean that everyone is happy about this. Hans Urs von Balthasar who, for his part, has given back to Evagrius the paternity of some *Selecta in Psalmos* formerly attributed to Origen, does not hesitate to write: "There is no doubt that the mysticism of Evagrius, carried to the strict conclusions of its premises, comes closer, by its essence, to Buddhism than to Christianity."[31]

For it is to Evagrius, rather than to Pseudo-Dionysius of whom we shall speak next, that we must attribute the first invasion of Christianity by what has been called the tendency to abstraction, and it must be admitted that this at first sight seems singularly

[28] *Nachrichten von der Gesellschaft der Wissenschaften zu Göttingen, Phil.-hist. Klasse*, N.F. XIII, 2, Berlin, 1912.

[29] Marcel Viller, "Aux sources de la spiritualité de saint Maxime: Évagre le Pontique", in *Revue d'Ascétique et de Mystique*, Toulouse, XI (1930), pp. 153–84, 239–68, 331–6.

[30] Irénée Hausherr, "Le Traité de l'Oraison d'Évagre le Pontique", *ibid.*, LXV (1934), pp. 34–93, 113–70, reprinted in *Les Leçons d'un contemplatif*, Paris, 1960. It was Wilhelm Bousset, we should remember, who first drew attention to the importance of Evagrius, by his *Evagrios Studien*, Tübingen, 1923.

[31] "Metaphysik und Mystik des Evagrius Ponticus", in *Zeitschrift für Aszese und Mystik*, XIV (1939), Innsbruck-Munchen, pp. 31–47. Also, "Die Hiera des Evagrius", in *Zeitschrift für katholische Theologie*, LXIII (1939), pp. 86–106.

foreign to the Gospel. Does it not wish to meet God in the voluntary forgetfulness of all created realities, including the humanity of the Saviour, in a cessation of all considerations of any distinct idea, including what is expressed in Christian dogma?

Whatever we must think of this complaint, to which we shall have to return later, this is how this personality presents itself to us today, with his work and his so strongly coordinated thought which is expressed with such unerring consistency.

Born around the middle of the fourth century on the shores of the Black Sea in the town of Ibora, Evagrius had the three Cappadocians as friends, one after the other or at the same time. Ordained lector by Basil, deacon by him or by Gregory of Nyssa, he became the companion of Gregory Nazianzen at Constantinople (and always considered him as his master, both in profane and sacred letters), before becoming the archdeacon of his successor Nectarius. Sozomenes and Palladius, the last with abundant details that need not be taken as guaranteed, tell us about the mischance which was the occasion for calling to the monastic life this man of high culture, and, we are told, great charm. Passionately enamoured of a great lady in the imperial city, he would have succumbed to temptation but for a warning dream which decided him to set out in haste for Jerusalem. There, near Melania and under her influence, he decided on the monastic life after many hesitations. He was to lead it, at first under the direction of Macarius of Scete, in Egypt where he settled until his death, which came in 399.

And so this man of letters, this philosopher, this theologian and dialectician exercised in the final struggle against the Arianism of Constantinople, came to transport to the Egyptian deserts, where monasticism had been born, the erudite spirituality for which the Cappadocians had provided the model. He owed a great deal to Gregory of Nyssa, above all in his ascetic views. But it was Origen above all, whom the Cappadocians had opened out to him but whom he read at first hand, who influenced him. He accepted him without the Cappadocians' particular reserves, but this did not prevent the spiritual system which he drew out of Origen, or rather constructed from him, from being very much his own.

He expressed it in numerous works, generally brief but very condensed. For, in addition to that of the letter, the literary form which he favoured and seems to have created—or at any rate to have assured its lasting success throughout the spiritual world of Byzantium—is the collection of lapidary sentences. Fr. Hausherr[32] admits the supposition of Wilhelm Bousett that Evagrius was in this

[32] Hausherr, *op. cit.*, pp. 34ff.

way at the origin of the collections of the *Apophthegmata Patrum* we have spoken of, which took their final form in the fifth century. We should be more inclined to see things the other way round. "Sayings" of "abbots" must have travelled around quickly through the monastic solitudes, and collections, continually added to, must have been circulated very early. However late their completion, these collections, which we find in their finished form towards the fifth century, are made up of materials betraying the fact that they were picked up here and there and then arranged more or less happily, or not arranged at all. On the contrary, the "century" or, more generally, the collection written and launched by Evagrius or his imitators, groups together sentences that have been artificially isolated. We have here pieces of an integral and very systematic thought that has been intentionally taken apart. The intellectual framework cannot be hidden between these sayings that mean to seem fragmentary, while it would have been impossible to construct a framework which would in any fashion unite organically the scattered observations of the very first monks.

Evagrius' Cosmology and Anthropology

For with Evagrius, cosmology, anthropology, asceticism and mysticism form a whole in which all the connections have been perfectly made. He borrowed from Origen, while transforming it a little, his vision of a universe that was originally wholly spiritual, in which matter is only the consequence of inattention to God, in other words, of sin. This does not in the least mean to say that, for him, matter is evil in itself or that God did not create it. But, with him as with Gregory of Nyssa, matter was created only in view of sin and, although the reparation of sin will not cause matter to disappear, properly speaking, it will spiritualize it to the maximum degree.[33]

So it can be said without contradiction, as he did, that all temptations come to us from evil spirits and, at the same time, from our flesh and from the world in which this flesh immerses us. They come to us not only from the demon in general, but from particular demons, specialized if one dare call them so, whether it is a question of the grossest temptations, such as carnal ones, or the subtlest, such as that to vainglory which threatens ascetics and even the most thoroughly tested contemplatives. But these temptations reach us through the *pathe*, the disordered affections which the body awakens in our soul and which disturb, or rather paralyse, the free play of the spirit in us.[34]

[33] *Ibid.*, p. 82.

[34] *Ibid.*, p. 71.

Our nature is, in fact, threefold and yet one. There is the spirit, more precisely the *nous* (intelligence)—Evagrius seldom speaks of the *pneuma*—which is the image of God in us. But, through the soul (*psyche*), this *nous* is bound to the body, descends into it. To free itself, to return to God and to his will by returning to itself—this is the task of the ascetic, of the man who is a monk not only as a man: that is, only by exterior practices, but in his spirit.[35]

Hence the precision which came to be given to a gradation in spiritual development, already sketched out, in the various ways we have seen, by Origen and by the Cappadocians.

The Stages of Spiritual Progress

Sometimes we find two divisions and sometimes three, under the pen of Evagrius. But, when the last two are distinguished, it is within the second term of the duality, which for him is basic, between "practice" and "gnosis".

Practice (simply *praktike*, and once or twice *praktike methodos*) is the domain of the virtues, of the commandments. It ends in *apatheia*, that is, liberation from the *pathe*, which have dominated us hitherto. At this moment can begin the development of gnosis (usually *gnosis*, or *gnostike*, *theoretike*, *theoria*).

This, however, is subdivided into two stages which must not be confused. In the first, we contemplate created, corporeal beings as well as incorporeal, by knowing them, no longer through the *pathe* of which they were hitherto the source, but through the *logoi*, that is a knowledge conformed to the divine reason, to the Logos who created all things. In the second stage, we go beyond all these multiple thoughts and leave them behind, just as, before and lower down, we have left the vices behind in order to contemplate God. And so we pass from *physike theoria* to *theologia*. "Theology", for Evagrius is always the supreme gnosis, what he calls "the gnosis of the Trinity": a knowledge of God brought about beyond all multiple knowledge, all distinct ideas.[36]

Virtues and Vices

Evagrius has very definite ideas on the virtues and the vices, their connection, their hierarchy. He was the first, it seems, to distinguish eight basic sins (the ancestors of our seven capital sins): gluttony, luxury, love of money, sadness, anger, acedia, vainglory, pride. His description of acedia, that is, disgust with spiritual things by

[35] *Ibid.*, p. 48 and p. 129.

[36] *Ibid.*, p. 131.

reason of weariness of the practices connected with them, remains famous:

> The demon of acedia, also called the midday demon, is the most oppressive of all the demons. He attacks the monk towards the fourth hour and besieges the soul until the eighth hour. He begins by giving the impression that the sun is hardly moving or not moving at all, and that the day has at least forty hours. After this, he continually draws the monk to his window; he forces him to go out of his cell, to look at the sun and calculate how much time still separates him from the ninth hour, and finally to look about here and there to see if some brother is not coming to see him.... This demon makes him disgusted with the place he is in, with his way of life, with his manual labour. Then he makes him think that the brothers are lacking in charity, that he has nobody to console him. And if anyone at such a time has given pain to the monk, the demon makes use of this to increase his hatred. Again he drives him to desire some other place, where he would easily find what he needs, where he could do some work that would be easier and more profitable. He adds that one can be pleasing to God anywhere. One can, in fact, adore Him everywhere. Together with this, he reminds the monk of his family and his previous way of life. He describes the long time that the monk still has to live and sets out before his eyes the efforts (*ponoi*) of asceticism; finally, so to say, he sets the machinery going that will drive the monk to leave his cell and flee from the arena.[37]

But it is his dynamic conception of the virtues and their development which is most interesting. It starts from the analyses of Clement of Alexandria, but it weaves them together, clarifies them, and gives them that strict coherence which is one of the most constant features of Evagrius' thought.

Faith is the starting-point. On it is built up the fear of God, from which flows *enkrateia*, the fundamental ascetic virtue of which continence is simply one particular form, consisting in resistance to all the impulses of the passions. On this is grafted patience, which causes us not only to resist the attractions of pleasure, but to bear everything that is painful. From this, finally, is born hope: the expectation of true goods, precisely those towards which faith directs us.

The result of all this chain is *apatheia*, and it is *apatheia* itself that engenders charity, *agape*.[38]

This explication is obviously of the greatest importance in

[37] *To Anatolos, On the Eight Thoughts*, VII; P.G., XL, 1273 BC.
[38] *Letter to Anatolos*, in the preface to *Practicos*, 47; P.G., XL, col. 1221.

locating, and so in rightly interpreting, *apatheia* as Evagrius conceived it.

Apatheia according to Evagrius

St Jerome, irreconcilably inimical to the whole group of ascetics connected with Rufinus and Melania and spurred on by the desire to clear himself at any cost of the suspicion of Origenism, grossly caricatured *apatheia* by reproaching Evagrius with wishing to make man "a stone or else God".[39] Actually, for Evagrius, *apatheia* is simply the domination of the passions in us that are opposed to charity. It withdraws us from the domination of demons to give us back to that of God. It suppresses nothing of the most natural human feelings, but it purifies them in taking away from them anything that is disordered, in submitting them to the *nous*, to what is most spiritual in us.

The signs that one has attained *apatheia* are the possibility of praying without distractions; peace of soul not only in the face of external things but in the face of our thoughts that recall them interiorly; the pacifying even of the deepest layers of our consciousness, which is translated into the calm we attain to even in dreams; and, finally, the ability to judge oneself objectively.[40] Evagrius explicitly states that this *apatheia*—which, moreover, has many degrees—can be lost, for temptations never disappear.[41] Conversely, it only flowers in charity, through what it prepares for: gnosis. In other words, however distinct, for the first time, is Evagrius' definition of successive stages in the spiritual life, he himself is never the prisoner of his outlines. Purification, as he understands it, must certainly precede contemplation. But it is completed only in and through contemplation.

> *Praktike*, he says, is a spiritual method (*pneumatike*) that purifies the sensible part of the soul. But the energies of the commandments do not suffice perfectly to heal the powers of the soul if contemplations for their part do not then take possession of the *nous*.[42]

This is so true for him that he goes so far as to say: "It is gnosis that heals the *nous*."[43]

On the other hand, he clearly proposes an idea of this gnosis that comes from the Alexandrians. But, by clarifications and distinctions

39 Jerome, *Epist*. 133, to Ctesiphon.

40 *Practicos*, II, 58; P.G., XL, 1248; cf. *Fifth Century*, 82; ed. Frankenberg, p. 355; *Practicos*, I, 35, 37, 41; P.G., LX, 1932, etc. See Viller, *op. cit.*, pp. 178ff.

41 *De Oratione*, 90; cf. Viller, *ibid.*

42 *Practicos*, I, 50 and 51; P.G., XL, 1233 B.

43 *Third Century*, 35; Frankenberg, p. 213.

of considerable further import, Evagrius causes us to pass on to a whole new phase in the history of Christian spirituality.

Gnosis according to Evagrius

We should note at the outset that, however intellectual may be the expressions used by Evagrius as by Clement, this gnosis never develops except within charity, as is also the case with Clement. Gnosis begins when charity can finally flourish on the soil of *apatheia.*

> Charity is the superior state of the reasonable soul (*nous*) in in which it is impossible to love anything in the world more than the gnosis of God.[44]

Gnosis, however, as we have said, is differentiated into two kinds, and these are separated by an abyss, even though one leads to the other. First comes the gnosis which is merely *physike theoria,* then comes the superior gnosis: *theologia.* This last is the "gnosis of the Trinity". But it is at the same time the discovery of ourselves, of our true self made to the image of God, which Evagrius understands, as does Gregory of Nyssa, as being like the image in a mirror, presupposing the effective presence of the archetype.

Physical contemplation is the knowledge of all beings through their "reasons", their *logoi,* which, since they exist only in the divine Logos, can be grasped only in the word in which he is himself expressed. In this physical understanding, Evagrius distinguishes four successive forms, which lead him to enumerate five kinds of gnoses, including the supreme gnosis, that of the holy Trinity.

> There are five fundamental gnoses that include all the others: the first is, as the Fathers say, the gnosis of the adorable Trinity; the second and the third are the gnosis of incorporeal beings and of corporeal beings; the fourth and the fifth, the gnosis of judgment and the gnosis of the providence of God.[45]

Another text, from the *Selecta in Psalmos,* for a long time attributed to Origen but restored to Evagrius by Hans Urs von Balthasar, explains clearly what is to be understood by the four different forms of *physike theoria.* Commenting on verse 16 of Psalm 138 (according to the Septuagint): "And all are written down in Your book", he says:

> The contemplation of corporeal and incorporeal beings is this book of God in which the pure spirit (*nous*) is inscribed by

[44] *First Century,* 86; Frankenberg, p. 123.
[45] *First Century,* 27; Frankenberg, p. 73; cf. *Letter,* 7; Frankenberg, p. 571.

> gnosis. In this book are written down also the *logoi* that concern providence and judgment, the book through which we know that God is Creator, wise, provident and Judge: Creator by reason of what has passed from nothingness to being, wise by the hidden reasons of these things, provident by the aids [that He has arranged] to lead us towards virtue and gnosis and, finally, Judge by the different bodies of reasonable beings, the different worlds and the different ages (*aionas*).[46]

This knowledge of the "eons", which he mentions again elsewhere and thus disquiets certain commentators as showing a trace of heretical "gnosticism", is, as can be seen here, the eschatological knowledge of the divine dispositions that lead all things, as Evagrius says a few lines further on, towards the knowledge of God. More generally, all physical contemplation, as we have already seen with the Alexandrians and with Gregory, culminates in an understanding of angelology. This causes us to discover how all creation and its history is a spiritual drama, at the heart of which the drama of man himself is naturally inserted. And so an understanding of the world is sketched out dominated by the understanding of the spiritual mysteries that explain it, and, above everything, of the great mystery of Christ, Saviour as well as Judge. We understand then how, while still being called rational (*logike*), this understanding is acquired in no other way than by meditation on the Scriptures in the light of the Logos made flesh.

But this itself, for Evagrius, is only preparatory to the supreme gnosis, that of the Holy Trinity. How are we to arrive at this last? He has not spared himself efforts to explain it, but it is not so easy for us to understand his explanations.

The "gnosis" or the "contemplation of the holy Trinity" which Evagrius opposes to the "contemplation of beings" has first a negative aspect. It presupposes, after the purification of the passions, a stripping off of all definite thoughts, even the highest to which "physical contemplation" has been able to lead us.

> The *nous* cannot see the place of God in itself if it is not raised above everything that dwells in things (*panton ton* [*noematon* is added by certain manuscripts] *en tois pragmasin*). But it is not raised above everything if it does not put away the *pathe* that hold it to sensible things by its thoughts, and it puts away the *pathe* by the virtues, and simple thoughts by spiritual contemplation, and this in turn is put off when that light manifests itself which, in the time of prayer, sculptures out (*ektupountos*) the place of God.[47]

[46] *Selecta in Psalmos* (attributed as a whole to Origen); P.G., XII, 1661 C.

[47] *Practicos*, I, 71; P.G., XL, 1244 AB; cf. *Fifth Century*, 21; Frankenberg, p. 441.

In this page are to be found many expressions typical of Evagrius, which we shall need to return to. Confining ourselves for the moment to the essential: the effacing of all thoughts, after domination has been acquired over the *pathe*, is necessary for that contemplation of the holy Trinity, that superior gnosis obtained in the highest kind of prayer, which Evagrius calls elsewhere pure prayer.[48]

As he says a few lines further on in the *Seventh Century*, the prayer in question is at once "the state of the soul illuminated by the one light of the holy Trinity [in ecstacy][49] "and the state of the soul that destroys all the reasonings (*logismoi*) of earth".[50]

A first question that presents itself on the subject of this pure prayer is whether man can attain to it by his own effort, by inhibiting in himself all distinct thoughts when he has arrived at the summits of the spiritual life, or whether, on the contrary, this is a grace that God gives him, coming on him independently of his will.

In favour of the first interpretation, all the texts might be invoked which speak of "keeping one's spirit without form (*aneideon*)", of maintaining it "above forms . . . during the time of prayer".[51] Above all, this sentence from the *De Oratione* seems to stand out:

> Do not represent the divinity in yourself when you pray, nor let your mind undergo the impression of any form: but as immaterial go to the immaterial, and you will understand.[52]

Yet in another place Evagrius states categorically:

> To have physical gnosis is within the power of the spirit, but to know the holy Trinity is not only beyond the power of the spirit but requires a superabundant grace from God.[53]

Still more precise on the point that now concerns us: the going beyond definite thoughts, is this other text:

> To remove the spirit from earthly things and lead it to the general knowing of all things is a charism of the sight of God.[54]

All the same, this last text clearly shows that the question did not present itself to Evagrius precisely as it does to us. For him, to say

[48] *Practicos*, I, 14 and 31; P.G., XL, col. 1225 and 1229; *Mirror for Nuns*, 38, ed. Gressmann (in *Texte und Untersuchungen*, 39, 4 Leipzig, 1913), p. 149; *Letters* 1 and 52; *Selecta in Psalmos*, P.G., XII, 1504 A.

[49] This addition is in the Syriac version, but the rediscovered Greek text does not have it (cf. Hausherr, *op. cit.*, p. 150, 11, i).

[50] *Seventh Century*, 29 and 30; Frankenberg, pp. 452–5.

[51] *Seventh Century*, 23; Frankenberg, p. 443.

[52] *De Oratione*, 66; trad. Hausherr, *op. cit.*, p. 114.

[53] *Fifth Century*, 79; Frankenberg, p. 425.

[54] *Seventh Century*, 2; Frankenberg, p. 425.

that attaining contemplation without forms is a grace does not exclude conscious effort on our part and may even imply it.

If we go on to the positive aspect of the superior gnosis, it appears that this gnosis is wholly luminous, in spite of the aspect of obscurity expressly attached to it, but precisely in that it goes beyond all forms. It is in this sense that the text of the *Third Century*, 86 is to be understood:

> Blessed is he who has arrived at infinite ignorance.[55]

The same thing is true of the "perfect amorphia" and the "perfect anaesthesia" of the *De Oratione*.[56] For this is its description in *Practicos*:

> When the *nous*, having stripped off the old man, has been reclothed with the man who comes from grace, then it will see its own state at the moment of prayer, like the colour of sapphire or of the sky, what Scripture calls the dwelling of God which was seen by the Ancients on Mount Sinai.[57]

This idea of the "dwelling of God" contemplated on the heights of prayer is dear to Evagrius.[58] Certainly, he brings out on occasion, as does everyone else, the fact that there is no "dwelling of God" in the usual sense of the expression.[59] But he says elsewhere that "we call peace the dwelling of God, but peace is the *apatheia* of the reasonable soul. He who desires that his God should dwell in him, then, must carefully purify his soul from all its passions."[60] More precisely, following the text of the *Practicos* quoted above, it is the light appearing to the soul in prayer which sculptures out in it the dwelling of God.

Here we are led towards a thought quite close to that of Gregory of Nyssa. On the one hand, Evagrius is categorical (and even more so than Gregory) about the vision of God to which we are called here below: "He who has not seen God cannot speak of him", he says in the *Fifth Century*.[61] To this text we could add the following from the *First Century*:

> Just as the light that shows us all things has no need of another light in order to be seen, so God who causes us to see

[55] The Greek text contains *agnosia*; cf. Hausherr, *op. cit.*, p. 149.
[56] *De Oratione*, 117 and 120.
[57] *Practicos*, 1, 71; P.G., XL, 1244 A.
[58] Cf. *De Oratione*, 57; where it is connected with the place of prayer which he has spoken of in the preceding verse.
[59] *First Century*, 62; Frankenberg, p. 103.
[60] *Seventh Century*, 28; Frankenberg, p. 453.
[61] *First Century*, 26; Frankenberg, p. 329.

all things has no need of a light in which we can see Him, and He is light by essence.[62]

Yet, in his thought, the vision of God is confused with the vision the *nous* has of itself:

> The naked nous [that is: stripped of all that is not its original pure spirituality] is that which is consummated in the vision of itself and has merited to communicate in the contemplation of the holy Trinity.[63]

This presupposes, as Evagrius teaches elsewhere, that the *nous* is once more rendered worthy, by asceticism, "of the perfect image of the holy Trinity from which it had fallen away".[64]

But for him, as for Gregory, this image is one that presupposes the living presence of the model. Evagrius says categorically that the *nous* is the image of God, not inasmuch as it is incorporeal, but inasmuch as it can receive the holy Trinity within it.[65] In other words, this image is a temple: man "is a perfect temple of God when he has received the gnosis of the holy Trinity."[66]

This contemplation, according to a pattern present throughout Evagrius' work, makes us like that which it causes us to contemplate, for the *nous* becomes what it knows: flesh when it lets itself be absorbed by the *pathe*, God when it sees him once more:

> When the *nous* is admitted to the gnosis of the holy Trinity, then, by grace, it is called God, as having arrived at the full image of its creator.[67]

The final question raised by Evagrius' work, evidently, is the sense in which the supreme gnosis is gnosis of the Trinity, when he has insisted so much on the fact that it is produced beyond all forms. It is most remarkable not only that he was the first to ask himself this question, but that it visibly embarrassed him. The proof of this is the answer addressed to him by Gregory of Nyssa (the manuscripts also attribute it to St Gregory Nazianzen).[68] But Evagrius himself has prepared the solution in his own letter (attributed to St Basil),[69] in insisting on the simplicity of God which

62 *First Century*, 35; Frankenberg, p. 79.
63 *Third Century*, 6; Frankenberg, p. 193.
64 *Third Century*, 28; Frankenberg, p. 207.
65 *Sixth Century*, 73; Frankenberg, p. 409; cf. *Third Century*, 69, and 32; *ibid.*, pp. 237 and 211.
66 *Fifth Century*, 84; Frankenberg, p. 359.
67 *Fifth Century*, 81; Frankenberg, p. 355; cf. *Fifth Century*, 51; *ibid.*, p. 293.
68 *Epist.* 26, also attributed to St Gregory Nazianzen under n. 243, but it seems clearly to be by Basil's brother.
69 *Epist.* 8, in the collection of St Basil's letters.

nothing can divide or multiply. Hence a distinction, of a distinctly Origenist flavour, between "the kingdom of Christ", which is "the contemplation that bears on all material beings", and "the kingdom of God, of the Father: the immaterial gnosis, which might be called the contemplation of the divinity itself".[70] This involves, as he tells us explicitly, going beyond the humanity of Christ in this superior gnosis. The *Sixth Century* explains to us again that the holy Trinity is not numerical, since it does not result from an addition, nor from a growth, and cannot undergo anything of the sort.[71]

Fr Hausherr[72] passes a severe judgment on these views:

> It must be said that Evagrius never integrated the theology of the Trinity in his mysticism. However often we may find in his Centuries the expression "contemplation of the holy Trinity", neither the Father as Father, nor the Son as Son, nor, above all, the Holy Spirit play any appreciable rôle in the ascent of the intellect. "Holy Trinity" is only the Christian way of speaking of the Divinity, of the "Monad". The *De Oratione,* by virtue of this same characteristic, wears the mark of its author. In spite of the theology which is its supreme goal, Evagrian mysticism remains more philosophical than properly theological.

This judgment explains the still more severe phrases of Hans Urs von Balthasar quoted above, emphasizing the absence of any specifically Christian character in Evagrius' mysticism.

Can we ratify these condemnations as given? We should hesitate a great deal to do so. It is true that Evagrius hardly speaks of our specific relations with the different divine Persons; it is true also that his insistence on going beyond all form in the higher kind of contemplation lends itself to the impression that he is actually tending, whether he knows it or not, towards going beyond the dogma of the Trinity itself. Yet, on this last point, we need to keep in mind a distinction which has been too greatly neglected, in connection with Evagrius as with many other mystics in his spiritual lineage, beginning with Meister Eckhart. Our intellectual representation of the Trinity obviously includes distinct forms. But the Trinity, in itself, certainly transcends all the forms in which we pretend to enclose it. An experience of the divine life could, then, very well be an experience of the Trinity, of God as he is in himself, of the life of the Trinity, as such, without including at the same moment an apprehension of the concept in which we express the God who is at once the one God and the consubstantial and indivisible Trinity.

[70] § 7.
[71] *Sixth Century*, 10–13; Frankenberg, pp. 367ff.
[72] *Op. cit.*, p. 117.

Conclusions

However, whatever precise meaning his own mysticism may have had for Evagrius, it would be difficult to deny that his expressions introduced a lasting threat into the Christian mystical tradition: the fatal attraction of pure abstraction. A neglect of Scripture, of dogma, in favour of a "contemplation" that runs the risk of being no more than a state of psychological vacuity is not, as experience has abundantly shown, for minds nourished on the tradition which we can now call Evagrian, a merely chimerical danger.

And there also may be a danger in the too neat distinction made between the three stages of the spiritual life. Even though with Evagrius himself the purification which, under one aspect, is preliminary to the development of gnosis, is not to be achieved except in and through the latter; even though he himself emphasizes the possibility that the superior gnostic may still succumb to the grossest temptations—yet the many dangers inherent in trying too neatly to distinguish successive stages in the spiritual life will none the less reveal themselves.

But, above all, it is the complete break which he was the first to formulate between what he calls "theology", that is the contemplation of God in himself, and the contemplations or purifications preceding it that has proved to be a two-edged sword. Following him, there has been only too great a tendency to detach the mystical experience, as it came to be called, from the whole ascetical and doctrinal substructure presupposed by it, reducing it finally to an extraordinary experience, distinguishable and, perhaps, even definable merely by certain mainly negative psychological criteria.

On the other hand, the complaint made against him in connection with *apatheia*, in the Origenist dispute, seems to be reduced to a gross misunderstanding. Nor is the importance he attached to the idea that pure prayer is a state (*katastasis*) to be forced in a quietist sense.

As it is, with its insufficiencies, its possible equivocations, but its unparalleled power of synthesis, the work of Evagrius has exercised a determining influence on certain of the most important later developments in Christian spirituality. In finally fixing the schema of the three ways, as they would be called; in systematizing the view of the vices and the virtues; above all, in preparing the radical distinction between what he calls pure prayer (that would soon be called mystical prayer or mystical experience) and every other form of prayer, Evagrius directed the explanation and even the conception of spirituality into decidedly new ways, and we are only now beginning to discover that everything about them is not equally essential.

It is most remarkable, as we have already pointed out, that certain of the works which exercised the greatest influence on the later development of monasticism and its spirituality accepted as a whole, often without knowing it, the entire framework of Evagrius' thought. This is true of Palladius, of John Climacus, of Hesychius of Jerusalem, as well as of a mind as powerfully original as that of St Maximus, with his whole Byzantine posterity. It is true also of the Syrians: Philoxenus of Mabbug, Isaac of Niniveh, Bar Hebraeus. And, finally, it is true of Cassian who exercised such a great influence on all Latin monasticism.

Yet the extent of Evagrius' radiation should not be exaggerated, and we cannot, for ourselves, completely agree with the viewpoint of Fr Hausherr, seeing in him, if not the father, at least the ancestor of Byzantine hesychasm. To the influence of Evagrius on this lasting tradition, we believe there should be added as being at least of equal importance that of the writings of Pseudo-Macarius, and, around these, a continuous influx of the evangelical vigour of the first monks of Egypt—a vigour which Evagrius himself had perhaps stifled a little in channelling it as perfectly as he did into an Origenism rethought, but strongly systematized and occasionally rigidified.[73]

[73] The most complete bibliography on the texts of Evagrius is in Viller-Rahner, *Aszese und Mystik in der Väterzeit*, Freiburg in Brisgau (1939), pp. 97ff. We should add to this J. Muyldermans, *Evagriana Syriaca*, Louvain, 1952, and A. Guillaumont, *Les six Centuries des "Kephalaia gnostica" d'Évagre le Pontique*, Patrologia Orientalis, XVIII, fasc. i, Paris, 1958.

XVI

PSEUDO-DIONYSIUS AND THE MYSTICISM OF THE FATHERS

With the writings of the Areopagite, we reach the third and last line in the spiritual posterity of the Cappadocians and of Gregory of Nyssa in particular, while Evagrius also seems to have left more than a trace, but a transfigured one, on the Dionysian *Corpus*.

One of the most notable characteristics of these writings, in fact, is precisely this: we can discern the marks of a whole series of influences, sometimes word for word, yet all, as with Evagrius, are recast into an astonishingly personal synthesis. In contrast to Evagrius' writings and their specious laconicism, here the rigorous articulations of thought, far from remaining underlying though still visible, are openly set out. Doubtless there is little spiritual (or even theological) writing which gives evidence of being so deliberate an expression of a thought intending to constitute a perfect system. This impression is strengthened by the extraordinary mastery with which a historical fiction is imperturbably developed, while a language and style completely *sui generis* remain unflinchingly faithful to a model conceived once for all.

We might say that these writings form a world apart, which, in spite of the materials that it uses very freely, never clearly indicates its relationship to anything. Hence the almost undecipherable enigma of their composition. Now if ever is the occasion to apply the whimsical statement of Fr Mandonnet saying that in every mystic there must be a mystifier.

The Historical and Literary Problem of the Areopagite Writings

The author of the Dionysian *Corpus* succeeded—in itself no mean achievement—in passing himself off as Dionysius the Areopagite, converted by St Paul according to the Acts of the Apostles. Later on, this original legend was elaborated with more or less fantastic combinations. The first Dionysius, with whom the author himself wished to be identified, was confused with the Dionysius who was Bishop of Athens in the second century. Then, following Hilduin, his translator and first propagator in the West, legend went so far as to make out that these were one with that other Dionysius (Denis) to whom the Parisian Church attributed its beginnings.

It seems superfluous to delay any longer over these last manipulations, the fantastic character of which at once leaps to the eye. But in return, in spite of the enormous effort of modern criticism since Valla to locate the precise place of the Dionysian writings in the body of Greek Patristics, it must be admitted that nothing decisive has as yet been produced, even though nobody now suggests that they go back further than the third century.

A triple barrage of dates[1] had been even considered as definitively established by Koch and Stiglmayr which forbad us to seek the place of our unknown author before the end of the fifth century. "Dionysius", in his description of the eucharistic liturgy, speaks of a "Catholic hymn" which, it seemed, could only be the Symbol of Nicea-Constantinople. And the introduction of this symbol into what we call the Byzantine liturgy is thought not to have taken place before 476. Furthermore, "Dionysius" seems to have a policy of balancing strictly Chalcedonian Christological formulas with Monophysite ones, which corresponds to the line traced out by the Henoticus of the emperor Zeno, a document which dates from 482. Finally, his theory concerning evil, as reduced to a mere privation, seems patterned on that of Proclus, who died in 487.

These considerations led Stiglmayr himself to propose Severus of Antioch as the possible author of the Dionysian *Corpus*. Does not the first known mention of our "Dionysius" consist in the bringing out of his texts by the Severian Monophysites? But Mgr Lebon seems to have made this attribution impossible by a close examination of the facts and dates in Severus' life, leaving no room for the composition of these writings where Stiglmayr wished to put them in.[2]

Fr Hausherr, however, basing his conclusions on a text of a

[1] The expression is that of Maurice de Gandillac, in his Introduction to the translation of the *Oeuvres complètes du Pseudo-Denys l'Aréopagite*, Paris, 1943. p. 22. The two chief works of Hugo Koch on this question are "Proklus als Quelle des Pseudo-Dionysius Areopagita in der Lehre von Bösen", in *Philologus*, LIV (1895), Göttingen, pp. 438–54, and *Pseudo-Dionysius Areopagita in seinen Beziehungen zum Neuplatonismus und Mysterienwesen*, Mainz, 1900. The thesis of J. Stiglmayr is most completely set forth in an article in the review *Scholastik*, of Fribourg, III, 1928: "Der sogennante Dionysius und Severus von Antiochen" (pp. 1–27 and 161–89).

[2] E. Lebon, "Le Pseudo-Denys et Sévère d'Antioche", in *Revue d'Histoire ecclésiastique*, Louvain, XXXVI (1930), pp. 880–915.

Syrian Nestorian of the eighth century, Joseph Hazzaya, which brings out the identity of style between the personal works of Sergius of Resaina and his Syriac translation (?) of "Dionysius", was to suggest that the said translation might, in this case, be the original text, with the Greek one being original also, since Sergius was bilingual.[3]

For his part, Hans Urs von Balthasar made the observation that the scholia of John of Scythopolis on the Dionysian *Corpus*, which are certainly anterior to 530, insist on its authenticity in a way that seems curious in a writer ordinarily so critical. Might he not be, if not the very author that he pretends to comment on, at least one of his friends?... Now, John and Sergius were connected with precisely the same group of Syrians who, remaining orthodox in the main current of their thought, were nevertheless tempted to retain several Monophysite formulas (this is what is called today Neo-Chalcedonianism).[4]

Another kindred hypothesis, which has enlisted the support of Charles Moeller, one of the best scholars on Severian circles, is the one developed by E. Honigmann.[5] According to him, the author of the *Corpus* would rather be Peter the Iberian, Prince of Georgia and Monophysite Bishop of Maiouma. This would also allow us to identify the "divine Hierotheos", to whom our "Dionysius" continually refers, as being Peter's friend, John the Eunuch. Visions attributed to these two personages do, in fact, seem to be very closely related to "Dionysius'" thought: that of Peter, with the development concerning the wheels of fire in the Celestial Hierarchy; and that of John concerning the whole conception of this hierarchy otherwise found as such only in "Dionysius" himself.

However, the famous triple barrage of dates, that led the majority of our contemporaries to look for "Dionysius" in this circle, improperly described as Monophysite, composed of Syrians of the beginning of the sixth century and their neighbours and friends, does not seem impregnable to everyone.

Mgr Athenagoras has observed that the "Catholic hymn" might be the *Gloria in excelsis* just as well as or better than the *Credo*, and that its place in that part of the eucharistic liturgy where

[3] Irénée Hausherr, "Doutes au sujet du 'Divin Denys'", in *Orientalia christiana periodica*, 1936, pp. 484–90.

[4] Hans Urs von Balthasar, "Das Scolienwerk des Johannes von Scythopolis", in *Scholastik*, XV (1940), pp. 16–38.

[5] E. Honigmann, "Pierre l'Ibérien et les écrits du Pseudo-Denys l'Aréopagite", in *Mémoires de l'Académie royale de Belgique, Classes des Lettres et des Sciences morales et politiques*, XLVII, fasc. 3, Brussels, 1952. Cf. Charles Moeller, "Du nouveau sur le Pseudo-Denys", in *Ephemerides theologicas lovanienses*, IV (1953), pp. 654–6.

"Dionysius" seems to locate it is vouched for precisely at an archaic period.[6]

Others, like Fr Ceslas Pera, O.P., have emphasized the fact that the reference to the Henoticus is actually merely an argument *e silentio*, which can equally well be turned against those who advance it. For, if "Dionysius" was influenced by this document, it is very strange that he never uses its characteristic terms, such as *homoousios* for the humanity of Jesus, and *theotokos* for the Virgin Mary. More curious still is the fact that he uses without any hesitation, in speaking of the Virgin, the term *theodokhos* which, after Nestorius, became suspect.[7]

Fr Elorduy calls in question the very argument, however topical it may seem, of "Dionysius'" literal dependence on Proclus with regard to his idea of evil as a privation.[8] Might not "Dionysius" and Proclus, here as elsewhere, have both depended on a tradition common in the Neo-Platonic school, which might go back much further than the sixth or even the fifth century?

What value is there, then, in the solutions proposed by the latter authors—which are the only ones up to now to suggest going back further than this period to merit discussion?

Fr Pera is the least ambitious, contenting himself with the end of the fourth century, and seeing the author of the *Corpus* as being a monk of Annesi, a faithful disciple of St Basil (whom we doubtless should see behind the figure of the "divine Hierotheos"). His positive arguments are of unequal value. The coincidence between the use of the term *theomakhia* in the *Corpus* and in the anti-Arian controversy is not very striking: the same vocabulary is to be found, used in an analogous way, in the struggle against all the ancient heresies. Much more impressive is the fact that the *Corpus* confines itself strictly, when speaking of the Holy Spirit, to the archaic formulas which Basil himself, in express opposition to St Gregory Nazianzen, never wished to go beyond.

Mgr Athenagoras, for his part, wishes to lead us back to the origins of the School of Alexandria. "Dionysius", would indeed be Dionysius, but the bishop of that city who was a contemporary of Clement's, the latter in this case filling the rôle of the "divine Hierotheos". It must be admitted that the arguments put forward for this hypothesis are not very convincing. To the extent that they are effective, they apply to any theological school largely informed

[6] Mgr Athenagoras, *A Liturgical Problem in connection with the great Problem of the Dionysian works* (in Greek), Alexandria, 1943.

[7] Ceslas Pera, "Denys le Mystique et la Theomachia", in *Revue des Sciences philosophiques et théologiques*, XXV (1936), pp. 5–75.

[8] See the studies of this author already mentioned above, p. 260, n.b.

by Greek thought and open to it, and, therefore, as well to the Cappadocia of the end of the fourth century as to the Alexandria of the beginning of the third.

More forceful, though paradoxical, certainly, is the argumentation of Fr Elorduy already mentioned. He also looks to Alexandria. But it is Ammonius Saccas whom he believes is to be seen under the mask of Dionysius. We have already mentioned his arguments. Even if they do not win our adherence to his thesis, they have the great merit of bringing into question for the first time the global view of Neo-Platonism as being practically immutable from one author to another. To make "Dionysius", identified with Ammonius Saccas, the source not only of Proclus but of Plotinus himself, is certainly to hold to a paradox which has hardly a chance of imposing itself, in the complete absence of any references to the *Corpus* before the sixth century. But this should not make us ignore the importance of certain observations formulated for the first time by Elorduy, in accurately locating the Greek Fathers and "Dionysius" in particular in relation to Neo-Platonism.

We have already brought out how much the Neo-Platonic notion of the divine transcendence—a transcendence that perhaps does not exclude any generous communication of God to his creatures (if one can so much as use this last term in such a context) and, particularly, in no way excludes a "knowledge" of God uniting us with him—indubitably owes to the biblical and even Christian ideas spread throughout the whole intellectual climate of Alexandria at the beginning of the third century.

We have also mentioned how probable, to say the least, was the influence of the Christian Trinity, as envisaged in the Alexandria of that period, on the Plotinian Triad. We now need to add that the many triads projected by Proclus, starting from this one, throughout the whole structure of his cosmos—equivalents of which have been found in "Dionysius"—could well have had the same origin. We do not mean only to say that, the Plotinian triad being patterned after the Christian Trinity, it was by way of this channel that the many triads of Proclus also flowed from the Christian Trinity. We would go further than this. The spiritual scheme underlying these triads with "Dionysius" is of directly Christian origin. For while the purification, illumination, and union with transcendence that define and animate these triads in his work are also found in Proclus, in the latter they are only the complementary aspects of a process of return to God, to the One, having no formal connection with the triad structure itself. With "Dionysius", on the contrary, these terms designate three successive activities, the structure of which corresponds to the *praktike*, the *theoria physike* and the "gnosis of the Holy Trinity" of Evagrius. This Evagrian division, however, proceeded from a distillation and a progressive clarification immanent to the Christian spiritual tradition: from Origen, then from monasticism as it took on little by little a reflex consciousness of itself and for this purpose directly seized on elements of Stoic thought, such as *apatheia*, the significance of which it furthermore completely transformed.

Under these conditions, it becomes very difficult to conclude that the parallelisms between "Dionysius" and Proclus are a proof of the dependence of the former on the latter. Even if we must admit (and is it so certain?) that "Dionysius" knew Proclus and borrowed certain of his formulations, it is possible that "Dionysius" may be the last link in an autonomous Christian tradition, to which Proclus, for his part, with the whole of later Neo-Platonism, would be tributary.

This, as we shall see later on, becomes still more probable when we undertake a rather strict lexicographical study of the related themes of "mysticism" and "divinization". It is a commonplace in all the handbooks that the dependence of the Greek Fathers with regard to Neo-Platonism is affirmed here more clearly than anywhere else. But a fact which nobody as yet seems to be aware of is this: the formation of the first of these terms, as the semantics involved bring it out with dazzling clarity, is purely Christian; of the second, sketches or echoes can be found in Hellenistic spirituality. But it was not here, and it was not under influences external to Christianity, that "divinization" attained its final definition: it was in a Christian environment, and starting from biblical elements.

Without adventuring further for the moment into these problems, let us try to draw the lesson from the preceding remarks in order to locate "Dionysius" to the extent that this is possible.

Pera's observations of his kinship with the Cappadocians are not to be neglected. They should even be completed and clarified by the history of the theme of darkness, so masterfully traced by H. Ch. Puech some years ago,[9] and recently discussed by Völker.[10] Here we have a whole body of evidence seemingly obliging us to place "Dionysius" in the direct line of Gregory of Nyssa, not without indisputable references to Evagrius. But this comes back to making him a disciple and a faithful continuator of the great Christian Alexandrians, however removed from them he may have been in time and place.

[9] H. Ch. Puech, "La ténèbre mystique chez le Pseudo-Denys l'Aréopagite et dans la tradition patristique", in *Études carmélitaines*, XXIII (2), Paris, 1938, pp. 33–53.

[10] Walther Völker, *Kontemplation und Ekstase bei Pseudo-Dionysius Areopagita*, Wiesbaden, 1958, particularly pp. 210ff.

Finally, the increasing evidence concerning the strong impregnation of the Syrian monastic atmosphere in the fifth century by Gregory's thought[11] would explain, if Stiglmayr and still more Balthasar and Hausherr (or perhaps Honigmann?) are right, how it was that the Dionysian *Corpus* happened to appear precisely there, while still being in so many respects very "Cappadocian" and even "Alexandrian"....

But, whatever his immediate origin, we must above all conclude from what has just been said, that, before studying "Dionysius" in function of philosophical themes and ideas current in non-Christian circles, it is necessary—as Völker has just done—to put him back into the context of Patristics and to study him first of all as a Christian theologian and spiritual writer.

Cosmos and Hierarchy

It is as such, moreover, that he presents himself, without in the least—quite the contrary, as his pseudonym proves—trying to dissimulate his impassioned concern for Greek philosophy and for everything that it might carry with it of spirituality, or at least the desire for it. But modern scholars, and even de Gandillac in his translation of the Dionysian *Corpus*, insist on turning things around by making his whole work rest on what seems to be most "philosophic" in it. According to this view, we should begin our study with the *Treatise on the Divine Names*, and then go on to the *Mystical Theology*, leaving as appendices, as secondary works, the *Celestial Hierarchy* and the *Ecclesiastical Hierarchy*. The reverse order, however, which is that of all the manuscripts, is quite clearly the one to be followed.

Far from starting from an abstract philosophic view of God, to come back somehow or other, later on, to traditional theology, "Dionysius" starts with the latter. His mysticism proceeds from the vision of the world and the Church which he draws from Scripture and the liturgy. And while, in the explication that he gives of his own thought, he has frequent recourse to the formulas of Greek thought, while, in particular, he manifests his close familiarity with that whole current to which the name of Neo-Platonism has been given—he remains no less basically Christian in his idea of the universe, of the God who made it, and of our possibility of attaining him.

[11] Cf. above, p. 351. On the vast literature concerning the Dionysian *Corpus* and the problems it raises, there is no better guide or more complete presentation than the work of Jean-Michel Hornus, "Les recherches récentes sur le Pseudo-Denys l'Aréopagite", *in Revue d'Histoire et de Philosophie religieuses*, Strasbourg, XXXV (1955), pp. 404–48, completed in vol. XLI (1961), pp. 22–81.

Certainly, his vision of the heavenly world—with its nine choirs of Angels arranged in three ordered triads—and then of the Church herself—similarly stratified, at first sight, from the Bishop, the summit of the initial triad, to the penitents, at the lowest grade of the ladder of the initiates—seems at first to be patterned on that of Proclus. Does it not present a world with a co-ordinated structure that is merely the fixation of a degradation of being, with successive emanations permanently separating the inferior beings from Being in its purity as much as, and more than, they connect them with it? And behind the cosmos of "Dionysius", as behind that of Proclus, is there not once more to be found, in the last analysis, the Stoic world, with its harmony testifying to the basic unity of being—a world where only a partial view distinguishes particular beings, which recover the total and one life only by the acceptance of fusing with and vanishing away in the unique Being? Do not the very terms "Dionysius" uses proclaim this dependence—*proodos* and *epistrophe*; "procession" (or emanation) and "conversion" (or, more precisely, return)—terms used by the Neo-Platonists to designate this diastole and systole of the great Being of which distinct beings are only the vestige?

Yet Dionysius' adoption of these images and this vocabulary should not conceal from us the fact that the images are reinterpreted and the vocabulary transposed according to the meaning that "Dionysius" wishes to attribute to them. We need to pay particular attention not merely to what he borrows from the surrounding atmosphere but also to what he adds to it, and we need to see the intention with which he does so.

Everyone is agreed on the fact that the key to his idea of the world is the term "hierarchy", and nobody seems to doubt that this word is his own creation. Yet, up to the present time, hardly any trouble has been taken to elucidate the sense he gives to it. It is admitted without any examination that with him the term is a mere equivalent of the terms *taxis* (order) and *seira* (ordered arrangement) in Proclus and, in consequence, that it implies a graduated universe in which, once again, the successive degrees are not so much links as accumulated barriers between the principle of all being and successive beings. But precisely the opposite is what "Dionysius" means by this word, "hierarchy". He himself defines it as:

> a sacred order, a science and an energy that assimilates as much as is permitted to the divine form (*taxis hiera kai episteme kai energeia pros to theoeides hos ephikton aphomoioumene*).[12]

[12] *Hier. celest.*; P.G., I, 164 D.

Further on he explains:

> The term "hierarchy" designates a certain ordering that is wholly sacred, image of the thearchic splendour, in orders and holy sciences, which carry out in a holy way (*hierourgousan*) the mysteries of the illumination (*ellampseos*) which is proper to it and assimilates as much as is fitting to its own principle.[13]

Hence the statement that "the end of hierarchy . . . is assimilation to and union (*henosis*) with God".[14]

These texts call for three main observations. The first is that hierarchy as such, for "Dionysius", is not the immutable order of beings, but quite the opposite; it is the circulation of knowledge and of life which, throughout the cosmic or ecclesiastical order, leads everything to God. The second is that hierarchy, as he understands it, is only a radiation throughout the world of the "thearchy" itself, that is, of the divine life as it flowers in the Trinity. The third and most important is that hierarchy, as a result, far from separating, in a world apparently complex but basically one, the superior beings from the inferior, is in reality what causes the superior beings to concern themselves exclusively, we might say, with reconnecting and bringing back the inferior beings to him who infinitely transcends them all.

"Dionysius" himself, after the Wisdom of Solomon, frequently takes up this idea that the highest creatures of God communicate what they have received from him "disinterestedly". The term, obviously, is taken from Platonic terminology, which describes the gods and the Good as being "disinterested".[15] But, with "Dionysius" this formula is now charged with a wholly new and wholly Christian positive content. The Greek gods, the Platonic Good, are "disinterested" in the sense that all beings share in the Good. But these beings in no way share in it in virtue of a love which the gods, and still less the Good, might have for them. "Disinterested", with the gods and with the Good, is only a synonym for the perfect indifference, nay even the total ignorance, of superior beings with regard to inferior. Love, that is, the *eros* made of desire, can exist in the latter only, as being the aspiration urging them to raise themselves towards what surpasses them. The love of God, in the universe of Platonism, of Aristotelianism and of their heirs, moves the whole universe: but it is the love *with which God is loved*:

[13] *Ibid.*, 165 B. [14] *Ibid.*, 165 A.

[15] Wisdom 6. 23. The Phaedrus (247 A) says that the divine choir is "without concern". The same thing is attributed to the demiurge by the *Timaeus* (29 d and e). On this theme, see observation of R. Roques, *L'universe dionysien*, Paris, 1954, p. 316, n. 1.

kinei hos eromenon. For God to love anything at all would be meaningless, since there is nothing that he can desire.[16]

For "Dionysius", on the contrary, the love that moves all beings is the love which is proper to God, to the Christian God: the *agape* with which he loves, pure gift, pure generosity. The *eros* of creatures, in his vision, is never, if it is pure, anything but a reascent of this *agape* towards its source. And, with them all, it can only bring them back effectively to the God from which they proceed by at the same time setting up within them that generous condescension of the divine *agape* which urges it to descend, in order to reach and lead back to itself what is farthest from it: its creatures, and even sinners.

In fact, far from the degrees of being in the Dionysian universe coming forth from one another by a successive generation, all immediately proceed from God alone, as creator.[17] They are not degraded forms of his being, but co-ordinated manifestations of the pure generosity of his love. If all together are reascending to him, it is not to be absorbed in him, but to attain their perfect flowering in him. And if they do this through, by means of, one another, this is because this flowering presupposes in those in whom it is produced the same givingness, the same generosity as with him who is its source. On all levels of being, the call to live the very life of God presupposes, at the same time as gratitude with regard to every superior being—which is superior only in opening itself out and giving itself to what it surpasses—the repetition and the extension of this openness and this giving.

The interest of the *Celestial Hierarchy* consists in tracing as it were the blue-print of this profound dynamism of a spiritual universe proceeding from the God-Spirit who wills to associate nothingness itself with his spiritual life, that is to say, with his life of generous love. But it is in the *Ecclesiastical Hierarchy* that this effective communication of the *agape-eros* is reunited, in all the concrete articulations of its historical realization for us, with the Incarnation and its consequences. The "hierarchy" of the Church, in fact, is manifested and realized in the communication of the truth by the proclamation of the divine word and in association, in the sacramental mystery, with the life which this truth proclaims.[18] With the ministers purifying, the priests enlightening, the bishop consummating in this unity which is perfection itself, the monks appear as those who have allowed themselves already here

[16] The formula quoted comes from Aristotle (*Metaphysics*, 1072 b, e). See Anders Nygren, *Agape and Eros*, Westminster, Phila., 1953, 363.

[17] See Roques, *op. cit.*, pp. 53 and 333.

[18] *Hier. eccl.*, I, 1; P.G., I, 369 D ff.

below to be consummated in this unity of love and of knowledge, the simple faithful as those who have already received its illumination, and the catechumens, energumens and penitents as those who are being purified in various ways to come or return to it.[19]

And behind both the one and the other hierarchy there is Christ —that is, the Logos in which is for ever proclaimed the mystery of unity of the divine thearchy, the mystery into which the angelic hierarchy was initiated by a primary and perpetual communication.[20]

Incarnated in the human world, the world of sin repaired, the Logos, in Jesus, becomes the content of the ecclesiastical preaching and of the liturgical celebration, in which the incorporeal hierarchies invisibly co-operate.[21] All this culminates in the Eucharist, which "Dionysius" usually calls the "synaxis"— in other words, the reassembling, the reuniting in God, through Christ, together with the intelligible universe, of the whole human universe.[22]

The "mystical theology" which is the subject of the last Dionysian book, is nothing other than the realization by man, to the extent to which it is accessible here below, of this profound reality of the divine thearchy, communicating itself to him, at his level, in the ecclesiastical hierarchy, which reflects and extends on earth the heavenly hierarchy. This book is given its necessary introduction in the exegeses of the *Treatise on the Divine Names,* which gives us understanding in faith of the truths proclaimed about God by the Church, in such a way that "mystical theology" effectively causes us to assimilate the divinizing mystery of the liturgy.

It is here in fact, and set out in this fashion, that we find in "Dionysius" the final flowering of the two interwoven themes of mysticism and of divinization. And it is by retracing this definitive flowering in his work that we can perceive the precise meaning of these themes for the whole of Greek Patristics and, at the same time, find the authentic key to "Dionysius'" own spirituality.

The Origin and the Nature of Mysticism in "Dionysius"

One of the commonest assertions among modern historians and one of the most generally accepted without anyone taking the trouble to prove it, is that any "mysticism" in the Fathers necessarily implies Greek and, more specifically, Neo-Platonic influence.

19 *Ibid.*, V, i, 2ff. and VI; col. 501 A ff. and 529 D ff.

20 Cf. *Hier. eccl.*, I, 1, col. 372 AB (also the last words of I, 2: "Jesus the principle and the end of all hierarchy", col. 373 B), with *Hier. celest.*, VII, 2, col. 208 C. See the commentary of Roques, *op. cit.*, p. 319 (it is to be noted that, unfortunately, the majority of references given in this particular place are inexact).

21 Cf. the text quoted in note 18. See Roques, *op. cit.*, pp. 323ff.

22 *Hier. eccl.*, III; col. 424 B ff.

Now, if "Dionysius" is, without any doubt, admirably informed in the developments of Neo-Platonism, and if he is not slow to speak its language and to borrow his favourite images from it—feeling free, once again, to transfigure all this by the use he makes of it—it is all the more remarkable that his use of the word *mysticos*, together with what is most characteristic of him in this use, is incorporated in a purely Christian and ecclesiastical context.

The fact is—and it cannot be said too often—in profane Greek speech, the word *mystikos* never had more than the general meaning of "hidden". Never had any properly religious sense been attached to it. Never, above all, do we find it used to designate and characterize a spiritual experience. The only uses of the word that we find in the Hellenistic world in connection with religious things concern the ritual of the "mysteries". But in this case they mean quite simply that the ritual is and must remain hidden. It is in this sense that Thucydides calls *ta mystika* the ceremonies of the mysteries and that Strabo applies the adjective to the initiates themselves: *hoi mystikoi*.

What was hidden in the Hellenistic mysteries was the rites and nothing but the rites. These did not include any "mystical" doctrine, for the very good reason that they did not include any doctrine at all. It was the philosophers, the poets, the literary men who delighted in finding deep meaning in the mysteries. But this meaning was never "hidden": anyone was free to develop it, even to invent it, according to his fancy, without running any risk at all of being accused of touching on the secret of the mysteries. In contrast, Alcibiades, in an evening of revelry, had only to parody the ritual to incur this accusation. The secret of the mysteries, what was *mystikos* about them, was, then, the rites in their materiality and nothing else.

However, the symbolic usage that literary men soon came to make of the images and formulas of the mysteries made ready for an intellectual and spiritual utilization of the term, but one which was only a special application of a multiform metaphorical use of it.

As to how commonplace this use had become, the only phrase characteristic of the language of the mysteries to be found in St Paul and the way in which he uses it are most revealing: "I have learned how (*memuemai*—I have been initiated) to eat for my hunger and to remain hungry."[23]

His contemporary, Philo, shows us how this vocabulary came to be used in the domain of philosophy: not in the least to designate particular teachings of spiritual experiences scarcely accessible to

[23] Phil. 4. 12.

the masses, but to signify any knowledge difficult to penetrate, such as the most academic and arid subtleties of Stoic physics or psychology.

It is in connection with this very loose and very commonplace usage that, also in Alexandria, the first Christian use of the word *mystikos* came to be introduced. It was used to describe what Clement and Origen considered the most difficult theological problem in Christianity: Scriptural exegesis as they understood it, that is, the discovery of the allegorical sense of the Scriptures. The result was the close association of this meaning of *mystikos* with the use St Paul had already made of the term *mysterion,* to designate Christ and his work, above all his cross, considered as the underlying reality and the ultimate key to the whole Bible. In this sense, for Clement, the Christian interpretation of the Scriptures is their "mystical interpretation", and Origen said that this interpretation is an "explication of the mystical sense (*mystikou nou*) brought out from the treasure of the [divine] words".[24]

In all the later Fathers (and even the Antiochenes), we find again this basic Christian use of the word "mystical" to designate a biblical exegesis centred on Christ and his mystery.[25]

Other doctrinal uses of the word "mystical" are encountered in the ancient Fathers to designate the teaching of the objects of faith in contrast to visible realities. All these uses might be said to be more or less coloured by the fundamental sense, as applying to the properly Christian understanding of revealed truths. Thus Eusebius of Caesarea, in his *Demonstratio Evangelica,* calls "more mystical" (*mystikotera*) the teaching that touches on the divinity of Christ, in comparison to what we know of his humanity.[26] It was in a kindred sense that Clement had previously described the divine name as the "mystical tetragram",[27] and also that Eusebius, St Cyril of Alexandria and many others later on would call the Christian Trinity the "mystical Triad" or its teaching a science "in a superior way, ineffable and mystical".[28]

From here we go on to a third sense in which mystical becomes merely a synonym for "spiritual" in contrast to "carnal". Thus Clement calls the teaching of Christ "mystical" in contrast to that of the Old Testament (and the same is true of Eusebius, Procopius

24 *V Stromata*, 6; P.G., IX, 64 A, and *Com. in Jo.*, I, 15; P.G., XIV, 49 B.
25 See, for example, Theodoret, *De Providentia*, 5; ed. Schulze, IV, p. 550.
26 Eusebius, *Demons. evang.*, 3, 7; P.G., XXII, 248 B.
27 *V Stromata*, 6; P.G., IX, 60 A.
28 Eusebius, *Contra Marcellum*, i, 1; P.G., XXIV, 716 C (cf. *De laudibus Constantini*, 6; P.G., XX, 1348 B; Cyril of Alexandria, *Fragm.*, 1; P.G., IX, 1424 A.

of Gaza, etc.)[29] And Clement also says that the kiss of peace ought always to be "mystical", that is, that it should not remain merely a formal gesture.[30]

All these texts in which "mystical" is used in the Fathers, in a biblical context, show us, then, that the word, in its Christian usage, is primarily connected with the divine reality which Christ communicates to us, which the Gospel reveals to us, which gives its whole meaning to the whole of Scripture. Hence we see how the word "mystical" came to be applied to any knowledge of the divine realities to which we have access through Christ, and then, by derivation, to these realities themselves. And, finally, the word is applied, in the same line of thought, to the spiritual reality of the "worship in spirit and in truth" as opposed to the emptiness of an external religion not vivified by the Lord's coming.

A text of St Cyril of Alexandria seems to give us a glimpse, as it were, of how the word "mystical" passed from this primary scriptural focus to a second liturgical and, particularly, Eucharistic one. In his *Commentary on Isaias*, he writes:

> We say that the sustenance of bread and water must be taken away from the synagogue. This word is mystical. It is to us, who have been called by faith to sanctification, that belongs the bread of heaven, Christ, that is, His body.[31]

The use of the term "mystical", then, came to pass from the Christian interpretation of the Scriptures to the content of the Christian sacraments. Here it designates at once the spiritual reality of the latter and the fact that this reality remains hidden. As one had to perceive "the Spirit", Christ as heralded, in the texts of the Old Testament, beyond what the Alexandrians called "history", that is the anecdote localized in time and space, so in the Christian sacraments, faith discovers something that sight does not. And this other reality, here again, is Christ: Christ actually given.

The Last Supper provides the occasion for a series of texts by the Fathers in which we see them actually going from the idea of the fulfilment of the Scriptures to that of the sacramental presence.

Thus the *Chronicon paschale* and the *Quaestiones evangelicae* of Hesychius of Jerusalem call the Supper a "mystical Passover".[32] Reciprocally, Eutychius, in his treatise on the Pasch, calls it "the first-fruit and the mystical pledge of the reality (*tou pragmatikou*)

[29] *VI Stromata*, 15; P.G., IX, 352 A. Cf. *Quis dives salvetur*, 5; *ibid.*, col. 609 C.

[30] *Paedagogus*, III, 11; P.G., VIII, 660 B.

[31] *Comm. on Isaias*, I, 1, second discourse; P.G., LXX, 96 C.

[32] *Chronicon paschale*; P.G., XCII, 548 C.—Hesychius of Jerusalem, *Quaest. evang.*, 34; P.G., XCIII, 1421 D.

of the cross.[33] The *Apostolic Constitutions*, in turn, contrast the Eucharist with bloody sacrifices as "the mystical sacrifice of his body and his blood."[34] St Nilus says that we are to approach it "not as mere bread but as mystical bread", explaining in another of his letters that we "eat the mystical body and we drink the blood" of Christ.[35] Eusebius and, later on, Theodoret, call the celebration, "liturgy" or "mystical hierurgy",[36] with the *Apostolic Constitutions* in turn speaking of the "mystical cult (*latreia*)",[37] St Gregory of Nyssa of "the mystical action" (*praxeos*),[38] and St Gregory Nazianzen calling the altar "the mystical table".[39]

The same way of speaking was extended to the other sacraments: for Eusebius, baptism is the "mystical regeneration",[40] and Gregory of Nyssa says that the baptized have been "regenerated by this mystical economy". He calls the baptismal water "mystical water",[41] and the adjective is also applied to the chrism by Eusebius, Epiphanius, Theodoret.[42]

To grasp properly the bearing of this new use of the word, we must not forget that the authors who present it continue also, a few lines or pages later, to use "mystical" as designating the ultimate meaning of the Scriptures in relation to Christ and his work. And for these same writers, every liturgical celebration is to be understood as a perpetual actualization of the "mystery of Christ" in the Paulinian sense recalled above. We might say, therefore, that, for the Fathers, the sacraments and, above all, the Eucharist, are "mystical" in that they envelop the reality of the "mystery" which the Gospel proclaims and unveils to the eyes of faith in the whole Bible.[43]

The first uses of the term which began to orient it towards designating a particular spiritual experience are visibly rooted

[33] *Treat. in Pascha*, 4; P.G., LXXXVI, 2397 A.

[34] *Const. apost.*, VI, 23, 4.

[35] *Epist.*, 3, 39 and 2, 23; P.G., LXXXIX, 405 and 320 C.

[36] Eusebius, *Vita Constantini*, IV, 71 and IV, 45; P.G., XX, 1225 A and 1196 B. —Theodoret, *Epist.* 146; ed. Schulze, IV, p. 1260, and *Hist. rel.*, XIII; Schulze, III, p. 1208.

[37] *Const. apost.*, VIII, 5, 11.

[38] *Orat. de Baptisma Christi;* P.G., XLVI, 581 A.

[39] *Orat.*, XL, 31; P.G., XXXVI, 404 A.

[40] *Contra Marcellum*, I, I; P.G., XXIV, 728 C.

[41] *Disc. cat.*, 34; P.G., XLV, 85 C; *ibid.*, 35, col. 92 C.

[42] Eusebius, *Demonst. evang.*, 1, 10; P.G., XXII, 89 D. Epiphanius, *Cont. Haer.*, XXX, 6; P.G., XLI, 413 D. Theodoret, *Comment. on Isaias*, LXI, 2; ed. Schulze, II, p. 383.

[43] It is in this sense that it is true to say that their vision of Christianity is dominated by the consideration of the "mystery" actualized through the liturgy. But the effort of Dom Casel to find in their texts his conception of a Kult-mysterium the notion of which had been derived from the mystery religions of antiquity seems to us to be the vain pursuit of a *Fata morgana.*

in these two primordial senses, themselves so directly related to one another. It is Origen who, in his Commentary on St John, shows us Jesus Christ as being "the high priest according to the order of Melchisedech, that is to say, our guide in mystical and ineffable contemplation."[44] The *theoria* he has in mind here is the profound understanding of the Scriptures, but we can see how this understanding, for him, is always more than a mere intellectual operation. This is confirmed by another use of the same adjectives, a little above in the same Commentary, when it is said that "ineffable and mystical visions (*theoremata*) rejoice and render enthusiastic".[45]

The same thing is found in a text of Gregory of Nyssa, strongly Origenist, where he speaks of the "mystical contemplation of the Canticle of Canticles".[46] Fr Daniélou asks himself whether by this expression Gregory means exegesis or mystical contemplation in the modern sense. The best answer certainly would be: both the one and the other, or the one in the other.[47]

This last text leads us directly towards the relatively numerous texts in the Dionysian *Corpus* which constitute the first decisive examples of a habitual use of the word to designate an interior experience. Two of the most characteristic of these, in fact, describing the experience and the teaching of the "divine Hierotheos", the supposed master of our author, again occur in an exegetical context.

The first, in the *Treatise on the Divine Names*, tells us, speaking of the loftiest Christian dogmas concerning the union in Christ of his divinity with his humanity:

> which we have received mystically (*mystikos pareilephamen*)... These things we have sufficiently explained elsewhere, and they have been supernaturally chanted by our renowned teacher in his *Theological Elements*, whether he received them from holy theologians, or whether he conceived them in wisely turning over the [divine] words, giving to them much effort and time, or whether he was initiated into them by some more divine inspiration, not only learning the things of God but experiencing them *me monon mathon alla kai pathon ta theia*), and through this sympathy with them, if we may say this, having been consummated in initiation into mystical union and faith in them, which cannot be taught.[48]

[44] *Comm. in Jo.*, XIII, 24; P.G., XIV, 440 C.
[45] *Comm. in Jo.*, I, 33; *ibid.*, col. 80 B.
[46] *First Hom. on the Cant.;* P.G., XLIV, 765 A.
[47] *Platonisme et Théologie mystique*, p. 192.
[48] *Nom. div.*, II, 9; P.G., III, 648 D.

In this text, we should notice exactly what distinctions "Dionysius" is making: all understanding of God, for him, comes from the Scriptures (the "holy theologians", in his writings, are the sacred writers); but this understanding is either found in the Scriptures ready to be discovered, or is disengaged by an effort of discursive reasoning, or else it is grasped by this "sympathy" with the realities the Scriptures speak of, a sympathy created in us by the very Spirit who inspired them. It is to this last mode of understanding that he applies here the expression, "mystical union and faith".

Another passage, still clearer, in the same treatise, concerning the divine Hierotheos, confirms our interpretation. For he is shown us as explaining the Scriptures, following the sacred writers themselves:

> wholly outside himself (*ekdemon*), in ecstasy (*existamenos*), and experiencing communion with what he was chanting, judged by all those who heard and saw him, whether they knew him or not, as one inspired by God and a divine hymnologue.

Taking up his theme, a few lines further on, of transmitting the teaching of the "divine Hierotheos" thus described, "Dionysius" calls this teaching: "Those mystical things, ineffable to the masses but known to you.[49]

These *mystika* are still, then, the final object of the Scriptures. And equally they remain the hidden content of the sacraments and chiefly of the eucharistic celebration. For this, as "Dionysius" explains at the heart of his *Ecclesiastical Hierarchy*, is the supreme initiation. We are told that it is called communion and synaxis,

> because it gathers together our divided lives in the one divinization (*eis enoeiden theosin*), and, by the godlike (*theoeidei*) gathering together of the separated, gives us the gift of communion and of union with the One.[50]

It is as being all this that "Dionysius" describes the eucharistic celebration, in a very characteristic association of terms, as "mystical distribution" carried out by the pontiff who himself has begun by "participating in the mysteries".[51]

If for him, then, the experience of the divine realities, *ta theia pathein*, is "mystical", we can say that it is such as being the experience of those truths of faith of which Scripture speaks, of that reality of faith which is communicated to us in the liturgical celebration of the Eucharist. What is hidden under the expressions

[49] *Nom. div.*, III, 2 and 3; *ibid.*, 681 D–684 A.
[50] *Hier. eccl.*, III, 1; *ibid.*, 424 C.
[51] *Hier. eccl.*, III, 111, 14; *ibid.*, 445 A.

of the one and under the sacramental symbols of the other is what is experienced in "mystical theology".

And here is how the latter is defined, at the beginning of the treatise that "Dionysius" devotes to it and names after it, in a prayer to the Trinity which is as it were its preface, almost in the liturgical sense of the term:

> O Trinity superessential, superdivine, supergood: ephoros of the theosophy of the Cherubim, lead us to that supreme height of mystical words that transcends understanding and manifestation, there where the simple, absolute, unchangeable mysteries of theology are unveiled in the superluminous cloud of silence that initiates into hidden things, super-resplendent in the deepest depths of darkness in a manner beyond any manifestation, which, wholly intangible and invisible, fills to overflowing with super-beautiful splendours our blinded spirits (*noas*). Such is my prayer, and you, my friend Timothy, applying yourself with all your strength to mystical contemplations (*peri na mystika theamata*), abandon the senses and the intellectual energies and everything that is sensible or intelligible, everything that is not and that is, and raise yourself in unknowing (*agnostos*) toward union, so far as this is permitted, towards what surpasses all essence and gnosis: indeed, it is purely by a free and absolute ecstasy out of yourself that you will be carried towards the superessential ray of the divine darkness.[52]

How are we to understand this identification of "mystical contemplations" with "unknowing", with the image of entering into the cloud, or into darkness?

Here again, "Dionysius" seems as it were the final product of the whole of Patristics. Already to be found in Philo, taken up by Clement and Origen, this theme of the cloud and the darkness in which contemplation, in the highest sense of the word, comes about, with Dionysius gives the impression of having been taken directly from Gregory of Nyssa and his *Life of Moses*. The third paragraph of the first chapter of his *Mystical Theology* seems to be an echo of Gregory's treatise and, as it were, a synthesis of it—which does not mean to say that "Dionysius'" interpretation of the events, which he classifies as did his predecessor, is not original—quite the contrary:

> The good principle of everything is at once abundant in words and concise, nay even mute (*alogos*), as if it had neither word nor thought, by the fact that it surpasses them all superessentially and that it manifests itself unveiled and truly only to those who have gone beyond everything that is evil and even everything

[52] *Theol. myst.*, I, 1; P.G., III, 997 A–1000 A.

that is pure, and who have surpassed all ascents and all the holy heights, leaving behind all the divine lights, the sounds and heavenly words, in order to enter into the cloud in which is in truth, as the [divine] words tell us, He who is above all things.

Indeed, the divine Moses was not only first called to purify himself, and then to separate himself from those who were not purified and, after all purification, to hear the blaring trumpets, to see the many lights shining with pure and multiple rays. But after all this, he was again separated from the multitude and, with the chosen priests, he came to the height of the divine ascents. But with all this he did not come close to God and he did not see Him, for He is invisible, but rather the place where He is.

I believe that this signifies that the divinest and highest of visions and thoughts are reasonings that subject [to our thought] what is subjected to Him who surpasses everything. Hereby is declared the presence of Him who surpasses all thought, advancing on the intelligible heights of the most holy places. Then [Moses] was detached from all things visible and from all seeings, and he entered into the cloud of truly mystical unknowing, in which he closed his eyes to all gnostic apprehensions and attained to what is beyond all, and in the cessation of all gnosis of anything whatever, of himself or of another, united in a superior way to Him who is unknowable, knowing beyond intelligence by the fact of knowing nothing.[53]

The interpretation of the cloud and the darkness provided by this text recalls Evagrius rather than Gregory of Nyssa; not the always unachieved pursuit of the inaccessible beyond everything that belongs to this world, but the encounter with the unknowable beyond all knowing according to our mode of understanding.

We might ask ourselves, however, if this text does not deliberately correct Evagrius on a whole series of definite points. Gnosis is no longer applied to God, but only to "beings" in the plural (and, "Dionysius" adds, to non-beings), which makes the object of the gnosis of a lower degree with Evagrius. God himself is attained only in "agnosia". Furthermore, the "place of God" reappears. However, it is no longer the object of the supreme vision, but only the prelude to it. At the same time, discreetly but very clearly, the Evagrian identification is denied between the soul's own vision of itself and its vision of God within it.

By contrast, the feature most strictly common to Evagrius and to "Dionysius", which they both owe to Gregory, is the statement that we know by the act of not knowing. But, far more with "Dionysius" than with his predecessors, this is not to be understood

[53] *Theol. myst.*, I, 3; *ibid.*, 100 C–10001 A.

as if the cessation of all distinct knowledge were in itself the divine knowing. As the context indicates, this abolition of all limited knowing is only an essential prelude or concomitant to the manifestation of him who is beyond everything created. With "Dionysius", the obscurity of mystical knowledge is to be understood only in relation to all knowledge drawn from this world, and perhaps (though this is less certain) in relation also to the disproportion always existing between him who thus comes to be known in mystical knowledge and those who are called so high. But the final reality is wholly luminous. What appears to us at first as darkness, starting from the kinds of knowledge to which we are accustomed, is in reality the inaccessible light in which God dwells. This is expressly stated in "Dionysius' " fifth letter:

> The divine cloud is that inaccessible light in which it is said that God dwells. Being invisible by the excess of its splendour, and inaccessible by the hyperbole of the superessential expansion of its light, whoever has been judged worthy to see God attains to this by the very fact of not seeing or knowing, having arrived truly in Him who is above all vision and gnosis, in knowing that He is above everything that is sensible or intelligible.[54]

All this is led up to and elucidated in advance by the treatise *On the Divine Names*. Examining one after the other the various concepts and images that Scripture applies to God, "Dionysius" explains that the knowledge they give us of him is never more than analogical. More precisely, cataphatic theology, which retains from these expressions everything about them that is positive and applies it to God in a supereminent way, must be always joined with apophatic theology, which denies all particular expression of his perfections, however lofty this may be, as being radically inadequate.[55]

Between these two ways, there is no room for choice, for even though apophatic theology approaches nearer to God in affirming his mystery, it would become simply empty of all substance if it were not constantly linked with cataphatic theology.[56] Yet its very vacuity prepares us for mystical theology in which God reveals himself to us, no longer by analogies that are necessarily inadequate and no longer by the simple supereminent negation of

[54] *Epist.* 5; P.G., III, 1073 A.

[55] See *Nom. div.*, I, 1 and 5; P.G., III, 585 B–588 B and 593 A–596 A, and, above all, *Theol. myst.*, III; *ibid.*, 1032 C ff.

[56] On the relationship between these two theologies, see R. Roques, pp. xxviff., of his Introduction to the edition of the *Hier. celest.*, in "Sources Chrétiennes", vol. 58, Paris, 1958. Also see Walther Völker, *Kontemplation und Ekstase*, pp. 185ff.

these analogies, but beyond negation as well as affirmation; in his presence and his direct communication of all that he is.[57]

It is here, as V. Lossky has strongly brought out, that the unbridgeable abyss is revealed separating the position of "Dionysius" from that of Plotinus and all Neo-Platonic spirituality. For Plotinus, God is beyond all particular affirmations because he is the One. For "Dionysius", he is equally beyond the One itself. The soul does not find him simply in itself, by stripping itself of all multiplicity, in unifying itself, by the rejection of all distinct thoughts. It finds him by going beyond itself as well as beyond all particular knowledge: not in simply becoming unified in itself, but in being united to him who transcends it, because he himself calls it to join him in the luminous darkness where he is and awaits it.[58]

It is on this summit of the religious thought of "Dionysius" that we understand to how great an extent, in spite of all analogies of vocabulary, he transcends Neo-Platonism in a wholly Christian way, in his idea of "conversion" as in that of "emanation".

For, at the starting-point, it was shown us that, in the Dionysian universe, God alone remains the Creator, immediately creating each being. Hence the universe is in no way a succession of waves proceeding from one another in a progressive degradation of the same being; it is a harmony of distinct beings designed to exchange between themselves as with God that creative *agape* which is to reascend as *eros* towards its source, without ceasing for all that to be pure generosity, pure communication.

And, at the final goal, it is revealed that—far from fixing the hierarchy of beings at their respective distances from the principle, or allowing them to be united with it only in an ecstasy that would annihilate their very distinction—this order constitutes for these beings the starting point of a unanimous ascent in which each being, with all and for all, immediately encounters, for its definitive flowering, him who equally transcends them all.

As Endre von Ivanka writes:

> The gradual succession of the communication of the divine, conceived by Neo-Platonism in such a way that the divine comes to be degraded and diminished from one degree to another, has become with Dionysius a multiplicity of forms of immediate participation in the divine, a participation that remains whole

[57] See the prayer mentioned above, p. 412. On the passive character of the very highest spiritual experience according to Dionysius, and how it is to be understood in the line of Gregory of Nyssa and Gregory Nazianzen, see Völker, *op. cit.*, pp. 206ff.

[58] Vl. Lossky, *Essai sur la théologie mystique de l'Église d'Orient*, pp. 28ff.

and perfect for each degree, although according to the nature of each one.[59]

However, in order fully to discover the basically Christian character of Dionysian mysticism as well as of its cosmology, we must go from the level of knowledge to that of ontology. For, in fact, assimilation to God is for him inseparably knowledge and communion. The divine *agape*, in reascending to God as *eros*, unites us with him and divinizes us. Here again, with "Dionysius" we find ourselves at the term of the development in Patristics of a theme currently presented as a typical borrowing from Hellenism. But a rigorous study of the lines of its development brings out the fact that, in the final analysis, this theme also is much more biblical and Christian than Hellenistic.

Union and Divinization

With "Dionysius", the theme of divinization is introduced in a hendyadis with that of union.

While union, or rather unification (*henosis*) is a specifically Plotinian theme, it must be emphasized that this theme, with Plotinus, covers a reality wholly immanent to the religious subject. In unifying itself, in withdrawing itself from all multiplicity, the soul becomes—or rather once more finds itself—divine. The Plotinian *henosis* then, has no objective complement. As taken up by "Dionysius", on the contrary, it always has one. For him, the question is not that of simply unifying oneself and thus regaining oneself in one's own being or, better, in the true being. It is that of going out of oneself, in order to be united to another, *as* other, to the supremely Other: it is the *henosis pros ton theon.*[60]

In other words, the Dionysian *henosis* presupposes faith (which, furthermore, is always expressly connected with it in his texts): belief in the transcendent God freely revealed, whose love rejoins us in order to draw us to him.

Henosis ends in *theosis*, the divinization which assimilates us to God not only on the plane of knowing but on that of being. This last theme is simply the final product of the biblical theme of the knowledge that unites and makes like. Platonism spoke of knowing God by the fact that one becomes or re-becomes like to him. The Bible, the teaching of the prophets, is on the contrary at the origin of the exactly contrary theme: that of the knowledge that makes

[59] Endre von Ivanka, "La signification du Corpus Areopagiticum", in *Recherches de Science religieuse*, Paris, XXXVI (1949), p. 18.

[60] See *Hier. celest.*, III, 2; P.G., III, 165 A.—*Hier. eccl.*, I, 3 and II, 1; *ibid.*, 376 A and 392 A.

us like to what we know. If this theme, amalgamated more or less successfully with the preceding one, made fleeting appearances in later Hellenism and particularly in Hermetism, this is only one more sign of the diffusion of a whole series of Jewish ideas in this environment. It was in order to translate into Greek terms this union, this assimilation to God, resulting from the wholly gratuitous revelation that he has made to us of himself, that the Greek Fathers used the terminology of divinization: *theosis* and *theoun*, or of deification: *theopoiesis* and *theopoiein*. But in the Greek authors whom we know to be free of any biblical or Christian influence there is no trace of any use of these expressions in such a sense.

In profane Greek speech, the rare appearances of these words designate either the making of idols or, much less frequently, the attributing by men of a divine character to certain beings (for this last meaning, it is rather *apotheosis* that is the technical term). Nowhere do we find the idea of a substantial transformation by which man would arrive at a participation in the divine essence. Apotheosis itself does not seem to have implied any ontological transformation, but merely the officially recognized accession of certain men to the rank of gods.

Clement is the first Christian author to use *theopoiein*. He does so precisely in the context of the biblical thought we have just recalled, saying that Christ "deifies man by a heavenly doctrine: *ouranio didaskalia theopoieon anthropon*."[61]

In his commentary on St John, Origen speaks in exactly the same way. Commenting on the Johannine texts on "knowing God" that we studied at length, he says that "the *nous* is deified in that which it contemplates": *en hois theorei thepoieitai*.[62]

The use of this vocabulary is, moreover, not specifically Alexandrian. We find it again in an author as distrustful of profane philosophies as Hippolytus of Rome and again in a context which testifies to the way in which the theme was born from that of our adoption, real and not fictive, in Christ.

> You who, living on this earth, have known the heavenly King, you will be the familiar friend of God and co-heir with Christ, being no more subject to the desires of the passions nor to maladies. For you have become God (*gegonas gar theoi*). All the trials you have endured, being man, God has sent to you because you are man; in return, all the goods that are natural to God, God has promised to give you when, engendered to immortality, you will be deified (*hotan theopoiethes athanatos*

[61] *Protrep.*, XI; P.G., VIII, 233 A.
[62] *Comm. in Jo.* XXXII, 17; P.G., XIV, 817 C.

gennetheis). By obeying His holy precepts, by rendering yourself good by the imitation of His goodness, you will be like Him, honoured by Him. For God is not poor, He who has made you God also in view of His glory.[63]

But the man whom we might call the doctor of our deification incontestably is St Athanasius. It is most interesting that he was the theologian who effected the master-stroke necessary to bring Christology, too permeated with Greek teachings on the Logos, back to complete fidelity to the biblical idea of God.[64] We can see also in his work how, on the other hand, this theme proceeds from Paulinian and Johannine ideas concerning our filiation in the Son and its full reality. And we can see here also the extent to which this theme was commonly admitted in traditional Christian teaching.

For it is the very heart of Athanasius' main argument against the Arians that Jesus, before deifying us by grace, must be God by nature. His *De Incarnatione*, even before the Arian crisis, contains the celebrated formula:

The Logos was made man so that we might be made God.[65]

This idea returns as a leitmotif in all his work for the defence of the faith of Nicea. Here is one text among many others:

> United to a creature, man would not have been once again deified, if the Son were not true God. Man would not have approached the Father, if He who took on the body had not been the natural and veritable Logos. And, just as we would not have been delivered from sin and from malediction if the flesh taken on by the Logos had not been a human flesh by nature—for we have nothing in common with a being that is foreign to us—in the same way, man would not have been deified if He who became flesh were not the issue of the Father by nature and His proper and veritable Logos. This is why the contact was made in this way, so that to the divine nature would be united human nature and so that the salvation and deification of the latter would be assured.[66]

A little later in the Macedonian controversy, the same line of reasoning is applied to the Holy Spirit. The *First Epistle to Serapion* says:

> For it is by the Spirit that we are all said to participate in God. . . . Now if, by the participation of the Spirit, we become participants in the divine nature, it would be foolish to say that the

[63] *Philosophoumena*, x, 34.

[64] See our work, *L'incarnation et l'Église-Corps du Christ dans la théologie de saint Athanase*, Paris, pp. 48ff.

[65] *De Incarnatione*, 54; P.G., XXV, 192 B.

[66] *I Contra Arianos*, 70; P.G., XXVI, 296 AB.

Spirit is of a created nature and not of the divine nature. This is also why those in whom He dwells are deified. Now, if He deifies, there is no doubt that His nature is that of God.[67]

The rest of the text expressly brings out how, for Athanasius, deification simply expresses the whole reality of our adoption in Christ according to the New Testament:

> It is in the Spirit, consequently, that the Logos glorifies creation and by deifying it and adopting it (*theopoion kai huiopoion*), leads it to the Father.[68]

This teaching was taken up literally by the Cappadocians. In his *Against Eunomius*, St Basil calls the Holy Spirit, "He who deifies others" and man "he who is deified by grace".[69]

It was St Gregory Nazianzen, on the other hand, who seems to have been the first to use *theoun* in the sense already traditional for *theopoiein.*

> If the Spirit, he says, is not to be adored, how does He divinize me by Baptism?[70]

Although he uses the substantive, *theosis*, he does not give it precisely the sense traditional for *theopoiesis*. Opposing the Arians in his discourse in praise of Heron the philosopher, he says that the divinity does not come from a mutation, nor *theosis* from a progress, wishing thereby simply to state the eternity of the divine paternity in God and of the divine filiation.[71]

It fell to Dionysius, therefore, to make *theosis* the technical term for our assimilation to God. He defines it in these terms:

> *Theosis* is assimilation to and union with God to the extent this is permitted. It is the common end of all hierarchy that a continual love (*prosekes agapesis*) of God and of divine things, carried out in a holy way in God and in unity, and, previously, the total and irreversible flight from what opposes it, the gnosis of what is as being, the vision and the science (*episteme*) of the holy truth, participation in God (*entheos*) in uniform perfection and in the One Himself so far as this is permitted, the satisfying intuition that nourishes intellectually whomever tends towards it.[72]

As a counterpart of this whole tradition, we can cite the only text which is not Christian, but certainly influenced by the religiosity of Alexandrian Judaism (and perhaps of primitive

[67] *Ist Ep. to Serapion*, 24; P.G., XXXVI, 588 A.
[68] *Ibid.*, 25; 589 B.
[69] *Cont. Eun.*, III, 5; P.G., XXIX, 665 BC.
[70] *Orat.*, XXXI (Fifth Theol.), 28; P.G., XXXVI, 165 A.
[71] *In laudem Heronis*, 16; P.G., XXXV, 1221 B.
[72] *Hier. eccl.*, I, 4; P.G., III, 376 A.

Christianity) in which *theoun* is taken in a kindred sense. This is the beautiful phrase of the *Poimandres*:

> For those who possess gnosis, the blessed goal is to be divinized (*theothenai*).[73]

As for Plato, he knew nothing but a "resemblance" to God, regained by the flight out of the sensible world and towards the intelligible.[74]

For Plotinus, since the soul is divine by nature, its ideal must be not only to escape from sin, but to regain this divine being (*theon einai*).[75] Thus, however, rather than becoming God, it gains (or regains) consciousness of being God: *theon genomenon, mallon de onta*.[76] This phrase, which might be considered the final word of the *Enneades*, shows us how completely foreign to them is any mysticism of divinization. As there is no place for mysticism and its darkness where there is nothing beyond that being which is ours and that of the world, so there is no place for a divinization where there is neither creature nor creator, but only the error to be surmounted of a partial being. To regain the one being, which is at the same time the universal being, it is enough, Plotinus believes, to renounce one's individuality.

This makes the difference between the ecstasy of Dionysius and that of Plotinus. While the one is a going out of oneself, a transport beyond oneself and the world, the other is the extinction of self which thinks to rejoin or, more exactly, to regain the divine existence by simply being absorbed in the world as indifferentiated unity.

Conclusions

In the final form it takes with "Dionysius" at the end of the whole effort of Greek patristics, this mysticism of divinization calls for two observations.

At first sight, it is equally surprising to see *apatheia*, the importance of which from Clement to Evagrius, was always being

[73] *Corpus hermeticum*, First Treatise, 26 (ed. Nock-Festugière), p. 16, 12). The context, in which God is called Father and in which there is question of the Powers, betrays a Philonian influence. In § 6 of the Tenth Treatise, we find a text which seems at first sight to give an analogous sense; *adunatos gar, o teknon, psuchen apotheothenai en somati anthropou theasamene to tou agathou kallos*. But the context does not seem to allow us to understand that the soul would be changed by contemplation in its profound nature, but merely that the soul, divine by essence, having become conscious of being divine, is promised, after death, "apotheosis" (ed. Nock-Festugière, pp. 116ff.; see note 27, p. 125).

[74] *Theetetus*, 176 B. Cf. *Republic*, X, 613.

[75] *Enneades*, IV, viii, 5, 24–7. Cf. Enneades, I, ii, 6, 2–3.

[76] *Enneades*, VI, ix, 59 (we are quoting the lines according to the ed. of Bréhier).

explained and affirmed, here disappearing, or almost so; while *gnosis*, if it has not disappeared, is at least considerably less emphasized.

In the Dionysian *Corpus*, the rare mentions of *apatheia*, when the term is not applied to the Angels, are generally found in a hendyadis with liberty. This is quite in conformity with the sense in which the term came to be adopted by Christian asceticism. As to this extreme discretion in its use, it is doubtless to be explained by the proximity of the Origenist controversy. The "purification" which, with "Dionysius", corresponds to the *praktike* of Evagrius, may be considered as an equivalent of the effort towards *apatheia* in the previous writers. However, the fact that he felt no necessity to assign a definite term to this effort brings out, perhaps, the extent to which, with him, mysticism, now standing out in full relief, absorbs all perspectives in itself. No repose now seems to be envisaged in the ascent towards God but that goal beyond any goal immanent to the religious subject.

It may be the same reason which in part explains the relative de-emphasis on gnosis. It appears as completely extrapolated in its summit which, paradoxically, is revealed as "agnosia", although this "agnosia" still corresponds quite closely to the "gnosis of the Trinity" in Evagrius. But to this we must add the use that "Dionysius" habitually makes of the term *episteme*, classic in Greek philosophy, almost as an equivalent to the specifically biblical and Christian term, *gnosis*. For him, in fact, *episteme* always has a directly religious meaning. It must even be said that *episteme*, as he conceives it, belongs primarily to God, and it is only on the heights of *theoria* that man truly participates in it. It belongs to the perfect.[77]

In spite of this, by the fact that he always considers it as being communicable in the hierarchic processions, "Dionysius" at least prepared the way for an opposition between this "science" and his purely ineffable "mystical theology". We might, therefore, ask ourselves whether the profound unity of the traditional gnosis, already split in two by Evagrius' distinction between "physical gnosis" and "gnosis of God", did not arrive with the Areopagitic writings at the verge of a break-up. This will be manifested in later developments. The opposition is now completely set up between a theology, henceforth conceived as a "science", human in all its procedures even though its sources and its formal objects are divine, and mysticism, wholly ineffable even though it proceeds from the faith which is systematized by theology.

[77] Roques, *op. cit.*, pp. 120ff.

XVII

DEVELOPMENTS AND COUNTER-CURRENTS

THE spiritual tradition which, in the fourth century, found its expression in the monastic movement and then was defined following the great Cappadocians, in a recourse to the religious thought of Origen, attained its last creative developments in the work of Pseudo-Macarius, Evagrius and Pseudo-Dionysius. Spiritual writers were very numerous in the East during the fifth and sixth centuries, and certain of them were masters whose influence was considerable throughout the whole later history of spirituality. But, in its great lines, a creative development seems now to have been completed. The results would be exploited, but no further progress made for the moment. It is only with St Maximus that a new departure was sketched out: that of the Byzantine spirituality of which he was the precursor and initiator of genius, while also being the last great writer representing the patristic era in the East.

Without neglecting a whole constellation of very interesting authors, we shall now go on to study them much more rapidly than we did their predecessors. The question is no longer that of seeing how the consciousness of the great elements of Christian spirituality was formed step by step, but only of going through the expositions of this consciousness which, although fed by both tradition and experience, do not contribute anything very new.

In this regard, and even though the authors whom we are now going to consider briefly witness to the decisive success both of the monastic movement and of its interpretation in the light of the Alexandrine theological tradition, we ought to complete our study of patristic spirituality by examining the various resistances encountered by this central line of tradition. These resistances often went so far as heresy, but none the less they constitute a very important witness to the complexity and wealth of the Catholic tradition which can never be limited to one single line of development.

Monastic Collections and Histories

The chief spiritual works left to us by the fifth century, in the line of the monastic spirituality the developments of which we have been tracing, are the collections of the sayings or great deeds of holy personages. The most valuable, equally from the historical and the spiritual point of view, are the *Apophthegms* of the Fathers, the value of which for any study of primitive monastic spirituality we have already brought out.

As we have them now, they are grouped in two different ways: either alphabetically (the series from Antony to Or, the Greek text of which Cotelier edited for the first time in the seventeenth century) or by topics, a series of which we have various forms in Latin traditions and which Rosweyde published in the last century. Wilhelm Bousset, who has compared the history of these "sayings" with that of the Gospel "logia", has studied their transmission and ordering in a very illuminating way, bringing out the substantial fidelity of these collections to the primitive form of the sentences thus preserved and collated.[1]

The various monastic "Histories", propagated at about the same time, adding to the words of the monastic Fathers a detailed account of their actions and, above all, of their ascetic practices, give evidence of a much greater degree of editorial intervention, in their glorification of one or another ideal ascetic.

The old *Historia monachorum*, according to Butler[2] translated (or rather adapted) into Latin by Rufinus of Aquileus from a Greek original, the author of which must have been a certain Timotheus, seems to be the most untouched by attempts at ordering, the most naïve. This does not in the least mean to say that it is "historical" in the strict sense we give to this word: marvellous things abound and so do various far too imaginative embellishments, such as the twenty thousand virgins and twelve thousand monks who are said to have peopled Oxyrrhincus at the end of the fourth century! But the account of the journey of seven monks of Jerusalem from Lycopolis to Diolkos, that is across all Egypt from the north to the south, between September 394 and January 395, swarms with concrete details that are entirely likely and too completely in agreement with our other sources to be dismissed as pious romances.

[1] The bibliographical references for the *Apophthegms* have already been provided above, p. 307.

[2] See the Introduction of Dom Cuthbert Butler to his edition of the *Historia lausiaca: The Lausiac History of Palladius*, 2 vols., Cambridge, 1891–1904. Some none the less maintain the originality of the Latin text. On the present state of the controversy, see A. J. Festugière, "Le problème littéraire de 'l'Historia monachorum'", in *Hermes*, Wiesbaden, 1955, pp. 257–85.

The *Historia Lausiaca*, by the Galatian bishop Palladius, the ardent partisan and historian of St John Chrysostom, was named after Lausus, the chamberlain of Theodosius II to whom it is dedicated, and has often been included among the manuscripts of the saint. Its author had passed some twelve years being initiated into Egyptian monasticism near Alexandria or at Nitria, when his health obliged him to give it up. Describing his stay, and other journeys to Jerusalem, in Syria, to Rome, etc., he continually mingles the accounts told to him with his own personal recollections. Clearly he was a disciple of Evagrius', and it was the pattern of the spirituality of the great teacher of Scete which he adopted, adapting words and deeds to it. But thereby he shows us all the better how the posterity of Evagrius had realized his ideal. Not hiding the weaknesses and the falls of his heroes, Palladius was dominated, even more than by admiration for a very rigorous asceticism, by an ideal of constant prayer directed towards "pure prayer".[3]

A little later, the *Religious History* of Theodoret of Cyrrhus describes the asceticism of the monks of Syria, with still more details, and an increased delight in the extraordinary penances which, as we have seen, very soon began to characterize these monks. But here also, it is prayer that appears as the supreme goal of the monk. But, rather than on prayer of the mystical kind dear to Evagrius, Theodoret, as was natural with an Antiochene, concentrates on a constant meditation of the Scriptures and an intense practice of Psalmody.[4]

At the end of the seventh century, John Moschus, a novice at the convent of St Theodosius, then a monk at Pharan, and later at Sinai, gives us one of the last collections of this type. His *Pratum spirituale* is the fruit of journeys to the places visited by Palladius a good century earlier. The taste for the miraculous, as we see in this work, still flourished there. But the traditions of the profound spiritual good sense of the first Fathers of the desert remained alive in spite of everything.[5]

[3] See the preceding note concerning Butler's edition. R. Draguet is preparing a new critical edition and a French translation (cf. his article "Un texte G de l'Histoire lausiaque dans le Lavra 333 F 93", in *Mélanges Lebreton*, II, Paris, 1954, pp. 107–15).

[4] For this work of Theodoret's we have only the Migne edition, P.G., XXXII, 1283–1496. See C. Cuthberlet, *Theodoret Monchgeschichte*, Munich, 1936, and M. Richard, "Théodoret, Jean d'Antioche et les moines d'Orient", in *Mélanges de Science religieuse*, Lille, 1946, pp. 147–56.

[5] The *Pratum spirituale* is found in Migne, P.G., XXXVI, 2581–3116. There is no modern critical edition. The translation and introduction by Fr. Rouët de Journel, in the collection "Sources chrétiennes", no. 12, met with a reserved welcome on the part of the Bollandists (see *Analecta Bollandiana*, 1947, pp. 286–8).

Letters and Conferences

A valuable complement to these accounts is to be found in the correspondence of a certain number of the great monks of the fifth and sixth centuries.

That of Isidore of Pelusium should first be mentioned, a cenobite in the Nile Delta, but more Antiochene than Alexandrian in inspiration, who died in 440. He appears as a forceful critic of all his contemporaries and correspondents, beginning with his bishop, St Cyril. His teaching, vigorous and sane, is not very original and remains on a rather elementary level. Its interest, perhaps, consists rather in the not very flattering picture he gives us of an ecclesiastical and monastic environment in which the almost universal conversion to Christianity and the widespread vogue for monasticism do not seem to have raised the general level to any great extent.[6]

Isaias of Scete, who died in revolt against Chalcedon in 488, presents in his discourses, obviously addressed to novices, a teaching akin to that of Isidore, in which the struggle against self-will holds the central place.[7]

St Nilus, superior of a monastery at Ancyra in Galatia at about the same period, has had an abundance of works attributed to him, including a spiritual treatise which is simply a plagiarized version of the *Manual* of the Stoic Epictetus and the *Treatise on Prayer* which everyone now agrees in restoring to Evagrius. St Nilus left a copious correspondence, quite analogous to that of Isidore, but still more extensive both as to the variety of correspondents and the number of letters. *Apatheia* is presented here as the goal of asceticism. There is great insistence on the imitation of Jesus, and the monastic ideal presented is clearly Basilian. The same thing is true of his *Ascetic Discourse*, which takes up the theme of the monastic life as the true philosophy. His treatise *On Voluntary Poverty* is interesting in that it indicates an already existing decadence of the institution of monasticism and does not hesitate to attribute this decadence to the too great possessions of the monasteries. He extols a moderate poverty, however, but still the laborious poverty of monks who gain by work from day to day the minimum needed to give themselves peacefully to meditation and prayer.

Mark the Hermit, superior of another monastery near Ancyra

[6] The correspondence of Isidore of Pelusium is given in Migne, P.G., LXXVIII, 177–1646.

[7] Migne only gives a Latin translation from Renaissance times of the twenty-nine *Discourses* of Isaias. The Greek text was published for the first time in Jerusalem in 1911, by a Greek monk, Fr Augustine.

who later withdrew into solitude, has for his part left us various spiritual *opuscula* in which a more personal thought comes to light, opposing to forgetfulness of God, the source of all sin, the thanksgiving for all things which should lead us back to him.[8]

The same tradition of cenobitic spirituality is developed and renewed by a first mystical renaissance in the first half of the sixth century in Palestine in the letters of the Barsanuphius (recluse of the monastery of Seridos) and of his disciple, John, as well as in the conferences of their correspondent Dorotheus, whom they directly influenced.[9]

At the period of the Persian invasions, we see a new genre appearing which was to have a great success in the Byzantine spirituality of the Middle Ages: that of spiritual *florilegia*. The monk Antiochus (of St Sabbas) collected the first, under the name of Pandectes, for the use of the dispersed monks, and addressed it to the superior of Attalina (near Ancyra in Galatia) where he must have begun his own monastic life.[10]

The tradition of these two centuries was finally crystallized in the Ladder of John the Scholastic, Superior of Sinai, who died in the middle of the seventh century. His treatise earned him the name of John Climacus, and it remains for Byzantine monasticism a compendium as it were of the old monastic teaching.[11] By thirty successive steps—as many, he tells us, as the years of our Lord's life before his baptism—he means to lead the monk from the novitiate to perfection, which, for him, is the same thing as perfect charity. Whether explicitly or not, almost all the monastic authors we have studied are cited here, even including the Latin Gregory the Great and not forgetting Cassian. The theme of the imitation of Christ is set up as the principle of everything else. In his analysis of the vices and the virtues, above all in his idea of the relationship between

[8] The correspondence of St Nilus is to be found in Migne, P.G., LXXIX, 81–282. On his real biography and the works that have been attributed to him, see Viller-Rahner, *Aszese und mystik in der Vaterzeit*, Innsbruck (1939), pp. 166–74. The works of Mark the Hermit also are in Migne, LXV, 903ff. These are intermingled with elements that are at least dubious, such as the *Capitula de Temperentia*.

[9] The correspondence of Barsanuphius and John has not as yet been edited except by St Nicodemus the Hagiorite, the renewer of Athonite spirituality (the edition that he prepared did not appear until seven years after his death, that is, in 1816). See the article "Barsanuphe" by I. Hausherr in *Dict. de Spiritualité chrétienne*. The Conferences of Dorotheus are given in P.G., LXXXVIII 1611–1838 (new edition in "Sources chrétiennes", n. 92, Paris, 1963, by L. Regnault and J. de Préville.

[10] The text of the *Pandectes* is to be found in P.G., LXXXIX, 1431–1850.

[11] Published by Migne, P.G., LXXXVIII, 691–1210, the text of the *Scala* (the title *Scala Paradisi* is found only in the Latin versions) has recently been given two Italian editions: P. Trevisan, *S. Giovanni Climaco Scala Paradisi*, 2 vols., Turin, 1946, and B. Ignesti, *La scala dei Paradiso*, 2 vols., Siena, 1953.

apatheia and charity, he is a particularly faithful echo of Evagrius. He insists greatly on prayer, which he defines in a way very close to Evagrius' as conversation and union with God, and divides, like the whole progress in the spiritual life, into three stages, corresponding somewhat to Evagrius' distinctions. All the same, he dilates much more on the conditions facilitating prayer than on its forms or its content.

The Syrian School: Isaac of Niniveh

The rebirth of a Syriac literature, soon a separatist one with regard to the Byzantine world and for that reason drawn either into Monophysitism or Nestorianism, produced at about this time a curious combination of products of the Greek tradition with a return to Semitic sources. This literature has certainly not yet gained the attention it deserves. Spirituality has a great rôle in it, but it is not always in this field that its originality is most perceptible. One writer, however, has made a very special place for himself. This is Isaac of Niniveh, whom the Byzantine world honours under the name of St Isaac the Syrian, without realizing that he lived as a Nestorian—a schism which in these regions was actually much more of a political than a doctrinal affair. His work was translated into all the languages of the Mediterranean basin. The vitality and warmth of his eloquence, very close to the Bible, retranslates the most traditional themes of monastic asceticism with a simplicity, a living humanity, that explains his extraordinary success.[12]

Throughout all the texts we have just mentioned, Syrian as well as Greek and even in the great book of John Climacus, although they are so rich in teaching because so largely formed by the whole monastic tradition, it is undeniable that we perceive as it were a progressive ebbing away of the mystical element, beginning at the end of the fourth century. This element, so evident although so slightly systematized in primitive monasticism, then brought out and methodically organized in what we have called erudite monasticism, later seems to recede in favour of a predominance of merely ascetic considerations.

Messalianism

Without doubt, one of the principal factors in this retreat of mysticism must be recognized as being the Euchite (or Messalian) heresy which deeply agitated and disturbed monasticism at this

[12] See the bibliographical references concerning Isaac of Niniveh in I. Ortiz de Urbina, *Patrologia syriaca*, Rome, 1958, pp. 135–6. An abundant collection of extracts translated into Latin can be found in Migne, P.G., LXXXVI, 811–88.

period (it is enough to read St Nilus to be aware of this fact). Under the one or the other name, Greek or Syriac, this heresy was named after the error of those who came to give so great a place to prayer that they devaluated work and even asceticism. We should realize that, while accusations or suspicions of Messalianism spring up everywhere in the fifth century, we find ourselves rather at a loss to define their errors. And so it is not astonishing that the hypothesis of Dom Villecourt, received favourably by Dom Wilmart,[13] was echoed so widely as for some time to seem definitive. The Homilies of Pseudo-Macarius were, according to these writers, we might recall, the manual of this sect. And, as has already been described, the discoveries of Dörries of the authentic text of the *Great Letter,* and of the *De Instituto* of Gregory of Nyssa by Jaeger's collaborators, have completely ruined this hypothesis.[14]

The most immediate result of admitting it had been formerly to render suspect of Messalianism almost all the spiritual writers of the Byzantine East, all manifesting to a greater or lesser extent the influence of the Homilies. This meant exaggerating things so much that most specialists of that period, such as Stiglmayr, even before the recent discoveries, could not accept the hypothesis of Dom Villecourt without many reservations.[15]

Was it really possible to find in these Homilies the errors stigmatized by St Epiphanius or Theodoret? It seemed the more difficult in that the spiritual work of Diadochus of Photike, certainly written with the struggle against Messalianism in mind, takes up for its part the majority of the themes stigmatized by Villecourt in Pseudo-Macarius, and even certain of the formulations judged the most characteristic of his terminology: the mysticism of light, insistence on spiritual experience (described by the words *en pase aisthesei kai plerophoria*), and even the coexistence in the soul of the influence of the demon and that of the Holy Spirit.

[13] Louis Villecourt, O.S.B., "La grande lettre grecque de Macaire, ses formes textuelles et son milieu littéraire", in *Revue de l'Orient chrétien*, Paris, XXII (1920), pp. 29–56, and "La date et l'origine des 'Homélies spirituelles' attribuées à Macaire", in *Comptes rendus des séances de l'Académie des Inscriptions et Belles-Lettres*, 1920, pp. 29–53. Cf. A. Wilmart, "L'origine veritable des homélies pneumatiques", in *Revue d'Ascétique et de Mystique*, Toulouse, I (1920), pp. 361–77.

[14] Cf. above, p. 352. Jaeger also makes the observation that Messalianism was condemned at the synod of Side, in 390, after having been vigorously attacked by Amphilocus of Iconium (friend of Gregory of Nyssa) at the Council of Antioch in 380. At this period, he proves, Gregory had certainly not yet written his *De Instituto christiano*. The Macarian writings, which have been made out to be the source of Messalianism, depending on the treatise of Gregory, could not, therefore, have been written until long after the condemnation of this heresy (*op. cit.*, p. 226).

[15] See J. Stiglmayr, "Pseudomakarius und die Aftermystik des Messalianer", in *Zeitschrift für Katholische Theologie*, XLIX, pp. 244–60.

It is true that there were found among our modern experts on heresy some minds sufficiently intrepid to maintain that their predecessor, Diadochus, doubtless less well informed than themselves, could have allowed himself to be captivated after all by the very errors that he meant to combat. Others struggled painfully to explain how the same teaching expressed in the same terms could be so obviously heretical with "Macarius" and indisputably orthodox with Diadochus. These exercises in involuntary comedy are now seen to have been completely useless. And the first-hand lights on Messalianism, thought at last to be in our possession, vanished at the same time.

Should the fact perhaps be recognized that this term, Messalianism, covered a complex reality which the zeal of the ancient heresy-hunters vainly tried to unify? First, about 480–90—in the Syrian centres where asceticism had taken on very early forms perhaps exaggeratedly spectacular—came the appearance of the movement of Adelphius, on the outskirts of regular monasticism. Then, in different monasteries, such as the famous community of the Acemetae of Alexander, at Constantinople, the experts on heresy perceived or thought that they perceived tendencies along the same lines.... Hence one of the first examples of those accusations, vague and thus the more difficult to dispose of—strikingly analogous to the Quietist affair in modern times—in which it is very difficult to estimate the precise degree to which the accusers themselves may have created the error they claimed to be searching out. The final result, as in the other case we have just recalled, was to cast a general discredit on all mysticism for several generations.

To the degree to which Messalianism had any real consistency, with Symeon of Mesopotamia or others, it seems to have been a kind of rigidified caricature of all the traits indicated in post-Gregorian mysticism. The vision of God here is interpreted as a physical vision, of a quasi-material light. The "spiritual senses" are conceived with a realism so gross that they cease to be spiritual at all. Not only does prayer, under the pretext that it is the superior activity of the monk, do away with every other activity, but it comes to be conceived as a means having a kind of mechanically infallible efficacy in leading to experience. The co-existence in the soul of the spirit of evil and the Spirit of God, the struggle between which is the very source of the spiritual combat, is degraded into a passivity of the so-called "spiritual man" towards all the impulses that go through him.[16]

[16] On Messalianism, see the two articles, "Euchites" et "Messaliens", by Mgr E. Amann, in *Dict. de Théol. cath.* In spite of their author's adherence, in the second of these articles, to the thesis of Dom Villecourt, they constitute a very clear exposition of all the elements of the problem.

Diadochus of Photike

The unprejudiced study of the *Hundred Chapters on Spiritual Perfection* by the Bishop Diadochus of Photike (about whom we know nothing more except, according to Photius, that he was one of the Fathers of the Council of Chalcedon) shows him to be an eclectic disciple both of Evagrius and of Pseudo-Macarius.[17] To the first he owes his conception of the relationship between *apatheia* and charity, his notion of contemplative gnosis culminating, in what he also, like "Dionysius", calls "theology". But from "Macarius", once again, he retains the whole mysticism of light, of experience, contenting himself with defining more precisely, in the face of contemporary errors, the way in which the two "spirits" act at the same time on the soul: the one has his throne there, the other only acting as it were from outside. It is the divine Spirit, obviously, which is established in the faithful soul, at least so long as it perseveres in the ascetic struggle, whatever the troubles that may still be roused within the soul by the evil spirit whose place the divine Spirit has taken.

> Others have imagined that grace and sin—that is to say, the spirit of truth and the spirit of error—are hidden at the same time in the depths of the *nous*. Hence, it is said, one of the two personages solicits the *nous* to goodness; the other to the direct opposite. For myself, the holy Scriptures and my own intellectual sense have made me understand that, before holy Baptism, grace exhorts the soul to goodness from without, while Satan coils himself in its depths, seeking to bar the way to all the efforts of the spirit to go out towards goodness; but, at the time of our regeneration, it is the demon who goes outside and grace enters within. We discover, then, that while formerly error reigned over the soul, in the same way, after Baptism, it is truth that rules over it. Nevertheless, Satan continues to act on the soul as formerly, and often in a worse way; not that he co-exists with grace—such a thought is far from me. But, by the humours of the body, it might he said that he disperses in the spirit the vapours of the sweetness of irrational pleasures; and this happens by the permission of God, so that in going through the storm and the fire of trial, man may arrive, if he wills it, at the enjoyment of the good. For it is said: "We have gone through fire and water, and you have led us out to refreshment."[18]

[17] See the edition and translation of his works by Rev. E. des Places, S.J., in the collection "Sources chrétiennes", no. 5 *bis*, Paris, 1955. The introduction, unfortunately, ignores the major work of Jaeger, which appeared in the preceding year.

[18] *76th Chapter on Spiritual perfection*, ed. des Places, pp. 134ff. The final quotation is from Psalm 65. 12.

The *Vision*, by the same Diadochus, devotes itself in an interesting way to reconciling the negativism of Evagrian "theology" and the luminous mysticism of the Homilies by introducing the idea of a vision, in glory, of the formless beauty of God.

> ...Those who are to be judged worthy of it are constantly in the light, always rejoicing, in glory, in the love of God, but incapable of conceiving wherein consists the nature of the light of God that enlightens them; in the same way, indeed, as God limits Himself as He wills while remaining unlimited, so also He allows Himself to be seen by remaining invisible.—And what are we to understand by the virtue of God?—A beauty without form that is known only in glory.[19]

Notable also, in spite of Diadochus' opposition to Messalian materialism, is the repeated statement that, while we can only fully grasp the heavenly vision after the transfiguration of the body, it is nevertheless reflected on the body when we approach it here below in gnosis:

> The very energy of our holy gnosis teaches us that there is one natural sense of the soul, later divided into two energies in consequence of Adam's disobedience, but that another sense is simple, that which comes to us from the Holy Spirit, which no one can know except those who willingly detach themselves from the advantages of this life in the hope of future blessings and who, by continence, scourge the appetite of the corporeal senses. Only in these does the *nous* move with complete vigour thanks to its detachment, and can sense the divine goodness in an indescribable way, following which it then communicates its own joy to its very body, according to the degree of its progress, exulting endlessly in its confession full of love: "In Him, says [the Psalmist], my heart has hoped, and my flesh has flourished again, and with all my will I shall confess Him." For the joy that then comes to soul and body is an infallible reminder of the incorruptible life."[20]

It has been rightly remarked that Diadochus, through the association of these different themes: of the formless beauty of the divinity, limiting itself in order to communicate itself to us while remaining itself unlimited, and of the union of the body with the divine vision, appears as one of the clearest precursors of Palamism. He is also the precursor of Hesychasm, which Gregory Palamas, in the fourteenth century, merely wished to justify in its ascetic practice and mystical orientation. For, not only are to be found in him the greater elements which in Pseudo-Macarius prepared the way

[19] *Vision*, 14th and 15th answers; *ibid.*, p. 173.
[20] *25th Chapter*, etc.; *ibid.*, pp. 96–7. Quotation from Psalm 27. 7.

for Hesychasm: *hesychia* itself,[21] the prayer of the heart, attentiveness to the Lord (which Diadochus calls the "memory of the Lord"), but he already explicitly centres all this on the constant invocation of the name of Jesus, and he expects from this practice to gain the vision of the interior light:

> The *nous* absolutely requires of us, when we close all its exits by the remembrance of God, a work that will satisfy its need for activity. We must therefore give it the "Lord Jesus" as the only occupation which completely answers its purpose. "No one, indeed, it is written, can say 'Jesus is the Lord', except in the Holy Spirit."[22] But at all times let it so exclusively contemplate this word in its own treasures that it does not turn away to any other imagination. All those, indeed, who meditate unceasingly, in the depth of their heart, on this holy and glorious name, will finally also be able to see the light of their own *nous*. For, maintained with close care by the thought, it consumes, in an intense sentiment, all the dirt that covers the surface of the soul and, indeed, "our God, as it is said, is a consuming fire".[23] As a result, henceforth, the Lord solicits the soul to a great love of His own glory. For when it persists, by intellectual memory, in fervour of heart, this glorious and so desirable name implants in us the habit of loving its goodness without anything henceforth opposing it. Here, indeed, is the priceless pearl that we can purchase by selling all our goods, in order, in its discovery, to rejoice in an ineffable joy.[24]

Origenism

After Messalianism, monasticism experienced a second doctrinal crisis with the more or less archaizing Origenism which made two successive appearances: one in Egypt and Palestine in the last years of the fourth century and the opening of the fifth; the other in Palestine a century later.[25] Confused by the many twistings and turnings of the principal protagonists, such as St Jerome and Theophilus of Alexandria, inflamed by the *rabies theologica* of Epiphanius of Salamis in its first phase and inextricably mingled with the Nestorian agitation in its second, this quarrel, we must admit, seems made up in great part of a litigation between tendencies and personal rivalries which doctrinal problems entered into as concealing rather than actually occasioning. However, behind all this went on the conflict between the old monastic tradition—weighted and nourished by Origenism since the time of the Cappadocians

[21] *30th* and *68th Chapters*, etc.
[22] 1 Cor. 12. 3.
[23] Deut. 4. 24.
[24] *59th Chapter*, etc.; trad. des Places, p. 119.
[25] See the article "Origénisme", by G. Fritz, in *Dict. de Théol. cath.*

and their disciple, Evagrius, and then become rigidified and exaggerated—and a more and more institutionalized monasticism, confined within a moralistic asceticism.

Here again, as with Diadochus when the anti-Messalian reaction was on the way to becoming purely and simply antimystical, a spiritual master arose who was able to take the part of the fire while salvaging the essential: in the present case, clearly to separate certain doubtful speculations and, more profoundly, an intellectualistic equivocation, from the positive wealth of the mysticism derived from Origen. This new master was Maximus of Chrysopolis, Maximus the Confessor as he was called, as the result of his trials and his death in exile for the definition and the defence of the Catholic faith against Mono-energism and Monothelism.[26]

Maximus the Confessor

An aristocrat of Constantinople, and, in 610, secretary to the emperor Heraclius, Maximus abandoned, a few years later, his pinnacle of honours and responsibilities to withdraw to the monastery of Chrysopolis on the other side of the Bosphorus. Driven into Africa by the Persian invasion of 626, he never regained his monastery. Whether in Africa or in Rome, he became the soul of the resistance to the Monothelism of the Emperor Constans II. Brought back to Constantinople to be tried and condemned in 643, together with the Pope St Martin I, he died two years later, exiled in Thrace, doubtless as the consequence of the tortures he had undergone.

St Maximus is the last great theologian of Greek patristics. We might say that he brought the Christology of the Fathers to its perfection, in elucidating as far as is possible the perfect integrity of Christ's human nature in the transcendent unity realized by his unique divine hypostasis. Thanks to this theological vision and to its definite affirmation that Christ is the ideal model of our perfection, Maximus can be considered as the doctor of divinization who clarified its meaning once for all.

Maximus showed that in Christ there could be no "gnomic will", that is any determination of the will by a deliberation resulting from limited and uncertain knowledge, as is the case with a merely human person. In his human nature is found only the "will of

[26] The study of this writer has been completely renovated by the works of Hans Urs von Balthasar, particularly his synthesis, *Kosmische Liturgie, Maximus der Bekenner*, Freiburg in Brisgau, 1941 (French translation, *Liturgie cosmique, Maxime le Confesseur*, Paris, 1947). See also the introduction of J. Pegon, S.J., to his translation of the *Centuries on charity*, "Sources chrétiennes", no. 9, Paris, 1943.

nature", that is the free tendency of that nature towards its good, towards the being that befits it. But this tendency, in the humanity of a divine person, always remains conformed to the divine will, divinized (*theothen*) according to the term of Gregory Nazianzen.

This is the ideal towards which every Christian ought to be oriented by charity: our freedom should wholly be moulded, by faith and hope, in adherence to the will of God. The sin of Adam came from *philautia*, from attachment to himself in consenting only to egoistic pleasure. From this attachment resulted sorrow and death for man. The acceptance of suffering and death in Christ will break up this *philautia*, re-establishing us in the charity that gives us wholly back to God. This is the core of Maximus' spirituality and soteriology.[27]

Inspired by Gregory of Nyssa, Maximus saw in sexual life, inextricably linked with the pleasure of the senses in which man is immersed, a providential disposition to keep sinful humanity alive, in spite of the death to which sin, allied with egoistic sensuality, had condemned mankind. But it is in virginity, linked up with faith and hope, and itself the principle of all asceticism, that man, by renouncing with Christ on the cross the life that is simply of this earth, regains the divine life communicated.[28]

On this basis, just as Diadochus effected a synthesis of Pseudo-Macarius and Evagrius, so Maximus synthesized in an even more personal way Evagrius and Pseudo-Dionysius. Commenting on the latter (and the interpretation that he gives determined his definitive integration with orthodox spirituality), Maximus fuses the Evagrian *ekdemia*, beyond all the *pathe* and distinct thoughts drawn from this world, with the Dionysian *extasis*: the escape from self of the *eros* of the soul which allows itself to be taken hold of and ravished in Christ by the divine *agape*. Adopting, as M. Viller has clearly shown,[29] almost all the formulations of Evagrius, Maximus definitely parts company with him in not seeing "theology" as the soul's knowledge of itself in which it knows God in recognizing itself as his image. Faithful to the Dionysian inspiration, he makes it a loss of the soul outside itself, a knowledge essentially obscure, not only in relation to knowledge drawn from this world, but in relation to all knowledge of self, in whatever way this be understood. As Hans Urs von Balthasar has

[27] See the lucid exposition of V. Grumel, in his article, "Maxime de Chrysopolis", in *Dict. de Théol. cath.*, which we have done no more than sum up in the preceding lines.

[28] See Hans Urs von Balthasar, *op. cit.*, pp. 127ff.

[29] Marcel Viller, "Aux sources de la spiritualité de saint Maxime: les œuvres d'Évagre le Pontique", in *Revue d'Ascétique et de Mystique*, 1930, pp. 153–84, 239–68, 331–6.

clearly shown, the death that is necessary for redemption after sin is only, according to this view, one manifestation of that death to self which is ineluctably present at the heart of every possible participation of the creature, even intact, in a love, in a life which are the very life and love of God.[30]

> When, in the transport of charity, the spirit emigrates towards God, it no longer retains any sense of itself or of any existing reality. Wholly illuminated with the infinite light of God, it becomes insensible to everything that only exists by virtue of this light. In the same way, the eye ceases to see the stars when the sun arises. . . .[31] The spirit is ravished, in the very upsurge of prayer, by the infinite light of God; it loses all sense of itself and of other beings, except of Him who, by charity, effects this illumination within it.[32]
>
> When it receives the representations of things, the spirit naturally models itself on each of them. When it contemplates them spiritually, it takes on various ways of being, according to the different objects of its contemplation. Arrived in God, it becomes perfectly without form and without figure, contemplating the Simple (*monoeide*), it becomes simple and wholly light.[33]

This complete extroversion of the soul possessed by the divine charity in no way means a destruction of its humanity, but rather its regeneration. For, in God himself, the divine charity is pure generosity with regard to creatures. And so, the man who is consummated in this charity which detaches man from himself loves all men in God, and even those who naturally seem the least lovable to him:

> God, by nature good and without passion, loves all men with an equal love, men who are the work of His hands: but He glorifies the just man, unites him intimately to himself in His will and, in His goodness, He has mercy on the sinner whom He seeks to convert in this life by His lessons. And so the man whose will has become good and free from passions loves all men with an equal love, the just for their nature and their good will, sinners for their nature and by that compassionate pity which one has for a foolish man who goes off into the night.
>
> Perfect charity does not admit, between men who are of the same nature, any distinction founded on the difference of characteristics. It never sees anything but this one nature; it attaches itself with an equal force to all men; to the good because

[30] *Op. cit.*, pp. 191ff.
[31] *First Century on charity*, ed. Pegon, p. 71.
[32] *Second Century on charity*, ch. VI; ed. Pegon, p. 95.
[33] *Third Century on charity*, ch. XCVII; ed. Pegon, p. 150.

they are friends, to the wicked because they are enemies in order to do them good, bearing with them, patiently enduring everything that they do to him, stubbornly refusing to see any malice in it, and going so far as to suffer for them if the occasion presents itself. And so sometimes perhaps he makes them friends; never, in the least, is he unfaithful to himself and, ceaselessly, to all men equally, he shows the fruits of his charity. Our God and Lord Jesus Christ, indeed, Himself showed His love in suffering for all mankind, and in freely giving to the whole world the possibility of one day rising again, each man remaining his own master in meriting glory or punishment.[34]

This synthesis of Maximus is of exceptional importance both for spirituality and for theology. Complete justice has not yet been done him—doubtless because his life, continually disturbed by circumstances quite independent of his will, allowed him to express his ideas only in brief, concise works that do not allow his thought to develop at leisure. He remains, however, one of those rare spirits who, synthesizing in intuitions of genius all the fruits of a tradition developed to the point of overloading, excel in refreshing this tradition by reimmersing it in its sources. He is certainly the most perfect fruit of the Alexandrian and Cappadocian tradition. But, in his struggle against Monothelism, he came to reintegrate with Alexandrianism almost all the wealth of human reality and concrete experience which justified the protestation of the school of Antioch against Alexandrianism. Above all, charity, which is the soul of all Christian spirituality, with him regains something of the first upsurge of the vigour of the Gospel.

In this respect, as St Maximus crowned the edifice of patristic thought, so he prepared the way for the great spiritual and intellectual rebirths of Byzantine Christianity.

The School of Antioch

This glimpse of his work invites us to penetrate the profound meaning of the irreconcilable protest of the School of Antioch against the School of Alexandria. Here we find illuminated in a special way that reaction in monasticism, so notable in the fifth and sixth centuries, from mysticism towards a rather moralistic asceticism. Historians, especially since the nineteenth century, tend to make much of and, still more, to falsify the opposition between Antioch and Alexandria. However, we must not forget that Lucian, the first Antiochene master of any renown and undeniably the inspirer of the whole group of Arianizing bishops who, in the fourth century, were described as "Collucianists", was closely

[34] *First Century on charity*, ch. XXV and LXXI; ed. Pegon, pp. 74 and 84.

dependent on Origen, as much for the inspiration of his theology as for that of his work in correcting and editing the text of the Bible.[35] Arianism might be said to have proceeded directly from what of Origen had been retained at Antioch, while it was refuted rather by what of Origen had asserted itself at Alexandria. Two centuries later, an archaizing Origenism was revived for one last time in Nestorian circles, as we mentioned above. But Nestorianism is a typical product of the School of Antioch in its opposition to the School of Alexandria.

The apparent paradox of these considerations, however indisputable, urges us to shade our judgments with a great deal of prudence. It is quite certain that from the time of Diodorus of Tarsus, in the second half of the fourth century, the school of Antioch became conscious of a certain opposition between its profound tendencies and those of Alexandria, more precisely in relation to Origenist exegesis. But there is hardly any doubt that the theological oppositions manifested in the Arian controversy set in motion a latent antagonism going far beyond problems of exegetical technique. In truth, it was the whole orientation of spirituality which was at stake.

It would be most helpful, however, to possess the lost treatise written by Diodorus, *On the Difference between Theory and Allegory*. For it must be admitted that this difference, with the great Antiochene exegetes or preachers who succeeded him—Theodore of Mopsuestia, St John Chrysostom, Theodoret—is not so easy to determine from their practice. We would be happy to know from its primary source the systematic theory of it which they themselves held.[36]

In any case, the simplicist view which still obtains everywhere, according to which the Antiochenes opposed the literal sense of Scripture to Origen's allegorism, is a caricature. It is even sometimes a complete contradiction. In the first place, for Origen—apart from certain very rare passages where there is no literal sense (or, it would be better to say, where the literal sense is itself symbolic, such as the Gospel parables)—the allegorical sense, far from excluding the literal sense, is entirely based on it. The first thing that the "spiritual" elucidation of the Scripture requires is, therefore, scrupulously to bring to light their literal sense.

And, it must be admitted, on this point Origen seems infinitely better equipped than the Antiochene exegetes. He knew Hebrew,

[35] See G. Bardy, *Recherches sur saint Lucien d'Antioche et son école*, Paris, 1936.

[36] Unfortunately, neither the *Adversus Allegoricos*, nor the *De obscura locutione* of Theodore have come down to us, any more than the basic work of Diodorus.

which none of them seemed to have concerned themselves with, and the rules of his textual criticism and his philological interpretation are in other respects more rigorous even than those of Theodore of Mopsuestia, the best among the Antiochenes in this regard.[37]

The latter, doubtless, appears in return as astonishingly open to the historical development of Israel, and notably careful, in order to understand the prophets, to locate them as precisely as possible in the context of their times. Equally, in connection with the psalms, though with much less assurance, he is one of the first, and perhaps the first, to try to perceive what circumstances, more or less ascertainable by date, could be connected with their composition. We should not forget, however, that he persisted in attributing them to David *en bloc* and that he saw in this adaptation only a very special case of prophetic foreknowledge.

To the extent that it can be defined, with him or with Theodoret, from the applications they made of it, the opposition of their "theory" to "allegory" remains in the line of Diodorus. "Theory" refuses to attribute to the biblical writer himself the formal intention of giving, under the veil of details concerning the history of Israel as to the letter, a teaching to be applied to the New Testament: to Christ, to the Church, to the Christian soul. But it is in the events, described without any further intention on the part of the writer, that God has again and again given us "types", images or, rather, anticipated sketches, of the Gospel events. This distinction is not without interest. And perhaps, in many cases, it may be closer to the proper thought of Origen than the simplistic notion of "allegory" which the Antiochenes themselves and modern scholars too easily attribute to him.

But in practice, it must be admitted, their search for "types", often seems neither more nor less arbitrary than Alexandrine allegory. In fact, with them at least as much as with Origen, in making these transpositions it frequently happens that the writer falls into a merely accommodated use of texts having nothing in themselves to orient them objectively towards the sense that he wishes to find in them. The real difference here between Antioch and Alexandria is not in the greater or lesser degree of fantasy in the transpositions thus made. It is rather that, in the school of Origen, the tendency is to find Christian dogma under its most metaphysical aspects, or Christian spirituality in its most mystical aspects (that is, what is connected with the life of Christ in us). In Antioch, on the contrary, the attempt was made to rather see either

37 See the article by Mgr Amann devoted to him in the *Dict. de Théol. cath.*, col. 248ff.

a sketch of the very events of the New Testament, in the detail of their historical unfolding, or a moralistic meaning.

There is no doubt that behind all this there is a stronger perception of the proper consistency of human history than at Alexandria and a greater esteem, perhaps, for creation in itself, apart from its capacity to symbolize the divine. But we are greatly deceiving ourselves if we suppose that the fantastic display of gratuitous exegeses, wholly subjective, would be for this reason better held in check. The sense of history, of its concrete reality, and the historic sense as we understand it today, do not always go together. Far from it! We should add that the sense of the Christian mystery, so strongly Paulinian, centred in Christ and his Cross, had grown quite weak in Antioch and, in virtue of this fact, too easily the search for "types" went astray in a superficial ingenuity: the wholly external analogy (and often how greatly forced) between situations directed attention towards what was accessory, while the great spiritual realities underlying the whole development of revelation were more or less lost to view. Under these conditions, we should not be too surprised that a Theodore of Mopsuestia was so easily able to discover his own Nestorianizing Christology in St Paul, nor that he remained so little aware of the mysterious depths of the Apostle's soteriology.

This tendency becomes aggravated, even more than in exegesis, in the explication of the liturgical rites. The mystagogic catecheses of the same Theodore of Mopsuestia, it must be admitted, too often betray a complete misunderstanding of the nature of the liturgical symbols. The infantile "historicism" of these catecheses caused them to see in the details of the rites a mere miming of the Gospel events. The absurdities of the *Expositiones missae* of the Medieval West, with the passage from the epistle to the Gospel recalling the transfer of Jesus from Annas to Caiphas, or the Lavabo signifying Pilate's washing his hands, are only a development of this type of "explanation". The school of Maria-Laach was particularly ill-advised when it took certain of his texts as a witness to the liturgical "mystery" (in Casel's use of the term).[38]

In fact, with Theodore of Mopsuestia, we are assisting at a first dissolution, or a first travestying, of the sacramental mystery in a dramatic conception of the rites that makes them, quite artificially and with no regard for their true historical origin, into a kind of

38 These *Catecheses* have been published in a Syriac translation rediscovered by Mingana (together with the English translation) in the *Woodbrooke Studies*, Cambridge, vols. V and VI, 1932 and 1933. The second volume, containing an explanation of the rites of Christian initiation, is particularly important in connection with Theodore's mystagogy.

didactic play-acting. Natural symbolism is degraded into flat and uninspired rationalism set out in an artificial cipher. And properly sacramental symbolism is therefore as it were stifled. There remains of the Eucharist hardly more than a pious "morality play" in the sense of the last centuries of the Latin Middle Ages.

On the other hand, with a personality as vivid as that of Theodoret,[39] this taste for the concrete, the human, has enriched us with innumerable historical observations and simple personal reflections which move us as few of the texts of antiquity succeed in doing, as Newman so well brought out. With St John Chrysostom,[40] this same tendency also produces a truthfulness of spiritual testimony, often disarming, as well as an attention to the practical problems in the life of his hearers or correspondents of which there are few other examples in this era. St Gregory Nazianzen alone is comparable to him in this regard. Rhetoric mars him even less than Chrysostom when it comes to these personal overflowings. But, again, Chrysostom surpasses him in his capacity to concern himself with other persons, even those very different from himself.

St John Chrysostom

Together with Theodore of Mopsuestia, St John began, however, once his classical studies were finished, by leading a quasi-monastic life in the famous *asceterion* of Diodorus, an advanced school in the fervent Christian life, it seems, rather than a monastery. Then, according to his biographer, Palladius,[41] he made an attempt at the cenobitic life and even the anchoritic. Returning to Antioch, he devoted himself to the ecclesiastical ministry, in the diaconate, the priesthood, and then in his episcopate at Constantinople where the fearless frankness of his preaching against Eudoxia was to earn him many trials, and even his death in the exile described in his letters to Olympias in a way that still moves us.[42]

[39] The volume of the *Dict. de Théol. cath.* containing the very important work of Mgr Amann on Theodore of Mopsuestia also contains a remarkable study by G. Bardy on Theodoret. A thesis, as yet unpublished, was presented in Paris in 1951 by Yvan Azéma, on *Théodoret de Cyr d'après sa correspondance*. See also the Introduction of P. Canivet, S.J., to his edition and translation of the *Thérapeutique des maladies helléniques*, of Theodoret, "Sources chrétiennes", no. 57, 2 vols., Paris, 1958. Bibliography in Quasten, *Patrology*, vol. 3. Works in P.G., XLVII–LXIV. Reprint by Vivès of the ed. Montfaucon, with French trans., by J. Bareille, Paris, 1865–73.

[40] See particularly Chr. Baur, *Johannes Chrysostomus und seine Zeit*, Munchen, 1929–30. J. Meyer, *Saint Jean Chrysostom, maître de perfection chrétienne*, Paris, 1933, should also be mentioned.

[41] *Palladii dialogus de vita sancti J. Chrysostomi*, ed. Coleman-Norton, Cambridge, 1928. This Palladius is the same as the author of the *Historia lausiaca* (in which a chapter is devoted also to Olympias, the friend of Chrysostom, ed. Butler, II, LVI).

[42] These have been edited and translated with a copious introduction by Anne-Marie Malingrey, "Sources chrétiennes", no. 13, Paris, 1947.

He remained to the end an ascetic far more austere for himself than for others. But we must admit that his justifications of asceticism, in the writings of his youth like the two books on *Compunction* or the three books *Against the Adversaries of the Monastic Life*, apart from the vehemence of a rhetoric of undeniable sincerity although marred for us by its outbursts, are of a distressing poverty. A Stoic ideal of sobriety, of independence with regard to the possible blows of fortune, seems to be Christianized only by an identification between the monastic life and the penitent life, doubtless very traditional, but limited to an almost entirely negative viewpoint. The Hellenistic theme of the "virtue" to be developed by asceticism had already, it is true, been used by the Cappadocians. But now it seems deprived of all mystical meaning and limited to a moralism, ardent certainly, but without great religious perspectives. A sincere love of Christ, borrowing from St Paul something of his fervour, fortunately comes to give warmth to all this,[43] but as if from outside.

The *Exhortation to Theodore after his Fall*, addressed, it may well be, to Theodore of Mopsuestia, tempted for a time to get married, is still more tiresome. Virginity is exalted here, certainly, but on the basis of a lowering of marriage, wherein the author seems to see nothing but the satisfaction of the flesh and the inconveniences and turmoil that it entails. What are we to think of an exhortation to the monastic life that has recourse to arguments like to this in order to turn an infatuated man away from a woman?

> Physical beauty is nothing other than phlegm, blood, humour, bile—in other words, the juice of decomposing elements.... Look at a piece of linen soiled with spittle and rheum, you would not want to touch it with the tip of your fingers, you would not even dare to look at it; and see, now you are in ecstasy before the impure receptacle of all these things, before this collective sickness.[44]

And this is perhaps still worse:

> Should I speak to you of the cares that a wife, children, slaves always bring with them? There are many drawbacks to taking a poor wife; there are no fewer in taking a rich one. In the one case, it is the resources, in the other, the freedom and authority of the husband that suffer. It costs a great deal when one has children; it is still more painful not to have any. To have none is to be deprived of the fruit that one expects from marriage; to have them is to be constrained to a rude slavery. When a child

[43] Ed. Vivès, I, Paris, 1865, pp. 217ff. and 80ff.
[44] *To Theodore after his Fall*, *ibid.*, p. 53 of Vivès.

is sick, it is an anxiety full of terrors. If he should die prematurely, it is a sorrow without consolation. As he grows up, there are new cares, new fears, new worries....[45]

In reading these two texts, one would believe that monasticism was merely a comfortable refuge for hardened egoists or mentally disturbed persons of a very suspect kind of misogyny. What follows, which unfortunately is the conclusion, seems to be a commentary on *Suave mari magno*.... It must be admitted that if poor Theodore had no better reasons for renouncing his Hermione, the spiritual profit that he could have expected from the monastic life would have been very meagre.

Doubtless we are to see here one of those crimes of rhetorical amplification committed by a very young man whose pious sophistry will use anything as a weapon. But we can also see here the extremes to which a monkish asceticism could tend when deprived of its mystical aspiration and reduced to a religious moralism and a conception of *apatheia* which, under these circumstances, falls back to the merely Stoic level: self-mastery, in view simply of escaping from subjection to external circumstances.

The *opusculum* on the *Comparison between a King and a Monk* again takes up from Stoicism the over-worked theme of the exaltation of the sage without causing it to undergo any appreciable transposition. The name of Christ is introduced only in an unimportant incident and, quite contrary to the old monastic texts, the vocation of the monk appears as a vocation to a continent wisdom having no essential connection with faith.[46]

The treatise *On Virginity*, which already seems of a somewhat later date, contains more positive elements: the affirmation that marriage is a good, and that it is precisely in considering it as a good and not an evil that virginity, by comparison, takes on all its excellence.[47] It presents above all an almost flawless exegesis of the words of St Paul connecting virginity with the eschatological expectation:

> ...If marriage does not go beyond the limits of the present life, if in the future life there is no question of marriage or espousal, if the present time is not distant from the end and if the day of the resurrection is about to dawn, we should be preoccupied not with marriage and the good things of the earth, but with detachment and the other virtues, the priceless advantages of which we shall then enjoy. Just as a young girl, so long as she remains at home with her mother, is vitally concerned with all the things of childhood, having nothing to take care of but the key of the little coffer which she has put in her little room and of all that it

[45] *Ibid.*, p. 8. [46] *Ibid.*, pp. 207ff. [47] *Ibid.*, pp. 462–5.

> contains, which she is mistress of, devoting herself to watching over these trifles with as much solicitude as is devoted to administering great houses—when at the last the time comes to choose a husband, and the state of marriage obliges her to leave her father's house, she must give up these insignificant and frivolous occupations in order to think of governing a house, possessions, many servants, of serving her husband, and other even more important cares; so we, once we have arrived at the perfect life and the age of maturity, should despise all the things of earth as so many childish playthings, and turn our thoughts towards heaven, to the splendour and the glory that await us there. We too, we have our Bridegroom, and He wishes so greatly to be loved by us that we must be ready, when there is need, to sacrifice for Him not only the things and trifles of earth, but our very life.[48]

It is unfortunate that pages such as these are only isolated incidents in the whole, and stop short at very general notions. The objection aroused by his customary considerations is so obvious that Chrysostom himself states it several times: "Is there then nothing to make us appreciate virginity other than the pains and worries of marriage?" On each occasion, he announces that he intends to go on to the positive riches of the ascetic life, but, after some generalities on the love of Christ and especially on the future reward, his habitual way of speaking might be said to be stronger than he, so that he cannot help falling again into a depreciation of marriage—which, nevertheless, he had previously proclaimed in the face of Encratist or Manichean errors to be good in itself.[49]

In fact, when, by an ingenuous sophistry, he has excluded the real purposes of marriage: the procreation of children, the family, the aid and mutual affection of husband and wife, there remains only a relative easing of concupiscence.[50] The misogyny, already visible elsewhere in the ascetical writings of this first period, goes beyond all bounds when we see him proving (?) that the help promised to man by the creator, in the person of woman, has in fact, been refused him by her sin.[51] And if, vaguely sensing his excess, he concedes all the same that woman can after all actually be a help to man in "the building up of the family, the struggle against the passions with which human nature is infected", he adds immediately this diatribe which would be stupefying if it were not simply funny:

> But when there is no longer any question of this life, or of the family, or of disordered passions, why speak to me of an aid like

[48] *Ibid.*, pp. 548–9.
[49] *Ibid.*, pp. 520ff.
[50] Cf. p. 504 and all the reasoning leading up to this conclusion.
[51] *Ibid.*, pp. 514–16.

this? Useful only for things of little importance, if [the woman] be called to share higher thoughts, not only is she no longer useful for anything, but she still raises obstacles by the cares of which she is the cause.[52]

It must be admitted that, in texts like these, this asceticism without mysticism not only reveals a hopeless aridity, but gives the impression that its tension with no sufficient objective could easily turn into obsession.

Did not Chrysostom sense this himself? We are told that he left his monastic retreat at the end of six years and went back to Antioch because he had ruined his health and, in particular, had disordered his digestion, in the exercises of solitary asceticism. Without casting doubt on these reasons, it is permissible to think that Chrysostom might equally have become aware, even though obscurely, that such a life, with the mentality that he had inherited from the school of Antioch, could not bring his Christian aspirations to fruition. It was only in an active existence in the service of Christ that they could be satisfied.

Chrysostom as Priest

The treatise *On the Priesthood*, which Chrysostom composed at Antioch at the time when he was passing from one orientation to the other, might be considered as the implicit avowal of this discovery. Here he multiplies the difficulties, which he admits frighten him, of undertaking a task bringing a weak and sinful man to frequent the most sacred mysteries, to take on himself the responsibility for the salvation of his brothers, above all to have to speak to them in the very name of God. But a cry from the heart, in the first pages where he sketches out the core of his subject, overcomes all this in advance:

What can be conceived of as more advantageous than to practise that which best proves our love for Christ, on the testimony of Christ Himself? Addressing Himself to the chief of the apostles, "Peter", He says, "Do you love Me?" And, on the formal declaration that he does, Christ adds: "If you love Me, feed my sheep". When the Master asks the disciple if He can count on his love, it is not to learn something unknown, for what could He learn, He who sees the secrets of all hearts? No, but He wishes to show us the esteem in which He holds the authority that is exercised over His flock.

Since there is no possible doubt in this regard, it is no less obvious that a great reward awaits him who has worked at a

[52] *Ibid.*, p. 516.

task so dear to Christ. We ourselves, when we see some of our servants watching with care over keeping our flocks, we see this solicitude as a proof of love for ourselves, even though all this is purchased for a sum of silver: how, then could He who redeemed us, not with gold or silver but at the price of His very life, giving His blood for the ransom of His flock—how could He not magnificently reward His shepherd? And so, as soon as the disciple had said: "You know, Lord, that I love You,"[53] thus calling to witness to his love the very One who was the object of it, the Saviour went still further and taught us what is the sign of love. He did not wish to establish by a new proof to what extent Peter loved Him, since this had already been demonstrated in a very obvious way: it was His own love for the Church that He wished to have shine out, both to Peter's eyes and to our own, so as to awaken a like ardour in our souls. Why did God not spare His only Son but delivered Him to death? To lead back to Himself those who had been taken away from Him by hatred, and to form a special people for Himself. Why did the Son shed His blood? To redeem the sheep that He entrusted to Peter and to his successors.

It was then with good reason that Christ said: "Who is the faithful and prudent servant that the Lord will set at the head of his house?"[54] Here again the phrase is a question, even though there was no doubt in the mind of Him who pronounced it. In the same way as when Jesus asked Peter if he loved Him, the question did not have as its purpose to establish the love of the disciple, but rather to manifest the greatness of the master's love; so, when He says, "Who is the faithful and prudent servant", it is not because He is in any doubt as to who is the servant endowed with these qualities; He wishes to show thereby how rare are such servants and how lofty their functions. And see also how He rewards them: "He will set them over all his possessions."[55]

Clearly these pages, in comparison with the preceding, strike a new note. It would not be going too far to say that the treatise *On the Priesthood* inaugurates, in the face of a monastic spirituality in the process of losing its objective and hardening in a kind of sclerosis, the beginnings of a completely different spirituality, properly sacerdotal. It does not, in fact, propose a definite spirituality. But it brings to light how, for realistic minds, attached to the concrete and drawn to contemplation little or not at all, only an ideal of generous service could prevent the asceticism exalted by the monastic movement from losing itself in irrealism.

The fact is that the practice of the priestly ministry came visibly

[53] John 21. 15ff. [54] Matt. 24. 45.

[55] *On the Priesthood*, bk. II, vol. II of the Vivès ed.

to give substance to the very ardent, but at the outset perhaps not very enlightened, Christianity of Chrysostom. Now we witness in him a flowering in charity of that humanity which his asceticism, hitherto, had limited itself to repressing, at the risk of deforming it. To realize this, it is enough to compare the preceding texts, the rather bitter fruits of his several years of solitude, with a text like the little work *To a Young Widow*, written when the care of souls had taken hold of him and when the men, the women that he speaks of, to whom he addresses himself, had ceased to be mere abstractions:

> ...You must have an ardent desire again to hear the voice [of Therasius] and to delight in loving him; your common life is lacking to you, and so also the honour, the radiance, the calm and the security which flowed over you from him: that all this has vanished, this is what casts trouble into your soul and spreads a cloud over your mind. But you can keep your love as well now as yesterday, with an inviolate fidelity. Such is the power of charity: it is not limited to persons who are present, to those who live beside us or who are under our eyes; it embraces those who are absent, it draws them and reunites them in its bosom; neither length of time, nor of distance, nor anything of the kind can break or weaken the ties of a friendship of souls. And if you wish to see him again face to face (I know well that this is what you desire above all)—well, then let no other man come near your bed, apply yourself to reproducing in yourself the examples of his life, and without doubt you will attain the same choir as he, and not for five years, as here, nor for twenty, a hundred, a thousand, two thousand, or even ten thousand and more, but you will live with him for innumerable ages without end.[56]

We have some difficulty in believing that the same pen, only a few years apart, could have written the preceding texts and this one. The exercise of the ministry, responsibility for souls, had made of a rather dried-up ascetic inclined towards a disquieting fanaticism, the precursor if not the initiator of a spirituality for the laity, full not only of understanding but of sympathy. Nothing is more striking in this regard than the twentieth of his Homilies on the Epistle to the Ephesians, wholly concerned with sentiments which ought to be those of Christian married people:

> Do you wish your wife to obey you as the Church obeys Christ? Be full of solicitude for her, as Christ is for the Church. If you had to give your life for her, to be cut in pieces, to suffer all torments, you would not recoil; and when you had done all that, you would have done nothing compared with what Christ

[56] Vol. I of the Vivès ed.

has done. You would do this for someone who is already united with you; He did it for her who had repulsed him and detested Him. By virtue of His solicitude, He triumphed over her aversion, her hatred, her misunderstanding, her flighty humour; He brought her to His feet, and it was not by threats, nor by harsh words, nor by fear nor anything of the like: act in the same way towards your wife. . . .

When a husband has such feelings, St John expects him to say to his young wife:

> A girl who is prudent and generous, who applies herself to devotion, is worth more than the whole universe. It is for this reason that I have chosen you, and I love you more than myself. The present life is nothing; I ask you then and I adjure you by every means in my power, that we should spend the time of the present life in such a way as to merit being reunited in the life to come, without any fear of then being separated. The time is short and strewn with difficulties and failures! If here we have been pleasing to God, then we shall go to live with Christ and we shall find one another together in eternal happiness. I prefer your love to everything and I could have no more mortal pain than to have to be separated from you. If I had to lose everything, to fall to the lowest depths of poverty, to suffer anything, all this would be bearable if only your feelings remain the same for me, and even children seem desirable to me only if you love me in this way. . . .

Concerning married people who have truly shared everything with one another, even to their life of prayer, he now does not hesitate to say:

> The man who takes a wife with all this in mind is hardly inferior to the solitaries, the man who is married in this way to him who is not married.[57]

All his public preaching insisted on the fact that perfection, in the final analysis, is proposed to all, those who are monks and those who are living in the world, and that all can attain it in the world if they attain the fullness of charity. All equally, he insists, should for this purpose nourish themselves with the word of God, by reading and personal meditation on Holy Scripture. This, for those who live in the world as for ascetics, is the primary source, together with the sacraments and particularly the Eucharist, of the life of Christ which should unfold within us.[58]

[57] Vol. XVIII of the Vivès ed.
[58] See the article by Denys Gorce, "Mariage et perfection chrétienne, d'après saint Jean Chrysostome", in *Études carmélitaines*, April 1936, pp. 245–84.

For this spiritual flowering, his own experience had taught him that the inevitable trials of life, accepted with a constancy sustained and animated by faith, could be as effective as the most severe ascetic practices. This is the very beautiful and simple lesson of his correspondence with Olympias, marking step by step that road of exile on which he was to die. When we think of the unconscious coarseness of his juvenile ascetic contempt for the poor female sex, we cannot help smiling when we read what Nicephorus Callistus tells us of the devotedness and little attentions lavished by this noble deaconess, so delicate and so generous, on the Archbishop of Constantinople at the height of his struggles and his apostolic frustrations.[59] We recall the humour with which the Fathers of the desert recounted the history of the solitary who detested women . . . and had to end his life in a monastery of virgins, completely bed-ridden and cared for like a baby by those he had so imprudently despised!

But we do not smile, but simply admire when, a little later, we see him as a proscribed old man, separated from his saintly friend by the ingratitude of those who had sent him to a solitary death, comforting her in her own trials by admitting so frankly how much he himself was suffering, and yet still unshakeable in the faith which made him able to repeat to the end his most beautiful words: "Glory to God for everything."

> Nothing, Olympias, is worth so much in commending us to God as patience in sufferings. This is the queen of blessings, the most beautiful of crowns and as it is superior to the other virtues, so in it the form of the others shines out the more resplendently.[60]

This experience of St John Chrysostom's is certainly worth reflecting on from many aspects. The enormous success of monasticism after the peace of the Church certainly did not take place without some unfortunate counterparts. An institutionalized monasticism, no longer having the wholly evangelical upsurge of the early days, inevitably ran the risk of artificiality, of in-humanity. For, even where it remained fervent, it is to be feared that its motivations became obscured or altered. On the other hand, however fruitful were the ways opened out by the Origenist tradition towards a definition of Christian mysticism, it seems undeniable that there was a part of human experience, certain legitimate and irrepressible forms of our access to reality, which this tradition was condemned from the outset to leave aside. Hence a crisis, which the compensatory instinct that emerged at Antioch against

[59] *Hist. eccl.*, XIII, 24; P.G., CXLVI, 1012.
[60] *17th Letter to Olympias.*

Alexandria may perhaps have contributed both to bring to a head and to overcome.

The crisis broke out where the mysticism expressed in the forms of thought inherited from Origen proved itself unassimilable. A fervent piety unsatisfied by mere moralism fell by the nature of things into a deceptive "asceticism". The healthy reaction was sought in the effort to impose a Christian form on the whole of human life, which is the key to the whole pastoral work of Chrysostom. But it may be that it was crowned with success less in the apparent achievements of those "Christian civilizations" of which Byzantium, before the Latin Middle Ages, was to present a first example, than in the drama discovered and lived by the saint himself: this new discovery of the cross in the life of a preacher of the integral truth in the midst of a world which ultimately could not adapt itself to this truth, or in the life of obscure and simple Christians, committed to living in this world as crucified with Christ, when, without abandoning the world, they desire not to abandon their Master.

Pelagianism and Naturalist Reactions

One of the last objective preoccupations which come to light in the correspondence of St John Chrysostom with Olympias is the concern he felt about the beginnings of the Pelagian heresy. Yet this heresy of ascetics too confident in their own asceticism was to seize on more than one of his texts, in which Stoic moralism did not always seem sufficiently open to the mystery of grace. But the confidence of Pelagius and his disciples in human nature, and in the possibilities of its freedom as always actual, quickly led them to an optimism that made all asceticism superfluous. Thus, with a Julian of Eclanum, the antipodes of the misogyny of the young Chrysostom were attained: an unreserved exaltation of marriage, a proclamation of the intact goodness of the natural instincts, even of the holiness of mere pleasure.[61]

Such a reversal of tendencies is not so surprising when we have noted the resistances, the repugnances that the monastic, or more generally the ascetic, ideal evidently met with, even among convinced Christians. Throughout the whole preaching of Chrysostom, we can sense them as secretly present everywhere.

We must certainly take into account here the very strong influence of pagan ways and their sensuality which seemed to be exasperated at this period. This influence was all the greater in that the adhesion of the masses to Christianity could not have been so

[61] See further on, pp. 482ff.

quickly accompanied by a change in the whole tone of public life, still less of its profound mentality. It is not certain, however, that the remains of paganism explain everything in these upshoots of "naturalism" which, in the fifth century and already in the fourth, began to come to light in opposition to monastic "supernaturalism". It was not only a mediocre Christian, like Ausonius, or men more or less clearly heretical such as Helvidius, Jovinian or Vigiliantius, who came to rise up, here and there, against what seemed to them an intolerable condemnation of creation. This resistance, more or less boldly stated, was the act even of minds perfectly accessible to the attraction of the purest Christian mysticism.

Synesius of Cyrene

There is doubtless no more interesting example of this reaction than that of Synesius of Cyrene. An aristocrat, a great landed proprietor, a lover of sports (in particular, an impassioned hunter), a philosopher and faithful disciple of the famous Hypatia and a refined poet, he describes himself in a correspondence which is one of the most endearing left to us by antiquity.[62] Here we find the self-portrait, without a trace of posing or of complacency, of one of the most honest, the most truly human men imaginable.

He loved solitude in order to read, to think, to raise himself to God, but was none the less the most sociable of men. Not concealing the fact that he was inclined to prefer his freedom to anything else, for the sake of the happily employed leisure it procured for him, he did not hesitate to put himself at the service of his fellow citizens when they asked it of him, undertaking difficult missions which must have been very tiresome to him but which he seems to have discharged more than honourably. At last, when he had only recently been converted, it seems, through a slow and progressive adherence to Christianity—to which his wife, probably related to Theophilus of Alexandria who had married them, could not have been a stranger—he had the bishopric of Ptolemais offered to him. The letter in which he sets out his scruples, even his repugnance, is most admirable in its frankness.[63]

It is very hard for him to have to abandon the life which had hitherto been his (he has a word of wry humour about his hunting dogs), but he would do so without hesitation if he believed himself worthy of the holy function offered to him and could render service in it. Two things stop him: he loves his wife, and he cannot bring

[62] See the article on him by G. Bardy in *Dict. de Théol. cath.* His work as a whole is in Migne, P.G., LXVI, 1053–1616.

[63] *Epist.* 105. This letter is addressed to his brother, and not, as M. Bardy wrote by an oversight, to Theophilus of Alexandria (*op. cit.*, col. 1998).

himself to resolve to have no more children by her other than the four sons they already have; moreover, his philosophic formation does not permit him, without a dishonesty which he cannot agree to, to allow the *vulgum pecus* to believe that he holds the pessimistic views on the sensible universe, or, towards the other extreme, the gross images of the resurrection which seem to him to be common among the Christians of his times.... We must believe that Theophilus, in spite of his *rabies theologica*, perhaps softened by age, was not dismayed by these difficulties and was able to banish these scruples.

For Synesius became bishop and exercised his episcopate, in those very troubled times, with a serenity and a courage that do him equal honour. At the time of a barbarian invasion, this intellectual sybarite did not hesitate to say:

> If I find myself in the city at the time of the assault, I will run straight to the church and not go away; I will not abandon it; I will take the holy font as my protection; I will embrace the holy pillars that support the inviolable table of the altar; it is there that I will stay as long as I live; it is there that I wish to rest after my death. I am the minister of God and the offerer of sacrifices to Him; it may be that I must offer Him my life in sacrifice. And certainly He will be touched to see the altar on which bloody victims are not offered to Him stained by the blood of the priest.[64]

It seems that, in spite of everything, he died peacefully some years later, about 413.

We must quote at least one of his hymns,[65] in which the best of Neo-Platonic spirituality seems to pass into a Christianity that is profoundly religious and even mystical but refuses to condemn in any way the world whose beauty it admires and the culture which has made him able to recognize and express this beauty:

When the dawn appears,
When the light grows,
When midday burns,
When has ceased
The holy light,
When the clear night comes;
I sing your praises, O Father,
Healer of hearts,
Healer of bodies,

[64] The last words of his *Catastasis*; P.G., LXVI, 1573 G.

[65] A recent edition of these Hymns has appeared in the *Scriptores latini et graeci* of the Académie des Lyncées, Rome, second printing, 1949. Its author, Nicolas Terzaghi, has provided it with notes of great interest in reconstructing the culture of Synesius.

Giver of wisdom,
Remedy of evil,
O Giver also
Of a life without evil,
A life not troubled
By earthly fear—
Mother of distress,
Mother of sorrows—
Keep my heart
In purity,
Let my songs speak
Of the hidden source
Of created things;
And, far from God,
Never let me drawn
Into sin.[66]

The fact that the populace of Alexandria, instigated by Cyril's monks, assassinated Hypatia in the name of Christianity a few years after the death of her disciple, enables us to evaluate everything that a personality like that of Synesius of Cyrene expresses in the way of intimate protest against an asceticism turning to hatred of creation and culture. A progressive narrowing of Christian perspectives, encouraged perhaps by the overly negative formulations of mysticism, and, above all, a rigidifying of the monastic ideal corresponding to its institutionalization become too oppressive and undermined by its own success, worked together more and more, first to leave aside as outside Christianity, and then to consider as simply hostile to its spirituality, too many elementary human values and positive products of culture. The inevitable consequence was that when attention was once again given to these too greatly neglected factors, it easily veered towards a nostalgia—one, moreover, often full of illusions—for ancient paganism.

Tertullian and the Rejection of the World

Behind all the types of fanaticism infesting the development of Christian asceticism and endangering the true bearing of its mysticism is hidden a tendency radically opposed to Christianity, to refuse the world as a whole, going so far as to suspect creation and to confuse it, in fact if not in theory, with sin itself. In Manicheanism[67] this tendency, already visible and active throughout the majority of the heretical gnoses of the first centuries, was to

[66] *Fourth Hymn.*
[67] Our knowledge of this strange heresy has been renewed by the discovery of its sacred books, some years ago.

find an expression openly at odds with the Church and Christianity. But, particularly in African Christianity, with Montanism, this tendency had too profoundly affected the meaning of the ascetic struggle for nothing to remain of it, even after open ruptures and condemnations.

Tertullian, the first Latin Christian writer, long before monasticism, had proclaimed better than anyone else this refusal of the world. And he can so little be rejected *en bloc* as a mere heretic that St Cyprian, the first and one of the greatest among the Latin Fathers, never denied what he owed him....

For, undeniably, Tertullian[68] expresses, in the face of all forms of naturalism, of "humanisms" Christian or christianized, the reality essentially contained in the Christian faith which refuses to lend itself to any compromise with the world, which cannot make a definitive and final peace with it. His extremism, which increased with the years, is obvious. But the tendency he represents, the tendency which his final secession did not cause to disappear from the Church, can no more be neglected or stifled than can the opposite tendency.

Between the love of the world as the divine creation and the hatred of the world as the instrument of the devil, it seems that Christian spirituality can neither settle down in any compromise nor make a choice. Synesius of Ptolemais represents, perhaps, a type of bishop who is too amiable, too human; Tertullian, for his part, is a type of priest whom we can easily find completely odious. The fact remains that both the one and the other incarnate something that cannot be eliminated from authentic Christianity and that cannot be complacently assumed as maintained in a stable equilibrium with the opposite element.

Long before Tertullian became a Montanist or was even tempted by Montanism, he breathes the rigour, the all-or-nothing mentality which are the inevitable consequences of the fact that Christianity is not of this world. However scholarly, however permeated with Roman juridicism, he expresses with a unique force of conviction the fact that the Gospel is imprinted on humanity from without, as the image on a coin, and so can neither be reduced to humanity nor even adapted to it. The fascinating attraction exercised on him by Montanism, with its claims to have conserved or regained the immediate experience of the Spirit, is the normal consequence of this intuition: the break with the world presupposes, unless it is

[68] Here again, the most recent study is an article in the *Dict. de Théol. cath.* by G. Bardy. Tertullian's work fills the first three volumes of the *Latin Patrology* of Migne. The *Corpus* of Vienna has as yet produced only two volumes (about half of the work), XX (1890) and XLVII (1906).

to lose itself in nothingness, the possibility of an experience of the other world as real in its way as that of this world to which we are accustomed.

Whatever the brutality, the narrowness of expression, given by Tertullian to these two inseparable convictions, it cannot be denied that he caused an irreducible element of the Gospel to spring up again. Here is the secret of the enduring attraction that his positions exercised on the whole later history of Christianity, and the deepest reason why, in spite of his indisputable errors, he cannot not be considered a Father of the Church.

We must equally admit that the Roman juridicism, which he was the first to put at the service of Christian theology and spirituality—although it has revealed itself as an equivocal acquisition, particularly in relation to the concept of merit which he defined and acclimated in a definitive way—has rendered too many services to the Church ever to be completely eliminated.

Where Tertullian's influence has proved most harmful is, perhaps, in the kind of polemics which he succeeded only too well in acclimating in ecclesiastic circles: combining an abstract and completely *a priori* logic with the supposition (candid or implied) that the adversary must be a fool or else dishonest.[69]

He is also, it seems, the first example of that eccentricity, so common among very austere Christian spiritual writers and moralists, of wishing to legislate in minute detail, starting from abstract principles, on matters such as the particulars of feminine dress, which it would certainly seem better to leave to the evaluation of the *vir bonus experienta praeditus* (and being such is something which an ecclesiastic, by definition, must renounce).[70]

These are defects or eccentricities which should lead us back continually to the fact that, while Christ judges the world by his very appearance within it, Christians—even the most eminent by reason of the sacred functions that have devolved upon them—should equip themselves with great prudence before themselves undertaking to play this transcendent rôle.

69 The *De praescriptione haereticorum* is the perfect example of such masterpieces of apologetics which are the joy of those already convinced but are liable completely to alienate everyone else.

70 The *De cultu feminarum* is in this regard involuntarily funny—and yet this same vein of exhortation has been continually exploited in ecclesiastical literature through the ages.

XVIII

THE LATIN FATHERS: FROM ST AMBROSE AND ST JEROME TO ST AUGUSTINE

WE should recognize the fact that, if St Augustine had not existed, Latin patristics—apart from Tertullian—would be reduced to works of translation, popularization or of adaptation of Greek patristics. As to his spirituality in particular, St Augustine himself is unthinkable without the whole spiritual heritage of the Christian East. But the way in which he synthesized it, rethought it, is often so personal, so creative, that his work was to be the starting-point for a renewed tradition. This needs to be understood in a double sense, however. The heirs of Augustine, that is to say almost the whole Latin Middle Ages, benefited for a long time from this source of new riches. But these same riches also constituted for the Middle Ages a screen, as it were, that did not always facilitate their acquiring the whole treasure of primitive tradition.

In this regard, nothing is more significant than a work like St Augustine's *De Trinitate* and the great success it came to have. By far the greater part of it is an inventory and an exposition, amazingly fertile, of nearly all the elements of tradition. Yet the Latin Middle Ages too frequently retained only those scintillatingly brilliant pages in which St Augustine presents his own personal illustration of this immense treasure, what is called the psychological theory of the Trinity, explaining the procession of the Son and the Spirit by analogy with the operations immanent to the human soul, of intelligence and will, on the basis of memory. As an incomparable transmitter of an immense deposit, but a thinker of still more astonishing originality and fecundity, St Augustine, by reason of his very genius, sometimes became for his successors the greatest obstacle standing in the way of any "return to the sources". We see this very clearly in the very fleeting success of spiritual renewals such as that of the twelfth century, or the difficulties encountered by an intellectual revolution like that of Thomism, a century later.

The work of St Augustine had its necessary preface, so to speak, in the works of two very prolific authors, themselves not without originality. But here the part given to the transmission of the Eastern tradition to the West is by far the most considerable. We mean the writings and the influence of St Ambrose and St Jerome.

St Ambrose

Born at Treves, it seems, about 330, of a father with an important public position, but brought up at Rome, Ambrose[1] represents the perfect fusion of the highest qualities of a man of the Roman State and of patristic Christianity. It is well known how, as governor of Liguria and Aemilia and called upon to intervene in the episcopal election at Milan, it was he himself who was elected, even though he was only a catechumen. Highly conscious of his duty as teacher as well as pastor, this improvised bishop, under the direction of a learned priest, Simplicius, who also was to succeed him, built up for himself a Christian culture drawn from the best Greek sources and made himself their popularizer in the West. His exegesis was derived from Origen and Philo, his theology the fruit of an attentive reading of St Athanasius and Didymus of Alexandria, the Cappadocians and St Cyril of Jerusalem.

His *De officiis ministrorum* provided the clerics to whom he directly addressed himself with the first treatise on Christian morals, patterned on the *De officiis* of Cicero, but completely transforming it. Of capital importance for the future of spirituality in the West was the way in which he took up the Stoic distinction between *kathekon* and *katorthoma* (*officium medium* and *officium perfectum*), and radically modified its meaning. This is not precisely the distinction between commandment and counsel, but a distinction between the perfection by which we imitate the heavenly Father, particularly in his mercy, and an average justice, which is as it were the minimum without which we exclude ourselves from eternal life.[2] To understand how he could transform Stoic morality while using its concepts, we find the key in his introduction of the theme of eternal life, to which alone belongs full

[1] A bibliography may be found in Berthold Altaner's *Patrology*, tr. by Hilda Graef (Herder & Herder, New York, 2nd printing, 1960), pp. 445ff. His work as a whole is given in Migne, P.L., XIV–XVII. The *Corpus* of Vienna has only published a part of it. The most recent synthesis is: H. Dudden, *The Life and Times of St. Ambrose*, 2 vols., Oxford, 1935. See also P. Courcelle, *Recherches sur les Confessions de saint Augustin*, Paris, 1950.

[2] *De Officiis ministrorum*, I, xii, §§ 36ff.; P.L., XVI, 37 D and 38.

beatitude. Hence the predominance given to virtue over a happiness that is immediately attainable and then, finally, over what is merely useful.[3]

It is this same consideration of eternal life that sustained all Ambrose's teaching on virginity. This insistence on eternal life, however, must not be understood to the detriment of the present life, as if asceticism, for St Ambrose, had no immediate counterpart. Quite the contrary, it is asceticism precisely that allows eternal life to be as it were inaugurated in the present life. Eternal life is manifested here and now to the extent that the presence of Christ in us is manifest.

The Meaning of Virginity

For virginity is a heavenly gift: "Here it is as a stranger, there it is at home."[4] In fact, it was not so much that Christ proceeded from the virginity of Mary, as that virginity came down from on high, from the Trinity itself, with the Son of God who made himself man. "Virginity belongs to Christ: and not Christ to virginity."[5] The virgin consecrated to Christ participates, then, in being his bride, in the supernatural fruitfulness belonging to the whole Church.

> So it is that the Church is immaculate in her union, fruitful in her childbearing, virgin in her chastity, mother in her children. Therefore as a virgin, she brings us forth, having conceived not by a man but by the Spirit. As a virgin she brings us forth, not in the pain of her members, but in the joy of the angels. As a virgin she nourishes us, not with a material milk but with the milk [of doctrine] of which the Apostle speaks (1 Cor. 3. 2), the milk which nourished the still frail infancy of the people [of God]. What wife has more children than holy Church, who is a virgin in her sacraments, a mother in her people, whose fruitfulness Scripture attests by saying: "The sons of her who was abandoned are more numerous than those of her who has a husband" (Isaias 54. 1)? It is to us that she belongs who has no [earthly] husband, but a [heavenly] Bridegroom, that is the Church for all peoples, the soul for each of us, who, by the word of God, without its chastity being harmed, is united with the eternal Bridegroom, free of all injury, spiritually fruitful.[6]

To this real union with Christ, according to the image of Mary, within the Church, Ambrose applies, as his own special contri-

[3] *Ibid.*, III, II–VIII; P.L., XVI, 156ff.
[4] *De virginibus*, I, v, § 20; P.L., XVI, 205 B.
[5] *Ibid.*, §§ 21 and 22; col. 205 C–206 A.
[6] *Ibid.*, VI, § 31; col. 208 B. The quotations are 1 Cor. 3. 2 and Isaias 56. 1.

bution, the images of nuptial mysticism already developed by Origen, in explicating Psalm 44 (Hebrew 45) or the *Canticle of Canticles*.[7]

The *De Virginitate* returns to the waiting for Christ which gives asceticism its whole meaning,[8] wherein hope, based on faith, finds here and now in charity the encounter and the union that it awaits.[9]

On the reality of the presence of Christ manifested to the soul who, relying on faith, has left everything for him, Ambrose uses expressions that already foreshadow St Bernard whom, furthermore, they directly inspired:

> Thus we have everything in Christ. Let every soul go to Him, whether it be sick from the sins of the body, or pierced with the nails of some desire of this age; or still imperfect—provided that it goes forward in persevering meditation, or is already perfect in many virtues: everything is within Christ's power, and Christ is everything to us. If you wish to be healed of your wound, He is the healer; if you burn with fevers, He is the fountain; if you are laden with iniquity, He is justice; if you have need of help, He is strength; if you fear death; He is life; if you desire heaven, He is the way to it; if you flee from darkness, He is the light; if you seek food, He is nourishment. "Taste, then, and see how good is the Lord: happy the man who hopes in Him."[10]

In the whole of Christian antiquity, there is certainly no other synthesis so successful as that found in all St Ambrose's writings on virginity between the nuptial mysticism of Origen and the ascetic ideal taking shape at this period in the rapid spread of the monastic movement.

However, what is truly the proper characteristic of St Ambrose is the wonderful humanity, the comprehensive delicacy that shows itself in so many pages of his biblical commentaries. It is thanks to this quality, as much as to his deeply evangelical spirit, that his exaltation of asceticism, however enthusiastic it may be, never has anything of the inconscious crudity or, quite simply, the coarseness, which mar or deform it in other writers of the same period. This aristocrat, this man of affairs, whose ecclesiastical policy was of an uncompromising rigour, as soon as he touches on the things of the soul and on human feelings, reveals to us, in the gentleness of his Christian urbanity, as very few and perhaps

[7] *Ibid.*, beginning with ch. VII, § 36; col. 209 D ff.
[8] *De virginitate*, IX; P.L., XVI, 293.
[9] *Ibid.*, XIII, § 77; col. 299 CD.
[10] *Ibid.*, XVI, § 90; col. 305 C. The final quotation is Ps. 33. 9.

no other writers of antiquity, the *humanitas et benignitas Salvatoris*.[11]

St Jerome

The same thing can hardly be said of St Jerome.[12] Born a little before the middle of the fourth century of a wealthy family of Strido near Aquilea, he went to Rome to carry on his studies, probably in 359. He was passionately devoted to literature (Virgil, in particular), and from that time on began to collect books and even to copy them out himself. And he had other passions as well, which seem to have shown themselves with all the violence proper to his character. He was to find it difficult to forget them, and he seems, on his own statement, to have been one of those personalities who can find salvation only in flight and in a rude rejection of all satisfaction given to the senses. Almost immediately after his baptism by Pope Liberius, he threw himself into the ascetic life. He led it first in his home country, at Aquilea, in a group of monks and of clerics attracted to monasticism, in company with his compatriot and co-disciple, Rufinus, whom he had come to know in Rome. From then on, having been introduced by Rufinus to the library of the old and erudite ascetic, Paul of Concordia, he combined asceticism with intellectual activity. He had not as yet given up profane authors, but he plunged into the study of Christian writers, attracted above all, already, by those who commented on the Bible.

A first quarrel, doubtless with his family, decided him to make the journey to the East so as there to know and live the monastic life at its source. Settling at some distance from Antioch, in the desert of Chalcis, he remained there for three or four years. The theological disputes of the monks who were his neighbours disgusted him and he was strengthened by contact with them and opposition to them in his conviction that the mind of a monk ought to be occupied with study. But soon his continued reading of the classics involved him, it seems, in disturbing fancies, and he decided, under the inspiration of a supernatural dream in which he heard Christ say to him: " You are not a Christian but a

[11] See in particular the very beautiful text of the *De fide ad Gratianum*, V, v, § 56; P.L., XVI, 688, with its reflections on the mother of James and John (it is read in the Roman Breviary, where it is given under a false reference, on the Wednesday of the second week in Lent).

[12] His work as a whole is given in Migne, P.L., XXII–XXX; *Corpus* of Vienna, LIV–LVII. Jérôme Labourt has published four volumes of the *Letters*, Paris, 1945–54, a critical edition with a French translation. Fr Cavallera has published two excellent volumes on his life: *Saint Jérôme, sa vie et son œuvre*, Louvain-Paris, 1922. For a more complete bibliography, see Altaner, *op. cit.*, pp. 465ff.

Ciceronian", to leave them aside in order to devote himself exclusively to biblical studies. Not content with accumulating all the commentaries he could get hold of, he set himself, not without difficulty, to learn Hebrew, having become aware of the uncertainty of the Latin versions. Completely disgusted with the desert by the monks who were his neighbours, he went back to Antioch where he had already been welcomed by the second Evagrius (the Latin translator of the *Life of St Antony*), a priest who was a great gentleman, an ascetic and also his friend. After following Apollinarius' lessons in exegesis, and beginning to frequent Jewish circles so as to develop his knowledge of Hebrew and of *judaica*, in 379 he went to Constantinople where the presence of Gregory Nazianzen drew and held him. It was Gregory, it seems, who won him over to Origen.

In 382, Paulinius of Antioch (who had ordained him priest much against his will before leaving that city) took Jerome with him to Rome.

This second stay in Rome, even though it lasted only three years, became the focus of his whole life. For one thing, Pope Damasus made Jerome his secretary. Discovering the already considerable biblical knowledge of this man of letters, he launched him into the work of revising the current Latin versions, the work that finally resulted in the Vulgate. For another thing, Jerome set himself, like Ambrose at Milan but in quite a different way, to propagating asceticism among the Roman aristocracy. In a very personal fashion, he combined vehement lessons in asceticism with an initiation into the Bible dominated by the scientific interests, more philological than theological, which had become his own.

St Jerome and Asceticism

Monastic asceticism had already had a great vogue in Rome at the period when St. Athanasius, the biographer of Antony, had spent some time there, accompanied by two Egyptian monks, Isidore and Ammonius. Later on, Peter of Alexandria, under analogous conditions, had renewed this interest. We can easily see how the presence of a personality so out of the ordinary as St Jerome would have brought curiosity to a high pitch, arousing it not less, perhaps, by the oppositions he caused to spring up as by the conversions. This odd type of Scythian who, whatever he might say, had lost nothing of his refined literary culture and not much of his native rusticity, must in every way have been the centre of attention in this Roman society. His project of correcting the biblical texts familiar to everyone from time immemorial would have been enough to set against him a clergy poorly disposed from the outset towards this intruder by whom Pope Damasus had let himself be bewitched. The stinging criticisms multiplied by this rustic against men of the Church who flattered themselves as being also men of the world, could not have helped to smooth things out. The asceticism that he extolled without the least moderation put the final touch to all this when it was clear that many of the ladies of the highest society had more taste for it than for the fine manners of these same good priests.

What is amusing about all this, is that it was Jerome himself who was the first to be surprised and, doubtless, the most sincerely disturbed by this kind of success. His misogyny was not, as was that of the young Chrysostom perhaps, based on ignorance. But the lovely ladies of the Aventine, beginning with the devout patrician, Marcella, knew how to do away with his distrust, which still believed itself to be well on guard. During his first stay in Rome, he had frequented pretty entertainers and little dancing-girls, and the inflammable Dalmatian knew himself to be helpless in such company. But he had not imagined that his austere intellectuality would have paved the way for stronger-minded women to gain different, but no less easy, victories over what he comically called his shyness or his modesty.[13] Marcella had held in reserve for a long time all the difficulties raised, in her singularly masculine mind, by a wholly personal reading of Scripture. In the face of such a temptation, Jerome was not even capable of opposing the flight that he recommended to others. And once he had been taken captive by a circle of biblical enthusiasts (we may imagine it as being a very earnest one), it was no longer very difficult to obtain from him the spiritual direction these same enthusiasts had sought in vain among the local ecclesiastics.

Marcella was immediately joined by Paula, a widow who could be consoled only by the asceticism to which Marcella had already won her over. But it was above all the latter's daughter, Blesilla, also a widow even though only twenty years old, who was to conquer the good Jerome by her exceptional intelligence (for, at heart, as these ladies had immediately perceived, he was a kind and even gentle man). Paula's second daughter, Paulina, was under a husband's control, being the wife of the Senator, Pammachius. Uniting in a very touching way a hope of motherhood, always frustrated by tragic accidents, with a respect for continence, she persevered in the vain hope of bringing forth a whole nursery of budding ascetics. Finally she died of a miscarriage, and had the

[13] *Epist.* 137, 7.

consolation thereby of bringing her senator husband to lead the life of a monk in the world. This Pammachius, an old acquaintance of Jerome's who had formerly been his companion in his literary studies and doubtless also in the less innocent distractions that these studies occasioned, was almost the only masculine recruit worthy of mention for this ascetic biblicism in which Jerome so decidedly specialized during these years.

The premature death of the frail Blesilla, attributed by pious souls to the intemperately ascetic kind of life to which Jerome had imprudently introduced her, unleashed the storm against him. Fortunately he had the compensation, about this time, of finding himself entrusted with the education of Blesilla's little sister, Eustochium. He formed her from a very tender age, in view of a kind of scholarly virginity—a formation that included Hebrew lexicons and exhortations to chastity, so precise and detailed as to make a legionary blush, and constituted, we must admit, certainly a very unusual kind of feminine education.

But Pope Damasus had died in the meantime, and, as Duchesne puts it, "there came a Pharaoh who had not known Joseph" in the person of Pope Siricus. Thereupon Jerome hastily made preparations for his return to the Holy Land. Paula and Eustochium joined him there, with a crowd of friends, followers and servants for whom, after they had made devout pilgrimages throughout Palestine, as many as three monasteries were founded at Bethlehem. Asceticism could thus be practised without intermingling persons of different social status: the first example (of which others will be seen in the course of the centuries!) of a feminine monastery where the renunciation of all things did not include forgetting either one's birth or, oddly enough, inequalities of wealth, even though the object of these inequalities had been lost.

One after the other, Helvidius, the Milanese layman who cast doubt on the perpetual virginity of Mary—so much had the exaltation of virginity grated on his nerves, and Jovinian, still a monk but one who had also come, by way of reaction, to deny that ascetics had any right to a better part in eternity than married men, had, during these last years, extorted from Jerome as well as from Ambrose justifications of virginity.[14] But those of the former, quite different in this from those of the latter, turned so easily into pamphleteering against marriage that they aroused concern even in St Augustine. Although his optimism on this subject was more than restrained, he wrote in reaction his *De bono*

[14] On this whole affair, see the study of Pierre de Labriolle on the antimonastic movement in the West, pp. 361ff., of vol. III of *Histoire de l'Église* of Fliche and Martin, Paris, 1936.

conjugali. We can judge from this how these final ascetico-polemical feats of Jerome had contributed to make the Roman atmosphere unbearable to him!

Rufinus had already given Jerome an example of such an exodus to the holy places on the part of a learned ascetic drawing rich and aristocratic foundresses after him, by bringing Melania the Elder there a few years earlier. Having established her at Jerusalem on the Mount of Olives, he went on to Egypt to familiarize himself both with the oldest monastic traditions and with the Origenist traditions retained by Didymus, before returning to rejoin Melania's foundation in a permanent way. The example of this friend and the lady whom he directed certainly attracted Jerome and his ladies; but he did not foresee that his first reunion with Rufinus in the country of the Bible would set the stage for the fiercest theologico-ascetical match of his whole existence, between himself and his old friend.

St Jerome and the Bible

In the course of the preceding years and also, it seems, from the first days of his installation in Palestine, Jerome remained faithful to the line of studies that he had laid out for himself first with St Gregory Nazianzen and then with St Gregory of Nyssa, at Constantinople. The reading (and even the translation—an undertaking requiring real enthusiasm) of Origen had turned him with renewed zeal towards the philological search for the literal sense, and towards allegorical commentary on it for the nourishment of the ascetic life. But now in 393 the old Epiphanius of Salamis made on the Holy Land one of those raids disguised as a crusade which he made a habit of. He discovered the new Origenist heresy; he smelled it out everywhere among the monks of Palestine; and he went on to wear out John, the bishop of Jerusalem, harassing him in vain against Rufinus. Jerome, who at heart was completely closed to theology under its metaphysical aspects but who had already seen life made unbearable by suspicions like this at Chalcis, not to mention his troubles in Rome, went at once to purchase peace for himself by a pitiful recantation that scandalized the honest Rufinus. Burning what he had adored, and far worse, trying to forget that he had adored it in order to persuade others that he had not, Jerome came more and more to nurse a grudge against his friend's too retentive memory. Theophilus of Alexandria, for once doing the work of a peacemaker—in a quarrel, however, which he had done a good deal to inflame—finally reconciled them in 397.

But then Rufinus, who had returned to Italy, published a

translation of the *Apology for Origen* by Pamphilus, and another translation, much softened for greater safety, of the *Peri Archon*. Jerome limited himself at first to opposing this with a literal translation (with little touches here and there which discreetly but effectively aggravated things). But he compromised himself more and more completely on the side of Theophilus in the struggle against a heresy that was in great part an imaginary one, to the point of going so far, in 406, as to translate the pamphlet of the Alexandrian bishop against Chrysostom.

What an uproar when, meanwhile, in 401, Rufinus published his *Apologia*, in which he set out with irrefutable proofs everything that Jerome had done and written that immersed him in Origenism, if there was such a thing as Origenism, no less than Rufinus himself!

It must be admitted that the saintly ladies attached respectively to one or other of these two devout and learned writers did not contribute very energetically—to say the least—to make it easy for Jerome and Rufinus to engage in private explanations that might have cleared up the situation. Henceforth, up to the death of Rufinus in 410, the year of the sack of Rome, the ex-friend became "the pig", the "scorpion", the "hydra with a hundred heads"; and the unfortunate old Melania, whom Jerome twenty years earlier had extolled to the skies in his *Chronicle*, heard it said of her, by a gallant play on words, that her name itself testified to the blackness of her soul.[15]

Pope Anastasius, Siricus' successor, allowed Theophilus to extort from him a condemnation of Origen's work as vague as it was general, which earned him praises from Jerome strictly proportionate to these insults. Anastasius' own successor, Innocent, was far less easy to interest in this deplorable quarrel. In its beginnings, it had caused St Augustine to write a fine epistle in the interests of peace which, unfortunately, remained a dead letter so far as Jerome was concerned, except in its too well justified prophecies of the scandal the quarrel was to cause.

J. Steinmann has recently taken a great deal of trouble to give Jerome a better rôle in this sad affair.[16] He would have had his eyes opened, by his own reflections as well as by the upsetting inquisition of Epiphanius, as to the profound error of Alexandrian exegesis. From this moment, he would have been converted to the unique value of the literal sense, and he must be forgiven if, in the ardour of this conversion, he could hardly believe that he could ever have been involved in a heresy like allegorism.

[15] *Epist.* 132, 3.
[16] See Jean Steinmann, *Saint Jérôme*, Paris, 1958.

This special pleading, unfortunately, is not much more convincing than the counter-apologies of Jerome himself at war with Rufinus, where the vigour of his protestations vainly spends itself against the exact facts recalled by the latter. Certainly, Jerome had become more and more attached to the *hebraica veritas*, that is, to a first-hand study of the Hebrew text with all the resources which Jewish grammarians and exegetes could put at his disposal. But precisely in this, he is nothing but Origen's greatest disciple.

It is true, for example, that the sense of history, with him as with the best of the Antiochenes, developed with the years. But the fantasy of his applications does not seem to have been particularly restrained for all that, except by considerations of prudence not having much to do with the great principles involved.

The programme of a purely biblical education, which he laid out for the upbringing of the second Paula, the granddaughter of the first, indicates an Origenism of fact no less obvious than his own earlier works.[17] During these years 400–02, he counselled Laeta, the wife of Toxotius and Paula's fortunate mother, to immerse the new-born child as soon as possible in the Proverbs of Solomon, then in Ecclesiastes; the only difference between his and Origen's programme of introduction to the spiritual life being that he suggests going on at once to the book of Job and reserving the Canticle of Canticles for the summit of initiation. But this is, if one may say so, to correct Origen in the spirit of Origen.

This formation of the little Paula was, we can sense, even dearer to the heart of the aged Jerome than, twenty years earlier, had been that of Eustochium. For, in this instance, he was given the opportunity to form to the Bible and, of course, to asceticism, a disciple taken from the cradle and not simply from her adolescence. Soon he began to insist that the still small child should be sent out to him, so that, formed to singing the psalms disguised as children's songs, she would run no risk of puerile distractions other than those of memorizing biblical genealogies, and, still more alluring, being initiated into Hebrew. And actually, her parents had the weakness or the simplicity to send her to him: it is true that her grandmother, Paula, near the end of her earthly life, and Eustochium, her aunt, were at hand to welcome her. But if Jerome imagined that he could perfectly succeed in moulding to his liking a clay still so pliable, it seems that he was labouring under some delusions. He had written to Laeta, with more enthusiasm than realism, as Gorce well says:[18] "If you send us

[17] See the delightful book of Denys Gorce, *Saint Jérôme et la lecture sacrée dans le milieu ascétique romain*, Paris, 1925, pp. 225ff.

[18] *Ibid.*, p. 230.

Paula, I pledge myself to be her father and her nurse. I will carry her in my arms and, old as I am, I will aid in forming her first prattlings."[19] But, soon after, the death of the grandmother, followed unexpectedly by that of the aunt, left him alone in charge of the child. Then came these piteous reflections in another letter to the new Pope Boniface: "I have the little Paula on my back, a load which I do not know whether I can carry, only the Lord knows, may the future not deceive me",[20] even though he had written superbly about her, but before he saw her, that he felt himself to be "far more glorious than any philosopher of this world, having to instruct, not a king of Macedonia destined to perish by poison at Babylon, but a servant and a bride of Christ called to reign in heaven".[21]

The truth seems to be that this intractable and fantastic old man was to find in this little piece of womanhood someone to complete his own education, if we can judge from the singularly more humane advice that he finally gave, thirteen years later, about the formation of another little girl, Pacatula, who had just been born to his friend Gaudentius. She must, certainly, learn the psalms to begin her education, but, to make her take to the sacred Scriptures, it would also be proper (who would have thought it!) to promise her cakes, honey candies, and even jewels and dolls!"[22]

The Cappadocians acquainted us with a new type of monasticism: a monasticism which was erudite, but in which learning, to use Bossuet's phrase, was wholly turned towards loving. True, it was this same end that the monastic learning of Jerome had in view but, we must admit it was not afraid of a rather roundabout road to it. What is very true in Steinmann's thesis is that any mysticism was so congenitally foreign to Jerome that with him the "mystical" sense of Scripture turned into pure intellectual virtuosity. Without doubt he must have felt this in some vague way, and this is not unrelated to the instinct that drove him to an increasingly close historical study of the inspired writings.

Thereby, indisputably, he rendered the greatest possible service to monastic culture, in showing by his own example how the biblicism which nourished it must be, not some vague subjective reverie on the surface of the texts, but an objective food which cannot be found and assimilated without rigorous intellectual effort. In return, he was also to be, although certainly without intending it, the initiator of that scholarly monastic learning in which pure intellectual research runs the risk of detaching itself from the

[19] *Epist.* 107, 13.
[20] *Epist.* 153.
[21] *Epist.* 107, 13.
[22] *Epist.* 128, 1.

spiritual quest. Turned into a mandarin-like occupation, it rescued the monk from laziness, without thereby always assuring him peace. It was to prove fatal when men came finally to ask themselves whether such activity of the mind could lead more directly to the heavenly vision than a more humble kind of activity exercised in the world, in the service of the Church and of men. . . .

St Augustine

Born at Tagaste, on the present Algerio-Tunisian frontier, in 354, Augustine[23] belonged to a family not too well off, as is shown by the financial difficulties his father experienced in connection with Augustine's pursuing higher studies. This father remained a pagan until just before his death. His mother, Monica, on the other hand, was a Christian, and a fervent one, although at that time perhaps not one of the most enlightened. She was still more desolated at seeing her son fall into Manicheanism than into debauchery. At the age of sixteen, a year of inaction precipitated him into both, while waiting for the material means to carry on the literary studies that attracted him. After some years at Carthage, he completed these studies at Rome, more and more immersed in that philosophy the materialism of which seems to have been what attracted him, in the feverish sensuality to which, from his first youth, he had completely given in.

Less contradictorily than it seems, perhaps, it was the misconduct of the leaders of the sect that began to turn him against it. In fact, however absorbed in sensuality he may have been at that time, he was secretly discontented and aspired to something different. The circumstances that led him, once his studies had been completed, himself to become a teacher in the chair of rhetoric at Milan were to lead him providentially to what he had been seeking without as yet knowing what it was.

His mother, Monica, joined him there. She laboured to bring him to the faith, and it was most probably at her insistence that he went to listen to St Ambrose. Augustine himself tells us what touched him in the words of the Bishop of Milan; together with the skill

[23] The Maurist edition is at the basis both of Migne (P.L., XXXII–XLVII) and of Vivès (32 vols., published in Paris, beginning in 1872, with a French translation). Since 1887, the *Corpus* of Vienna has given a new critical edition of a good part of St Augustine's work.

Every attempt at a bibliography on such a subject is discouraging. Fr. Cayré, who has devoted so many and such worthy efforts to popularize the thought of St Augustine, and to whom we owe the very useful *Bibliothèque augustinienne* (texts, translations and notes, Paris, beginning in 1939) gives from pages 683ff. of his *Patrologie*, vol. I, Paris, 1953, well classified references that are very valuable. See also Altaner, *op. cit.*, pp. 487ff.

and the culture they manifested, it was what he calls Ambrose's gentleness: doubtless that outstanding humanity we mentioned. Augustine's mother, in the meantime, tried to get him married. But, far from urging him to regularize the more or less stable union he had contracted with a young woman (moreover a Christian, but about whom we know practically nothing more except that she was the mother of his son, Adeodatus), Monica tried to separate him from her. Undoubtedly she did not consider the girl as belonging to a class in keeping with the ambitions she still entertained for "the son of so many tears", according to the much-quoted saying of a good bishop.

Augustine seems to have let himself be persuaded to abandon the girl, with even less resistance than he put up against going to hear Ambrose. Was he really so indifferent to this woman? Nowhere in the Confessions do we find him admitting to any affection for her. It seems that, in his own case at least, he never saw anything but the physical in the union of the sexes. Later on, as bishop, he made loyal efforts to give a higher view of it to his Christians. But it must be admitted that the result was never to be very convincing.

The phases of his conversion, or of his return to the faith of his childhood revivified, were so progressive that it is difficult to determine the truly decisive moment. In 386, he considered himself again a catechumen. In 387, at the beginning of Lent, after the famous scene in the garden recounted in the *Confessions*, where he heard the child's voice repeating: *Tolle, lege* . . . as an inspiration from on high, he decided at last to be enrolled among the candidates for baptism. He received it at Easter, in the seclusion of Cassiciacum, living with some friends in a villa where they meditated together.

Christianity and Neo-Platonism in Augustine's Conversion

But here we have a new problem: what was Augustine really converted to? Prosper Alfaric has maintained that, in spite of the baptism taking place in the middle of all this, it was actually a conversion to Neo-Platonism and not to Christianity properly speaking.[24]

The fact is that Augustine does not conceal the decisive rôle played by the reading of the "Platonic" books that came into his hands in the course of that winter. And even at Cassiciacum, if we

[24] Prosper Alfaric, *L'évolution intellectuelle de saint Augustin*, Paris, 1918. Alfaric's thesis was immediately disputed by Ch. Boyer, *Christianisme et néo-Platonisme dans la formation de saint Augustin*, Paris, 1920. See also the work of Courcelle mentioned above, p. 456.

can judge from the *Soliloquies* and the other writings of that period, it cannot be denied that philosophical considerations, and of a philosophy at least very Platonizing, continued to absorb him. The very mysticism reflected in the pages of the *Confessions* during the months that followed was developed in the same atmosphere. Even the vision of Ostia, during a conversation with Monica a little before her death, can be read either in the one or the other register, Neo-Platonic or Christian.[25]

However, there are other factors to be taken into consideration: the part played in his conversion by the echoes of that of Marius Victorinus, the rhetor and philosopher thanks to whose translations Augustine read Plotinus—the rôle also of the *Life of Antony*, in which monasticism is presented in a light so purely that of the Gospel.... But two things above all must not be forgotten: however Neo-Platonic St Augustine's religion may seem during these years, it is still clear that his God is the Christian God: God the creator, the personal God.

The fact is, first of all, that Neo-Platonism providentially came Augustine's way at the time when he was again turning to the Church. To such an intellectual, of an instinctively philosophical turn of mind, but with an African sensuality which as much and even more than his Manichean lines of thought enclosed him in the sensible, this encounter was doubtless necessary so that the religion of the spirit could become acceptable to him, because comprehensible. But at this point the attraction of an ascetic, monastic Christianity is no less important. It has been noted that, once he was converted, Augustine thought of no possible form of life other than the ascetic. However, while this presented itself to him under the cloak of monasticism, it was not in monasticism properly speaking, not in any case under any of the forms it had taken hitherto, that he was to carry it out.

We should, at this central point in his education, try to put together all the factors which came into play at the same time.

Although his conversion was effected on the basis of an abandonment of Manicheanism, we should certainly not neglect the spiritual pattern it had left him with: a dualism of substantial oppositions, hence an all-or-nothing spirituality: to yield to the attractions of the flesh, or else completely to exclude them. Doubtless, monastic Christianity had given an entirely different motivation to this scheme: it showed him that a decisive sacrifice could be the surest way of regaining his freedom to follow Christ. Neo-Platonism, then,

[25] See in particular Paul Henry, *La vision d'Ostie*, Paris, 1930, and A. Hendrikx, *Augustins Verhältnis zur Mystik*, Würzburg, 1936.

came to be inserted just at this point to assure him that the renunciation of the sensible is the necessary, if not the sufficient, condition for a discovery and living apprehension of the spiritual.

All this is what is woven together in the famous prayer at the beginning of the *Soliloquies*:

> O God, creator of the universe, grant me first of all to pray rightly to You, and to make me worthy to be heard, and finally to be delivered . . . O God, Father of truth, Father of wisdom, Father of the true and sovereign life, Father of beatitude, Father of the good and the beautiful, Father of the intelligible light, Father of the awakening and the clarity of our spirit, Father of the promises that encourage us to return to You: I invoke You, O God of truth in whom, because of whom, and through whom everything is true that is true: God, Wisdom, in whom, because of whom, and through whom everything is wise that is wise; God, the true and sovereign life in whom, because of whom, and through whom everything lives that participates in the true and sovereign life: God, Blessedness, in whom, because of whom, and through whom everything is happy that is happy; God, Goodness and Beauty, in whom, because of whom, and through whom everything is good and beautiful that is good and beautiful; God, the intelligible light, in whom, because of whom, and through whom everything that is knowable has the intelligible light: God, whose kingdom is the world that our senses know nothing of. . . .
>
> O God, faith leads us to You, hope gives us trust in You, charity unites us with You. . . .
>
> . . . Grant, O Father, that I may seek You and keep me from error: that in my search nothing but You yourself will be presented to me. If it is true that I desire nothing other than You, grant, I pray, O Father, that I may find You. And if there still is in me any superfluous desire, be pleased to strip me of it Yourself, and make me capable of seeing You.[26]

The intellectual material used in the expression of this prayer is obviously wholly Neo-Platonic. And, according to what he confides to us in the *Confessions*, it was Neo-Platonism again that awakened in him the desire with which the prayer ends: to see God. But a biblical inspiration breathes throughout, not only in the focal mention of faith, hope and charity, but above all in the trustful expectation, the suppliant hope, of a personal intervention of God: of his grace. Hence the Platonic themes are arranged in a progression clearly evangelical, leading us from the graces of light to those of life and, in life, having us once again find the light, but a light which is no more that of this world.

[26] *Soliloquies*, I, I, II and VI; ed. Vivès, II, pp. 566ff.

The Vision at Ostia

In the account of the vision, or more precisely of the conversation at Ostia, in which the ninth book of the *Confessions* reaches its climax, the predominance of Christian themes is still more evident. But if we analyse the elements of its thought and the dialectic that guides them, the Neo-Platonic impression is perhaps even stronger.

> The day now approaching whereon she was to depart this life (which day Thou well knewest, we knew not), it came to pass, Thyself, as I believe, by Thy secret ways so ordering it, that she and I stood alone, leaning in a certain window, which looked into the garden of the house where we now lay, at Ostia; where removed from the din of men, we were recruiting from the fatigues of a long journey, for the voyage. We were discoursing then together, alone, very sweetly; and forgetting those things which are behind, and reaching forth unto those things which are before, we were enquiring between ourselves in the presence of the Truth, which Thou art, of what sort the eternal life of the saints was to be, which eye hath not seen, nor ear heard, nor hath it entered into the heart of man. But yet we gasped with the mouth of our heart after those heavenly streams of Thy fountain, the fountain of life, which is with Thee; that being bedewed thence according to our capacity, we might in some sort meditate upon so high a mystery.
>
> And when our discourse was brought to that point, that the very highest delight of the earthly senses, in the very purest material light, was, in respect of the sweetness of that life, not only not worthy of comparison, but not even of mention; we, raising up ourselves with a more glowing affection towards the "Self-same," did by degrees pass through all things bodily, even the very heaven whence sun and moon and stars shine upon the earth; yea, we were soaring higher yet, by inward musing, and discourse, and admiring of Thy works; and we came to our own minds, and went beyond them, that we might arrive at that region of never-failing plenty, where Thou feedest Israel for ever with the food of truth, and where life is the Wisdom by whom all these things are made, and what have been, and what shall be, and she is not made, but is, as she hath been, and so shall she be ever; yea rather, to "have been," and "hereafter to be," are not in her, but only "to be," seeing she is eternal. For to "have been," and to "be hereafter," are not eternal. And while we were discoursing and panting after her, we slightly touched on her with the whole effort of our heart; and we sighed, and there we left bound the first fruits of the Spirit; and returned to vocal expressions of our mouth, where the word spoken has beginning and end. And what is like unto Thy Word, our Lord,

who endureth in Himself without becoming old, and maketh all things new?

We were saying then: If to any the tumult of the flesh were hushed, hushed the images of earth, and waters, and air, hushed also the poles of heaven, yea the very soul be hushed to herself, and by not thinking of self surmount self, hushed all dreams and imaginary revelations, every tongue and every sign, and whatsoever exists only in transition, since if any could hear, all these say, We made not ourselves, but He made us that abideth for ever—If then having uttered this, they too should be hushed, having roused only our ears to Him who made them, and He alone speak, not by them but by Himself, that we may hear His Word, not through any tongue of flesh, nor Angel's voice, nor sound of thunder, nor in the dark riddle of a similitude, but might hear Whom in these things we love, might hear His Very Self without these (as we two now strained ourselves, and in swift thought touched on that Eternal Wisdom which abideth over all);—could this be continued on, and other visions of kind far unlike be withdrawn, and this one ravished, and absorb, and wrap up its beholder amid these inward joys, so that life might be for ever like that one moment of understanding which now we sighed after; were not this, Enter into thy Master's joy?[27]

This text has undergone so many commentaries and such contradictory ones that we cannot help feeling some hesitation at undertaking one. We shall simply try to disengage the various lines of thought that compose its substance, at first sight so smooth, so unified.

What could be more Christian than the general pattern of this elevation? Creatures evoke the thought of God, precisely as Creator. Then the soul collects itself in expectation of the personal word by which He will reveal Himself to it, as He from whom all things proceed but who transcends them all, the soul as well as everything else. . . .

This is true, but the way in which the transition is carried out, it must be recognized, directly recalls the Plotinian "purification". It is the soul itself, we should notice, that causes all beings, all distinct thoughts, to fall silent. . . . Then, it seems, as the mere converse of this abolition of the multiple and the imperfect, the Presence is to be revealed which everything else witnesses to and also veils. . . .

If we had only texts like these, this contemplation at Ostia, it must be admitted, would be no less capable of being read in the sense of a Neo-Platonism borrowing Christian expressions as in

[27] *Confessions*, I, IX; ed. Vivès, II, pp. 266ff. (The translation given here is taken from the classic one by Edward Pusey, available in the *Pocket Library* editions.)

that of a Christianity formulated in terms taken from Plotinus. The impression is confirmed in the first sense if we compare with the text we have just read the graph of the progress of the soul towards God as described in the *De quantitate animae* almost immediately after Augustine's baptism.

The De Quantitate Animae and the True Sense of Augustinian Mysticism

In this treatise, we see how the soul is progressively purified by locating itself in turn at seven successive levels of its activity, passing from the simple animation of the body to sensibility, then to intellectual knowledge, whence comes virtue, then the interior repose which this assures, preparing it to enter into the divine light. When its eyes are accustomed to this light, then it is seized by contemplation, entirely immersed in God and forgetful of everything else. The desire to die dominates it, so that nothing will ever be able to separate it or distract it from God in whom it is henceforth established in a permanent way, but whose presence and whose beauty can be perceived here below only in an evanescent manner.[28]

Later on, however, Augustine expresses in quite different terms the same experience of the experimental discovery of God and of our union with Him. Henceforth, he uses completely biblical expressions to characterize this quest and its end. Must it be said, as has so often been said and repeated, that this is merely the product of a slow working towards a Christian manner of expression, which should not deceive us as to the nature of an experience that remained essentially unchanged? It seems to us that this interpretation involves a double misunderstanding. In the first place, it neglects the presence—so clear even in the first and most philosophic expressions of Augustinian mysticism—of those themes so profoundly foreign to Neo-Platonism; of God the creator, of the God who draws the soul to speak to Him with no intermediary. But what proves that from the outset these themes actually are the support and constitute as it were the impulse of all the rest is the way in which later they are so naturally, so progressively, completely absorbed, completely assimilated.

We should take into account, it seems, the ignorance of the young Augustine, even after his conversion, with regard to the whole biblical and traditional deposit. On the other hand, he was saturated with Neo-Platonic thought, and it would be only too

28 *De quantitate animae*, xxxiii, 70–26; ed. Vivès, III, pp. 80ff.

natural that he would seek and find in it a first expression of his spiritual experience. Yet, however this may have been facilitated by the teaching of Platonizing spirituality, from the outset, as we see it, this experience was set in motion by the bringing forward in the preaching of Ambrose reawakening all the memories of his early Christian education, of themes basically biblical and evangelical. To the extent to which Augustine familiarized himself with the Bible and with Christian writers, then, it was these themes that dominated him to the point of more or less eliminating all the others.

The question that immediately arises after this is, therefore, if, as we see it, the mystical experience of Augustine was authentically Christian, how could Neo-Platonism have been so easily capable of providing him with an expression of it? This gives us a last opportunity to repeat: this fact simply witnesses to what, in Plotinus particularly but also in the whole Neo-Platonic school, and even in its opposition to Christianity, actually comes from Christianity. When we study Neo-Platonism in a Christian like Augustine who, indisputably, was influenced by it, it reveals its true nature perhaps better than in mixed cases, like that of Pseudo-Dionysius. In the latter, we would hesitate to decide what he received from the Neo-Platonic tradition, what he had in common with it by way of a language and representations wherein Christianity and Neo-Platonism meet in a common development, and what, if not Dionysius himself, at least his immediate Christian predecessors themselves may have contributed to Plotinus or to his disciples. But it is obvious that Augustine received a great deal from "Platonists" as he calls them, without being able to give them anything. And so his example shows the extent to which the whole of Neo-Platonic "mysticism" is obscurely oriented towards the meeting with a personal God, attracted, so to say, by the pre-perception of a supra-cosmic being of whom pristine Hellenism never seems to have had the slightest suspicion. However Greek, therefore, all the elements may be from which Neo-Platonism is constructed, what motivates the construction is certainly no longer Greek. There is no cause for astonishment, then, that such a synthesis should have lent itself so easily to a transfer: in fact this transfer is only its completion or the making explicit of what was already present, but as it were latent.

In this respect, the same thing is true of Neo-Platonism as of those pagan religions that Julian tried to galvanize into life: to make them possible rivals of Christianity, the only means was somehow or other to infuse into them some Christian elements. But when these latter were not immediately devitalized, they could not but lead back to their biblical source, as in the case of Plotinus read and relived by Augustine.

Augustine's Mysticism in the Enarrationes

We can judge the truth of this last statement from the final expression of his mysticism which Augustine gives, for example, in the *Enarrationes in Psalmos*, after he had gone back to Africa, where he became a priest in 391 and then Bishop of Hippo, four years later. Fr Maréchal has rightly pointed out, from the point of view which is ours at the moment, the exceptional importance of the *Enarratio* on Psalm 41 (42 in the Hebrew).[29]

> ... "As the deer longs for the watersprings, so, O my God, my soul longs for You." Who is it, then, who speaks in this way? If we wish it, it is we ourselves who speak this language. And what need have you to ask who is speaking, when it is within your power to be him whom you ask about? Yet it is not one man alone: it is one body, the body of Christ, the Church. Now, this holy desire is not found in all who enter into the Church; yet, let those who have tasted the sweetness of God and who, in this chant, recognize this sweetness that they love—let them not believe themselves alone in tasting it, and let them be persuaded that a like seed is spread throughout the field of the Lord, through the whole world, and that this word: "As the deer longs for the watersprings, so, O my God, my soul longs for you" is that of a certain Christian unity.

This first paragraph is of the very greatest importance because of the way in which it locates Augustine's mysticism within the Church, making it the realization by certain of the faithful, precisely because they see themselves as integrally faithful, of the aspiration which is that of the whole Church. This invites us to locate what follows in the context of all the *Enarrationes*: a dialogue between the Church and Christ, between the Church as the Bride and Christ as the Bridegroom, between the Church considered as speaking in the Psalms as the body of Christ, and Christ as the Head of this body.

> And we would not be deceived [St Augustine continues] if we believe [this word] to be the expression of the desire of catechumens, hastening to attain the grace of holy baptism. This is why this Psalm is solemnly chanted, so that they may long for the font of the remission of sins, as the deer longs for the watersprings. May this be true, and may the truth of this interpretation

[29] See J. Maréchal, *Études sur la psychologie des mystiques*, vol. 2, Paris, pp. 180ff.

> be given a solemn consecration in the Church. However, my brothers, it seems to me that baptism itself is not enough to arouse in the faithful such an ardent desire. But if they realize the exile wherein their life must be passed and the place which they are to attain, then perhaps they will be seized with such great fervour.

In other words, what baptism causes us to possess, we must desire to make our own, and this cannot be done fully except in eternity. The mysticism of Augustine the bishop is made up wholly of this desire to assimilate, to interiorize, everything that has been given us at baptism. This is what he expresses a little further on in the same *Enarratio* by contrasting the desire to drink of these waters with the desire simply to bathe in them.

What follows immediately after the preceding paragraph, by means of an allegorical exegesis of the name of the "sons of Core" explained as "the sons of Calvary", explains how the desire in question is indeed the desire proper to those who have been reborn by the virtue of the Cross:

> The children of the Bridegroom, the children of His Passion, the children ransomed by His blood, the children of His cross, who wear on their foreheads what the enemies of Christ planted on the place of Calvary—these call themselves the children of Core: this psalm is sung to them for the sake of understanding. Arouse yourselves, then, to the desire to understand. What understanding shall we have of it? What are we to comprehend in singing this psalm? I dare to answer: "The invisible perfections of God have become visible, since the creation of the world, by the understanding of them which is given us by the things that He has made."[30] O my brothers, be eager with me, share with me this desire; let us love together; let the same thirst devour us; let us run together to the spring of understanding. Without speaking, then, of that spring to which those aspire who are to be baptized for the remission of their sins, let us, who are already baptized, desire like the deer, desire the spring of which it is said in another passage of Scripture: "For in you is the fountain of life", for God Himself is the fountain and the light, because "in Your light we shall see light".[31]

Thanks to the mystery of the Cross into which, as St Paul says, we have been engrafted by baptism, we are now, therefore, to attain to that inseparable light and life the source of which is in God. Augustine again insists on the fact that—once we are in the Church—it is all together, as supporting one another, that we are

[30] Rom. 1. 20. [31] Ps. 35. 10.

to tend towards, and help one another to tend towards, that source. Then he resumes his basic theme:

> To say: "As the deer longs for the watersprings, so, O my God, my soul longs for you" is the same thing as to say: "My soul thirsts for the living God". But "what is this thirst?" When shall I come and when shall I appear before the face of God? I am thirsty on my journey, I am thirsty as I run: I shall be satisfied when I arrive. But "when shall I come?" What is swift for God is slow in coming for him who desires. When shall I come and when shall I appear before the face of God? This same desire causes him to cry out, in another psalm: "One thing have I asked of the Lord; and I will ask it of Him again: to live in the house of the Lord all the days of my life."[32] And why? "To contemplate, he says, the joy of the Lord". "When shall I come and when shall I appear before the face of God?"

This thirst for the manifested presence of God is, then, what animates the Christian in the present life, and makes it impossible for him to settle down in any of the joys of this world.

> "And each day they say to me: where is your God?" What if this question is put to me by a pagan, I cannot say to him in turn: "Where is your God?" For he can show me his god by pointing to him. He holds his fingers out towards some stone and says: "There is my God! . . . Where is your God?" If I laugh at that stone and the man who has shown it to me begins to blush, he turns his eyes from the stone, looks at the sky and, perhaps, pointing out the sun, says again "There is my God! . . . Where is your God?" He finds what he can show to the eyes of the body: but as for me, it is not that I have nothing to show him; he does not have the eyes by which he could see what I would show him. He can indeed point out the sun, which is his God, to the eyes of my body, but with what eyes can he perceive Him who made the sun?

Here, undeniably, we touch on one of the constants in Augustine's religious life, as he went from Manicheanism to Christianity by way of Neo-Platonism. Buried in the carnal, he preserved the living aspiration towards the divine vision, but he then sought to find this vision in a luminous apparition, like that promised by the Manicheans to their adepts. Neo-Platonism made him understand that the light of God is nothing like this. But then, as he himself does not fail to bring up later on in his *Retractationes*, he was certainly tempted to let himself be deceived and to believe that it was enough to close his eyes to sensible lights for the intelligible light to become manifest. Fully christianized, he came to recognize

[32] Ps. 26. 4.

the futility of this too facile spiritualism. Then he gives the following image of the quest for God and of his imperfect discovery of it here below—an image much more subtly worked out :

> Since the invisible wonders of God are understood and perceived by the aid of the visible wonders that He has created, what shall I do to find my God? I will consider the earth: the earth that has been created. Great is the beauty of this earth, but the earth has someone who made it. Great are the marvels of seeds and generations; but all these things have a creator. I contemplate the immensity of the seas surrounding the lands; I am astounded, I admire them, and I seek for Him who made them. I lift my eyes to the sky, towards the magnificence of the stars; I admire the splendour of the sun that can produce the daylight, and of the moon that consoles the darkness of night. All these things are wonderful; they are worthy of all praise or, rather, they confound our mind; they no longer belong to the earth, these are already things wholly of heaven. And yet my thirst has still not been quenched: I admire these beauties, I praise them, but I thirst for Him who made them. I return to myself, I seek what I am, the self that examines all these wonders; I find that I possess a body and a soul: a body that I must guide, a soul that is to guide me; a body to serve, a soul to command. I perceive that my soul is something superior to the body and, in the faculty that carries out these different quests within me, I recognize my soul and my body; and yet I recognize that it is with the aid of the senses of my body that I have examined all the things that I have gone through.

At this point, very typically Augustinian, the transcending of the material in the spiritual takes the specific form of an interiorization.

> ... The eyes are members of the flesh; they are the windows of the spirit: the spirit, that sees through these windows, is within: and, when it is absent, absorbed by some thought, the eyes are useless even though open. My God, who made all these things that my eyes see is not to be sought by these same eyes. It must be, then, that the spirit sees something by itself ... or something that I see interiorly? What thing has no colour, no sound, no smell, no taste; what is neither hot nor cold, nor hard nor soft. If someone says to me, for instance, what colour is wisdom! ... There is, therefore, something that is seen by the spirit, the ruler and guide of the body that it inhabits; something that it perceives, not with the eyes of the body, nor with the ears, nor the nostrils, nor the palate, nor the mouth, but by itself and always better by itself than by means of its servant. It is certainly like this, for the spirit sees itself and it sees itself as soon as it knows itself. And never in order to

see itself does it need the help of the eyes of the body: rather it withdraws itself from all the senses of the body as constituting so many impediments the noise of which troubles it; and it withdraws within itself to see itself in itself, and to know itself in itself.

But here we come to a decisive turning-point, where Augustine the Christian very consciously takes precedence over Augustine the Neo-Platonist. Can the soul see God simply by seeing itself, doing away with everything corporal that limits and distracts it? Not at all.

> But, is the God for whom it seeks something like its own spirit? Certainly, we can see God only by means of the spirit; and yet, God is not what our own spirit is. For the spirit of the Prophet seeks something that is God, so that, having found Him, he will no longer be exposed to the scorn of those who say to him: "Where is your God?" He seeks an unchangeable truth, a substance that nothing can alter. And our spirit is not like this: it undergoes change and it progresses; it knows and it is ignorant; it remembers and it forgets; and now it sees something and now it does not see it. This instability does not exist in God....
>
> Seeking my God in visible and corporal things, and not finding Him; seeking His substance in myself, as if He were something similar to what I am, and not finding Him; I perceive that my God is something superior to my soul. Then, to succeed in attaining to Him, "I meditated on these things and I poured out my soul above myself". How, indeed, can my soul attain what it must seek above itself if my soul does not pour itself out above itself? If it remains within itself, it will see nothing but itself, and in itself it will not see its God.... "I have poured out my soul above myself" and there remains nothing more to lay hold of other than my God. Indeed, it is there, it is above my soul, that the house of God is. There He dwells, thence He sees me, thence He created me, thence He rules me, thence He sees my needs, thence He arouses me, thence He calls me, thence He directs me, thence He guides me, thence He will lead me to the port.

God being above the soul itself, it seems, then, that it can find him only if he himself comes to it, to lead it to himself. This is what is shown in what follows. God has as it were to leave his inaccessible dwelling to make himself a tabernacle on earth, the Church. In this tabernacle, he himself prepares the way for our final ascent to his heavenly mansion.

> For He who possesses, beyond the highest heavens, an invisible mansion, has also a tent on the earth. His tent is His Church, still on pilgrimage. It is here that we must seek Him, because in the tent we shall find the way that leads to the house.

Indeed, when I have poured out my soul above me, why have I done so? "So that I may enter into the place of the tabernacle," I will enter into the place of the tabernacle, the wonderful tabernacle, even to the house of God.... The tabernacle of God on earth is made up of faithful men. I admire in them the way in which their members are subject to them, because sin in no way rules in them to enslave them to the desire of evil, and because they have not given over their members to sin as the instruments of iniquity, but they offer them to the living God through their good works.[33]

...Thus I admire these virtues in the soul, but I am as yet only in this place of the tabernacle. I pass on, and however wonderful this tabernacle may be, I am amazed when I arrive at the house of God....

How is this transition to come about? Augustine tells us by referring to a phrase from Psalm 72. 16.

This is what the prophet knew in the sanctuary of God; he received the understanding of the last times. He went up into the tent, and from there he went on to the house of God. While he admired the saints, who are as it were the different parts of this tent, he was led to the house of God, by following the attraction of a certain sweetness, of I know not what secret delight; as if there escaped from the house of God the delicious sounds of some ravishing instrument: he went into the tent when, hearing this interior melody the sweetness of which attracted him, he set himself to follow what he had heard, by withdrawing himself from all the noise of blood and flesh, and he arrived even at the house of God. He himself recounts both his journey and this mysterious leading; as if he had said to him: You admire the tent that is on earth; how did you attain even to the secret of the house of God? "In the midst, he says, of the songs of joy and praise, in the midst of the concerts that celebrated the joy of feasting." When, amongst us, some splendid feast is celebrated, it is customary to place in front of the house, instrument-players, singers, or musicians, employed at feasts to arouse the guests to pleasure. And when we hear them, what do we say as we go by? What is happening here? And someone tells us that there is some feast... a birth, or a wedding is being celebrated. So the songs do not seem to us out of place, and pleasure finds its excuse in the feast being celebrated. In the house of God, it is a continual feast. But here nothing transitory is celebrated. The eternal feast is celebrated by the choir of the angels, and the face of God, seen openly, causes a joy that nothing can alter. This feast day has no beginning; no end that can terminate it. From this eternal and perpetual feast escapes I know not what sound that echoes sweetly in the ears of the heart, provided that no human noise be

[33] Rom. 6. 12.

intermingled with it. The harmony of this feast enchants the ear of the man who goes into that tent, and who contemplates the marvels that God has wrought for the redemption of the faithful; and it draws the deer towards the watersprings.

If we really understand these images, it is, therefore, the experience of life in the Church, of effective participation in the victory of grace over sin within us, that equally awakens within us some pre-perception of eternal life, where we shall be satisfied with the face of God contemplated unveiled. How this is to come about is explained to some degree, without dissipating its mystery, by reflecting on these evanescent experiences of it.

But, my brothers, because we are journeying far from God, so long as we are in this mortal[34] body; because this body devoted to corruption, weighs on the soul, and because this earthly dwelling lowers the spirit troubled by its many thoughts;[35] even though we sometimes attain, by going forward under the impulse of the desire that dissipates the images around us, to hear these divine sounds, in such a way as to grasp, by our efforts, something of the house of God; yet, overcome by the weight of our weakness, we soon fall back into our usual ways and we let ourselves be involved in our customary life. And in the same way as in approaching God we have found joy, so in falling back to earth, we find reason for groaning.... Here we are—we who have already enjoyed a certain interior sweetness; who have, in the highest part of our spirit, been able to perceive, even though scantily and as it were by stealth, something unchangeable: "Why then do you still trouble me?" Why are you sad, O my soul? Indeed, you have no doubt of your God. You do not lack a reply to make to those who say to you: "Where is your God?..." Already I feel as it were a foretaste of that which is unchangeable; why do you still trouble me? "Hope in God." And his soul answers him in secret: Why then do I trouble you, if not because I am not still in the abode in which that sweetness is tasted, to the heart of which I had been already transported, but as if in passing? At the present time, do I drink at that spring without fearing anything? At the present time, do I fear no scandal? Am I, here and now, in safety against all my lusts, as if they were put down and conquered? The demon, my enemy, does he not spy on me? Every day does he not hold out to me his treacherous snares? And you do not want me to trouble you, when I am in the midst of the world, still exiled from the house of God! Then, to his soul that troubles him and gives him an account, as it were, of that trouble, in exposing to him the evils with which the world is filled, he answers: "Hope in God." In waiting, dwell here below in your hope. "For the hope of the things we see is no

[34] 2 Cor. 5. 6.

[35] Wisdom 9. 15.

longer hope; but if we hope in what we do not see, we wait for it in patience."[36]

"Hope in God" Why: Hope? "Because I shall confess to Him." What will you confess to Him? That He is my God, the salvation of my countenance". My salvation cannot come from myself; I say it, I will confess it: "My God is the salvation of my countenance. . . ."[37]

Thus, finally, these foretastes of the eternal beatitude that we can have here below, living in the Church and living the life of holiness that Christ communicates to her—these foretastes simply nourish hope, a hope, that is, of attaining to the full and stable possession of what we know here below only in an ephemeral way and still from afar, a hope that no longer rests on ourselves, but only on God.

Mysticism and Grace of Charity

The Pelagian controversy evidently led Augustine to insist on this last note. And thus his mysticism appears more and more clearly as being simply our becoming conscious of grace, of its sovereignty in our salvation, a consciousness brought about to the degree to which we give ourselves up to this grace that solicits us. At the same time, Augustine was led to explain what there could be in common between our Christian experience here below and the experience of heaven. He affirms that it is charity, which for him is simply grace as penetrating us, assimilating us to the very love with which God, precisely, has graced us.

It was doubtless his meditation on another conflict with which, as bishop, he was taken up for a long time—the Donatist affair—that gave him the fully developed vision of this charity which characterizes the works of his maturity, like the *Enarrationes* or the *Tractatus in Johannem*. His final and deepest perceptions, which are at the same time the most profound view he has left us of his conception of Christianity itself, are set down in the *De Trinitate*. At the end of his life, in the face of the breakup of the Roman empire, his anxious meditation on human history, in the *De Civitate Dei*, is resolved in the conviction of the final victory of that city which has charity as its foundation over the city which has tried to build itself up on concupiscence. It was then that he found the ultimate definition of these two loves, the conflict between which dominates the history of the world and the history of each man:

> Two loves have made these two cities: the earthly, the love of self carried so far as contempt of God; but the heavenly, the love of God carried so far as contempt of self.[38]

[36] Rom. 8. 24. [37] *Enarratio in Ps. 51.*
[38] *De civitate Dei*, XIV, xxviii; Vivès, XXIV, p. 240.

St Augustine's own experience after his conversion, without doubt, taught him that the hope of a perfection accessible here below, in a fixed contemplation of the one divine beauty, was a chimera by which Neo-Platonism had charmed him, but of which a realistic Christianity should have relieved him. His reaction against Pelagius and his disciple Celestius, and then against their rather paradoxical but unusually penetrating epigone, Julian of Eclanum, was therefore a very lively one, from the very fact that it led him to make the first retractations which he felt to be a duty imposed upon him.

The substantially concordant information furnished us by St Augustine and St Jerome as to the ideas of Pelagius are not, perhaps, sufficient proof of the complete objectivity of their interpretation. For instance, they quarrel with Pelagius and his disciples for teaching that all sins are equally mortal; but we now know that the letter to the virgin Demetriades, insisting on the possibility and the necessity of a constant progress, attributed to St Augustine for a long time and considered particularly characteristic of his doctrine[39] ... is actually by Pelagius. This fact alone invites us to introduce some nuances into our understanding of a doctrine which its adversaries, as so often happens, may have viewed more in relation to the consequences that they saw flowing from it than in its original tenor.

Pelagius,[40] a Breton monk, energetic and austere, began simply by rigidifying the theme traditional in the Greek theories of asceticism which we have seen expressed particularly by St Gregory of Nyssa: asceticism and its fruits are within the power of every man, provided that he makes uses of his free will; if we make an effort on our part, relying on faith, God will not allow this effort to be in vain. From the idea that God neither asks nor could ask the impossible, Pelagius drew the consequences that, if man takes the ascetic means necessary to dominate his passions, he can attain the condition of sinning no more. Having acquired *apatheia* by his own powers, the ascetic—that is to say, every serious Christian—will then merit by himself the crown promised by God to the victor.

Forced to the wall, the Pelagians had no hesitation, it seems, in declaring that Adam's sin had left human nature unchanged in such a way that it had only to follow the example given by Christ in order to be saved. To Augustine's eyes, on the contrary, it was obvious that concupiscence, as we all experience it, can be nothing

[39] In ed. Vivès, VI, pp. 339ff.

[40] On Pelagius and the Pelagians, see the section by G. de Plinval in vol. IV of *Histoire de l'Église*, by Fliche and Martin, Paris, 1937, pp. 79ff.

other than a consequence of original sin, not to be uprooted without an interior intervention of divine grace.

But what is concupiscence? It is the disordered inclination of fallen man towards the pleasure of the senses and, more particularly, carnal pleasure. This disorder, according to Augustine, is manifested on the occasion of every act of generation, and thus it is that original sin is transmitted together with life itself.[41]

All asceticism consists in the struggle against concupiscence.[42] This is a combat that can know no relaxation, that cannot be halted; to cease to make progress is infallibly to regress. Here, let us repeat, Augustine is quite in accord with Pelagius. Where he separates from him is on the necessity for divine grace, without which, after original sin, this struggle is condemned to remain a vain one.

Doubtless, all the acts of fallen man, without grace, are not mortal sins. But he cannot for long avoid falling into such faults, and always something sinful is intermingled even in his apparently good acts. It is in this sense that man's freedom, after sin, no longer exists. His free will, that is, the radical power of choosing between good and evil, is not destroyed: grace will reanimate it; but, without grace, it remains ineffective, incapable of effectively willing the good, which is the only true liberty.[43]

These first declarations, against Pelagius or Celestius, frightened a number of ascetics: both at Hadrumetum, in Africa, and in the monasteries of Lérins and Marseilles, inspired by Cassian. Doubtless, they said, man cannot overcome sin without grace, but still, for grace to act in him, he must open himself to it. Must there not remain in man, even after original sin, an ineradicable capacity to turn himself towards God? At least a desire for faith, making him accessible to the grace offered him?[44]

This objection arose, evidently, from the obvious opposition between the language now used by Augustine and the language already made customary by Gregorian synergism. More profoundly, these monks were motivated by a fear, which was not to prove entirely chimerical, that the conclusion would be drawn from Augustine's formulations that, since all efforts are vain, there is nothing to do but remain passive under the action of grace.

Augustine tried to reply to the criticism of those who are usually called semi-Pelagians, at the same time as to the dangerous interpretations of his own teaching which they were objecting to. On the

41 *De peccatorum mer. et. rem.*, II, XXIII, 37; Vivès, XXX, p. 88.
42 *Contra Julianum op. imp.*, II, 47; Vivès, XXXII, p. 26.
43 *Contra 2 epist. pel.*, i, 5: Vivès, XXXI, p. 6.
44 *De gratia et libero arbitrio*, V; Vivès, XXXI, pp. 474ff.

one hand, grace is purely gratuitous; it cannot be merited as such. The first thought of conversion, the first inclination to return to God, comes from him, just as the perfect carrying out of the good. But, on the other hand, grace itself solicits our co-operation and makes this possible. Far from grace suppressing the necessity for the spiritual combat, for effort and progress, it is grace that underlies them.

The first grace, in fact, is that which urges us to prayer. And it is in prayer that we gain the power of acting and, finally of persevering in grace.

So long as we are here below, even with grace, we cannot certainly avoid all venial sin, for:

> We shall not have perfect health, until we have perfect charity . . . but we shall have perfect charity when we see God as He is.[45] For there will be nothing more that can be added to our love when we have attained vision.[46]

Is there, then, no perfection here below? Only a relative one:

> Be always discontented with your state if you wish to attain a more perfect one. For as soon as you are complacent about yourself, you cease to make progress. If you say: I have attained perfection, you will have lost everything.[47]

And here is his final word:

> It is the property of perfection to recognize that it is imperfect.[48]

This progress, however, is not simply a negative one: merely the progressive disappearance of sins. Doubtless Augustine defines it as such when he says:

> To advance without stain may perhaps be said without absurdity of the man who is not yet perfect, but who runs without reproach towards perfection itself, avoiding (*carens*) damnable sins and not neglecting to purify himself by almsgiving from venial sins themselves.[49]

But the mention of almsgiving, for him the special manifestation of charity, shows clearly that our progress towards purity, by an increasing mastery exercised over concupiscence, can only be a progress in charity.

[45] 1 John 3. 2.
[46] *De perfecta justitia hominis*, III, 8; Vivès, XXX, p. 256.
[47] *Sermon 169*, 18; Vivès, XVII, pp. 578–9.
[48] *Sermon 170*, 8, Vivès, II, p. 585.
[49] *De perfecta just. hom.*, ch. x, 20; Vivès, XXX, p. 265.

As he says and repeats elsewhere:

> The more you love, the more you will be raised up.[50]

And again:

> As charity grows, cupidity diminishes.[51]

For man always loves something, the whole question is whether he loves what he should love:

> By its nature, love (*dilectio*) cannot remain slothful. For what is actually the cause of every human act, even bad ones, but love (*amor*)? Show me a slothful love, an inactive love. Crimes, adulteries, misdeeds, homicides, all kinds of debauchery—is it not love that produces them? Then purify your love: the water that runs into the gutter—turn it into the garden. Those impetuous impulses that it has towards the world, it should have towards the author of the world. Would anyone tell you: Love nothing? No, certainly not. If you were to love nothing, you would be among those men who are inert and dead, detestable and contemptible. Love, but be careful what you love. The love of God, the love of neighbour, is called charity; the love of the world, the love of this age, is called cupidity. Restrain cupidity, excite charity.[52]

But what is charity? How is it distinguished from cupidity, and opposed to concupiscence, produced in Adam and the source of sin in us?

St Augustine tried to explain this by the distinction between *frui* and *uti*: to enjoy or to use some good. To enjoy something, he says, is to love it in such a way that we are attached to it, that we delight in it for itself, that we make it the end, that is, the repose of our happiness. To use something is simply to make it serve as a means to attaining what we want to enjoy.[53] Lust goes astray in placing, or rather wishing to place, *frui* somewhere other than in God alone. Charity takes its place in consenting only to *uti* in any love that bears us towards creatures and to *frui* in the love of God alone.[54]

> We use, indeed, what we have need of; we enjoy what gives us joy. [God] has, therefore, given us all temporal things so that we may make use of them, but Himself for us to enjoy.[55]

[50] *Enarratio in Ps. 82*, 10; Vivès, XII, p. 529.
[51] *Enchiridion*, CXXI, 32; Vivès, XXI, p. 362.
[52] *Enarratio in Ps. 21*, 5; Vivès, XII, p. 9.
[53] *De doctrina christiana*, I, III, 3; Vivès, VI, pp. 445–6.
[54] *Ibid.*, 4; p. 446. Cf. *De civit. Dei*, XI, XXV; Vivès, XXIV, pp. 110–11.
[55] *Sermon 177*, 8; Vivès, XVII, p. 624.

The corollary of this statement is that we ought to love God for himself, simply for the joy of knowing and loving him, and not for any other good that his friendship might procure for us:

> He who asks another recompense from God and wills to serve God for that recompense gives more value to what he wants to receive than to the God from whom he wants to receive it. What then? Has God no reward [for us]. It is nothing other than Himself. God's recompense is God. Here is what [a chaste heart] loves, what it holds dear. If it holds anything else dear, its love will no longer be chaste.[56]

This text is revealing. It translates what is most fundamentally biblical and Christian into the Augustinian *caritas*. This is the love of God that recognizes in him the being who merits to be loved for himself and in himself, as Someone supreme and unique.

But, at the same time, it expresses that love in terms that do not explicitly include the personal existence of the supreme object of charity and that run the risk of ignoring it in its secondary objects.

It is very notable that St Augustine was the first, even if perhaps in a rather confused way, to sense the inadequacy in this regard of the distinction he himself drew between *frui* and *uti*. On the one hand, he maintains it for its usefulness even in the *City of God*. But, on the other hand, he had hardly formulated it when he was concerned to provide it with all kinds of correctives.

The love of neighbour, indeed, if it is a true love, cannot be reduced to *uti*. Augustine was led, therefore, to superimpose on the first distinction a second one that does not coincide with it: instead of the opposition between *frui* and *uti* he brings in the idea of an "order of love", allowing us to love our neighbour not only as a means but as an end, provided that it be a relative end, itself always referred to God.[57]

Taken up with this line of "retractation", Augustine went still further and conceded that even corporal goods, in this "ordered" fashion, might be the object of a true love, a true delight. He multiplies concrete examples in one sermon:[58] the great spectacles of nature, a psalm beautifully sung, flowers and their scent; he even went so far as to add "*conjugales amplexus*". As Burnaby brings out, this last addition must have cost him dear, he who had not been afraid to write, in the first fervour of his Platonising

[56] *Enarratio in Ps. 72*, 32; Vivès, XIII, p. 329.
[57] *De doctrina christiana*, I, xxi, 22; Vivès, VI, p. 456.
[58] *Sermon 159;* Vivès, XVII, p. 493.

ultra-spiritualism: *"nihil mihi tam fugiendum quam concubitum esse decrevi"*.[59]

This change of mind is certainly moving in this man who had been a Manichean and who, hearing himself reproached, not without some pertinence, by Julian of Eclanum for still being one, conscientiously tried to give no further basis for such a reproach. But, whatever the extreme towards which the pendulum swung, with him such discussions always give the renewed impression that what we love, in charity, is an abstract good. For he always comes back to ordering the love of persons and of things under the same head, whether it is to exclude all creatures from the love with which something is loved for itself, or to give it to them all *en bloc*.

Charity and the Life of Christ Communicated in the Church

There are other texts, however, that bring us out of this painful dilemma. In these, charity is revealed as being not only the love of the only true good, but the love of this good recognized as the good of all men: not only the good that can be possessed by many persons, without any of them thereby suffering any deprivation, but the good that can only be possessed by all together.

Here again, the material of his thought is Platonic: it is the idea of the *bonum diffusivum sui*, but this time the thought is none the less wholly Christian. Considered in this way, charity is explicitly, for St Augustine, the charity of which the whole Church is the subject, which we possess only by being incorporated into the Church. It is the love with which the Bride of Christ loves her Bridegroom; and it can only subsist in the common love that her members have for one another. It is the love that unites the members of the body of Christ in a single community of love in him.

These themes gain all their clarity and force in Augustine's mind on the occasion of the struggle against the Donatists, who pretended to make sanctity the possession of some pure persons separated from the mass of the people. The *Enarrationes in psalmos* delight in dwelling on the fact that he who excludes his brother, even a sinner, from his love cannot pretend to love God in Christ:

> All run in the race, says St Paul, but only one receives the prize,[60] and the others go away vanquished. But, for us, it is not

[59] *Soliloquies*, I, XI, 17; Vivès, II, p. 579. See Burnaby, *Amor Dei*, London, 1938 (2nd printing 1947), p. 113. This work is certainly the best existing study of Augustinian *caritas*.
[60] 1 Cor. 9. 24.

> like this. All those who run, provided that they run to the end, receive it and he who has arrived first awaits for the last in order to be crowned with him. For this contest is the act of charity and not of cupidity: all those who run love one another mutually, and it is this love that is their course.[61]

This is because this love which is ours flows from the love of Christ for us, and this is nothing other than a desire to share his own inheritance. This is explained in the *Enarratio in psalmum XLIX*, in a magnificent text which is one of the rare ones in which Augustine takes up the theme of deification, dear to the Greek Fathers, in order to illuminate it in reference to grace and charity in Christ:

> It is obvious that God has given the title of gods to those men deified by His grace and not born of His own substance.[62] For He alone can justify who is just in Himself and not by the good deed of another; in the same way, He alone can deify who is God of Himself and not by participation in the divinity of another. Now He who can justify is the same as He who deifies, because He makes those whom He justifies children of God. For He has given them power to become sons of God."[63] If we have become children of God, we are thereby become gods, but by a grace of adoption and not by the nature of our generation. For the Son of God is unique, one God with the Father, Our Lord and Saviour Jesus Christ, Word from the beginning, Word with God, Word-God. The others who become gods become such by His grace: they are not born of His substance to be what He is, but to attain Him by His goodness, to be co-heirs with Christ. How great, indeed, is the charity of this Heir who desires to have co-heirs? What avaricious man would wish to have others inherit with him? But if one were found willing, he would share his inheritance with others and, in sharing it, would have less than if he possessed it wholly himself. On the contrary, the inheritance in which we are co-heirs with Christ is not diminished by the great numbers of those possessing it, and it is not lessened by the great number of co-heirs; but it is as great for many as for a small number and as great for each one in particular as for all together.[64]

The same *Enarratio* draws from this the conclusion that we cannot recognize grace in ourselves without at the same time recognizing it in others.[65] The *Enarratio* on Psalm 121, goes still further, stating that love makes it possible for a man who is not personally

[61] *Enarratio in Ps. 39*, 12; Vivès, XII, p. 276.
[62] An allusion to Ps. 81. 6: "I say: You are gods . . ."
[63] John 1. 12.
[64] *Enarratio in Ps. 49*, 2: Vivès, XII, p. 459.
[65] *Ibid.*, 30.

capable of heroic virtue to possess it none the less, in those who, in the communion of the same Catholic Church, have attained it.[66] Indeed, explains the *Tractatus 67 in Johannem*, God will be finally all in all in such a way that:

> charity will make common to all what each one possesses. For each one, when he loves in another what he does not have himself, possesses it himself: there will therefore be no envy for an unequal glory, since the unity of charity will reign in all.[67]

This prepares for the final vision of the tenth book of the City of God, where the sacrifice offered to God will be:

> the whole redeemed community, the congregation and the communion of saints offered to God by the High Priest who offered Himself in suffering for us, so that we might be the body of so great a Head.[68]

But these supreme perspectives which Augustine opens out to us on charity needed first to be prepared by the great meditation of the *De Trinitate*.

Charity and the Trinity

For it is here that Augustine, without thereby abandoning the not merely experimental but psychological orientation of all his spirituality, comes to consider charity not primarily in us, but in God, in the Trinity. Thence, by means of his very personal mode of speculation on the divine image in us, precisely as the image of the Trinity, he finally succeeded in regarding charity in us as a participation in the charity proper to God, as love of the love with which we have been loved.

Behind Augustine's psychological interpretation of the Trinity from the starting-point of the human soul, its image restored by grace, Burnaby has rightly seen the Johannine triad of Life, Light and Love.[69] So it is that the soul is, knows, and wills. Its "memory" —that is, the self-consciousness, logically anterior to all activity, which yet does not grasp itself except in its activity—is the basis on which its knowledge and its will stand out. I am, I know, I will, that is to say, I am a being that knows and wills; that knows and wills its being, its knowledge and its will. In the same way, the Father, in knowing himself, produces his Son, and, in finding in him his dilection, the Holy Spirit.[70]

66 *Enarratio in Ps. 121*, 10; Vivès, XV, p. 33.
67 *Tractatus 67 in Joh.*, 2: Vivès, X, p. 217.
68 *De civit. Dei*, X, VI; Vivès, XXIV, p. 38.
69 Burnaby, *op. cit.*, p. 147.
70 *De Trinitate*, XV, VIII, 12; Vivès, XXVII, pp. 358ff.

And this same love, in which the life proper to God in himself finds its end, is the sole principle of the communication of life to all his creatures, but eminently in those whom he has created to his image: to be, to know, to will, that is, in him, by knowing in his truth, by loving in his love.

Recognizing God as such by faith, loving him by charity, it is therefore only through this love in which his life opens out that we love. And we love him as love itself: He who is eternally love, who has created us through love, redeemed us through love....[71] Thereby we understand how we love all things in his love. It is in this way that the *City of God*, at the end of Augustine's life, defined charity as the love of God carried to contempt of self, as opposed to concupiscence, love of self carried to contempt of God. Such a love is the fulfilment and not the destruction of self, because it is love of the very love from which all love and life proceed.

Augustinian Wisdom

Throughout all these developments, so full of potentialities, Augustinian spirituality remains obviously impressive in its unity. We can understand how it could impose itself on the whole Latin Middle Ages as a quasi-definitive Summa.

This unity, as we have seen, does not exclude changes of mind, which were the object of the "retractations" with which Augustine concerned himself at the end of his life, with a lucid honesty that does him the greatest credit. But it is actually the unity of an original orientation which was affirmed at the time of his conversion, and then never ceased to correct, to complete, to perfect its expressions and its very design. This labour was marvellously furthered by the great Pelagian and Donatist controversies, and by the whole pastoral as well as the most personal experience of the saint. This work is the elaboration and the focusing of what St Augustine himself defined as wisdom (*sapientia*) in contrast to science (*scientia*).

Science, for him, is only the knowledge of the goods of this world, of the useful. Wisdom, on the contrary, is concerned with the ultimate end of man, with what makes him happy by leading him towards that for which he is made: *Fecisti nos ad te et inquietum cor nostrum donec requiescat in te*, says the first page of the *Confessions*, in a formula that not only sums up the Confessions, but also the whole of Augustinian wisdom.

Augustine first thought that he had found the essence of this wisdom in Neo-Platonic philosophy, as the philosophy of the spirit,

[71] *De Trinitate*, XIII, I; Vivès, XXVII, pp. 438ff.

of its absolute and unique value. ... But, without ever denying the intuitions that had so keenly struck him—and not that he had not coloured them from the outset with what of Christianity he carried within him even before his conversion—he progressively came to see here not spiritual reality itself, but a kind of abstract draft of it, so to speak. Reality: the true good which is not only the object of speculation but of experience, he came more and more explicitly to think, is given us by Christian revelation alone, and the life of the Church, in the Church, is its realization, as perfect as can be known here on earth. Here only, in fact, do we know and love the true good, for here only, in Christ, is it communicated to us by his sovereign grace. Here only does man discover a wisdom that is a true participation in the wisdom proper to God, in the renewal in man of that image of the Holy Trinity according to which he was created, but which sin had irremediably obscured.[72]

Is this Augustinian wisdom precisely contemplative? There is no doubt that it is such in the Neo-Platonizing writings of Cassiciacum. But this is far less clear in what follows. The progress of Augustine's experience came to assure him that the vision of God, in the strict sense, like the perfection in charity which is inseparable from it, is only accessible in the world to come; when man will finally be freed from the weight of the flesh of sin.

Here below, he recognized, contemplation is never given except in a way that cannot be grasped, a way that impels us, by its very instability, to struggle and so to spiritual progress. Such contemplation will be the ceaselessly renewed reward for this combat and progress, but also one that is continually taken away, and thereby is an incitement precisely never to halt or to take rest before the entrance into eternal blessedness.

We might say that Augustine, from the beginning to the end of his Christian career, went from a mysticism more speculative than experimental, even though experience certainly had its part in it, to what Fr Cayré has happily called a "mystical moralism".[73] We should understand this to mean a development of charity in which an asceticism increasingly dominated by the pastoral care for the salvation of his brethren, inseparable in the Church from his own salvation, remains none the less, for Augustine, moved by the mystical aspiration: to see God, and to find blessedness in love, charity, perfect and satisfied in this very vision.

[72] *De Trinitate*, VIII, VIII, 12; Vivès, XXVII, pp. 358ff.
[73] See his article in *Mélanges Lebreton*, I, Paris, 1951–52, pp. 443–60.

Conclusions on St Augustine

It would be futile to try to sum up in a few general ideas the influence of a writer and a personality like Augustine. His idea of wisdom, however, affords a viewpoint sufficiently revealing to give us an appreciation of what he must have contributed to the Christian West. For, whatever may be the importance of the elements that Augustine took from the Greek Fathers in order to plant them in the Latin world, this idea of wisdom brings out the fact that he did not transmit one of the most basic, the most traditional structures of Greek spirituality. We mean gnosis, as we have seen it defined little by little under our eyes, especially, but not exclusively, at Alexandria.

Augustinian wisdom, in spite of certain affinities, is something other than the gnosis of the Greek Fathers. It is distinguished particularly by its psychological, reflexive orientation: it is not the mystery of God in Christ that it has directly in view, but the mystery of ourselves, which God, which Christ, aid us to unravel. Thereby, it must be recognized, whatever may be the material place that the meditation of holy Scriptures retains in Augustinian spirituality, the sense of this meditation has been changed. An element, we should not say precisely of subjectivism, or of immanentism—this would be to force things unduly, but certainly of anthropocentrism and, if we dare to formulate it, of psychocentrism, has been introduced. Its emergence, perhaps, will trace out the main line of the progressive alienation of the Latin West with regard to the ancient tradition—that is, what we now call the Eastern tradition.

The gains which have been procured by this change of orientation must not be ignored. The interiorization of all Christianity is the first consequence of it. A new interest given to the human, in its concrete quality, was to be a later result, even though with Augustine himself it is scarcely indicated. But when man, in his experience of God, comes to fix his attention primarily on his own experience, it is foreseeable that, sooner or later, his experience alone will be enough to captivate him, whatever the object of it may be. It is precisely at this moment that subjectivism, immanentism, are introduced. It would be foolish to make Augustine either into a Protestant or a modern Idealist in advance. It remains true that neither Protestantism nor the idealistic religious philosophies would have been even conceivable in a world in which the influence of St Augustine had not been practically predominant.

To this, one last characteristic must be added, one that may seem secondary but that has had a later influence which, perhaps, has not as yet been sufficiently appreciated. This is, furthermore, connected with the preceding one. If we consider the ancient type of asceticism, doubtless precisely because it was the work of minds radically objective in their orientation, it is striking to observe the extent to which it is positive in its motivations: the question is that of freeing oneself completely from what is not God *for God*. With the young Chrysostom, still more with Jerome, we have seen an asceticism introduced that tended to justify itself by a disgust of the world, of the body, and, what is even more serious, of woman seen simply as the intermediary by which the religious man finds himself wholly absorbed in the body and as it were nailed to the world. Augustine should be given the credit for having tried as well as he could, and increasingly so, to react against the Manicheanism latent in this way of looking at things. Unfortunately, neither his own temperament nor his experiences as a young man, nor, above all perhaps, grafted on all this, his tendency to lift introspection into the very heart of wisdom, helped to make his reaction on this point a very effective one.

XIX

LATIN MONASTICISM FROM ST AUGUSTINE TO ST GREGORY

THE work of Augustine directly related to spirituality should not be considered apart from what might be called his work with regard to institutions, particularly in the domain of the monastic life. There is no doubt that this allows us to observe a mutation which the monastic life was to undergo in passing from the East into the West, a mutation so basic that the Easterners soon came to question whether it was not a complete metamorphosis.

This mutation, it should be clearly understood, was not without precedents in the East. Nor was it to be universal in the West. Moreover, it cannot be said without qualifications that Augustine was the author of it. But what had been, in the East, a form occasionally taken on by monasticism came to correspond, in the West, to a more or less generalized tendency, and to become the object of more or less formal systematizations. Augustine's example, even more than his works directly connected with these problems, provides an expression, an illustration of everything we have just mentioned.

For here we need to distinguish between the writings by St Augustine or attributed to him, and the monastic or quasimonastic life which he himself exemplified.

The Monastic Writings of St Augustine

In patristic studies today, there are few literary problems so intricate as that of the documents which have been called "Rules of St Augustine".

Everyone agrees on the fact that the *Regula prima* is not by St Augustine, but is a product of Spain and, perhaps, Priscillian.[1] The

[1] See Dom Patrice Cousin, *Précis d'Histoire monastique*, p. 113.

Regula secunda (or *De ordine monasterii*),—in spite of Fr Mandonnet who saw it as being the real "Rule" written for monks by St Augustine,[2] seems to be no more than an exhortation, a preface to the *Regula tertia* (or *Regula ad servos Dei*), as Dom Cyrille Lambot claims.[3]

As to this *Regula tertia* itself, since the labours of the Maurists, it would seem to be established that it is only an adaptation to monasteries for men of Letter 211, written by St Augustine to the superior who succeeded her own sister in conducting the monastery of women founded by the latter. But Dom Lambot seems also to have established the fact that, if Letter 211 is authentically Augustinian, the adaptation may not be: we should rather see it as being the later work of an abbot of southern Italy.[4]

However, Fr Merlin maintains, quite the contrary, both the authenticity of the *Regula tertia* and its anteriority in relation to Letter 211.[5] On his part, Fr Hümpfner does not hesitate to attribute the letter itself, not to St Augustine, but to St Fructuosus of Braga.[6] We should finally quote Fr Verheijen who, after having maintained the non-authenticity of the *Regula tertia* and the only partial authenticity of Letter 211, has returned to his earlier opinion, but becoming much more radical in the process: for him, now, it is the *Regula tertia* that is Augustinian and the Letter is only a later adaptation (from the end of the sixth century) made in Spain by St Leander. . . .[7]

These discussions have no major interest for our present study, for, whatever theories or hypotheses one may adopt, apart from some influences of the *Regula ed servos Dei* doubtless to be discerned in some ancient rules such as that of St Cesarius of Arles or that of the monastery of Tarnat, these "Rules of St Augustine" actually had no great vogue until the twelfth century. It was during the renewal of canonical institutions characteristic of that period that these texts first attracted attention, And it was at that time that the *Regula ad servos Dei* was adopted as an actual rule, first by the Dominicans, then by the Premonstratensians, and all kinds of other modern orders in turn. But this is not our field.[8]

[2] *Saint Dominique, l'idée, l'homme, l'œuvre*, Paris, 1938, II, pp. 103–62.

[3] See his article from the *Revue bénédictine*, 1941, pp. 41–58: "Saint Augustin a-t-il redigé la Règle pour moines qui porte son nom?"

[4] *Ibid.*

[5] "Un exemple typique d'un préjugé littéraire: le texte primordial de la Règle de saint Augustin", in *Analecta Praemonstratensia*, Louvain, 1948, pp. 5–19.

[6] W. Hümpfner, *Die grossen Ordensregeln*, Einsiedeln, 1948, pp. 5–19.

[7] Cf. M. Verheijen, "La Regula Sancti Augustini", in *Vigiliae Christianae*, 1953, pp. 27–56, and his contribution to *Augustiniana*, Louvain, 1954, pp. 42–52.

[8] See Cousin, *op. cit.*, p. 110.

Moreover, both the Letter and the Rule hardly go beyond devout exhortation to a common life, in real poverty, fraternal charity, and an obedience founded on humility. It would be difficult to draw from these generalities, framed to suit almost any circumstances (since they apply equally well to nuns and to religious clerics) any very well-defined teaching on the monastic life. As to practical directives, these are so vague that, from the time of the first medieval religious groups which adopted this "rule", it has been necessary to complete it by more precise "constitutions".

St Augustine's Monasticism

What should rather hold our attention is the kind of "monastic" life that St Augustine himself led or recommended. From this point of view, we should distinguish four stages in his life: at Cassiciacum; when he returned to Tagaste; when he lived at Hippo before he was made bishop; and after he became bishop.

The villa at Cassiciacum, belonging to Verecundus, one of Augustine's friends, where he lived from October 386 to May 387, had nothing monastic about it. Neither could the existence, withdrawn and meditative, that Augustine lived there with some friends or young disciples be in any way described as monastic. But this semi-solitude, in which instructing the young Adeodatus and other adolescents, and conversing with some disciples like Alypius, Licentius and Tregetius, were intermingled with personal reflection in the presence of God, was certainly to put its special stamp on Augustine's subsequent experiences of a retired life lived with several other persons.

Two years later, when he had returned to Africa, in his native town of Tagaste, it was now a kind of a sketch of a monastery, more or less organized, that Augustine formed around himself, but one in which the completion of Adeodatus' education and studies pursued in common with friends continued to occupy an important place.

When he became a priest at Hippo in 391 (forced to do so, as is well known, by popular pressure, when the Bishop Valerius publicly complained about his lack of helpers), Augustine was at first dismayed at having to break with the kind of life that suited him so well: a life of meditation turning spontaneously into conversation with friends and disciples, in a solitude that was frugal, monastic if you will, but above all a retreat for devout and serious intellectuals. He soon succeeded, however, in reconciling his pastoral obligations, which won him over more and more as he experienced them, with his old kind of life. At Hippo, the more or less academic "monastery" of Tagaste was refashioned, but it soon took on the air of a seminary in which many of Augustine's intimate friends were prepared for the episcopate or the priesthood, friends who had followed him thus far and did not wish to abandon him in his new public duties.

It was as a fruit of this last experience and the reflections it inspired in him, doubtless, that, when Augustine had become bishop, succeeding Valerius in 396, he undertook to organize the whole life of the clergy around him in a quasi-monastic fashion.[9]

In doing so, Augustine was not an innovator, properly speaking. At that period, the tendency was increasingly appearing, not only to select bishops by preference from among monks (which was soon to become the general rule in the East), but, at least in the West, to expect priests in any case to practise ascetic continence from the time of their ordination. The opposition aroused by Vigilantius, a Spanish priest, about this time, against the progressive introduction of this new custom was to unloose various controversies, in which the old Jerome, off in Palestine, was to take part with his usual impetuosity. The movement seems to have been furthered rather than restrained thereby.[10]

It was, however, to take a further step in the "monasticizing" of the clergy to impose on them, as Augustine did, together with the common life, its obligations of poverty and obedience, even though these did not have at that period the canonical precision to be given them later on. All the same, even here Augustine had had a predecessor in Italy, since 363, where Eusebius of Vercelli had had the clerics of his cathedral live in a real clerical monastery, the first known to history. St Ambrose at Milan, the priest St Paulinus at Nola, perhaps St Victricius at Rouen had made analogous attempts, more or less effectively promoted, more or less crowned with success.

But it seems indisputable that the example of Augustine had the very greatest effect in accrediting, defining and propagating this new type of monasticism, clerical monasticism.[11] Sermons 355 and 356 tell us about its realization at Hippo.[12] We should note here first of all the insistence on the common life as such, after the image of the primitive community at Jerusalem. The developments that follow are concentrated on the common sharing of all possessions and on poverty. Here we can see clearly the repugnance felt by many clerics to accept this requirement, Augustine's own evasive

[9] See M. Mellet, *L'itinéraire et l'idéal monastique de saint Augustin*, Paris, 1934.
[10] See F. Cavallera, *Saint Jérôme, sa vie, son œuvre*, I, pp. 306ff.
[11] See Cousin, *op. cit.*, pp. 106 and 117.
[12] *De vita et moribus clericorum suorum*, ed. Vivès, XIX, pp. 229–47.

statements as to how rigorously it should be enforced, and finally (perhaps particularly) the suspiciousness of the faithful. It is clear that the practical realization of this idea came up either against their scepticism or their fear lest all this would actually result in an accumulation of possessions in the hands of the bishop and some priests. . . .

These texts show that the resemblances between what was now happening and what had already been observed in eastern Syria or, again in Gaul with St Martin (of whom we shall speak again) are misleading. In all these latter cases, the question was that of an accidental clericalization of monasticism, called for by the needs of evangelizing a still pagan country lacking in clergy. Here, it was rather, to repeat, a "monasticizing" of the clergy that was being attempted.

But, in fact, the chief result was to detach from the organic unity of ancient monasticism the particular practices of poverty, chastity, and obedience, which were thus brought into the foreground, to be reunited by the Middle Ages in a new synthesis. The idea of the common life, for the moment, came to be the binding force, evidently vivified by Augustine's very ecclesiastical vision of *caritas*.

On the other hand, although Augustine himself was not entirely aware of it, as a result of the progressive enlistment of himself and his group of friends in the work of the clergy, this common life little by little abandoned its contemplative purpose to become directed towards an ideal of pastoral service. Once again, no more than in the personal ideal of St Augustine did this signify any real renunciation of the mystical search. But, here again, from a mysticism that was much more intellectualist than had been, even in the East, that of the erudite monasticism we have studied, a transition was very definitely made to a "mystical moralism". There is no doubt that what the clerical monasticism desired by St Augustine tended towards was the "Religious", in the sense that the Latin Middle Ages were to give to the term; and this is no longer in any way the monk in the primitive and Eastern sense.

Ancient Monasticism Passes into the West

In the West, however, side by side with this new monasticism, the older type was propagated. Another of Augustine's writings, like the *De opere monachorum*, testifies to the permanence of monasteries of laymen, strangers both to the care for intellectual culture that had always been his and to the pastoral cares added later on.

In Italy and in Gaul, monasteries of this kind were multiplied, naturally under influences from the East, from the fourth century on, and the movement did not cease in the fifth or even in the sixth century. Treves seems to have been the first centre of diffusion. It was in Gaul, in fact, that there took place the first great spread of monasticism in true continuity with primitive monasticism, even though there it took on particular characteristics of its own.[13]

Three great figures stand out in succession: St Martin at Marmoutier, Cassian at Marseilles and St Cesarius (more than St Honoratus) first at Lérins and then at Arles.

Martin's work[14] as bishop, apostle and missionary is more important than his work as monk. This convert soldier of Pannonian origin began about 363, with St Hilary of Poitiers, at Ligugé, to lead the classic form of eremitic life. It drew disciples as usual. Elected Bishop of Tours, Martin simply took his monastic life with him to Marmoutier. Some of his disciples whom he associated in his ministry formed a clerical core in a monastery (more a laura than a cenobium) that remained none the less of the traditional type.

Equally, it was a laura of the Palestinian type that Honoratus founded at Lérins about 310, on an island near Cannes.[15] Even though it soon constituted a nursery of bishops for the whole region, it still did not abandon this original pattern. The eremitic life was reserved for the tried monks and the novices prepared for it in a cenobium, following a very elastic formula, the members becoming Cassian's disciples when he settled down not far away.

And it was Cassian, more than any other writer, whose task it became to transmit to the West, not only the monastic practices and types of organization first developed in the East, but the best distillation of the teaching of the Eastern monks.

Cassian

In spite of a whole series of scholarly works that he has recently inspired,[16] Cassian still remains a very imperfectly known figure.

[13] See Cousin, *op. cit.*, pp. 106 and 115.

[14] See Cousin, *op. cit.*, pp. 116–17. Our source is Sulpicius Severus, *Vita Martini*, with the three epistles and the dialogues accompanying it, in Migne, P.L., XX, 95–248.

[15] See Cousin, *op. cit.*, p. 120. Migne gives the *Vita Honorati*, by Hilary, the monk of Lérins, later Bishop of Arles; P.L., I, 1249–78.

[16] See particularly Owen Chadwick, *John Cassian, A Study in Primitive Monasticism*, Cambridge, 1950, and the introduction of Dom E. Pichery to his edition and translation of the *Conferences* in the collection "Sources chrétiennes", Paris, no. 42, 1945, no. 54, 1958 and no. 64, 1959. Cassian's works, given in Migne, P.L., XLIX and L, have been completely edited in the *Corpus* of Vienna, the *Conferences* in vol. XIII (1889) and the rest of his work in vol. XVII (1888).

Even though he was finally drawn to Provence, he does not seem to have been a Provençal. Gennadius, around the end of the fifth century, calls him a Scythian, which would explain his almost equal mastery of Greek and Latin. Very early, with his inseparable friend, Germanus, he went to Palestine, attracted by the examples of monasticism to be found there as much as by the holy places. He must then have been about seventeen or eighteen years old. Since he stayed at Bethlehem, but does not seem personally to have known Jerome, whom he admired a great deal without admiring Rufinus much less, this stay must be dated around 383, a little before the arrival of the holy and irascible Dalmatian.

But soon Cassian and his companion, attracted by anchoritism, set off for Egypt. Arriving by sea in the Delta, at Thermesus, they first stayed in the environs of Panephysis, then at Diolkos, before going on to Scete, where they made contact with Paphnucius, the Origenist. There they settled down, breaking their long stay by a journey to Bethlehem, to settle their affairs with their superiors. They also made an excursion to the Cells and to Nitria.

When the Origenist affair broke out, they were among the number of the religious who set off for Constantinople with the Longi Fratres. Chrysostom ordained Germanus priest and Cassian deacon, winning the latter's affection and filial admiration. After the Synod of the Oak, where Theophilus of Alexandria obtained Chrysostom's deposition, it was Germanus and Cassian who were entrusted with taking to Rome the protest of the clergy remaining faithful to the archbishop.

They arrived in Rome in the spring of 405, and it seems that it was there that Cassian in turn was elevated to the priesthood. He stayed there for ten years, becoming a friend of the future St Leo. His inseparable companion having died, it is thought, he set out again, this time for Provence. It is possible that some ecclesiastics there had got wind of his competence in monasticism and called him expressly to undertake the work of founder and reformer. In any case, he established two monasteries at Marseilles, one for men and the other for women. The Bishop of Apt, Castor, asked him to describe the institutions of the East, especially those of Egypt. Then he urged him to give ten further conferences on the Fathers of Scete. These were followed by another series, of seven conferences, on the Fathers at Panephysis, dedicated to St Honoratus of Lérins and his disciple Eucherius, the future bishop of Lyons. Seven more conferences finally completed the series, dedicated this time to the abbots of four monasteries of the islands of Hyères.

Cassian, as we have already said, was at the centre of the opposition to the too trenchant formulas of Augustine against

Pelagianism. Here he reveals, we must admit, that speculative theology was not his strong point, nor indeed abstract thinking in general.

But he comes into his own when there is question of expressing all the riches of the monastic tradition. He was able to compose a final synthesis of it in which the most attractive humaneness is allied with the most austere ascetic ideal. Everything is illuminated with a spiritual aspiration in which fervour and discretion go hand-in-hand. Cassian remains the great inspirer of the properly monastic tradition in the West. It would be extremely difficult to succeed better than he did in transmitting in an assimilable form the best of Egyptian monastic experience, enlightened by a distilled Evagrianism and an Origenism stamped with the very greatest moderation.

The *Institutions*, having spoken of the monk's habit, of prayer, of psalmody, then of ascetic institutions properly so called, studies the eight principal vices distinguished by Evagrius. The three series of *Conferences* allow the great abbots whom he had known to speak for themselves, in the freest and most familiar fashion, about the meaning of the monastic life, discretion, the three renunciations, the powers that incite us to evil and, above all, the very positive elements of the monastic life: prayer, the ideal of perfection, chastity, spiritual knowledge, charisms, etc.

On the cenobitic and the anchoritic life, Cassian makes himself the interpreter, though as always a very perspicacious one, of the consensus which had at that period become almost unanimous among the monks of the East. To say monasticism is to say anchoritism, entering into complete solitude with God. In actual fact, however, all men are not able to bear such a testing; above all, there is hardly anyone able fruitfully to undertake it unless he has first exercised himself for a long time in the cenobitic life. Without abating any of his enthusiasm for the great solitaries of Egypt, Cassian lets it be seen very clearly that he accuses himself, retrospectively, of some presumption in having wished to attempt this life after spending only a few years in the cenobitic life.[17]

As to the goal of the monastic life, the first conference, with the Abbot Moses, describes it after the manner of the Gospel, not without some reflection of Evagrius running through. Throughout the whole work of asceticism, the monk is not to seek anything but the Kingdom of God. He will attain to this Kingdom by purity of heart. But this purity is not in the least negative. It is at once the condition and the counterpart of the full development of charity

[17] See E. Pichery, *op. cit.*, I, pp. 51ff.

within us. Never, certainly, has the conviction been more strongly expressed that all the renouncements of asceticism are vain if they do not bear fruit in charity:

> ...Many, who have abandoned with contempt large fortunes, enormous sums of gold and silver and magnificent estates, let themselves, a little later, be troubled about an eraser, a stylus, a needle, a reed to write with. If they look constantly to purity of heart, they will never fall on account of such trifles, after having preferred to strip themselves of great and valuable goods rather than find in them the occasion of precisely similar faults.
>
> Men are to be found who are so jealous of a manuscript that they cannot endure another person even to cast his eyes on it or to take it up in his hand; and this encounter, which invites them to gain gentleness and charity as its reward, becomes for them an occasion of impatience and death. Having distributed all their riches for the love of Christ, they retain their old passion and let it go after trifles, ready to defend them angrily. Since they do not possess the charity that St Paul speaks of, their life is struck down by complete sterility. The blessed Apostle foresaw this misfortune in spirit: "Although I distribute all my goods to feed the poor, and deliver my body to the flames, if I do not have charity this will prove useless to me"—an obvious proof that we do not reach perfection at one stride simply by nakedness, the renouncement of all wealth, if we do not unite with it that charity of which the Apostle describes the various members. Now this is only to be found in purity of heart. For to know neither envy, nor conceit, nor anger; never to act out of frivolity; not to seek our own interests; not to take pleasure in injustice; not to take account of evil and the rest: what is this but continually to offer to God a perfect and very pure heart, and to guard it intact from any movement of passion?
>
> Purity of heart is, then, the unique end of our actions and our desires. It is to gain this that we should embrace solitude, suffer fastings, vigils, work, nakedness, devote ourselves to reading and to the practice of other virtues, having no other purpose, through all these things, than to make and to keep our heart invulnerable to all wicked passions and to mount, as by so many degrees, even to the perfection of charity.[18]

This fine text gives us Cassian's procedure: to begin with a concrete remark, showing refined psychological insight and superior spiritual good sense, in order to arrive at the most profound principles.

It is to be noted that Cassian's prudence kept him from ever mentioning *apatheia*, now that the term had aroused the opposition of the anti-Origenists and the Pelagians had succeeded in

[18] *First Conference*, VI and VII.

compromising it. But the last paragraphs are enough to establish very clearly the fact that under the term, purity of heart, he is teaching the essence of the Evagrian *apatheia*. The close relationship uniting both the one and the other to charity is precisely the same. Like the Evagrian *apatheia*, purity of heart, according to Cassian, tends to be established in a relatively stable state:

> A vice that is only contained with difficulty will indeed allow the fighter some transient truce but not the security and the lasting repose that follow on the labour. On the contrary, when it is completely vanquished, by a virtue that penetrates into the very depths of the whole being, it will henceforth be quiet, without giving the least sign of revolt, and allow its conqueror to enjoy a peace that is tranquil and secure.[19]

As this *Twelfth Conference on Chastity* clearly indicates, Cassian even believes in the possibility of attaining a mastery, at least in part, of the unconscious. But no more than Evagrius did he fall thereby into any illusions of our becoming inaccessible to temptation. On the contrary, he is no less categorical than Augustine in declaring impossible here below any mastery over sin which would be complete, still less secured once and for all.[20]

The way whereby asceticism is to lead to the perfection of charity, is, however, doubtless Cassian's most original and happiest contribution. Here again we see, more clearly than ever, how to him asceticism is only a means. We have seen sketched out, with the *De officiis* of St Ambrose, the pattern which, throughout the whole of the Latin Middle Ages, was to become set: of a virtue as it were with a higher and a lower floor, according to whether or not a person practises the evangelical counsels. No author is further from such an orientation than Cassian. For him, there is only one perfection, that of charity, itself flourishing in and above all the virtues. The counsels, in themselves, in no way constitute a superior degree of virtue, but rather the most effective means of realizing as directly as possible the only perfection known to the Gospel.

But Cassian does describe the progress of the monastic life in three successive stages constituted by three successive renunciations, each leading to the next: the renunciation involved in asceticism, the renunciation of vices, the renunciation of everything that is not God and the things of God. We should give particular attention to this order: the ascetic renunciation is not placed above the renunciation of sin, as a superior stage. On the contrary, it is the basis of a renunciation of sin which will thereby

[19] *Second Conference*, X.
[20] Cf. *ibid.*, XVI; still more categorically, *Eleventh Conference*, IX.

be made as effective as possible, and it is this other renunciation which is its purpose.

The initial renunciation is the deprivation, the effective deprivation, of all the material goods, all the conveniences that engulf us and enchain us. It is on this basis that we go on, by humility and patience, to rid ourselves of bad habits and passions. Humility is found in submission to the judgment of our elders. Patience is the constancy obtained in the persevering struggle against everything that disturbs us. Its acquisition is therefore already the acquisition of peace, of tranquillity (here once again we find *hesychia*). It is at this point that charity is developed in the soul, inseparably from what Cassian calls *actualis scientia*, which is his equivalent for gnosis, but he emphasizes that this is simply charity tending towards its complete development.

The third renunciation, by which we lift our gaze towards the eternal dwelling, banishing even the memory of present things, assures our being wholly possessed by this contemplative charity. But, far from being a goal, this only means entering on a progress that can have no limits, since henceforth it tends with no further hesitations towards the very perfection of the Father.[21]

While it is by these three successive renunciations that Cassian lays out the monk's progress, what has already been said about his so perspicacious condemnation of any asceticism seeking its purpose in itself enables us to foresee that he will take great care to bring out the positive reality which is the reverse of the renunciations. It might even be said that he states it as a principle that there can be no lasting renunciation unless there is a compensating reality which the renunciation itself simply permits us to adhere to. In his *Institutions*, he already writes:

> It is impossible to despise the pleasures of the mouth if the soul, attached to contemplation, does not find greater delights in the love of virtues and in the beauty of heavenly things. The hour when we disdain as valueless the things of the present is also that in which the look of the spirit is inseparably fixed on those that are unchangeable and eternal.[22]

In the *Twelfth Conference*, he says in a still more generalized and still more precise way:

> The vital force of the soul does not allow it to rest without some feeling of desire or of fear, of joy or of sadness: we must then give it the right occupation. We desire to drive from our heart the lusts of the flesh: let us unrestrainedly make room for

[21] We have already quoted this text on p. 327.
[22] *Institutions*, V, XIV.

spiritual joys. Let us not imagine that we can in any way master or banish the desire of present things unless, in place of these tendencies which we desire to cut off, we place good ones.[23]

We can see, then, what a considerable place is to be given to contemplation. Under one aspect, this appears as the fruit of asceticism or, at least, as made possible by it. But, under another aspect, it is contemplation itself that nourishes and animates the spiritual ascent.

Reading and Contemplation

For this contemplation has many degrees and, above all, many forms. But always, for Cassian, here deeply Origenist but in the best sense of the term, it proceeds from Holy Scripture, continually read by the monk, meditated, more deeply understood, assimilated. The Abbot Nestorius says, in the *Fourteenth Conference*:

> Having banished all earthly cares and thoughts, strive to apply yourselves assiduously and, how shall I say it, constantly, to holy reading, so that this continual meditation finally impregnates your soul and forms it, so to say, to its own image. It makes the soul in some way the ark of the covenant, enclosing within in the two tables of stone, that is to say, the eternal strength of the one and the other Testament; the golden urn, symbol of a pure and stainless memory that always contains the hidden treasure of the manna—understanding by this the eternal and heavenly sweetness of spiritual thoughts and the bread of the angels; the rod of Aaron, that is to say the standard, the saving sign, of our sovereign and true pontiff, Jesus Christ, always flowering anew in an undying memory. . . . All these things are covered over by two cherubim, that is the fullness of historical and spiritual knowledge. For cherubim signify fullness of knowledge. Continually they cover the propitiatory of God, that is, the tranquillity of your heart, and protect it against evil spirits. Your soul, thus becoming by its love of purity the ark of the divine Testament and the priestly kingdom, absorbed in some way in spiritual understandings, carries out the commandment given to the pontiff by the lawgiver: "He is not to go out of the sanctuary, lest he profane the sanctuary of God", that is, his heart, where the Lord promises to make His abiding dwelling-place.[24]

Dom Pichery, in his commentary on this beautiful text, rightly emphasizes the presence of the mystical theme, underlying the scriptural one: impregnation, illumination, absorption of the soul, the divine presence established in the heart. . . .[25] The same author

[23] *Twelfth Conference*, V.
[24] *Fourteenth Conference*, X.
[25] See Int., trad. Pichery, I, p. 38.

also insists for good reason on the fact that with Cassian as with Clement (and we should add: with Pseudo-Macarius) there is question only of light: in his teaching we need not look for any mysticism of obscurity as accompanying or extending the mysticism of daylight.[26] But we do not think that this justifies us in accusing Cassian of intellectualism. The summits of his mysticism are, in fact, described by him as a prayer, a constant prayer, a prayer of fire, wholly inspired by the Gospel.

This prayer is born of constant meditation on the Scriptures and, still more precisely, it is a perfect assimilation of psalmody, the practice of which Cassian, at the beginning of his *Institutions*, explains so carefully. Never has anyone so well expressed the meaning and the purpose of this constant recitation of the Psalter which became so early as it were the structure and, above all, the source of monastic prayer. Later on, came the tendency to oppose mental prayer to vocal prayer, or at least to find a problem in the question of their relationship. Here, on the contrary, we see the most mystical prayer taking its flight from psalmody, and alone capable of revealing its whole meaning:

> God Himself will enlighten the monk with His light, to cause him to ascend to the multiform science of His being; and He will satisfy him with the sight of the most sublime and most hidden mysteries, as the prophet says: "The high mountains are for the deer...."
>
> ...The living ardour of his soul will make him resemble, indeed, a spiritual deer, who feeds on the mountains of the prophets and the apostles, that is, who is filled with their most sublime and mysterious teachings. Vivified by this food on which he continually feeds, he is permeated to the point that all the sentiments composed in the psalms he recites henceforth seem, not as if they had been composed by the prophet, but as if he himself were their author, and as his personal prayer, in sentiments of the most profound compunction; at least he will think that they were composed expressly for him and he will know that what they express was not only realized long ago in the person of the prophet, but still finds its realization in him every day. For indeed the divine Scriptures open out to us the more clearly and it is their heart in some way and their core that are manifested to us, when our own experience not only allows us to become conscious of this, but brings it about that we go ahead of this knowledge, and that the sense of the words is not opened out to us by some explanation, but by the experience that we ourselves have had of it. Permeated with the same sentiments as those with which the psalm was sung or composed, we become,

[26] *Ibid.*, pp. 38–9.

as it were, its authors, and we go ahead of its thought, rather than following it; we grasp the meaning before knowing the letter. These are memories, if I may say so, which the holy words awaken in us, memories of the daily assaults that we have sustained and still sustain, of the effects of negligence or of the conquests of our zeal, of the blessings of divine providence and the deceits of the enemy, of the misdeeds of forgetfulness, so subtile and so quick to slide into our soul, of the stains due to human weakness and the blindness of an unforeseeing ignorance. We find all these sentiments expressed in the psalms; but because we see very clearly, as in a pure mirror, everything that is said to us, we have a much more profound understanding of it. Taught by what we ourselves sense, these are properly speaking no longer things that we learn by agreeing with them, but we handle, so to say, their reality, so as to reach their depths; they no longer have the effect on us of having been memorized, but we bring them forth from the depth of our heart as sentiments that are natural to us and form part of our being; it is not reading that makes us penetrate the sense of words, but rather acquired experience.

By this road, our soul will arrive at the purity of prayer which was the subject which our preceding conversation tried to clarify, according to the grace the Lord was pleased to bestow on us. This prayer is not taken up with the consideration of any image; further, it does not express itself by speech or by any words; but it springs up in an impulse wholly of fire, an ineffable transport (*cordis excessus*), an insatiable impetuosity of spirit. Ravished out of our senses and everything visible, it is by ineffable groanings and sighs that the soul pours itself out towards God.[27]

In this last paragraph we may have recognized more than one reminiscence of the "pure prayer" of Evagrius, with perhaps a new and more exact echo of Pseudo-Macarius. But the delicacy with which Cassian locates these formulas in a context in which they are no longer in the least misleading is entirely his own. Nowhere else, perhaps, is the juncture so perfectly natural between the most transcendent mysticism and the simple "knowledge of God" fed by the Scriptures.

This prayer of fire is clearly a theme that fascinated Cassian. He returns to it often and cannot, it seems, finish speaking of its ineffable nature.

It surpasses all human sensing. Not the sound of the voices, nor movements of the tongue, nor articulate word. The soul, wholly bathed in the light from on high, no longer makes use of human speech, always so weak. But it is within it like a wave mounting up from all holy affections at once: a superabundant

27 *Tenth Conference*, XI.

source, from whence its prayer springs and overflows and spreads out in an ineffable way towards God. It says so many things in this brief moment that it cannot easily express them nor even go over them in its memory when it returns to itself.[28]

Cassian tells us again that this prayer, concentrating our gaze on God, is the conflagration of love:

> It is a gazing on God alone, a great fire of love. The soul here is buried and engulfed in holy dilection, and converses with Him as with a Father, most familiarly and tenderly.[29]

Elsewhere, he says that this prayer is simply the fruit of Christ's prayer, that the divine love, in us, may produce perfect unity:

> Then, do we see the full realization of the prayer that our Lord made to His Father for His disciples: "So that the love with which You have loved me may be in them, and they in us. . . . So that all may be one, as You, Father, are in me, and I in you, that they also may be one in us." The perfect love with which God has first loved us passes into our heart by the virtue of this prayer, the prayer which our faith tells us cannot be in vain. And here are the signs of it: God will be our whole love and all our desire, all our search and the soul of all our efforts, all our thought, our life, our speaking and our very breathing. The always existing unity of the Father with the Son and of the Son with the Father will flow out into the intimate depth of our soul; and as God loves us with a true and pure charity, one that never dies, so we shall be united with Him by the indissoluble bond of an unfailing charity: so attached to Him that He will be all our breathing, all our thinking, all our speaking.[30]

For Cassian, such a prayer is clearly the goal towards which all the efforts of the monk are to be oriented. Conversely, it will only flourish in a life fully attuned to God by asceticism:

> The whole edifice of the virtues has only one end, which is to attain to the perfection of prayer; but, without this crown, which assembles the various parts of it in such a way as to form a self-subsistent whole, it has neither solidity nor permanence. Without the virtues, the constant tranquillity of prayer that we have been speaking of can neither be acquired nor consummated, but, in return, the virtues which serve it as assistants will not achieve their perfection without it.[31]

[28] *Ninth Conference*, XXV. [29] *Ibid.*, XVIII, p. 55.
[30] *Tenth Conference*, VII. The quotation from memory of John 17. 26 and 21 should be noted, unconsciously rearranging the text.
[31] *Ninth Conference*, II.

Without knowing any method of prayer, in the modern sense of the word, Cassian none the less gives us, in order to attain to this ardent prayer by constant prayer, a counsel which is one more fruit of the Eastern tradition, but one on which he has put his own stamp. We have already mentioned how the monastic mysticism of the East, since the patristic age, was directed towards the *monologistos* prayer, concentrated on one single formula, and then simply on the name of Jesus. Perhaps Macarius the Egyptian had already taught it. Pseudo-Macarius tends towards it. With Diadochus of Photike, we find it explicitly proposed. And Cassian points out to us as the ideal means for arriving at the prayer of fire, starting from psalmody and meditation on the Scriptures, the constant repetition of the formula:

O God, come to my assistance,
Lord, make haste to help me.

This is the great theme of the tenth conference, put on the lips of the Abbot Isaias, and this is the conference in which is to be found the wonderful unfolding of the prayer of the psalms, meditation and mystical prayer just quoted.[32]

It has often, and rightly, been brought out that this spirituality, so strong, so realistic, so healthy and yet so mystical in inspiration and therefore so positive in its asceticism, is dominated by the notion of discretion. This seemed so important to Cassian that he made it the subject of his whole second conference.[33] The need and the difficulty of discretion are enough to explain his insistence on a lengthy and fruitful passage through the cenobitic life before attempting anchoritism. Without discretion, in fact, the most heroic efforts will be ill-directed and unregulated and therefore futile. This is the virtue which always keeps in sight the purpose of all asceticism, not only as a point of view, but as the inspiration effectively and efficaciously incarnated in all ascetic practices. Lacking this, once again, these practices no longer have any value.

In the Western environment in which the asceticism of the East, transferred with such enthusiasm, had been so quickly threatened with losing the clear understanding of its primitive meaning, it is good finally to find once again this lucidity, at once wholly supernatural and realistic, which at the same time affirms the distinctly eschatological and mystical perspectives without which the purest and most intense essence of monasticism evaporates. Happily, all these characteristics were soon to inspire the greatest lawgiver of Western monasticism: St Benedict.

[32] *Tenth Conference*, X. [33] *Second Conference.*

Western Monasticism before St Benedict

It clearly appears, in fact, that at this period the institution of monasticism, as adopted in the West, suffered from the lack of the line of great and inspiring figures which it had known and continued to know in the East.

In Spain, with Priscillianism, ascetic inspiration came definitely to turn towards a Neo-Manicheanism.[34] Elsewhere, it exhausted itself in attempts that were fruitless or, in any case, short-lived because poorly directed. The need for a strongly defined teaching came to make itself felt so strongly that the practical tendency of the Westerners impelled them to formulate it in a "rule" rather than in a systematic teaching. But, among many other attempts, the successful rules were those taking their substance from the teaching of Cassian.

The first that should be mentioned in this regard are those of St Cesarius,[35] a monk of Lérins although coming originally from Burgundy, who became Bishop of Arles in 502. His very brief *Regula monachorum* (twenty-four articles directly inspired by Scripture) was doubtless written for the reorganization of a monastery at Arles, the Hilarianum, the reform of which had been entrusted to him three years before his elevation to the episcopate. Later on, in 512, he founded at Aliscamps a monastery for women, soon flourishing under the direction of his sister, Cesaria. It was for this other foundation, dedicated to St John, that he wrote the *Regula ad virgines,* much more profound and detailed than the first (in a form completed in 534, it includes sixty-five articles).

Even though he was passionately Augustinian in his teaching on grace, Cesarius retained the greatest admiration for the ascetic teaching of Cassian. On his second rule in particular, the influence of the *Institutions* is frequently visible, along with that of the various Augustinian texts on monasticism we have indicated.

The great innovation of Cesarius, however, heralding and preparing for the work of St Benedict, was, together with strictly requiring an effective community of all goods in the monastery, that of stability. Thereby, for the first time, was checked the unregulated efflorescence of multiplied but ineffective attempts to lead the monastic life which hitherto had been allowed to dissipate so much of the energy of Western monasticism.

The rules of Cesarius, the second in any case, were to be

[34] See the study of P. de Labriolle, in vol. III of *Histoire de l'Église* by Fliche and Martin, Paris, 1936, pp. 385ff.

[35] On Cesarius, see Dom Patrice Cousin, *Précis d'Histoire monastique*, pp. 121–2. His life and rules are given in vol. II of his *Opera omnia*, ed. by Dom G. Morin (Maredsous, 1942).

distributed quite widely. The famous monastery of Sainte-Croix, founded by Queen St Radegonde and made illustrious by the relic of the True Cross praised by Venantius Fortunatus, was among those that adopted it and kept it for a long time.

We have already mentioned the rule of Tarnat (the place in question has not been identified, maybe somewhere in the Rhone valley); it also was adopted in other places, combining, together with Cesarius' sources, Cesarius himself.[36] Still other rules that depend on him have come down to us, like that of Aurelian, Cesarius' successor, for the new monastery of SS. Peter and Paul founded by Childebert, or that of St Ferreolus of Uzes.[37] But we must wait for the Benedictine rule to find a legislative text which was to have a lasting and truly universal success, at least in all the monasticism of the West faithful to the traditional inspirations of the East.

St Benedict and his Rule

There is no personality nor text in the history of monasticism that has occasioned more studies than that of St Benedict and his Rule.[38] And neither is there any that raises such delicate problems, nor problems the solution of which is so controversial.

The first of these problems is that the portrait of St Benedict given us in the *Dialogues* of St Gregory the Great (our only source on the patriarch of Western monks) does not seem, at least at first sight, to be easily reconcilable with the impression given by the rule which has always been attributed to him. The St Benedict of the *Dialogues* is a solitary, only with difficulty persuaded to concern himself with cenobites and leaving them several times. On occasion he is a missionary. Above all, he is a wonder-worker and a mystic. The St Benedict of the Rule is—quite the contrary, we are tempted to write—a prudent legislator, who does not in the least exclude the anchoritic ideal but who holds for his part to a well-regulated cenobitism, a mind wholly impregnated with moderation and discretion.... On the other hand, we find no trace in him of the pastoral concerns which led, with Augustine, to such a mutation in the very idea of what a monk should be.

The second problem is that raised during the last twenty years by a comparison of the Rule attributed to St Benedict with another document which has drawn more and more attention from scholars, called the Rule of the Master: *Regula Magistri*. Its composition

36 Cousin, *op. cit.*, p. 122.

37 *Ibid.* These Rules, as well as that of Tarnat, are given in Migne, P.L., LXVIII, 385–406, and LXVI, 959–86.

38 See the well-classified bibliography in Cousin, *op. cit.*, pp. 148ff.

had been for a long time placed in the seventh century, and its frequent parallels with the *Regula monasteriorum*, as the Rule of St Benedict is entitled, seen as so many marks of dependence. A more attentive study has led to the idea that the dependence might well be the other way round. In this case, what remains of real originality in him whom the monks of the West have always considered to be their great legislator and inspiration?

The St Benedict of the Dialogues

To understand something of the figure of the St Benedict of St Gregory's *Dialogues*,[39] we must not lose sight of the purpose of these writings. Their introduction states it in its own terms: the purpose is to gather together, in order to console the Pope's contemporaries afflicted by so many catastrophes of all kinds, the miracles recently accomplished by men of God: thus it will be established that, however things may seem, God has not abandoned his own today any more than in the first ages of the Church.

Like many other pious writers, Gregory, although on the level of principles not lacking in a critical sense, when it comes to collecting the *mirabilia* that have been reported to him does not seem inclined to apply these principles very strictly. This does not prevent the fact that Benedict was almost his contemporary, nor that Gregory had direct relations with the monks of Monte Cassino. Whatever we may think of the profusion of extraordinary facts he reports, there seems, therefore, no reason to doubt the outline of the biography in which these facts are inserted.

Born in Nursia, that is in the Sabinian mountains of the North (in 480, as is generally said; nearer 470, according to the opinion of Cardinal Schuster), Benedict studied rhetoric for some time at Rome. Then, frightened or disgusted by the corruption of the student environment, he withdrew into solitude near the lake of Anio, at Subiaco. Another solitary, Romanus, who had settled there before him, gave him the monastic habit. His preaching to some shepherds and his miracles made him famous. The neighbouring monks of Vicovaro asked him to be their abbot. But, faced with his strictness, they soon changed their minds and even tried to poison him. He returned to Subiaco, and soon had disciples coming to him. He gathered them in twelve little monasteries, each having a superior, and he himself, in a thirteenth, reserving for himself the task of forming the novices.

39 Given in Migne, P.L., LXVI, 125–204, the *Dialogues* have been the subject of a critical edition, provided by U. Moricca, *Dialogi sancti Gregorii*, Rome, 1924.

This time, it was the hostility of a neighbouring pastor, Florentius, that led him to depart, with some faithful followers. Going southwards, he noticed the high hill dominating the town of Cassinum. He destroyed the temple of Jupiter which crowned it and replaced it with a church dedicated to St Martin. There a new cenobium was organized, which Benedict concerned himself with, also preaching to the country people, without mentioning the neighbouring monastery for women, governed by his sister, Scholastica. Later on, he made another foundation, at Rome, St Pancratius of the Lateran, and still another not far from Monte Cassino, at Terracina. He died on 21 March (547?).

In this whole account (we have passed over the innumerable miracles which occupy by far the most space in it), Gregory has only these few words to say about the Rule:

> In the midst of such miracles, by which this man of God had been made famous throughout the world, he shone no less by the word of his teaching. For he wrote a rule for monks remarkable for its discretion and most pleasingly written (*discretione praecipuam, sermone luculentam*). And if anyone wishes to know more details about his ways and his life, he can find in the teaching of this very rule all the actions that Benedict taught, for a holy man cannot teach otherwise than as he lives.[40]

Once again, not to speak of the literary talent said to be evidenced by the Rule, this perfect homogeneity between it and the life recounted by Gregory, even if mentioned for stylistic effectiveness, leaves us somewhat embarrassed. The Rule begins by "excoriating" the wandering type of monk, and one of its most formal prescriptions, made the object of a solemn engagement at the time of profession, is stability. This is, perhaps, not a characteristic we would have inferred from St Gregory's account.

Whatever the facts may be on this point, and on many others scarcely more concordant, as we have already observed, with the portrait provided by Gregory, at least we have the Rule itself, and we can judge it on its own account.

The Benedictine Rule

It is certainly not only a very remarkable document, but one that must be called quite unique. No other text of the same kind, in fact, so successfully unites general principles which are very clear but permeated with breadth and flexibility, a spiritual exhortation both precise and fed with doctrine, details of organization clearly the fruit of a very rich experience and one enlightened by

[40] *Dialogi*, II, xxxvi; P.L., LXVI, 200 B.

wide reading, the whole being put together with an exceptional sagacity.[41]

In the prologue, the idea of the reign of God (doubtless taken from Cassian's *Conferences*) dominates the monastic ideal and its realization: more precisely, the idea of the kingdom of Christ at whose service the monk is to put himself. The first chapter then states, after a very unflattering portrait of the types of monks current at the time, that the author is going to write for cenobites. The sarabaites, pure individualists, the gyrovagues, continually on the road from one monastery to another, having been stigmatized, the cenobites are stated to be "*fortissimum genus*".

These are put first; what follows holds the possibility of anchoritism in reserve, but only for those who have been well formed in cenobitism. As to this last, the definition given of it at the outset must be kept in mind: it is the type of monasticism which is developed in a monastery, "fighting under a rule, under an abbot". What follows seems to indicate that *sub regula vel abbate* should be understood to mean: "under the rule of an abbot".

For from the second chapter, it appears that the abbot is the keystone of cenobitism as the Rule conceives it.[42] The abbot is all-powerful, his authority is to be exercised on everyone and in everything. But he is to take counsel with the elder monks in important decisions; he must see himself as the father of all the monks, with the responsibility this implies, and the author of the Rule does not fail to remind him that he ought to be the first to submit himself to the rule which he imposes, and that he has a formidable account to render to the Lord, for himself and for his monks.

Modern writers, both monastic and otherwise, take pleasure in comparing the Benedictine abbot to the Latin *paterfamilias*. The extent of his power approaches that of the latter. But this comparison was unknown to all antiquity. The fact is that there is one essential difference: it is only the necessity inherent in a spiritual mission that gives him such a wide power over things and persons in the monastery.

We should see him much more as being above all the spiritual master: the "doctor". The abbot, as his name indicates, is a father, and his fatherhood is affirmed above all in his teaching. The prologue, we should never forget, has defined the monastery as a "school of divine service". This school, true enough, is a practical more than a speculative one. But the fact remains that the abbot is above everything else the spiritual educator, he who is to form

[41] In what follows we have made use of a thesis by Dom Adalbert de Vogüé, on the rôle of the abbot in the Rule of St Benedict.

[42] On the abbot, see ch. II, III, LXIIIff.

his monks to perfection, and the Benedictine monastery is the place in which everything is ordered so that he can do this effectively.

In this respect, it should be emphasized—for the whole later history of Benedictine monasticism was to feel its effects—that the abbot as the Rule describes him presents two irreducible aspects, which flow no doubt from the mature and considered intention of St Benedict. On the one hand, as abbot, he is the heir of the great charismatics, the "spiritual fathers" of the tradition of the Fathers of the desert, so well expressed by Cassian. In other words, he needs to be a man fully experienced in monastic teaching and life, and one filled with the Spirit so as to lead others to the goal he has already himself attained. On the other hand, he is, if one may say so, a public personage, juridically fortified with definite powers that place him at the head of a society in order to rule it, temporally as well as spiritually, as a whole as in each of its members.

There are two suppositions implicit here: that the ideal "spiritual father" be chosen as abbot—that he also reveal himself capable of skilfully administering the common life. Obviously, it is understood that this life ought itself to be wholly at the service of the fatherly aspect of the abbot's work, that of engendering and educating men to the life of perfection. But this does not prevent two questions from arising: can one hope regularly to find men who are at once consummate spiritual men and prudent administrators? —can one hope above all that a function as charismatic as that of "spiritual father" can be institutionalized without, by the very nature of things, being changed thereby?

On the first point, Benedict had so few illusions that his whole Rule, or at least by far the greater part of it, seems written with the idea of teaching the abbot how to administer wisely and well, with an administration wholly inspired by the ideal of the *schola divini servitii*. On the second point, it is clear that the solution, for him, lies in the judicious choice of an abbot.

Yet he was so convinced that stability is a condition *sine qua non* of the monastic life as he understood it that, in spite of the possible dangers which he must have been well aware of, he wishes the abbot to be elected for life, just as the postulant is to commit himself for life to "fight" under his leadership.

In fact, this last feature, that of stability,[43] characterizes the Rule no less deliberately than the firm teaching and clearly defined prescriptions concerning the abbot.

Not only is stability one of the most striking novelties of the Rule (although already present with St Cesarius), but we must say

[43] See ch. LXIII.

that it seems to go against one of the themes of the older asceticism. This other theme was to be given a last outlet in Irish spirituality, but it could not hold out for long against Benedictine stability. We mean here the *xeniteia*, the character of "strangers and travellers on the earth", which the monks of old, abandoning their homeland and their family, were conscious of assuming, in an endless wandering, after the example of Abraham, in search of the heavenly homeland.[44] The very remarkable combination of the spirituality of the ascetic with the spirituality of the pilgrim which we have seen in Rufinus, in Jerome, in Cassian, doubtless in Evagrius and, more or less, with all the Palladiuses, the Moschos and their imitators, are revealing. Perhaps Benedictine stability did not stifle this theme, but it constrained it to a radical interiorization. For stability is the condition of obedience, and it is obedience that the Rule caused to be recognized as the great means of detachment. Here is found the very principle of the school which the monastery is to be, and the stability, of the abbot as of the monk, is its safeguard.

Only obedience will form the monk to the basic virtue, which now appears as humility. This primordial importance given to humility is also a legacy from Cassian. Benedict's whole doctrine of spiritual progress consists in his teaching on the degrees of humility.[45] Humility, which is openness to grace, perfect disposability to the divine will, manifested in all things, become the mother of perfection itself, that is, of the flowering of true charity.

Stability, obedience, humility, are at the service of an ideal which certainly goes back to the very first beginnings of the monastic life, an ideal which is purely biblical: that of a life in which faith, faith in Christ and his rule, subjects all life to itself. The application, and above all the concrete pursuit of this ideal in the context of the Benedictine cenobium is itself a product of experience, very personally thought out. But this development, however considerable, is certainly connected, without any break or artificial suture, with the very earliest tradition.

The importance given to the abbot, to complete submission to his authority, should not make us ignore other aspects of the cenobium, aspects on which St Benedict does not insist so much but which are no less important in his eyes. The abbot is not only to nourish direct relationships, vertical so to say, with each of his monks. He is to organize and maintain the cenobium as such. In the context of this cenobium, fraternal relationships, carefully hier-

44 See what was said above on this theme, pp. 326–7.

45 *Rule*, ch. VII, to be connected with ch. V, on obedience.

archized, between the monks themselves, form an element of the *schola* that should not be neglected.[46]

If we go on to concrete details of legislation, three things are particularly to be noted.

The monastery is to form a society which is as complete in itself, as independent of the outside world, as possible.[47] Obviously, the insecurity of the times in which Benedict lived and produced his Rule has something to do with this. But it results, above all, from the conviction that everything, in the life of the monk, must be able to be organized in function of the purpose of his association with his brothers: the reign of Christ over them.

The second point is the discretion which has been praised so often, marked by the constant care to make a lucid and comprehensive charity the basis of all existence and, above all, of all mutual relationships.[48] The division of the community into decanies, the abbot's assistants whose rôle is laid out in great detail[49]—these characteristics among others seem intended in order to avoid making the community in any way like a barracks, to safeguard between the abbot and his monks relations that are truly filial, and fraternal between themselves.

The third point is the "theocentric" character of this service of God, of this quest for God—and whether it is really this quest that attracts the postulant is what must be carefully ascertained. Indeed, the aspect of praise, of the glorification of God: *"ut in omnibus glorificetur Deus"*, as the Rule says,[50] is, sometimes discreetly but always constantly, present. It is present as much in manual labour, the instruments of which, like every possession of the monastery, are to be respected as God's property, as in the Opus Dei *par excellence*, the recitation of the Office. More precisely, work and prayer are to saturate the monk's life with an atmosphere in which service is glorification and in which glorification impregnates the whole of life with service.

Prayer is evidently the soul of all this, even though little is said about it outside the Office: a prayer which, just as with Cassian, who is expressly invoked at this point, is fed on *lectio divina*, exercised by psalmody, and prolonged and assimilated in those frequent but brief prayers which are particularly recommended.[51]

The final touch must neither be overemphasized nor minimized.

[46] See in particular ch. LXVIIIff.

[47] Ch. LXVI.

[48] This is as marked in the chapters on the abbot and his assistants as in those concerning the relationships of the monks between themselves in general.

[49] Ch. XXI, LXIV, LXV.

[50] 1 Peter 4. 11, quoted at the end of ch. LVII.

[51] See ch. VIII–XX, on the Divine Office and prayer, XLVIII and CXXIII on *lectio*.

Benedict was conscious of having done nothing but establish a firm basis, a basis that would be realizable in all times and places, on which the ascent to God, a work necessarily individual and interior, however effectively fostered by the community and guided from without by the abbot, was to be (and henceforth could be) carried out with security.[52]

The Rule of St Benedict and the Rule of the Master

What are we to think about the immediate origins of this document, with its admirable balance and perceptiveness? A comparison with the *Rule of the Master* obviously gives the impression that we have in the latter a rather incoherent confusion, with attempts to systematize which hardly seem capable of standing up under experience; in the former, on the contrary, everything is distilled, the explanations are never useless or fantastic, the "nothing too much" can be sensed everywhere, and yet no truly pure aspiration feels itself restrained.

In the *Rule of the Master* do we have, then, a sketch which experience later ordered and focused, or an amplification not without its own riches, but, in spite of everything, rarely a very happy one? It was on the latter point of view that attention formerly rested. Recent research and discussions incline us, however, towards the former.

The question was first raised by Dom A. Genestout, a monk of Solesmes, in 1940, in an article in the *Revue d'Ascétique et de Mystique*.[53] For him, the Rule of the Master, which up to that time had been placed in the seventh century, would go back to the beginning of the fifth, in the surroundings of Nicetas of Remesiana.

[52] See the conclusion, in ch. LXXXIII.

[53] Dom Augustin Genestout, "La Règle du Maître et la Règle de saint Benoît", in *Revue d'Ascétique et de Mystique*, Toulouse, XXI (1940), pp. 51–112. Note that there exist two critical editions of the Rule of St Benedict: those of Dom Cuthbert Butler, *S. Benedicti Regula monachorum*, Freiburg, 1912 (3rd ed. in 1935), and that of Dom Linderbauer, *S. Benedicti Regula monasteriorum cum dissertatione philologica*, Metten, 1922 (2nd ed., Bonn, 1928). As to the *Regula Magistri*, published for the first time by Holstenius in 1661 it has recently been the object of an edition by H. Vanderhoven, F. Masai and P. B. Corbett, *Regula Magistri, Edition diplomatique des manuscrits latins, 12205 and 12634 de Paris*, Paris, 1953. We should also point out the very practical edition by Dom Gregorio Penco, Florence, 1958, with a preface and notes containing very useful materials for the study of the question. Here we should mention also the excellent handbook edition of the Rule of St Benedict by Dom Ph. Schmitz (2nd ed. Maredsous, 1955) and his French translation: *La Règle des moines*, Maredsous, 1948, as well as that of Dom Augustin Savaton, Saint-Paul-de Wisques, 1950 Many English translations are available (including one in pamphlet form, tr. by Leonard Doyle, Liturgical Press, Collegeville, Minn.) and also commentaries, both for the use of monks and of oblates.

Others, like Dom Cappuyns,[54] supported by Dom Vandenbroucke,[55] while bringing it back very nearly to the time of the Benedictine Rule, suggest seeing it as the rule composed by Cassiodorus for his monastery at Vivarium, and so coming after St Benedict's.

On the contrary, F. Masai, basing himself on the respective lengths of the two rules (that of the Master is three times that of the other), refuses to see in the *Regula monasteriorum* anything but "a mere reworking", and thinks that we must give up "the concept of St Benedict as a profound and original thinker".[56]

Dom Froger, however, observing that the description given by St Gregory applies better to the *Regula Magistri* (but what are we to think, then, of the *"discretione praecipua"*?), does not hesitate to see in the *Rule of the Master*, at least in a shorter form, the true Rule of St Benedict. He himself, or one of his successors, would have first developed it, but what we today call "The Rule of St Benedict" would be only a "Gallican rule of the first half of the sixth century", adapting the preceding ones.[57]

Conversely, for Dom Renner, it is in the *Regula Benedicti* that we must distinguish two successive versions: one of them brief and anterior to the *Regula Magistri*, and a long one, the one we now possess, posterior to the latter and dependent on it.[58]

It must be repeated that, in general, the analysis, whether of the parallel doctrinal sections or practical prescriptions of the two Rules makes less comprehensible the supposed process of amplification that would have produced the *Rule of the Master* by starting with the Rule said to be by St Benedict, than the converse process of simplification and adjustment.[59]

However, only a close analysis of the language of the two texts, like those in which Christine Mohrmann specializes, might perhaps

[54] See in his article in *Recherches de Théologie ancienne et médiévale*, 1948 Louvain, pp. 209–68; "L'auteur de la Regula Magistri: Cassiodore".

[55] See his article, *ibid.*, 1949, pp. 186–226; "Saint Benoît, le Maître et Cassiodore."

[56] F. Masai, "La Règle de saint Benoît et la 'Regula Magistri'", in *Latomus*, VI (1947), p. 229.

[57] J. Froger, "La Règle du Maître et les sources du monachisme bénédictin", in *Revue d'Ascétique et de Mystique*, XXX (1954), pp. 275–88. Note that as early as in 1950 O. J. Zimmermann had proposed seeing the *Regula Magistri* as a first rule written by St Benedict at Subiaco ("The Regula Magistri: the Primitive Rule of St. Benedict", in the *American Benedictine Review*, I, 1950, pp. 11–36).

[58] F. Renner, "Textschichten und Entstenungphasen der Benediktusregel", in *Benedictus, Vater des Abendländes*, München, 1948, pp. 397–474.

[59] On this whole discussion, see Ezio Franceschini, "La questione della Regola di san Benedetto", in *Il Monachesimo nell'alto medioevo e la formazione della civilta occidentale*, Spoleto, 1957, pp. 222–56. See also the introduction by Dom Penco to his edition mentioned above.

give us some certainty about their relative place in time.[60] But so long as a rigorous examination of the manuscript tradition for the *Rule of the Master* has not been carried out, it will be difficult to arrive by this road at any definitive conclusions.

In any case, it is certain that the success of the *Regula monasteriorum*, of which St Benedict or some anonymous genius was the author, was not instantaneous. St Gregory the Great has generally been seen as its propagator. But actually, neither in the monastery established in the house of Coelius to which the Roman magistrate withdrew before becoming deacon, then ambassador and, finally, supreme pontiff, nor in the other monasteries of the city at his time, nor even in the monasteries which Augustine, his prior, established in England, as centres of the mission that took him there, do we have any certain proof that the Benedictine Rule was applied at that time. At the most, we can conjecture that its influence, or that of the *Rule of the Master*, must have made itself felt.

In fact, the centuries that followed were to see the monasticism of the West submerged by a wholly new and extremely original current, that of Irish monasticism. It was only in the ninth century, in the Carolingian renaissance, with St Benedict of Aniane, that the current began to flow the other way. At this time, the Benedictine Rule, not without adaptations in practice, was to be promoted in the West and have an almost universal success.

It is from this period on that "Benedictine", in the West, was to become practically synonymous with "monk".

This most remarkable synthesis, nourished as to its details by St Basil as well as St Augustine, but in which everything is dominated by the very early primitive ideal transmitted by Cassian, was then, for many centuries, to reveal itself both fertile in creative developments and capable of serving as a springboard for various "returns to the sources". Does it not end in a conclusion of a breadth and balance equalled only by its humility, but a humility wholly permeated with the single desire for God?

> "We have set out this Rule so that, carrying it out in monasteries, we may see that there is amongst us some rightness of manners and some beginning of observance. But if anyone tends to the perfect life, he has the teachings of the saints the practice of which leads man to the summit of perfection. For is there any page of holy Scripture, whether of the Old or the New Testament, which is not a very right and perfect rule for the

60 Christine Mohrmann, "Regula Magistri, A propos de l'édition diplomatique des mss. lat. 12205 et 122634 de Paris", in *Vigiliae Christianae*, VIII (1954), pp. 239–51.

conduct of our life? And is there any page of the holy Catholic Fathers that does not teach us the means of attaining speedily by a straight path to our creator? And still more, the *Conferences* of the Fathers, their *Institutions* and their *Lives*, and also the Rule of our Father St Basil—what are they but examples of monks of good life and exact in obedience, and excellent instructions in practising the virtues? And this should be a subject of shame and confusion to us who live in so much laxity, disorder and negligence. Whoever you be, then, you who desire to advance towards the heavenly homeland, strive, with the help of Jesus Christ, to keep this little rule in which we have set out the beginning of the religious life and, having done this, you will then go on with the help of God to study the sublime instructions and to practise the eminent virtues that we have just mentioned.[61]

[61] Ch. LXXXIII of St Benedict's Rule.

GENERAL CONCLUSION ON THE PRIMITIVE AND PATRISTIC PERIOD: LOVE AND KNOWLEDGE OF GOD

THE life and work of St Gregory the Great stand out against a background of catastrophes. The Vandals already were besieging the city when Augustine died. Benedict's retreat was disturbed by the invasion of Totila. The Vivarium of Cassiodorus was to be no more than an oasis already condemned, where for a time both the prayer and the culture of antiquity survived. And Gregory saw the Roman Empire and its civilization dying under his eyes.

He himself, even when an ambassador at Constantinople, had never learned Greek. And his Latin, like that of Benedict, shows quite strongly his lack of culture.

The earthly city in which the heavenly city had at first appeared to be incarnated once and for all was no more, in the West, at least. Upon the heritage, chiefly of St Augustine, to which that of St Benedict was soon added, Gregory was one of the first to attempt to construct as it were a city of refuge, while awaiting the final catastrophe that would cause us to pass from time to eternity. Actually, without knowing it, he began the building of a new Christianity, which was to be that of the Latin Middle Ages.

A first age had arrived at its end. It is time to pause, to turn back and to evaluate the road travelled since the apostolic period.[1]

Monasticism and the Church: the Spirituality of the Liturgies and the Catecheses

From the moment when the persecutions ceased and martyrdom was no longer so much an actual ideal, it was monasticism that condensed all the progress, or we might say more simply the development of Christian spirituality. As we have said, this did not take place without provoking various resistances, not without giving rise, above all in the West, to some one-sided or even frankly erroneous emphases.

[1] The spirituality of St Gregory the Great will be studied at the beginning of the next volume.

But however great this preponderance, the whole Church did not become monastic, and it might be well, in conclusion, to locate the impulse towards monastic spirituality in its context in the ordinary life of the Church. It must not be forgotten that it was in the Church, and in the common life of the truth in the Church, that monasticism, like martyrdom before it, was nurtured. Reciprocally, the great spiritual geniuses who expressed and built up the spirituality of monasticism did not fail to leave some imprint on the institutions and the teaching which are the common possession of the whole Church.

We have seen Christian spirituality born in the liturgy, fed with the Word of God in the one and the other Testament. It is in this context, or rather as drawing from these enduring sources, that was formed the spirituality increasingly centred on monasticism. It is interesting to ask ourselves what transformations these developments, along with the struggle against heresies and the final victory over paganism, contributed to the organism within which they themselves were produced.

When we examine the Christian liturgy as it presents itself at the end of the patristic age, we may first be impressed by the cultural creation which seems, in some few centuries, to have built up a whole new edifice. Above all in the Greek East, much less at Rome, more in other Latin countries in which Eastern influences, Hellenic or Syrian, were felt more strongly, a double development is indicated, the two branches of which, moreover, are related to one another.

The liturgical formularies have gained a new precision through which runs, together with the mark of heresies overcome, the trace of an effort of thought nourished by Hellenism. But, even more, the literary and artistic context of the celebration has become as it were a final and magnificent product of ancient culture as rectified and made fruitful by Christianity.

When we go deeper than certain externals, however, what is new strikes us much less than what has remained the same. The Benedictine school of Maria-Laach believed that it had found in the *Kultmysterium* (the "cultic Mystery") the great cultural and religious creation of the period we are concerned with. This school hailed in this creation the depositing of the new Christian reality in the lines, the moulds, already prepared by a pre-Christian religious effort: those mysteries of the last Hellenistic paganism which attempted to bring out a hope of immortality for man by his cultic participation in the death of gods continually re-born. It must be admitted that this idea is something of an optical illusion.

Certainly, the mystery of St Paul, the mystery of the Cross of Jesus, of his Cross as the power of resurrection, of new and eternal life, is at the heart, or rather remains at the heart, of the patristic liturgy. But, precisely, it was already at the heart of the liturgy of the New Testament. And here, it is quite certain that it owed nothing at all to Hellenism, but everything to that flowering, in Christ and in the new-born Church, of the divine seeds already planted in Judaism.

After the victory of Christ over the Greek gods or the oriental divinities that had attempted, almost at the same period, to invade what we call the ancient world, that is, the Roman empire civilized by Greece, doubtless the Church did not fail to borrow certain symbols from them, those which were richest in human resonances. In the same way, she took on, together with the language, something of the forms of thought of Hellenism, although not without submitting them to vigorous refashioning. But nothing of all this touches the content of Christian revelation nor the profound spiritual realities that it alone can arouse and create in the human soul. At the most, the access to all this, and so the response to it, was thereby made easier.[2]

In fact, the Eucharist of the fourth, of the fifth, or of the sixth centuries, the other sacraments and the divine office, manifest, in their basic structure, an astonishing permanence in relation to the first century, and this continuity remains perceptible even so far as external forms are concerned, despite a varnish of Hellenism. Whether they are Greeks, Romans or, soon, barbarians, Christians remain, in their worship, in their prayer and in the common life of their faith, "spiritual Semites". The divine "Word", our "eucharistic" response to it, as the spirituality of a Cassian still indicates, this is the profound line of force of the most personal prayer, and as such it remains always visible in the worship from which piety had to draw before giving back to it what it had received from it and made its own.

It is most remarkable that a collection of prayers as archaic as that of the *Apostolic Constitutions* could still have been put together towards the end of the patristic age, and that it should harmonize so well, as the great eucharistic Christian prayer included in it demonstrates, with the creations or reworkings which took their final form at this period, such as the liturgies called those of St Basil or of St John Chrysostom.[3]

[2] For a discussion of this whole question, may we refer the reader to our book, *Liturgical Piety* (Notre Dame Press, 1955). We hope soon to publish a semantic study on *Mysterion in the Religious Literature of Antiquity*.

[3] In Migne, P.G., I, 555–1156. Critical edition by F. X. Funk, *Didascalia et Constitutiones Apostolorum*, 2 vols., Paderborn, 1905.

Nothing is more revealing in this respect than the catecheses that have come down to us, generally from the end of the fourth or the beginning of the fifth century, whether they are by St Cyril (or John?) of Jerusalem, Theodore of Mopsuestia, St John Chrysostom, Narsai, St Ambrose (or some other preacher perhaps covered by his name).[4] In spite of secondary marks of different schools of thought or personalities, not only are these all profoundly in accord with one another, but they all remain Paulinian and Johannine in substance. The Cross of Christ, our association in his victory, our incorporation in Christ himself—this is the baptismal initiation. The life of Christ in us, the consummation of his sacrifice in the union of all his own with him and their reunion, by the Spirit, in his own recapitulation in the bosom of the Father—this is the Eucharist.

Christian asceticism, in monasticism as previously in the preparation for martyrdom, is never anything other than a realization, an actualization of this sacramental union, through faith, with Christ crucified. And mysticism, let us recall, in its very concept and designation, was born of the experience made by faith, in the heart of the Church, of our union, itself already actual, with the risen Christ, God all in all.

What the living tradition that disengaged itself little by little, above all in monasticism, developed and elucidated speculatively while carrying it out in practice, is simply something of what this "knowledge of God" can be which the New Testament proclaims. Fully communicating in the mystery of Christ, here it discovers itself as being one with the recognition of love, of the divine *agape*: "God has shown his love in that he delivered his Son to death for sinners.... In this we have known *agape*, in that he has given his life for us."[5]

Certain modern studies, brilliant, filled with illuminating intuitions, but too regimented by a systematization that history knows nothing of and it is useless to try to impose on it, have tried to characterize the development of patristic spirituality as being a

[4] Cyril of Jerusalem, *Catecheses*, P.G., XXXIII, 331–1180. (J. Quasten has given a critical edition in the series *Florilegium Patristicum*, 1936; the handbook edition of F. I. Cross, London, 1951, follows the English translation by Church.) Theodore of Mopsuestia, *Catecheses*, ed. Mingana and Tonneau-Devreesse (see p. 439). Chrysostom, *Huit catéchèses baptismales*, ed. and tr. by A. Wenger, A.A., no. 50 in the collection "Sources chrétiennes", Paris, 1957. Narsai, *Liturgical Homilies*, English translation by Dom R. H. Connolly, in the collection "Texts and Studies, etc.", vol. VIII, no. I, Cambridge, 1909. Ambrose, *Des Sacraments et Des Mystères*, ed. and French tr. by Dom Bernard Botte, in the collection "Sources chrétiennes", no. 25, Paris, 1950. The attribution of both the last two texts to St Ambrose still raises many difficulties.

[5] Romans 5. 8 and 1 John 3. 16.

passage from the prophetic religion to a mystical religion.[6] The progressive immersion of the Gospel theme of *agape* in the Hellenic theme of *eros* is denounced, mysticism and Hellenism being supposed *a priori* to be the same thing.[7]

Our study of the very origins of the idea and the reality of Christian mysticism should be enough to dissipate the prejudice which is at the basis of this whole construction. If we follow, on the other hand, the development in the Greek Fathers or in St Augustine of the idea, so specifically Christian, of the *agape* of God poured out in our hearts by the Holy Spirit, what strikes us here is not how the *agape* became diluted or dissipated in the pre-Christian *eros*, but rather how the latter was transformed and finally broke apart, to be reborn under the radiation of the *agape*.

The whole of the Christian asceticism of the patristic era, in spite of the risks of deviation continually threatening it, remains basically simply the concrete realization of that cross which the Servant of Yahweh invited his disciples to take up and to carry after him. The mysticism of the Fathers is only the fruit of the "knowledge of God", knowledge in the Scriptures, by the faith that takes hold of the whole of life, the faith to which God reveals himself in Christ as *agape*, while he pours out precisely this *agape*, through the Spirit of Christ, into the hearts of those who give themselves up unreservedly to the mystery of his Cross. Such remains the teaching of the last great bishops and doctors.

St Cyril of Alexandria

At least as much as with St Athanasius, the concern to preserve, by dogmatic exactitude, the integrity, the authenticity of spirituality is revealed in one of the most combative of his successors in the episcopal see of Alexandria, the archbishop Cyril. Athanasius had defended the full divinity of the Saviour in the name of the reality of the "deification" that he brings us.[8] Against Nestorius, it was for the same reason that Cyril maintained the true union in Christ's Person of the divinity with the humanity. On this basis, he reaffirmed, in terms of definitive precision, the Pauline doctrine of the Church as the body of Christ and the Johannine doctrine of our union with his very flesh in the Eucharist, as the two premises of our own divinization in the Spirit.

In fact, the incarnation, as Cyril conceived it, making the humanity of Christ the humanity of the Son of God, gives him a

[6] See Freidrich Heiler, *Prayer* (ed. by McComb and Park, paper, Oxford, 1958).
[7] See Anders Nygren, *Agape and Eros* (Westminster, Phila., Pa, 1953).
[8] Cf. above p. 416.

transcendent unity which allows him to gather us all together so that we may all be adopted in him.

> We all, indeed, were in Christ and it is the common person of humanity that is reformed in Him. The Logos has dwelt in all through one alone: one alone having been constituted Son of God in power according to the Spirit of holiness, this dignity is communicated to the whole human race, so that, through one of us, this word reaches us, us also: "I have said, you are all gods and sons of the Most High."[9]

Less than ever, with Cyril, is it possible to interpret this as if it were a question of salvation by the fact of the incarnation alone, independent of the Cross. On the contrary, as he himself says in the most categorical fashion: if Christ takes our body, it is in it to conquer our death by his own:

> The Logos was made flesh and dwelt among us uniquely in order to undergo the death of the flesh and thereby to triumph over the principalities and powers, and to reduce to nothingness him who himself held the power of death, that is Satan, to take away corruption, and with it to drive out the sin that tyrannizes over us and thus to render inoperative the ancient curse which the nature of man had undergone in Adam, as in the first fruits of the race and in its first root.[10]

It is, then, on the basis of this offering of himself to the cross that Christ came to sanctify us all in himself. But he did this because at the Supper, inseparably, he offered himself to the cross in giving himself to us in the Eucharist.

> To fuse us into unity with God and among ourselves, even though we each have a distinct personality, the only Son invented a wonderful means: by one body, His own, He sanctifies His faithful in the mystical communion, making them one single body with Him and among themselves. No division can come within Christ; all united with the one Christ by His own body, all receiving it—it being one and indivisible—into our own bodies, we are the members of this one body, and thus it is for us the bond of unity.[11]

In this one body, then, the one Spirit consummates our union:

> In the same way, indeed, as the power of His holy flesh makes concorporal (*syssomous*) with Him those in whom He is, so, if I am not deceived, the one Spirit of God, dwelling in an indivisible way in all, leads us ineluctably to spiritual unity.[12]

And he insists on the reality of this spiritual unity in ourselves, as in Jesus, a unity that surpasses the mere union of wills to attain

[9] *Comm. in Johan.*, I; P.G., LXXIII, 161 C.
[10] *Comm. in Rom.*, V, 3; P.G., LXXXIV, 781 D.
[11] *Comm. in Johan.*, XVII; P.G., LXXXIV, 560 and the whole context.
[12] *Ibid.*

a transforming participation of our nature in the divine nature itself:

> There is no union with God except through the participation of the Holy Spirit, infusing us with the holiness of His own nature; remodelling human souls in His own life, He imprints them with a divine likeness and sculptures out in them the image of that substance which is the most perfect of substances.[13]

He is not afraid to explain more precisely what must be understood by this, some lines away, by images that will be taken up by the mystics most insistent on the reality of our divine life:

> It is false that we cannot be one with God except by an accord of wills. For above this union, there is another more sublime and far superior, which is effected in us by a communication of the divinity to man, who, while still conserving his proper nature, is transformed, so to say, into God, in the same way as iron that is plunged into the fire becomes fiery and, while still remaining iron, seems changed into fire. This is the kind of union with God that our Lord asks for His disciples, through their receiving and participating in the divinity.[14]

St Leo the Great

If we must give one last name summing up both this development proper to the patristic age and that permanence of the primitive deposit, always faithful to itself, in a spirituality lived by the whole Church and proposed to all its members, we can perhaps make no better choice than St Leo the Great. Pope Gregory is as it were the first face of medieval Christianity; Pope Leo (400?–61?) in some way immortalizes that of patristic Christianity.[15] Under a language and a style still magnificent, he expresses in his liturgical homilies, just as St Gregory Nazianzen does in his but even better than he, a spirituality of incorporation into Christ, by faith and the sacraments. The great themes of our divinization, counterpart of the incarnation; of the cross of Christ, our victory; of his resurrection and ascension, the principles of our new life, here set out one last time, in the face of the heresies that had threatened to alter them, a Paulinianism formulated in the context of the ancient liturgy.

[13] *Ibid.*, col. 553.

[14] *Ibid.* Cf. H. du Manoir, *Dogme et spiritualité chez saint Cyrille*, Paris, 1944, pp. 289ff.

[15] See the collection of his *Sermons* in vol. LIV of the Latin Patrology of Migne. Dom René Dolle has undertaken a translation, to accompany the re-editing of this text for the collection, "Sources chrétiennes", with an introduction by Dom Jean Leclercq. Of the four volumes announced, two have appeared so far (no. 22, Paris, 1949, and no. 49, 1957). On St Leo and his work, see T. Jalland, *The Life and Times of Saint Leo the Great*, London-New York, 1941. We should also mention G. Hudon, *La perfection chrétienne d'après les Sermons de saint Léon*, Paris, 1959.

The actuality of the life of Christ in the Church, according to St Leo, is to be realized in each of us by an asceticism proposed to all Christians, monks or not. The two fundamental practices, closely connected with one another—as in primitive monasticism: remember the *Vita Antonii*—are fasting and almsgiving. Fasting frees us from our attachments to the world so that we may belong to Christ, and fasting, while it facilitates our adherence to God in Christ, offers both the occasion and the material wherewithal for almsgiving. Thus faith in the coming of Christ to the world, within the Church celebrating the Eucharist, within each of those who celebrate it together, reaches, *hic et nunc*, so far as this is possible, its realization.

In terms accessible to all, Leo proposes to the faithful substantially the same asceticism, the same basically scriptural mysticism which his friend Cassian had for one last time set out for monks:

> Our Saviour, dearly beloved, is born today: rejoice! For it is not fitting that we give any place to sadness when Life is born, the Life which, consuming the fear of death, has filled us with joy because of the eternity He promises. No one is excluded from this gladness. One reason for joy is common to all, since Our Lord, the destroyer of sin and death, as He found no one free from sin, came to deliver us all. The saint is to exult, for he is nearing his palm. The sinner is to rejoice, for he is invited to forgiveness. The pagan is to take courage, for he is called to life....
>
> ... And so, dearly beloved, we are to give thanks to God the Father, through His Son, in the Holy Spirit, to Him who, in the abundant mercy with which He has loved us, has had pity on us, and "when we were dead in our sins, has brought us to life together with Christ", so that we may be in Him a new creature,[16] a new work. Let us, then, take off the old man with his works, and become partakers in the generation of Christ, renouncing the works of the flesh. O Christian, realize your dignity: you are associated with the divine nature, do not turn back to your past base condition by a degenerate way of life. Remember that you have been rescued from the power of darkness, you have been transported into the light and the kingdom of God. By the sacrament of Baptism, you have been made the temple of the Holy Spirit. Do not make such a guest take flight by perverse actions nor submit yourself again to the devil's slavery, for you have been redeemed by the blood of Christ, for He will judge you in truth, He who has redeemed you in mercy, He who lives and reigns with the Father and the Holy Spirit for ever and ever. Amen.[17]

[16] Eph. 2. 5.

[17] *Sermon* xx, the first for the Nativity.

INDEX OF SUBJECTS

BIBLICAL INDEX

Old Testament

New Testament

INDEX OF ANCIENT AUTHORS

INDEX OF MODERN AUTHORS

BOOKS OF SIGNIFICANT AND ENDURING SCHOLARSHIP
FROM THE SEABURY PRESS

Bernard Lonergan
METHOD IN THEOLOGY
"Outstanding . . . it presents an original and internally consistent theory, systematically constructed according to a fully articulated philosophy of human knowing." —Avery Dulles in *Theological Studies*
Pbk 424pp

Harvey H. Guthrie, Jr.
ISRAEL'S SACRED SONGS:
A Study of Dominant Themes
"An excellent study of dominant themes in the psalter. . . . Little space is wasted in this compact volume. The author makes his way in orderly fashion, showing an admirable acquaintance with ancient Near Eastern literature. . . . His chapters are truly thematic, but at the same time the obvious product of careful research." —Ignatius Hunt
Pbk 256pp

R. M. French, Translator
THE WAY OF A PILGRIM
***and* THE PILGRIM CONTINUES HIS WAY**
"Unique among devotional books. . . . The pilgrim's spontaneous ministry to his fellow men, his earnest wrestlings with the problem of how to pray continually, his humble receptiveness to the promptings of God, become a shared religious experience with the reader." —Edmund Fuller
Pbk 256pp